Trade Finance

Trade Finance

Technology, Innovation and Documentary Credits

Edited by
CHRISTOPHER HARE AND DORA NEO

OXFORD
UNIVERSITY PRESS

OXFORD
UNIVERSITY PRESS

Great Clarendon Street, Oxford, OX2 6DP,
United Kingdom

Oxford University Press is a department of the University of Oxford.
It furthers the University's objective of excellence in research, scholarship,
and education by publishing worldwide. Oxford is a registered trade mark of
Oxford University Press in the UK and in certain other countries

First Edition published in 2021
Impression: 1

Published in the United States of America by Oxford University Press
198 Madison Avenue, New York, NY 10016, United States of America

British Library Cataloguing in Publication Data
Data available

Library of Congress Control Number: 2020952641

ISBN 978–0–19–885447–0

DOI: 10.1093/law/9780198854470.001.0001

Printed and bound in the UK by
TJ Books Limited

Preface

The collection of essays focuses on an area that, whilst fundamentally important in practice, has received relatively limited academic airtime. This is surprising given the knotty doctrinal, conceptual and practical difficulties that the trade finance area can throw up. This collection of essays could easily have focused upon just the traditional form of trade finance (namely, the documentary letter of credit) and still have had plenty to say that was original and cutting-edge. However, the range of essays recognizes that, whilst still a dominant force, the documentary letter of credit has struggled in recent times to maintain its market share. The documentary letter of credit is increasingly criticized for being slow, complex and expensive. The rise of technology has fueled demands for digital letters of credit and other electronic forms of payment, whilst concerns over cost and increased compliance have driven trade parties to find other ways of paying for their goods. Trade finance is accordingly at a crossroads: the fundamental difficulties associated with traditional trade finance and the (still dominant) documentary letter of credit remain to be worked through, yet there is an increasing focus on technological and innovative trade finance solutions that are yet in their infancy.

This pivotal moment for trade finance led to the holding of a symposium entitled *Trade Finance for the 21st Century*, in March 2018. This event was hosted and funded by the Centre for Banking & Finance Law at the Faculty of Law, National University of Singapore. Speakers were invited to present papers relating to topics such as persistent difficulties in traditional trade finance and to consider technological and innovative ways of developing trade finance mechanisms. The presentations were followed by responses from invited commentators with expertise in different aspects of trade financing, and discussion amongst the participants. These papers have been further developed and updated since the symposium and comprise the majority of the chapters in this volume. They are joined by a few new chapters, resulting in wider and more holistic coverage.

The symposium highlighted six core themes relevant to modern trade finance. The first theme was the impact of technology and digitization, both in relation to traditional forms of financing (such as the documentary letter of credit) and newer solutions (such as the bank payment obligation). Increased use of technology has given rise to other issues regarding the application of domestic law principles and the role and significance of the conflict of laws. The second theme concerned the reform of the frameworks within which trade finance operates. In particular, whilst the UCP regime has undoubtedly been successful, there are some persistent issues (such as the meaning of 'negotiation', the standard of documentary compliance or the form required of transport documents) that should be remedied through a further revision of the UCP 600. Unfortunately, this looks increasingly unlikely. Accordingly, there is need to find alternative frameworks, whether legal, contractual or technological, within which trade finance activity can operate. The third theme related to financial innovation, whether the development of the BPO, the use of blockchain technology for trade finance or the use of supply-chain financing, syndication or securitization structures to provide liquidity and manage risk. The fourth theme concerned the role that national law still plays in trade finance, despite the harmonizing tendency of the UCP regime. Accordingly, national law still has to determine such important issues as the contractual nature of the letter of credit, whether nominated and other banks qualify as agents and how one determines the law applicable to a particular letter of credit. This stems from the fact that the UCP regime represents a restatement of international banking *practice*, rather than international banking *law*, so that, without the underpinnings of domestic law, traditional trade finance structures would be inoperable. The fifth theme concerned the impact of financial regulation on trade finance activity. There can be no doubt that, when the UCP regime was first conceived, international banking law was largely the law of the jungle, but increasingly international initiatives have been developed to control funds representing the proceeds of crime or intended to fund terrorism, to ensure banks' capital adequacy or to sanction certain regimes for violating perceived norms of good international behaviour. Whilst it is difficult to argue against the good sense underlying these international initiatives, they do present a real problem for trade finance: traditional trade finance can no longer rely upon banks simply checking the documents' face, but nowadays banks have to investigate the details of the underlying transactions; and technological trade finance solutions may become slower and more expensive as a result of having to carry out initial and ongoing compliance checks. The final theme concerned the role of party autonomy and the extent to which this might be limited. In particular, there may be concerns as to whether "soft clauses" should be used in letters of credit or "*Asplenium* clauses" might be used in performance bonds. Whilst there can be no doubt that party autonomy should give way to larger public policy concerns, there is a more difficult issue of whether trade finance parties should be protected from themselves.

The chapters in this volume were accordingly drafted in light of these six symposium themes, which in turn informed this volume's overall structure. Part I focuses upon traditional trade finance mechanisms, such as the documentary letter of credit and performance bond. Whilst these mechanisms are undoubtedly facing challenges from technology and innovation, they remain (and are likely to continue to be) the most significant aspect of the trade finance landscape. That said, traditional trade finance faces a number of persistent problems: the difficulties of keeping the UCP regime relevant and workable; the fundamental nature of the letter of credit; and the problems of documentary compliance, fraud, "soft clauses" and foreign stop orders. Part II focuses on the challenges of technology. One of the most significant barriers to technological solutions is the need to digitize documents, whether the bill of lading, bill of exchange or insurance documents. There seems little likelihood, however, of trade actors making this shift until there are sufficiently reliable and robust legal and technological frameworks in place. Whilst the advent of distributed-ledger technology may provide a solution to the latter problem, trade finance must be careful not to get overly caught up in the excitement that has surrounded the use of blockchain. Undoubtedly, digitization would allow current trade finance operations to operate more efficiently. There is, however, an alternative. Part III considers trade-finance innovation. This involves developing new trade finance instruments (such as the bank payment obligation or sharia-compliant structures) or re-purposing existing structures (as occurs with supply-chain finance or countertrade) to meet the current needs of the trading community.

Whilst constant innovation is important, its limits must be recognized: for every innovative success, there will be countless failures. Accordingly, some of the forms of innovation considered in this volume may take root and become a dominant force in trade, others may disappear into obscurity.

Indeed, the tripartite structure of this volume is itself innovative in the academic trade finance field. Whilst there are authoritative academic publications dealing with letters of credit and (to a lesser degree) performance bonds, little academic attention has been given to the place of those traditional trade finance instruments within the broader, developing trade finance context. Indeed, the academic conversation in the trade finance area has become rather muted since the advent of the UCP 600. This volume will hopefully show that the letter of credit remains an important (but not the only) player in the trade-finance game and retains an academic vibrancy that is worthy of further critical investigation. If this volume re-ignites an academic conversation around the principles and practice of letters of credit and ignites an academic discussion about innovations in trade finance more broadly, then it will have achieved its aim.

We would like to thank the contributors for their interesting and informative chapters, and our publishers, Oxford University Press, for their support and hard work on this volume. We would also like to thank the participants and commentators at our symposium for their helpful contributions to the development of the chapters in this volume. We are grateful to the Centre for Banking & Finance Law at the Faculty of Law, National University of Singapore, for funding this research project.

Christopher Hare and Dora Neo

Table of Contents

PART II: TRADE FINANCE TECHNOLOGY

PART III: INNOVATION AND TRADE-FINANCE CHALLENGERS

List of Contributors

Ebenezer Adodo, Associate Professor of Commercial Law and Director, Leicester LLM Programmes, University of Leicester, UK.

Sandra Booysen, Associate Professor and Deputy-Director, Centre for Banking & Finance Law, Faculty of Law, National University of Singapore.

James E Byrne, Founder and Former Director, Institute of International Banking Law and Practice, USA.

Soh Chee Seng, Technical Consultant on Trade Finance Issues, Association of Banks in Singapore.

Alan Davidson, Senior Lecturer, TC Beirne School of Law, University of Queensland, Australia; Solicitor and Barrister.

Martin Davies, Admiralty Law Institute Professor of Maritime Law, Tulane University Law School, USA.

Nelson Enonchong, Barber Professor of Law, University of Birmingham, UK.

Jonathan Ercanbrack, Senior Lecturer in Transnational Financial Law; Director, Centre for Islamic and Middle Eastern Law, SOAS, University of London, UK.

Xiang Gao, Professor of Law, China University of Political Science & Law, China; Professor of Law (part-time), Faculty of Law, University of Technology Sydney, Australia.

Benjamin Geva, Professor of Law, Osgoode Hall Law School of York University, Toronto, Canada.

Miriam Goldby, Professor in Shipping, Insurance and Commercial Law, Queen Mary University of London, UK; Director, Insurance, Shipping and Aviation Law Institute; Co-Academic Director, Institute of Transnational Commercial Law.

Christopher Hare, Travers Smith Associate Professor of Corporate and Commercial Law, University of Oxford; Tutorial Fellow, Somerville College, UK.

Agasha Mugasha, Professor of Law, Bishop Stuart University, Mbarara, Uganda.

Dora Neo, Associate Professor and Director, Centre for Banking & Finance Law, Faculty of Law, National University of Singapore.

Toh Kian Sing SC, Senior Partner, Rajah & Tann Singapore LLP.

Jane K Winn, Professor, University of Washington Law School, USA; Adjunct Professor, UW Human Centered Design and Engineering, College of Engineering; Adjunct Professor, UW Jackson School of International Studies.

Chen Zhida, Associate Director, Helmsman LLC, Singapore; Adjunct Assistant Professor, Faculty of Law, National University of Singapore.

List of Abbreviations

AAOIFI	The Accounting and Auditing Organization for Islamic Financial Institutions
ACH	Automated Clearing House
ASYCUDA	UNCTAD's Automated System for Customs Data
BAFT	Bankers Association for Finance and Trade
BBL	Bolero Bill of Lading
BCMP	Bolero Core Messaging Platform
BEA	Bills of Exchange Act 1882 (UK)
BiTA	Blockchain in Transport Alliance
Bolero	Bill of Lading Electronic Registry Organization
BPAs	Banking Practice Agreements
BPO	bank payment obligation
DHS	Department of Homeland Security
DLPC	Distributed Ledger Payment Commitment
DLT	distributed-ledger technologies
DOCDEX	Documentary Instruments Dispute Resolution Expertise
DPC	Deferred Payment Credit
DPU	Deferred Payment Undertaking
ECCHO	Electronic Check Clearing House Organization
ECJ	European Court of Justice
EFT	electronic funds transfer
EPO	Electronic Payment Order
eUCP	Uniform Customs and Practice for Documentary Credits for Electronic Presentation
FATF	Financial Action Task Force
GFC	Global Financial Crisis
GSCFF	Global Supply Chain Finance Forum
GTM	global trade management
ICC	International Chamber of Commerce
IGP&I	International Group of Protection and Indemnity Clubs
IMF	International Monetary Fund
ISBP	International Standard Banking Practices
ISP98	International Standby Practices
ITDS	International Trade Data System
LC	letter of credit
LEC	UNCITRAL Model Law on Electronic Commerce
LETR	UNCITRAL's Model Law on Electronic Transferable Records
MENA	Middle East and North Africa region
ML-EC	UNCITRAL Model Law on Electronic Commerce
ML-ETR	Model Law on Electronic Transferable Records
NACHA	National Automated Clearing House Association
OIC	Organisation of Islamic Cooperation
SaaS	software as a service
SCF	Supply Chain Finance
SMEs	small- and medium-sized enterprises

SWIFT	Society for Worldwide Interbank Financial Telecommunication
TBML	trade-based money laundering
TSMT	ISO 20022 Trade Services Management
TSU	SWIFTNet Trade Services Utility
UCP	Uniform Customs and Practice for Documentary Credits
UCTA	Unfair Contract Terms Act 1977
UNCITRAL	United Nations Commission on International Trade Law
UNECE	United Nations Economic Commission for Europe
URBPO	Uniform Rules on Bank Payment Obligations
URDG	The Uniform Rules for Demand Guarantees
URF 800	Uniform Rules for Forfaiting
WCO	World Customs Organisation
WTO TFA	World Trade Organisation Trade Facilitation Agreement

Table of Cases

UNITED KINGDOM

EUROPEAN UNION

AUSTRALIA

CANADA

CHINA

HONG KONG

IRELAND

NORTHERN IRELAND

SINGAPORE

SOUTH AFRICA

MALAYSIA

NEW ZEALAND

UNITED STATES

Table of Legislation

UNITED KINGDOM STATUTES

STATUTORY INSTRUMENTS

OTHER LEGISLATION

Australia

Canada

China

Egypt

Hong Kong

Singapore

United States

EUROPEAN REGULATIONS

INTERNATIONAL INSTRUMENTS

INTERNATIONAL CHAMBER OF COMMERCE

PART I

LEGAL AND PRACTICAL CHALLENGES TO TRADITIONAL TRADE FINANCE

Part I considers the modern challenges presented to traditional trade finance instruments, namely documentary letters of credit and performance bonds. The first challenge involves identifying the relevant legal framework for such instruments: on one level, it has become increasingly difficult to accommodate documentary trade finance within domestic contract law; whereas, on another level, the international framework provided by the 'UCP' and analogous default rules has become increasingly out of date and difficult to update. Without either framework, it is unclear how documentary trade finance can continue to develop and serve the trading community effectively. Even within the principles governing such traditional documentary instruments a number of uncertainties and challenges have arisen, including the use of soft clauses in letters of credit; the role of nominated banks; the determination of compliant presentations; and the impact of fraud, unconscionability and foreign stop orders. Given that documentary trade has always pursued the twin aims of providing certainty of payment to the beneficiaries of such instruments and reducing the administrative burden on issuing and confirming banks, uncertainty regarding the applicable legal framework and its operation can only undermine the utility of documentary trade finance. This is not just a challenge; it is a matter of survival.

1

The UCP Regime

Past, Present, and Future

James E Byrne, Soh Chee Seng, and Christopher Hare*

'Those who cannot remember the past are condemned to repeat it.'[1]

I. Introduction

For many years, documentary letters of credit have been the pre-eminent way of financing international sales. This chapter offers a centennial perspective on the UCP regime, which has long provided the framework of principles within which letters of credit operate.[2] Given its centenary, it is timely to consider the impact that the UCP regime has made and may potentially continue to have in the future. In that regard, this chapter focuses on the timeline representing the letter of credit's and the UCP regime's historical development and its potential future development. Accordingly, this chapter's tripartite structure reflects its threefold aims: to act as a reminder of the rich history underlying the UCP regime, to examine its current operation in the trade finance sphere, and to offer some perspectives upon its future prospects. In relation to the last issue, the discussion will consider both the likelihood of there being a further revision to the UCP regime and the types of issue that any revision process should address. **1.01**

II. The Historical Perspective

There was life before the UCP regime.[3] There is evidence to suggest that instruments analogous to letters of credit were used in ancient Egypt and Babylon, as the University Museum of Philadelphia contains a clay promissory note dating from 3,000 BC providing for repayment with interest.[4] A cuneiform tablet found in Egypt is the earliest extant example of a letter of credit.[5] Other examples of promissory and negotiable instruments **1.02**

* This chapter incorporates Professor Jim Byrne's keynote address (by video conference) at the Trade Finance for the 21st Century Symposium held at the Faculty of Law, National University of Singapore (8 March 2018). As this chapter was finalised after Professor Byrne passed away, the views expressed may not always represent his position.

[1] George Santayana, *Reason in Common Sense* (ἡ γὰρ νοῦ ἐνέργεια ζωή) (Charles Scribner's Sons 1905) 284.

[2] The UCP regime is also applicable to standby letters of credit. As these are functional equivalents to traditional guarantees operating upon an obligor's default, they are less directly concerned with international trade and are not considered further.

[3] Carl A Mead, 'Documentary Letters of Credit' (1922) 22 Columbia Law Review 297, 298.

[4] Rufus James Trimble, 'The Law Merchant and the Letter of Credit' (1948) 61 Harvard Law Review 981, 982 (hereafter Trimble, 'The Law Merchant').

[5] ibid 984, referring to 'Comment' (1926) 36 Yale LJ 245, 248–49.

from that period also exist.[6] Furthermore, there is evidence to suggest that Phoenician merchants used letters of credit when trading with Mediterranean cities and that banks in Ancient Greece prepared 'letters of credit on correspondents with a view to obviating the actual transport of *specie* in payment of accounts'.[7] Given the reception of many Ancient Greek concepts into Roman Law, it can be 'surmise[d] that Roman commerce required something in the nature of the letter of credit'.[8] Indeed, as Usher has stated, '[t]here was nothing in the formal rules of law to prevent a banker from recognizing a written order of payment as an appointment of the person named as agent of the principal for that specific act'.[9] Following the collapse of the Roman Empire and a period of degeneration in banking activity,[10] it was the rise of the Italian city-states, such as Genoa, Venice, and Florence in the twelfth and thirteenth centuries, together with the increasing levels of trade between European nations, that saw the genesis of modern instruments resembling the letter of credit.[11] Indeed, by the fourteenth century, letters of credit were used freely across continental Europe[12] and in England.[13] Whilst the legal concepts underlying letters of credit were received in a relatively straightforward manner in civil law jurisdictions,[14] the English common law had more difficulty reconciling the irrevocability and enforceability of letters of credit with traditional doctrines, such as consideration.[15] This issue was overcome in *Pillans v Van Mierop*,[16] in which Lord Mansfield pithily stated that 'a *nudum pactum* does not exist in the usage and law of merchants'. Whilst the English courts sought to row back from Lord Mansfield's view in later years,[17] letters of credit continued to be used during the eighteenth and ninteenth centuries and their legal validity has never since been explicitly doubted. Indeed, as Goode has stated, 'to this day there is no reported English case which directly holds that a letter of credit becomes binding on receipt despite the lack of consideration in the ordinary sense ... But there are dicta in several cases in which the courts have taken it for granted that letters of credit are enforceable undertakings and any argument to the contrary would be likely to receive short shrift at the hands of the judiciary'.[18] Indeed, the legal validity of letters of credit has only belatedly been acknowledged judicially in England.[19]

[6] William L Westermann and Casper J Kraemer, *Greek Papyri in the Library of Cornell University* (Columbia University Press 1926) 32; John Henry Wigmore, *A Panorama of the World's Legal Systems* (West Publishing Company 1928) 69.

[7] Trimble, 'The Law Merchant' (n 4) 984.

[8] ibid 985.

[9] Abbott P Usher, *The Early History of Deposit Banking in Mediterranean Europe* (Harvard University Press 1943) 11.

[10] ibid.

[11] Trimble, 'The Law Merchant' (n 4) 982.

[12] Bensa Enrico, *Francesco di Marco da Prato; Notizie e Documenti Sulla Mercatura Italiana Del Secolo* (Treves 1928) 386.

[13] Gerard Malynes, *The Ancient Law Merchant* (Adam Islip 1622) 76.

[14] Omer F Hershey, 'Letters of Credit' (1918) 32 Harvard Law Review 1.

[15] William Holdsworth, 'The Origins and Early History of Negotiable Instruments' (1916) 32 LQR 20, 28.

[16] (1765) 3 Burr 1664, 1669. See further Garard McMeel, '*Pillans v Van Mierop* (1765)' in Charles Mitchell and Paul Mitchell (eds), *Landmark Cases in the Law of Contract* (Hart Publishing 2008) 23.

[17] *Rann v Hughes* (1778) 4 Brown PC 27.

[18] Goode, 'Abstract Payment Undertakings' in P Cane and J Stapleton (eds), *Essays for Patrick Atiyah* (OUP 1991) 218–19. See further ch 2 (Booysen) in this volume.

[19] *Taurus Petroleum Ltd v State Oil Marketing Company of the Ministry of Oil, Republic of Iraq* [2018] AC 690 (SC) [25], [95], [100]. See also *Simic v New South Wales Land and Housing Corporation* [2016] HCA 47 [34]–[37] (hereafter *Simic v NSWLHC*).

The legal force given to letters of credit in *Pillans* is, however, only part of the narrative; there can be little doubt that letters of credit would not have had quite the same success story had it not been for the impetus given by the International Chamber of Commerce ('ICC'). The ICC was founded in the immediate aftermath of the First World War, when there was no global system of rules governing international trade or its financing. Given that many of the major state-based actors were focusing upon re-building their economies, it fell to a group of entrepreneurs, driven by the view that the private sector was best placed to establish universal business standards, to create an institution representing international trade and global business interests. Following its inception in 1919, the ICC quickly established its significance by inaugurating the International Court of Arbitration in Paris, which still functions as one of the pre-eminent centres for international commercial arbitration today. **1.03**

From its earliest days, the ICC recognised that the facilitation of international trade depended upon the availability and security of finance and credit. During the 1920s, banks in a number of European countries had adopted embryonic versions of the UCP, and by 1927 a consensus had started building around a set of principles and guidelines followed by banks in New York. It was this version that was subsequently adopted by the ICC in its Uniform Regulations for Commercial Documentary Credits in 1929, which sought to unify 'the commercial documentary credit regulations previously adopted and published by banking associations in various countries'.[20] This initial instrument was, however, replaced only four years later with the Uniform Customs and Practice for Commercial Documentary Credits in 1933.[21] There have subsequently been six revisions to the UCP regime since its adoption,[22] with the coverage and detail progressively increasing with each revision.[23] Both the original version of the UCP and its subsequent revisions represent the product of a concerted and coordinated effort on the part of bankers, traders, and lawyers (increasingly mediated nowadays through the ICC's various committees and sub-committees), albeit that the representation of bankers increasingly overshadows the other interested constituencies. **1.04**

In terms of its timeline, the UCP's greatest popularity was arguably during the period between the 1970s and the 1990s when the UCP 400 and 500 were in effect. As a letter of credit is a proxy for counterparty trust, it is unsurprising that the UCP saw its greatest success during periods of global economic and political instability, with oil crises in the 1970s, the Cold War in the 1980s, and the collapse of the Soviet Bloc in the 1990s[24] (indeed, there was a marked uptick in letter of credit use between 2009 and 2013 following the Global Financial Crisis,[25] and a similar phenomenon is predicted in the wake of the **1.05**

[20] International Chamber of Commerce ('ICC'), 'Uniform Regulations for Commercial Documentary Credits' (1929), Introduction.

[21] ICC, 'Uniform Customs and Practice for Commercial Documentary Credits' (1933), ICC Brochure No 82 of 1933.

[22] These revisions took place approximately every ten years in 1951 (UCP 151), 1962 (UCP 222), 1974 (UCP 290), 1983 (UCP 400), 1993 (UCP 500), and 2006 (UCP 600).

[23] Whilst the length of the UCP had been gradually increasing with each subsequent revision, the latest version is considerably shorter than its predecessor, as a result of leaving entirely to domestic law any matters related to the issuing bank-applicant relationship.

[24] Christopher Hare, 'Consolidation and Disintegration in Trade Finance' in Djakhongir Saidov, *Research Handbook on International and Comparative Sale of Goods Law* (Edward Elgar Publishing 2019) ch 16 (hereafter Hare, 'Consolidation and Disintegration').

[25] ICC, 'Rethinking Trade and Finance' (July 2017) (hereafter ICC, 'Rethinking Trade') 89, figures 40–41.

coronavirus pandemic).[26] Over that time, the UCP regime's achievements have been significant. Principally, it has led to a harmonisation in the banking practices and customs applicable to letter of credit operations and, such has been its level of acceptance, that it is unusual to find a letter of credit that is not subject to the UCP, a bank that does not operate according to its guidance, or a jurisdiction that is not prepared to give effect to its tenets. Indeed, as an exercise in international harmonisation, the UCP regime's reach and impact are largely unparalleled. That said, the UCP regime is not law and its drafting indicates that the UCP was never intended to have mandatory application or to have the force of law;[27] instead, the various UCP revisions have generally only applied to particular letters of credit to the extent that the relevant version of the UCP had been incorporated into the text of the instrument itself.[28] Whilst civilian jurisdictions have been more willing to treat the UCP (or at least its more fundamental principles) as having achieved a more normative status,[29] or as having developed into a set of 'rules'[30] taking effect as a 'universally accepted mercantile usage',[31] the notion that the UCP remains nothing more than an optional regime has certainly persisted in England[32] (despite the English courts occasionally applying the UCP to letters of credit without their incorporation).[33] Accordingly, the UCP regime establishes little more than a default set of contractual terms that can be incorporated by reference into the letter of credit, although those default provisions differ from ordinary contractual terms by virtue of the judicial approach to their interpretation,[34] implication,[35] and vitiation.[36]

1.06 The UCP's modest legal status, however, belies its success; it is an exemplar of the superiority of private ordering over mandatory regulation. That said, the ICC has provided more than just the framework of principles in the UCP, but has been instrumental in developing the accompanying apparatus to support the UCP's operation. There are four key elements. First, following the formation of the Society for Worldwide Interbank Financial

[26] ICC, 'Trade Register Report' (May 2020) 8, 16: 'The risk mitigating properties of documentary trade may grow in popularity (reversing the ongoing shift to open account trade), although this may be less pronounced than in previous crises as more attention has been placed on how to apply risk mitigation to SCF.'

[27] Peter Ellinger, 'Rejection of Documents Tendered under a Letter of Credit' [2013] LMCLQ 1, 4 (hereafter Ellinger, 'Rejection of Documents').

[28] See, for example, ICC, 'Uniform Customs and Practice for Documentary Credits' (ICC Publication No 500, 1993) (hereafter 'UCP 500') art 1, which only applied its terms to a letter of credit 'where they are incorporated into the text of the Credit'.

[29] Frans P De Rooy, *Documentary Credits* (Kluwer Law and Taxation Publishers 1994) 16, suggesting that certain principles (notably the autonomy doctrine) have risen above the essentially contractual status of the UCP regime. See also Ramandeep Chhina, 'Unconscionability as an Exception to the Autonomy Principle: How Well Is it Entrenched in Singaporean Jurisprudence?' [2016] LMCLQ 412.

[30] See ICC, 'Uniform Customs and Practice for Documentary Credits' (ICC Publication No 600, 2007) (hereafter 'UCP 600') art 1, referring to its principles as 'rules'.

[31] Peter Ellinger, 'The Uniform Customs and Practice for Documentary Credits (UCP): Their Development and the Current Revisions' [2007] LMCLQ 152, 172–73 (hereafter Ellinger, 'The UCP').

[32] *M Golodetz & Co Inc v Czarnikow-Rionda Co Inc* [1980] 1 WLR 495 (CA) 509, 517, 519. See also *Mitsui & Co Ltd v Beteiligungsgesellschaft LPG Tankerflotte MBH & Co KG* [2017] UKSC 68, [41]: '[The UCP depends] wholly on contractual incorporation for their binding force. But they are designed to create a body of principle applicable internationally in a uniform way . . .'.

[33] See, for example, *Siporex Trade SA v Comdel Commodities Ltd* [1986] 2 Lloyd's Rep 428 (QB).

[34] *Fortis Bank SA/NV v Indian Overseas Bank* [2010] 2 All ER (Comm) 28 (QB) [43] (hereafter *Fortis Bank v IOB* (QB)), aff'd on this issue: [2011] 2 All ER (Comm) 288 (CA) [72] (hereafter *Fortis Bank v IOB* (CA)).

[35] *Fortis Bank v IOB* (CA) (n 34) [55]. See also *Deutsche Bank AG, London v CIMB Bank Berhad* [2017] EWHC 1264 (Comm) [37].

[36] For example, the security features of the SWIFT messaging system largely preclude any assertion based upon the issuing bank's lack of authority to issue a letter of credit: see *Standard Bank London Ltd v The Bank of Tokyo Ltd* [1995] 2 Lloyd's Rep 169 (QB); *Industrial and Commercial Bank Ltd v Banco Ambrosiano Veneto SpA* [2003] 1 SLR(R) 221 (HC).

Telecommunication (SWIFT) in 1973, and the subsequent development of the SWIFT inter-bank messaging network from 1977, letters of credit could be *inter alia* issued, advised, amended, confirmed, and transferred on templates that sought to standardise the format, data, and layout of credits. Secondly, in the absence of any supra-national judicial authority over the UCP, the ICC's Banking Commission developed a mechanism for responding to individual queries from its banking members about the application of the UCP to letter of credit disputes facing them.[37] Whilst this jurisdiction was designed to provide guidance on the resolution of *particular* disputes, the ICC Commission on Banking Technique and Practice ('ICC Banking Commission') on several occasions chose to intervene in a more general way by drafting position papers when a perceived error in the UCP's interpretation had developed at national level,[38] or when it became apparent that divergent domestic banking practices had developed. Indeed, the ICC's dispute-resolution function has been cemented with the development of the 'Documentary Instruments Dispute Resolution Expertise' ('DOCDEX'), which is a non-binding system whereby appointed experts issue opinions on letter of credit disputes that are published by the ICC to produce a body of persuasive determinations on the proper application of the UCP.[39] By these various adjudicatory mechanisms, the ICC has been able to maintain and strengthen the consolidating effect of the UCP on international payments in the long period between the various revisions. Thirdly, in an effort to reduce discrepancies between banking centres in terms of the applicable standards for documentary compliance,[40] the ICC developed the 'International Standard Banking Practices' as a supplement to the UCP regime, thereby providing international banks with a common frame of reference for their document-checking role.[41] The latest version was published in 2013 as 'ISBP 745'. Fourthly, in anticipation of there being a mass migration towards the digitisation and electronic presentation of documents under letters of credit, the ICC introduced an electronic supplement to the UCP regime in the form of the 'e-UCP'.[42] Despite this failing to have the intended impact, as considered further below, the ICC has attempted to keep the UCP relevant by updating the electronic supplements regularly.[43] The institutional framework developed around the UCP regime has been as much a reason for its success, as the rules themselves.

Accordingly, it is clear that the twentieth century represented the letter of credit's heyday and it was this success that drove the drafting and adoption of the UCP's current version, **1.07**

[37] For an early example of the activities of the ICC Commission on Banking Technique and Practice ('ICC Banking Commission') in this regard, see, for example, G Collyer and R Katz (eds), *ICC Banking Commission Collection Opinions 1995–2001* (ICC Publication No 632E 2002).

[38] See, for example, ICC Banking Commission, 'Position Papers Nos 1–4 on UCP 500' (1 September 1994); ICC Banking Commission, 'When a Non-bank Issues a Letter of Credit' (30 October 2002) (hereafter ICC, 'Non-bank Issue').

[39] See, for example, ICC, *Collected DOCDEX Decisions 1997–2003* (ICC Publication No 665E, 2004).

[40] Ellinger, 'The UCP' (n 31) 159.

[41] ICC, *International Standard Banking Practice for the Examination of Documents under Documentary Credits* (ICC Publication No 645 2002). For subsequent revisions, see ICC, *International Standard Banking Practice for the Examination of Documents under Documentary Credits* (ICC Publication No 681 2007) (hereafter 'ISBP 681'); ICC, *International Standard Banking Practice for the Examination of Documents under UCP 600* (ICC Publication No 745E 2013) (hereafter 'ISBP 745'). For judicial use of the ISBP see, for example, *Credit Industriel et Commercial v China Merchants Bank* [2002] EWHC 973 (Comm) (hereafter *CIC v China Merchants Bank*).

[42] ICC, 'Supplement for UCP for Electronic Presentation, Version 1.0' (ICC Publication No 500/3, 2002).

[43] ICC, 'Supplement for UCP for Electronic Presentation, Version 1.1' (ICC Publication No 639, 2007); ICC, 'eUCP Version 2.0' (2019) (hereafter ICC, 'eUCP Version 2.0').

the UCP 600. The issue is whether the twenty-first century will treat the letter of credit as kindly.

III. The Present Context

1.08 In light of the UCP 500's roaring success in facilitating trade finance, a new revision was always going to prove a long and arduous process given the many disparate interests across the trade, carriage, banking, insurance, and logistics sectors that rely upon the UCP framework. Indeed, it took over three years for the UCP 600 to reach its final form following the work of the ICC's UCP Drafting Group, UCP Consulting Group, Commission on Banking Technique and Practice, and 130 National Committees worldwide.[44] The resulting document has a number of notable features. First, after a series of revisions that had increased the overall length and complexity of the UCP, the UCP 600 was notable for its overall reduction in length and the succinctness of its drafting. In part, the reduction in length resulted from a decision to exclude from the UCP's ambit issues relating to the relationship between the applicant and the issuing bank: given that these parties will almost invariably be located in the same jurisdiction, the form and nature of the applicant's instructions and the applicant's obligation to reimburse the issuing bank are properly the concern of the law applicable to the banker-customer relationship between those parties. Accordingly, the UCP 600's focus is upon the inter-bank relationship, the beneficiary's obligations with respect to presentation, and the banks' role in examining the documents. Similarly, the UCP 600 improved the position with respect to some common problems that had arisen under the UCP 500. These included reversing the decision of the English Court of Appeal in *Banco Santander SA v Banque Paribas*,[45] by deeming that the issuing bank has conferred authority upon a nominated bank to discount its deferred payment undertaking;[46] by allowing a document to be treated as the original if it bears an 'apparently' original signature,[47] 'appears' to be written under the issuer's hand,[48] or 'appears' to be on the issuer's original stationery;[49] and by attempting a clearer definition of 'negotiation' to mean 'the purchase by the nominated bank of drafts (drawn on a bank other than the nominated bank) and/or documents under a complying presentation, by advancing or agreeing to advance funds to the beneficiary on or before the banking day on which reimbursement is due to the nominated bank'.[50]

[44] For the true scale of the revision process, see ch 5 (Adodo) in this volume.

[45] [2000] All ER (D) 246 (CA) (hereafter *Banco Santander*).

[46] UCP 600, art 12(b). Whilst this provision reverses the narrow holding in *Banco Santander* (n 45), it does not deal with the situation where the issuing bank discounts a deferred paying undertaking or the impact vis-à-vis the beneficiary of the nominated bank's discounting.

[47] ibid art 17(b). Under UCP 500, art 20(b), there was significant judicial confusion surrounding what constituted an 'original' document when it was produced by 'reprographic, automated or computerized systems': see *Glencore International AG v Bank of China* [1996] 1 Lloyd's Rep 135 (CA); *Kredietbank Antwerp v Midland Bank plc* [1999] 1 All ER (Comm) 801 (CA). The ICC sought to remedy the confusion by issuing guidance: see ICC Banking Commission, 'The Determination of an "Original" Document in the Context of UCP 500 sub-Article 20(b)' (12 July 1999) (hereafter ICC, 'The Determination of an "Original"'). This appeared to have the desired effect: see *CIC v China Merchants Bank* (n 41).

[48] UCP 600, art 17(c)(i).

[49] ibid art 17(c)(ii).

[50] ibid art 2. For the difficulties under the UCP 500, see ICC Banking Commission, 'UCP 500 sub-Article 10(b)(ii): Negotiation', Position Paper No 2 on UCP 500 (1 September 1994) (hereafter ICC, 'Negotiation').

Despite these improvements, the UCP 600 faces the existential threat that, whilst documentary letters of credit still remain 'important to about 10% of global merchandise trade',[51] there is no doubt that the percentage of trade covered by a letter of credit has been dropping for some time and continues to do so.[52] That said, the data are not uniform: there are variations in the letter of credit's continued popularity depending upon the particular trade sector[53] and geographical region, with traditional trade finance mechanisms being far more prevalent in the Asia-Pacific region (in particular China, India, and Korea), much less popular in South America (especially Mexico), and Europe (led by Italy) falling somewhere between the two.[54] As well as economic factors playing their role, the letter of credit's use may depend upon geographical factors (such as the distance to major commercial centres or trading partners)[55] and upon the presence (or otherwise) of international banks in a particular jurisdiction.[56] Accordingly, there may be isolated instances where the volume of letters of credit continues to hold steady, or even increase, but the overall picture for the UCP 600 is an increasingly bleak one. A combination of four factors may explain the letter of credit's dimming star. **1.09**

A. Reliability

The first factor is that letters of credit are becoming increasingly unreliable payment instruments for sellers and accordingly the UCP regime is considered more and more as something that creates obstacles to payment in international trade, rather than facilitating it. Once a payment instrument loses the trust and confidence of the market that it is designed to serve, it is unsurprising when it goes into terminal decline. The source of the problem lies in the fact that, even at the UCP 600's advent, there were a high number of discrepancies in presented documents under letters of credit with the result that rejection rates were higher than might otherwise have been desirable from a payment instrument that supposedly guaranteed the seller payment.[57] So severe has the problem become that the presumption of payment under a letter of credit has been replaced with a counter-presumption that no payment will be forthcoming: a joke long doing the rounds is that 'UCP stands for "You Cannot Pay"'! Whilst the requirement of strict documentary compliance was originally intended to smooth the passage of the documents by making the banks' role essentially mechanical, this **1.10**

[51] ICC, 'Rethinking Trade' (n 25) 21.

[52] SWIFT messaging volumes associated with documentary credits dropped by 5% in volume in 2015 and a further 4.7% in 2016: see ICC, 'Trade Register Report' (February 2018) (hereafter ICC, 'Trade Register (2018)') 15.

[53] For example, there is evidence of parties in the oil trade using the 'irrevocable payment undertaking' as a mechanism to ensure payment directly to the supplier's bank: see *Totsa Total Oil Trading SA v Bharat Petroleum Corp Ltd* [2005] EWHC 1641; *Raiffeisen Zentralbank Österreich AG v China Marine Bunker (Petrochina) Co Ltd* [2006] EWHC 212 (Comm).

[54] Bank for International Settlements, 'Trade Finance: Developments and Issues' (January 2014) 9, 16 (hereafter BIS, 'Trade Finance'). This is a report submitted by a Study Group established by the Committee on the Global Financial System.

[55] Friederike Niepmann and Tim Schmidt-Eisenlohr, 'Banks in International Trade Finance: Evidence from the US' (Federal Reserve Bank of New York Staff Report No 633, 2013) (hereafter Niepmann and Schmidt-Eisenlohr, 'Banks').

[56] BIS, 'Trade Finance' (n 54) 11–12.

[57] Just before the UCP 600 was adopted, average rejection rates were between 52% and 56% for import and export letters of credit respectively: see Institute of International Banking Law and Practice, 'DC-PRO 2005 LC Market Intelligence Survey', in James Byrne and Christopher Byrnes (eds), *Annual Survey of Letter of Credit Law and Practice Handbook* (The Institute of International Banking Law & Practice 2006) 231.

has increasingly given banks a discretion (often acting upon their customer's instructions) whether or not to honour the presentation. Indeed, it would be an unusual set of documents that did not contain even the slightest error, no matter how minor.[58]

1.11 The UCP 600 aimed to address this problem, but its provisions dealing with the requirements of documentary presentation and examination were either overly complex (in the case of the carriage documents) or elliptical (in the case of the requirement that documents be examined in the light of 'international standard banking practice'). Whilst the ICC certainly sought to address the latter concern by subsequently developing guidance concerning 'international standard banking practice', so that document-checkers in different jurisdictions would adopt a consistent approach to the identification of discrepancies, 'the ICC's attempt to introduce uniformity as regards details of compliance—made in the International Standard Banking Practice (known as ISBP)—has not achieved its object'.[59] Accordingly, rejection levels have remained stubbornly elevated under the UCP 600 and the letter of credit's basic machinery appears slowly to be grinding to a halt.

B. Competition

1.12 The second factor is that, as a result of the falling levels of trust in the letter of credit and the high bank fees associated with letter of credit operations, legal Darwinism has allowed cheaper, quicker, and better-adapted competitor payment mechanisms to gain market share. The most obvious response was for traders to eschew banks altogether and it is accordingly no surprise that there has been an exponential growth in trading on 'open account' terms (when shipment is to occur before payment) or on 'cash-in-advance' or 'prepayment' terms (for the converse situation).[60] There has also been a renewal of interest in countertrade activities, which are simply not dependent upon banks,[61] and more specialised trade finance mechanisms that banks may not be best placed to deliver.[62] Before the Global Financial Crisis (GFC), there were indications that 'open account' trading accounted for up to 60% of global trade payments,[63] although some surveys put the figure even higher at 70%[64] or 80%.[65] While these figures appeared to dip during the GFC, they appear to represent the new normal.[66] Open account financing will be particularly attractive where the trade parties have dealt with each other successfully on previous occasions, already have an established and ongoing legal relationship, and/or for some other reason trust each other (whether as a result of the size or nature of the counterparty's enterprise or the type of jurisdiction in which it is based).[67] In some instances, commercial standby letters of credit or

58 *Moralice (London) Ltd v ED&F Man* [1954] 2 Lloyd's Rep 526 (QB).
59 Ellinger, 'Rejection of Documents' (n 27) 3.
60 See ch 14 (Hare) in this volume.
61 See ch 16 (Hare) in this volume.
62 For the growth in Islamic trade finance, see ch 15 (Ercanbrack) in this volume.
63 International Monetary Fund ('IMF') and Bankers Association for Finance and Trade ('BAFT'), 'IMF-BAFT Trade Finance Survey. A Survey Among Banks Assessing the Current Trade Finance Environment' (2009); IMF and BAFT, 'A Survey Among Banks Assessing the Current Trade Finance Environment. Trade Finance Services: Current Environment and Recommendations: Wave 3' (2010).
64 BIS, 'Trade Finance' (n 54) 9.
65 ICC, 'ICC Global Trade and Finance Survey' (2009).
66 ICC, 'Rethinking Trade' (n 25) 21.
67 Unsurprisingly, data reveal that the parties are more likely to resort to payment mechanisms that interpose a bank when involved in a newly formed trade relationship: see Niepmann and Schmidt-Eisenlohr, 'Banks' (n 55).

demand guarantees are used to mitigate the non-payment or non-performance risks under an open-account arrangement. Open-account or pre-payment trading is not, however, a panacea, as it leaves traders with the cash-flow problem of turning illiquid receivables into liquid funds. As letter of credit fees have dried up, banks have seized the opportunity to continue earning fees through 'Supply Chain Finance' or 'SCF', which seeks to provide working capital liquidity to traders by receivables financing, inventory financing, and extensions of credit.[68] Indeed, data suggest that banks view SCF as the area with the greatest potential for future growth, largely at the expense of traditional financing methods.[69]

This trend in 'do-it-yourself' trade finance may effectively render the UCP regime, and by association the ICC's trade finance role, otiose. Appreciating the risk of being sidelined from trade finance activity, the ICC fought a rearguard action by introducing the eUCP to allow presentation of electronic documents and inventing a complete alternative to letters of credit, namely the 'bank payment obligation' or 'BPO', which seeks to replace payment against documents with payment against electronic data. As the BPO has proved too expensive and sophisticated to have much impact, neither initiative has halted the steady march of open-account and SCF at the expense of the letter of credit. **1.13**

C. Technology

The third factor, linked to the increased competition from challenger payment mechanisms, is that the growth of technology has cast an increasingly strong light upon the fact that presentation of paper documents reduces transaction speed, whilst increasing the costs of compliance. As indicated above, the ICC has made two attempts to capture some of the electronic market. The first attempt was to introduce the eUCP,[70] which extended the ambit of the UCP regime to enable beneficiaries to present digitised documents in place of their paper counterparts. Despite the obvious attraction of this solution, the UCP regime has to date proved largely incapable of accommodating e-commerce within its paper-based philosophy. The principal reason for this failure is that there seems to be little point allowing for electronic presentation of documents until documents are routinely capable of digitisation, which has proved difficult due to fears of increased fraud and the need for bills of exchange and lading to be transferable.[71] Whilst there are increasingly legal[72] and technological frameworks[73] that might allow for the digitisation of bills of exchange,[74] bills of lading, and cargo insurance certificates,[75] these are still at a relatively early stage of their development. Indeed, even if these digital documents perform their intended function at all,[76] there is the risk that the general trend towards open-account, prepayment, and supply chain financing **1.14**

[68] ICC, 'Rethinking Trade' (n 25) 21.
[69] ICC, 'Trade Register (2018)' (n 52) 15.
[70] For the current version, see ICC, 'eUCP Version 2.0' (n 43).
[71] Ellinger, 'The UCP' (n 31) 158.
[72] See ch 11 (Davidson) in this volume.
[73] This may result from the re-purposing of existing technological solutions, rather than developing entirely new solutions: see ch 12 (Winn) in this volume.
[74] See ch 9 (Geva) in this volume.
[75] See ch 10 (Goldby) in this volume.
[76] For a sceptical view of the transformative nature of blockchain technology, see ch 12 (Winn) in this volume.

has gone past the point where traders are likely to return to paying the fees associated with letters of credit as a payment mechanism, even in a new digital form.

1.15 The second attempt was to introduce an entirely new form of payment mechanism, the BPO,[77] replacing the transfer of documents with the transmission of the data that they contain and replacing document-checking with the verification of the transmitted data against an electronic baseline. The BPO was introduced with much fanfare.[78] Unfortunately, the adoption of the BPO by banks 'has been lower than expected ... because it depends on acceptance of the instrument by a "critical mass" of banks',[79] which has not yet to date occurred. Accordingly, the BPO has been compared to being the first owner of a mobile phone; the technology works, but there is nobody to call.[80] The reasons for this slow adoption might be linked to early confusion about the treatment of BPOs for bank capital adequacy purposes and their pricing structure;[81] SWIFT's pricing model 'making it nigh-on impossible for peripheral banks to join BPO';[82] the high costs on the part of banks and traders in investing in new technology and infrastructure to support a new payment mechanism; and the fact that those banks that initially invested heavily into BPO subsequently abandoned the project when the uptake amongst other banks appeared 'sluggish',[83] and there was little chance of a return on investment. Whilst there has recently been an attempt to reinvigorate the BPO by a consortium of international banks, without broader adoption by banks and a greater realisation on the part of traders as to the potential benefits of the BPO, it is unclear how much more traction it is likely to gain in the future.

1.16 Given the simplicity, speed, and cost-effectiveness of open account trading, the fact that banks can now earn their fees through SCF and the availability of distributed ledger technology that does not rely upon a central registry or the ICC to provide the legal or technological framework, the letter of credit's demise is only likely to accelerate.

D. Language, Development, and Regulation

1.17 The final factor is that a number of issues persist with the way in which the UCP 600 operates. First, the language of the UCP 600 remains too technical, with a number of the terms and concepts dating back to the nineteenth century, in particular the continued reference to the use of 'drafts' and the language of negotiation. Accordingly, in order to understand

[77] See ch 13 (Mugasha) in this volume.

[78] SWIFT, Corporate and Supply Chain Team, 'Market adoption of BPO' (August 2015) <https://www.tradefinance.training/library/files/BPO%20Market%20Adoption%20Aug2015.pdf> accessed 15 August 2020.

[79] Commerzbank, 'The Bank Payment Obligation: Leading the Path of Digital Evolution' (2018) Introduction <https://www.tradefinanceglobal.com/wp-content/uploads/2019/02/WhitepaperBPO.pdf> accessed 22 February 2021. See also Commerzbank, 'Bank Payment Obligation Can Act as a Gateway for Further Trade Finance Technologies, Says New Commerzbank Whitepaper', Press Release (31 January 2019) <https://www.commerzbank.com/en/hauptnavigation/presse/pressemitteilungen/archiv1/2019/quartal_19_01/presse_archiv_detail_19_01_78730.html> 22 February 2021.

[80] Eleanor Wragg, 'Why some banks still back BPO' *Global Trade Review* (London, 25 February 2019) (hereafter Wragg, 'Bank Payment Obligation') <https://www.gtreview.com/news/fintech/why-some-banks-still-back-bpo/> 22 February 2021.

[81] See 'BPO pricing crucial to its success' *Global Trade Review* (London, 5 December 2012) <https://staging.gtreview.com/news/global/bpo-pricing-crucial-for-its-success/> 22 February 2021.

[82] Wragg, 'Bank Payment Obligation' (n 80).

[83] ibid.

the concepts, structure, and operation of the UCP regime, it is often necessary to delve into its history to uncover the issues that the language was seeking to address, rather than being able to deal with the UCP 600 on its own terms. For example, without understanding the law of bills of exchange, it is difficult for banks or traders to operate the acceptance or negotiation mechanisms successfully. Moreover, the UCP 600 often employs legal language to describe issues that are essentially a matter of banking practice, rather than banking law; the language accordingly lacks the precision of an international legal text or domestic legislation, leaving too much scope for reasonable disagreement as to its true meaning.

Secondly, in such cases of ambiguity in the UCP's text, the UCP regime appears to be interpreted and operated in an unnecessarily pro-bank manner. In *Fortis Bank SA/NV v Indian Overseas Bank*,[84] Hamblen J stated that the UCP 600 requires a 'purposive approach to construction' and indicated that this approach should 'reflect "the best practice and reasonable expectations of market practitioners"'. Similarly, on appeal in *Fortis Bank*,[85] Thomas LJ indicated that '[c]ourts must therefore interpret [the UCP 600] in accordance with its underlying aims and purposes reflecting international practice and the expectations of international bankers and international traders so that it underpins the operation of letters of credit in international trade'. This view has subsequently been endorsed by the Singapore Court of Appeal.[86] Whilst these statements appear innocuous enough on their face, the suggestion that ambiguities in a document drafted by bankers should be interpreted in their favour does seem odd. Not only is it inconsistent with the basic *contra proferentem* approach to interpretation adopted in other contexts, but an interpretation of the UCP 600 that prefers banks' interests, rather than prioritising those of beneficiaries, risks undermining the attractiveness of letters of credit to traders generally. Certainly, there should be limits to the extent that banks can rely upon their own practices to cure their own drafting infelicities.[87] **1.18**

Thirdly, the mechanisms for amending or supplementing the terms of the UCP 600 are cumbersome. As stated above, a full revision of the UCP regime is a lengthy process requiring 'not only a minimum 3-year commitment, but also a regular meeting schedule between Working Group participants. An effective Working Group will require 6–8 participants available for frequent meetings, travel, phone conferences and independent work outside the meetings and calls.'[88] Other techniques fare no better. Whilst it is possible for the ICC Banking Commission to issue opinions on controversial matters, there are only two meetings per annum; the drafting of the opinion tends to be dominated by those at the top of its hierarchical structure; no opinion will be issued if there is no consensus as to the appropriate response; and there is a self-denying ordinance when the request for an opinion concerns the terms of a particular letter of credit, rather than the operation of a particular provision of the UCP 600. Even when such opinions are issued, their impact upon national courts is variable, with some opinions being followed wholesale at a domestic level[89] and **1.19**

84 *Fortis Bank v IOB* (QB) (n 34) [43].
85 ibid [72].
86 *Grains and Industrial Products Trading Pte Ltd v Bank of India* [2016] 3 SLR 1308 (CA) [84]–[91].
87 *Turner v Royal Bank of Scotland* [2000] BPIR 683 (CA).
88 ICC Banking Commission, 'Recommendation of the ICC Banking Commission Executive Committee in Respect of a Revision of UCP 600' (October 2016) 2 (hereafter ICC, 'Revision').
89 See, for example, *CIC v China Merchants Bank* (n 41), applying ICC, 'The Determination of an "Original"' (n 47).

others being almost totally ignored.[90] Even the ICC's guidance on 'international standard banking practice' is problematic,[91] as there is no allusion to that guidance's existence in the UCP 600 itself, so that an ingénue may be totally unaware of its existence. Worse still, there are instances when the UCP 600 and the ISBP actually conflict. For example, Article 14(d) of the UCP 600 makes clear that '[d]ata in a document … must not conflict with … any other stipulated document or the credit',[92] but the ISBP provides that '[w]hen the amount in words and figures are in conflict, the amount in words is to be examined as the amount demanded'.[93] Similarly, Adodo has highlighted another example of such a conflict:[94] the UCP 600 requires that a bill of lading be signed by the carrier or its agent,[95] whilst the previous version of the ISBP indicated that '[w]here copies [of a transport document] are presented, they need not evidence signatures, dates, etc'.[96] Nor is it clear that this position has been remedied under the more recent ISBP 745.[97] Accordingly, the manner in which the UCP regime develops is at best not particularly clear, and at worst is a recipe for confusion.

1.20 Fourthly, the regulatory environment in which banks operate nowadays has altered radically, even when compared with the situation that pertained at the UCP 600's introduction. There are three particular sources of regulatory difficulty for banks. The first problem is that there has been some confusion as to how letters of credit should be treated for a bank's capital adequacy purposes: the more costly an instrument in capital terms, the less likely that banks are likely to become involved in that type of transaction.[98] Whilst the Basel Banking Committee has recently indicated that it would adopt from 2018 a more favourable approach to trade-finance instruments for the purposes of regulatory capital,[99] this may have all come a little too late: as a result of the uncertainty, traditional banks have abandoned letters of credit and investment banks, insurance companies, pension funds, export credit agencies, and other shadow banks (which are not directly affected by the capital adequacy, liquidity, and leverage ratios) are filling the void left behind.[100] This is not promising for the UCP regime, which only governs bank-issued letters of credit.[101] The second problem concerns the impact upon the letter of credit of sanctions imposed by the United Nations, the EU Council, or individual countries to achieve political and economic ends.[102] To avoid the criminal penalties resulting from violating such sanctions, banks issuing and confirming letters of credit may no longer just deal with the documents alone (as stated in the UCP

[90] See, for example, *CIC v China Merchants Bank* (n 41); *Korea Exchange Bank v Standard Chartered Bank* [2006] 1 SLR(R) 565 (HC), ignoring ICC Banking Commission, 'Position Paper No 3: UCP 500 sub-Article 13(c) on Non-documentary Conditions' (1 September 1994).
[91] For the current version, see ISBP 745 (n 41).
[92] UCP 600, art 14(d).
[93] ISBP 745 (n 41) [B14].
[94] See ch 5 (Adodo) in this volume.
[95] UCP 600, art 20(a).
[96] ISBP 681 (n 41) [20].
[97] ISBP 745 (n 41) [A31].
[98] For a discussion of the changing approach to trade-finance instruments for the purposes of bank regulatory capital, see Hare, 'Consolidation and Disintegration' (n 24).
[99] Marc Auboin and Isabella Blengini, 'The Impact of Basel II on Trade Finance: The Potential Unintended Consequences of the Leverage Ratio', CESIFO Working Paper No 4953, 7. See also Basel Committee on Banking Supervision, *Basel III: Finalising Post-crisis Reforms* (December 2017) Annex: Leverage Ratio [13].
[100] Duygu Tavan, 'Basel III Reshapes Trade Finance' *The Banker* (London, 1 March 2013) <https://www.thebanker.com/Transactions-Technology/Trading/Basel-III-reshapes-trade-finance?ct=true> 22 February 2021.
[101] See ICC, 'Non-bank Issue' (n 38).
[102] See Hare, 'Consolidation and Disintegration' (n 24).

600),[103] ignoring all other matters. Instead, banks must nowadays inform themselves about the details of the underlying sales transactions, including the ultimate destination of the underlying goods or the funds to be disbursed under the credit, in order to decide whether or not a complying presentation should be honoured.[104] Indeed, the ICC has expressed concerns that clauses inserted into a letter of credit to protect banks from the consequences of violating sanctions might undermine the irrevocable nature of the credit, in particular when the clause either purports to confer a discretion upon the issuing or confirming bank as to whether or not to honour its commitment in light of relevant sanctions regimes[105] or allows such banks to decline payment by reference to their 'internal sanctions-related policy'.[106] The third problem concerns banks' obligations to comply with anti-money laundering and terrorist financing legislation.[107] As well as conducting the usual 'know your customer' checks required for all forms of trade finance in relation to an instructing party,[108] the issuing and confirming banks are required to look out for certain 'red flags' relating to the underlying transaction that might indicate the existence of trade-based money laundering.[109] Given that banks must nowadays carry out checks into the underlying sale transaction, the letter of credit's foundational autonomy principle[110] effectively becomes a mirage.

IV. Towards UCP 900?

The quote at the outset from Santayana's philosophical writings is particularly apt when considering the future of the UCP regime, given that there have been a number of successes and failures during its evolution. Learning the lessons from those previous experiences holds the key to producing a successful new UCP revision. That moment may, however, be some time away. On 6 October 2016, the ICC Banking Commission issued an initial communication setting out its position that 'there is insufficient justification for the significant time and cost of a revision [to the UCP 600]'.[111] In that regard, the ICC Banking Commission made clear that a revision would only be possible when it had been 'clearly demonstrated that the existing UCP is no longer benefitting the trade finance community'.[112] Whilst the Commission indicated that '50% of the problems [with letters of credit] apply to the presented documents', particularly the transport documents, it saw the solution to this problem in 'a greater understanding of ISBP 745'.[113] As regards the other 50% of problems, the Commission considered it difficult 'to see how a revision of UCP would 1.21

[103] UCP 600, art 5.
[104] Consider BAFT, 'Guiding Principles for Sanctions Issues Related to Shipping and Financial Products' (February 2017).
[105] ICC, 'Guidance paper on the Use of Sanctions Clauses in Trade Finance-Related Instruments Subject to ICC Rules' (Document No 470/1238, 2014) [2.4], [3.1(c)], [4.1]–[4.2].
[106] ibid [2.5], [3.1(b)], [4.1]–[4.2].
[107] See generally Financial Action Task Force, 'International Standards on Combating Money Laundering and the Financing of Terrorism and Proliferation' (October 2003).
[108] See The Wolfsberg Group, International Chamber of Commerce and the Bankers Association for Finance and Trade, 'Trade Finance Principles' (2017) [1.5], Appendix IV.
[109] BAFT, 'Guidance for Identifying Potentially Suspicious Activity in Letters of Credit and Documentary Collections' (March 2015).
[110] UCP 600, art 4.
[111] ICC, 'Revision' (n 88) 3.
[112] ibid 1.
[113] ibid 2.

make much of a material difference'.[114] Despite its initially negative assessment, the ICC Banking Commission invited ICC national committees to indicate whether they disagreed with that view and, if so, to send 'a detailed business case and rationale that supports consideration of a revision'.[115] In this regard, two meetings were held with ICC national committee representatives in Rome on 8 November 2016 and Paris on 23 November 2016. Despite some counterviews, those meetings generally indicated support for the ICC Banking Commission's initial position. Accordingly, the ICC Banking Commission confirmed its initial view in a communiqué on 19 December 2016 and again at the Banking Commission Annual Meeting in Jakarta on 6 April 2017. This process concluded with a formal decision issued by the ICC Banking Commission on 15 June 2017, which stated:

> The overwhelming response revealed that a revision of UCP 600 was not required. The prime objective of a revision is to address developments in the banking, transport and insurance industries. Significant feedback evidenced that *any problems lay not with the rules themselves, but with the application, i.e. practice* ('international standard banking practice') of the rules. An analysis of the revision explanatory notes (which covered over 70 issues including comments received from National Committees) did not provide a compelling enough rational, nor sufficient support, to justify a revision of UCP 600 at this stage.

1.22 Whilst it is clear from this decision that a new UCP is not at present imminent, the concluding three words suggest that the ICC Banking Commission has not entirely ruled out a new revision at some point in the future. If such a revision were ever promulgated, it is unlikely to follow the current sequence of UCP 400, UCP 500, and UCP 600 by being termed the UCP 700; the ICC's publications have already passed this number (such as the ISBP 745), so that any revision is likely to be termed the 'UCP 900' or later. This in itself may be a point of confusion for the trade finance industry. Putting that issue aside, the possibility of UCP 900 raises two issues: namely should there be a revision (the procedural question) and, if so, what should it look like (the substantive question).

A. The Procedural Question

1.23 As regards the procedural question, the question posed by the ICC is whether there is a 'business case' for a further revision. On the cost side, most letters of credit are issued, advised and amended on SWIFT formats, which will be difficult, time-consuming, and expensive to change. Furthermore, the ICC has envisaged a lengthy and costly process to produce any new revision.[116] Moreover, it will not only be the ICC and SWIFT involved in expense, but banks, traders, and all those involved in letter of credit transactions will also have to change their operations to respond to any further UCP revision. Accordingly, the collective costs are high.

1.24 The better view is that these costs are unlikely to justify the limited benefits of any revision. For example, the transport provisions of the UCP 400 were revised in the UCP 500 and 600 in order to make their presentation and examination under letters of credit more efficient

[114] ibid.
[115] ibid 3.
[116] ibid 2.

and straightforward. Unfortunately, as indicated above, there has been no real change in the number of discrepancies related to the transport documents under letters of credit. This is unsurprising given that the position under the UCP 400 was more straightforward: if a bank was unable to determine the precise nature of the transport document presented under a letter of credit, the UCP 400 nevertheless contained minimum criteria that a bank could apply to determine whether or not to accept the document as compliant.[117] This commonsense position was altered under the UCP 600, with banks needing now to determine whether the transport document qualifies as an ocean bill of lading, a charterparty bill of lading, or some other type of document. As there was no residual category of transport document in the UCP 500 or 600, a bank that was unable to classify the particular transport document was left with little option but to reject the whole presentation. There was little principled basis or justification for altering the UCP 400 in this regard and the minimal (if any) practical benefits of the alteration did not justify the costs associated with revising the UCP regime. This is not a solitary example.

Ultimately, if there is no sound business case for revising the UCP 600, then there may be **1.25** a more cost-effective way of achieving the functionally equivalent result to a full revision, namely by developing standard-form documentation for letters of credit and the documents to be presented thereunder. Whilst a degree of standardisation has already been achieved for the letter of credit itself through the development of SWIFT formats, this is less true of letter of credit documentation. Such standard-form documents have already been developed under the equivalent rules for standby letters of credit, namely the International Standby Practices 1998 ('ISP98'),[118] and there is no reason why greater standardisation might not be attempted in the letter of credit context. Moreover, such an approach could lead to the development of a simplified form of letter of credit, which requires the beneficiary to provide the nominated bank with a single document containing all the data relevant to the underlying sale and a certification or undertaking from the beneficiary that the goods have been shipped and the relevant documents sent directly to the issuing bank. Provided the certificate contains all the information required from the beneficiary, the nominated bank can pay safely and seek reimbursement from the issuing bank. In effect, the letter of credit would operate as a paper-based BPO and, if electronic presentation of such a document were permitted, the letter of credit would be indistinguishable from the BPO. Indeed, by amalgamating the letter of credit and BPO, this may pave the way for saving both by making the new hybrid instrument more attractive to beneficiaries. That said, there is no escaping the fact that, by allowing the beneficiary to present a simple pro forma certificate (in a manner similar to on-demand undertakings), the risks associated with letters of credits for issuing banks would increase. Whilst an issuing bank would always be entitled to recover the funds from the beneficiary on restitutionary or tortious grounds should the beneficiary's certificate prove false (because, for example, the documents were never forwarded to the issuing bank), if beneficiaries are unwilling to pay the higher fees associated with riskier products and banks are unwilling to issue riskier letters of credit for capital adequacy reasons, then this proposal may ultimately struggle to gain traction. The longer term

[117] International Chamber of Commerce, 'Uniform Customs and Practice for Documentary Credits' (ICC Publication No 400, 1983) (hereafter 'UCP 400') art 25.

[118] International Chamber of Commerce, 'International Standby Practices' (ICC Publication No 590, 1998) (hereafter ICC, 'ISP 98').

costs for banks may, however, be far greater if the letter of credit as an institution ultimately founders.

B. The Substantive Question

1.26 As regards the substantive question, assuming that the ICC chose to develop the UCP 900, a revision would be timely, as there are a number of changes that the UCP 600 requires. First, to avoid the future risk of inconsistency, the guidelines on what counts as 'international standard banking practice' for document-checkers should be merged into the text of the UCP 900. This would strengthen the role played by 'international standard banking practice'; would clarify that practice and make it more accessible to non-bankers; and permit the UCP 900 to focus on letter of credit *practice*, rather than letter of credit *law*, as the latter is properly the domain of judicial and arbitral bodies.

1.27 Secondly, the requirement in UCP 600 that the presented documents must 'not conflict with' should be clarified, so that banks and other parties understand the relevant standard of documentary compliance that they have to meet. In this regard, the UCP 600 appears to establish a higher standard before documents can be rejected than existed under the equivalent UCP 500 provision, which required that the documents not 'appear on their face to be inconsistent with one another';[119] yet the number of discrepancies and rejections has not been dramatically affected by that change. As indicated above, this problem is exacerbated by the ISBP 745 being drafted in inconsistent terms. This confusion is part of a larger debate concerning the appropriate standard for documentary compliance and whether banks and courts should insist upon strict compliance,[120] commonsense compliance,[121] or some other more liberal standard. Without resolution of this fundamental issue, rejection rates under UCP 900 are unlikely to fall.

1.28 Thirdly, the UCP 600's provisions on transport documents are simply too complicated and represent the primary reason for the continued high rejection rates.[122] For example, the UCP 600 places significant emphasis on the on-board notation appearing on ocean bills of lading in determining the document's date of issue;[123] yet the ISBP 745 highlights the complexity of the issue and raises the question of whether a bill of lading issued on the same date as the onboard notation, but without an issue date, may nevertheless be treated as non-compliant under the UCP 600. Similarly, whilst the buyer will undoubtedly need to clear the goods through customs, so that timely arrival of the documents will be commercially necessary in order to avoid charges, the ICC Banking Commission has never explained the justification behind the requirement that the original transport document be presented

[119] Charles Debattista, 'The New UCP 600—Changes to the Tender of the Seller's Shipping Documents under Letters of Credit' [2007] JBL 329.

[120] *Equitable Trust Co of New York v Dawson Partners Ltd* (1927) 27 Lloyd's Law Rep 49. See Uniform Commercial Code, s 5–108(a).

[121] *Hing Hip Hing Fat Co Ltd v Daiwa Bank Ltd* [1991] 2 HKLR 35 (SC); *United Bank Ltd v Banque Nationale de Paris* [1991] 2 SLR(R) 60 (HC); *Seaconsar Far East Ltd v Bank Markazi Jomhouri Islami Iran* [1993] 1 Lloyd's Rep 236 (CA); *Bulgrains & Co Ltd v Shinhan Bank* [2013] EWHC 2498; *Simic v NSWLHC* (n 19) [99]. See also Peter Ellinger, 'New Problems of Strict Compliance in Letters of Credit' [1988] JBL 320.

[122] Anna Mari Antoniou, 'New Rules for Letters of Credit: Time to Update the UCP 600' (2017) 32 Journal of International Banking Law & Regulation 128 (hereafter Antoniou, 'New Rules').

[123] UCP 600, art 20(a)(ii).

within twenty-one calendar days of shipment[124] given modern, efficient forms of communication; yet this unnecessary twenty-one-day requirement remains a trap for the unwary, especially as this time frame could be further curtailed by the credit's expiration.[125] A more straightforward solution would simply be to let the parties to the sale transaction negotiate their own time frames (whether seven or fourteen days) without the UCP regime having to become involved at all. In light of these and other issues, the transport provisions in the UCP 600 would require drastic simplification in any new revision. The UCP 900 should, like the UCP 400,[126] contain a common set of core requirements relating to transport that must be set out by the beneficiary in a pro forma document to qualify as a valid presentation to a nominated bank, whilst the transport document itself is sent directly to the issuing bank. Those criteria might include the need for a signature, the dates of the relevant carriage, the points between which carriage is to occur, and the identity of the carrier and vessel. Such transport neutrality would obviate the need for the nominated bank to distinguish between different types of transportation, each with their own unique requirements. Potentially the rate of discrepancies would fall if the bank only needed to check the pro forma document's contents. Whilst this would have the downside for the nominated bank of not having any security over the underlying goods, it is unclear how significant this loss would be in practice when it has a right of reimbursement against a well-capitalised bank. The issuing bank's rights as pledgee need not be impacted, however, if the documents are sent straight to that bank.

Fourthly, the possibility of presenting a draft or bill of exchange under a letter of credit has been a source of some confusion, since it is not a document that the applicant relies upon for completion of the sale contract, but instead simply represents part of the process whereby the bank's obligations can be placed in a form that facilitates transfer to third parties. If the letter of credit does not stipulate for a draft, the UCP 600 requires the bank to ignore the document.[127] The applicant should, therefore, follow suit. The reality is that applicants frequently invoke discrepancies in the draft, or are asked to waive such discrepancies, despite the document's obvious lack of utility to the applicant; and banks frequently reject presentations on the basis that the draft has not been properly indorsed. Conversely, even where a letter of credit does require the presentation of a draft, the English courts have been prepared to read down that stipulation on the basis that the draft simply concerns the means by which the bank performs its undertaking.[128] Accordingly, to resolve this difficulty, the UCP 900 should reduce the four types of letter of credit under the UCP 600, namely letters of credit 'available by sight, deferred payment, acceptance or negotiation',[129] to just two: payment by sight of conforming documents or payment on a deferred basis. This would reduce the complexity of the UCP 900 by breaking the historical link between letters of credit and bills of exchange. Indeed, given that drafts may attract stamp duty and that domestic laws regulating bills of exchange are perceived as complex,[130] the number of letters of credit **1.29**

[124] ibid art 14(c).
[125] ibid.
[126] UCP 400, art 25.
[127] UCP 600, art 14(g).
[128] *CIC v China Merchants Bank* (n 41).
[129] UCP 600, art 6(b).
[130] Complexity arises from determining the relevant legal system whose bills of exchange legislation will be applicable to the particular dispute (see, for example, UK Bills of Exchange Act 1882, s 72); the fact that many jurisdictions still require the physical presentation of bills of exchange for acceptance or insist upon subordinate

involving drafts has already seriously declined. Whilst drafts can admittedly still perform an important function for the seller/beneficiary in managing its cash flow, the availability of other SCF techniques (as well as the possibility of a transferable letter of credit) means that the beneficiary would not be left without options if drafts were to disappear from the letter of credit landscape.

1.30 Fifthly, there has been almost perpetual confusion over the concept of 'negotiation'. Such was the issue under the UCP 500 that the ICC issued a separate position paper on the point, since 'a number of banks fail to understand the meaning of the term "negotiation" in connection with the availability of a documentary credit'.[131] Despite this being a major aspect of the UCP 600's revision, the position has improved little given that negotiability is a concept steeped in the history of the bill of exchange. If, as suggested above, the UCP 900 reduced the types of credit available (to sight and deferred payment credits only), the concept of 'negotiation' could be excised from the UCP's text altogether.

1.31 Sixthly, letters of credit often stipulate for the presentation of documents bearing the number associated with the letter of credit, as well as the original letter of credit itself, yet neither the UCP 600 nor the ISBP 745 contains any provision dealing with such stipulations. Nevertheless, the failure to comply with such requirements has been a source of many alleged discrepancies, despite the fact that this requirement is generally for the purpose of the bank's own internal housekeeping. As such a stipulation has little to do with the credit's operation, it should be abandoned as a basis for rejecting presented documents.

1.32 Seventhly, the UCP 600 contains a *force majeure* clause that is likely to be given legal effect by national courts.[132] The significance of such a provision is self-evident during a global pandemic that has shut down supply chains.[133] Such a clause is, however, hardly likely to inspire confidence in the letter of credit as an institution, given that the provision covers a wide variety of potentially frustrating events, including 'any other cases beyond [the bank's] control', and potentially terminates entirely (rather than simply suspends) the banks' obligations to pay if the credit expires whilst the frustrating event is still extant. Such a provision should be removed entirely, with the matter being left to the relevant contract's applicable law, or significantly softened to become more beneficiary-friendly. Indeed, given the absence of any choice of law rule in the UCP 600 (and the fact that letters of credit rarely contain a choice of law), it is odd that the UCP seeks to deal with such an overtly legal issue when the impact of frustration or *force majeure* on the banks' undertakings will depend so heavily on the approach taken by the particular applicable law. If the *force majeure* provision is to be retained, it should at least be redrafted to deal with the problem of sanctions, which was considered above.

legislation before electronic presentation is permitted (see, for example, UK Bills of Exchange Act 1882, ss 89A–F); and the fact that a bill of exchange may be invalidated by formal defects (as in China).

131 ICC, 'Negotiation' (n 50).

132 UCP 600, art 36.

133 OECD, *Covid-19 and International Trade: Issues and Actions* (12 June 2020) <http://www.oecd.org/coronavirus/policy-responses/covid-19-and-international-trade-issues-and-actions-494da2fa/> 22 February 2021. See also ICC, *Trade Financing and Covid-19* (May 2020).

Eighthly, the inter-relationship between a letter of credit's transfer and its assignment is a source of confusion. In particular, the UCP 600 makes clear that an assignment of proceeds is permissible (provided that it is valid by reference to its applicable law), but that 'the assignment of the right to perform under the credit' is not.[134] Not only is it often difficult, as a matter of interpretation, to determine whether a particular assignment concerns the right to performance or the fruits of performance, but the validity of non-assignment clauses in domestic law is fraught with difficulty.[135] Accordingly, it would be preferable if the UCP 900 dealt solely with the procedures for transferable credits, omitting issues relating to assignment altogether. Indeed, as with the case of *force majeure*, it is surprising that the UCP attempts to deal with such questions at all, given that an assignment's validity will depend so heavily on the relevant applicable law. **1.33**

Ninthly, rather than electronic presentation being covered by a distinct set of principles as a mere adjunct to the UCP 600,[136] such issues should be placed up-front and centre in the text of the UCP 900 itself. Whilst this change may appear cosmetic, when compared to what currently exists under the UCP 600 and e-UCP, it would send the strong message that the ICC is serious about adapting the UCP regime to e-commerce. **1.34**

Finally, when drafting the UCP 900 greater thought should be given to whether the text should continue to govern default payment undertakings, such as standby letters of credit, given that there are separate principles and rules available for such instruments.[137] Once standby credits are removed from the UCP regime's scope, the UCP 900 would have to address more explicitly the inter-relationship with other international instruments (such as ISP98) and domestic legislation (notably Article 5 of the Uniform Commercial Code). **1.35**

V. Conclusion

The UCP regime has clearly been successful, but its time may be over. Whilst there can be no doubt that there are significant defects in the UCP 600, it is difficult to justify a full-blown revision either in terms of the time and costs that would be involved or in terms of the benefits that would accrue: the documentary letter of credit is being eclipsed by more nimble competitors, is difficult to justify in an electronic world, and is nowadays operating in a more hostile legal, regulatory and commercial environment. If the letter of credit is to have a future, alternatives to revising the UCP 600 may need to be considered. Better education about the letter of credit's merits and wider access to letter of credit resources might be a starting point. **1.36**

134 UCP 600, art 39.
135 Gregory Tolhurst and John Carter, 'Prohibitions on Assignment: A Choice to be Made' (2014) 73 CLJ 405.
136 ICC, 'eUCP Version 2.0' (n 43).
137 ICC, 'ISP 98' (n 118). See also Antoniou, 'New Rules' (n 122).

2

The Letter of Credit as a Contract

*Sandra Booysen**

I. Introduction

2.01 Commercial letters of credit have been used for nearly 200 years to finance international trade transactions.[1] They solve the common problem facing a buyer and seller of goods when neither wishes to perform first, whether by making payment or shipping the goods. The letter of credit evolved to resolve this impasse by introducing a reliable middleman into the equation. The middleman, typically a bank,[2] undertakes to pay the seller on the production of specified documents that evidence, at a minimum, that the goods have been shipped, how much is owed and that the goods correspond with their description. These documents will commonly be a bill of lading, the seller's invoice, and a certificate of quality and/or quantity issued by an expert appointed by the buyer. The arrangement assures the seller of being paid for the goods once they have been shipped, and gives the buyer some assurance that it will receive the goods contracted for. Such, at least, is the theory although in practice the mechanism may not always operate so smoothly.[3] In addition to functioning as a payment mechanism, the letter of credit also serves a financing function by enabling a buyer to purchase the goods with the support of the bank that issues the credit. The funding is often secured by the bank having the right to possession of the letter of credit documentation, which will include a document of title to the goods. The credit may also serve a financing function for the seller who may be able to realise payment in advance of the maturity of the credit by negotiating it.[4]

2.02 Letter of credit transactions are commonly, but not necessarily, governed by the Uniform Customs and Practice for Documentary Credits ('UCP'), a model law produced by the International Chamber of Commerce ('ICC').[5] An alternative framework to the UCP is Article 5 of the Uniform Commercial Code ('UCC') of the United States.[6] China has also

* I am grateful to Dora Neo for her editing suggestions and for the comments received from Barry Crown, Peter Ellinger, Deborah Horowitz, Helena Whalen-Bridge, and the participants in the Trade Finance Symposium hosted by the Centre for Banking and Finance Law at the National University of Singapore, 8–9 March 2018.

[1] See, for example A G Guest (gen ed), *Benjamin's Sale of Goods* (7th edn, Sweet & Maxwell 2006) para 23-001; F R Sanborn, *Origins of the Early English Maritime and Commercial Law* (The Century Company 1930) 347.

[2] The UCP 600 envisages the issuer to be a bank, see art 7, but the ICC Banking Commission Opinion TA 537 indicated that it is not a violation of the UCP to have a non-bank issuer, see Gary Collyer, *Commentary on UCP 600* (International Chamber of Commerce 2007) 21 (hereafter *ICC Commentary on UCP 600*).

[3] For example, the obligation of the bank to pay on compliant documents can be manipulated through misuse of the doctrine of strict compliance, discussed in ch 5 (Adodo) in this volume.

[4] See, for example, *Ng Chee Chong, Ng Weng Chong, Ng Cheng and Ng Yew (a firm trading as Maran Road Saw Mill) v Austin Taylor & Co Ltd* [1975] 1 Lloyd's Rep 156 (QB) 157.

[5] For a discussion of the history of the UCP, see E P Ellinger, 'The Uniform Customs—their Nature and the 1983 Revision' [1984] LMCLQ 578; and E P Ellinger, 'The UCP-500: Considering a New Revision' [2004] LMCLQ 30.

[6] For further discussion, see James E Byrne, 'Contracting Out of Revised UCC Article 5 (Letters of Credit)' (2006) 40 Loyola of Los Angeles Law Review 297.

produced provisions relating to letters of credit.[7] This chapter is written from the perspective of a letter of credit that is governed by the UCP. The UCP was first promulgated in 1933 and is currently in its sixth revision—the UCP 600. The UCP is a set of standard terms that is incorporated into the letter of credit, preferably expressly,[8] but potentially also on the basis of a previous course of dealing. The UCP's goal was to facilitate international commerce by promoting uniformity in letters of credit which are used by persons in various jurisdictions with diverse legal systems.

A buyer of goods is typically obliged by its contract with the seller to open a letter of credit in the seller's favour on certain terms and within a certain time. The buyer, now termed the applicant, will apply to its bank, known as the issuing bank, to issue a credit in favour of the seller, now called the beneficiary. At its simplest, therefore, three parties are involved: the buyer-applicant, issuing bank, and seller-beneficiary. In this chapter, the terms buyer, seller, and issuing bank will be used. The seller will often insist in its underlying sale contract with the buyer, on the appointment of a correspondent bank in its own jurisdiction for convenience, or the issuer may for convenience elect to do so, and in practice such a fourth party is commonly involved.[9] The correspondent may be asked to notify the seller of the credit, in which case the correspondent is called the advising bank.[10] Not uncommonly, the correspondent bank assumes a greater role by adding its own commitment to the seller, thereby becoming the confirming bank.[11] The correspondent may, in addition, be nominated in the credit to make payment to the seller, in which case it is also known as the nominated bank.[12] Other banks may be nominated to pay the seller too, including the seller's bank. A nominated bank that acts in this way will, in turn, claim payment from the issuer. The seller is not obliged to deal with the nominated bank and may always choose to present the documents to the issuer or confirmer.[13] **2.03**

The letter of credit contains the promise of payment made by the issuing bank to the seller. The UCP indicates that a credit can be 'available', ie realised, in four ways: 'sight payment, deferred payment, acceptance or negotiation'.[14] The first three options make up the meaning of 'honour' in the UCP, ie they are the recognised methods by which the seller obtains payment.[15] Sight payment refers to a credit that is payable on production of the stipulated documents.[16] Deferred payment refers to a credit that is payable at a future date on production of the stipulated documents, such as ninety days after the documents' acceptance or simply at a stipulated date hence. Acceptance refers to a credit that achieves a similar result **2.04**

[7] The Provisions of the Supreme People's Court on Some Issues Concerning the Trial of Cases of Disputes over Letter of Credit, 1 January 2006.

[8] See UCP 600, art 1; Peter Ellinger and Dora Neo, *The Law and Practice of Documentary Letters of Credit* (Hart Publishing 2010) 43–46 (hereafter Ellinger and Neo, *Law and Practice of Documentary Letters of Credit*). See also Chia-Jui Cheng (ed), *Clive M Schmitthoff's Select Essays on International Trade Law* (Martinus Nihoff Publishers/ Graham & Trotman 1988) 449, 455–58.

[9] See, for example, *United City Merchants (Investments) Ltd v Royal Bank of Canada* [1983] 1 AC 168 (HL) 182–83 (hereafter *UCM v RBC*).

[10] See UCP 600, art 2.

[11] ibid art 2.

[12] ibid art 2

[13] ibid art 6(a).

[14] ibid art 6(b).

[15] ibid art 2.

[16] See, for example, *Midland Bank Ltd v Seymour* [1955] 2 Lloyd's Rep 147 (QB) 165 (hereafter *Midland Bank v Seymour*).

to the deferred payment credit but through the use of a bill of exchange which is drawn by the seller usually on the issuer or confirmer.[17] Negotiation is not considered a method of honour but is, rather, a form of financial accommodation. The deferred payment credit and the acceptance credit reflect different usages. The commitment of the issuing/confirming bank under a deferred payment credit is to pay at some time after the presentation of conforming documents, while for an acceptance credit it is to accept and, in due course, to pay a bill of exchange drawn on it by the seller,[18] provided that it is accompanied by the requisite documents. The ICC has issued guidance discouraging the use of bills of exchange with letters of credit, preferring instead the deferred payment credit.[19]

2.05 The seminal House of Lords decision in *United City Merchants (Investments) Ltd v Royal Bank of Canada*, articulated the accepted view of the letter of credit as a composite structure comprising distinct but interlinked contractual relationships.[20] Section II gives an overview of the relationships that typically arise in a letter of credit transaction other than the relationship between the issuing bank and the seller which is examined in section III and is the main focus of this chapter. Section III explores the contractual nature or otherwise of the relationship, a question which has long interested scholars. The existence of a binding obligation between these two parties is crucial to the letter of credit fulfilling its purpose.[21] The debate is an old one,[22] and this chapter revisits it in the light of developments in the law in recent decades. The view supported here is that, to the extent that the requirements for a contractual obligation are absent, they are supplemented by commercial custom to nevertheless create a binding contractual obligation. The chapter is written from a common law perspective, with reference to cases from a range of jurisdictions including Australia, Canada, Hong Kong, Singapore, the United Kingdom, and the United States.

II. Overview of the Letter of Credit Contractual Relationships

A. Buyer and Issuing Bank

2.06 The relationship between the buyer and issuer is relatively straightforward. There is usually an underlying bank-customer relationship pursuant to which the issuer agrees with the buyer to establish a credit in the seller's favour and notify the seller of the credit. The notification will usually be sent via a secure network, such as SWIFT, to the correspondent bank

[17] See, for example, *Midland Bank v Seymour* (n 16) 165. In some jurisdictions, the practice developed of the seller drawing a bill of exchange on the buyer, with the issuer/confirmer promising in the credit to purchase the bill on presentation of conforming documents. However, UCP 600, art 6 (c) disallows this practice. The reason appears to be the muddying of the issuer's irrevocable undertaking, see *ICC Commentary on UCP 600* (n 2) 34.

[18] Such bills of exchange did not normally qualify as cheques, defined as a bill of exchange drawn on a bank and payable on demand, because although commonly drawn on a bank, they would commonly be payable at some stipulated future time, see Bills of Exchange Act 1882, ss 3 and 73.

[19] See International Chamber of Commerce, 'Guidance Paper—The use of drafts (bills of exchange) under documentary credits' (8 January 2019). The reason is to avoid complications that can arise when negotiable instruments law is brought to bear on agreements relating to letters of credit.

[20] *UCM v RBC* (n 9), 182–83.

[21] Letters of credit are typically irrevocable. Revocable letters of credit are unlikely to satisfy a seller and the UCP 600 does not entertain revocable credits, see arts 2 and 3.

[22] For a thorough examination of the question, see E P Ellinger, *Documentary Letters of Credit: A Comparative Study* (University of Singapore Press 1970) chs III and IV (hereafter Ellinger, *Documentary Letters of Credit: A Comparative Study*). The discussion that follows draws on this work.

in the seller's jurisdiction for advising or confirmation. Thereafter, the issuer's primary duty is to pay the seller or the nominated bank on the presentation of complying documents.[23] Provided it has adhered to its instructions, the issuer is entitled to reimbursement from the buyer. Often that reimbursement comes from the sale proceeds of the goods that have been bought and the issuer will commonly take security over the goods, for example, via a trust receipt.[24] The contract between buyer and issuer is likely to be governed by standard terms and conditions that, amongst other things, may seek to protect the issuing bank in the event that it pays on non-complying documents, ie breaches the doctrine of strict compliance.[25] The validity of such provisions may be governed by the mechanisms used in the applicable jurisdiction to control contractual unfairness.[26]

B. Issuing Bank and Correspondent

As noted in summary above, the correspondent bank may assume a variety of roles including: advising bank, confirming bank, and negotiating bank. Multinational banks will, where possible, use their own overseas offices as correspondent banks. The UCP treats the branches of a bank in different countries as separate banks,[27] which facilitates the advising or confirmation by a local entity. An advising bank incurs minimal responsibility to the seller, its main obligations being to satisfy itself that the credit is authentic and to advise the terms of the credit accurately.[28] It has no obligation to pay or negotiate the credit.[29] The confirming bank incurs obligations to the seller similar to the issuer, as discussed below. **2.07**

C. Buyer and Correspondent

It is well-established that the buyer and correspondent are not usually in a contractual relationship.[30] As a result, any default by the correspondent is not actionable by the buyer as a breach of contract and the buyer would have to resort to tort if it wished to pursue the correspondent directly. At common law such a tort claim is, however, unnecessary as the issuing bank is accountable to its customer for the defaults of the correspondent.[31] The issuer, **2.08**

[23] UCP 600, arts 7(a) and 8(a). See, for example, *Midland Bank v Seymour* (n 16) 165; *UCM v RBC* (n 9) 182–83.
[24] See, for example, *Midland Bank v Seymour* (n 16) 165.
[25] See ch 5 (Adodo) in this volume.
[26] For example, the UK's Unfair Contract Terms Act 1977, applicable in similar terms in Hong Kong (Control of Exemption Clauses Ordinance (Chapter 71)); and Singapore (Unfair Contract Terms Act (Chapter 396, 1994 Revised Edition)).
[27] UCP 600, art 3.
[28] ibid art 9(b).
[29] ibid art 9(a).
[30] See, for example: *Mackersy v Ramsays, Bonars & Co* (1843) 8 ER 628 (hereafter *Mackersy v Ramsays*); *Equitable Trust Co of New York v Dawson Partners* (1927) 27 Lloyd's Rep 157 (HL) (hereafter *Equitable Trust Co v Dawson Partners*); *Calico Printers v Barclays Ltd* (1931) 36 Com Vas 71 (QB) 77–80 (hereafter *Calico Printers v Barclays*); *Royal Products Ltd v Midland Bank* [1981] 2 Lloyd's Rep 194 (QB) 198 (hereafter *Royal Products v Midland Bank*); *A A Valibhoy & Sons v Habib Bank Ltd* [1983–1984] SLR(R) 219 (HC) [47], [53] (hereafter *A A Valibhoy v Habib Bank*); *A A Valibhoy and Sons (1907) Pte Ltd v Banque Nationale de Paris* [1994] 2 SLR(R) 14 (HC) [42] (hereafter *A A Valibhoy v BNP*).
[31] See *Equitable Trust Co v Dawson Partners* (n 30); also *Mackersy v Ramsays* (n 30); *Calico Printers v Barclays* (n 30); *Royal Products v Midland Bank* (n 30) 198; *A A Valibhoy v Habib Bank* (n 30) [47], [53]; *A A Valibhoy v BNP* (n 30) [42].

in turn, has recourse against the correspondent. In an era of standard terms and conditions, however, this solution is routinely compromised by the ubiquitous use of exemption clauses exonerating the issuing bank from liability for the correspondent's defaults. As referred to earlier, such exemptions may be subject to statutory controls on unfairness in the governing jurisdiction.

D. Collecting Bank and Seller

2.09 The collecting bank, often the seller's own bank, presents the documents to the confirmer or issuer on behalf of the seller, and thus acts as an agent of the seller. The seller's bank is likely to be financing the seller, in which case it has an interest, formal or otherwise,[32] in the credit proceeds, which is one reason why it may wish to be involved as a collecting bank. The seller and its bank will have a bank-customer relationship very similar to that of the buyer and the issuer.

III. Issuing/Confirming Bank and Seller

2.10 The UCP 600 is the first version of the UCP to state that the issuer is irrevocably obliged *from the time the credit is issued*,[33] to honour the credit in one of the three ways discussed above, and the confirmer is irrevocably obliged to honour or negotiate the credit *from the moment it confirms*.[34] The time of issuance and confirmation are not defined but the prevalent view appears to be that issuance occurs 'when the credit leaves the operational control of the issuer', and similar for confirmations.[35] Before the UCP 600, the weight of older authority supported the view that the credit became binding once it was communicated to the seller.[36] In other words, under the UCP 600 the credit becomes binding earlier than previously thought as the dispatch of the credit logically precedes receipt by the seller.

2.11 The liability created by the letter of credit is superficially contractual, and it is generally labelled as contractual,[37] but a granular analysis suggests a problem with the requirements for the formation of a contract. The remainder of this chapter is directed at this debate. Few cases have disputed the contractual nature of the issuing bank's liability and such a dispute is likely to be roundly dismissed, yet there are circumstances in which it could be raised. The most obvious is where the issuer is in liquidation. A liquidator has different incentives from

[32] See, for example, *Midland Bank v Seymour* (n 16) 165.

[33] UCP 600, art 7(b),.

[34] ibid art 8(b).

[35] See James E Byrne, *The Comparison of UCP 600 & UCP 500* (The Institute of International Banking Law & Practice 2007) 87 (para 10), 93 (para 10) (hereafter Byrne, *The Comparison of UCP 600 & UCP 500*); M G Bridge (gen ed), *Benjamin's Sale of Goods* (10th edn, Thomson Reuters 2017) para 23-073.

[36] See, for example, *Bunge Corporation v Vegetable Vitamin Foods (Private) Ltd* [1985] 1 Lloyd's Rep 613 (QB) 617; Ellinger and Neo, *Law and Practice of Documentary Letters of Credit* (n 8) 9–10; also Ellinger, *Documentary Letters of Credit: A Comparative Study* (n 22) 9–12.

[37] See, for example, *Sinotani Pacific Pte Ltd v Agricultural Bank of China* [1999] 2 SLR(R) 970 (CA) [14]; *Bank of Credit and Commerce Hong Kong Ltd (in liquidation) v Sonali Bank* [1995] 1 Lloyd's Rep 227 (QB) 237; *UCM v RBC* (n 9) 182–83; *European Asian Bank AG v Punjab & Sind Bank (No 2)* [1983] 1 WLR 642 (CA) 651 (hereafter *European Asian Bank v Punjab & Sind Bank (No 2)*); *Donald H Scott & Co Ltd v Barclays Bank Ltd* [1923] 2 KB 1, 14.

a going concern and need not worry about reputational damage. A recent case confirming that this issue remains alive, and still merits attention, is *Taurus Petroleum Ltd v State Oil Marketing Co of the Ministry of Oil, Republic of Iraq* (*Taurus Petroleum*).[38] Taurus sought to execute an arbitration award in its favour against the State Oil Marketing Company of Iraq ('SOMO') by attaching monies owed under a letter of credit to SOMO by a third party issuer. In these less usual circumstances, a strategic argument was aired that the issuing bank's promise to pay was unenforceable for want of consideration.

As discussed by Professor Peter Ellinger, attempts to demonstrate the contractual nature of the obligation between issuer/confirmer and seller broadly take one of three forms: one is to reason from first principles and suggest how the letter of credit can meet the requirements for contract formation; another is to characterise the letter of credit as an example of one of a number of existing contract types; and the third is to fall back on custom and usage to overcome any defects in the formation requirements.[39] The second approach, termed the 'classification' approach by Professor Ellinger,[40] apparently has prospects in civilian systems but is generally doomed in the common law since it begs the question whether there is a contract in the first place. It will, accordingly, be considered only in overview following a more detailed examination of the requirements for contract formation and how they operate in the letter of credit context. Before considering custom and usage, the contract alternatives of trust, deed, and estoppel will also be discussed, as well as possible recourse to legal fiction. **2.12**

A. The Letter of Credit and the Requirements for Contract Formation

Whether the letter of credit is a contract sui generis, as has been suggested,[41] or it falls into a recognised contract type, it must meet the requirements for contract formation: offer and acceptance, consideration, certainty of terms, and an intention to enter into legal relations. The most elusive are offer and acceptance, and consideration, which will be considered in more detail below.[42] The remaining two elements are less problematic. The terms on which the issuing bank makes the promise of payment are generally standard and certain,[43] and there is little doubt that the issuing bank and seller intend to have a legal commitment. **2.13**

1. Offer and Acceptance

In common law contract theory, a matching offer and acceptance are needed in order to bring a contract into being. This so-called mirror image approach requires the offer to be accepted by the person to whom it is addressed. The acceptance must be communicated to the **2.14**

[38] [2018] AC 690 (SC) (hereafter *Taurus Petroleum*). I am grateful to Nelson Enonchong for referring me to this case. See also *Dexters Ltd v Schenker & Co* (1923) 14 Lloyd's Rep 586 (KB).

[39] Ellinger, *Documentary Letters of Credit: A Comparative Study* (n 22) 42–43.

[40] ibid 44.

[41] See *Bank of Nova Scotia v Angelica-Whitewear Ltd* [1987] 1 SCR 59, [16]; *Alaska Textile Co v Chase Manhattan Bank* 982 F 2d 813 (2nd Cir 1992) 816; *Simic v New South Wales Land and Housing Corporation* [2016] HCA 47, [37] (hereafter *Simic v NSW Land and Housing Corp*).

[42] The discussion that follows draws in part from Ellinger, *Documentary Letters of Credit: A Comparative Study* (n 22) ch IV.

[43] Although there are likely to be variations between the usages of different issuers, or adaptations for different circumstances.

offeror unless it is a unilateral offer which is accepted by performance, thereby dispensing with the need for a communicated acceptance. The latter typically arises when the offer is made to a large group of people as happens in reward cases and competitions. Acceptance, whether communicated or taking the form of performance, must be in response to the offer—it cannot be a coincidence. The offer and acceptance model does not dictate which party makes the offer and who accepts it and, in the event of a dispute, it is left to a court to decide what role the parties assumed.

2.15 The issue of a letter of credit by a bank might instinctively be viewed as an offer—an offer to pay in certain circumstances. The problem is that the promise to pay is regarded as being binding either from the moment of issue under the UCP 600, and hence before the seller is aware of it, or from the time of communication to the seller who has yet to signal any acceptance.[44] One attempt around that problem is to view the seller's forbearance from selling the goods elsewhere as acceptance. The immediate objection to this analysis is that acceptance must generally be communicated to the offeror. Silence can, unusually, constitute an acceptance and the letter of credit might be just such an unusual situation since the issuer arguably does not expect to receive an acceptance from the seller whose primary focus is the obligation of supply owed to the buyer. However, it cannot explain how the letter of credit can be binding from the moment of issue or communication, which precedes any forbearance. It also doesn't help to view the forbearance as dating back to the conclusion of the sale contract as that would mean that the acceptance is not made in response to the offer.

2.16 An alternative explanation views the credit as a unilateral offer by the issuer which is accepted by the seller's performance, but it too struggles with the time at which the credit is considered to be irrevocable.[45] Another attempt to deal with this timing problem is to characterise the seller as making an offer to the issuer, which is accepted by the issue of the credit.[46] This offer, it is said, is made in the sale contract with the buyer. One might see the offer as a promise to supply goods to the buyer in return for payment from the issuer. The analysis is, however, unattractively artificial since it means the offer is made via the buyer, and it jars with the autonomy principle that governs letters of credit, ie that the issuer's obligation to pay is independent of the underlying sale contract.[47]

2. Consideration

2.17 The second big challenge for viewing the letter of credit as a contract is the doctrine of consideration, a controversial doctrine of the common law which has generated much debate.[48] This doctrine dictates that one-sided promises are not enforceable—it requires an exchange of value between the parties. Superficially, in the letter of credit context, there is an exchange: money for goods. However, between the issuer/confirmer and seller there is neither a supply, nor a promise to supply, by the seller.

[44] See UCP 600, arts 7(b) and 8(b).
[45] An analysis suggested by A G Davis, see Ellinger, *Documentary Letters of Credit: A Comparative Study* (n 22) 82–91.
[46] An analysis suggested by P H Thayer, see ibid 77.
[47] UCP 600, art 4,.
[48] See, for example, B Coote, 'Consideration and Benefit in Fact and in Law' (1990) 2 JCL 23; P Atiyah 'Consideration: A Restatement' in P Atiyah (ed), *Essays on Contract* (OUP 1986); G Treitel 'Consideration: A Critical Analysis of Professor Atiyah's Fundamental Restatement' (1976) 50 ALJ 439.

One suggestion is that the seller's forbearance constitutes consideration.[49] The forbearance might take the same form as that discussed under acceptance—the seller's forbearance after receiving the credit from selling the goods elsewhere. The forbearance might, alternatively, take the form of refraining from seeking payment from the buyer. Both of these versions of forbearance fail, however, to explain the time at which the credit becomes binding on the issuer, since the forbearance is logically after the issue or communication of the credit. Forbearance in seeking payment from the buyer also does not reflect the dynamics behind the issue of the letter of credit which is used precisely because the seller does not wish to rely on the buyer for payment—a far cry from forbearing to sue the buyer. Another possibility is that the seller provides consideration in the form of submitting the documents to the bank, which is a requirement under the credit. This possibility is not satisfactory either, because the seller does not promise to furnish any documents to the issuer, and if s/he does not, there is no breach as far as the issuer is concerned. **2.18**

An additional difficulty in finding consideration in the letter of credit context is that the doctrine of consideration requires the seller's promise or performance to be given in exchange for the promise by the issuer, not merely in reliance on it.[50] This requirement means that the issuer must expressly or impliedly request the supply of the goods. In reality, the seller's shipping of the goods is done in performance of the sale contract, and the issuer does not request the supply. Hence, dating the seller's forbearance to the time of concluding the goods contract doesn't solve the problem. The buyer requests the supply but an attempt to view the buyer's promise of payment as consideration does not suffice since consideration must come from the promisor,[51] and it disrespects the autonomy doctrine. **2.19**

The twentieth century saw two significant developments concerning the doctrine of consideration in the UK, although it seems that neither assists in the letter of credit context. The first is the recognition of practical benefit, which substantially modifies the requirement of fresh consideration for contract variations. Practical benefit was first recognised in an agreement to pay more for the same services—the benefit resided in securing the completion of work that otherwise was in danger of not being done.[52] Since then, the concept has been applied to agreements to accept less in settlement of a debt.[53] Both decisions are Court of Appeal decisions in England and Wales, and the UK Supreme Court has yet to rule on the matter—the latter decision was taken to the Supreme Court which disposed of the appeal without ruling on the consideration aspect.[54] Although the issuer may have an economic interest in the financial wellbeing of the buyer, there seems to be little prospect of arguing that the seller receives a practical benefit by securing the seller's supply of the goods to the buyer. The main problem with such an argument is that practical benefit has only been recognised in the context of contract variations, and current authorities do not suggest that it can bring a wholly new contractual obligation into being. **2.20**

[49] Ellinger, *Documentary Letters of Credit: A Comparative Study* (n 22) 100–04.
[50] *Combe v Combe* [1951] 2 KB 215 (CA) 221, 223, 226–27.
[51] See *Dunlop Pneumatic Tyre Co v Selfridge* [1915] AC 847 (HL).
[52] *Williams v Roffey Bros & Nicholls (Contractors) Ltd* [1991] 1 QB 1 (CA).
[53] *MWB Business Exchange Centres Ltd v Rock Advertising Ltd* [2017] QB 604 (CA).
[54] *MWB Business Exchange Centres Ltd v Rock Advertising Ltd* [2019] AC 119 (SC) [18], [20].

2.21 The second notable development is the doctrine of promissory estoppel,[55] which is an equitable estoppel that operates when a one-sided promise without consideration varies the terms of a contract. The promise cannot be broken if it would be inequitable to do so and provided other requirements are met: a clear and unequivocal promise that the promisee relied on. In the posited scenario, the requirement of reliance means the promise can only be relied on after it is communicated and acted on in some way, which does not explain why the issuer is bound on issue or communication of the credit. There is another problem—we are seeking to explain how the seller acquires the right to payment from the issuer, but the creation of new rights is beyond the orthodox scope of promissory estoppel, as captured by the maxim that it operates as a shield not a sword.[56]

3. Discussion

2.22 The fact that the letter of credit does not fit comfortably or perfectly into the offer and acceptance model of contract does not necessarily scupper the view that the letter of credit creates a binding contract between the issuer and the seller. Lord Denning famously said in *Gibson v Manchester City Council*: '[i]t is a mistake to think that all contracts can be analysed into the form of offer and acceptance'.[57] On appeal, the House of Lords accepted that exceptionally, some contracts 'do not fit easily into the normal analysis of a contract as being constituted by offer and acceptance'.[58] The case law also shows that binding agreements have been recognised despite the absence of offer and acceptance in the conventional sense. A good example for the present context is *The Satanita*.[59] The owner of a yacht was held liable in damages to the owner of another yacht that had been sunk in a racing competition. There was no agreement between the two parties but they had each agreed with the competition organiser to be bound by certain rules and to be liable in damages for their breach. Lord Herschell said: 'The effect of their entering for the race, and undertaking to be bound by these rules to the knowledge of each other, is sufficient, I think, where those rules indicate a liability on the part of the one to the other, to create a contractual obligation to discharge that liability.'[60] The Court of Appeal in the same case indicated that the contract between the yacht owners was formed when they started sailing; another contract came into being between each yacht owner and the race organisers when the competition form was signed.[61] While it is only exceptionally that a contract will be recognised in the absence of an accepted offer, it is plausible to claim that the letter of credit is such an exception.

2.23 As international instruments, letters of credit have been influenced by various legal systems including those of civilian systems that articulate the requirements for contract formation differently. The promulgator of the UCP, the ICC, has arguably been influenced more by the civil law than the common law, and hence has shown less concern for the English doctrine of consideration.[62] The doctrine insists on reciprocity before agreements will be

[55] The doctrine can be traced to *Hughes v Metropolitan Railway Co* (1877) 2 App Cas 439, but it was raised to prominence by the later decision of Lord Denning in *Central London Property Ltd v High Trees House Ltd* [1947] 1 KB 130.

[56] But see the Australian High Court decision of *Walton's Stores v Maher* (1988) 164 CLR 387.

[57] [1978] 1 WLR 520 (CA) 523.

[58] [1979] 1 WLR 294 (HL) 297.

[59] [1897] 1 AC 59 (HL) (hereafter *The Satanita*).

[60] *The Satanita* (n 59) 63.

[61] [1895] P 248 (CA) 255–56, 262.

[62] See F M Ventris, *Banker's Documentary Credits* (Lloyds of London Press Ltd 1980) 55 (hereafter Ventris, *Banker's Documentary Credits*). The UK banking industry only started adopting the UCP in their letters of credit

enforced. Viewed in isolation there may be no direct reciprocity between the issuing bank and the seller. But viewed in its broader context, the arrangement does not lack reciprocity and no one disputes that letters of credit should be binding. In the US, the problem of an absence of consideration has been removed by the UCC which provides: 'Consideration is not required to issue, amend, transfer, or cancel a letter of credit, advice, or confirmation.'[63] Some support for a special approach for letters of credit in the common law can be found in *Dexters Ltd v Schenker & Co* in which Greer J considered, obiter, an argument of an absence of consideration to be without merit.[64] Recent common law developments regarding practical benefit also suggest an increasingly liberal view of the doctrine. Such a more expansive approach to consideration, it is submitted, should be able to recognise consideration in the unique circumstances of the letter of credit bearing in mind its place amongst a number of connected contracts.

B. Fitting the Letter of Credit into an Existing Legal Category

It has been variously suggested that the letter of credit is an example of a guarantee, an assignment, a novation, or an agency,[65] all being recognised sources of obligation of a contractual nature. Leaving aside the formidable point that any contract, irrespective of its classification, must satisfy the contractual requisites discussed above, an objection to many of the suggested classifications is that they fail to deal with the fact that the issuer/confirmer's obligation is primary and independent of the contract between the buyer and the seller or the buyer and the issuer.[66] **2.24**

Guarantees, also sometimes termed suretyships,[67] are secondary obligations and hence are inapposite to describe letters of credit which are primary obligations. Indeed, it is a key feature of the credit that the issuer's obligations are independent of the contract between the buyer and the seller. The alternative possibility, of categorising the letter of credit as an indemnity, ie a primary liability, encounters the main problem that crucial formation elements for a contract are missing, as discussed earlier. The assignment argument posits that the buyer assigns his/her rights in the contract with the issuer to the seller. One of the flaws with this suggestion is that it would render the seller vulnerable to any defences and equities which the issuer can raise against the buyer, which is incompatible with how letters of credit operate and does not reflect the intentions of the key actors. Alternatively, in a novation of parties, the buyer would drop out of the equation but that does not explain why the buyer remains secondarily liable to the seller if the issuer does not pay. The agency **2.25**

after the 1962 Revision, see E P Ellinger 'The Uniform Customs—Their Nature and the 1983 Revision' [1984] LMCLQ 578; and E P Ellinger 'The UCP-500: Considering a New Revision' [2004] LMCLQ 30.

[63] Uniform Commercial Code, § 5-105.

[64] (1923) 14 Lloyd's Rep 586 (KB) 588.

[65] All of these possibilities are discussed in more detail in Ellinger, *Documentary Letters of Credit: A Comparative Study* (n 22) Ch III.

[66] Ellinger notes in *Documentary Letters of Credit: A Comparative Study* (n 22) that the 'abstract promise' (at 72–75) recognised in German law can explain irrevocable credits and to a lesser extent so can the French *delegation imparfaite* (at 59–62). However, neither offers a common law explanation (at 75).

[67] As opposed to demand guarantees such as standby letters of credit or performance bonds. For a discussion of primary/secondary liability in this context, see Deborah Horowitz, *Letters of Credit and Demand Guarantees: Defences to Payment* (OUP 2010) paras 1.06 and 5.05–5.06.

classification treats the buyer as the seller's agent in procuring the credit, but it does not reflect the reality of the arrangement which is that issuer and seller deal with each other as principals. For similar reasons, viewing the issuer as an agent of the buyer when it issues the credit is unsatisfactory as the entire point of introducing the issuing bank into the equation is to give the seller an independent claim against a more trusted party.[68]

2.26 It has also been argued that the promise of payment in the letter of credit constitutes an advance or anticipatory acceptance of any bill of exchange that will be drawn by the seller pursuant to the credit. This suggestion can, at most, explain letters of credit that utilise negotiable instruments—and not all do—and it will not work where bills of exchange legislation requires an acceptance to be written on the bill itself, as is typical in the common law world.[69]

2.27 Another possibility that must be mentioned is the letter of credit as a contract for the benefit of a third party. The argument would be that the contract between the buyer and the issuer is for the benefit of the seller. At one time, third parties had limited scope to claim rights from a contract in the common law. This position has now changed with similar legislation found, for example, in the UK,[70] Singapore,[71] and Hong Kong.[72] The UK legislation provides that a third party can enforce a contract where it expressly provides for third party enforcement or, which is more likely, where it purports to confer a benefit on the third party. This requirement is designed to distinguish between intended and incidental benefits. The third party must be identified or identifiable from the contract and, importantly, the statute states that the failure of the third party to provide consideration is not a bar to her/his claim. While in theory the seller could utilise this legislation to enforce the promise of payment made by the issuer to the buyer, for a number of reasons it may not assist: the provisions of the legislation can be excluded, and such exclusion is boilerplate in bank documentation—notably the UCP says that a seller cannot claim under the contract between the buyer and the issuer.[73] The Hong Kong Ordinance providing for third party rights of enforcement specifically excludes letters of credit from its ambit.[74] The privity legislation also does not explain the common law position which is that a seller enforces its right to payment as principal and not as a third party—if the seller is enforcing a right in the contract between the buyer and the issuer, the letter of credit is superfluous.

C. Contract Alternatives

2.28 This section discusses non-contractual bases on which the issuing bank's liability to the seller under the letter of credit can be placed. The three possibilities that will be considered are that the letter of credit constitutes a trust, a deed,[75] or that it gives rise to an estoppel.

[68] See Ellinger, *Documentary Letters of Credit: A Comparative Study* (n 22) 66.

[69] Bills of Exchange Act 1882, s 17. As noted earlier, this legislation has been implemented in numerous former British colonies.

[70] Contracts (Rights of Third Parties) Act 1999.

[71] Contracts (Rights of Third Parties) Act (Chapter 53B, 2002 Revised Edition).

[72] Contracts (Rights of Third Parties) Ordinance (Chapter 623).

[73] UCP 600, art 4a.

[74] Contracts (Rights of Third Parties) Ordinance (Chapter 623), s 3(2)(f).

[75] I am grateful to Christopher Hare for highlighting this possibility to me.

1. The Letter of Credit as a Trust

The agreement between the buyer and the issuing bank for the credit to be issued arguably creates a trust with the buyer as the settlor, the bank as the trustee, and the seller as the beneficiary.[76] The trust explanation is, however, unpersuasive: there must be an intention to create a trust,[77] a requirement which is almost certainly missing in the letter of credit context, and a trust requires certainty of property,[78] yet such property is frequently absent as the issuing bank typically pays the seller from its own funds and recoups from the buyer in due course. Yet another problem is that a seller enforcing its rights under a credit sues as a party to the credit and not as a beneficiary of a trust created between the buyer and the bank. 2.29

2. The Letter of Credit as a Deed

Deeds have been said to be 'the most solemn act that a person can perform with respect to a particular piece of property or other right.[79] They were historically divided into two types: indentures and deeds poll, a distinction which was based on the physical differences between the two, a difference that is no longer particularly significant.[80] As regards function, indentures are agreements between two or more parties and are used when a binding commitment is desired but a contractual element is missing, typically consideration. Deeds poll are used for one-sided announcements, and are today synonymous with name changes.[81] Deeds, even when not legally required, have also been used out of habit and caution. As a matter of practice, they are/have been used for a variety of purposes, including to: create a trust over property,[82] grant a power of attorney,[83] effect bank guarantees,[84] convey land,[85] and effect name changes. 2.30

In the present context, the question is whether the letter of credit can be cast as a deed. A problem with casting the letter of credit as an indenture between the seller and the issuing bank is similar to one of the problems seen with the contractual analysis—an indenture is essentially an agreement, yet the problem we are trying to solve is that in a letter of credit there is no assent from the seller by the time the credit is regarded as binding. Thus, while casting the credit as a deed by way of indenture can avoid the problem of consideration, the absence of a consensus remains. Since the letter of credit is a one-sided act when viewed in isolation, the deed poll may be a better fit than the indenture. One-sided declarations can be binding if contained in a deed, thus avoiding both the requirements of offer and acceptance, and consideration. Although particularly associated with name changes, the deed poll can 2.31

[76] In some circumstances the beneficiary of a trust can enforce its terms and hence trusts are an exception to the rule that a third party cannot acquire enforceable rights from an agreement to which they are not a party.

[77] See, for example, *Re Schebsman* [1944] 1 Ch 83 (CA) 89–90, 104; *Paul v Constance* [1977] 1 WLR 527 (CA); *Cytec Industries Pte Ltd v Asia Pulp & Paper Co Ltd* [2009] 2 SLR(R) 806 (HC) [4] (hereafter *Cytec Industries v Asia Pulp*).

[78] See, for example, *Palmer v Simmonds* (1854) 2 Drew 221, 61 ER 704.

[79] *Manton v Parabolic Pty Ltd* (1985) 2 NSWLR 361 (NSWSC) 367–68.

[80] See *Halsbury's Laws of England* (5th edn, LexisNexis 2012) vol 32, para 203 (hereafter *Halsbury's Laws of England*). See also *Re A & K Holdings Pty Ltd* [1964] VR 257, 261.

[81] See *Halsbury's Laws of England* (n 80) vol 32, para 203; *Halsbury's Laws of Australia* (Butterworths 1991) paras 140-1–140-20. See also *Re A & K Holdings Pty Ltd* [1964] VR 257 (VSC) 261.

[82] Most trusts do not require the use of a deed, although statute may dictate otherwise, see, for example, UK Law of Property Act 1925, s 53; Singapore Civil Law Act (Chapter 43, 1999 Revised Edition), s 7.

[83] See, for example, the UK's Powers of Attorney Act 1971, s 1.

[84] Presumably to avoid any problems with consideration.

[85] Law of Property Act 1925, s 52 (England); Conveyancing and Law of Property Act (Chapter 61, 1994 Revised Edition), s 53 (Singapore).

be used to make other important declarations. For example, in Hong Kong it is used to partition land,[86] in England it is apparently used by clergy to renounce their ordination,[87] and in Australia it has been used by an insurance company to assume liabilities under certain policies issued by another insurance company.[88]

2.32 The problem with viewing letters of credit as deeds poll or indentures, is non-compliance with the formalities needed for a deed. Historically deeds were required to be signed, sealed, and delivered,[89] although these formalities have been altered by statute in different jurisdictions. The requirement of signature is probably unproblematic as letters of credit are always in writing and will be signed in some way by the issuer/confirmer. The requirement of a seal, traditionally a red disk of paper or wax, has been watered down in many jurisdictions,[90] and is practically or legally no longer a requirement in many circumstances.[91] For corporates, it has been replaced by the signatures of designated office-holders in the company. For example, the UK's Companies Act 2006 does away with a seal if the document is executed by a director and the secretary, two directors, or a single director in the presence of an attesting witness.[92] In Singapore, the Companies Act was similarly amended in 2017 but also requires the document to be described as, or expressed to be, a deed.[93] In letter of credit practice, these requirements are almost certainly not met.

2.33 Delivery remains a requirement for a deed, for example, in England and Singapore but it does not require parting with possession of the deed in the ordinary sense. *Xenos v Wickham* shows, rather, that the requirement of delivery for a deed is some act that confirms the seriousness of the commitment being undertaken.[94] One way of doing this is to exhibit or publicise the deed in some way, for example by distributing copies to those who have an interest in its contents. The requirement of delivery is potentially also problematic if we seek to characterise the letter of credit as a deed since the letter of credit under the UCP 600 is considered binding from the moment of issue. If issue occurs on leaving the control of the issuer, at that point there may not yet be an act that can satisfy the requirement of delivery. In summary, the formalities for the creation of a deed at common law or as modified by statute are probably not met by letters of credit since the requirements of a seal or signature by designated bank officers, and delivery may not be satisfied.

3. The Letter of Credit as an Estoppel

2.34 Estoppel is another possibility that might explain why the letter of credit binds the issuer. There are different species of estoppel, two of which will be considered here. Equitable

[86] See Lawrence Wai-chung Lai and Daniel Chi-wing Ho, *Change in Use of Land: A Practical Guide to Development in Hong Kong* (3rd edn, Hong Kong University Press 2017) 70.

[87] See 'Deed Poll' at Wikipedia, online.

[88] *Re Wily as Liquidator of Anglican Insurance Ltd* [2009] NSWSC 696, [6]–[8]. See also *Sunderland Marine Insurance Co v Kearney* (1851) 16 QB 925, 938; 117 ER 1136, 1141.

[89] See *Scook v Premier Building Solutions Pty Ltd* (2003) 28 WAR 124 (WACA) [22] (hereafter *Scook v Premier Building Solutions*). For a fuller discussion, see Edwin Peel, *Treitel: The Law of Contract* (14th edn, Sweet & Maxwell 2015) paras 3-170–3-173.

[90] See *First National Securities v Jones* [1978] Ch 109 (CA); *Cytec Industries v Asia Pulp* (n 77) [4].

[91] See Australia: Corporations Act 2001, s 127; Hong Kong: Companies Ordinance (Chapter 622), s 127(5); Singapore: Companies Act (Chapter 50, 2006 Revised Edition), s 41B; UK: Companies Act 2006, s 44(4), Law of Property (Miscellaneous Provisions) Act 1989, s 1(1)(b).

[92] Companies Act 2006, ss 44(1)–44(4).

[93] Companies Act, (Chapter 50, 2006 Revised Edition), s 41B(1).

[94] (1867) LR 2 HL 296, 309.

promissory estoppel, mentioned earlier, does not assist a seller seeking to enforce a bank's promise of payment since the doctrine is generally seen as operating defensively and not allowing the acquisition or creation of new rights—it acts as a shield and not a sword.[95] Another option is estoppel by representation. This common law estoppel requires a statement of past or present fact, and reliance by the recipient to her/his detriment.[96] A point to note about this estoppel is that it does not uphold promises about the future, such as a promise to pay on the presentation of conforming documents. As such, it is ill-suited to the current context, and the requirement of reliance faces similar problems as in promissory estoppel, which was discussed earlier.

D. Legal Fiction

A different argument is that the existence of a contract between the issuer and seller is based on a fiction that the requisite requirements for contract formation are met. Legal fictions are not unfamiliar in banking law. It is well-established, for example, that the true owner of a converted bill of exchange can sue in conversion for the face value of the bill, notwithstanding that the piece of paper that is converted has only nominal value, and the bill's real value derives from it being a chose in action which, to this day, cannot be converted.[97] The right to sue for the face value of the instrument is an acknowledged fiction.[98] There are numerous other examples of legal fiction in common law systems, including the fiction of lost modern grant for property rights acquired by prescription;[99] the fiction of a licence to avoid the legal consequences of trespass in some circumstances;[100] the fiction that an insurance broker has paid an insurance premium to an underwriter;[101] the fiction that unborn children are treated as born to enable them to take a benefit they would have if born;[102] the fiction that judicial acts, notably judgments, are considered effective from the start of the day on which they occur;[103] and the fiction that transitory acts committed abroad can be treated as local for the purposes of giving a domestic court jurisdiction.[104] **2.35**

In the English case of *Clarke v Bradlaugh*, Denman J in the Divisional Court stated that fictions exist in order to do justice.[105] That rationale would hold in the letter of credit context since it is universally accepted that the issuer should be bound by the promise made in the credit, and should not escape on the grounds of a technicality. On the other hand, legal fictions should be a last resort in a legal system as their use can undermine established **2.36**

[95] But see the Australian High Court decision of *Walton's Stores v Maher* (1988) 164 CLR 387.

[96] See, for example, *Greenwood v Martins Bank Limited* [1933] 1 AC 51 (HL) 57; *Pertamina Energy Trading Limited v Credit Suisse* [2006] 4 SLR(R) 273 (CA) [72].

[97] See the seminal decision in *OBG Ltd v Allan* [2008] 1 AC 1 (HL).

[98] See, for example, *Smith v Lloyds TSB Group Plc* [2000] 3 WLR 1725 (CA) 1731, 1738.

[99] See, for example *Bakewell Management Ltd v Brandwood* [2004] 2 AC 519 (HL); *Yong Joo Lin, Yong Shook Lin and Yong Loo Lin v Fung Poi Fong* [1941] MLJ 63 (Straits Settlements SC); *Charles Dalton v Henry Angus & Co* (1881) 6 App Cas 740.

[100] *British Railways Board v Herrington* [1972] AC 877 (HL).

[101] *Heath Lambert Ltd v Sociedad de Corretaje de Seguros* [2004] 1 WLR 2820 (CA).

[102] *Elliot v Lord Joicey* [1935] 1 AC 209 (HL).

[103] *In re Palmer* [1994] 1 Ch 316 (CA); *Clarke v Bradlaugh* (1881) 8 QBD 63.

[104] *The British South Africa Company v Companhia De Mocambique* [1893] 1 AC 602 (HL).

[105] (1881) 7 QBD 151, 153, Watkin Williams J concurred. The decision was affirmed on appeal without contradicting the statement, see *Clarke v Bradlaugh* (1881) 8 QBD 63.

legal doctrine and hence the certainty of the law. For this reason, fictions cannot simply be concocted to sidestep legal doctrine and, while the binding obligation on the issuer to pay the seller could be explained as another legal fiction, there is little or no judicial support for such an explanation.

E. Custom and Usage

2.37 The final option that will be considered is that that the issuer's obligation to the seller is based on mercantile custom. This argument is another attempt to show that the relationship is contractual. Custom and usage is more typically used to imply terms into an extant contract or to shed light on the construction of an extant contract, so in the current context it would be operating in a more fundamental way to create a contractual obligation.[106] The major obstacle to such an expansive application of usage is that modern usage (eg that an issuer/confirmer incurs a binding obligation to the seller) cannot be used to contradict established law (the contract formation requirements).[107] There is an exception for so-called ancient mercantile usage but the usage associated with letters of credit is considered modern.[108] Although this restriction is at first blush problematic, Professor Ellinger points out that it depends on how one interprets the restriction.[109] A fundamentalist interpretation would not allow modern usage ever to operate contrary to the common law, but a more compromising interpretation allows for modern usage to depart from the norm so long as the common law has not previously nullified it. Since the common law has not previously nullified the custom that the letter of credit gives rise to a binding obligation between the issuer and the seller, it has done quite the contrary, the conclusion is that there is no restriction on recourse to modern usage.

2.38 There is strong support for this approach in the related context of negotiable instruments which have also developed from established modern usage. Although now codified in many countries,[110] the law governing negotiable instruments was once governed by the common law. Negotiable instruments flouted the common law in numerous ways: by recognising past consideration as being good consideration,[111] by allowing for the transmission of the right to payment contained in the bill,[112] and for giving a better title to the transferee in some situations.[113] The case of *Goodwin v Robarts* is instructive. In the

[106] I am grateful to Michael Bridge for making this point.

[107] See *Goodwin v Robarts* (1875) LR 10 Ex 337, 357, aff'd (1876) 1 App Cas 476, 490, 496.

[108] See Ellinger, *Documentary Letters of Credit: A Comparative Study* (n 22) 105–08.

[109] ibid 109–10.

[110] It is regarded as a particularly successful codification of the common law, see *Bank Polski v K J Mulder and Co* [1942] 1 KB 497 (CA) 500; J Milnes Holden, *The History of Negotiable Instruments in English Law* (Wm W Gaunt & Sons 1993) 201–02; A R Coleman, *The Cheques and Payment Orders Act 1986* (Longman Professional Statute Guides 1987) 3; Charles L McKeehan 'The Negotiable Instruments Law' (1902) 50 Am L Reg 437, 438; Benjamin Geva, 'The Modernization of the Bills of Exchange Act: A Proposal' (2011) 50 Can Bus LJ 26.

[111] Codified in the Bills of Exchange Act 1882, s 27(1)(b), see Ellinger, *Documentary Letters of Credit: A Comparative Study* (n 22) 115, citing inter alia *Poirier v Morris* (1853) 2 EL & Bl 89, 118 ER 702; *Currie v Misa* (1875) LR 10 Ex 153, (1876) 1 App Cas 554.

[112] Codified in the Bills of Exchange Act 1882, s 38, see Ellinger, *Documentary Letters of Credit: A Comparative Study* (n 22) 115.

[113] This privilege goes to the holder in due course, ie a person who purchases a bill without notice of any irregularities or defects, codified in the Bills of Exchange Act 1882, ss 29 and 38(2).

Exchequer Chamber, Cockburn CJ rejected the argument that only instruments recognised by the ancient law merchant could be negotiable by usage.[114] He stated that courts recognise the usages that attach to trade, such that what was once mere usage, becomes 'engrafted upon, or incorporated into, the common law, and may thus be said to form part of it'.[115] In the same case, in the House of Lords, Lord Cairns said that instruments would be treated as negotiable upon proof of such a usage by banks, money dealers, and stock exchanges for over fifty years.[116] The letter of credit is an instrument developed by the usage of banks and traders for about two centuries to meet the needs of international trade,[117] such that the binding nature of the issuer's promise to the seller is surely established by such usage.

In his last discussion of the issue, Professor Ellinger stated that the letter of credit as a binding obligation is 'supported by "mercantile usage" all over the world,' and that it is so regarded by the courts.[118] Samples of that judicial support include the following cases. First, *International Banking Corporation v Barclays Bank Ltd*, where Atkin LJ said:[119] **2.39**

> I think it may be said that the law relating to such transactions is not at the present moment crystallized that it is not dependent upon proof of custom. In any case it is clear that it is emphatically the kind of transaction where commercial usage when proved will eventually govern the legal rights between the parties ...

Secondly, *Hamzeh Malas & Sons v British Imex Industries Ltd*, where Jenkins LJ said:[120] **2.40**

> [T]he opening of a confirmed letter of credit constitutes a bargain between the banker and the vendor of the goods, which imposes upon the banker an absolute obligation to pay.... An elaborate commercial system has been built up on the footing that bankers' confirmed credits are of that character, and ... it would be wrong for this court ... to interfere with that established practice.

Thirdly, in relation to performance bonds,[121] *Simic v New South Wales Land and Housing Corporation*, Gageler, Nettle, and Gordon JJ in the High Court of Australia said:[122] **2.41**

> They are contracts, although of a specific kind. When and how a contractual promise to pay, not under seal, in favour of a named principal establishes a binding contract has been the subject of debate and discussion since at least the first half of the 20th century. For present purposes, however, that debate and discussion may be put to one side. Consistent

[114] (1875) LR 10 Ex 337 at 355–56, see also 357 (hereafter *Goodwin v Robarts*).
[115] ibid 346, aff'd (1876) 1 App Cas 476, 490, 494 (hereafter *Goodwin v Robarts (HL)*). See also Bertram Jacobs, *A Short Treatise on the Law or Bills of Exchange, Cheques Promissory Notes, and Negotiable Instruments Generally* (2nd edn, Sweet & Maxwell Ltd 1924) 8.
[116] See *Goodwin v Robarts (HL)* (n 115) 490, read with 478. See also *Bechuanaland Exploration Co v London Trading Bank Ltd* [1898] 2 QB 658.
[117] See, for example, Ellinger, *Documentary Letters of Credit: A Comparative Study* (n 22) ch II.
[118] Ellinger and Neo, *Law and Practice of Documentary Letters of Credit* (n 8) 111.
[119] (1925) 5 Legal Decisions Affecting Bankers 1, 4.
[120] [1958] 2 QB 127 (CA) 129. See also *Stein v Hambros Bank of Northern Commerce* (1921) 9 Lloyd's Rep 433 (KB) and 507 (CA); *UCM v RBC* (n 9) 182–83.
[121] The obligations assumed by a bank under a performance bond are analogous to those assumed by the issuer or confirming bank under a letter of credit.
[122] *Simic v NSW Land and Housing Corp* (n 41) [77].

with established banking practice, no party contended that the Undertakings were to be construed otherwise than in accordance with ordinary principles of contract construction.

2.42 To the extent that the requirement of offer and acceptance, and consideration are not met in an attenuated sense, as argued earlier, it is submitted that custom and usage remedies the deficiency such that the issuer's promise to the seller is indeed contractual.

IV. Conclusion

2.43 In disputes between the issuing/confirming bank and the seller, defences based on the absence of a contractual nexus are rarely raised. As noted earlier, a recent exception is *Taurus Petroleum*,[123] where, for strategic reasons, it was argued that an issuer's promise pursuant to a letter of credit was unenforceable for want of consideration. The issue did not, ultimately, have to be decided but Lord Clarke endorsed Moore-Bick LJ's view in the Court of Appeal that he would be 'loath to hold, particularly in a commercial context, that a promise which both parties intended should be relied on was unenforceable for want of consideration'.[124] Lord Mance, dissenting on the outcome, said it would be inconsistent with established principles to deny consideration or the binding nature of the promises between the three parties.[125] These dicta reinforce the unlikelihood of naysayers ever succeeding with an argument that the issuer's promise to pay in a letter of credit lacks contractual force, for to hold otherwise would be to destabilise international trading transactions. As an international instrument, developed from the custom of merchants from different parts of the world trading with each other, pragmatism rather than legal doctrine drove its development. It is unsurprising, therefore, that it transcends domestic legal doctrine.

2.44 It has been argued here that while the relationship between the issuing/confirming bank and the seller of goods does not fit the orthodox mould for contract formation, it does so in an attenuated sense. Other features of the parties' relationship align strongly with it being a contract: the context is trade and commerce where relationships are primarily governed by contract, and the contractual mesh surrounding the letter of credit lends support to the contractual analysis: the buyer and seller of the goods contract for the seller to be paid by a letter of credit which indicates the seller's advance acceptance of/desire for that method of payment; the issuing bank and the buyer contract that the former will incur a payment obligation to the seller on particular terms; and while the seller may not provide consideration to the issuing bank, it does provide consideration to the buyer. Taken as a whole, the requisite elements of contract formation are present.

2.45 Although the doctrine of autonomy requires that the letter of credit be considered without regard to the underlying transaction, the purpose of the doctrine is to strengthen the seller's rights to payment and to leave disputes about the goods to be resolved later. In other respects, however, the underlying transaction is key to the letter of credit and is surely able to plug doctrinal gaps.[126] Such a view is supported by statements in *New Zealand Shipping*

[123] *Taurus Petroleum* (n 38).
[124] ibid [25].
[125] ibid [95].
[126] See also Ventris, *Banker's Documentary Credits* (n 62) 55.

Co Ltd v A M Satterthwaite & Co Ltd,[127] albeit not a letter of credit case. Lord Wilberforce endorsed an approach that looks at the big picture when the contractual nature of an arrangement is in doubt. He said: 'The whole contract is of a commercial character, involving service on one side, rates of payment on the other, and qualifying stipulations as to both. The relations of all parties to each other are commercial relations entered into for business reasons of ultimate profit.' In the same case, Lord Wilberforce reminded us that numerous commonplace arrangements struggle to fit into the orthodox contract mould: 'sales at auction; supermarket purchases; boarding an omnibus; purchasing a train ticket; tenders for the supply of goods; offers of rewards; acceptance by post; warranties of authority by agents; manufacturers' guarantees; gratuitous bailments; bankers' commercial credits.'[128] In these situations, he pointed out, the orthodox requirements are implemented with some pragmatism.

The subject of this chapter has been not so much whether letters of credit are enforceable by a seller—their enforceability has never been in doubt as attested to by the longevity of the instrument. Rather the focus has been on whether the credit's enforceability is contractual in nature. The latest reference to that issue by the UK Supreme Court in *Taurus Petroleum* supports the view taken here that the promise contained in the latter of credit is indeed to be regarded as contractual, even if the elements for contract formation are met in an unorthodox way. **2.46**

[127] [1975] 1 AC 154 (HL) 167.
[128] ibid.

3

Soft Clauses in Letters of Credit

Martin Davies

I. Introduction: A Rod for the Beneficiary's Own Back

3.01 'Soft clauses' in letters of credit are sometimes known, even more disparagingly, as 'joker clauses'.[1] They are clauses that require the beneficiary of the credit to present a document issued or signed by the applicant (or someone in the applicant's country) in order to secure payment from the issuing, confirming, or nominated bank under a letter of credit. One obvious consequence is that the applicant has within its control the means of preventing payment to the beneficiary, because the doctrine of strict compliance is unforgiving in its insistence that the beneficiary is not entitled to payment without presentation of a document that conforms exactly to the requirements of the soft clause. The beneficiary cannot cure any discrepancy in the documents, as it might be able to do with documents produced in its own country at its own request, because it has no control, direct or indirect, over the production of the 'soft clause' document.

3.02 The International Standard Banking Practice ('ISBP') document produced by the International Chamber of Commerce as a companion to the Uniform Customs and Practice for Documentary Credits ('UCP 600') is almost brutally unsympathetic to a beneficiary who has agreed to be paid under a letter of credit including such a clause. The 2007 version ('ISBP 681') stated:

> A credit should not require presentation of documents that are to be issued or countersigned by the applicant. If a credit is issued including such terms, the beneficiary must either seek amendment or comply with them and bear the risk of failure to do so.[2]

3.03 The 2013 version ('ISBP 745') is a little less harsh, but the message for the beneficiary is much the same: if you accept such terms you are making a rod for your own back:

> A credit or any amendment thereto should not require presentation of a document that is to be issued or countersigned by the applicant. If, nevertheless, a credit or amendment is issued including such a requirement, the beneficiary should consider the appropriateness of such a requirement and determine its ability to comply with it, or seek a suitable amendment.[3]

[1] See Tradefinance.training blog, 'Joker clauses' (*Tradefinance.training*, 18 October 2017) <https://www.tradefinance.training/blog/articles/joker-clauses/> accessed 4 February 2021.

[2] International Chamber of Commerce, *International Standard Banking Practice for the Examination of Documents under Documentary Credits, 2007 Revision for UCP 600* (ICC Publication No 681E, 2007) Preliminary Considerations, para (iv) (hereafter 'ISBP 681 (2007)').

[3] International Chamber of Commerce, *International Standard Banking Practice for the Examination of Documents under UCP 600* (ICC Publication No 745E, 2013) Preliminary Considerations, para (vii) (hereafter 'ISBP 745 (2013)').

That may be easier said than done, of course. The applicant may have a legitimate reason for insisting on the inclusion of such a term, particularly if it relates to the condition or conformity of the goods on arrival in the applicant's country. Nevertheless, the applicant's ability to control, directly or indirectly, the release of funds may provide it with an irresistible temptation if the market value of the goods or services in the underlying contract falls. The English case of *The Messiniaki Tolmi*[4] is both a good example of a case where there was a legitimate reason for inclusion of a soft clause, and also an illustration of the difficulties that the doctrine of strict compliance creates for a beneficiary who has agreed to be paid under a letter of credit requiring presentation of documents to be produced in the applicant's country, beyond the beneficiary's ability to cure any possible discrepancies. **3.04**

In *The Messiniaki Tolmi*, a Panamanian shipowner agreed to sell its ship to a Taiwanese buyer to be scrapped in Taiwan. The buyer's bank in Taiwan issued a letter of credit in favour of the seller/beneficiary, which was later confirmed by a London bank, as the seller/beneficiary had requested. The sale contract specified that the ship should be delivered in Taiwan with a valid gas-free certificate 'to be approved by the Taiwan Authorities' so that 'hot work' could be done on the ship during scrapping. The sale contract also stipulated that the buyer would not accept delivery of the ship without that certificate. Accordingly, the letter of credit required presentation of the following documents (among others): **3.05**

> [A] copy of the valid Gas-Free Certificate for hot work, which Certificate to be approved by the Taiwan Authorities, together with a copy of the notice of readiness countersigned by the Kaohsiung Harbour Master or Lloyds Agents in Taiwan ... confirming the safe arrival of the vessel inside Kaohsiung Harbour and accepted and signed by the Purchasers ...[5]

Clearly, the applicant/buyer had (or at least ostensibly had) a legitimate reason for asking for inclusion of the soft clause in the letter of credit, as the ship could not be scrapped safely if it had not been gas-freed properly. However, the clause also gave the applicant/buyer effective control over the release of the funds by the banks, and thus the ability to take advantage of any changes in the market value of scrap metal. In such circumstances, even the most scrupulous of buyers might find itself just a little tempted if the market moved against the seller before performance was completed. **3.06**

When the ship arrived at Kaohsiung, the Harbour Master did not sign the gas-free certificate indicating his approval, and the buyer refused to accept and sign the notice of readiness. To cut a long story short,[6] the confirming bank in London refused to accept the documents presented by the seller/beneficiary because the gas-free certificate did not bear any endorsement indicating approval by the Taiwanese authorities.[7] The ship eventually left Taiwan and **3.07**

[4] *Astro Exito Navegacion v Chase Manhattan Bank (The Messiniaki Tolmi)* [1988] 2 Lloyd's Rep 217 (CA) (hereafter *The Messiniaki Tolmi (1988) CA*).

[5] ibid 218–19 (per Lloyd LJ).

[6] The transaction occurred in 1980; the final decision in the litigation did not occur until 1988. At interlocutory stages, the case went to the Court of Appeal three times and to the House of Lords once: see *Astro Exito Navegacion v Chase Manhattan Bank (The Messiniaki Tolmi)* [1983] 2 AC 787 (HL) (hereafter *The Messiniaki Tolmi (1983) HL*), where the House of Lords ordered that a Supreme Court master should countersign the notice of readiness because the buyer had ignored the lower court's order that it should do so. The decision referred to in *The Messiniaki Tolmi (1988) CA*) (n 4) was the fourth visit of the case to the Court of Appeal.

[7] Not surprisingly, there were allegations that the buyer/applicant had tried to persuade the harbour authorities in Kaohsiung not to accept the validity of the gas-free certificate: see *Astro Exito Navegacion, v Chase Manhattan Bank (The Messiniaki Tolmi)* [1986] 1 Lloyd's Rep. 455 (QBD) 456 (per Leggatt J).

was sold to a new buyer in Hong Kong at a considerable loss, as the market price of scrap metal had fallen from US$212.50 per ton at the time when the original contract was made to about US$150 per ton.[8] It is impossible now to know whether the refusal of the Taiwanese buyer to accept the ship was driven by its genuine concern for the safety of the scrapping process, or by its desire to take advantage of the steep fall in the scrap value of the ship, but it is tempting to think that there was at least a little of both reasons. Nevertheless, no matter what the buyer's motive, the end result of the case was that the English Court of Appeal held, perhaps not surprisingly, that the confirming bank was entitled to refuse to accept the documents as a conforming tender under the letter of credit, because they did not comply strictly with the requirement of approval by the Taiwanese authorities.[9] The seller/beneficiary had put itself in the position of having to present documents the production of which it could not control, and so had made itself vulnerable to a change in position at the applicant's end of the transaction. In short, it had made a rod for its own back.

II. Little Sympathy for Beneficiaries

3.08 The bleakly unsympathetic attitude of the ISBP is largely mirrored by the response of courts that have been called on to consider the effect of soft clauses in letters of credit. We have already seen that the English Court of Appeal in *The Messiniaki Tolmi* used the traditional strict-compliance doctrine to deny payment to a beneficiary who could not comply with a soft clause. Some examples from the United States illustrate a variety of different, fairly typical, soft clauses, all of which produce the same result: difficulty for the beneficiary to present strictly conforming documents in order to get paid.

3.09 In *Eximetals Corp v Guimaraes SA*,[10] an importer in New York agreed to buy steel flanges from an exporter in Brazil. Payment was to be made by two letters of credit issued by New York banks, both requiring presentation of (among other things) an 'inspection certificate verified by and countersigned by Mr. Gang,' who was the president of the applicant/buyer corporation. One bank rejected the inspection certificate first presented by the Brazilian beneficiary on account of a discrepancy that had nothing to do with the requirement for countersignature; it also rejected a later tender that cured the original discrepancy because the certificate had not been countersigned by Mr. Gang. The other bank rejected the inspection certificate, even though it appeared to have been signed by Mr. Gang, because it had not been signed by the person who had conducted the inspection.[11] The Appellate Division of the New York Supreme Court held that both issuing banks were

[8] *The Messiniaki Tolmi (1983) HL* (n 6) 796 (per Lord Roskill).

[9] See *The Messiniaki Tolmi (1988) CA* (n 4). Although the Court of Appeal's decision is consistent with earlier English authority to the effect that certification of approval must, by implication, take documentary form—see *Banque de L'Indochine et de Suez SA v J H Rayner (Mincing Lane) Ltd* [1983] QB 711 (CA)—it should be noted that ISBP 745 (2013) (n 3) para A 26 states that: 'When a credit contains a condition without stipulating a document to indicate compliance therewith ("non-documentary condition"), compliance with such condition need not be evidenced on any stipulated document.'

[10] 422 NYS 2d 684 (App Div NY, 1979) (hereafter *Eximetal Corps v Guimaraes SA*).

[11] The applicant actually claimed that Mr. Gang's signature on this certificate had been forged, but the court assumed for purposes of these proceedings that the signature was genuine, because the matter came before the court on an application for summary judgment by the issuing banks: see ibid 527. On an application for summary judgment, the court views all disputed facts in the light most favourable to the non-moving party, which in this case was the beneficiary and the banks.

entitled to refuse to pay because in neither case did the inspection certificate comply strictly with the terms of the credit. The inspection certificate that had not been signed by Mr. Gang was not a conforming presentation for that reason alone. The inspection certificate that was signed by Mr. Gang but not the inspector was not 'countersigned' by Mr. Gang; 'countersigned' meant that his signature should be added to someone else's.

In *Marino Industries Corp v Chase Manhattan Bank NA*,[12] there were three different soft clauses, each of which caused problems for the beneficiary. The plaintiff, an American manufacturer, contracted with a German company to send construction materials to a job site in Saudi Arabia. Payment was to be made under two letters of credit issued by a German bank, both of which were confirmed by the defendant bank in the United States, naming the American seller as beneficiary: 40% of the price was to be paid on shipment and 60% when the goods were received. The seller/beneficiary shipped all the goods to Saudi Arabia as required, but the confirming bank refused to honour the seller/beneficiary's three separate presentations, claiming in each case that the documents were discrepant because of their failure to comply strictly with the soft clauses in the letter of credit. (It may or may not have been a coincidence that the confirming bank's rejection of the documents occurred after the German buyer went into bankruptcy.) Each of the three refusals was for a different reason; all three turned on a soft clause in the letters of credit. 3.10

The first refusal related to a requirement in the letter of credit that the beneficiary should present (among other things) a certificate showing that the goods had been received in Saudi Arabia. The certificates of receipt were to be signed by a representative of the Saudi Arabian joint venture that was to receive the goods, or a notarised signature of the freight forwarder arranging transportation of the materials to Saudi Arabia. The German issuing bank had sent three signature samples to the American confirming bank, but the confirming bank did not tell the beneficiary that only those three signatures would be acceptable, or that other signatures would be acceptable only if they identified the signer as a representative of the Saudi joint venture. On the first presentation, the beneficiary presented a certificate of receipt that had been signed, but the signature was not one of the three authorised ones. The confirming bank rejected the presentation on account of that discrepancy. The beneficiary cured the discrepancy by securing a notarised signature of the freight forwarder, but was not able to present the revised document before the credit expired. The US Court of Appeals for the Second Circuit held that the letter of credit itself did not make any mention of the fact that only three signatures were acceptable (which is often done in soft clauses of this kind). If it had, the doctrine of strict compliance would have required the beneficiary to present a certificate of receipt bearing one of the approved signatures. Because there was no mention in the credit itself of the requirement for one of the approved signatures, the certificate of receipt would be an acceptable tender if the signature that it originally bore was that of a representative of the Saudi joint venture.[13] 3.11

The second refusal related to a requirement in the letter of credit that the beneficiary present a copy of a telex to the German applicant/buyer confirming that various 'legalized' documents, including a packing list, had been sent to the buyer's representative in Riyadh, 3.12

[12] 686 F 2d 112 (2nd Cir 1982) (hereafter *Marino Industries v Chase Manhattan*).

[13] The identity of the signer had not been determined as fact at first instance, so the court remanded the case to the court below to determine as fact whether the signer was a representative of the Saudi joint venture: see ibid 117.

Saudi Arabia, and also to a customs agent at the port of destination. The telex that the beneficiary presented to the confirming bank confirmed that a packing list had been sent, along with the other documents, but not that the packing list had been 'legalized.' 'Legalization' required the document to be stamped by the consulate of the country of destination, Saudi Arabia, which had not been done in relation to the packing list. The US Court of Appeals for the Second Circuit held that the confirming bank was entitled to reject the presentation because it did not conform strictly to the credit.

3.13 The third refusal related to a requirement in the letter of credit that the certificate of receipt should show that freight charges had been prepaid for carriage all the way to the Saudi jobsite. The certificates of receipt stated nothing about prepayment of freight charges, but they did contain the words 'ACCOUNT: CASH' with the word 'CASH' crossed out. Apparently, the crossing-out of the word 'CASH' reflected a practice in the freight forwarding industry of recording that freight had been prepaid, but nevertheless the confirming bank rejected the document. The US Court of Appeals for the Second Circuit held that the confirming bank was entitled to reject the presentation. The confirming bank could not properly be expected to know what the crossing-out of the word 'CASH' signified; the certificate of receipt did not bear a notation indicating that freight had been prepaid, so it did not conform strictly to the requirement in the letter of credit.

3.14 In retrospect, it is difficult to know why the seller/beneficiary accepted such far-reaching 'soft clauses' in the *Marino Industries* case, although it was probably a consequence of the parties' relative bargaining power in the underlying transaction. That may also have been the explanation for the willingness of the beneficiary to accept soft clauses in the Canadian case *Nareerux Import Co v Canadian Imperial Bank of Commerce* ('*Nareerux*').[14] A Thai shrimp producer agreed to sell shrimp to an American buyer for eventual on-sale to Sam's Club, a division of Wal-Mart. The buyer applied to its bank in Canada to issue letters of credit to the Thai seller. Initially, the credits included the 'soft' provision that payment would not be made until the issuing bank had received documentary proof that the shrimp had cleared inspection by the US Food and Drug Administration. The seller/beneficiary later agreed to an additional, even 'softer', condition, which was that payment would not be made until the bank had received from the applicant a signed purchase order from Sam's Club and delivery receipts showing that the shrimp had actually been received by one of Sam's Club Distribution Centres. By agreeing to such terms, the Thai seller was knowingly taking the risk of handing over possession of the shrimp to the ultimate buyer, Sam's Club, before payment was made. The case reports give no indication of why the seller was prepared to take such a commercial risk, but one can speculate that the size and market share of the final customer, Sam's Club, were large enough that it could dictate terms both to the American wholesaler and the Thai seller. A division of America's largest retailer certainly had a legitimate reason for wanting to satisfy itself that the shrimp it would be putting on its shelves were fit for human consumption, and, unlike most buyers, it had the market muscle to ensure that payment was not released to the producer until it had satisfied itself of that fact.

3.15 Whatever the reason for the Thai seller/beneficiary's acceptance of the risk of non-payment in the *Nareerux* case, the soft clauses made an apparently irrevocable letter of credit into

[14] (2009) 312 DLR (4th) 678 (hereafter *Nareerux*).

something very like a revocable one, where the applicant could secure the withholding of payment simply by refusing to produce the required receipts from its customer—which is exactly what it eventually did. One writer has gone even further in his description of the parties' arrangements in *Nareerux*, arguing that this was, in effect, no longer a letter of credit at all, because the beneficiary could only hope to secure payment by trusting in the applicant's cooperation, which meant that it had given up on the letter of credit as its security in the transaction.[15] Whether or not one accepts that rather extreme characterisation, there is no doubt that letters of credit with soft clauses do not conform readily to the stereotype upon which UCP 600 and traditional letter of credit law are built. The payment mechanisms set up in *The Messiniaki Tolmi*, *Eximetals*, and *Marino Industries* did not secure payment to the seller because of the traditional doctrine of strict compliance. That doctrine would also have denied payment to the seller in *Nareerux*, but for court intervention that will be described in the next section. If letters of credit with soft clauses are not to be treated as an entirely different payment instrument, which seems excessive,[16] and if the UCP is not going to be amended to accommodate this type of banking practice, which seems highly unlikely, then some other means must be found within the existing legal framework to avoid abuses by unscrupulous applicants.

III. Fraud in the Underlying Transaction, Unconscionability, Good Faith: A Sword Instead of a Shield?

Although, as noted above, the applicant may originally have a legitimate reason for including a soft clause in the letter of credit, its refusal to produce a document required for payment, such as a signed certificate of receipt or countersigned certificate of inspection, may ultimately be driven by a desire to avoid its obligation to pay under the underlying transaction, perhaps because that transaction no longer provides at the time of performance the benefits that it appeared to promise at the time the contract was made, such as when the market price falls before payment is due in a contract for the sale of goods. This is one of the principal underlying fears in relation to soft clauses, namely that they can be used as vehicles for fraud by an unscrupulous applicant.[17] To apply the fraud exception in cases such as this would be to extend it far beyond its traditional operation as a shield restraining payment by the bank to make it into a sword requiring payment by the bank. Such a development is admittedly very unlikely, but the possibility nevertheless warrants consideration. **3.16**

The autonomy principle enshrined in UCP 600, arts 4(a) and 5 requires banks to pay against conforming documents regardless of what may be going on in the underlying transaction, **3.17**

[15] Bradley Crawford, QC, '*Nareerux Import Co. Ltd v. Canadian Imperial Bank of Commerce*: A New Implied Duty of Good Faith for Banks Issuing Letters of Credit?' (2010) 49 Canadian Business Law Journal 130 (hereafter Crawford, 'Implied Duty of Good Faith').

[16] There is US authority for the proposition that a document ceases to be a letter of credit, even if so described on its face, if the substantive provisions require the issuer to deal not simply in documents alone, but in facts relating to the performance of a separate contract: see *Wichita Eagle & Beacon Pub Co Inc v Pacific Nat Bank of San Francisco* 493 F 2d 1285 (9th Cir 1974). Even by this standard, it would seem that a letter of credit with a 'soft' clause is still a letter of credit, as it requires no more of the bank than consideration of the documents presented.

[17] See, for example, Yanan Zhang, 'Can Soft Clauses in Letter of Credit Transactions Be Considered Letter of Credit Fraud in China?' [2011] 2011:1 Nordic Journal of Commercial Law 1 (hereafter Zhang, 'Soft Clauses in Letter of Credit Transactions').

because, as art 5 puts it: 'Banks deal with documents and not with goods, services or performance to which the documents may relate.' Although UCP 600 makes no mention of an exception in cases of fraud, most countries have as part of their national law a fraud exception that allows a defrauded applicant to restrain payment by the issuing, confirming, or nominated bank in the event of fraud by the beneficiary.[18]

3.18 In many countries, the fraud exception extends only to documents that have been fraudulently produced, which is generally referred to as 'fraud on the documents'. That is the position in the UK[19] and other common law countries that have historically followed UK law, such as Australia[20] and Singapore.[21] In countries such as these, the fraud exception would be of no assistance in the reverse situation under consideration here, in which the beneficiary is unable to present conforming documents because of the applicant's refusal to provide some of the documents stipulated in the soft clause of the letter of credit, such as a signed certificate of receipt. The document has not been fraudulently produced to secure payment; it is merely non-conforming or absent altogether.

3.19 In other countries, by contrast, the fraud exception extends to 'fraud in the underlying transaction', which requires the court to look at whether the presentation of documents under the letter of credit is being used to effect fraud in the underlying transaction, even if the documents themselves are not fraudulently produced. This broader version of the fraud exception forms part of the law in the United States,[22] Canada,[23] and China,[24] among others. In countries such as these, an extended version of the fraud exception could conceivably be of assistance to a beneficiary who is unable to present conforming documents because of the applicant's deliberate inaction or positive misconduct in relation to the production of documents required by the soft clause.

3.20 For example, if the soft clause in the letter of credit requires signature by a representative of the applicant that matches a specimen sent to the issuing and/or confirming bank, the applicant may get the required representative to sign if the market has gone up since the contract was made, but may get another person to sign if the market has gone down.[25] In the latter situation, the applicant would be well aware that the doctrine of strict compliance should, and most probably would, lead to the result that the issuing, confirming, or nominated bank

[18] Professor Xiang Gao has published an invaluable comparative analysis of the operation of the fraud exception under different national laws. See Xiang Gao, *The Fraud Rule in the Law of Letters of Credit: A Comparative Study* (Kluwer Law International 2002) (hereafter Xiang Gao, *Fraud Rule*) and ch 6 of this volume which focuses on the operation of the fraud exception in the twenty-first century.

[19] *United City Merchants (Investments) Ltd v Royal Bank of Canada* [1983] AC 168 (HL) (hereafter *United City Merchants v Royal Bank of Canada*).

[20] *Inflatable Toy Co Pty Ltd v State Bank of New South Wales Ltd* (1994) 34 NSWLR 243.

[21] *Brody, White and Co Inc v Chemet Handel Trading (S) Pte Ltd* [1992] 3 SLR(R) 146 (CA); *Beam Technology (Mfg) Pte Ltd v Standard Chartered Bank [2003] 1 SLR(R) 597* (CA). See also *Mees Pierson NV v Bay Pacific (S) Pte Ltd and others* [2000] 2 SLR(R) 864 (HC) 878–82 (per S Rajendran J); *Lambias (Importers & Exporters) Co Pte Ltd v Hong Kong and Shanghai Banking Corp* [1993] 1 SLR(R) 752 (HC).

[22] See, for example, *Mid-America Tire Inc v PTZ Trading Ltd* 768 NE 2d 619 (Ohio, 2002).

[23] *Bank of Novia Scotia v Angelica-Whitewear Ltd* [1987] 1 SCR 59 (SCC) (hereafter *Bank of Nova Scotia v Angelica-Whitewear*).

[24] *Zuigao Renmin Fayuan Guanyu Shenli Xinyongzheng Jioafu Anjian Ruogan Wenti De Guiding* (*Provisions Concerning Certain Issues in Hearing Letter of Credit Cases*), an interpretive document promulgated by the Supreme People's Court of the PRC in September 2001, described by Xiang Gao in Xiang Gao, *Fraud Rule* (n 18) 183–87.

[25] Zhang, 'Soft Clauses in Letter of Credit Transactions' (n 17) 10, fn 57, citing Xu Junke, *Study on International Trade Law Special Topics: New Development under WTO Framework* (China Legal Publishing House 2007) 99.

would quite properly reject the document as non-conforming and so would withhold payment. Such conduct could, if proven, amount to fraud in the underlying transaction: the applicant would be acting deliberately to ensure that the beneficiary would not get paid.

Even if a fraud of this kind in the underlying transaction could be proved (which is, in itself, a very big if), the fact remains that even this broader version of the fraud exception has traditionally been a vehicle for restraining payment, rather than a means of demanding payment. In the United States, the doctrine of fraud in the underlying transaction has a statutory basis in § 5–109 of the Uniform Commercial Code, which by its terms refers only to circumstances in which the issuing bank may refuse to honour a presentation, or may be enjoined from doing so by a court.[26] In other words, the statutory 'fraud in the underlying transaction' doctrine in the United States is a shield, not a sword. In contrast, the 'fraud in the underlying transaction' doctrine in Canada is based on common law principles rather than the provisions of a statute and so could conceivably be argued to be of general application whenever fraudulent conduct is to be found in the underlying transaction. Nevertheless, the question arises in both countries (and in any others, like China, with a 'fraud in the underlying transaction' exception): what can be done if it is the *applicant* who is guilty of fraud in the underlying transaction, rather than the beneficiary? Can the doctrine be turned into a sword requiring payment to a beneficiary, rather than a shield preventing payment at the applicant's request? **3.21**

The short answer to that question seems to be 'No', but the idea that unfair conduct unravels the banks' obligations under the letter of credit does seem to be gaining some ground in recent years. Several countries, including Singapore[27] and Australia,[28] have expanded the grounds for restraining payment to include unconscionability, ie the situation where the beneficiary is acting unconscionably, rather than fraudulently, in drawing on a letter of credit or performance guarantee.[29] This development has been aptly described as fairness at the expense of commercial certainty,[30] and it is significant that it has occurred in countries that confine the fraud exception to fraud on the documents. Both the unconscionability doctrine and the 'fraud in the underlying transaction' doctrine recognise that unfair **3.22**

[26] UCC § 5–109(a),(b). Until 1995, the relevant provision was UCC § 5–114(2). The numbering was changed when the UCC was revised in 1995.

[27] *Bocotra Construction Pte Ltd v Attorney General* [1995] 2 SLR(R) 262 (CA); *Dauphin Offshore Engineering & Trading Pte Ltd v Private Office of HRH Sheikh Sultan bin Kalifa bin Azyed al Nahyan* [2000] 1 SLR(R) 117 (CA); *Eltraco International Pte Ltd v CGH Development Pte Ltd* [2000] 3 SLR(R) 198 (CA).

[28] In Australia, the unconscionability ground is based on the statutory prohibition against acting unconscionably in trade or commerce now contained in the *Australian Consumer Law* (Cth), ss 20–22. See *Olex Focas Pty Ltd v Skodaexport Co Ltd* [1998] 3 VR 380; *Boral Formwork & Scaffolding Pty Ltd v Action Makers Ltd* [2003] NSWSC 713; *Clough Engineering Ltd v Oil & Natural Gas Corp (No 2)* (2008) 24 BCL 35; [2007] FCA 927; *Clough Engineering Ltd v Oil & Natural Gas Corp* [2008] FCAFC 136; *Ottoway Engineering Pty Ltd v Westpac Banking Corp (No 2)* [2017] FCA 1500.

[29] It should be noted that most of the Singaporean cases in which unconscionability has led to an injunction restraining payment have been in relation to performance guarantees or standby letters of credit, rather than 'commercial' letters of credit. The doctrine has been trenchantly criticised by one of the contributors to this volume, Professor Nelson Enonchong: see Nelson Enonchong, *The Independence Principle of Letters of Credit and Demand Guarantees* (OUP 2011), esp at [7.32]–[7.35] Professor Enonchong's critique was considered at some length by the Singapore Court of Appeal in *BS Mount Sophia Pte Ltd v Join-Aim Pte Ltd* [2012] 3 SLR 352 (CA). Because the Australian doctrine of unconscionability is statutory, it applies to 'commercial' letters of credit as well as performance guarantees.

[30] Roger Johns and Mark Blodgett, 'Fairness at the Expense of Commercial Certainty: The International Emergence of Unconscionability and Illegality as Exceptions to the Independence Principle of Letters of Credit and Bank Guarantees' (2011) 31 Northern Illinois University Law Review 297.

behaviour (to put it deliberately broadly) in the underlying transaction is a reason for breaking through the wall that traditionally separates the letter of credit transaction from the underlying transaction. An applicant's deliberate refusal to provide the documents required by a soft clause seems just as unfair or unconscionable as, for example, a beneficiary's attempt to draw on a standby letter of credit when it knows that there is a genuine dispute about its entitlement to draw the claimed amount.[31]

3.23 The problem, of course, lies in the fact that there is no real mechanism for treating fraud in the underlying transaction or unconscionable behaviour as a sword rather than a shield. Two possible solutions suggest themselves. The first would be for the court to order the bank to disregard the absence or non-conformity of the document required by the soft clause if the court were sufficiently persuaded that the applicant was acting fraudulently (or unconscionably) in making sure that the beneficiary did not have a conforming document to present. In the context of the 'regular' fraud exception, courts in both the UK[32] and Canada[33] have held that a beneficiary should not be prevented from receiving payment when it presents a document fraudulently prepared by someone else without the beneficiary's knowledge. An extension (admittedly, a very large extension) of this principle would say that a beneficiary should not be prevented from receiving payment when it either fails to present a document, or presents a non-conforming document, because of fraudulent (or unconscionable) conduct on the part of someone else (the applicant or someone in the applicant's country acting at the applicant's behest), over whom it has no control.

3.24 The second possibility would be for the court to order the applicant to sign (or countersign) the missing or discrepant document. That was done in *The Messiniaki Tolmi* litigation,[34] where the High Court ordered the applicant to countersign the notice of readiness, and then ordered that a Supreme Court master should countersign it when the applicant ignored the court's order; the House of Lords later confirmed that the High Court had jurisdiction to make such orders.[35] This expedient would work if the fraudulent or unconscionable withholding were being done by the applicant itself, but not if it were being done by a third party. The beneficiary in *The Messiniaki Tolmi* ultimately failed to recover under the letter of credit, despite the countersignature that was eventually put on the notice of readiness, because the Taiwanese authorities did not indicate their approval of the gas-free certificate.[36]

3.25 Another possible sword for the beneficiary might be the development of a doctrine of good faith, which might preclude a bank from relying on the doctrine of strict compliance if it would not be acting in good faith when doing so. That was the result in the *Nareerux* case, described above.[37] Sam's Club began to refuse to take delivery of the shrimp from Thailand, so the American wholesaler (the first buyer) began to sell the shrimp to other customers. When it deposited the proceeds of sale into its bank—the issuing bank under the letter of credit—the bank applied the balance to reducing the wholesaler's line of credit, rather than paying it to the Thai seller/beneficiary under the letter of credit. The Ontario Court of

[31] See, eg *Boral Formwork & Scaffolding Pty Ltd v Action Makers Ltd* [2003] NSWSC 713.
[32] *United City Merchants v Royal Bank of Canada* (n 19).
[33] *Bank of Nova Scotia v Angelica-Whitewear* (n 23) [20] (Le Dain J).
[34] See nn 4–9.
[35] *The Messiniaki Tolmi (1983) HL* (n 6).
[36] See nn 4 and 9.
[37] *Nareerux* (n 14).

Appeal ultimately held that although the documents presented by the Thai seller/beneficiary did not conform strictly to the terms of the credit, the bank was precluded by the doctrine of good faith from relying on the doctrine of strict compliance. The court held that the bank had 'knowingly contributed to, or acquiesced in, the circumstances that undermined the prospect of strict compliance'.[38]

3.26 The *Nareerux* decision has been roundly criticised in Canada,[39] and it seems that it has never yet been followed by another Canadian court. John Dolan suggested that the new Canadian principle of good faith should be confined to the situation where the issuer's own actions render compliance impossible.[40] If confined in such a way, the principle would be of no assistance to a beneficiary when the issuing bank is merely aware that the applicant is withholding crucial documentation, but does nothing to inform the beneficiary. In any event, there are several conceptual difficulties with the imposition of a duty of good faith on an issuing bank. The Ontario Court of Appeal held that the duty was implied in the contract between issuing bank and beneficiary,[41] but it is questionable in many common law countries whether the relationship between those two is, indeed, contractual.[42] Even in the United States, where a duty of good faith is imposed on issuing banks by section 1-304 (formerly § 1–203) of the Uniform Commercial Code ('UCC'), it is not settled whether the duty is an implied contractual term,[43] or an extra-contractual duty imposed as a result of the contractual relationship.[44] A detailed consideration of these issues goes beyond the scope of this chapter: it is sufficient for present purposes simply to note that any development of a general doctrine of good faith on the part of an issuing bank might not be sufficient to solve the beneficiary's problems in relation to soft clauses, and would inevitably raise difficult questions of choice of law. The actions of the issuing bank under scrutiny would usually take place in a country different from that where their effect is felt: should the relevant law be that of the issuing bank's country, on the basis that that was where the conduct occurred, or that of the beneficiary's country, on the basis that that was where the bank's conduct had its effect?

3.27 At the end of the day, it seems very unlikely that any of these legal devices—the 'fraud in the underlying transaction' doctrine, the unconscionability doctrine, or a good faith doctrine—can be pressed into service to rescue a beneficiary who has difficulty in complying with a soft clause because of difficulty in presenting documents to be produced by the applicant or in the applicant's country. In this context, it is worth recalling that in the context of sale of goods, at least, a refusal by the bank to make payment under

[38] ibid [44] (per R A Blair JA).

[39] Crawford, 'Implied Duty of Good Faith' (n 15); John Dolan, '*Nareerux* Redux: The Ontario Court of Appeal Fashions Novel Letter of Credit Law' (2010) 25 Banking & Finance Law Review 535 (hereafter Dolan, 'Novel Letter of Credit Law').

[40] Dolan, 'Novel Letter of Credit Law' (n 39) 544.

[41] *Nareerux* (n 14) [69] (per R A Blair JA).

[42] See Crawford, 'Implied Duty of Good Faith' (n 15); ch 2 (Booysen) in this volume. In *Bhasin v Hrynew* 2014 SCC 71, [2014] 3 SCR 495, the Supreme Court of Canada held that the doctrine of good faith operates as a matter of law, rather than as an implied term in a specific contract, which might provide scope for future development even if the relationship is not regarded as contractual.

[43] *Fleet Bank of Maine v Druce* 791 F Supp 14 (D Me 1992); *Esso Petroleum Canada, Division of Imperial Oil, Ltd v Security Pacific Bank* 710 F Supp 275, 282 (D Or 1989).

[44] *Schmueser v Burkburnett Bank* 937 F 2d 1025, 1029–30 (5th Cir 1991); *Ward Petroleum Corp v FDIC* 903 F 2d 1297, 1300 (10th Cir 1990).

a letter of credit does not relieve the buyer of its contractual obligation to make payment for the goods in question.[45] The seller's cause of action for breach of the sale contract by the buyer may be much less secure than its hoped-for right to collect on the letter of credit provided on the buyer's application, but it does still have a cause of action for non-payment against the buyer. For example, in *The Messiniaki Tolmi*,[46] the Panamanian shipowner obtained a large arbitration award in its favour for breach of the sale contract by the Taiwanese buyer, but it still continued to try to enforce payment by the confirming bank under the letter of credit because the award could not be enforced effectively against the Taiwanese buyer.[47] Similarly, the seller/beneficiary might have a cause of action against the buyer/beneficiary under the sale contract for the latter's refusal to issue or sign a document required for presentation by the soft clause, either because the parties so stipulate in the sale contract, or because of an implied obligation of good faith and fair dealing in the sale contract.[48]

IV. What Are the Beneficiary's Alternatives?

3.28 The harsh truth seems to be that nothing can be done for a beneficiary who is advised of a letter of credit with soft clauses, except to counsel it, as ISBP does, to demand amendments or refuse to accept the credit as a valid discharge of the applicant's payment obligation. This presupposes, of course, that beneficiaries are sufficiently sophisticated to be able to identify soft clauses, or sufficiently wary to seek advice about the provisions of a letter of credit of which they have been advised. There is a considerable academic literature in China devoted to the pitfalls of soft clauses and means of avoiding them, which seems to be premised on the idea that Chinese beneficiaries are prone to exploitation by unscrupulous foreign applicants.[49] If identifying or objecting to soft clauses is a problem in practice, what are the alternatives for a wary or well-informed exporter, short of insisting on deletion of the soft clause? Because the alternative payment mechanisms are fairly well-known, and because some are covered in more detail in other chapters of this book, I will outline them only briefly here, focusing on those situations where the party who would be the applicant under a letter of credit (eg the buyer under a sale of goods contract) would have a legitimate reason for wanting a soft clause. For the sake of convenience, the subsections that follow use the common example of payment instruments in international sale of goods contracts, although that is obviously not their only use.

[45] *E D & F Man Ltd v Nigerian Sweets & Confectionery Co Ltd* [1977] 2 Lloyd's Rep 50 (QBD); *North Western Shipping & Towage Co Pty Ltd v Commonwealth Bank of Australia* (1993) 118 ALR 453 (FCA).

[46] *The Messiniaki Tolmi (1988) CA* (n 4).

[47] ibid 218 (Lloyd LJ). Taiwan was not, and still is not, party to the United Nations Convention on the Recognition and Enforcement of Foreign Arbitral Awards 1958 (the New York Convention).

[48] The implication of a duty of good faith and fair dealing in international sales contracts is another large topic beyond the scope of this chapter. See generally Steven D Walt, 'The Modest Role of Good Faith in Uniform Sales Law' (2015) Boston University International Law Journal 37.

[49] See Zhang, 'Soft Clauses in Letter of Credit Transactions' (n 17), which collects references to the literature on this point.

A. Documentary Collections and Bills of Exchange/Time Drafts: Back to the Future?

The use of documentary collections and bills of exchange (called time drafts in North America) is generally regarded as rather old-fashioned because it does not provide the exporter with any certainty (as a letter of credit does, or should) that it will be paid by a solvent entity if it sends the goods and documents to the importer's country. An immediate retort to this objection is that the use of a documentary collection and bill of exchange/time draft is no less secure from the exporter's point of view than is a letter of credit with a soft clause, which can, as we have seen, lead to the result that payment is easily subverted by the applicant's refusal to issue the relevant documents. There may, however, be other advantages in returning to this supposedly old-fashioned method of payment as a means of avoiding the pitfalls of soft clauses in letters of credit. **3.29**

The use of bills of exchange/time drafts saw something of a resurgence in the wake of the decision in *Banco Santander SA v Bayfern Ltd*,[50] where the English Court of Appeal held that deferred payment letters of credit cannot be assigned free of any defect in the transferor's title, as can bills of exchange, by virtue of the Bills of Exchange Act 1882 (UK), s 38(2), which allows the holder in due course of a bill of exchange to enforce payment under the bill free of any defect of title of prior parties.[51] The resulting chill on the liquidity of the market for discounting deferred payment letters of credit was supposedly remedied by the inclusion in 2007 of art 12(b) of UCP 600, which provides that by nominating a bank to incur a deferred payment undertaking, an issuing bank authorises the nominated bank to prepay or discount the deferred payment undertaking. To the extent that the art 12(b) 'fix' works at all, it works only in relation to discounting by the nominated bank, and does nothing to protect the position of third-party forfaiters, at least in countries that have no legislation protecting their position, as does the United States.[52] For that reason alone, bills of exchange/time drafts may be a more desirable means of payment than deferred payment letters of credit, because they are more readily marketable to third-party forfaiters. Their attractiveness may be enhanced yet further as they make the transition to electronic form, as considered by Professor Benjamin Geva in a subsequent chapter.[53] **3.30**

For present purposes, however, perhaps the more significant feature of the use of documentary collections is that the collection instruction describing the documents to be presented in return for payment or acceptance of the bill of exchange/time draft is prepared by the seller/principal and not by the buyer/drawee, pursuant to the Uniform Rules for Collections (1995) ('URC 522'). If the buyer/drawee has a legitimate reason for making payment contingent upon the production of some document in the buyer's country, as the buyer did (at least initially) in *The Messiniaki Tolmi*,[54] it must specifically ask for the document to be included in the list of documents enclosed with the collection, as required by art 4(b)(v) of **3.31**

[50] [2001] 1 All ER (Comm) 776 (CA).

[51] The Singapore Court of Appeal came to a similar conclusion in *Credit Agricole Indosuez v Banque Nationale de Paris* [2001] 1 SLR(R) 285 (CA).

[52] UCC 600, art 5-109(a)(1)(iv) provides the same protection to the holder in due course of a deferred payment letter of credit as the UK Bills of Exchange Act 1882, s 38(2) does to the holder in due course of a bill of exchange.

[53] See further ch 9 (Geva) in this volume.

[54] *The Messiniaki Tolmi (1988) CA* (n 4).

URC 522. At the very least, then, the 'softness' of the payment obligation must be brought squarely to the seller/principal's attention. This mechanism would not protect against an unscrupulous refusal by the buyer/drawee to produce the document in question—perhaps nothing can do that—but it would at least avoid one of the problems that apparently exists with soft clauses in letters of credit, namely that the seller/beneficiary is unaware of the 'softness' of the obligation undertaken by the issuing or confirming bank.

B. Open Account/Standby Letter of Credit: Not Really the Future at All?

3.32 Although letters of credit supposedly provide the seller/beneficiary with security that it will be paid by a solvent party if it sends the goods to the other side of the world, that security comes at a price: banks typically charge about 1% of the face value of the credit as their fee, or possibly more, depending on the applicant's country. For repeat business, fees of this size can accumulate to a commercially unacceptable level if they must be paid on every single shipment of goods. For that reason, contracting parties who have some degree of trust and confidence in one another, and/or some reliable information about each other's creditworthiness, tend to prefer to trade on an open account basis, under which the exporter sends goods to the importer without any guarantee of payment for each particular shipment, but with the importer's contractual obligation to pay for the goods secured by a standby letter of credit on which the exporter can draw in the event of non-payment by the importer. Open account may even be offered to new customers by an exporter trying to break into a new or competitive market by offering attractive payment terms, although in such a case the exporter's collateral security (often a stand-by letter of credit) takes on extra significance.

3.33 Nothing about this mechanism for payment is new or forward-looking, but it does at least avoid the problems of soft clauses in letters of credit, because the seller/beneficiary's right to payment is not dependent on presentation of any commercial documents such as bills of lading, packing lists, or the kinds of certificate of receipt called for by soft clauses. The seller/beneficiary presents no commercial documents of any kind; it need only present a beneficiary's certificate in the event of non-payment, and so is not at the mercy of the requirements of any soft clauses or uncooperative actions by an unscrupulous buyer trying to take advantage of a change in market price. Of course, parties who have no pre-existing trading relationship of trust and confidence may be reluctant to contract on open account terms from the beginning of their relationship, but it is clearly better from the seller/beneficiary's point of view than a commercial letter of credit with soft clauses.

C. Blockchain: The Real Future?

3.34 In chapter 12 of this volume, Professor Jane Winn expresses some scepticism about whether blockchain technology will actually deliver on the expectations people presently have for its transformative potential.[55] A thorough examination of the ways in which blockchain

[55] 'Will Blockchain Transform Trade Finance?'.

technology might possibly transform trade finance in the future is well beyond the scope of this chapter. For present purposes, it suffices to say that the promise of blockchain is that it will finally replace the use of paper documents in trade finance transactions, a result that has been an apparently impossible desideratum throughout the previous thirty years or so in which electronic communications have been the norm in other aspects of business and daily life. More than $4 trillion in goods are shipped each year, and the cost of required trade documentation is estimated to be as much as 20% of the physical transportation costs; blockchain technology may be able vastly to reduce that number, leading to a significant increase in global trade.[56] With blockchain, there will be no need for the production of any soft-clause-type document such as a signed certificate of receipt or countersigned certificate of inspection, because no part of the transaction will depend on the production of paper documents. Of course, the unscrupulous buyer who wants to take advantage of favourable market movements under the guise of reluctance to certify its acceptance of the goods may still be able to do so by illegitimately refusing to add its block to the chain, but the speed and transparency of the blockchain transaction should produce the result that the seller should no longer be so vulnerable to the risk of deliberate manipulation of the process by the buyer.

Previous attempts to replace paper documents with electronic ones in trade payments, such **3.35** as the proprietary BOLERO or SeaDocs experiments, have relied on the use of some form of central registry recording successive transactions with the relevant commercial documents. They have not been successful, despite decades of effort, partly because of commercial parties' mistrust of central registries, and partly because of the systems' reliance on technology that was not widely or cheaply available. Because it decentralises the payment process and makes it available to anyone with a simple internet connection, blockchain may be the future of trade finance. If it is the future, it is likely to provide a sweeping solution to soft clauses in letters of credit by transforming the structure of international payment systems completely.

V. Conclusion

Soft clauses in letters of credit may be an example of the maxim: 'Fool me once, shame on **3.36** you; fool me twice, shame on me.' Any beneficiary who does not object to the presence of a soft clause in a letter of credit may find itself in a similar position to the beneficiaries in the *Messiniaki Tolmi*, *Marino Industries*, and *Nareerux* cases, struggling to achieve a complying presentation in circumstances where it is impossible for them to cure any documentary non-conformity themselves. Presumably, any beneficiary who suffers through this experience will vow never to put itself in such a weak position again—unless it has to because the nature of the trade means that the applicant can dictate the terms. As for the applicant, even if it originally has a legitimate reason for including the soft clause, a change in market conditions may put it in the situation of the fictional Lord Darlington in Oscar Wilde's play *Lady Windermere's Fan*: 'I can resist anything except temptation.'

[56] A P Moller, 'Maersk and IBM Expand Blockchain Offerings' (*The Maritime Executive*, 16 January 2018) <https://www.maritime-executive.com/article/maersk-and-ibm-expand-blockchain-offerings> accessed 4 February 2021.

3.37 It seems that little can be done to alleviate the position of the beneficiary if the applicant becomes uncooperative in production of the documents required by the soft clause—indeed, some would say that nothing should be done to remove the rod that the beneficiary put on its own back. To date, courts have been stern in their application of the doctrine of strict compliance in soft clause cases to rebuff beneficiaries who have tried to present documents that are 'almost the same'.[57] Perhaps the creeping intrusion of fairness at the expense of commercial certainty may see a change in letter of credit law in the future,[58] but unless and until there is some relaxation in the standards of strict compliance, either generally or specifically in relation to soft clauses, exporters would be well advised to suggest an alternative method of payment if their importers propose inclusion of a soft clause.

57 As Viscount Sumner famously observed in *Equitable Trust Co. of New York v Dawson Partners Ltd* (1927) 27 Ll L Rep 49 (HL) 52: 'There is no room for documents which are almost the same, or which will do just as well.'

58 See section III of this chapter.

4

Perspectives on the Role of the Nominated Bank in a Letter of Credit

Toh Kian Sing and Chen Zhida

I. Introduction

A nominated bank plays a crucial role in the performance of the issuing bank's promise to the beneficiary to honour the credit, as it is typically the bank with which a letter of credit is available. The nominated bank's treatment of documents presented under a credit will not only be relevant to its rights and liabilities towards the issuing bank, but will also affect the rights and liabilities of the issuing bank towards the beneficiary. Further, the nominated bank may, in certain circumstances, attract rights and liabilities vis-à-vis the beneficiary. **4.01**

The provisions of the Uniform Customs & Practice for Documentary Credits ('UCP 600') address many but not all of these rights and liabilities. For example, what happens if a nominated bank declines to act on the nomination? In this situation, what, if any, obligation does it owe towards the issuing bank or the beneficiary? Would common law rules, such as the rules of agency, apply to govern the relationship between the nominated bank and the issuing bank? This chapter will examine these questions against the backdrop of the decision by the Singapore Court of Appeal in *Grains and Industrial Products Trading Pte Ltd v Bank of India and another*,[1] in which the facts bring these issues into sharp focus. Following this introduction, section II explains the findings in the *Grains* case, where it was decided that even where a nominated bank declines to act on its nomination, it nevertheless owes duties to the issuing bank, and further, its actions or inaction could trigger the issuing bank's obligations towards the beneficiary under the credit. Section III discusses the practical implications of these findings from the perspective of the three principal players in a letter of credit, namely, the issuing bank, the nominated bank, and the beneficiary. Section IV critically explores the conceptual implications of attributing an agency relationship to the nominated bank in its dealing with the issuing bank.

II. Decision in *Grains*

The Singapore Court of Appeal decision in *Grains* involves a claim brought by the Singapore beneficiary of the letter of credit (allegedly issued for a synthetic transaction in which only copies of bills of lading had to be presented) against the issuing bank, Indian Bank, which in turn brought an indemnity claim against the nominated bank **4.02**

[1] [2016] 3 SLR 1308 (CA) (hereafter *Grains*).

in Singapore, Bank of India, if the beneficiary's claim was successful. The nominated bank had kept the conforming documents presented under the letter of credit for a substantial period (longer than the five banking days allowed under art 16(d) of UCP 600) before forwarding them to the issuing bank. During this period, the nominated bank was deciding on whether to provide 'negotiation' to the beneficiary against the documents, which it eventually refused to do. After deciding against 'negotiation', the nominated bank forwarded the documents to the issuing bank. The issuing bank rejected the documents so received because the documents arrived after the letter of credit had expired. It bears noting that the letter of credit provided that Bank of India was the bank with which the credit was available 'by acceptance' and not 'by negotiation'[2] and that the Court of Appeal expressly indicated that it was using the terms 'negotiate' and 'discount' interchangeably to describe the purchase of the credit by a correspondent bank.[3]

4.03 At the first instance, the High Court Judge allowed the beneficiary's claim against the issuing bank and dismissed its claim against the nominated bank.[4] In essence, the Judge found that the issuing bank was liable to honour the credit pursuant to art 7(a)(iv) of UCP 600 because the beneficiary made a timely, complying presentation to the nominated bank.[5] The Judge dismissed the issuing bank's indemnity claim against the nominated bank because he found that the nominated bank did not act upon or accept its nomination, such that no contract arose between them and thus no liability was owed by the nominated bank to the issuing bank.[6] The issuing bank filed an appeal and the beneficiary filed a cross-appeal (against the dismissal of the claim against the nominated bank and on the issues of interests and costs) against the Judge's decision.[7]

4.04 The Court of Appeal, upholding the first instance judge in both appeals, allowed the beneficiary's claim under the letter of credit against the issuing bank and rejected the issuing bank's indemnity claim. Notably, while the Court of Appeal was unanimous in respect of the outcome of the beneficiary's appeal, Chan Sek Keong SJ disagreed with the reasoning adopted by Sundaresh Menon CJ and Andrew Phang JA on a number of points, which will be discussed below.

4.05 In arriving at its conclusion to allow the beneficiary's claim against the issuing bank and refusing the latter's claim for indemnity against the nominated bank, the Court of Appeal (in the majority opinion delivered by Menon CJ) laid down the following salient legal principles:

[2] ibid [11] and [203].

[3] ibid [8]. That having been said, this chapter focuses on negotiation credits, which are more frequently encountered in practice than acceptance credit.

[4] See the High Court decision reported as *Grains and Industrial Products Trading Pte Ltd v Bank of India* [2015] 1 SLR 1213 (hereafter *Grains HC*). The essential grounds of decision of the High Court Judge can be found in *Grains* (n 1) [28].

[5] *Grains HC* (n 4) [77]–[87]. Art 7(a)(iv) of UCP 600 states: 'Provided that the stipulated documents are presented to the nominated bank or to the issuing bank and that they constitute a complying presentation, the issuing bank must honour if the credit is available by: ... (iv) acceptance with a nominated bank and that nominated bank does not accept a draft drawn on it or, having accepted a draft drawn on it, does not pay at maturity....'

[6] *Grains HC* (n 4) [95]–[99].

[7] *Grains* (n 1) [5] and [6].

(a) When the documents are presented under a letter of credit to the nominated bank, the latter acts as an agent of the issuing bank in receiving the documents even if it does not negotiate or discount the documents.[8]

(b) A beneficiary can present documents to either the nominated bank or issuing bank under art 7(a) of UCP 600. If the beneficiary makes a timely and conforming presentation to the nominated bank, the liability of the issuing bank to honour or pay under the letter of credit may still be engaged if the nominated bank does not pay at sight, incur a deferred payment undertaking, accept a draft or negotiate against the documents, as the case may be, depending on the type of credit involved. In other words, it does not matter, so far as the issuing bank's liability under the letter of credit is concerned, that the nominated bank does not act on the nomination. If the nominated bank does act on the nomination, then it is entitled to seek reimbursement from the issuing bank under art 7(c) of UCP 600.[9]

(c) If the nominated bank fails to check the documents for conformity with the terms of the letter of credit and/or rejects the documents for discrepancies, art 16(f) of UCP 600 operates to preclude the issuing bank for rejecting the documents vis-à-vis the beneficiary. The issuing bank becomes bound to pay the beneficiary under the letter of credit under art 7(a) of UCP 600. The issuing bank is liable notwithstanding the fact that it is the omission of the nominated bank (as opposed to the issuing bank) to check the documents or to give a notice of refusal according to art 16.[10]

(d) If the conforming documents are received by the nominated bank before the letter of credit expiry date, they would have been presented on time vis-à-vis the issuing bank, even if the issuing bank receives them after that date.[11]

(e) If an issuing bank wants the beneficiary to make a direct presentation of documents to itself in the event that the nominated bank does not negotiate or discount documents presented thereunder, it can (and should) expressly provide for that event under the terms of the letter of credit, thereby departing from the default position in art 7(a) that it is bound by a timely and conforming presentation to the nominated bank.[12]

(f) The fact that a beneficiary presents documents to the nominated bank with the intention that the nominated bank is to negotiate or discount the documents, does not preclude the possibility that the documents are also presented to that bank in its capacity as the nominated bank. The documents would still be considered to have been presented by the beneficiary to the nominated bank under art 7(a) of UCP 600, thereby triggering off the undertaking of the issuing bank to honour the letter of credit.[13]

(g) If a nominated bank, acting as the issuing bank's agent, wrongly accepts the documents which are non-complying, such an act will bind the issuing bank vis-à-vis the

[8] ibid [56], [59], and [60].
[9] ibid [50]–[55].
[10] ibid [73]–[75].
[11] ibid [47]–[57]. An exception, though not articulated by the Court as it does not arise on the facts, is where the letter of credit expires at the counter of the issuing bank.
[12] ibid [75].
[13] ibid [60].

beneficiary even though the issuing bank may be able to sue the nominated bank for failing to act properly and carefully in the examination of documents or reject the non-complying documents in accordance with the rejection procedure prescribed in art 16(c) of UCP 600.[14]

(h) A nominated bank may be authorised by the issuing bank to perform various tasks, including receiving, examining, and where appropriate rejecting documents presented, advising the beneficiary of the credit, negotiating, or confirming the credit. The extent of the nominated bank's authority depends on the terms of the letter of credit and the provisions of UCP 600.[15]

(i) A bank which does not wish to act upon the nomination of the issuing bank should inform the issuing bank as well as the beneficiary, directing the latter to present the documents directly to the former.[16]

(j) A nominated bank, having examined and found the documents presented to be complying, should *promptly* forward the documents to the issuing bank (even if it does not negotiate/discount the documents). (This is so even though art 15 of UCP 600 does not expressly cover this situation.) In the absence of any compelling reasons for the delay, this should be done by the end of the next banking day after the nominated bank determines that the documents are complying. A nominated bank which unreasonably delays the forwarding of documents to the issuing bank may be liable for the losses suffered by the latter arising from or caused by the delay.[17] (On the facts of *Grains*, this was not proved by the issuing bank which led to the eventual dismissal of its indemnity claim.)[18]

4.06 This chapter focuses on the agency reasoning adopted by Menon CJ and Phang JA in *Grains*, and flowing from that, the result that even if the nominated bank presented with documents under the credit declines to negotiate or discount the same, it can still be an agent of the issuing bank for the purpose of receiving, examining, and handling of the presented documents.[19] As alluded to earlier, Chan SJ issued a separate opinion[20] in which his Honour disagreed with the reasoning adopted by Menon CJ and Phang JA and offered an *alternative* analysis which avoids the agency reasoning altogether. In fact, his Honour opined that there is no need to employ agency reasoning to describe the legal relationship between a nominated bank and an issuing bank.[21] Instead, his Honour considered that the rights and obligations were (and ought) to be governed by and flowed from the articles of the UCP 600 which operate as contractual provisions incorporated into the letters of credit[22] as well as the terms of the letters of credit, without having to overlay the same with principles of agency law.

14 ibid [56] and [69].
15 ibid [71]–[72].
16 ibid [77].
17 ibid [92]–[108].
18 ibid [114] and [118].
19 ibid [69]–[71], [77], and [80].
20 ibid [158]–[290].
21 ibid [186]–[195].
22 ibid.

III. Practical Implications of the Decision in *Grains*

As would be apparent from the foregoing distillation of the principles established in the decision, the role of the nominated bank (and performance of that role) can critically affect the rights and liabilities of the issuing bank vis-à-vis the beneficiary as well as the nominated bank itself. As the case law that applies in Singapore (alongside the UCP 600) to letters of credit is derived from the principles of the English common law, the principles established in the *Grains* decision have potential relevance in other common law jurisdictions. Banks must therefore be alive to the practical implications that application of these principles may have on their practices, regardless of whether they are acting as issuing bank or nominated bank. Some of these practical implications and suggestions to ameliorate their impact on banks are discussed in the subsection that follows, starting with the perspective of an issuing bank before turning to consider the perspective of a nominated bank. **4.07**

A. Practical Implications from Issuing Bank's Perspective

1. Choice of Nominated Bank

Under UCP 600, if the credit does not narrow the nomination to a named bank, any bank operating in the beneficiary's jurisdiction can potentially be a nominated bank.[23] This potentially exposes the issuing bank to the risk of any failure by a bank (whose identity may be unknown to the issuing bank beforehand) to which documents are presented by the beneficiary and which does not expressly decline to receive the documents or refuse to accept the nomination. On the majority reasoning of *Grains*, such a bank may be considered the agent of the issuing bank under art 7(a) of UCP 600. Its acts and omissions in relation to the handling of the presented documents therefore binds the latter. Accordingly, one important aspect for banks (acting in their capacity as issuing banks) to consider is whether (and under what circumstances) would they be prepared to issue a credit that is available with any bank, which by its nature, attracts the risk described above. One possible strategy is to limit the banks with which the credit is available to the advising bank; after all, the choice of the advising bank is something an issuing bank can decide for itself. For this purpose, a provision entitling the issuing bank to restrict nomination to a bank of its choice in the beneficiary's jurisdiction (overriding any conflicting express instructions from the beneficiary to issue a credit available with any bank if necessary) may have to be included in the letter of credit application form. **4.08**

2. Direct Presentation by Beneficiary to Issuing Bank

A nominated bank may reject the documents without fully complying with the rejection procedure in art 16(c) of UCP 600. Arising from such failure, the issuing bank will be bound to accept the documents or be said to have lost its right of rejection under art 16(c)—that **4.09**

[23] See definition of 'nominated bank' UCP 600, art 2 which reads: 'Nominated Bank means the bank with which the credit is available or any bank in the case of a credit available with any bank.' This can be contrasted with the position under UCP 500, where the term 'nominated bank' appears parenthetically in art 10(b)(i), which states: 'Unless the Credit stipulates that it is available only with the Issuing Bank, all Credits must nominate the bank (the "Nominated Bank") which is authorised to pay, to incur a deferred payment undertaking, to accept Draft(s) or to negotiate. In a freely negotiable Credit, any bank is a Nominated Bank.'

was what happened in *Grains* itself. To protect its interests, an issuing bank may wish to make it clear to the beneficiary that if documents which are initially received by the nominated bank are subsequently refused by the latter whether on account of discrepancies or a refusal to negotiate the documents, the beneficiary has to present the documents *directly* to the issuing bank and that the issuing bank is not bound by the acts or omission of the nominated bank in its receipt and handling of the documents. This requires the inclusion of an appropriately worded provision in the credit. The reason a provision making clear the above should be included is that otherwise—in the event that the nominated bank fails to properly handle the documents presented to it while not acting on the nomination to pay or negotiate the credit—all that the issuing bank is left with is a negligence claim against the nominated bank. The issuing bank is still exposed to a claim by the beneficiary for what the nominated bank does or fails to do in handling the documents presented.

3. Release of Security and Scope of Applicant's Indemnity

4.10 In some instances, an issuing bank takes security from the applicant before it agrees to issue a letter of credit. If documents do not arrive at the bank's counter by the expiry date of the letter of credit, the issuing bank may assume that the documents have either not been presented at all or that the documents presented have been rejected by the nominated bank. It may be recalled that in *Grains*, the documents arrived at the issuing bank after the expiry date but the issuing bank was still found to be liable. Thus, an issuing bank should consider if it wants to release the security it holds back to the applicant only after it has ascertained that either no documents have been presented to the nominated bank, or if documents have been presented, they have in fact been found to be discrepant and rejected. However, this practice would only be feasible practically if nomination is restricted to a particular bank. Further, issuing banks may also wish to expand the scope of the applicant's indemnity to the bank (usually set out in the bank's letter of credit application terms and conditions) to cover any loss which the issuing bank suffers from as a result of the acts or omission of the nominated bank in the receipt, examination, handling, and forwarding of documents presented by the beneficiary.

B. Practical Implications from Nominated Bank's Perspective

4.11 The foregoing points pertain to the rights and obligations of a bank where it acts as the issuing bank. The implications from *Grains* are somewhat different in relation to a nominated bank.

1. Refusing to Negotiate, Discount, or to Act as Nominated Bank

4.12 When presented with documents which are complying but which the nominated bank does not wish to negotiate or discount, it should promptly forward these documents to the issuing bank. That would in the absence of extenuating circumstances be the banking day following the day examination of documents is completed. Further, if a bank does not wish to accept the role of a nominated bank (especially where nomination is restricted to it), the bank should inform the issuing bank and the beneficiary immediately when the latter presents the documents to the bank, as well as promptly return the documents so presented to the beneficiary. Even if the nominated bank refuses to negotiate or discount ie act on the nomination, it may still be requested by the beneficiary to send the documents to the issuing bank by way of collection on the beneficiary's behalf. If that is the case and the bank agrees to do so, the bank's role should be clearly stated in the collection schedule to be sent to the issuing bank.

2. Agreeing to Act on the Nomination

If a nominated bank does act on its nomination and pays or otherwise extends financing against a conforming set of documents according to the availability of the credit, it becomes entitled to reimbursement from the issuing bank when the documents are forwarded to the issuing bank. The nominated bank's officers need to be made aware that any negligence or fault on their part in the receipt, examination, and handling of the presented documents may result in the bank being exposed to the issuing bank and/or the beneficiary. In practice, some banks have already introduced provisions in the letters of credit that they issue which expressly oblige the nominated bank to take certain steps, like forwarding of documents expeditiously, in light of the decision in *Grains*. The nominated bank's officers must be alerted to such provisions, which means that a close scrutiny of the letter of credit terms is called for. **4.13**

IV. Conceptual Implications of Treating Nominated Bank as Issuing Bank's Agent

The foregoing section examines the practical implications of the decision in *Grains* on banking practice and puts forward some suggestion on how banks, in their respective role, as issuing banks and nominated banks, can protect themselves. The rest of this chapter will be focused on a separate question, that is, how well do the principles of agency law function in the context of the relationship between a nominated bank and an issuing bank? A survey of the pre-UCP 600 cases as well as the views of commentators on the UCP 600 reveals a lack of support (and indeed justification) for a general role of agency on the part of the nominated banks vis-à-vis the issuing bank. This suggests that a narrow reading of *Grains* should be adopted. **4.14**

A. The Nominated Bank as Defined in UCP 600

Historically, before modern technology made it possible (and economical) for banks to set up branches in key trading hubs around the world, banks involved in cross-border trade financing had to rely on banks in jurisdictions where the credit's beneficiaries were located. Correspondent banking, it is said, is one of the 'most important features of the international banking system' without which beneficiaries would lose the ability to work with a local bank who is empowered to act on the credit.[24] The correspondent bank usually played an advising role[25] as well as a negotiating/confirming function if authorised under the credit. **4.15**

[24] Byrne et al, *UCP600: An Analytical Commentary* (Institute of International Banking Law and Practice 2010) 171 (hereafter Byrne et al, *UCP600: An Analytical Commentary*).

[25] *Equitable Trust Company of New York v Dawson Partners Ltd* (1927) 27 LIL Rep 49 (HL) for an early example of such arrangement.

4.16 The term 'nominated bank' was not in common usage in documentary credit law or practice in the early days. A definition of a 'nominated bank' was only introduced in art 2 of UCP 600. A nominated bank is in fact 'the bank with which the credit is available or any bank in the case of a credit available with any bank.' In UCP 500 the nominated bank is mentioned, perhaps oddly, in parenthesis in art 10(b)(i) which deals with 'Types of Credit'.[26] Once nominated, the nominated bank becomes a party to the credit and is authorised to act under the credit.[27] This notion of nominated bank evolved in the UCP in order to 'categorise *all* banks named to act in the credit except the issuer and advising bank'.[28] It includes, inter alia, a confirming bank and a negotiating bank.

4.17 By nominating a bank as the bank with which the credit is available, an issuing bank invites and authorises the nominated bank to receive and examine documents and to honour or negotiate, as the case may be.[29] Further, the issuing bank agrees to honour the credit as long as a timely and complying presentation is made *to the nominated bank* by the beneficiary whether or not the nominated bank acts upon its nomination and even if the nominated bank wrongfully refuses to accept the documents.[30] An issuing bank or a confirming bank may be precluded from claiming that the documents presented are discrepant if they fail to act in accordance with the rejection procedure prescribed in art 16 of UCP 600.

4.18 To the extent that a nominated bank is able, pursuant to the articles in the UCP 600, to act in a manner that affects the rights and obligations of the issuing bank vis-à-vis a third party, ie the beneficiary, its role does resemble that of an agent. This may provide some justification for characterising the relationship between the issuing bank and the nominated bank as one of agency. This notion of agency, however, finds no express grounding in the articles of the UCP 600.[31] Neither will one be able to find a principled (or even a consistent) basis in the case law prior to UCP 600 (which will be discussed below) for the proposition that a negotiating/confirming bank is an agent of the issuing bank.

1. Pre-UCP 600 Cases

4.19 The pre-UCP 600 cases do not speak with a consistent voice as regards the role of a negotiating or confirming bank acting as agent of the issuing bank.

4.20 In respect of negotiating banks, they are not generally regarded as agents of the issuing bank, a view which finds support in *European Asian Bank AG v Punjab and Sind Bank (No. 2)*.[32] In that case, the English Court of Appeal rejected the appellant's argument (relying on the well-established principle in *Ireland v Livingstone*)[33] that, as the letter of credit was ambiguous in its terms (specifically as to whether they were authorised as negotiating bank), the respondents (as issuing bank) could not deny that the appellants were authorised to act as negotiating bank.[34] Goff LJ held that, on the facts of the case, that the appellants (negotiating

[26] See n 23.
[27] Byrne et al, *UCP600: An Analytical Commentary* (n 24) 173.
[28] James E Byrne, *The Comparison of UCP600 & UCP500* (Institute of International Banking Law and Practice 2007) 38.
[29] Ali Malek and David Quest, *Jack: Documentary Credits* (4th edn, Tottel Publishing 2009) (hereafter Malek and Quest, *Jack: Documentary Credits*) 142, citing arts 6 and 12 of UCP 600.
[30] UCP 600, art 7(a). This is, as would be recalled, the basis of the Court's reasoning in *Grains* (n 1).
[31] As observed by Chan Sek Keong SJ in *Grains* (n 1) [189].
[32] [1983] 1 Lloyd's Rep 611 (hereafter *European Asian Bank v Punjab and Sind Bank*).
[33] (1872) LR 5 HL 395.
[34] *European Asian Bank v Punjab and Sind Bank* (n 32) 617 (col 2).

bank) cannot be regarded as agent of the respondents (issuing bank).[35] Significantly, his Lordship went on to state, as a matter of general principle, that a negotiating bank cannot be regarded as an agent of an issuing bank,[36] and on that basis, held that the principle as stated in *Ireland v Livingstone* could not be applied.[37] This statement also coheres with the role of the negotiating bank prior to UCP 600. A negotiating bank did not have to examine the documents presented by the beneficiary for compliance. It may decide to negotiate but is not obliged to do so. It may even negotiate a set of documents with discrepancies 'under reserve'.[38] In the event that the negotiating bank decides not to negotiate, it would owe no duty to the issuing bank.

As for confirming banks, they are sometimes characterised by bankers as agents of the issuing bank and this notion (or misconception)[39] is perhaps partly due to the fact that the confirming banks are traditionally regarded as doing in the jurisdiction of the beneficiary what the issuing bank is supposed to do (but could not do because the issuing bank is not present in the jurisdiction). Indeed, it is convenient for bankers and lay persons to view the role of the confirming bank as one of 'extending' the presence of the issuing bank into the jurisdiction where the beneficiary is operating its business, the purpose of which is to mitigate the risks that come along with the fact that the issuing bank is not local to the beneficiary.[40] **4.21**

This notion that a confirming bank is an agent of the issuing bank (at least in this limited way) finds support in pre-UCP 600 cases such as *Bank Melli Iran v Barclays Bank (Dominion, Colonial & Overseas)*[41] and *The Bank of Baroda Ltd v The Vysya Bank Ltd*,[42] where the English courts took the view that the confirming bank and the issuing bank are in a relationship of agency, albeit only for the narrow function envisaged in the UCP. Indeed, as Mance J explained in *Bank of Baroda v Vysya Bank*, the relationship of agency between the confirming bank and the issuing bank is consistent with the language of authorisation and request used in the UCP,[43] and is also shown by **4.22**

[35] ibid 618.
[36] ibid.
[37] ibid.
[38] See Malek and Quest, *Jack: Documentary Credits* (n 29) 121–24 discussing, inter alia, UCP 500, art 14(f) and *Banque de l'Indochine et de Suez SA v J H Rayner (Mincing Lane)* [1983] QB 711 (CA).
[39] See Byrne et al, *UCP600: An Analytical Commentary* (n 24) 106, where the learned commentators consider that it is a mistake to characterise the relationship as one of agency.
[40] See, generally, ibid 102.
[41] [1951] 2 Lloyd's Rep 367 (KB).
[42] [1994] 2 Lloyd's Rep 87 (QB) (hereafter *Bank of Baroda v Vysya Bank*).
[43] ibid 91 (col 1) referring, in particular, to UCP 400, art 10(b) (1983 Rev) which reads: 'When an issuing bank authorizes or requests another bank to confirm its irrevocable credit and the latter has added its confirmation, such confirmation constitutes a definite undertaking of such bank (the confirming bank), in addition to that of the issuing bank, provided that the stipulated documents are presented and that the terms and conditions of the credit are complied with' and UCP 400, art 11(d) (1983 Rev) which reads: 'By nominating a bank other than itself, or by allowing for negotiation by any bank, or by authorizing or requesting a bank to add its confirmation, the issuing bank authorizes such bank to pay, accept or negotiate, as the case may be, against documents which appear on their face to be in accordance with the terms and conditions of the credit, and undertakes to reimburse such bank in accordance with the provisions of these articles.' See also *Ng Chee Chong, Ng Weng Chong, Ng Cheng and Ng Yew (a firm t/a Maran Road Saw Mill) v Austin Taylor & Company Limited* [1975] 1 Lloyd's Rep 156 (QB) at 161, where Ackner J having considered the wording of the UCP 222 (1962 Rev) stated that whereas the non-confirming bank is the agent of the issuing bank for the purpose of advising the credit, it acts as a principal vis-à-vis the beneficiary and is under no duty to negotiate.

the language used in the correspondence in that case when the confirming bank was instructed.[44]

4.23 On the other hand, a different (and perhaps more nuanced) view was taken by the English Court of Appeal in *Credit Agricole Indosuez v Muslim Commercial Bank Ltd*.[45] Even though the Court held that there is '*not in law an agency relationship between an issuing bank and a confirming bank*', nevertheless Christopher Staughton LJ considered that the principle in *Ireland v Livingstone* would apply as between a confirming bank and an issuing bank:

> But in terms of commerce the confirming bank is the correspondent of the issuing bank, and acts for the issuing bank in order to do what the issuing bank is not present to do for itself. That is in my respectful *opinion sufficient to attract the rule that an agent is to be excused for acting on a reasonable, even if ultimately wrong, interpretation of his principal instructions.*[46]

4.24 In the recent Hong Kong case of *So Sau Lai Connie t/a Wing Fung Trading Co v DBS Bank (Hong Kong) Ltd*,[47] the Court took a more 'conventional' view that the confirming bank acts as agent for the issuing bank, but only with regard to the obligations of the issuing bank, citing *Jack: Documentary Credits*.[48] *Jack* suggests that the position of the confirming bank is that, in carrying out its function, where appropriate, it will act in a 'dual capacity' (ie, principal/agent). In other words, it acts as a principal 'in relation to its obligations as confirming bank' vis-à-vis the beneficiary but acts as agent for the issuing bank 'with regard to the obligations of the issuing bank'.[49]

4.25 As can be seen from the discussion above, the state of law as regards whether, and if so, to what extent there exists a relationship of agency between a confirming/negotiating bank on the one hand and an issuing bank on the other in the pre-UCP 600 cases is one of some uncertainty. The cases are not only inconsistent, but also lack in-depth reasoning as to how they reached the conclusion as to whether a confirming/negotiating bank is or is not an agent of the issuing bank. To the extent that the confirming bank performs the role of the issuing bank in the place where the beneficiary carries on business, ie receiving presentation of documents under the credit and honouring it if the presentation is conforming, it can be said to replicate the role of the issuing bank in the beneficiary's jurisdiction. To that extent, the agency characterisation appears to be attractive. But there is a limit to this characterisation. The confirming bank has a self-standing contractual obligation to honour a conforming presentation by the beneficiary unlike a conventional agent who drops out once the principal and third party enter into a contractual relationship.

4.26 The justification for not describing a negotiating bank as an agent is perhaps easier to explain. The negotiating bank has no obligation to discount or give value to a set of conforming documents; it is performing the role of the issuing bank in the beneficiary's place of

[44] *Bank of Baroda v Vysya Bank* (n 42) 91 (col 1). The instructions were communicated via telex, using the words 'We have now established the above LC ... We now request you to add your confirmation and advise the beneficiary.'

[45] [2000] 1 Lloyd's Rep 275 (CA).

[46] ibid 280 (col 1) (emphasis added).

[47] [2017] HKCU 82.

[48] ibid [60], citing Malek and Quest, *Jack: Documentary Credits* (n 29) paras 6.22 to 6.24.

[49] Malek and Quest, *Jack: Documentary Credits* (n 29) para 6.24.

business. However, if it decides to do so, then it acquires an independent right of reimbursement against the issuing bank.

2. Under UCP 600

As observed by Chan SJ in *Grains*, the articles in UCP 600 make no mention of agency.[50] It follows that there is no clear articulation in the UCP 600 as to the scope of any relationship of agency between an issuing bank and the nominated bank. In the absence of any clear authority, the preponderantview among commentators is against any *general* role of agency. **4.27**

According to Byrne et al, *UCP 600: An Analytical Commentary*, the nomination of a bank does not confer a *general* agency status on the nominated bank with respect to the issuer or confirmer even if it elects to act pursuant to the nomination, unless otherwise expressly provided.[51] In the similar vein, the authors of Ellinger & Neo, *The Law and Practice of Documentary Letters of Credit*, note that the precise legal position *depends on the role that the bank is asked to play*. In their view, a bank that is nominated to negotiate documents and/or drafts under the credit does so in its own capacity and is not an agent of the issuing bank.[52] As for a confirming bank, their view is that it is sometimes said to be an agent of the issuing bank but that is only in one aspect of its legal position, ie it has mandate to honour or negotiate the credit for which it will be entitled to claim reimbursement, and further, where it honours or negotiates the credit, it might be seen as acting on behalf of the issuing bank in the sense that it discharges the issuing bank's obligation to the beneficiary.[53] **4.28**

Insofar as some of the commentators seem to take a contrary view (such as John Dolan and *Jack*),[54] they appear to refer to *specific acts* contemplated under the provisions of UCP 600 and not to general agency (as noted by Chan SJ in his separate judgment in *Grains*).[55] Moreover, both Dolan and *Jack* can be understood to be merely *describing* the operation of the relevant articles in UCP 600 and referring to the relationship as one that is *analogous* to that of an agency relationship.[56] **4.29**

B. A Narrow Reading of *Grains*

The role of the nominated bank as an agent of the issuing bank should be confined to a situation where, for example, the nominated bank is timeously[57] presented with a set of conforming documents by the beneficiary which it does not negotiate (where the credit is available by negotiation) or where it does not accept a draft drawn on it (where the credit is available by acceptance). Where such a presentation is made to the nominated bank, the obligation of the issuing bank is triggered. To that extent only, the nominated bank assumes **4.30**

[50] *Grains* (n 1) [189].
[51] Byrne et al, *UCP 600: An Analytical Commentary* (n 24) 181.
[52] Peter Ellinger and Dora Neo, *The Law and Practice of Documentary Letters of Credit* (Hart Publishing 2010) 176.
[53] ibid.
[54] John F Dolan, 'The Correspondent Bank in the Letter-of-Credit Transaction' (1992) 109 Banking LJ 396; Malek and Quest, *Jack: Documentary Credits* (n 29) 142–43, 155. Both views were cited by Menon CJ and Phang JA in *Grains* (n 1) at [73]–[74].
[55] *Grains* (n 1) [186].
[56] ibid [189]–[190].
[57] ie before the expiry of the credit.

the capacity of an agent of the issuing bank. On the other hand, if the nominated bank negotiates the conforming documents,[58] it acts as a principal in its own right, both vis-à-vis the beneficiary and the issuing bank of the credit.[59] As against the beneficiary, it discounts the documents presented by imposing its own terms (including interest that it charges and any negotiation commission) without having to consult the issuing bank as regards these terms. Having negotiated the documents presented, it acquires a right of reimbursement vis-à-vis the issuing bank under art 7(c) of UCP 600 (which, it is noted, bears some similarity to the right that an agent has against a principal under agency law). The contractual relationship between the issuing bank and the nominated bank and the right of reimbursement thereunder comes into effect by the acceptance by the nominated bank of an offer contained in the credit to negotiate the conforming documents presented by the beneficiary.

4.31 Even on this narrow reading of the nominated bank's role as agent, several potential difficulties arise.[60]

1. A Freely Negotiable Credit

4.32 In a freely negotiable credit, which in practice is more frequently encountered than a credit in which negotiation is restricted to a specified bank, any bank operating in the jurisdiction of the beneficiary can be a nominated bank.[61] It is conceivable that a beneficiary may present a set of documents to a bank that has no relationship with the beneficiary, requesting the bank to negotiate. If the bank refuses to negotiate, thereby declining to act on the nomination, the issuing bank is put at risk if that bank does not reject the documents within the maximum five-day period and/or in accordance with the rejection procedure prescribed in art 16(c) of UCP 600. Likewise, if the bank examines the documents negligently and misses a discrepancy or conversely wrongfully rejects documents that turn out to be compliant, the issuing bank is similarly at risk.

2. The Beneficiary's Request to Negotiate—A Residual Duty

4.33 In documentary credit practice, a beneficiary when requesting a bank to negotiate a set of documents is usually required to complete a form setting out the terms and conditions imposed by the bank for that purpose. The intention of the beneficiary is to offer to the bank the opportunity to negotiate based on the latter's terms. If the bank refuses to negotiate for one reason or another, it simply does not accept the offer to do so. The impact of *Grains* is that the bank (that refuses to negotiate at the request of the beneficiary) nonetheless comes under a duty vis-à-vis the issuing bank to receive and examine the documents as well as to notify the beneficiary in accordance with the rejection procedure of art 16 of UCP 600 if the documents do not conform to the credit. If it performs this task negligently, and the beneficiary brings a successful claim against the issuing bank, the latter has a potential claim for negligence against the nominated bank. Thus, the bank's involvement does not end simply when it refuses to negotiate—the implied duty which arises when it is deemed to have acted

[58] Or, depending on the availability of the credit, the nominated bank accepts a draft drawn on it or incurs a deferred payment undertaking.

[59] As discussed in section IV of this chapter, the negotiating bank is generally not regarded as an agent of the issuing bank.

[60] These difficulties pertain to situations that go beyond the facts of *Grains* (n 1) and hence were not considered by the Court in that case.

[61] See definition of 'nominated bank' in UCP 600, art 2.

on the nomination, for which it is not even paid, to examine and handle the documents as required under UCP 600, presents a trap for the unwary. A bank is well advised then to notify the beneficiary and the issuing bank expeditiously of any decision to decline to act on the nomination as well as to return the documents to the former expeditiously.

From the beneficiary's perspective, things look considerably better in such a situation. What might have started out as a request to negotiate (which is also regarded as a presentation to the bank in its capacity as nominated bank) in fact yields four options if the nominated bank refuses to negotiate: **4.34**

(a) Retrieve the documents and present directly to the issuing bank.
(b) Retrieve the documents and approach another bank for negotiation (assuming the credit is freely negotiable).
(c) Unless the documents are rejected in accordance with art 16 of UCP 600 by the nominated bank, after refusal to negotiate, claim against the issuing bank under the credit.
(d) Request/demand that the bank forward the documents to the issuing bank on a collection basis.[62]

3. Scope of the Agency—Does and Should it Go Beyond UCP 600?

Agency in this context, it is suggested above, should not be understood in the wide common law sense. The agency in *Grains* is one inferred from the provisions of UCP 600, particularly, arts 7 and 16, ie it is confined to receiving, examining, and depending on whether the documents comply, forwarding them to the issuing bank with reasonable expedition[63] if they do, and following the rejection procedure in art 16 if they do not.[64] There should, however, be little or no scope to go beyond the prescribed duties under arts 7 and 16 of the UCP 600. Principles such as fiduciary duty, good faith, apparent authority, ratification, etc, while well established as a matter of common law of agency, might be alien to a nominated bank operating in a jurisdiction with a civil, rather than common law, tradition. It would not be reasonable or fair to expect such a bank to behave in accordance with the standards of an agent at common law. **4.35**

Reasonableness and fairness aside, there is a principled basis to avoid such a result, applying choice of law rules. As between an issuing bank on the one hand and the confirming/negotiating bank on the other, their relationship is governed by the law of the place where the latter carries out its business, in the absence of express choice of law clause.[65] While it is not settled by case law whether the relationship between an issuing bank and a nominated bank which does not act on the nomination is governed by the same choice of law, there is a fairly convincing case to be made in favour of such an extension. The performance of the nominated bank's duties in receipt, examination, and handling of documents presented under the credit is performed in the jurisdiction in which it carries on business. Such **4.36**

[62] Compared with the third option, this may be less acrimonious and is less likely to cause problems to the buyer due to the non-arrival of the documents.
[63] Even so, the duty to forward documents with reasonable expedition is implied.
[64] This is assuming that the credit does not contain express duties that the nominated bank has to perform.
[65] See, for instance, *Mizuho Corporate Bank Ltd v Cho Hung Bank* [2004] 4 SLR(R) 67 (HC) [7], citing *European Asian Bank AG v Punjab and Sind Bank Ltd* [1981] 2 Lloyd's Rep 651 (QB), and *Kredietbank NV v Sinotani Pacific Pte Ltd (Agricultural Bank of China, third party)* [1999] 1 SLR(R) 274 (HC).

performance is the focus of the relationship between the two banks. As such, the law of the place of such performance should have a strong claim as the law governing that relationship. On the assumption that nominated bank operates in a civil law jurisdiction, the outcome of applying the laws of that jurisdiction is that the common law principles associated with agency may be displaced.

4.37 Applying choice of law rules to avoid such an outcome, however, is not without its perils. It can, in other situations, lead to unacceptable consequences. There may, for instance, be a shorter limitation period under the laws of the place where the nominated bank carries on business or there may be statutory exclusion or limitation of liability that banks in that jurisdiction may enjoy. Thus, inasmuch as a nominated bank operating in a civil law jurisdiction may be caught off guard by common law notions of agency, likewise an issuing bank operating in a common law jurisdiction may find itself having to deal with any quirks in the laws of the place where the nominated bank is based.

4. Implied Obligations

4.38 The appellate courts in England and Singapore have read into the provisions of UCP 600 implied terms concerning the disposal of documents presented under a credit.

4.39 In *Fortis Bank SA/NV and another v Indian Overseas Bank* ('*Fortis Bank*'),[66] Indian Overseas Bank ('IOB') issued five letters of credit (L/C 1 to 5), each subject to UCP 600 and contained a request for Fortis Bank ('Fortis') to act as a confirming bank. L/C 1 to 3 were confirmed by Fortis. The beneficiary presented documents under L/C 1 to 3 which Fortis accepted and paid, and the documents were then forwarded to IOB by Fortis. The documents presented under L/C 4 and 5 (which were not confirmed) were subsequently forwarded by Fortis to IOB. IOB rejected the documents presented under L/C 1 to 5, and refused to reimburse Fortis (for L/C 1 to 3) or pay the beneficiary (for L/C 4 and 5). It gave notice under art 16(c)(iii)(c) of UCP 600 stating that it was returning the documents in respect of all the presentations (except for presentations under L/C 3 where IOB stated that it exercised the option under art 16(c)(iii)(a) to hold pending further instructions from the presenter). Further instructions were given by Fortis in January 2009 to return the documents, but IOB did not return any of the documents until 16 February 2009. One of the issues raised was whether there is an implied obligation on the issuing bank to return the documents in accordance with the 'return' notice (*per* art 16(c)(iii)(c)) or 'hold' notice (*per* art 16(c)(iii)(a)), and if so, whether it has to do so with 'reasonable promptness'. On this issue, Hamblen J held that a term that the documents should be returned within a reasonable period of time to Fortis should be implied, and a reasonable time in the context should refer to '*reasonable promptness*'.[67] This was upheld on appeal by the English Court of Appeal.[68]

[66] [2011] 2 Lloyd's Rep 33 (CA) (hereafter *Fortis CA*); [2010] 1 Lloyd's Rep 227 (HC); [2010] 2 Lloyd's Rep 641 (HC) (hereafter *Fortis HC 2*).
[67] *Fortis HC 2* (n 66) [75].
[68] Fortis CA (n 66) [68]–[70].

Like the English courts, the Singapore Court of Appeal also came to the view that it is possible to imply terms into the provisions of the UCP 600. Having considered the decisions in *Fortis Bank*, the discussions in Byrne et al, *UCP 600: An Analytical Commentary*[69] as well as having examined the duty of an *agent* to forward documents under common law,[70] the Singapore Court of Appeal in *Grains* held that a nominated bank owes an implied obligation to forward the documents with reasonable promptness to the issuing bank *whatever course it should decide to take in relation to the credit* by virtue of its having accepted its nomination.[71] **4.40**

The implication of terms—a technique with a quintessentially common law flavour—into the provisions of UCP 600 in these cases does not sit very well with the English Court of Appeal's observation that the domestic canons of construction should not be applied to the UCP 600 because of its international usage. However, the prompt disposal of documents, whether by way of forwarding them to the issuing bank or returning them to the presenting bank, is something that banks would expect of each other in documentary credit practice.[72] To that extent, the technique of implying a duty is nothing more than a convenient way of reaching a result that accords with international standard banking practice. Notably, neither court had to deal with any argument that such implied terms are not permitted by any applicable foreign systems of law. **4.41**

The question that remains to be answered is the readiness with which such a technique will be used by the courts in the future. It is suggested that judicial appetite for implication of duties into UCP 600 should be modest for a number of reasons. First, as a matter of common law, the implication of terms into a contract is governed by strict requirements. Second, as explained above, over-zealous use of a common law technique may sit uneasily with principles that operate in civil law traditions. Third, the document itself, ie UCP 600 is meant to be used internationally and was not drafted with any notions or premises of the common law in mind. Fourth, there is always the possibility that the governing law, derived from a choice of law analysis, does not recognise this technique of implication at all. **4.42**

V. Conclusion

Given the importance and prevalence of nominated banks in letter of credit transactions, it is rather surprising to find a lack of clarity on the nature of a nominated bank's relationship with the other key actors, namely, the issuing bank and the beneficiary. Perhaps this stems from the widespread (and possibly universal) usage and acceptance of UCP 600, which sets out many of the rights and obligations of the nominated bank vis-à-vis the issuing bank and the beneficiary (but not the nature of the relationship), such that there is seldom a need to go beyond the text of UCP 600. Where UCP 600 is **4.43**

[69] *Grains* (n 1) at [84]–[91] (on the *Fortis* decisions) and [92]–[103] (on the observations in *Byrne* et al, *UCP600: An Analytical Commentary* (n 24) which the Court of Appeal recognised as one of the 'leading treaties on the construction of UCP 600': see *Grains* (n 1) [51]).

[70] *Grains* (n 1) [104]–[107].

[71] ibid [101].

[72] See the unanimous views of the two experts called in *Fortis HC 2* (n 66) at [19]–[21], [52], and [76].

silent, however, issues arise. In that regard, to the extent that it is necessary to resolve the issues at hand, the Singapore and English courts have been prepared to go beyond the text of UCP 600 (as in *Fortis Bank* and *Grains*), but such endeavours should, for the reasons stated above, be only where absolutely necessary and consistent with the terms of UCP 600.

5

Determining a Complying Presentation in Letter of Credit Transactions

A Principled Appraisal of Current Requirements and Challenges

*Ebenezer Adodo**

I. Introduction

Following the commencement of the latest version of the Uniform Customs and Practice for Documentary Credits ('UCP 600'),[1] it has been settled that a letter of credit constitutes an irrevocable undertaking by the issuing bank (and by the confirming bank in the context of a confirmed credit) to honour[2] a complying presentation. The condition for performance of the banks' undertaking is beyond doubt, but determining when a presentation is complying comprises the core of letter of credit operations, and all too often forms the subject of serious disputes potentially involving protracted and costly litigation. Difficult issues of considerable commercial and doctrinal importance arise in ascertaining the conformity of tendered documents. What approach should be adopted when construing and applying the UCP? To what aids may appropriate recourse be had when interpreting a provision of a code of banking practice, such as the UCP? Under the UCP, a credit must not be issued available by a draft drawn on the credit applicant; but an inexperienced bank may nevertheless issue a credit of that very sort: would it be competent for the bank to insist on presentation of the draft despite the obviously odd stipulation? How about the legal effect of an unstipulated document appearing among the stipulated documents that are presented? A directive in the UCP's rules of banking practice demands that unstipulated documents be 'disregarded'. Is there some limit to compliance with that codified instruction? Pursuant to the UCP regime, a place for presentation of documents, other than the issuing bank's counters, counts as an additional place for documentary presentation: can the beneficiary ignore the place specified in the credit for the submission of the documents and remit the documents directly to the issuing bank? Does the beneficiary have a discretion to do so? Consideration of these 5.01

* I would like to express my gratitude to Christopher Hare for the extremely thorough editing of an earlier draft of this chapter. At various places the discussion benefited greatly from his meticulous attention to detail. His observations and suggestions enabled me to update the material as necessary.

[1] International Chamber of Commerce (ICC), 'Uniform Customs and Practice for Documentary Credits' (ICC Publication No 600, 2007) (hereafter UCP 600).

[2] The mode of honour depends on the availability of the credit, which may take the shape of an engagement by the bank, upon being furnished a complying presentation, to pay at sight, which requires payment of cash or remittance of the sum to a nominated bank account; to incur a deferred payment undertaking and pay that stated sum at the maturity date of the credit; or to accept a bill of exchange drawn by the beneficiary and pay the draft at maturity: see ibid art 2. Alternatively, a letter of credit may be issued available by negotiation with a nominated bank or with any bank: see ibid art 7(a)(v).

issues, from an Anglo-American perspective, comprises the main purpose of this chapter. Before proceeding further, however, some introductory observations are desirable.

5.02 Letters of credit have a long-established reputation as essential, flexible payment and financing instruments in international sale of goods transactions. The flexibility of this financing device enables the buyer and seller to agree in their sales contract on a letter of credit suitable for their business needs. Proper performance of the buyer's obligations under the contract of sale typically results in the buyer's bank issuing the required letter of credit in favour of the seller, as the credit beneficiary. The establishment of the letter of credit gives rise to two contracts, namely an irrevocable undertaking by the issuing bank to honour[3] a complying presentation and an engagement by the buyer to reimburse the issuing bank as promisee for payment made in accordance with the credit. The issuing bank's undertaking in turn generates two contracts: one with the seller, and the other with a nominated bank, both parties thereby becoming promisees of the undertaking. All three promisees (the issuing bank, the seller, and the nominated bank) face a common daily problem in letter of credit operations: the seller's right to payment under the credit depends on his making a 'complying presentation'[4] at the counters of the issuing or nominated bank; for the issuing or nominated bank to obtain reimbursement of the sum disbursed under the credit, it must have honoured a 'complying presentation'[5] and forwarded the documents to its promisor (the buyer vis-à-vis the issuing bank; the issuing bank vis-à-vis a nominated bank). The standard of documentary conformity with the credit required for the presentation to each promisor is strict.[6] Strict compliance does not translate into a test of mirror image, literal compliance in all circumstances, and for every tendered document. Minor discrepancies between the documents and the credit's terms, or inconsequential irregularities within a set of the documents, afford no valid ground for the presentee to refuse the presentation.[7] A discrepancy that calls for an inquiry, invites litigation, or casts doubts upon the sufficiency of contractual performance evidenced by the document would render the presentation non-conforming and unacceptable. A perennial practical problem lies in the fact that document-checkers, including established documentary credit practitioners, do not always find it possible to distinguish trivial variations from material deviations with mathematical precision.

5.03 Usually, the engagement of the buyer to reimburse the issuing bank is contained in an application form for the opening of the requisite letter of credit. Specific sections of the credit opening agreement set out the buyer's instructions to his bank. In the ordinary course of things, those instructions should be reproduced faithfully in the letter of credit itself. Ordinarily, the credit will contain a clause incorporating the UCP 600 by reference. In the US, Revised Article 5 of the Uniform Commercial Code ('Revised Article 5') applies to letters of credit, if the credit is issued anywhere in the US or, in the case of a credit issued

[3] The mode of honour depends on the type of letter of credit involved: see ibid.

[4] ibid art 2.

[5] ibid.

[6] *JH Rayner & Co Ltd v Hambro's Bank Ltd* [1943] KB 37 (CA) 40; *English, Scottish and Australian Bank Ltd v Bank of* South Africa (1922) 13 Ll L Rep 21 (KBD) 24; *Kumagai-Zenecon Construction Pte Ltd (in liquidation) v Arab Bank plc* [1997] 2 SLR(R) 1020 (CA) [16] (hereafter *Kumagai-Zenecon v Arab Bank*).

[7] *Kredietbank Antwerp v Midland Bank* [1999] 1 All ER (Comm) 801 (CA) 806; *Banque l'Indochine v JH Rayner Ltd* [1983] QB 711 (CA) 721 (hereafter *Banque l'Indochine v JH Rayner*); *Golodetz & Co Inc v Czarnikow-Rionda Co Inc* [1980] 1 WLR 495 (CA) 510.

abroad, if it is governed by the law of a US state, as determined by that state's choice of law rules. Accordingly, both Revised Article 5 and UCP 600 can govern such a credit. However, the latter is far more comprehensive than the former and takes precedence[8] in the event of a conflict between them.

Under both codes and at common law, a complying presentation requires the presentee-promisor to discharge its payment or reimbursement undertaking to the presenter-promisee. The various contracts are distinct and separate from one another[9] by reason of the doctrine of autonomy. A decision by the issuing bank that the set of documents it has honoured complies with the credit's terms does not bind the applicant to whom the issuing bank tenders the documents for reimbursement. Similarly, as discussed below,[10] a nominated bank's acceptance of a presentation will not operate to make the issuing bank liable to honour the documents, unless the nominated bank acted as the issuing bank's agent.[11] Under the autonomy principle, the presentee-issuing bank cannot assert against the presenting party (whether the seller or a nominated bank) any defences that the issuing bank may have against the buyer,[12] or any defences that the buyer may have against the seller under the sale contract. Similarly, a presentee-buyer may not deny reimbursement to the presenting issuing bank because of information that the buyer makes available to the bank about the seller's non-performance or defective performance of the sale contract. If the issuing or nominated bank has honoured a non-complying presentation, either because it did not notice that the documents materially differ in some respect from a stipulation in the letter of credit or the UCP 600, it usually has no right of reimbursement against the presentee party. **5.04**

Non-complying presentations often leave the presenting promisee in an extremely difficult situation, particularly if the price of the underlying goods has collapsed. Occasionally, the presenter of the validly rejected imperfect documents will be an issuing bank or a non-recourse nominated bank and would be obliged to request the buyer to take the merchandise at a discount or arrange for their resale. Where the promisee is the seller and the irregularity in the documents cannot be rectified before the credit expires, he tends to be at the mercy of the buyer, who may be seeking any opportunity to renegotiate the price or escape the contract of sale altogether. Alternatively, the seller may have to meet huge storage charges in respect of the goods or cover other financial losses. On the other hand, the opening of the letter of credit stipulated in the sale contract operates only as conditional rather than absolute payment for the relevant goods, unless the parties to the contract expressly or by necessary implication agreed otherwise.[13] It merely suspends, rather than extinguishes, the buyer's payment obligation under the contract of sale. Accordingly, the seller's inability to receive payment under the credit simply restores the buyer's liability for the price, but only in exceptional circumstances.[14] As the buyer has incurred fees in establishing the credit, **5.05**

8 Uniform Commercial Code, rev art 5, § 5–116(c).
9 UCP 600, art 4(a).
10 See section IV of this chapter.
11 *Southern Ocean Shipbuilding Co Pte Ltd v Deutsche Bank AG* [1993] 3 SLR(R) 86 (HC) [39]-[40] (hereafter *Southern Ocean v Deutsche Bank*).
12 UCP 600, art 4(a).
13 *Re Charge Card Services Ltd* [1987] Ch 150, 166.
14 *Maran Road Saw Mill v Austin Taylor & Co Ltd* [1975] 1 Lloyd's Rep 156, 159; *Alan (WJ) & Co Ltd v El Nasr Export & Import Co* [1972] 2 QB 189, 210, 220; *Soproma SpA v Marine & Animal By-Products Corp* [1966] 1 Lloyd's Rep 367, 386-87.

the seller cannot simply resile from the credit and demand payment from the buyer by presenting documents to him save, for example, where the credit fails to provide the promised payment because of the issuing bank's insolvency.[15] In that event, the buyer's obligation to pay the seller revives on the basis that the buyer undertook to pay by means of a letter of credit with a reliable paymaster, rather than a letter of credit that would not result in payment owing to the issuing bank's insolvency.

5.06 In many cases, a non-conforming presentation stems from an improper understanding of the ways in which the requirements of a letter of credit interact with the UCP 600's provisions. This chapter provides a principled evaluation of the prevailing approach to that interaction in the Anglo-American courts. Since the UCP 600's requirements are at the core of the parties' various undertakings in the credit transaction, the inquiry necessarily begins by surveying the principles applicable to interpreting such a code. It then considers specific types of problem relating to credit stipulations calling for a draft drawn in a stated form. The final part of the chapter examines the practical implications of the place for documentary presentation under article 6 of the UCP 600.

II. Proper Approach to Interpretation of the UCP 600 as to Documentary Compliance

A. Background to the UCP Regime

5.07 The UCP regime has been the linchpin of letters of credit for nearly a century. It originated with its modern form in the late 1920s, simultaneously with the increased use of documentary credits in an unprecedented era of international sales. Credit transactions involved various banking associations in the US[16] and Continental Europe[17] formulating and promoting their individual practices for credit operations. Each group insisted that beneficiaries presenting documents under credits issued by a member bank of the group, or involving a member as correspondent bank, had to observe its published guiding provisions and regulations. This insistence resulted in widespread disparities in banking practice regarding the acceptable form of shipping documents. At that time, it was common for a nominated bank located abroad, say on the Scandinavian peninsular, to honour a bill of lading that complied with the terms of the credit pursuant to its own adopted practice, but for an issuing bank in the US to consider the document non-conforming and accordingly refuse to reimburse the nominated bank for the sum paid to the beneficiary. Frequently, there was also a marked lack of uniform understanding among bankers operating in different trade finance centres within the same country, such as in the US, about the meaning and effect of important commonplace stipulations in a credit.[18] The variations in banking practice pertaining to credit operations caused mostly nominated banks and credit beneficiaries

[15] *ED & F Man Ltd v Nigerian Sweets & Confectionery Co* [1977] 2 Lloyd's Rep 50.

[16] Early drive for uniformity occurred in 1920, with a set of regulations adopted by a group of thirty-five banks in New York for their application to letters of credit operations.

[17] They mostly consisted of banks in France, Norway, Czechoslovakia, Italy, the Netherlands, Sweden, and Denmark.

[18] Wilbert Ward and Morris S Rosenthal, 'The Need for the Uniform Commercial Code in Foreign Trade' (1950) 63 Harvard Law Review 589.

enormous financial losses and significant practical problems regarding the resale of goods covered by rejected documents.

As part of its commitment to facilitate international trade and foster the employment of letters of credit in sales transactions, the International Chamber of Commerce ('ICC'), headquartered in Paris, launched the Uniform Regulations for Commercial Documentary Credits in 1929 to unify 'the commercial documentary credit regulations previously adopted and published by banking associations in various countries'.[19] This was replaced four years later with the Uniform Customs and Practice for Commercial Documentary Credits.[20] Further revisions of the code at substantially regular intervals[21] have enabled the UCP to retain its international currency by keeping abreast of new developments in the global practices relating to letter of credit operations, the nature and form of shipping documents, and marine insurance policies, as well as gaining the acceptance of banks in more than 180 countries—the UCP thus crystallised into a worldwide code of uniform banking practice, embodying since 1962 the standard criteria for establishing conformity of documents tendered under credits.[22] **5.08**

Over the years, the revision process has culminated in successive updated editions of the UCP, which have adopted a drafting style that seeks to ensure a uniform understanding, interpretation, and application of the UCP in determining documentary compliance. The UCP 600 itself is the fruit of dozens of negotiations, seminars, workshops, and discussions about the shortcomings of the UCP 500,[23] spanning more than three years and unarguably a product of the most extensive revision initiative in the annals of updating the code. The drafting process involved the establishment of a Drafting Group, which had a membership unparalleled in the history of the UCP, both in terms of size and composition—the members were highly regarded professionals drawn from the banking, trade finance, transport, and insurance communities. The process also entailed the circulation of fifteen successive drafts among some 150 ICC national committees, as well as individual banks throughout the world. The Drafting Group sifted through more than 5,000 assorted comments and suggestions on the drafts; regularly sought and obtained advice from a Consulting Group, consisting of forty bankers and other experts from twenty-six countries; undertook in-depth consideration of decisions issued by DOCDEX panels on documentary credit disputes;[24] **5.09**

[19] ICC, *Uniform Regulations for Commercial Documentary Credits* (1929), Introduction.

[20] ICC, *Uniform Customs and Practice for Commercial Documentary Credits* (1933), ICC Brochure No 82 of 1933.

[21] The revisions occurred in 1951, 1962, 1983, 1993, and 2006.

[22] Bernard S Wheble, 'Uniform Customs and Practice for Documentary Credits 1971 Revision' (1971) 4 Cornell International Law Journal 97, 98; Peter Ellinger, 'The Uniform Customs—Their Nature and the 1983 Revision' [1984] LMCLQ 578; Christopher Axworthy, 'The Revision of the Uniform Customs on Documentary Credits' [1971] JBL 38.

[23] ICC, 'Uniform Customs and Practice for Documentary Credits' (ICC Publication No 500, 1993) (hereafter 'UCP 500').

[24] DOCDEX is an anacronym for Documentary Instruments Dispute Resolution Expertise, pursuant to which the ICC provides an arbitration mechanism for the settlement of disputes arising out of transactions involving documentary credits, standby letter of credits, bank-to-bank reimbursements, documentary collections, demand guarantees or counter-guarantees, or any other trade-finance-related instrument, undertaking, or agreement: see 'DOCDEX' <https://iccwbo.org/dispute-resolution-services/docdex/> accessed 26 August 2020. For the ICC's rules and procedures governing the submission of a claim for a DOCDEX, see 'DOCDEX Rules' <https://iccwbo.org/dispute-resolution-services/docdex/docdex-rules/> accessed 26 August 2020; 'DOCDEX Procedure' <https://iccwbo.org/dispute-resolution-services/docdex/procedure/> accessed 26 August 2020. Previous decisions are published periodically: see, for example, Gary Collyer and David Meynell (eds), *Collected DOCDEX Decisions 2013–2016* (ICC Publication No 786 2017).

and a meticulous review by 400-odd members of the ICC's Commission on Banking Technique and Practice of approximately 488 official opinions, position papers, and guidelines of the Commission.

B. Contractual Interpretation of Letters of Credit and the UCP 600

1. General Principles of Contractual Interpretation

5.10 Documentary letters of credit and the underlying credit-opening (or indemnity) agreement customarily contain clauses that incorporate the UCP 600 by reference. With such incorporation, the provisions of the UCP become integrated into the contracts arising from the credit and the indemnity agreement. As considered further below, the UCP 600 is the result of successive international meetings, conferences, workshops, seminars, and worldwide consultations and represents an agreed global response to common problems perceived or experienced in letter of credit operations. Where English domestic law is applicable to the relevant contractual relationship,[25] an issue arises as to the extent to which the recently reaffirmed[26] 'common sense' and 'plain meaning' domestic principles of contractual interpretation apply to letters of credit and the UCP 600. In particular, are there any limits to the application of those principles, having regard to the unique international aims of the UCP and the autonomous nature of letters of credit? The answer is explored next.

5.11 Under Anglo-American law, the doctrine that parties are free to contract on whatever lawful terms they think fit is based on the fundamental premise that the law will give effect to the parties' mutual intention as expressed in the terms of their contract. To discover their common intention, the common law's policy has been to adopt an objective standard of interpretation and generally to reject evidence of the parties' subjective or actual intentions.[27] Traditionally, the pertinent case law is marked by an insistence on the literal meaning of words. Nevertheless, a significant line of weighty dicta adopted an alternative approach which entailed placing a business sense construction on commercial contracts and business instruments in order to identify the meaning of the contract's words that most closely accords with the parties' intentions.[28] The modern technique of interpretation drew inspiration from the balanced approach in influential early cases and effectively started life with Lord Wilberforce's observations in *Prenn v Simmonds*[29] and *Reardon Smith Line Ltd v Hansen-Tangen*.[30] These were subsequently developed, applied,[31] and lucidly re-formulated in *Investors Compensation Scheme Ltd v West Bromwich Building Society*,[32] which was in

[25] A contract's applicable law includes only the relevant jurisdiction's domestic law principles, but not its conflict of laws principles, since *renvoi* is generally excluded: see *Amin Rasheed Shipping Corp v Kuwait Insurance Co (The Al Wahab)* [1984] AC 50 (HL).

[26] *Wood v Capita Insurance Services Ltd* [2017] AC 1173 (SC) (hereafter *Wood v Capita Insurance*).

[27] *Inland Revenue Commissioners v Raphael* [1935] AC 96 (HL) 142; *Prenn v Simmonds* [1971] 1 WLR 1381 (HL) 1384 (hereafter *Prenn v Simmonds*).

[28] *Glynn v Margetson & Co* [1893] AC 351 (HL) 355–56, 358; *Robertson v French* (1803) 4 East 130, 135; 102 ER 779.

[29] *Prenn v Simmonds* (n 27) 1383–84.

[30] *Reardon Smith Line Ltd v Hansen-Tangen* [1976] 1 WLR 989 (HL) 995–96 (hereafter *Reardon v Hansen-Tangen*).

[31] *Miramar Martime Corp v Holborn Oil Trading Ltd* [1984] AC 676, 682; *Antaios Compania Naviera SA v Salen Rederierna AB* [1985] AC 191, 201; *Mannai Investment Co Ltd v Eagle Star Life Assuarance Co* Ltd [1997] AC 749.

[32] *Investors Compensation Scheme Ltd v West Bromwich Building Society* [1998] 1 WLR 896 (HL).

turn substantially reaffirmed in a series of decisions by the House of Lords and UK Supreme Court.[33] To summarise: in construing a written contract or contractual document, the court's concern is to identify the parties' intentions by reference to what a reasonable business person would have understood the parties to have meant by the language that they employed in the contract. For these purposes, the reasonable person is deemed to have all the background knowledge that was reasonably available to the parties at the time they made their bargain. The construction exercise essentially comprises an iterative process: it requires the court to check each of the rival meanings advanced by the litigants against the contractual provisions and their commercial consequences. To qualify as a potentially valid interpretation, a competing meaning must have some basis in the contract's words and the wider context of the parties' transaction.[34] A choice between two or more possible constructions is to be made by having regard to the relevant background and by adopting the construction that is more consistent with business common sense or achieves the more reasonable result.[35] Applied to the UCP, the interpretation of the code requires the meaning of its provisions to be ascertained by reference to what they would convey to a reasonable reader in the class of persons to whom the UCP is addressed. The addressees notionally consist of international bankers, exporters, importers, and trade finance professionals that habitually engage in documentary credit operations. For these purposes, the 'relevant background' refers to anything the reasonable reader would have considered necessary to ascertain the reasonable meaning of the UCP's provisions at the time of their incorporation into the relevant letter of credit. Examples of relevant background material include applicable elements from the case law; existing statutory instruments or regulatory enactments; identifiable banking practices prevalent in the locality of the document-examining bank; and the identifiable commercial object of the UCP's provisions. This 'contextual' approach to interpretation clearly represents the prevailing view and should be regarded as the governing principle on questions of interpretation of the terms and explicit requirements of letters of credit.

Despite this shift towards 'contextualism', the English courts have continued to emphasise 5.12
that loyalty to the text of the contract or contractual document (known as 'textualism') is of paramount importance in identifying the parties' common intention.[36] Admittedly, the starting point in the construction process must be the ordinary meaning of the contract's words because the natural import of what a person says usually affords a useful guide to what he means.[37] Textualism produces difficulties, however, when the words are unambiguous, but their literal construction leads to an improbable commercial result. Must the literal outcome be denied effect in favour of a construction that appears from the contract's contextual setting to be commercially and reasonably preferable? Would a departure from the uncommercial result be justified? To beging with, the relevant background could lead

[33] *Sirius Insurance Co v FAI General Insurance* [2004] 1 WLR 3251 (HL) [15]–[19]; *Rainy Sky SA v Kookmin Bank* [2011] 1 WLR 2900 (SC) [14], [18]–[30] (hereafter *Rainy Sky v Kookmin Bank*); *Arnold v Britton* [2015] AC 1619 (SC) [15]–[23], [76]–[79], [108]–[112] (hereafter *Arnold v Britton*); *Wood v Capita Insurance* (n 26).

[34] *Arnold v Britton* (n 33) [77].

[35] *Barclays Bank plc v HHY Luxembourg SARL* [2011] 1 BCLC 336 (CA) [26]; *Attica Sea Carriers Corp v Ferrostaal Poseidon Bulk Reederei GmbH* [1976] 1 Lloyd's Rep 250 (CA) 253.

[36] *BCCI v Ali* [2002] AC 251 (HL) 269. See also Johan Steyn, 'Contract Law: Fulfilling the Reasonable Expectations of Honest Men' (1997) 113 LQR 433, 441.

[37] *Arbuthnott v Fagan* [1995] CLC 1396 (CA) 1400.

the court to detect a mistake in the drafting of the particular UCP requirement (or in its application to the particular credit) and conclude that 'something must have gone wrong with the language' in terms of the words or syntax used in the clause.[38] Such an error can be addressed by the process of construction: the language of the code, albeit precise and wholly unambiguous, will be substituted with what presents itself as the meaning that the reasonable addressee of the UCP would understand the clause to mean. As succinctly observed by Lord Diplock in *Antaios Compania Naviera SA v Salen Rederierna AB*,[39] 'if detailed semantic and syntactical analysis of words in a commercial contract is going to lead to a conclusion that flouts business commonsense, it must be made to yield to business commonsense'.[40] *Antaois* involved the meaning and effect of a clause in a charterparty providing that 'on any breach of this charterparty the shipowners shall be at liberty to withdraw the vessel from the service of the Charterers'. The phrase 'any breach' was construed as limited on commercial grounds to a repudiatory failure to perform the charterparty, rather than intended to carry its literal meaning that would embrace *every breach* of the charterparty, no matter how minor.

5.13 Conversely, in *Rainy Sky SA v Kookmin Bank* ('*Rainy Sky*'),[41] which concerned the correct construction of certain clauses in six advance payment bonds, Sir Simon Tuckey in the Court of Appeal[42] stated that, if the plain language of the bonds leads clearly to the conclusion that one or other of the proposed constructions is the correct one, the court must give effect to that interpretation, however surprising or unreasonable the result might be. Patten LJ, however, took a different view. In his Lordship's opinion, 'unless the most natural meaning of the words produces a result which is so extreme as to suggest that it was unintended, the court has no alternative but to give effect to its terms'.[43] Lord Clarke, with whom the other Supreme Court Justices concurred, decisively rejected Patten LJ's suggestion and declared that 'where the parties have used unambiguous language, the court must apply it'. In support of this conclusion, Lord Clarke referred to Lord Reid's observations in *Wickman Machine Tools Sales Ltd v L Schuler AG*:[44] 'The fact that a particular construction leads to a very unreasonable result must be a relevant consideration. The more unreasonable the result, the more unlikely it is that the parties can have intended it, and if they do intend it the more necessary it is that they shall make that intention abundantly clear.'[45] Reliance was also placed on *Co-operative Wholesale Society Ltd v National Westminster Bank plc* ('*Co-operative Wholesale*'),[46] in which a commercial landlord advanced a construction of four rent-review clauses that the Court of Appeal found to produce improbable commercial results. In applying the rules of construction for commercial contracts to the standard-form rent review clauses, Hoffmann LJ cited Lord Diplock's statement of principle in *Antaois*

[38] It might be thought that a court would rarely be prepared to consider that 'something has gone wrong' with the language of a code that was the outcome of a detailed and extensive drafting process. In *Re Sigma Finance Corp* [2010] BCC 40 (SC) [12] (hereafter *Re Sigma*), Lord Mance clarified that a meticulous contractual drafting process was not itself sufficient to prevent the court taking due account of the equally important reality that even the most skilful contract draftsman is at the end of day fallible and sometimes fails to see the wood for the trees.

[39] *Antaios Compania Naviera SA v Salen Rederierna AB* [1985] AC 191 (HL).

[40] ibid 201.

[41] *Rainy Sky v Kookmin Bank* (n 33).

[42] *Rainy Sky v Kookmin Bank* [2010] EWCA Civ 582, [2011] 1 All ER (Comm) 18 [19].

[43] ibid [42].

[44] *Wickman Machine Tools Sales Ltd v L Schuler AG* [1974] AC 235 (HL).

[45] ibid 251.

[46] *Co-operative Wholesale Society Ltd v National Westminster Bank plc* [1995] 1 EGLR 97 (CA).

and commented: 'This robust declaration does not however mean that one can rewrite the language which the parties have used in order to make the contract conform to business common sense. But language is a very flexible instrument and if it is capable of more than one construction, one chooses that which seems most likely to give effect to the commercial purpose of the agreement.'[47] All three Lords Justices in substance pointed out that only the most unambiguous clause could support the landlord's proposed construction, but nevertheless upheld one of the clauses that did 'unambiguously ... achieve the improbable result for which the landlord contended'.[48]

As interpretation aims to determine the parties' intentions, it is probably unrealistic to expect contracting parties, as rational actors, to intend the unreasonable result of their unambiguous contractual language. Whilst textualism and the 'natural meaning' approach may well remain a canon of contractual interpretation in English law, given its approval in *Co-operative Wholesale* and *Rainy Sky*, there is little room for such an approach when applying the UCP's requirements for a complying presentation or interpreting express stipulations in a letter of credit that incorporates the UCP or some other code of banking practice. Ascertainment of the meaning of a given provision or term requires an examination of what the clause in question would convey to a reasonable document-checker having the relevant background knowledge of how letters of credit operate. Interpretation of the UCP provisions should take care to eschew literalism. **5.14**

The application of these principles in the context of the UCP 600 is considered next. **5.15**

2. Interpretation of UCP 600

Upon its incorporation into a documentary credit, the UCP 600 has the unique standing of being a hybrid, international set of standard-form contractual terms and conditions. As a result of the intensive and exhaustive revision process described above, the UCP 600 can also be considered a unique product of seasoned international trade-finance professionals, reflecting global best practice in trade finance and the reasonable expectations of experienced international bankers and traders.[49] As an international banking code designed to achieve uniformity in letter of credit operations generally, and more specifically in the criteria for determining documentary compliance, the UCP 600 has a justifiable claim to be treated like other international commercial conventions when it comes to the question of its interpretation. Examples of such instruments include the various Hague regimes on bills of lading,[50] the Warsaw Convention,[51] and the CMR Convention.[52] These conventions are intended to have a unifying effect upon the specified international rules falling within their scope. In the interest of achieving a uniform application across the various contracting states, it has been long-settled that those conventions should be interpreted 'unconstrained **5.16**

[47] ibid.

[48] ibid.

[49] See, for example, *Glencore International AG v Bank of China* [1996] 1 Lloyd's Rep 135 (CA) 148.

[50] International Convention for the Unification of Certain Rules of Law relating to Bills of Lading 1924 (hereafter 'Hague Rules'), as amended by the Brussels Protocol 1968 (hereafter 'Hague-Visby Rules'), implemented in the UK by the Carriage of Goods by Sea Act 1971.

[51] International Convention for the Unification of Certain Rules Relating to International Carriage by Air 1929 (hereafter 'Warsaw Convention'), which is scheduled to the UK Carriage by Air Act 1961.

[52] International Convention on the Contract for the International Carriage of Goods by Road 1956, implemented in the UK by the Carriage of Goods by Road Act 1965.

by technical rules of English law, or by English legal precedent, but on broad principles of general acceptation',[53] as appropriate to their international mercantile subject-matter.[54] In essence, such conventions require a purposive internationalist construction: an English judge is entitled to avail himself of any aid to interpretation available to foreign courts, except that he should not engage in speculation about the interpretation that those courts are likely to adopt in relation to the relevant provision.[55]

5.17 An issue concerning the construction of the UCP 600 arose in *Fortis Bank SA v Indian Overseas Bank* ('*Fortis Bank*').[56] Primarily, it concerned the scope and content of the obligations imposed on an issuing bank by article 16(c) of the UCP 600 towards a presenting nominated bank when sending a rejection notice to the latter bank following a non-conforming presentation. Article 16(c) imposes no explicit obligation on the issuing bank to return the discrepant documents to the presenting bank following service of the rejection notice. This omission is further complicated by article 16(e), which provides that the rejecting bank, after sending the above-mentioned notice, 'may ... return the documents to the presenter at any time'. Judging by the literal import of the words 'may' and 'at any time', returning the documents is left to the rejecting bank's discretion, but it is unclear if this was the intended meaning of articles 16(c) and (e) when read together. This narrow issue developed into a wider argument in *Fortis Bank* about how an English court should interpret the UCP 600 or whether further requirements might be implied into the UCP. All the judges at first instance[57] and in the Court of Appeal[58] in *Fortis Bank* acknowledged the UCP's uniqueness as an international code of banking practice, settled by experienced trade-finance professionals with the aim of achieving common and definite standards of conduct for banks, applicants, and beneficiaries in documentary credit operations throughout the world. All four judges also accepted that a purposive construction of the UCP was appropriate and that a court should accordingly give due consideration to the code's overriding objective of maintaining good practice consonant with the reasonable expectations of international bankers and international traders. In particular, Thomas LJ in *Fortis Bank* emphasised[59] that the court must recognise the UCP's international nature when interpreting its terms. In that regard, his Lordship stated that the UCP 'is intended to be a self-contained code for those areas of practice which it covers and to reflect good practice and achieve consistency across the world. Courts must therefore interpret it in accordance with its underlying aims and purposes reflecting international practice and the expectations of international bankers and international traders so that it underpins the operation of letters of credit in international trade. A *literalistic* and national approach must be avoided.'[60]

[53] *Stag Line Ltd v Foscolo Mango & Co* [1932] AC 328 (HL) 350; *James Buchanan & Co Ltd v Babco Forwarding & Shipping (UK) Ltd* [1978] AC 141 (HL) 152 (hereafter *James Buchanan v Babco Forwarding*); *Ulster-Swift v Taunton Meat Ltd* [1977] 1 WLR 625 (CA) 628; *The Kapitan Petko Voivoda* [2003] 2 Lloyd's Rep 1 (CA) 12 (col 2).

[54] *JI MacWilliam Inc v Mediterranean Shipping SA (The Rafaela S)* [2005] 2 AC 423 (HL) [44] (hereafter *The Rafaela S*).

[55] *James Buchanan v Babco Forwarding* (n 53) 153.

[56] *Fortis Bank SA/NV v Indian Overseas Bank* [2010] 2 All ER (Comm) 28 (QBD) (hereafter *Fortis Bank v Indian Overseas* (HC)).

[57] ibid [43].

[58] *Fortis Bank SA/NV v Indian Overseas Bank* [2011] 2 All ER (Comm) 288 (CA).

[59] ibid [29].

[60] ibid [30] (emphasis added).

Whilst, as considered above, Thomas LJ was correct to eschew a literal or textual approach to the UCP 600, the suggestion that a 'national approach' must be avoided is confusing and too widely stated to be an appropriate guideline. Where the law governing an issuing bank's engagement under the credit is English law, the prevailing principles for construction of commercial contracts, as discussed above, will apply to determine the bank's rights, obligations, and liabilities to the beneficiary or a nominated bank located in a foreign jurisdiction. Those principles, albeit influenced to some degree by developments in the New York Court of Appeals,[61] are simply part of English domestic law. English law does not have a body of special interpretational rules for dealing with international standard-form contractual terms any more than it has specialised principles for the interpretation of private law treaties or international commercial conventions implemented into UK law by a statute. Accordingly, it is difficult to see how a 'national approach' can be avoided. In approaching the UCP 600, an English court would consider all the relevant contextual background, which would include decisions of foreign courts; ascertained international standard banking practice; expert evidence concerning the existence and scope of any particular banking practice relevant to the litigation; and the reasonable expectations of the class of international commercial actors and letter of credit practitioners to whom the UCP is addressed. A national approach involving due consideration of all the material elements of the relevant background may very well represent an interpretative breakthrough as to the proper meaning of a given UCP provision, leading the way for courts and arbitrators abroad to follow. 5.18

Given such a contextual approach to the interpretation of the UCP 600, a particular issue that arose in *Fortis Bank* concerned the materials to which an English court might make reference as part of the interpretative exercise. Before Hamblen J, the claimant nominated bank sought to rely on the UCP 600 Drafting Group's Commentary on UCP 600 ('the Commentary')[62] to contend that articles 16(c) and (e) should be interpreted as requiring the rejecting bank to return the documents to the presenter reasonable promptly, and that the presenter's failure to do so had engaged the 'preclusion rule' in article 16(f) of the UCP 600. Hamblen J doubted that the Commentary was analogous to the *travaux préparatoires* (preparatory works) underlying an international convention or treaty. His Lordship concluded that the 'comments made are of interest, but ... do not ... have an evidential status'.[63] The Court of Appeal made no pronouncement regarding this specific point. 5.19

Hamblen J's conclusion appears suspect, as it betrays an unduly narrow approach to what counts as admissible extrinsic evidence. Ample authoritative guidance on the use of *travaux préparatoires* as an interpretative aid was provided by the House of Lords in *Fothergill v Monarch Airlines Ltd* ('*Fothergill*'),[64] which was cited to the court in *Fortis Bank*. *Fothergill* concerned the meaning of the word 'damage' in article 26(2) of the Warsaw Convention,[65] 5.20

[61] Pronouncements of Cardozo J in *Utica City National Bank v Gunn*, 222 NY 204 (NYSC, 1918) were discussed and then adopted in *Prenn v Simmonds* [1971] 1 WLR 1381, 1384 and *Reardon v Hansen-Tangen* [1976] 1 WLR 989, 996.

[62] UCP 600 Drafting Group & ICC Banking Commission, *Commentary on UCP 600: Article-by-Article Analysis* (ICC Publication No 680, 2007) (hereafter ICC, *Commentary*).

[63] *Fortis Bank v Indian Overseas* (HC) (n 56) 44.

[64] *Fothergill v Monarch Airlines Ltd* [1981] AC 251 (HL) (hereafter *Fothergill v Monarch*).

[65] According to Art. 26(2) of the Warsaw Convention (n 51), '[i]n the case of damage to any registered baggage, the person entitled to delivery must complain to the carrier forthwith after the discovery of the damage, and, at the latest, within seven days from the date of receipt in the case of baggage'.

and the legitimacy of resorting to the *travaux préparatoires* contained in the minutes of meetings concerning the negotiation of the Hague Protocol of 1955 to that convention.[66] A majority of the House of Lords in *Fothergill*[67] accepted that, when determining what the delegates at an international conference decided by their majority vote in favour of a particular convention text, regard should be had to *any material* that was available to those delegates when clarifying any textual ambiguities. Indeed, the United States Court of Appeal for the Second Circuit in *Day v Transworld Inc*[68] has expressed a similar view and was prepared to consider the minutes of a drafting committee for the Warsaw Convention, although ultimately this provided little assistance in the particular circumstances of the case before the court.[69] Whilst accepting their relevance, these decisions (i.e. Forthergill and Transworld) also establish that such material as is readily or reasonably accessible to those involved in negotiating or drafting international conventions cannot be treated as the gospel truth or in any way conclusive; rather, that the material should be used cautiously for the purpose of resolving any ambiguity in the treaty. In the context of the UCP 600, the Drafting Group prepared the Commentary in question to enlighten practitioners in documentary credit operations about 'a number of the thought processes behind the changes in each article and to explain why a change was introduced, why no change was made, why some issues may appear new but are [in fact] not ... and to suggest the way the wording in UCP 600 should be understood and applied'.[70] The content of the Commentary does not represent the official opinion of the ICC Commission on Banking Technique and Practice ('ICC Banking Commission'). However, a published official statement, opinion, or decision of the Commission itself *can* command a highly persuasive status before the Anglo-American courts.[71] Similarly, the Commentary considered in *Fortis Bank can* provide valuable assistance in determining the correct meaning of a UCP 600 provision and ought not to be excluded from the interpretation of such an international code simply because some antediluvian local precept apparently denies its evidential character. Utility and substance, rather than fastidious adherence to antequated formalism, should govern resort to such preliminary material.

3. Implication of Terms into UCP 600

5.21 One further point remains for consideration in light of *Fortis Bank*: can a judge, or an arbitrator hearing letter of credit submission under the DOCDEX Rules, imply a requirement into the UCP 600? The primary contention of the claimant nominated bank in *Fortis Bank* was that article 16(c)(iii) imposes a duty on the rejecting issuing bank to return the rejected documents upon sending a rejection notice, and that such an obligation could be imposed by implying a term, as an alternative to interpreting the UCP 600's language. This approach

[66] Protocol to Amend the Convention for the Unification of Certain Rules Relating to International Carriage by Air 1955.

[67] For Lord Fraser's dissent, see *Fothergill v Monarch* (n 64) 287.

[68] 528 F 2d 31 (1975).

[69] *Day v Trans World Airlines Inc*, 528 F 2d 31 (2nd Cir, 1975) 34–5.

[70] ICC, *Commentary* (n 62) 8.

[71] See, for example, *Western International Forest Products Inc v Shinhan Bank*, 960 F Supp 151 (SDNY, 1994) 154 (clarifying that the opinions of 'the ICC Banking Commission Group of Experts, of course, are not law, but they are entitled to some persuasive weight in interpreting the UCP'); *Credit Agricole Indosuez v Credit Suisse* [2001] 1 All ER (Comm) 1088 (QBD) [23]; *Credit Industriel et Commercial v China Merchant Bank* [2002] CLC 1263 (QBD) 1269; *Korea Exchange Bank v Standard Chartered Bank* [2006] 1 SLR(R) 565 (HC) (hereafter *Korea Exchange v Standard Chartered*) 570.

gained favour with Hamblen J. The judge recognised that the English courts had been prepared to make such an implication on three previous occasions[72] (albeit without specifically considering the propriety of doing so). But Thomas LJ found it unnecessary to provide a concluded view on the issue, not least because he had already dismissed the appeal on the key issue of article 16(c)(iii)'s proper construction. Insofar as the processes of implication and interpretation differ, his Lordship did, however, raise serious concerns about using domestic implication principles as the basis for writing an obligation into the UCP.

Those misgivings might appear understandable and do echo the occasional objection[73] to the tendency of some English judges to construe the provisions of the UCP according to traditional domestic canons of interpretation. The objections, however, need to be kept in perspective. To start with, the relevant letter of credit contracts in *Fortis Bank* were subject to English law. Pursuant to article 12(1) of the Rome I Regulation,[74] when English law applies to a letter of credit contract, that law governs the 'interpretation' of the UCP when incorporated by reference into the credit. In English law, the process of interpretation differs from the implication exercise. Whilst interpretation and implication were conflated by Lord Hoffmann in *Attorney General of Belize v Belize Telecom Ltd*,[75] this was firmly rejected by Singapore's apex court.[76] The rejection was endorsed by the UK Supreme Court in *Marks & Spencer plc v BNP Paribas Securities Trust Co (Jersey) Ltd*.[77] This now represents English law. Indeed, Sir Thomas Bingham MR, in *Philips Electronique v British Sky Broadcasting Ltd*,[78] captured the essential distinction between interpretation and implication thus: 'The courts' usual role in contract interpretation is, by resolving ambiguities or resolving apparent inconsistencies, to attribute the true meaning to the language in which the parties themselves have expressed their contract.' That process is iterative, involving checking each of the rival meanings against other provisions of the contractual document and investigating its commercial consequences.[79] In contrast, 'the implication of contract terms involves a different and altogether more ambitious undertaking: the interpretation of terms to deal with matters for which, *ex hypothesi*, the parties themselves have made no provision'. Essentially, construction is a non-intrusive exercise, while interpolation in a contractual provision entails 'the supplying'[80] or 'adding'[81] of a term or a requirement in respect of which the contract is silent, and therefore operates as an ad hoc gap-filler,[82] namely filling up identified interstices in the express clauses of the contractual document.[83] **5.22**

[72] *The Royan* [1987] 1 Lloyd's Rep 345; *Bankers Trust v State Bank of India* [1991] 1 Lloyd's Rep 587; *Seaconsar v Bank Markazi* [1999] 1 Lloyd's Rep 36.

[73] See for example Michael Brindle and Raymond Cox (eds), *Law of Bank Payments* (5th edn, Sweet & Maxwell 2017) [7–005].

[74] Council Regulation (EC) 593/2008 of 17 June 2008 on the Law Applicable to Contractual Obligations [2008] OJ L177/6 (hereafter 'Rome I Regulation'). The Rome I Regulation establishes the choice of law rules in the EU for determining the law applicable to contracts having an international element that were concluded after 18 December 2009.

[75] *Attorney General of Belize v Belize Telecom Ltd* [2009] 1 WLR 1988 (PC).

[76] *Sembcorp Marine Ltd v PPL Holdings Pte Ltd* [2013] 4 SLR 193 (CA).

[77] *Marks & Spencer plc v BNP Paribas Securities Trust Co (Jersey) Ltd* [2016] AC 742 (SC) (hereafter *M&S v BNP Paribas*).

[78] *Philips Electronique v British Sky Broadcasting Ltd* [1995] EMLR 472 (CA).

[79] *Re Sigma* (n 38) [12]. For the view of Lord Neuberger in the Court of Appeal, see *Re Sigma Finance Corp* [2009] BCC 393 (CA) [98], [115], [131].

[80] *Liverpool City Council v Irwin* [1977] AC 239 (HL) 253.

[81] ibid.

[82] *Equitable Life Assurance Society v Hyman* [2002] 1 AC 408 (HL) 459.

[83] *Luxor (Eastbourne) Ltd v Cooper* [1941] AC 108 (HL) 140.

Compared with construction, implication into a document runs a greater risk of violating the cardinal principle that judges have no right to make or improve the parties' contract. For these reasons, the court should only exercise this extraordinary power if the proposed term, satisfies very strict criteria.

5.23 As well as possibly implying a term by custom, it is conceivable that a term may be implied 'in fact' into a particular letter of credit on a 'one-off' basis,[84] provided that the implication is necessary to give business efficacy to the credit.[85] When the issue concerns whether to imply a term into the UCP, as in *Fortis Bank*, the issue concerns whether it is necessary to imply a term 'in law' into a whole category of contracts. In this situation, implication is approached differently, involving wider considerations, such as the overriding objective of the UCP and the standard of practice expected of banks in the documentary credit community and the reasonable expectations of experienced practitioners in the marketplace. Given the need for such implication to be 'necessary', the misgivings articulated in *Fortis Bank* about implying terms into the UCP can hardly be justified. A court applying English law to the UCP should encounter little difficulty if it pays proper regard to the above principles.

C. Treatment of Expert Testimony

5.24 An important yardstick for determining the conformity of documents presented for payment under a letter of credit is 'international standard banking practice'. This requirement first appeared in article 13(a) of the 1993 UCP Revision (UCP 500), which provided that the compliance of documents, on their face, with the terms and conditions of the credit, 'shall be determined by international standard banking practice as reflected in these Articles'. This requirement attracted widespread controversy, generating significant uncertainty in the trade-finance community. The choice of words in article 13(a) was generally, and rightly, considered unwise, seeing that the UCP cannot seriously profess to define 'international standard banking practice' exhaustively. The concept has now been suitably expressed as part of the definition of 'complying presentation' in article 2 of the UCP 600. To assist appropriate understanding of 'international standard banking practice', there exists a set of ICC Banking Commission guidelines, the 'ISBP'.[86] Unfortunately, the current experience suggests that the ISBP's precepts only provide a limited helping hand to document-checkers examining a documentary presentation to determine its regularity; partly because, no doubt owing to resource and budget constraints, the ISBP's content was not the product of an in-depth survey of documentary credit practices currently prevalent among banks in different regions and trade finance centres around the world. Accordingly, the ISBP does

[84] *Forefront Medical Technology (Pte) Ltd v Modern-Pak Pte Ltd* [2006] 1 SLR(R) 927 (HC) [41]. See also Andrew Phang, 'The Challenge of Principled Gap-Filling—A Study of Implied Terms in a Comparative Context' [2013] Queensland Legal Yearbook 351, 355–56.

[85] *M&S v BNP Paribas* (n 77); *Mediterranean Salvage & Towage Ltd v Seamar Trading* [2009] 2 Lloyd's Rep 639 (CA).

[86] ICC, *International Standard Banking Practice for the Examination of Documents under Documentary Credits* (ICC, 2003) (ICC Publication No 645), which applied to the UCP 500. The publication was updated in June 2007 (ICC Publication No 681). For the latest edition of the ISBP for the UCP 600, see ICC, *International Standard Banking Practice for the Examination of Documents under UCP 600* (ICC, 2013) (ICC Publication No 745E) (hereafter 'ISBP 745'). In its Introduction, the ISBP's drafters state that the current edition is a 'necessary companion to the UCP for determining compliance of documents'.

not necessarily reflect a universal consensus regarding international banking practice, albeit that the ISBP was an initiative commendably intended to explain the workings of certain requirements articulated in the UCP.

As to letter of credit litigation or arbitration, this much seems generally accepted: the compliance of a documentary presentation with 'international standard banking practice' may be established to the satisfaction of the court or arbitrator by expert testimony. The American Uniform Commercial Code Revised article 5 is very explicit on this point: section 5-108(e) provides that '[a]n issuer shall observe standard practice of financial institutions that regularly issue letters of credit. Determination of the issuer's observance of the standard practice is a matter of interpretation for the court. The court shall offer the parties a reasonable opportunity to present evidence of the standard practice.' That provision appears to have been applied unsatisfactorily by the Appellate Division of the New York Supreme Court in *Blonder & Co Inc v Citibank NA*.[87] An issuing bank honoured a letter of credit relating to the sale of a quantity of scrap nickel and subsequently claimed reimbursement of its payment from the credit applicant, who was buying the goods. The reimbursement arrangement between the issuing bank and applicant provided that the issuing bank should only make payment if the documents presented at its counters were in 'substantial compliance' with the terms and conditions of the credit. When the scrap nickel failed to arrive in Rotterdam, the applicant refused the issuing bank payment on the basis that the documents were 'fake' and that the bank had failed to exercise reasonable care to ensure that the presented documents 'complied substantially' with the terms of the credit. In particular, the issues arose as to whether the bills of lading and other documents conformed with 'international standard banking practice' in circumstances where they omitted the consignee's name and arguably bore conflicting dates, as well as the pre-printed inspection certificate referring to 'Leon, Nicaragua' in the box marked 'port of loading' (rather than 'Corinto Port, Nicaragua' as required by the credit). Normally, a claim for reimbursement should succeed insofar as the bills of lading and other documents *on their face* constitute a complying presentation,[88] but not where the documents are apparently irregular. In that regard, the applicant adduced expert testimony attesting that, in the deponent's thirty years of documentary credit experience, he had never seen a bill of lading of the sort in question and that the document was unacceptable as a bill of lading according to international standard banking practice. Accordingly, the applicant contended that the irregularities on the face of the documents should have alerted the issuing bank to the need to seek a waiver of those discrepancies before making payment against the obviously non-conforming presentation. The bank adduced no opposing expert evidence, relying straightforwardly on the argument that the documents substantially complied with the credit and the reimbursement arrangements between the parties for the setting up of the credit. **5.25**

Nevertheless, Andrias J, delivering the majority judgment, affirmed that the relevant banking usages and practices are embodied in the UCP and that the court, rather than the expert witness, is the sole determinant of compliance with that code. Their Honours in effect substituted their own opinion of what counts as a proper document in international standard **5.26**

[87] *Blonder & Co Inc v Citibank NA*, 808 NYS 2d 214 (NYSC, 2006).

[88] *Commercial Banking Co of Sydney Ltd v Jalsard Pty Ltd* [1973] AC 279; *Gian Singh & Co Ltd v Banque de l'Indochine* [1974] 1 WLR 1234 (PC).

banking practice for the thirty years of experience possessed by the credit applicant's expert witness. Professor Byrne lamented this type of undesirable substitution by pointing out that '[j]udges deceive themselves if they think that their legal training qualifies them to understand the UCP without resort to expert guidance'.[89] The principal difficulty with the majority approach in *Blonder* stems from their characterisation of 'international standard banking practice' as a trade usage that is exclusively articulated in the UCP, so that the expert testimony in that case was an attempt to 'usurp [the court's] function' of determining the bank's observance of relevant banking practice. In effect, their Honours seem to have been misled by the wording of article 13(a) of the UCP 500 into thinking that 'international standard banking practice' cannot be determined beyond the four corners of that code. On the other hand, their Honours inexcusably failed to give any proper meaning to the critical requirement in section 5-108(e) of revised article 5, which also applied on the facts, that the 'court shall offer the parties a reasonable opportunity to present evidence of [an alleged] standard practice'. A knee-jerk rejection of unchallenged expert testimony signifies non-adherence to section 5-108(e) and represents a regrettable error. It is suggested that expert evidence concerning a party's compliance or otherwise with 'international standard banking practice', or as to the meaning of a UCP provision, should normally receive careful judicial consideration and be accepted by the court, unless to do so would be inconsistent with the fundamental principles underlying documentary credits. If rival expert evidence is adduced, then whichever testimony appears more compelling, considering the specific necessities of the trade-finance facility, is entitled to judicial recognition and enforcement.

5.27 Putting aside the court's problematic approach to the expert evidence in *Blonder*, it is submitted that the bill of lading in that case was non-conformity as a matter of legal principle. A bill of lading is either a negotiable bill[90] (whether a bearer or order bill) or a non-negotiable or straight bill. Both are documents of title to the goods mentioned therein and they customarily contain a series of numbered boxes on their front page.[91] Negotiability of a bill of lading often depends primarily on the form of the typewritten entries in the information box headed 'Consignee'. The relevant information in most negotiable bills of lading consists of a specific name followed by the time-honoured words 'or order'. Variations may have the wording 'to order' or 'order or assigns'. By contrast, non-negotiable bill of lading has the name of the consignee alone, without adding such words. The information box under consideration performs yet another important function: it enables the carrier to identify the person to whom the goods are deliverable and makes it possible for the named consignee to use the document as evidence of his entitlement to delivery of the cargo at the port of destination, or as security for an advance. A major drawback of the straight bill of lading lies in its inability to be transferred by endorsement and delivery to a sub-buyer in a string of sub-sales or some other third party. For this reason, a presenting beneficiary usually has no discretion over the form of the bill of lading to be tendered to the bank for payment. There

[89] James Byrne, 'Letter of Credit Trends' *Letter of Credit Update* (January 1997) 3, 5.

[90] In this context, negotiability merely refers to the bill of lading's transferability from the shipper or the consignee to some third party, such as a sub-buyer in a chain of sales contracts. Negotiability in this context does not mean the same as in the context of a bill of exchange, under which the transferee can acquire a better title than the transferor possesses: see *APL Co Pte Ltd v Voss Peer* [2002] 2 SLR(R) 1119 (CA) [19]–[20] (hereafter *APL v Voss*).

[91] The Singapore Court of Appeal in *APL v Voss* (n 90) recognised a straight bill of lading as a document of title and the House of Lords followed suit in *The Rafaela S* (n 54) 449, 458, 462.

is a strong presumption in the UCP[92] that a stipulation in a credit requiring presentation of a bill of lading signifies a negotiable bill of lading (termed an 'ocean bill' in previous editions of the UCP). Accordingly, presentation of a non-negotiable bill would not conform to the UCP and would be at variance with the credit's terms.[93] On the basis of these considerations and the expert evidence, what the issuing bank honoured in *Blonder* and what the buyer was requested to accept belonged to none of the established classes of bill of lading, as no consignee was indicated in the 'bills of lading' which the bank honoured. Separately, the inspection certificate appeared to state a port of loading (Leon, Nicaragua) that was at odds with the letter of credits explicit requirement of '1 copy of bill of lading evidencing freight prepaid and shipment from Corinto Port, Nicaragua to Rotterdam, Netherlands'. No document-checker acting with reasonable care and diligence ought to have accepted such a bill of lading or inspection certificate, and it was arguably wrong that the credit applicant in *Blonder* be obliged to reimburse the issuing bank in such circumstances. Any suggestion that the reference to 'substantial compliance' in the reimbursement arrangement effectively relieved the issuing bank of its obligation to check the tendered documents with reasonable care should be rejected; if the parties had intended those words to have such an exclusionary effect, then long-established principles instruct that clearer and more precise wording was required to achieve that result.

Slightly different problems, but with much the same significance, arose in *Mago International LLC v LHB Internationale Handelsbank AG*.[94] The beneficiary of a standby letter of credit incorporating the UCP 600 sought to obtain payment for large consignments of poultry, beef, and other meat products that had been shipped to buyers in Kosovo. To that end, the beneficiary presented a set of shipping documents to LHB, the confirming bank, in New York a couple of days prior to the credit's expiry. As is customary, the credit was issued on a SWIFT format and Field 46A called for a 'photocopy of B/L (bill of lading) evidencing shipment of the goods to the (credit) applicant'. Among the tendered documents was a copy of an unsigned bill of lading. The confirming bank rejected that document on the ground that the credit and the UCP required a copy of a signed bill of lading. Subsequently, the seller managed to procure the requisite copy of the signed bill and re-tendered the documents, together with various sight drafts, but by that time the credit had lapsed; payment was refused. The lateness of its final presentation left the seller with no choice, but to insist that its initial presentation (including the copy of the unsigned bill of lading) constituted a complying presentation. Nevertheless, McMahon J in the Southern District Court of New York ruled that, to conform to Field 46A, the requisite shipping document had to be a photocopy of a signed original bill of lading, rather than the copy of an unsigned, non-negotiable bill of lading that was actually presented. The Court of Appeal for the Second Circuit agreed with the trial judge.[95] **5.28**

[92] This presumption is evident in the reference to 'Marine/Order Bill of Lading' in the heading of UCP 500, art 23. It clearly excludes negotiable (straight) bills of lading. The corresponding provision in UCP 600, art 20, does not have the same heading, but the omission is doubtless insufficient to indicate a shift away from the old requirement applicable to any document purporting to be a bill of lading for presentation under a credit.

[93] *Soproma SpA v Marine and Animal By-Products Corp* [1966] 1 Lloyd's Rep 367 (QBD) 388.

[94] *Mago International LLC v LHB Internationale Handelsbank AG*, WL 4653229 (SDNY, 2015).

[95] *Mago International LLC v LHB Internationale Handelsbank AG*, 833 F 2d 270 (2nd Cir, 2016).

5.29 The ICC Banking Commission's 'ISBP' guidelines under the UCP 600, which were designed to assist document-checkers in deciding whether a documentary presentation accords with 'international standard banking practice', might have caused both courts in *Mago* a complicated dilemma, but their Honours fortunately took no serious notice of these. The version of the ISBP applicable at the time that the documentary examination in *Mago* provided that '[w]here a credit allows for the presentation of a copy transport document rather than an original, the credit must explicitly state the details to be shown. Where copies (non-negotiable) are presented, they need not evidence signature, dates, etc.'[96] This ill-conceived provision unfortunately misinformed the seller about his rights and caused him to advance the wholly unsustainable argument that the initially presented (unsigned) copy document was a complying bill of lading. To satisfy a credit calling for a copy of a bill of lading, the relevant document must be a photocopy of a bill of lading that itself complies with the requirements for valid transport documents in the UCP 600. According to article 20(a)(i) of the UCP 600, signature is an essential feature of bills of lading. In particular, the signature on the bill of lading 'must appear to indicate the name of the carrier and be *signed* by the carrier or a named agent for or on behalf of the carrier, or the master or a named agent for or on behalf of the master'.[97] A carrier's, master's, or agent's signature 'must be identified as that of the carrier, master or agent'.[98] Moreover, an agent's signature 'must indicate whether the agent has signed for or on behalf of the carrier or for or on behalf of the master'.[99] In maritime practice,[100] the box headed 'signature' on the shipping document (usually in the lower part of the document's front page) will be signed (upon receipt of the goods for shipment or the completion of the shipment) by means of a handwritten name or a manually applied stamp or symbol. The signature box identifies the carrier[101] and serves two crucial commercial purposes: to identify the party who witnessed the shipment of the goods or their receipt for shipment in a specified condition; and, more crucially, to establish the party who has undertaken to perform the carriage contract from the designated port of loading to a stated port of discharge, and who accordingly bears contractual responsibility for loss of, damage to, or delay in carrying, the goods to the stipulated destination. An unsigned original bill of lading effectively means that the cargo owner will have no carrier to sue under the bill in the event of, for instance, misdelivery or mishandling of the goods; a photocopy of such a bill should afford the cargo owner no different legal protection than the original document. In contrast, if the bill of lading is properly signed, a copy of that signed bill in the cargo owner's

96 ICC, *International Standard Banking Practice for the Examination of Documents under Documentary Credits* (ICC Publication No 681 2007) [20]. There is no direct equivalent of this provision in ISBP 745 (n 86). Nevertheless, ISBP 745 (n 86) [A31(b)] does provide that '[c]opies of documents need not be signed nor dated'.

97 UCP 600, art 20(a)(i) (emphasis added).

98 ibid.

99 ibid.

100 See, for example, bills of lading issued in the form used by the Baltic and International Maritime Council ('BIMCO'), which is the world's largest international association of shipowners, headquartered in Copenhagen, Denmark.

101 The carrier is usually the shipowner, but may well turn out to be a charterer. An enormous body of case law exists on questions concerning the identity of the carrier: see *Homburg Houtimport BV v Agrosin Private Ltd (The Starsin)* [2004] 1 AC 715 (HL), overruling *Fetim BV v Oceanspeed Shipping Ltd (The Flecha)* [1999] 1 Lloyd's Rep 612 (QBD); *MB Pyramid Sound NV v Briese Schiffahrts GmbH (The Ines)* [1995] 2 Lloyd's Rep 144 (QBD); *The Hector* [1998] 2 Lloyd's Rep 287 (QBD); *Universal Steam Navigation Co Ltd v James McKelvie & Co* [1923] AC 492 (HL); *The Berkshire* [1974] 1 Lloyd's Rep 185 (QBD); *The Okehampton* [1913] P 173; *Tillsman v SS Knutsford* [1909] AC 406; *Wilston SS Co Ltd v Andrew* (1925) 22 Ll L Rep 521 (KBD); *Kruger v Moel Tryvan Ship* [1907] AC 272 (HL). These cases are the consequence of the imperfect, slovenly form in which signatures appear on many bills of lading.

hands would provide him as 'holder' with certain proprietary and contractual rights. The courts in *Mago* were, therefore, correct to brush aside counsel's suggestion for the seller that the presentee bank should have accepted copy of the unsigned bill of lading.

An important salutary lesson from the *Mago* litigation is that credit-litigants should tread carefully when relying on the ISBP and related ICC publications to contest the validity of a refusal of their documents. Banks and beneficiaries under letters of credit should only exceptionally regard the guidance offered by such material as furnishing a foolproof interpretation of what amounts to a conforming document, especially for the purpose of deciding whether to initiate or defend a claim asserting the compliance or non-compliance of a documentary presentation. **5.30**

D. Credit Stipulations Tying Payment to Performance of the Underlying Contract

Article 4(a) of the UCP 600 articulates the fundamental autonomy doctrine by providing that '[a] credit by its nature is a separate transaction from the sale or other contract on which it may be based. Banks are in no way concerned with or bound by such contract, even if any reference whatsoever to it is included in the credit.'[102] The separation between the credit and the underlying contract is augmented in articles 4(b) and 5 of the UCP 600. Article 5 makes clear that the letter of credit is a document-based transaction: 'Banks deal with documents and not with goods, services or performance to which the documents may relate.'[103] This provision reflects the common law understanding of the bank's role dating back to 1922,[104] and differs materially from the corresponding article 4 of the UCP 500, in that article 5 of the UCP 600 replaces the word 'parties' with 'banks'. That replacement is justified and commendable. As a practical matter, in letter of credit operations, neither the credit applicant/buyer nor the beneficiary/seller can be accurately regarded as dealing only in documents.[105] In the context of a credit covering a shipment of goods, for example, upon the discovery of a discrepancy in the documents, the issuing bank will often refer the matter to the buyer to waive the discrepancy. The bank has no general contractual obligation to do so,[106] but instead consults with the buyer as a matter of standard banking practice when handling apparently irregular documents. Although this practice is recognised in the UCP 600,[107] the bank's consultation with the buyer is often driven by commercial considerations, not least the desire to strengthen banking relationship with its customers. In deciding whether or not **5.31**

[102] See also Uniform Commercial Code, Revised Article 5, § 5–103 (d): 'Rights and obligations of an issuer to a beneficiary or a nominated person under a letter of credit are independent of the existence, performance or non-performance of a contract or arrangement out of which the letter of credit arises or which underlies it, including contracts or arrangements between the issuer and the applicant and between the applicant and the beneficiary.'

[103] UCP 600, art 5.

[104] *National City Bank v Seattle National Bank* 121 Wash 476 (US, 1922) 483.

[105] cf the age-old controversy over the characterisation of cif contracts, originating with Scrutton J's description of such a contract as a sale of documents, rather than a sale of the goods mentioned in the documents: see *Arnhold Karberg & Co v Blythe Green Jourdain & Co* [1915] 2 KB 379 (KBD) 388. In the Court of Appeal ([1916] 1 KB 495 (CA) 510), Bankes LJ disagreed with Scrutton J's view.

[106] Nevertheless, an application to open a letter of credit may expressly impose a duty on the issuing bank not to reject a non-complying presentation without prior consultation with the applicant. A well-advised applicant would include a stipulation of that sort.

[107] UCP 600, art 16(b).

to waive a non-conforming presentation, the buyer typically looks at the nature and materiality of the irregularity in the documents, as well as any additional information concerning the conformity of the goods with the sales contract. Similarly, the seller's performance of the sales contract naturally involves his dealing in the goods forming the subject-matter of that contract, as well as the shipping documents, which, if they involve a bill of lading, will represent the goods and serve as a key to the warehouse in which the consignment are stored.[108] It follows that neither buyer nor seller deals solely with documents.

5.32 The autonomy doctrine, therefore, primarily seeks to prevent the banks becoming embroiled in disputes between the credit applicant and the beneficiary over performance or non-performance of obligations embodied in the sales contract underlying the credit.[109] The corollary is that the beneficiary's right to payment under the credit depends *absolutely* on his presentation of the documents stipulated in the credit. The autonomy principle also forbids the courts from looking at the contractual arrangements underlying the credit when judging compliance of the documents with the terms of the credit.[110] Consistently with these propositions, article 4(b) of the UCP 600 requires an issuing bank to 'discourage any attempt by the applicant to include, as an integral part of the credit, copies of the underlying contract, proforma invoice and the like'.[111] As banks deal only in documents, however, what is the position where a credit nevertheless contains a stipulation conditioning payment upon the proper performance of the underlying contract? Can a nominated bank that has honoured a set of documents by reference to article 4(b) claim to be in no way bound by the credit's reference to the due performance of the underlying contract? Conversely, would the issuing bank be entitled to refuse reimbursement or payment by insisting that the documentary presentation must conform to the express clause outlawed under article 4(b)?

5.33 Considered from the perspective of article 4(b) of the UCP 600, it is certainly arguable that the reference in a credit to the underlying transaction ought to be treated as straightforwardly invalid, or alternatively, that the relevant clause might constitute a non-documentary condition and therefore liable to suffer the fate reserved for such eventuality pursuant to article 14(h) of the UCP 600 – the subarticle provides that '[i]f a credit contains a condition without stipulating the document to indicate compliance with the condition, banks will deem such condition as not stated and will disregard it'.[112] The former approach was adopted in *Pringle-Associated Mortgage Corp v Southern National Bank of Hattiesburg*.[113] The beneficiary was to draw upon the credit 'only after the credit extended under (a stated) First Mississippi National Bank letter of credit in the amount of . . . has been exhausted'. The principal issue concerned the effect of the reference in the credit to another contract, and whether this had expressed a condition for payment. In line with the autonomy doctrine,

[108] *Sanders Bros v Maclean & Co* (1883) 11 QBD 327 (CA) 341.

[109] *Frey & Co v Sherburne* 193 App Div 849 (NYSC, 1920) 853: 'It is equally clear here that the bank issuing the letter of credit is in no way concerned with any contract existing between the buyer (credit applicant) and seller (beneficiary).' See also *Lamborn v Lake Shore Banking and Trust Co* 196 App Div 504 (NYSC, 1921), affirmed 231 NY 616 (1921); *United City Merchants (Investments) Ltd v Royal Bank of Canada* [1983] AC 168 (HL); *Angelica-Whitewear v Bank of Nova Scotia* [1987] 1 SCR 59 (SCC).

[110] *Andy Marine Inc v Zidell Inc* 812 F 2d 534 (1987) 537.

[111] UCP 600, art 4(b). This sub-article replaces Article 5 of the UCP 500, which primarily requested banks to discourage the inclusion of excessive detail in letters of credit.

[112] ibid art 14(h).

[113] *Pringle-Associated Mortgage Corp v Southern National Bank of Hattiesburg*, 571 F 2d 871 (5th Cir, 1978) (hereafter *Pringle-Associated v Southern National*).

the Court of Appeal for the Fifth Circuit intimated that general references to an underlying sale contract in a credit are surplusage and should not be considered in deciding whether the beneficiary has tendered documents conforming to the letter of credit's terms. Ultimately, the court in *Pringle-Associated* ruled in favour of the beneficiary, who in the event filed an affidavit attesting that the funds available under the Mississippi bank letter of credit had in fact been withdrawn, as required by the credit in dispute. The bank's dishonour of the presentation was thus wrongful and liable in damages to the beneficiary. That said, it always remains possible for a credit explicitly to make compliance with another contract a condition for honouring the drafts and documents presented to the bank. An example is provided by the District Court of Utah in *Newvector Communications Inc v Union Bank*.[114] At issue was a letter of credit expressed 'available by sight draft(s) as per Resellers Agreement on past due accounts'. Thomas Greene J stated that the reference to the 'Resellers Agreement constituted a sufficiently clear documentary requirement, or a sufficiently clear non-documentary requirement, which in either case would require presentation of the document for examination of the written representations contained therein'.[115] In the result, the bank was entitled to decline payment under the credit unless the beneficiary produced the referenced 'Resellers Agreement'.[116]

An alternative objection to a credit that references the performance of the underlying contract as a precondition for payment is that such a payment instrument should not be characterised as a letter of credit at all, since it makes payment dependent upon the existence of facts, rather than documents evidencing the existence of those facts. *Wichita Eagle & Beacon Publishing Co v Pacific National Bank*[117] instructs that an instrument that labels itself as a letter of credit may cease to be so, if it 'strays too far from the basic purpose of letters of credit', namely an assurance of payment upon presentation of specified documents. Such an instrument may, instead, be characterised as an ordinary contract of guarantee that obliges the bank-issuer to pay if the beneficiary establishes the actual existence of the stipulated condition (usually a breach of the underlying contract). The instrument in *Wichita* promised payment of a stated amount in the event of a named lessee failing to perform the terms of the lease and neglecting to remedy that default. The Court of Appeal for the Ninth Circuit denied that the document was a letter of credit because its substantive provisions required the issuing bank to deal not simply in documents alone, but in facts relating to the performance of the underlying lease. This was inconsistent with the autonomy principle: the bank is a paymaster that must determine whether or not a documentary presentation is conforming within a short five-day window,[118] rather than a self-appointed adjudicator over disputes arising out of the underlying transaction. 5.34

Nevertheless, *Wichita* probably no longer offers, if it ever did, a reliable guide as to how the courts would nowadays deal with the type of clause that might have traditionally 5.35

[114] *Newvector Communications Inc v Union Bank* 663 F Supp 252 (DC Utah, 1987) (hereafter *Newvector Communications v Union Bank*).

[115] ibid 257–257.

[116] In the event, summary judgment was denied because of a factual issue about the existence of the 'Resellers Agreement'.

[117] *Wichita Eagle & Beacon Publishing Co v Pacific National Bank* 493 F 2d 1285 (1974).

[118] UCP 600, art 14(b) provides that the set timeframe is 'a maximum of five banking days following the day of presentation'. For the equivalent period at common law, see *Hansson v Hamel and Horley Ltd* [1922] AC 36 (HL) 46.

disqualified an instrument from being a letter of credit. In the several decades that have elapsed since that decision, the law in the US,[119] England, and Singapore pertaining to the construction of non-documentary clauses in letters of credit has not stood still; but, on the contrary, progressed considerably. Just as the UCP 600's provisions are to be interpreted in an international spirit by reference to generally accepted principles and free from the rigid constraints of domestic precedents, so too the express clauses in letters of credit should be interpreted in a manner that promotes uniformity.[120] The courts increasingly appreciate that express clauses in letters of credit are not drafted in the classic mould of Chancery solicitors, but habitually by clerks in a bank's trade finance department with little or no training in the niceties of legal drafting. When a court is asked to interpret inapt language or provisions in letters of credit, it should strive to adopt a construction that makes the performance of the bank's payment or reimbursement undertaking dependent upon the presentation of complying documents to the bank. In this way, a non-documentary stipulation in a credit is construed as calling for any document that would reasonably enable the document-checker to determine whether or not the particular stipulation had been fulfilled.

5.36 The English case of *Astro Exito Navegacion SA v Chase Manhattan Bank* ('*Astro Exito Navegacion*')[121] provides an authoritative illustration of the proper method for interpreting non-documentary clauses in letters of credit. Taiwanese buyers agreed to purchase from Panamanian sellers a Greek vessel, *The Messiniaki Tolmi*, for delivery at Kaohsiung harbour, and accordingly furnished the sellers with a letter of credit, confirmed by Chase Manhattan Bank, London ('Chase'), to secure payment of the price. The buyers intended to dismantle the vessel and recycle her parts on sale to sub-buyers. It was thus vital that the vessel be safe for 'hot work' upon its arrival. To this end, the credit stipulated for presentation of 'a valid gas free certificate approved by the Taiwan authorities'. A certificate tendered to Chase had an indecipherable imprint of an approval stamp. Chase rejected the certificate and refused payment, drawing the beneficiary's attention to the deficiency. No difficulty arose with the word 'valid' in the credit: at the very least, this requirement signifies that a document purporting to be a gas-free certificate should carry a recent date of issue. The parties (namely, the banks, buyers, and sellers) equally had little problem about what 'Taiwan authorities' denoted: they understood that term to mean the Harbour Bureau at Kaohsiung. The main dispute concerned the need for the certificate to be 'approved' and whether the confirming bank (pursuant to its obligation towards the issuing bank) was entitled to demand from the presenting beneficiary documentary evidence of the Harbour Bureau's approval of the certificate. If so, the issue arose as to what type evidence would suffice.

5.37 Both Leggatt J[122] and the Court of Appeal (Sir Nicolas Browne-Wilkinson VC, Dillon, and Lloyd L JJ) in *Astro Exito Navegacion*[123] concluded that the confirming bank was entitled to demand documentary confirmation of the certificate's approval by the relevant authority. In

[119] See, for example, *Pringle-Associated v Southern National* (n 113); *Newvector Communications v Union Bank* (n 114).

[120] This point does not seem to have been reflected in the UK Supreme Court decision of *Taurus Petroleum Ltd v State Oil Marketing Co* [2018] AC 690 (SC).

[121] *Astro Exito Navegacion SA v Chase Manhattan Bank NA (The Messiniaki Tolmi)* [1988] 2 Lloyd's Rep 217 (CA) (hereafter *The Messiniaki Tolmi* (CA)).

[122] *Astro Exito Navegacion SA v Chase Manhattan Bank* [1986] 1 Lloyd's Rep 455 (QBD) (hereafter *The Messiniaki Tolmi* (HC)).

[123] *The Messiniaki Tolmi* (CA) (n 121).

coming to this conclusion, their Lordships found valuable support in *Banque de L'Indochine et de Suez SA v JH Rayner (Mincing Lane) Ltd* ('*JH Rayner*'),[124] which had been decided several years earlier. In *JH Rayner*, the letter of credit stated that shipment was to be effected on a 'Conference Line' vessel, but the bills of lading and other documents presented under the credit did not evidence in a reasonably clear manner that the vessel used for shipment of the goods belonged to a member of the relevant shipping conference. Accordingly, the bank requested that the beneficiary provide documents evidencing that the shipment had in fact been made on the type of vessel specified in the credit. Parker J accepted that the bank's request was justified. His Lordship said:

> [S]ince the credit expressly stipulated for shipment on ... 'a Conference Line Vessel' the [banks] were both entitled and obliged to ensure that the stipulation was complied with. No specific documentary proof was called for by the credit but, since parties to documentary credits deal only in documents, the bank[s] were ... entitled to insist upon, and the [beneficiaries] were obliged to provide, reasonable documentary proof. The request for a certificate was ... a reasonable requirement and accordingly the bank[s] were entitled to regard its absence as a valid ground for refusing payment even if, as was in fact the case, the vessel was a Conference Line vessel.[125]

All eight judges in both English cases substantially recognised that in documentary credit operations, banks deal solely with documents and have no ready means themselves of establishing the beneficiary's compliance with an explicit stipulation in a credit, other than by way of documentary evidence provided by the beneficiary. At the same time, their Lordships also appreciated the potential commercial consequences of denying any effect to such a non-documentary clause simply because it omitted, whether accidentally or carelessly, to specify the documents required to evidence fulfilment of its conditions. There can be no doubt as to the vessel purchaser's objective in insisting that the credit in *Astro Exito Navegacion* contain a stipulation that the Harbour Bureau approve the required gas certificate: that approval was intended to provide independent confirmation of the vessel's gas-free status in readiness for 'hot work'. Accordingly, a certificate without the necessary approval would undermine the buyer's fundamental purpose in entering the transaction in the first place. Thus, if the Court of Appeal in *Astro Exito Navegacion* had not permitted the bank to probe the contents of the presented documents (or alternatively if the court had refused to give effect to the non-documentary condition at all), then the buyer in that case risked having to reimburse the bank for accepting a certificate that the Harbour Bureau would not have considered satisfactory and would therefore have rejected. Clearly, the commercial justification for the law recognising a bank's entitlement to insist upon presentation of a reasonable documentary evidence showing compliance with a non-documentary clause is to protect the buyer from the potential losses that it might otherwise suffer. **5.38**

The issue does not, however, rest there. *Astro Exito Navegacion*, *JH Rayner*, and the US cases were decided under the UCP 290, which was introduced in 1974, whereas article 14(h) of the UCP 600 now instructs banks in a mandatory tone to 'disregard' any credit term that 'contains a condition without stipulating the document to indicate compliance with the **5.39**

124 *Banque l'Indochine v JH Rayner* (n 7).
125 ibid 719.

condition'.[126] On its face, the UCP 600 would appear to reverse the effect of those earlier decisions. In *Korea Exchange Bank v Standard Chartered Bank* ('*Korea Exchange Bank*'),[127] Andrew Ang J in the Singapore High Court demonstrated that this is not necessarily the case, since an express non-documentary clause would effectively create an irreconcilable inconsistency with article 14(h) of the UCP 600 with the result that the latter term, which was only incorporated by reference, should give way to the credit's express terms.[128] Such reasoning might be potentially problematic, however, in light of article 1 of the UCP 600, which states that the UCP's provisions only apply to a credit that incorporates them 'unless expressly modified or excluded by the credit'.[129] In *Korea Exchange Bank*, however, Andrew Ang J clarified the meaning of the identical phrase in article 1 of the UCP 500.[130] In that regard, his Honour indicated that the words 'unless expressly modified or excluded by the credit' are not to be 'interpreted so stringently as to mean that only an express exclusion of any particular provision of the UCP ... will have effect. It is enough if an express provision in the [credit] stipulates a requirement which is clearly at odds with a provision in the UCP ... in circumstances where an implication may be drawn that the intention was to exclude the operation of the UCP provision in question. In such an event, the express provision will override the provision of the UCP incorporated by reference'.[131] On that basis, then, notwithstanding the literal effect of article 1 of the UCP 600, a non-documentary condition in a letter of credit inherently excludes renders nugatory the attempt to invalidate that condition in article 14(h) of the UCP 600. Hence, the latter subarticle has effectively become something of a dead-letter. Nor would it be justifiable, as a matter of current international standard banking practice, to accord the prescriptive language in article 14(h) a literal meaning. According to the ISPB, 'data contained in a stipulated document are not to be in conflict with a non-documentary condition'.[132] If the true import of article 14(h) of the UCP 600 is that non-documentary conditions are indeed deemed not to be stated in the credit, so that no account should be taken of them during the document-examining process, why should banks also ensure the consistency of the presented documents with such non-documentary conditions by virtue of the ISBP? The apparent inconsistency of approach between article 14 (h) of the UCP and ISBP is regrettable. It therefore deserves pointing out that current banking practice reflected in the latter code and cases such as *Astro Exito Navegacion* make clear that a non-documentary condition or stipulation in a letter of credit normally requires presentation of a document reasonably showing its satisfaction before a tendered set of documents under the credit can be accepted and honoured.

5.40 It is submitted that the same conclusion applies to article 14(g) of the UCP 600, which provides that a 'document presented but not required by the credit will be disregarded and may be returned to the presenter'.[133] As considered above, when interpreting this provision a court should consider the meaning that the language would convey to a reasonable person

[126] UCP 600, art 14(h).
[127] *Korea Exchange v Standard Chartered* (n 71).
[128] *Thomas (TW) & Co Ltd v Portsea Steamship Co Ltd* [1912] AC 1 (HL); *Hamilton & Co v Mackie & Sons* (1889) 5 TLR 677; *Modern Building Wales Ltd v Limmer & Trinidad Ltd* [1975] 1 WLR 1281 (CA) 1289.
[129] UCP 600, art 1.
[130] UCP 500, art 1 although UCP 600, art 1 is in the same terms.
[131] *Korea Exchange v Standard Chartered* (n 71) [32], following *Kumagai-Zenecon v Arab Bank* (n 6).
[132] ISBP 745 (n 86) [A26].
[133] UCP 600, art. 14(g).

having all the relevant background knowledge that was reasonably available to the credit applicant, issuing bank (including any nominated bank participating in the transaction) and the beneficiary at the time of the credit's issuance. In essence, the reasonable person is deemed to understand the operation of the letter of credit market, standard banking practice as embodied in the UCP and ISBP, and the legitimate expectations of different market participants. In the ordinary runs of events in credit operations, the reasonable merchant or banker would know that data in a tendered document 'must not conflict with' data in that document or in any other tendered stipulated document.[134] Critically, such a person would also understand that a presented unstipulated document that helps to clarify an apparent contradiction between tendered stipulated documents (and accordingly removes the ostensible documentary conflict) is not within the category of unstipulated documents liable to be disregarded under article 14(g).[135] Rather, that provision should be interpreted as prohibiting unstipulated documents that prove to be unhelpful in resolving such conflicts.

Upon their proper construction, then, the reach of both articles 14(g) and (h) of the UCP 600 is far more limited than their literal interpretation might at first suggest. Presentee banks and presenting parties would be well-advised to apply the subarticles in terms which accord due consideration to their substance as discussed in the foregoing. **5.41**

III. Effect of a Draft Drawn on the Credit Applicant

Under article 6(c) of the UCP 600, a 'credit *must* not be issued available by a draft drawn on the applicant'.[136] This provision reaffirms the spirit of the second sentence of article 9(a)(iv) of the UCP 500; but, presumably in an attempt to emphasise the prohibition, the UCP 600 has dropped the further provision found in the UCP 500 to the effect that, when a credit expressly requires a draft to be drawn on the applicant, the draft would be treated as an additional document.[137] The reason underlying the UCP's proscription is to remind the parties to a letter of credit calling for a draft drawn on the applicant that a credit involves *only* the bank's irrevocable undertaking to honour drafts against complying presentation. Yet, in practice, it is common to see credits stating in relevant part, '[w]e hereby issue in your favour this irrevocable documentary credit which is available by your drafts at sight drawn on XYZ Pte Ltd (the applicant) for full invoice value accompanied by the following documents'.[138] A typical variant on this wording is that '[t]his irrevocable letter of credit is **5.42**

[134] ibid art 14(d).

[135] See generally *Uniloy Milacron Inc v PNC Bank*, WL 1830939 (DC Kent, 2008), holding that information in a covering letter, which was an unstipulated document, operated to cure deficiencies in the presented stipulated documents.

[136] UCP 600, art 6(c) (emphasis added).

[137] ICC, *Commentary* (n 62) 34.

[138] For examples of credits containing this wording, see *Kydon Compania Naviera SA v National Westminster Bank Ltd (The Lena)* [1981] 1 Lloyd's Rep 68 (QBD) 70 (col 2) (hereafter *The Lena*); *Computer Place Services Pte Ltd v Malayan Banking Bhd* [1996] 2 SLR(R) 455 (HC) (hereafter *Computer Place v Malayan Banking*); *Credit Agricole Indosuez v Banque Nationale de Paris* [2001] 2 SLR 1 (CA) 11. Such credits will also almost invariably include an engagement by the issuing bank that 'drafts/documents drawn in conformity with the terms of the credit will be duly honoured on presentation at our counter'. See further *Union Bank of Switzerland v Indian Bank* [1993] 3 SLR 371 (HC) 373.

available by acceptance of your drafts on (openers) XYZ Pte Ltd . . . at 90 days sight for 100% invoice value'.[139]

5.43 In a credit of the first type, which is essentially a credit available by sight payment, the requirement that the draft be drawn on the applicant does not usually present any practical problems or conceptual difficulties. Under such a credit, the issuing bank undertakes to make payment immediately, provided that a draft drawn in the required form is presented along with the other stipulated documents. Thus, as long as the draft is tendered in precisely the specified form, it is conforming and has to be paid forthwith. At one time, however, it was believed that, where a credit required sight drafts to be drawn on the applicant, an issuing bank's omission to include those drafts in its presentation to the credit applicant would not render the documents non-conforming, so that the applicant would still have to reimburse the bank.[140] The justification for this position was that the drafts served no real commercial purpose for the applicant. Unsurprisingly, this proposition has never been accepted judicially,[141] as the commercial utility of a stipulated document is not an acceptable basis for determining the conformity or otherwise of a documentary presentation. Credits calling for sight drafts are fairly straightforward and give rise to little controversy about the apparent irregularity in a presentation which does not include the required drafts.

5.44 In contrast, the second type of credit, which expresses itself available by the acceptance of time drafts drawn on the applicant, presents considerable problems. Particularly unappealing is the fact that a time draft accepted by the applicant, unlike a draft drawn on a bank for acceptance, is not readily discountable in the financial market.[142] Furthermore, in practical terms, such a documentary requirement brings the applicant into the credit settlement process and puts him in a position to manipulate the performance of the issuing bank's undertaking under the credit, notwithstanding that the issuing bank has received an otherwise complying presentation. According to such a credit's terms, the bank's undertaking is simply to obtain acceptance of the beneficiary's draft by the applicant and then to ensure its payment at maturity.[143] In contradistinction to its traditional undertaking in a credit, the issuing bank's primary liability is thus not immediately engaged. Indeed, where the applicant, for reasons best known to himself, declines to accept the draft, the issuing bank may then

[139] See, for example, *Forestal Mimosa Ltd v Oriental Credit Ltd* [1986] 1 WLR 631 (CA) (hereafter *Forestal Mimosa v Oriental Credit*). Under such a credit, it is usual to find this undertaking: 'We [ie issuing bank] hereby engage with drawers and/or bona fide holders that drafts accepted within the terms of this credit will be duly honoured at maturity'. See also *Sinotani Pacific Pte Ltd v Agricultural Bank of China* [1999] 4 SLR 34 (CA) 37.

[140] See Richard King (ed), *Gutteridge & Megrah's Law of Bankers' Commercial Credits* (8th edn, Europa 2001) [4–93].

[141] *Computer Place v Malayan Banking* (n 138) 295, holding that the issuing bank could not recover against the buyer because it honoured a tender without the required sight draft drawn on the applicant. See also *The Lena* (n 138), in which Parker J held that the issuing bank was justified in refusing payment because the sight draft was drawn on the issuing bank, rather than the applicant as required in the credit. In *The Messiniaki Tolmi* (HC) (n 122) 457 (col 2), Leggatt J held that, as the relevant letter of credit called 'for a sight draft, the presentation of documents which did not include it was not such as to satisfy the requirements of the credit'.

[142] Peter Ellinger, 'The Uniform Customs and Practice for Documentary Credits—The 1993 Revision' [1994] LMCLQ 377, 387.

[143] This reflects UCP 400, Arts 10(a)(iii), 10(b)(iii), on which see *Forestal Mimosa v Oriental Credit* (n 139). For a refreshing discussion of Sir John Megaw's judgment in *Forestal*, see Peter Ellinger, 'The Uniform Customs and Practice for Documentary Credits (UCP): Their Development and the Current Revisions' [2007] LMCLQ 152, 176–77(hereafter Ellinger, 'UCP'). For much earlier notes, see Peter Ellinger, 'Effect of Incorporation of UCP and Question of Leave to Defend Action to Enforce Documentary Credit' [1986] LMCLQ 420; Frank R Ryder, 'A Documentary Credit Acceptance' [1986] JBL 311.

be tempted to sit on its hands and justify its refusal to honour the presentation by asserting the non-acceptance of the draft.[144] In that event, what options are open to the beneficiary? Article 6(c) of the UCP 600, which states that a credit 'must not be issued available by a draft drawn on the applicant', offer no further answers and provides no clue as to what should happen in the event of a failure to observe its directive in a credit. Nevertheless, two possibilities suggest themselves.

Under the first possibility, provided the credit has not expired, the beneficiary may apply to a court in his own jurisdiction for a mandatory order requiring the applicant to accept the draft tendered.[145] Notably, a successful application may be of little value: the stated route entails the beneficiary prosecuting a potentially expensive action to obtain the relief; the accepted bill of exchange does not translate into actual cash unless and until discounted by a willing forfeiter; and the applicant's acceptance of the draft exposes the beneficiary to the applicant's shenanigans or insolvency at the draft's maturity date, which is the very evil from which the letter of credit device is supposed to protect the beneficiary. The second possibility would be to require the issuing bank to honour the credit by its permitting the beneficiary to draw his bill of exchange directly on that bank for the same amount and tenor as the draft that the credit requires to be drawn on the applicant.[146] This seems a preferable solution, as it conforms with the fundamental premise that modern letters of credit, as understood by the global banking community, represents the bank's (rather than the applicant's) undertaking to provide payment against conforming documents. According to this approach, even when the bank's undertaking appears to be conditioned by the acceptance of a draft by the very party on whose behalf the credit is issued (rather than simply the bank's receipt of apparently regular documents), the bank's obligation should nevertheless still be viewed as one to pay against conforming documents, irrespective of whether the applicant accepts the draft or not. In that sense, it is to be hoped that judges will be willing to uphold the validity of letter credits requiring an applicant to accept a draft, rather than re-classifying the credit as some other form of non-autonomous payment undertaking.[147] **5.45**

IV. Implications of the Place for Documentary Presentation

The nominated bank 'with which [the credit] is available',[148] or which the credit designates to receive the stipulated documents, is normally the bank to which the beneficiary must make a presentation. Such a bank may be the issuing bank's correspondent operating in the beneficiary's jurisdiction; but may equally be any bank in that jurisdiction where the credit 'is available with any bank'.[149] A significant number of credits have the latter feature. On **5.46**

[144] This might arise, for example, where the bank's own financial interests are at stake because the applicant is insolvent or facing winding-up proceedings, so that reimbursement looks unlikely.

[145] Senior Courts Act 1981, s 39 (formerly s 47, Supreme Court of Judicature (Consolidation) Act 1925, which was considered and applied in *Astro Navegacion SA v Southland Enterprise Co (The Messiniaki Tolmi) (No 2)* [1983] 2 AC 787 (HL)). For the position in Singapore, see Supreme Court of Judicature Act, s 14 (Cap 322, 2007 rev edn).

[146] For a similar suggestion, see James E Byrne, *The Comparison of UCP 600 & UCP 500* (Institute of International Banking Law & Practice 2007) 82.

[147] Consider, for example, *Venizelos SA v Chase Manhattan Bank*, 425 F 2d 461 (2nd Cir, 1970) 466; *Corporacion de Mercadeo Agricola v Mellon Bank International*, 608 F 2d 43 (2nd Cir, 1979).

[148] UCP 600, art 6(a).

[149] ibid.

its face, the nomination of a bank in this way is usually for the beneficiary's convenience. Nevertheless, the beneficiary for its own business reasons may prefer to use its own bank to make the tender to the issuing bank, especially where the bank identified by the issuing bank under the credit is *merely* to receive the documents, examine them for compliance and then forward them to the issuing bank for payment.

5.47 Important questions arise as to whether the beneficiary has a choice between utilising his own bank or the bank named in the credit to make presentation to the issuing bank. Does the beneficiary have the discretion to deviate from what the credit has expressly directed it to do? A combined reading of articles 6(a)[150] and (d)(ii)[151] of the UCP 600 appears to confer upon the beneficiary the option of presenting his documents to the issuing bank without going through the bank specifically nominated in the credit.[152] This reflects the ICC Banking Commission's stance over many years: its published official opinions enunciate that, where the issuing bank has nominated another bank and documents are not presented to that nominated bank, but are instead presented to the issuing bank whether directly or through a third bank, the issuing bank must still pay against a complying presentation.[153]

5.48 The Banking Commission's stance is puzzling: how can a presentation be in compliance with the credit when it fails to adhere to what the credit has stipulated? The issuing bank's undertaking in a letter of credit is to 'honour a complying presentation'. According to article 2 of the UCP 600, 'a complying presentation means a presentation that is in accordance with the terms and conditions of the credit, the applicable provisions of the [UCP] rules and international standard banking practice'.[154] In relation to these three criteria for establishing the conformity of a presentation, it is widely acknowledged in the banking world (and long recognised by the courts as a matter of contract law) that the express stipulations in a credit will override the UCP's provisions or relevant banking practice in the event of any irreconcilable conflict. It is suggested that, when a letter of credit expressly requires the stipulated documents to be delivered to the issuing bank via a designated bank, article 6(a) of the UCP will effectively be displaced insofar as it otherwise purports to entitle the beneficiary to shun that nominated bank and present the documents directly to the issuing bank.

5.49 On this approach, a direct tender to the issuing bank will inevitably be non-conforming and in breach of the credit's terms as to the place of presentation. Support for this view can be found in *Kredietbank NV v Sinotani Pacific Pte Ltd*,[155] in which a Chinese bank issued an unconfirmed letter of credit subject to the UCP 500 in favour of a Singapore beneficiary. The credit required that the documents 'be presented to Royal Bank of Canada Singapore branch, which holds special arrangements for … document forwarding'. In the event, the

[150] UCP 600, art 6(a) provides that a 'credit available with a nominated bank *is also* available with the issuing bank' (emphasis added).

[151] ibid art 6(d)(ii) provides that '[t]he place of the bank with which [a] credit is available is the place for presentation. … A place for presentation *other than* that of the issuing bank is *in addition* to the place of the issuing bank' (emphasis added).

[152] See, for example, Ellinger, 'UCP' (n 143) 161; cf Raymond Jack, Ali Malek, and David Quest (eds), *Documentary Credits*, (4th edn, Informa 2001) [6–19].

[153] Bernard Wheble (ed), *Opinions of the ICC Banking Commission: on Queries Relating to Uniform Customs and Practice for Documentary Credits (UCP) 1987–1988* (ICC Publication No 469) R150. See also ICC Banking Commission, 'UCP 500 sub-Article 10(b)(ii): Negotiation' (Position Paper No 2 on UCP 500, 1 September 1994).

[154] UCP 600, art 2.

[155] *Kredietbank NV v Sinotani Pacific Pte Ltd* [1999] 1 SLR(R) 274 (HC) (hereafter *Kredietbank v Sinotani Pacific*).

beneficiary bypassed the stipulated bank and instead presented the documents to its own bank for onward transmission to the issuing bank in China. Chan Seng Onn JC expressed the view that the presentation was irregular because it did not comply with the directions specified in the credit.[156] That said, a beneficiary is at liberty to take his documents straight to the issuing bank's counters where the nominated bank is unwilling to negotiate the documents, provided of course that the time for presentation in the credit has yet to expire.[157] Furthermore, where the beneficiary presents the documents to a nominated bank that has not confirmed the credit, a decision by the nominated bank to accept or reject[158] the documents will bind the issuing bank, if in the circumstances the nominated bank appears to be acting as the issuing bank's agent. In this regard, in *Grains & Industrial Trading Pte Ltd v Bank of India*,[159] Sundaresh Menon CJ (with whom Andrew Phang Boon Leong JA agreed) confirmed that if the 'issuing bank nominates a bank in accordance with the UCP, then as between the beneficiary and the issuing bank … the latter's liability is engaged as long as the beneficiary makes a valid and complying presentation to the nominated bank. For this purpose, it is immaterial whether the nominated bank has expressly agreed to honour the credit or to act on its nomination.' In other words, the tender of the documents to a nominated bank is effectively treated as a tender to the issuing bank. This point will have some significance in a situation where the beneficiary tenders documents to the nominated bank on the last day of the period for presentation. In a situation of that type, the tender will be regarded as timely. However, the risk of late presentation is heightened when a beneficiary chooses to use his own bank, rather than the nominated bank, to deliver the requisite documents under a credit. That said, should a beneficiary insists on using his own bank in any event, he could always request an amendment to the credit from the buyer, who would then instruct the issuing bank to effect the changes as appropriate.

V. Conclusion

The use of documentary credits to finance international sales transactions has been declining steadily in recent years.[160] In some regions, such as South America, continental Europe, and the UK, use of this instrument as a means of obtaining payment continues to stagnate. Part of the reason for the dwindling interest in the letter of credit appears to derive from the unsatisfactory approach to the interpretation and application of certain UCP provisions and common credit terms. As discussed above, both the UCP and letters of credit themselves are international contractual documents, so that complex issues of interpretation can arise. These can be overcome. The starting point entails a proper appreciation of the predominant object of construction, namely ascertaining the meaning that the credit's **5.50**

[156] The evidence established, however, that the issuing bank had waived the irregularity: see *Kredietbank v Sinotani* Pacific (n 155) [55], [63]–[64].

[157] *Amixco Asia (Pte) Ltd v Bank Bumiputra Malaysia Bhd* [1992] 2 SLR 943 (HC) 947, 955–56.

[158] Either way the act of the nominated bank will be imputed to the issuing bank, so that, if it is wrongful, the beneficiary may utilise the preclusion rule under UCP 600, art 16(f) to recover against the issuing bank under the credit. See generally *Southern Ocean v Deutsche Bank* (n 11) [39]–[40], where Coomaraswamy J expressed the view that a presentation to such an agent is presentation to the issuing bank as principal.

[159] *Grains & Industrial Products Trading Pte Ltd v Bank of India* [2016] 3 SLR 1308 (CA) [55]–[56]. For a detailed analysis of the nominated bank's role, see ch 4 (Toh and Chen) in this volume.

[160] ICC Banking Commission, 'ICC Global Survey on Trade Finance' (July 2020) 38–41 <https://iccwbo.org/publication/global-survey/> accessed 18 August 2020.

terms (including those UCP provisions that are incorporated by reference) would convey to a reasonable person in the class of persons likely to participate in the operation of the credit, such as international bankers, experienced international merchants, and trade-finance professionals. Accordingly, the UCP 600 should be construed purposively and in an international spirit in order to inject sustainable life and meaning into its provisions. Conversely, provincial banking practice and textualism should be avoided where possible. Applying the principles of contractual interpretation also involves a recognition that the codified rules of banking practice in the UCP have no freestanding, self-executing statutory flavour; they need incorporation into a credit in order to govern the parties' rights and obligations (albeit that, even absent incorporation, the UCP may have limited application to a credit as evidence of the prevailing practice regarding the examination and handling of documents tendered for payment). As the UCP is effectively a set of standard terms incorporated by reference into a credit, it only applied to the extent that its provisions advance the ostensible commercial purpose of the credit's express terms; in the event of inconsistency, the UCP is disregarded. Ultimately, the UCP aims to serve the objectively ascertainable business interests and expectations of the parties to the credit, not any separate intention disclosed by the code's literal wording.

5.51 Much the same suggestion applies to ICC publications, which are released to assist document-checkers handling documents in banks' trade-finance departments. Prudent and cautious use should be made of this published guidance when dealing with the requirements of the UCP 600. Presenting nominated banks and beneficiaries need to eschew unthinking employment of their precepts. From the beneficiaries' perspective, it is clear that overconfident reliance on this secondary material as the foundation for claims asserting the wrongful dishonour of a presentation is fraught with considerable litigation risk. From the nominated bank's perspective, an over-reliance on the express words of the UCP and inadequate attention to the secondary material may cause a bank to take a course that would result in liability. For example, the course of action prescribed by article 14(h) of the UCP 600, when an examining bank is confronted with a non-documentary stipulation, is expressed in the clearest words. An examining bank would, however, be well-advised to give due attention to the current version of the ISBP.[161] In substance, this supports the view that non-documentary conditions cannot just be ignored outright, but actually demand careful consideration from the document-scrutineer: it is only the absence of reasonable documentary proof regarding compliance with a non-documentary condition that furnishes a valid ground for the document-checker to reject the tendered documents and refuse payment. Merchants who have the contractual advantage of an absolute promise of payment against complying documents must be alive to the requirements of the credit they seek to enforce and cannot blame such rejection on anyone else.

[161] ISBP 745 (n 86) [A26].

6

The Fraud Rule in the Law of Letters of Credit Revisited

*Xiang Gao**

I. Introduction

The fraud rule in the law of letters credit[1] means that, although documents presented are facially in strict compliance with the letter of credit, payment under the letter of credit may be stopped if fraud is found before payment is made, provided that the presenter is not an innocent third party. The fraud rule has been recognised worldwide since the landmark case of *Sztejn v J Henry Schroder Banking Corp*[2] was handed down in 1941 in the US.[3] **6.01**

However, the fraud rule in the law of letters of credit is still developing and has proven to be 'the most controversial and confused area',[4] mainly because fraud is an 'inherently pliable concept',[5] and different courts or jurisdictions have given different interpretations of the concept. After decades of reckoning and development, the current international rules and national laws and decisions by most of the courts in many jurisdictions, such as the US and the UK, emphasising that the letter of credit is a unique commercial device and must be protected from simple contractual disputes because it is often not easy to distinguish simple contractual disputes from certain fraud claims,[6] have taken the position that the fraud rule must be applied in a strict fashion, or in cases where only 'clear', 'established', 'egregious', or 'material' fraud is involved.[7] However, in other jurisdictions, such as Australia and Singapore, a more flexible approach has been taken, where unconscionable conduct can trigger the application of the fraud rule.[8] **6.02**

* The author is grateful to Professor Dora Neo of University of Singapore for her kind invitation to attend the Trade Finance for the 21st Century Symposium held in Singapore on 8–9 March 2018 (then the author was the Dean of the College of Comparative Law at CUPL), her thoughtful and thorough editing of this chapter, and the experts for their comments on the draft of this chapter provided at the Symposium. All errors and omissions are the author's own.

[1] Unless the context requires otherwise, the term 'letter of credit' is used broadly in this chapter to include commercial letters of credit, standby letters of credit, and independent guarantees.

[2] (1941) 31 NYS 2d 631.

[3] For a comprehensive discussion about the fraud rule in the US, the UK, Australia, and Canada, see Xiang Gao, *The Fraud Rule in the Law of Letters of Credit: A Comparative Study* (Kluwer Law International 2002).

[4] 'Fraud in the Transaction: Enjoining Letters of Credit during the Iranian Revolution' (1980) 93 Harvard Law Review 992, 995.

[5] Gerald T McLaughlin, 'Letters of Credit and Illegal Contracts: The Limits of the Independence Principle' (1989) 49 Ohio State Law Journal 1197, 1203 (hereafter McLaughlin, 'Letters of Credit and Illegal Contracts').

[6] McLaughlin, 'Letters of Credit and Illegal Contracts' (n 5).

[7] See Gao Xiang and Ross P Buckley, 'A Comparative Analysis of the Standard of Fraud Required under the Fraud Rule in Letter of Credit Law' (2003) 12 Duke Journal of Comparative and International Law 293.

[8] See Dee Felicity Monteiro, 'Documentary Credits: The Autonomy Principle and the Fraud Exception: A Comparative Analysis of Common Law Approaches and Suggestions for New Zealand' (2007) 13 Auckland University Law Review 144, 159–61 (hereafter Monteiro, 'Autonomy Principle and the Fraud Exception: Comparative Analysis'). It should be noted that, in Australia and Singapore, the test of unconscionability

6.03 The reason for the divergence of the views has been succinctly expressed in the Canadian case of *Bank of Nova Scotia v Angelica-Whitewear Ltd*,[9] reflecting the tension between two different policy considerations:

> the importance to international commerce of maintaining the principle of the autonomy of documentary credits ... and the importance of discouraging or suppressing fraud in the letter of credit transaction.[10]

6.04 On the one hand, if fraud is defined too widely, the fraud rule may be applied too often and abused by an applicant who does not want the issuer to pay under the credit simply because it will not profit from the underlying transaction. If obstruction of payment of a letter of credit is repeated too often, business confidence in letters of credit as effective assurances of performance will be destroyed.[11] On the other hand, if fraud is defined too narrowly and the fraud rule cannot be applied in cases even though fraud has been clearly established, the effectiveness of the fraud rule, and the values embodied in the law against fraud, will be compromised. It may also discourage the use of letters of credit by applicants and ultimately harm the commercial utility of letters of credit.[12] Moreover, it may also encourage fraudulent conduct by beneficiaries, which should not be allowed in any legal system under any circumstances, because it works against the values and the basis of the law. Unfortunately, increased occurrences of fraud have become a problem, and that is the focus of this chapter.

6.05 This chapter consists of four sections. Following this introduction, the second section will introduce the current status of the fraud rule and the problem arising therefrom. The focus will be on the current position of the fraud rule in international rules and conventions and in the US, the UK, and China. The third section will argue why and how the current fraud rule in some jurisdictions should be refined. The last section will conclude the chapter by advocating a bifurcated approach to solve the problem.

II. The Current Status of the Fraud Rule

6.06 This chapter will present the current position of the fraud rule in international rules and conventions and also in the jurisdictions of the US, the UK, and China. These international rules and selected jurisdictional rules are important in terms of practice as well as legal development of the law of letters of credit. A number of cases illustrating the problem arising out the current fraud rule will also be analysed.

has been applied in the context of an application for an injunction to stop payment on a performance bond until a final resolution of the dispute between the parties. In my view, both letters of credit (including standby letters of credit) and independent guarantees, including performance bonds, are documentary transactions, so the same rules should be applied. Therefore, in this chapter, when I discuss the fraud rule in the law of letters of credit, I also cover the law of independent guarantees.

[9] (1987) 36 DLR 4th 161 (hereafter *Nova Scotia v Anglica-Whitewear*).

[10] ibid 168.

[11] Robert Jay Gavigan, '*Wysko Investment Company v Great American Bank*: A New Attack on the Usefulness of Letters of Credit' (1993)14 Northwestern Journal of International Law and Business 184, 202 (hereafter Gavigan, '*Wysko Investment Company v Great American Bank:* New Attack on Usefulness of LCs').

[12] cf Stephen J Leacock, 'Fraud in the International Transaction: Enjoining Payment of Letters of Credit in International Transactions' (1984) 17 Vanderbilt Journal of Transnational Law 855, 899.

A. International Rules and Conventions

1. ICC Rules

The Uniform Customs and Practice for Documentary Credits ('UCP') published by the International Chamber of Commerce ('ICC') is silent with respect to the issue of fraud and the fraud rule. The reason is that the UCP is simply designed to provide a contractual framework for dealings between issuers and beneficiaries, and issuers and correspondent banks. It is not concerned with the rights and duties of parties to the underlying contract, nor is it the function of the UCP to regulate issues which are the proper province of national law and national courts.[13] Similarly, the ICC's special rules for standby letters of credit, the International Standby Practices ('ISP98'), takes a similar approach and leaves the issue of fraudulent or abusive drawing or 'defences to honour based on fraud, abuse or similar matters ... to applicable law'.[14] The Uniform Rules for Demand Guarantees ('URDG') published by the ICC are also silent on the fraud rule, leaving it to the courts of the various jurisdictions.[15] **6.07**

Both the content and the interpretation of all of the ICC rules are influenced by the fact that 'their function is to serve as rules of best banking practice, not rules of law',[16] and the issue of fraud is considered as 'the province of the applicable law and of the courts of the forum'.[17] Any injunctive relief on the ground of fraud by the beneficiary should therefore be dealt with by national laws. In other words, although '[t]he ICC drafters are clearly aware of the fraud issue',[18] and have implicitly recognised the existence of the fraud rule in various jurisdictions,[19] they have deliberately left it out.[20] **6.08**

2. UN Convention

Unlike the ICC rules, the United Nations Convention on Independent Guarantees and Standby Letters of Credit ('the Convention') has made an effort to address the issue of fraud. First, the Convention puts up a general requirement in article 15(3) in relation to beneficiary demands for payment, providing that '[t]he beneficiary, when demanding payment, is deemed to certify that the demand is not in bad faith and that none of the elements referred **6.09**

[13] Ross P Buckley, 'The 1993 Revision of the Uniform Customs and Practice for Documentary Credits' (1995) 6 Journal of Banking and Finance Law and Practice 77, 95ff.

[14] International Chamber of Commerce, 'International Standby Practices' (ICC Publication No 590, 1998) (hereafter ICC, 'ISP 98') Rule 1.05(c).

[15] RIVF Bertrams, *Bank Guarantees in International Trade* (2nd edn, Kluwer Law International 1996) 25 (hereafter Bertrams, *Bank Guarantees in International Trade*).

[16] Roy Goode, 'Abstract Payment Undertakings and the Rules of the International Chamber of Commerce' (1995) 39 St Louis University Law Journal 725, 727.

[17] ibid.

[18] J F Dolan, 'Commentary on Legislative Developments in Letters of Credit Law: An Interim Report' (1992) 8 Banking & Finance Law Review 53, 63.

[19] This is evidenced by the *Opinions of the ICC Banking Commission (1980–1981)* (No 399, International Chamber of Commerce, ICC Banking Commission 1982), where it was asked by a bank in Bangladesh whether a negotiating bank, which had paid and been reimbursed, was liable to refund the money to the issuing bank when the bill of lading tendered was found to be forged. The Commission replied at page 27:

> [T]he negotiating bank passing forward what proved to be a forged bill of lading was protected by Article 9 [equivalent of Article 34 of UCP 600] unless it was itself a party to the fraud, or it had knowledge of the fraud prior to presentation of the document, or unless it had failed to exercise reasonable care, eg, if the forgery were apparent 'on the face' of the document.

[20] K A Barski, 'Letters of Credit: A Comparison of Article 5 of the Uniform Commercial Code and the Uniform Customs and Practice for Documentary Credits' (1996) 41 Loyola Law Review 735, 751.

to in subparagraphs (a), (b) and (c) of paragraph (1) of Article 19 are present'. Article 19(1) provides that the guarantor/issuer has a right, as against the beneficiary, to withhold payment if one of the following is 'manifest and clear':

(a) Any document is not genuine or has been falsified;
(b) No payment is due on the basis asserted in the demand and the supporting documents; or
(c) Judging by the type and purpose of the undertaking, the demand has no conceivable basis. . . .

6.10 While paragraph (a) focuses on fraud in the documents, paragraphs (b) and (c) are related to fraud in the underlying transaction. Paragraph (2) of article 19 explains the meaning of the term 'no conceivable basis' as follows:

(a) The contingency or risk against which the undertaking was designed to secure the beneficiary has undoubtedly not materialised;
(b) The undertaking obligation of the principal/applicant has been declared invalid by a court or arbitral tribunal, unless the undertaking indicates that such contingency falls within the risk to be covered by the undertaking;
(c) The underlying obligation has undoubtedly been fulfilled to the satisfaction of the beneficiary;
(d) Fulfilment of the underlying obligation has clearly been prevented by wilful misconduct of the beneficiary; or
(e) In the case of a demand under a counter-guarantee, the beneficiary of the counter-guarantee has made payment in bad faith as guarantor/issuer of the undertaking to which the counter-guarantee relates.

6.11 Paragraph (3) of article 19 further provides that, if fraud is involved, not only can the issuer refuse payment, but also the applicant can take court measures against the beneficiary by stating that 'in the circumstances set out in subparagraphs (a), (b) and (c) of paragraph (1) of this article, the principal/applicant is entitled to provisional court measures in accordance with article 20'.

6.12 Under the Convention, the fraud rule can be briefly summarised as the following: if it is 'manifest and clear' that fraud or abusive drawing under standby letters of credit or independent guarantees is established, the fraud rule can be applied, no matter whether fraud is involved in the documents, as stated in paragraph (1) (a) of article 19, or is related to the underlying transaction, as stated in paragraphs (b) and (c) of article 19(1).

B. National Laws

1. United States

6.13 The current fraud rule in the law of letters of credit in the US is provided in s 5–109 of Article 5 of the Uniform Commercial Code ('UCC'),[21] which reads:

[21] UCC, art 5 was first promulgated in 1950s, and thoroughly revised in 1995. In this chapter the revised version will be referred as the 'revised UCC article 5', and the previous version will be referred as 'prior UCC article 5'.

(a) If a presentation is made that appears on its face strictly to comply with the terms and conditions of the letter of credit, but a required document is forged or materially fraudulent, or honour of the presentation would facilitate a material fraud by the beneficiary on the issuer or applicant:

(1) the issuer shall honour the presentation, if honour is demanded by (i) a nominated person who has given value in good faith and without notice of forgery or material fraud, (ii) a confirmer who has honoured its confirmation in good faith, (iii) a holder in due course of a draft drawn under the letter of credit which was taken after acceptance by the issuer or nominated person, or (iv) an assignee of the issuer's or nominated person's deferred obligation that was taken for value and without notice of forgery or *material fraud* after the obligation was incurred by the issuer or nominated person; and

(2) the issuer, acting in good faith, may honour or dishonour the presentation in any other case.

(b) If an applicant claims that a required document is forged or materially fraudulent or that honour of the presentation would facilitate a material fraud by the beneficiary on the issuer or applicant, a court of competent jurisdiction may temporarily or permanently enjoin the issuer from honouring a presentation or grant similar relief against the issuer or other persons only if the courts find that:

(1) the relief is not prohibited under the law applicable to an accepted draft or deferred obligation incurred by the issuer;

(2) a beneficiary, issuer, or nominated person who may be adversely affected is adequately protected against loss that it may suffer because the relief is granted;

(3) all of the conditions to entitle a person to the relief under the law of this State have been met; and

(4) on the basis of the information submitted to the court, the applicant is more likely than not to succeed under its claim of forgery or material fraud and the person demanding honour does not qualify for protection under subsection (a)(1).

As can be seen, in order for the fraud rule to apply in the US, 'material fraud' is needed. **6.14**
Since 'material fraud' is a generic term, like the term 'no conceivable basis' provided in article 19 of the Convention, and it is not defined in the s 5–109 of the UCC itself, efforts have been made to explain the concept in the second paragraph of the Official Comment of the article, which states:

> Necessarily courts must decide the breadth and width of 'materiality'. The use of the word requires that the fraudulent aspect of a document be material to a purchaser of that document or that the fraudulent act be significant to the participants in the underlying transaction. Assume, for example, that the beneficiary has a contract to deliver 1,000 barrels of salad oil. Knowing that it has delivered only 998, the beneficiary nevertheless submits an invoice showing 1,000 barrels. If two barrels in a 1,000 barrel shipment would be an insubstantial and immaterial breach of the underlying contract, the beneficiary's act, though possibly fraudulent, is not materially so and would not justify an injunction. Conversely, the knowing submission of those invoices upon delivery of only five barrels would be materially fraudulent.

6.15 The example set out in the paragraph above seeks to explain what the term 'material fraud' means in a scenario of a commercial letter of credit. As for standby letters of credit, it has stated:

> Material fraud by the beneficiary occurs only when the beneficiary has no colourable right to expect honour and where there is no basis in fact to support such a right to honour ...[22]
>
> We have said throughout that courts may not '*normally*' issue an injunction because of an important exception to the general 'no injunction' rule. The exception, as we also explained in Itek, 730 F.2d at 24-25, concerns 'fraud' so serious as to make it obviously pointless and unjust to permit the beneficiary to obtain the money. Where the circumstances '*plainly*' show that the underlying contract forbids the beneficiary to call a letter of credit, Itek, 730 F.2d at 24; where they show that the contract deprives the beneficiary of even a 'colourable' right to do so, id., at 25; where the contract and circumstances reveal that the beneficiary's demand for payment has 'absolutely no basis in fact,' id.; *Dynamics Corp. of America*, 356 F Supp. at 999; where the beneficiary's conduct has 'so vitiated the entire transaction that the legitimate purposes of the independence of the issuer's obligation would no longer be served,' Itek, 730 F.2d at 25 (quoting *Roman Ceramics Corp. v. Peoples National Bank*, 714 F.2d 1207, 1212 n. 12, 1215 (3d Cir. 1983) (quoting *Intraworld Indus.*, 336 A 2d at 324-25); *then* a court may enjoin payment.[23]

6.16 As can be seen, to apply the fraud rule in the US, 'material fraud' is required. For commercial letters of credit, material fraud 'requires that the fraudulent aspect of a document be material to a purchaser of that document or that the fraudulent act be significant to the participants in the underlying transaction.' Further, the 'beneficiary's act, though possibly fraudulent, would not justify' the application of the fraud rule if it is not materially fraudulent. Even if the beneficiary *knowingly or intentionally* delivers fewer goods than contracted or commits fraud, the fraud rule cannot be applied if the fraudulent act is 'an insubstantial and immaterial breach of the underlying contract.' For standby letters of credit, the fraud involved should be 'so serious as to make it obviously pointless and unjust to permit the beneficiary to obtain the money.' In summary, under revised UCC article 5 in the US, even if fraud is clear and established, the fraud rule cannot be applied if the fraud is not 'material.'

6.17 The fraud rule in the US has been tested in many cases. It has generally been a success story.[24] However, in some cases, the application of the rule has raised serious questions. The typical example in the US is *Al Makaaseb General Trading Co v United States Steel International Inc*[25] decided in 2006 by the US District Court for the Western District of Pennsylvania. In the case, Vijaya Gajapathy Engineers ('VG'), an Indian company, entered into a contract of sale with the defendant, United States Steel International ('USSI'), a US company located in Pittsburgh, for the purchase and transport of 756 metric tons of seamless steel pipes to be delivered to the dock at the Port of Mobile, Alabama. On the eve of delivery of the pipes to the dock, VG discovered that it was unable to obtain the letter of credit as required, and

[22] Official Comment of s 5–109 of revised UCC article 5, [3] (1st sentence).

[23] *Ground Air Transfer v Westate's Airlines*, 899 F 2d 1269 (1st Cir, 1990), 1272–73.

[24] cf Huiwen Li, *The Standard of 'Material Fraud' in the Law of Letters of Credit in the United States of America* (LLM Thesis, China University of Political Science and Law 2016) (written in Chinese with title translated by the author, who was her supervisor) [unpublished], online: <http://epub.cnki.net/kns/brief/result.aspx?dbPrefix=CDMD>.

[25] 412 F Supp (2d) 485 (WD Pa 2006).

made a deal with the plaintiff, Al Makaaseb General Trading ('AMGT'), a company headquartered in the United Arab Emirates, for the plaintiff to act as the financier on the letter of credit, for which it became the applicant. One of the documents required for the payment of the letter of credit was a dock receipt. When a dispute rose, AMGT sued USSI, alleging, among other things, fraud and forgery in connection with the letter of credit and moved for summary judgment.

AMGT alleged that the 28 February 2004 dock receipt was 'fraudulent' because it erroneously indicated that all 184 pieces of pipe had been unloaded at the designated pier on or before Saturday, 28 February 2004, when in fact, thirty-two pieces of pipe contained in two railroad cars which were physically at the port were not actually physically unloaded by the stevedore until 3 March 2004. Although the dock receipt was dated 28 February 2004, it was not signed until 3 March 2004, when all of the thirty-two remaining pieces had been unloaded. **6.18**

The Court rejected the claim and held: **6.19**

> What plaintiff does not demonstrate, even under the broadest reading of the above facts, is how these events could 'so vitiate the underlying transaction' as to constitute a material fraud. See *Intraworld Industries, Inc. v. Girard Trust Bank, 461 Pa. 343, 336 A.2d 316, 324-325 (Pa. 1975)*.The Official Comments to *Section 5109* of the U.C.C. explain that 'material fraud' would not include petty or inconsequential discrepancies, that the courts must examine the underlying transaction when there is an allegation of material fraud, and that material fraud by the beneficiary occurs only when the beneficiary has no colorable right to expect honor and where there is no basis in fact to support such a right to honor. *Vol. 2B Uniform Commercial Code (U.L.A.) § 5-109 (Master Edition)*. Even accepting *plaintiff's* position that the facts of a discrepancy is not disputed, the Court does not see how this discrepancy amounts to a fraud at all, much less a 'material fraud,' such that USSI had no colorable right to expect honor.
>
> As discussed above, plaintiff alleges that the dock receipts contained untruthful representations. The dock receipt is the presentation document submitted pursuant to a L/C presentment, and accordingly, even if the minor delay in unloading could be construed to render the receipt false, the warranty of presentment was not breached because veracity was not a condition of the letter of credit. *PNC Bank, National Ass'n, 912 F. Supp. 169; Farmers-Merchants Bank & Trust Co. v. Travelers Indem. Co., 791 F. Supp. 150, 153 (W.D. La 1992)*. Accordingly, accepting plaintiff's position that there is no dispute of material fact on this issue, defendant USSI is not liable for breach of the warranty of presentment as a matter of law.[26]

The facts of the case are clear. That is, the dock receipt stated that all 184 pieces of pipe were unloaded at the designated pier on or before 28 February 2004, but thirty-two pieces of pipe were actually not unloaded until 3 March 2004. The dock receipt, which was a required document for the payment under the letter of credit, was *not* telling the truth. The beneficiary was not honest. It had lied or committed fraud in relation to the dock receipt. However, because the dock receipt did not affect the value of the goods, the court took the **6.20**

[26] ibid 496 (footnotes omitted).

view that the beneficiary's dishonest behaviour did not '*so vitiate the underlying transaction as to constitute a material fraud*'. Therefore, the fraud rule was not applied and payment was not stopped.

6.21 The consequence of the judgement is this: because the beneficiary had lied or acted fraudulently, it presented 'complying documents' and obtained payment; if it had acted honestly or not lied or not committed fraud, it could not have presented complying documents and obtained payment. It is obviously a very strange and unfair result! Is it good law?

2. United Kingdom

6.22 The fraud rule is recognised in the UK, but only in cases, not in statutes, as there is no statutory law in this area in the UK.

6.23 The English courts 'have traditionally been very reluctant'[27] to interfere with the payment of a letter of credit and have adopted an inflexible and narrow approach towards the application of the fraud rule.[28] They have saddled plaintiffs with a great burden of proof, requiring them to establish the existence of clear or obvious fraud known to the issuer in order to apply the fraud rule. The oft-quoted passage is the following statement of Kerr J in *R D Harbottle (Mercantile) Ltd v National Westminster Bank Ltd*:[29]

> It is only in exceptional cases that the courts will interfere with the machinery of irrevocable obligations assumed by banks. They are the life-blood of international commerce. Such obligations are regarded collateral to the underlying rights and obligations between the merchants at either end of the banking chain. Except possibly *in clear* cases of fraud of which the banks have notice, courts will leave the merchants to settle their disputes under the contracts by litigation or arbitration as available to them or stipulated in the contracts.... Otherwise, trust in international commerce could be irreparably damaged.[30]

6.24 The difficulty to establish 'clear' fraud in English courts has been well demonstrated by the first English case to cite *Sztejn* with approval:[31] *Discount Records Ltd v Barclays Bank Ltd*,[32] where the plaintiff, an English buyer, contracted with a French seller, Promodisc, to buy 8,625 discs and 825 cassettes. The buyer instructed the defendant to issue a documentary credit in favour of the seller. The seller shipped goods purporting to be those ordered and presented a draft with documents regular on their face to the confirming bank in Paris and the documents were accepted. When the goods arrived, the buyer inspected them in the presence of a representative of the issuer and found that 'there were 94 cartons, but of these two were empty, five were filled with rubbish or packing, twenty-five of the record boxes and three of the cassette boxes were only partly filled, and two boxes labelled as cassettes were filled with records; instead of 825 cassettes, as ordered, there were only 518 cassettes and 25 cartridges ... Out of the 518 cassettes delivered, 75% were not as ordered ... out of

[27] Pugh-Thomas A, 'Letters of Credit—Injunctions—The Purist And The Pragmatist: Can A Buyer Bypass The Guarantor And Stop The Seller From Demanding Payment From The Guarantor?' (1996) 11 Journal of International Banking Law 210, 210.

[28] Bertrams, *Bank Guarantees in International Trade* (n 15) 266.

[29] [1977] 2 All ER 862 (QB).

[30] ibid 870 (emphasis added).

[31] G A Fellinger, 'Letters of Credit: The Autonomy Principle and the Fraud Exception' (1990) 1 Journal of Banking and Finance Law and Practice 4, 17.

[32] [1975] 1 All ER 1071 (Ch) (hereafter *Discount Records Ltd v Barclays Bank Ltd*).

the 8625 records ordered, only 275 were delivered as per order. The rest were not as ordered and were either rejects or unsaleable'.[33]

Relying upon *Sztejn*, the buyer attempted to enjoin the issuer from honouring the drafts drawn upon the letter of credit, alleging that the seller was guilty of fraud. Megarry J of the Chancery Division rejected the buyer's claim and said: 6.25

> [I]t is important to notice that in the *Sztejn* case the proceedings consisted of a motion to dismiss the formal complaint on the ground that it disclosed no cause of action. That being so, the court had to assume that the facts stated in the complaint were true. The complaint alleged fraud, and so the court was dealing with a case of established fraud. In the present case there is, of course, no *established* fraud, but merely an allegation of fraud. The defendants, who were not concerned with that matter, have understandably adduced no evidence on the issue of fraud. Indeed, it seems unlikely that any action to which Promodisc was not a party would contain the evidence required to resolve this issue. Accordingly, the matter has to be dealt with on the footing that this is a case in which fraud is alleged but has not been established.[34]

Despite the fact that the buyer in the case obtained its evidence in the presence of the issuer, showing that a great proportion of the shipment was either rubbish or empty cartons, the court ruled that there was 'no established fraud, but merely an allegation of fraud', because the seller was not involved with the proceedings. 6.26

The leading case in the UK is *United City Merchants (Investments) Ltd v Royal Bank of Canada*,[35] where Glass Fibres and Equipment Ltd ('GFE'), an English company, entered into a contract selling glass fibre-making equipment with a Peruvian company named Vitrorefuerzos SA ('Vitro'). Payment was to be made by an irrevocable letter of credit issued by Banco Continental SA of Peru and confirmed by Royal Bank of Canada ('RBC'). GFE assigned their rights, entitlements, and benefits due under the letter of credit to United City Merchants ('UCM'), and notice of the assignment was given to the banks. Shipment was to be from London to Callao on or before 15 December 1976. The goods were nevertheless shipped by the loading broker on 16 December, not on 15 December as required. When documents were presented to RBC for payment, they were rejected on the basis that, among others, 'information in our possession suggests that shipment was not in fact effected as it appears by the bill of lading'.[36] 6.27

The beneficiary sued the confirming bank for wrongful dishonour, and won the case when it went on appeal to the House of Lords. The House of Lords approved of the trial judge's reasoning that the fraud was committed by a third party without the involvement or knowledge of the beneficiary, and should therefore not prevent the beneficiary from being paid on the letter of credit. This decision is consistent with the rationale behind the fraud rule in the English courts, which is that 'fraud unravels all': The courts will not allow their process 6.28

[33] ibid 1073.
[34] ibid1074 (citations omitted, emphasis added).
[35] See the case reports at first instance [1979] 1 Lloyd's Rep 267 (QB) (hereafter *United City Merchants (at first instance)*); before the Court of Appeal [1981] 1 Lloyd's Rep 604 (CA) (hereafter *United City Merchants (CA)*); and before the House of Lords [1983] AC 168 (HL) (*hereafter United City Merchants (HL)*).
[36] *United City Merchants (at first instance)* (n 35) 272.

to be used by a dishonest person to carry out a fraud.[37] The beneficiary in this case was not affected by the fraud rule as it had not been dishonest.

6.29 When considering the issue of third party fraud, Lord Diplock touched upon the kind of fraud that could invoke the fraud rule and said:

> To this general statement of principle [of independence] as to the contractual obligations of the confirming bank to the seller, there is one exception: that is, where the seller, for the purpose of drawing on the credit, fraudulently presents to the confirming bank documents that contain, expressly or by implication, *material* representations of fact that to his knowledge are untrue.[38]

6.30 As can be seen, according to Lord Diplock, 'material misrepresentation' of the fact can invoke the fraud rule in the UK. As to what the term 'material' means, Lord Diplock rejected two propositions by the counsel for the confirming bank. The first is 'a misstatement of a fact which if the true fact had been disclosed would have entitled the buyer to reject the goods'[39] because it 'is to destroy the autonomy of the documentary credit which is its *raison d'etre*; it is to make the seller's right to payment by the confirming bank dependent upon the buyer's rights against the seller under the terms of the contract for the sale of goods, of which the confirming bank will have no knowledge'.[40] The second is 'material to the price which the goods to which the documents relate would fetch on sale if, failing reimbursement by the buyer, the bank should be driven to realise its security'[41] because 'the realisable value on arrival at Callao of a glass fibre manufacturing plant made to the specification of the buyers could not be in any way affected by having been loaded on board a ship at Flexistowe on December 16, instead of December 15, 1976'.[42]

6.31 Lord Diplock himself did not provide an answer to the question. However, it may be assumed from the judgment of the case that predating of bills of lading as occurred in the case can be taken as 'material misrepresentation' because the House of Lords never denied the existence of fraud in the case. In fact, all of the three levels of the courts, the first instance, the Court of Appeal, and the House of Lords handled the case on the basis of letter of credit fraud. Therefore, it can be said that predating of bills of lading is taken as fraud in the law of letters of credit and can trigger the application of the fraud rule in the UK.

3. China

6.32 In China, the fraud rule is provided in the *Rules of the Supreme People's Court Concerning Several Issues in Hearing Letter of Credit Cases* ('Chinese LC Rules') published in late 2005.[43] Article 8 of the Chinese LC Rules provides:

> Any of the following shall be considered as letter of credit fraud:

[37] *United City Merchants (HL)* (n 35) 184.
[38] ibid 183 (emphasis added).
[39] ibid 185
[40] ibid 185.
[41] ibid 186.
[42] ibid 186.
[43] Adjudication Committee of the Supreme People's Court of the People's Republic of China, *Zuigao Renmin Fayuan Guanyu Shenli Xinyongzhen Jiaofeng Anjian Ruogan Wenti De Guiding* (24 October 2005, became effective on 1 January 2006).

(i) The beneficiary has forged documents or presented documents containing fraudulent information;
(ii) The beneficiary has intentionally failed to deliver goods or delivered goods with no value;
(iii) The beneficiary has conspired with the applicant or a third party and presented fraudulent documents whereas there is no actual underlying transaction; or
(iv) Other circumstances that constitute letter of credit fraud.

Subsection (i) deals with fraud in the documents. It covers two types of situations: one is that the document does not exist at all but is simply forged by the beneficiary; the other is that the document exists but the information contained therein is fraudulent. **6.33**

Subsection (ii) deals with fraud in the underlying transaction. Where fraud is alleged to have been involved in relation to the underlying transaction or goods, the fraud rule in the PRC can only be applied in circumstances where no goods have been delivered or where goods have been delivered but without any value. Other situations, such as where goods are of low quality or a lesser quantity is delivered than the contractual amount, cannot be treated as fraud. **6.34**

Subsection (iii) deals with the situation where no genuine underlying transaction is involved. From time to time, cases are reported in the PRC where the beneficiary and the applicant are in collusion to defraud the bank or to avoid the rules of foreign exchange control by making false contracts. Strictly speaking, it is not the type of fraud normally considered under the fraud rule of letters of credit. **6.35**

Subsection (iv) is a catch-all clause to cover anything that might have been left over by subsections (i), (ii), and (iii). It is to serve as a safety valve to prevent any fraudulent acts from falling through the net. Again, strictly speaking, this is not the type of fraud normally considered under the fraud rule of letters of credit. **6.36**

Accordingly, though there are four sections under article 8 of the Chinese LC Rules, only subsections (i) and (ii) are relevant to illustrate, in the context of this chapter, the type of fraud that can invoke the fraud rule in the PRC. The fraud rule in China is different from that provided under s 5–109 of the revised UCC article 5 in the US or the position in the UK, where a catch all standard of fraud, or 'material' fraud or misrepresentation, is used. The fraud rule provided under the Chinese LC Rules is a two-point or bifurcated standard of fraud system: **6.37**

(1) For fraud in documents, as long as the documents are forged or fraudulent, the fraud rule can be triggered.
(2) For fraud in the underlying transaction, if the transaction is for the sale of goods, it is only when goods have not been delivered or have been delivered but without any value that the fraud rule will be triggered. In other words, disputes over quality or quantity of goods cannot invoke the fraud rule at all in the PRC.

However, it is worth mentioning a Chinese case where the influence of US law can clearly be seen. In the case of *Industrial Bank of Korea Seoul v Lianyungang Kuchifuku Foods Co Ltd*,[44] decided by the Jiangsu High People's Court ('JHC') in 2003 under the guidance of the Supreme People's Court of the PRC ('SPC'), the appellant, Industrial Bank of Korea Seoul **6.38**

[44] (2003) *Su Min San Zhong Zi No 052* ((2003) 苏民三终字第052号) (hereafter *Lianyungang Kuchifuku Foods*).

('IBK') issued an irrevocable letter of credit in favour of Lianyungang Kuchifuku Foods Co Ltd ('LKF') on 24 April 2002. The latest loading date was 31 May 2002. When the documents were presented, they were rejected by the issuer on the basis of fraud, as the goods were not loaded on board the ship until 4 am 1 June 2002, four hours later than the latest time permitted for loading under the letters of credit. The beneficiary sued the issuer for wrongful dishonour in the Nanjing Intermediate People's Court, which ruled in favour of the beneficiary on the basis that the issuer's claim of fraud was not proven. The issuer appealed on the basis that the beneficiary had presented a bill of lading that was predated, which is a fraud in the law of letters of credit. The JHC ruled in favour of the beneficiary by saying:[45]

> 1. LKF had no intention of fraud. Evidence presented has illustrated that LKF had prepared the goods before the date of loading, transported the goods to the designated place and went through customs' formalities. IBK has no evidence to show that the goods prepared by LKJ are without value or inferior in quality, and no other evidence to show LKJ is using the predated bill of lading to commit fraud. 2. Although IBK is claiming that the goods arrived late because of the predating of bills of lading, it has not provided evidence showing that the applicant has suffered substantial loss due to the goods loaded one day late (in fact 4 hours).

6.39 The case was handed down by the JHC, but it so ruled under the guidance of the SPC of the PRC. Before handing down the judgment, the JHC went through the special internal court procedure and applied for an opinion from the SPC because there were two different opinions within the JHC:[46]

6.40 The first opinion (majority view) was that the Korean bank cannot refuse payment on the basis of predating of bill of lading because:

> 1. Key elements for fraud under letters of credit. According to laws and court cases of other countries, letter of credit fraud should meet the following criterion: (1) fraud must be committed by the beneficiary or the beneficiary must have taken part in the fraudulent activity. Normally fraud relating to bills of lading refers to the beneficiary's tampering with the content of the bills of lading or conspiring with the carrier so the carrier issues a bill of lading with material fraudulent information; (2) the fraudulent act has caused the applicant (the buyer under the underlying contract) material damage, that is, the beneficiary's fraudulent act has fundamentally broken the underlying contract. As for fraud in relation to predating bills of lading, material fraud arises when the underlying transaction is involved with seasonal or fresh goods, when the price of the goods changes dramatically or when the seller's delayed loading may have caused the buyer to breach its resale contract with its buyer, because the buyer will treat the seller's predating of bill of lading as a gross breach of the contract.
>
> ...
>
> 3. Looking at the causes and the consequences in the current case, the reason why the goods were not loaded timely was somewhat related to the fact that the applicant hindered the loading of the goods by the initial carrier. Further, the predating was only for

[45] Quotation from ibid (translated by the author).

[46] Quotation from the internal report by the JHC to the Supreme People Court of the PRC [unpublished] (translated by the author).

4 hours, and the Korean bank has no evidence to show that the buyer has suffered material loss due to the predating.

The second opinion was: 6.41

> There are no provisions in China as to whether predating can be considered as fraud, and whether the issuer can refuse payment. Predating a bill of lading may normally harm the security of the transaction, and the issuer may refuse payment because the documents are in fact not in compliance with the terms and conditions of the letter of credit, no matter whether the beneficiary has taken part in predating the bills of lading or not.

The SPC issued a reply to the JHC and agreed with the first opinion, saying:[47] 6.42

> Predating bills of lading does not necessarily constitute fraud. Neither does it necessarily give the issuer the right to refuse payment. It should be dealt with according to different circumstances. If predating of bills of lading is caused by the beneficiary's intentional fraud arising out of ill will, predating as a means of fraud shall be regarded as fraud even if predating is perpetrated by the carrier. In such a case, the bank can refuse payment on that basis. If predating of bills of lading is not caused by the beneficiary's intentional fraud arising out of ill will, and the interest of the applicant is not damaged due to predating bills of lading, it shall not be regarded as fraud, and the bank cannot refuse payment on that basis. Looking at the circumstances of the case, KFJ should not be held as fraudulent, and the Korean bank is not entitled to refuse payment based on predating bills of lading.

On the face of the judgment, no fraud was found in the case by the JHC, which followed the opinion of the SPC that 'Looking at the circumstances of the case, KFJ should not be held as fraudulent, and the Korean bank is not entitled to refuse payment based on predating bill of lading.' It is likely that the judgment was heavily influenced by the US position of 'material fraud', as the JHC prefaced the first view by stating that this was 'according to laws and court cases of other countries'. 6.43

The result of this case is the similar to that of the US case *Al Makaaseb General Trading Co v United States Steel International Inc* discussed above. That is, if the beneficiary had acted honestly and had not lied nor predated the bills of lading, it could not have presented complying documents and obtained payment. When it lied or acted dishonestly, it presented complying documents and obtained payment! This case was decided in 2003, which was before the Chinese LC Rules were promulgated. How the Chinese courts will react to similar cases after the Chinese LC Rules have been published remains to be seen. 6.44

III. Refining the Current Fraud Rule

A. The Rationale

As has been seen, under the position of the current fraud rule in the US, only 'material fraud' can invoke the fraud rule. Following this approach, in some cases, as illustrated by the 6.45

[47] (2003) *Min Si Ta Zi No 33* ((2003) 民四他字第33号) (translated by the author).

two cases in the US and China, even if fraud has been clearly established, if the fraud is not regarded as 'material', the fraud rule cannot be applied.

6.46 The application of the fraud rule in such a way has led to a very strange and unfair result: if the beneficiary behaves honestly, it cannot present complying documents, and therefore cannot be paid; if it behaves dishonestly, it can present complying documents and get paid! This should not be allowed. More importantly, the application of the fraud rule in such a way is against the fundamental values or the common basis of the general law against fraud. It is well known that 'fraud unravels all'.[48] 'There is as much public interest in discouraging fraud as in encouraging the use of letters of credit.'[49] The fraud rule is part of a sound legal system safeguarding the public policy of control of fraud. It is not good law nor good public policy to openly allow fraud which is not 'material' to be committed under the law of letters of credit. Fraud is wrong and should be prohibited and prevented in any case. When fraud is obvious, whether it is 'material' or not, the fraud rule should be applied.

6.47 Moreover, this application of the fraud rule is against the two basic principles of the law of letters of credit. First, it is against the principle of independence. Because of the separation of transactions and the practice of letters of credit, how could the issuer know whether the predating in the cases discussed above so vitiates the underlying transaction as to constitute a material fraud or not? Secondly, it is against the principle of strict compliance, under which documents tendered for payment under a letter of credit must be in strict compliance with the terms and conditions of the credit. If the letter of credit specifies, for example, that the bill of lading must evidence shipment on or before 31 May as in the case of *Lianyungang Kuchifuku Foods*, but the bill of lading tendered shows that the goods are shipped on 1 June, the bank is bound to refuse to honour the letter of credit unless the discrepancy is waived. If the bank pays out, the buyer will not be obliged by a court to reimburse a bank that has not strictly obeyed its instructions. In *Lianyungang Kuchifuku Foods*, if the bills of lading had not been fraudulently predated (ie if the beneficiary had tendered one bearing the true date of loading), the bank could have relied on the principle of strict compliance and simply refused to honour the presentation. In such a situation, the beneficiary would not even have had a case!

B. The Way Out

6.48 How to refine the fraud rule? A two-point standard of fraud or bifurcated standard of fraud should be adopted.

1. Simple Fraud for Fraud in Documents

6.49 For fraud in the documents, a clear simple fraud should trigger the fraud rule. Normally, fraud in documents is obvious and easy to establish, as shown in the cases discussed above. Therefore, it is not necessary to take great pains to ascertain if fraud is involved. When fraud

[48] *United City Merchants (HL)* (n 35) 184 (*per* Lord Diplock). See also *United Trading Corporation v Allied Arab Bank Ltd* [1985] 2 Lloyd's Rep 554 (CA); *Contronic Distributors Pty Ltd v Bank of New South Wales* [1984] 3 NSWLR 110; *Hortico (Australia) Pty Ltd v Energy Equipment Co (Australia) Pty Ltd* [1985] 1 NSWLR 545.

[49] *Dynamics Corp of America v Citizens & Southern Nat'l Bank* (1973) 356 F Supp 991 (ND Ga 1973) 1000 (per Edenfield J).

is clear and established, the fraud rule should be applied and payment should be stopped. Therefore, in relation to fraud in the documents, a simple fraud should trigger the application of the fraud rule, as provided in subsection (i) of Chinese LC Rules. This is clearly supported by the Court of Appeal in the case of *United City Merchants*,[50] where Ackner LJ stated:

> [T]he buyer, unless otherwise agreed, cannot be deemed to have authorised the banker to pay against documents which are known to be forged. If the documents are forged, then obviously they are not valid.... The banker's authority or mandate is to pay against genuine documents and that is what the bank has undertaken to do.[51]

Griffith LJ observed: **6.50**

> The latest date for shipment of the machinery was Dec. 15, 1976. The machinery was in fact shipped on Dec. 16, 1976, and if the bill of lading had shown that date the bank would have refused to pay upon presentation of the documents because of the strict rule that the documents must comply in every respect with the terms of the letter of credit ... [I]t would be a strange rule that required a bank to refuse payment if the document correctly showed the date of shipment as Dec. 16, yet obliged the bank to make payment if it knew the document falsely showed the date of shipment as Dec. 15 and that the true date was Dec. 16.[52]

Secondly, it is also in line with the documentary nature of the letter of credit, or the centrality of the documents in letter of credit transactions. The genuineness of the documents is the foundation of the success of letters of credit, because '[b]anks deal with documents and not with goods, services or performances to which the documents may relate'.[53] Only genuine documents can meet the bargain of the parties and be accepted by issuers and applicants, whose interests otherwise will not be properly protected. Trusting that genuine documents will be tendered, the applicant authorises the issuer to pay the beneficiary, and the issuer agrees to pay the beneficiary when documents conforming on their face to the terms and conditions of the letter of credit are received. So, if documents cannot be taken to mean what they say, the commercial foundation of letters of credit will vanish. Although it is not explicitly stated in every letter of credit that the documents should be genuine, it is logically and generally recognised that there is an implied warranty by the beneficiary that documents tendered are genuine.[54] **6.51**

The key argument or the reason to tolerate fraud in the documents is that it seems unfair to the beneficiary to refuse payment where the fraud involved is merely of a technical nature. For example, in either the Chinese case of *Industrial Bank of Korea Seoul* or the US case of *Al* **6.52**

[50] It should be noted that, although the decision of the Court of Appeal was overturned by the House of Lords, the point illustrated here should still be valid. Further, as discussed above, although the House of Lords used the term 'material representation' when discussing the fraud involved in the case, it may be assumed from their judgment of the case that predating of bills of lading, a simple fraud in the documents, can be taken as 'material misrepresentation' because they never denied the existence of fraud in the case. In other words, the position in the UK is different from that of the US, although both countries have used the word 'material' to refer the standard of fraud.

[51] *United City Merchants (CA)* (n 35) 628–29.

[52] ibid 632.

[53] UCP 600, art 5.

[54] See eg A G Guest (gen ed), *Benjamin's Sale of Goods* (5th edn, Sweet & Maxwell 1997) 1715; H Harfield, *Bank Credits and Acceptances* (5th edn, Ronald Press Co 1974) 80; Reade H Ryan Jr, 'Who Should Be Immune from the "Fraud in the Transaction" Defense in a Letter of Credit Transaction' (1990–1991) 56 Brooklyn Law Review 119, 126.

Makaaseb General Trading discussed above, the fraud was only related to the dating of the bill of lading or the dock receipt, and the fact that false dates were stated in the documents would seem to have made little difference with regard to the value of the goods. There were no disputes over the quality or quantity of the goods involved. How can such an insignificant misconduct lead to non-payment of a significant amount of money?

6.53 When these cases are looked at ad hoc, it does seem to be unfair. Nonetheless, when they are looked at in the context of the overall legal system, it is not unfair at all. Firstly, the law cannot encourage fraud, no matter how minor it is. Secondly, a letter of credit is, after all, an instrument of payment. It is designed to facilitate the underlying transaction between the applicant and the beneficiary. If the beneficiary fully performs its obligations under the underlying contract, it can obtain complying documents evidencing its full performance of the underlying contract, present the required documents, and promptly get paid. If it cannot present complying documents, it means that the beneficiary hasn't fully performed its obligations under the underlying contract, or has broken the contract. For example, in the Chinese case of *Industrial Bank of Korea Seoul*, the beneficiary did not load the goods on board the ship on or before 31 May 2002 as required in the underlying contract. When the beneficiary has broken the contract, who should bear the consequence? Naturally it should be the beneficiary.

6.54 One of the functions of the letter of credit is to allocate risks. In the normal course of business, if the beneficiary can fully perform its obligation under the contract, it has less risk than the applicant. However, if it cannot fully perform its obligation under the contract to present complying documents and breaks the contract, the risk should be kicked back to the beneficiary. Under such circumstances, if the non-compliance is insignificant, it can ask the applicant, through the issuer, to waive the discrepancies in the documents. If the applicant permits the waver, the beneficiary can still get paid through letters of credit. If the beneficiary cannot get the waver, it can get paid through the underlying contract, though it may have to bear the risk of reduced payment or even non-payment because the applicant may suffer loss or even become bankrupt due to the beneficiary's fault or other causes. Even if the beneficiary cannot get paid, it is not unfair because this is due to its own fault or breach of the contract.

2. High Standard for Fraud in the Transaction

6.55 For fraud in the transaction, the standard of fraud should be high. The reasons are obvious. The first reason is a legal and commercial one, ie to minimise the application of the rule and maintain the principle of independence and the commerciality of letters of credit. 'Fraud is, in practice, virtually the only defence available when one seeks to escape payment'[55] in many jurisdictions. If fraud is defined too widely, the fraud rule may be abused by the applicant who does not want the issuer to pay simply because it cannot profit from the underlying transaction. If the fraud rule is abused and obstruction of payment of a letter of credit is repeated too often, the inherent commercial functions of letters of credit such as prompt

[55] Bertrams, *Bank Guarantees in International Trade* (n 15) 257. Illegality may be another one, but cases are scarce in this respect. See eg *United City Merchants (at first instance)* (n 35); *United City Merchants (CA)* (n 35); and *United City Merchants (HL)* (n 35). In Australia and Singapore, another defence—unconscionable conduct—has become available recent years. See Monteiro, 'Autonomy Principle and the Fraud Exception: Comparative Analysis' (n 8) 159–61.

payment and allocation of risks will disappear, the business confidence in letters of credit as effective performance assurances will be destroyed,[56] and eventually the principle of independence and the commercial utility of the letters of credit themselves will be harmed. The second reason is a technical one, ie fraud in the transaction is not clear and obvious, unlike fraud in the documents. In many cases, it is very hard to distinguish fraud from breach of contract. To maintain the commerciality of letters of credit, the standard of fraud must be set high to prevent disputes related to breach of contract from becoming disputes involving letter of credit fraud.

Therefore, for fraud in the underlying transaction, a very high standard of fraud is necessary and favourable. The current standard of 'material' fraud adopted in s 5–109 of revised UCC article 5 in the US or the standard of 'non-delivery' or 'no value' provided under subsection (ii) of article 8 of the Chinese LC Rules are adequate and appropriate. **6.56**

IV. Conclusion

The fraud rule in the law of letters of credit is a difficult and developing area. Currently, at the international level, it is silent in all ICC rules but has been provided in the UN Convention, where it requires 'manifest and clear' fraud for the application of the fraud rule. At the national level, in the leading countries such as the US and the UK, the standard of 'material' fraud, is required to apply the fraud rule, although the word 'material' may mean different things. In China, before the Chinese LC Rules were promulgated in 2006, cases were influenced by the position of the US. After the Chinese LC Rules were promulgated, how similar cases for fraud in the documents will be decided still remains to be seen. **6.57**

Unfortunately, applying the US standard of 'material' fraud in cases of fraud in the documents, where fraud is clear and obvious but not regarded as 'material', has led to an unfair and strange result. To solve the problem, it has been proposed that the fraud rule should be refined and that a bifurcated standard of fraud should be adopted. That is, for fraud in the documents, a clear and simple fraud should be able to trigger the application of the rule; for fraud in the transaction, a high standard of fraud should be adopted. **6.58**

[56] Gavigan, '*Wysko Investment Company v Great American Bank:* New Attack on Usefulness of LCs' (n 11) 202.

7

Letters of Credit and Stop Payment Orders Made in the Issuer's Country

*Nelson Enonchong**

I. Introduction

7.01 It is well known that the principal purpose of a letter of credit is to provide the exporter with assurance that the importer's payment obligation under the underlying contract of sale will be honoured by a reliable paymaster, namely a bank. This assurance of payment is underpinned by the principle of autonomy or independence, which shields the bank's undertaking to pay the exporter from disputes between the importer and the exporter relating to the underlying contract of sale. However, difficulties arise where, after the exporter has supplied goods to the importer, a court or other authority in the issuing bank's country makes an order prohibiting the bank from making payment under the credit (a 'stop payment order'). Such an order made by a local court at the request of the importer in connection with its claim against the exporter for breach of the underlying contract of sale strikes at the independence of letters of credit.[1] Nevertheless, in such a case, the issuer, observing the terms of the order, will refuse to make payment under the credit, thus presenting a serious problem for the beneficiary or a bank that has paid the beneficiary pursuant to the credit and is claiming reimbursement from the issuer (a 'claiming bank').

7.02 The question whether, and to what extent, a foreign stop payment order can constitute a defence to a claim against the issuer in a court outside the issuer's home jurisdiction has presented itself to courts in various jurisdictions[2] and to the International Chamber of Commerce (ICC) Banking Commission[3] over many years. However, this question has

* I am grateful to Professor Michael Bridge for his comments on the version of this chapter that was presented at the Trade Finance for the 21st Century Symposium, National University of Singapore (8–9 March 2018). I would also like to express my thanks to Christopher Hare for all his work as the editor in charge of this chapter. I remain solely responsible for any remaining errors.

[1] This chapter is focused on cases where the foreign stop payment order is based on a claim by the importer relating to the underlying contract and where the issuing bank has no other defence to payment that is recognised under the law of the forum, such as fraud, illegality, including violations of United Nations or other sanctions that are enforceable in the forum.

[2] See, for example, *Power Curber International Ltd v National Bank of Kuwait* [1981] 1 WLR 1233 (CA) (hereafter *Power Curber v National Bank of Kuwait*); *National Infrastructure Development Co Ltd v BNP Paribas* [2016] EWHC 2508 (Comm) (hereafter *NIDCO v BNP Paribas*); *National Infrastructure Development Co Ltd v Banco Santander* [2017] EWCA Civ 27, [2017] 1 CLC 37 (hereafter *NIDCO v Banco Santander*). See also, in Hong Kong, *Cooperative Centrale Raiffeisen-Boerenleenbank BA v Bank of China* [2004] 3 HKC 119 (hereafter *Cooperative Centrale v Bank of China*); in Singapore, *Agritrade International Pte Ltd v Industrial and Commercial Bank of China* [1998] 1 SLR(R) 322 (HC) (hereafter *Agritrade International v ICBC*); and, in the US, *Cantrade Privatbank AG Zurich v Bangkok Bank Pub Co Ltd*, 256 AD 2d 11 (NYSC, 1998) (hereafter *Cantrade Privatbank v Bangkok Bank*).

[3] See, for example, *Opinions of the ICC Banking Commission* (hereafter *ICC Opinion*), R519 / TA556; *ICC Opinion*, R629 / TA672rev; *ICC Opinion*, R779 / TA736rev.

attracted very little, if any, academic attention.[4] This chapter examines this under-explored issue. It shows that in the case of proceedings by a claiming bank, as opposed to the exporter, a stop payment order made in the issuer's home country rarely gives the issuer a good ground for resisting payment in England or in some other common law jurisdictions. The position is different, however, in a claim by a beneficiary under an unconfirmed credit where documents are to be presented to, and payment made at, the issuing bank's office in its home country. In such a case, a stop payment order made in the issuer's country normally constitutes a good defence to the beneficiary's claim in England and in some other common law jurisdictions. However, in the more usual case where documents are to be presented to, and payment made at, another bank in a different country, stop payment orders made in the issuer's home jurisdiction have had a more limited reach under the common law rules in England[5] and in other common law jurisdictions, such as Hong Kong and Singapore.

The chapter argues that the outcome has been the same under the rules of the Rome Convention[6] ('the Convention'), which in England applied to credits issued between 1 April 1991 and 16 December 2009.[7] This result is attributable to the courts' practice of invoking article 4(5) of the Convention to displace the law of the issuer's country, as the law prima facie applicable to the contract between the issuer and the beneficiary (under article 4(2)), in favour of the law of the country of performance. Since stop payment orders had a very limited reach at common law and under the Convention, attempts to rely on such orders to defeat the issuing bank's payment obligation have been rare. **7.03**

However, that state of affairs may change under the Regulation (the Regulation),[8] which applies to credits issued from 17 December 2009.[9] Amendments to the structure and language of article 4 of the Regulation, compared to article 4 of the Convention, mean that the threshold required to displace the applicable law designated by the basic rule appears higher **7.04**

[4] Commentators have focused instead on the circumstances when a stop payment order may be granted by a court. See, for example, Ali Malek and David Quest, *Jack: Documentary Credits* (4th edn, Tottel Publishing 2009) ch 9. See also A D Barclay, 'Court Orders against Payment under First Demand Guarantees Used in International Trade' (1989) 4(3) J Int Banking Law 110; Jurgen Dohm, 'Enjoining Payment of Demand Guarantees: A Synthesis of the Case Law and Legal Writings from Selected European Countries' [1992] Int Business LJ 887.

[5] The English common law rules apply to credits issued before 1 April 1991.

[6] Convention 80/934/EEC of 19 June 1980 on the Law Applicable to Contractual Obligations [1980] OJ L266/1 (hereafter 'Rome Convention').

[7] Contracts (Applicable Law) Act 1990, s 4A.

[8] Council Regulation (EC) 593/2008 of 17 June 2008 on the Law Applicable to Contractual Obligations [2008] OJ L177/6 (hereafter 'Rome I Regulation').

[9] The Rome I Regulation (n 8) is of course European Union ('EU') legislation and, therefore, its status in the UK has changed after the UK's exit from the EU ('Brexit'). While the UK formally withdrew from the EU on 31 January 2020, under the Agreement of 12 November 2019 on the Withdrawal of the United Kingdom of Great Britain and Northern Ireland from the European Union and the European Atomic Energy Community [2019] OJ CI384/1 (hereafter 'Withdrawal Agreement'), art 127, the Rome I Regulation continued to apply to, and within, the UK during the transition period (to 31 December 2020). Further, after 31 December 2020, the Rome I Regulation continues to apply in the UK to contracts concluded before 31 December 2020: ibid art 66. Thirdly, in relation to cases where, after 31 December 2020, the Rome I Regulation will not apply in the UK, as EU legislation, the UK Parliament has passed legislation (European Union (Withdrawal) Act 2018, as amended) that incorporates directly into UK domestic law from 'exit day' certain EU legislation (including the Rome I Regulation) operative immediately before exit day. This is subject to some amendments, designed to adjust the Rome I Regulation for application in the UK as UK domestic legislation: see the Law Applicable to Contractual Obligations and Non-Contractual Obligations (Amendment etc) (EU Exit) Regulations 2019, SI No 834 which has further been amended by the Jurisdiction, Judgments and Applicable Law (Amendment) (EU Exit) Regulations 2020, SI No 1574. The result of all this is that, after 31 December 2020, the retained Rome I Regulation applies in England to determine the law applicable to contractual obligations, subject to any changes that the UK Parliament may introduce in the future.

under article 4(3) of the Regulation than under article 4(5) of the Convention. This chapter further explores the question whether this apparently higher threshold means, as some suggest,[10] that courts would no longer be able to displace the law of the issuing bank's country in favour of the law of the country of performance in situations where it was possible to do so under the Convention. If there has been such a shift in the law, then under the Regulation, the law governing the contract between the issuing bank and the beneficiary will be the law of the issuing bank's country in many cases where under the Convention it would be the law of the place of performance. Consequently, under the Regulation, a stop payment order made in the issuing bank's country would constitute a good defence to a beneficiary's claim in England in many cases where it would not have been a defence under the Convention. This would be a significant departure from the position under both the Convention and at common law. It would strike at the established policy of English law that a letter of credit 'should be honoured—and not nullified by an attachment order at the suit of the buyer'.[11]

7.05 After explaining the role of choice of law rules in this context, in section II, the chapter discusses the reach of stop payment orders in the context of unconfirmed credits, both at common law, in section III, and under the Convention, in section IV. The extent to which stop payment orders may now give the issuing bank a good defence under article 4 of the Regulation is examined in section V. Section VI explores the question whether the court can use the public policy exception as a ground to refuse to give effect to a foreign stop payment order. This is followed by a discussion, in section VII, of the reach of foreign stop payment orders in claims by banks seeking reimbursement from the issuing bank. The conclusions are stated in section VIII.

II. The Role of Choice of Law Rules

7.06 A beneficiary or a claiming bank faced with an issuer's refusal to honour the credit because of a stop payment order made in the issuer's country may consider a number of options. First, where the credit is subject to the ICC Uniform Customs and Practice for Documentary Credits, 2007 Revision (UCP 600), the beneficiary or the claiming bank may argue that, by virtue of the principle of independence of letters of credit enshrined in the UCP 600,[12] the issuer should nevertheless honour the credit.[13] However, that argument is unlikely to persuade the issuer to make payment, since it cannot ignore the stop payment order.

7.07 The alternative response is to persuade the issuer to make an application to the local court for the order to be discharged. However, whilst in some cases the issuer may be willing to do so, this may not always be the case. Moreover, even if the issuer intervenes to request that the order be set aside, success is not guaranteed.[14]

[10] See, for example, Jonathan Hill and Maire Ni Shúilleabháin, *Clarkson & Hill's Conflict of Laws* (5th edn, OUP 2016) 233–35 (hereafter Hill and Shúilleabháin, *Conflict of Laws*).

[11] *Power Curber v National Bank of Kuwait* (n 2) 1241.

[12] International Chamber of Commerce ('ICC'), 'Uniform Customs and Practice for Documentary Credits' (ICC Publication No 600, 2007) (hereafter UCP 600) arts 4(a), 5.

[13] ibid arts 7(a), 15(a).

[14] See, for example, *Power Curber v National Bank of Kuwait* (n 2), where the issuing bank's application to the local court in Kuwait to set aside a stop payment order was dismissed and the refusal was upheld on appeal. Compare *Fortis Bank (Nederland) NV v Abu Dhabi Islamic Bank*, 32 Misc 3d 1232(A) (NYSC, 2010), where a

A further option is for the claimant itself to petition the court in the issuer's country for the order to be discharged and for summary judgment to be entered against the issuer. However, whilst such a claim may be successful in some countries,[15] in other jurisdictions the prospects of success may be negligible. **7.08**

Therefore, in many cases, the claimant is left with no option but to institute legal proceedings against the issuing bank in the claimant's own country (or in a third country). In those proceedings, the issuing bank would raise the stop payment order as a defence and the court would have to decide whether or not to give effect to that order. Whilst, in raising that defence, the issuing bank could potentially rely on the rules for the recognition of foreign judgments, in practice that option is normally eschewed. A number of factors account for this. First, in some cases the stop payment order is issued by the government or an administrative (as opposed to a judicial) authority and therefore it cannot be recognised as a judgment. Secondly, even where the order is made by a court, if the issuing bank seeks to rely on the rules for the recognition of foreign judgments, it would encounter a number of formidable obstacles where recognition is sought under the common law rules.[16] The first difficulty is the requirement that for the English court to recognise a foreign judgment, it must be final and conclusive on the merits.[17] In the case of stop payment orders, this requirement will not be satisfied in most cases because the orders are normally only provisional (interim), pending trial of the underlying dispute. The second difficulty is that recognition of a foreign judgment for purposes of a defence or estoppel is based on the principle of discouraging re-litigation of matters already judicially decided as between the same parties.[18] Where, as in many cases, the claiming bank is not a party to the foreign proceedings between the importer and the issuing bank or the underlying proceedings initiated by the importer against the exporter, it is doubtful whether the foreign order, issued in the course of those proceedings, can be recognised as having already determined the matter in the forum as between the issuing bank and the *claiming bank*. **7.09**

stop payment order obtained by the confirming bank in the issuing bank's country (Bahrain), restraining the confirming bank from making payment under the credit, was later set aside by the court.

[15] See, for example, *First Commercial Bank v Gotham Originals Inc*, 475 NE 2d 1255 (NY Ct App, 1985) (hereafter *First Commercial Bank v Gotham Originals*), where a paying bank in Taiwan successfully applied to the courts in New York to discharge a stop payment order issued in New York restraining the issuing bank in New York from making payment under the letter of credit.

[16] In England, prior to the UK's withdrawal from the EU, separate rules applied where the judgment was made in a country that was an EU Member State, to which Regulation (EU) 1215/2012 of 12 December 2012 on Jurisdiction and the Recognition and Enforcement of Judgments in Civil and Commercial Matters [2012] OJ L351/1 (hereafter 'Brussels I Recast') applied or a country to which the Lugano Convention on Jurisdiction and the Recognition and Enforcement of Judgments in Civil and Commercial Matters 2007 (hereafter the "Lugano Convention") applied. Whilst the United Kingdom formally withdrew from the European Union on 31 January 2020, the Brussels I Recast continues to apply in the UK (and in the other member states of the EU) to the recognition and enforcement of judgments given in legal proceedings instituted before the end of the transition period of 31 December 2020: see Withdrawal Agreement (n 9) art 67(2)(a). Following the UK's withdrawal from the EU, the Brussels I Recast and the Lugano Convention no longer apply in England to the recognition and enforcement of judgments given in proceedings commenced on or after 1 January 2021. Therefore, the common law rules discussed in the text now have greater significance in practice.

[17] *Black-Clawson International Ltd v Papierwerke Waldhof-Aschaffenburg AG* [1975] AC 591 (HL); *The Sennar (No 2)* [1985] 1 WLR 490 (HL). By contrast, under the Brussels I Recast, judgments entitled to recognition include provisional measures ordered by a court: see Brussels I Recast (n 16) art 2(a).

[18] *Carl Zeiss Stiftung v Rayner & Keeler Ltd (No 2)* [1967] 1 AC 853 (HL); *Airbus Industrie GIE v Patel* [1996] ILPr 465 (CA) [28].

7.10 Thirdly, even in the case where the matter in the foreign court is deemed to be one between the same parties as involved in the English proceedings, there is a further obstacle. At common law, the English courts will not recognise a foreign judgment unless, in the eyes of English law, the foreign court had jurisdiction over the defendant in the foreign proceedings (the claimant in the English proceedings).[19] In the case of a judgment *in personam*, at common law, the English courts would recognise a foreign court as having jurisdiction only where according to English law the defendant was present in the foreign country at the time the foreign proceedings were instituted; prior to the commencement of the proceedings in the foreign country, the defendant had agreed to submit to the foreign court's jurisdiction in respect of the subject matter of those proceedings; the defendant submitted to that foreign court's jurisdiction by voluntarily appearing in the proceedings; or the defendant claimed or counterclaimed in the foreign proceedings.[20] In the context of stop payment orders, even if the English court considers the underlying claim by the importer in the issuing bank's country against the beneficiary/exporter (rather than the claim for a stop payment order between the importer and the issuing bank), it is unlikely that any of these bases of jurisdiction would be satisfied in most cases.

7.11 Confronted with these difficult, if not insuperable, hurdles, issuing banks seeking to rely on foreign stop payment orders as a defence normally choose the alternative route. This is to request the court to give effect to the order simply as a prohibition under the law of the issuer's country that has rendered further performance of the issuer's obligation under the credit illegal and, therefore, unenforceable. This is based on the principle that the English court will not compel performance of a contract where performance is unlawful under the law that governs the contract,[21] or where performance is unlawful under the law of the country where the obligation is to be performed.[22] Thus, where the law of the issuing bank's country is the law that governs its undertaking under the letter of credit, or where the issuing bank's payment obligation is to be performed in its home country, the English court will give effect to a stop payment order made in that country and the claim against the issuing bank will be defeated. However, such an order affords the issuing bank no defence against a claim in England where the governing law is not that of the issuing bank's country, the credit is valid and enforceable under its governing law, and performance of the bank's payment obligation is not illegal in the country of performance.[23] Of course, the answer to the question whether the law that governs the issuer's undertaking under the credit is the law of the issuer's home country, or the law of a different country, depends on the choice of law rules of the forum

[19] *Sirdar Gurdyal Singh v The Rajah of Faridkote* [1894] AC 670 (PC). By contrast, under the Brussels I Recast, the jurisdiction of the court of origin may not be reviewed: see Brussels I Recast (n 16) art 45(3).

[20] See Lord Collins et al (eds), *Dicey, Morris and Collins on the Conflict of Laws* (15th edn, Sweet & Maxwell 2018), vol 1, rule 43 (hereafter *Dicey, Morris and Collins on the Conflict of Laws*). The grounds are similar for recognition of foreign judgments under the Foreign Judgments (Reciprocal Enforcement) Act 1933, ss 4(1)(a)(ii), (2)(a).

[21] *Ralli Bros v Compania Naviera Sota Y Aznar* [1920] 2 KB 287 (CA); *Kahler v Midland Bank Ltd* [1950] AC 24 (HL); *Zivnostenska Banka National Corporation v Frankman* [1950] AC 57 (HL) (hereafter *Zivnostenska Banka v Frankman*).

[22] *Kleinwort, Sons & Co v Unarische Baumwolle Industrie Aktiengesellschaft* [1939] 2 KB 678 (CA) 694; *Zivnostenska Banka v Frankman* (n 21) 78; *Mackender v Feldia AG* [1967] 1 QB 590 (HL) 601. See also Rome I Regulation (n 8), art 9(3). The position is similar in Singapore: see *Peh Teck Quee v Bayerische Landesbank Girozentrale* [1999] 3 SLR(R) 842 (CA); *Brooks Exim Pte Ltd v Bhagwandas* [1995] 1 SLR(R) 543 (CA). See also *Singapore Finance Ltd v Soetano & Ors* [1992] 1 SLR(R) 645 (HC).

[23] See, for example, *Power Curber v National Bank of Kuwait* (n 2). See also *National Infrastructure Development Co Ltd v Banco Santander SA* [2016] EWHC 2990 (Comm), aff'd [2017] 1 CLC 37; *NIDCO v BNP Paribas* (n 2).

where the dispute is being heard.[24] In England, these have evolved from common law rules, through the rules of the Convention to the current regime in the Regulation. It is, therefore, helpful to start with the position at common law.

III. Stop Payment Orders at Common Law

The general rule at common law is that, in the absence of an express or implied choice of law by the parties, the law applicable to a contract is the law of the country with which the contract has the closest and most real connection.[25] In determining that country, the court looks at connecting factors, such as the place of residence or business of the parties, the place where the contract was made, the place of contractual performance and the connection between the contract in question and other related contracts. However, in financial transactions, where a place is chosen for performance, that is normally an important, often decisive, factor.[26] Little importance is attached to the place of residence of the party making the payment.[27] The discussion in this chapter shows that in the context of letters of credit, the place of contractual performance, and the connection between the contract in question and another contract in the chain of interconnected contracts in a letter of credit transaction, are the dominant factors. In determining the place of performance under an unconfirmed credit, it is helpful to distinguish between cases where under the credit documents are to be presented to the issuing bank in its home country (where payment is also to be made) and cases where under the credit documents are to be presented to, and payment made at, a nominated bank in a different country. **7.12**

A. Where Documents Are to Be Presented Directly to the Issuer

Where, under the credit, documents are to be presented directly to the issuing bank in exchange for payment by the issuing bank, the place of performance is the country where the issuing bank is located, and the law of that country is the law governing the contract between the issuing bank and the beneficiary.[28] Consequently, a stop payment order made in that country will be effective to defeat a claim by the beneficiary against the issuing bank, as performance of the issuing bank's payment obligation will have become illegal under the law that governs the credit. The position is similar in some other common law jurisdictions, such as Singapore[29] and Hong Kong.[30] **7.13**

[24] This chapter focuses on situations where the parties have not chosen the applicable law, for at least two reasons. First, in practice, most letters of credit do not include a choice of law clause. Secondly, in the rare cases where the parties have made a choice of governing law, there is usually no difficulty. The courts will give effect to that choice, subject to limited exceptions, such as under the Rome Convention (n 6) art 3(3) and the Rome I Regulation (n 8) art 3(3).

[25] *Bonython v Commonwealth of Australia* [1951] AC 201 (PC) 219.

[26] ibid 219–20.

[27] *Samcrete Egypt Engineers and Contractors SAE v Land Rover Exports Ltd* [2002] CLC 533 (CA) [39].

[28] cf *Banco Amazonas SA v BNP Paribas (Suisse) SA*, 2005 WL 59599993 (NYSC) (hereafter *Banco Amazonas v BNP Paribas*).

[29] See, for example, *Kredietbank NV v Sinotani Pacific Pte Ltd (Agricultural Bank of China, third party)* [1999] 2 SLR(R) 970 (CA) (hereafter *Kredietbank NV v Sinotani Pacific* (CA)), giving effect to a stop payment order issued in China.

[30] See, for example, *Cooperative Centrale v Bank of China* (n 2) 119, giving effect to a stop payment order issued in China.

B. Where Documents Are to Be Presented to Another Bank

7.14 However, where, under the credit, documents are to be presented to, and payment made at, another (nominated) bank, the place of performance of the contract is the country where the nominated bank is located. This is the case where the credit is available at the nominated bank by drafts drawn on the nominated bank,[31] or where the nominated bank is authorised to honour or negotiate a complying presentation.[32] Therefore, the law that governs the contract in such a case is the law of the nominated bank's country. Consequently, if performance is not unlawful in that country, a stop payment order made in the issuing bank's country is no defence to the beneficiary's claim in England. In the well-known case of *Power Curber International Ltd v National Bank of Kuwait SAK* ('*Power Curber*'),[33] a bank in Kuwait issued a credit to an exporter in the US, payable through an advising bank in North Carolina. At the request of the importer, a Kuwaiti court issued an injunction restraining the issuer from making payment under the credit. The beneficiary brought an action in England, where the bank had a branch, to enforce the bank's obligation to pay under the letter of credit. The Court of Appeal held that the credit was governed by the law of North Carolina, where payment was to be made against presentation of documents. Consequently, the illegality of performance in Kuwait, due to the injunction by the Kuwaiti court, did not affect the issuer's obligation under the credit.

7.15 Courts in some common law jurisdictions have also adopted the view that, in cases where documents are to be presented to and payment made at a nominated bank, the law that governs the contract is the law of the country where the nominated bank is located.[34] Accordingly, in such cases, courts in Singapore[35] and the US[36] have refused to give effect to stop payment orders made in the issuer's country.

7.16 It is perhaps worth observing that, at one point, some courts in the US adopted a different view. They held that, where documents were to be presented to and payment made at a nominated bank (that did not confirm the credit or undertake to make payment to the beneficiary), the place of performance was still the country where the issuing bank was located and the law of that country governed the contract between the issuing bank and the beneficiary.[37] The consequence was that a stop payment order made in the issuer's country

[31] *Offshore International SA v Banco Central SA* [1977] 1 WLR 399 (QB).

[32] See, for example, *Agritrade International v ICBC* (n 2), where the nominated bank actually negotiated the draft. See also *PT Pan Indonesia Bank Ltd TBK v Marconi Communications International Ltd* [2007] 2 Lloyd's Rep 72 (CA) [43] (hereafter *PT Pan Indonesia Bank v Marconi Communications*), a case decided under the Rome Convention (n 6), where the nominated bank did not negotiate the credit, although authorised to do so.

[33] *Power Curber v National Bank of Kuwait* (n 2).

[34] See, for example, *Bank of Cochin Ltd v Manufacturers Hanover Trust*, 612 F Supp 1533 (SDNY, 1985) 1542, aff'd 808 F 2d 209 (2nd Cir, 1986); *Consolidated Aluminium Corp v Bank of Virginia*, 544 F Supp 386 (D Md, 1982), aff'd 704 F 2d 136 (4th Cir, 1983); *H Ray Baker Inc v Associated Banking Corp*, 592 F 2d 550 (9th Cir, 1979) 553; *Empire Abrasive Equipment Corp v Watson Inc*, 56 F 2d 554 (3rd Cir, 1977); *Optoptics Laboratories Corp v Savannah Bank of Nigeria Ltd*, 816 F Supp 898 (SDNY, 1993).

[35] See, for example, *Agritrade International v ICBC* (n 2).

[36] *J Zeevi and Sons, Ltd v Grindlays Bank (Uganda) Ltd*, 333 NE 2d 168 (1975), cert denied 423 US 866 (1975) (hereafter *J Zeevi v Grindlays Bank*).

[37] *RSB Mfg Corp v Bank of Baroda*, 15 Bankruptcy Reports 650 (DCNY, 1981); *Sabolyk v Morgan Guaranty Trust Co of New York*, 1984 WL 1275 (SDNY, 1984); *Chuidian v Philippine National Bank*, 734 F Supp 415 (CD Ca, 1990),

gave the issuer a good defence to a claim in the US.[38] This approach gave stop payment orders a much longer reach than under the English common law approach.

7.17 The English approach restricted the reach of such orders even in cases where the nominated bank neither confirmed the credit nor undertook to make payment to the beneficiary, and was simply acting as an assistant or agent of the issuing bank. In *Power Curber*,[39] for example, the fact that the draft was to be drawn on the issuing bank in Kuwait and the nominated bank in North Carolina did not negotiate the credit,[40] but simply forwarded the documents it received in North Carolina to the issuing bank in Kuwait, did not alter the position. It was sufficient that, under the letter of credit, payment was to be made in North Carolina by the nominated bank on behalf of the issuing bank against presentation of documents.[41] Griffiths LJ stated that:

> Under the letter of credit the [Kuwaiti] bank accepted the obligation of paying or arranging payment of the sums due in American dollars against presentation of documents at the [nominated] bank in North Carolina. The [issuing] bank could not have discharged its obligation by offering payment in Kuwait.[42]

7.18 Since, under most unconfirmed credits, documents are to be presented to, and payment made at, a nominated bank in the beneficiary's country, stop payment orders made in the issuer's country generally had very little effect at common law on claims against issuers.

IV. Stop Payment Orders under the Rome Convention

7.19 It is submitted that, under the Convention, stop payment orders made in the issuing bank's country do not have a longer reach than at common law. To be sure, in the case of an unconfirmed credit, the presumption in article 4(2) leads to the law of the issuing bank's country applying to the contract between the beneficiary and the issuing bank, even where documents are to be presented to, and payment made at, a bank in a different country. This would allow stop payment orders from the issuer's country to constitute a good defence to the beneficiary's claim in England. However, that result was avoided by the English courts' practice of relying on the 'escape clause' in article 4(5) to displace the law of the issuer's country as the applicable law in favour of the law of the country of performance.

aff'd 976 F 2d 561 (9th Cir, 1992) (hereafter *Chuidian v Philippine National Bank*); *Averbach v Vnescheconombank*, 280 F Supp 2d 945 (ND Cal, 2003).

[38] See, for example, *Chuidian v Philippine National Bank* (n 37).

[39] *Power Curber v National Bank of Kuwait* (n 2).

[40] The law report is not entirely clear as to whether the bank in North Carolina was authorised to negotiate the credit.

[41] *Power Curber v National Bank of Kuwait* (n 2) 1240.

[42] ibid 1242. The position is different where the court finds that, in presenting documents to a bank in his own country, the beneficiary was using the bank only as his or her own agent for collection. See, for example, *Kredietbank NV v Sinotani Pacific* (CA) (n 29), affirming *Kredietbank NV v Sinotani Pacific Pte Ltd* [1999] 1 SLR(R) 274 (HC) (hereafter *Kredietbank NV v Sinotani Pacific* (HC)); *Cooperative Centrale v Bank of China* (n 2).

A. Article 4(2) Points to the Law of the Issuer's Country

7.20 Article 4(1) of the Convention provides that in the absence of choice of law by the parties, a contract is governed by the law of the country with which the contract 'is most closely connected'. This is essentially the same general principle as that of the common law, as discussed above. However, the general principle in article 4(1) is followed by a presumption in article 4(2) to the effect that:

> [T]he contract is most closely connected to the country where the party who is to effect the performance which is characteristic of the contract has, at the time of conclusion of the contract, his habitual residence, or, in the case of a body corporate or unincorporated, its central administration. However, if the contract is entered into in the course of that party's trade or profession, that country shall be the country in which the principal place of business is situated or, where under the terms of the contract the performance is to be effected through a place of business other than the principal place of business, the country in which that other place of business is situated.

7.21 In the case of an unconfirmed letter of credit, the performance that is characteristic of the contract between the issuing bank and the beneficiary is that of the issuing bank in honouring its undertaking to make payment in accordance with the terms of the credit.[43] Consequently, under article 4(2), the law that governs the contract is the law of the country where the issuing bank has its principal place of business.[44]

7.22 Therefore, if article 4(2) is applied then, unlike the position at common law, stop payment orders made in the issuer's country would be effective in England to defeat the beneficiary's claim. For example, *Power Curber* would be decided differently under article 4(2) of the Convention, since the applicable law would be the law of Kuwait, as the issuer's home country. However, it is submitted that the English courts would avoid that result by invoking article 4(5) to displace the law of the issuing bank's country in favour of the law of another country that is more closely connected to the contract.

B. Displacing the Law of the Issuer's Country under Article 4(5)

7.23 In general, when applying article 4 of the Convention, the court must first determine the applicable law on the basis of article 4(2) before moving on to determine, under article 4(5), whether the applicable law identified under article 4(2) must be disregarded.[45] A court is not required to go through the two stages in every case. It may stop at the first stage. However, a court cannot go to the second stage without first completing stage one. Where a court proceeds to the second stage, it will likely take into account a wide range of factors in determining whether the contract is more closely connected with the law of a country other

[43] *Taurus Petroleum Ltd v State Oil Co of Iraq* [2016] 1 Lloyd's Rep 42 (CA) (hereafter *Taurus Petroleum v State Oil Co of Iraq*) [35]. This issue was not raised on appeal to the Supreme Court: [2018] AC 690.

[44] ibid.

[45] *Haeger & Schmidt GmbH v MMA IARD* [2015] QB 319 [46]–[48]; *Intercontainer Interfrigo SC (ICF) v Balkenende Oosthuizen BV* [2010] QB 411 [62]–[64] (hereafter *Intercontainer Interfrigo v Balkenende Oosthuizen BV*).

than that identified in stage one. In the context of letters of credit, two factors appear to be of particular significance for the English courts: the place of contractual performance and the connection with other contracts in the chain of contracts.

1. The Weight of the Place of Performance

Where the issuing bank's country is different from the country of performance, the English courts usually resort to article 4(5) to displace the law of the issuing bank's country as the applicable law (designated pursuant to article 4(2)) in favour of the law of the place of performance.[46] In *Marconi Communications International Ltd v PT Pan Indonesia Bank Ltd* (hereafter *Marconi Communications*),[47] the English Court of Appeal stated that in the case of letters of credit the result arrived at under article 4(2) 'will usually be displaced where the documents are to be presented to, and payments made by, an advising bank in another jurisdiction'.[48] **7.24**

Thus, whereas under article 4(2), the presumption is that the law applicable to a contract is the law of the country where the characteristic performer is located, in the case of letters of credit, the English courts have in effect replaced that presumption with a counter-presumption that the applicable law is the law of the country of performance. Therefore, under the Convention, in the case of an unconfirmed credit, where documents are to be presented to and payment made by a nominated bank in a different country, the applicable law is the law of the country where the nominated bank is located. Consequently, in such a case, a stop payment order made in the issuer's country gives the issuer no defence to the beneficiary's claim. Therefore, the ultimate outcome under the Convention is the same as under the common law. For example, *Power Curber* would be decided the same way under the Convention, since the law of the issuing bank's home country (Kuwait), applicable under article 4(2), would be displaced (pursuant to article 4(5)) in favour of the law of the place where documents were to be presented and payment made (North Carolina). **7.25**

2. Closely Connected Contracts

The other factor that has weighed heavily with the English courts when applying the 'escape clause' in article 4(5) of the Convention is the need to avoid contracts that are closely related being governed by different laws. This is a particular concern in the case of letters of credit where there are multiple autonomous, but interconnected, contracts. Considered separately, each of the contracts might have a different applicable law. However, as Mance J explained in *Bank of Baroda v Vysya Bank Ltd* (hereafter *Bank of Baroda*),[49] it would be commercially undesirable for the confirming bank's obligation to the beneficiary to be governed by one law (under which the confirming bank may be liable to pay), whilst its right to reimbursement from the issuing bank is governed by a different law (under which the confirming bank may not be entitled to reimbursement even though it has paid the beneficiary as instructed by the issuing bank).[50] To avoid **7.26**

[46] See, for example, *Bank of Baroda v Vysya Bank Ltd* [1994] 4 CLC 41 (QB) 48 (hereafter *Bank of Baroda v Vysya Bank*). See also *Filatona Trading Ltd v Navigator Equities Ltd* [2019] EWHC 172 (Comm) [328].

[47] *PT Pan Indonesia Bank v Marconi Communications* (n 32).

[48] ibid [49].

[49] *Bank of Baroda v Vysya Bank* (n 46).

[50] It is also undesirable that the beneficiary's right to payment under the letter of credit should vary depending on whether the claim for payment is made against the confirming bank (in which case the law of country A applies) or against the issuing bank (in which case the law of country B applies).

that undesirable result, the courts take into account the fact that a particular contract arising under the letter of credit is closely connected to another contract or contracts in the chain of contracts arising under the same arrangement.[51] In *Bank of Baroda*, the contract between the beneficiary and the confirming bank, located in England, was governed by English law.[52] That was a relevant factor leading Mance J to conclude that English law also governed the related contract between the beneficiary and the issuing bank (in India). This outcome also avoided the undesirable result where the beneficiary's contract with the confirming bank would be governed by one law (English law) and its contract with the issuing bank would be governed by a different law (Indian law).

7.27 In *Bank of Baroda*, the letter of credit was confirmed. However, Mance J expressly stated that he 'should not be taken as suggesting that the conclusion would be any different if the credit had been an unconfirmed credit' to be advised on the Indian issuing bank's behalf by a bank in England and available for negotiation in England.[53] In such a case, the law of the issuing bank's country, which would be the law applicable to the contract between the issuing bank and beneficiary under article 4(2), would be disregarded under article 4(5), in favour of the law governing the beneficiary's contract with the negotiating bank (namely, English law).[54] Consequently, in such a case, a stop payment order from the issuing bank's country would afford the bank no defence to a beneficiary's claim in England.

7.28 Under the Convention, therefore, stop payment orders made in the issuing bank's country had no more effect in England than at common law. This perhaps explains why attempts to rely on such orders as a defence have been extremely rare under the Convention.

V. The Rome I Regulation: Has it Opened a Door to Stop Payment Orders?

7.29 Turning to the position under the Regulation, the question is whether the amendments to article 4 have increased the likelihood that the English courts would give effect to stop payment orders made in the issuing bank's country. If, under article 4(1) or (2), the law of the issuing bank's country is the law applicable to the contract between the issuing bank and the beneficiary and if that law cannot be displaced pursuant to article 4(3), then such orders would indeed constitute a good defence to a beneficiary's claim. If so, then in effect the Regulation has opened a door to stop payment orders where, in English law, it was shut under the Convention.

[51] The approach of the English courts, in taking into account the connection between the contract in question and other contracts in a chain of contracts, was confirmed by the ECJ in *Haeger & Schmidt GmbH v MMA IARD* [2015] QB 319 (ECJ) [49].
[52] Rome Convention (n 6) art 4(2).
[53] *Bank of Baroda v Vysya Bank* (n 46) 49.
[54] See also *PT Pan Indonesia Bank v Marconi Communications* (n 32).

A. Does the Law of the Issuer's Country Apply under Article 4(1) or (2)?

Under the Regulation, in the absence of a choice of law, the law applicable to the contract between the issuing bank and beneficiary under an unconfirmed credit would be determined by the rule in article 4(1)(b), if that contract is classified as 'a contract for the provision of services'. If the contract is not one for the provision of services, however, then the applicable law would be determined under article 4(2). The Regulation does not define the concept of 'provision of services' in article 4(1)(b) and the European Court of Justice (ECJ) has not yet provided a definition of the concept. So, it is not entirely clear whether the contract between an issuing bank and a beneficiary would fall within that provision. The editors of *Dicey, Morris & Collins on the Conflict of Laws* have suggested that, although the issuing bank-beneficiary contract may be classified as one for the provision of a payment service within article 4(1)(b), it is 'more likely' to be regarded as a contract other than one for the provision of services.[55] However, it is submitted that the contract should be classified as one for the provision of services within article 4(1)(b) and that the issuing bank is the party providing the services. This view derives support from the ECJ's interpretation of the concept of 'provision of services' in article 5(1)(b) of the Brussels I Regulation,[56] now article 7(1)(b) of the Brussels I Recast Regulation.[57] Recital 17 of the Rome I Regulation states that the concept of 'provision of services' in article 4(1)(b) should be interpreted in the same way as it is interpreted under what is now article 7 of the Brussels I Recast Regulation.[58] **7.30**

In *Falco Privatstiftung v Weller-Lindhorst*,[59] the ECJ held that 'the concept of service implies, at the least, that the party who provides the service, carries out a particular activity in return for remuneration'.[60] Further, in *Corman-Collins SA v La Maison du Whisky SA*,[61] the ECJ clarified that the first criterion set out in the *Falco* case, namely the existence of 'a particular activity', requires the performance of positive acts, rather than mere omissions,[62] and that the second criterion, namely the 'remuneration' paid as consideration for that activity, is not to be understood strictly as payment of a sum of money.[63] The notion of 'remuneration' is given an expansive meaning. All advantages that 'represent an economic value' for the party carrying out the activities may be regarded as constituting remuneration.[64] More recently, in *Kareda v Benko*,[65] the ECJ held that a credit agreement between a credit institution and a borrower is a contract for the provision of services within article 7(1)(b) of the Brussels Recast Regulation. In such a contract, 'the supply of services lies in the transfer of a sum of money by the credit institution to the borrower, in return for fees paid by the borrower, in principle, in the form of interest'.[66] **7.31**

[55] *Dicey, Morris and Collins on the Conflict of Laws* (n 20) vol 2 [33–317].

[56] Council Regulation (EC) 44/2001 of 22 December 2000 on Jurisdiction and the Recognition and Enforcement of Judgments in Civil and Commercial Matters [2001] OJ L12/1.

[57] Brussels I Recast (n 16) art 7(1)(b).

[58] See also *Koelzsch v Grand Duchy of Luxembourg* [2011] ECR I–1595 (ECJ).

[59] *Falco Privatstiftung v Weller-Lindhorst* [2009] ECR I–3327 (ECJ).

[60] ibid [29]. *Falco* was followed in *Krejci Lager v Olbrich Transport* [2014] ILPr 139 (ECJ) [26].

[61] *Corman-Collins SA v La Maison du Whisky SA* [2014] QB 431 (ECJ) (hereafter *Corman-Collins v La Maison du Whisky*).

[62] *Corman-Collins v La Maison du Whisky* (n 61) [38], followed in *Granarolo SpA v Ambrosi Emmi France SA* [2016] ILPr 32 (ECJ) [37].

[63] *Corman-Collins v La Maison du Whisky* (n 61) [39].

[64] ibid [40].

[65] *Kareda v Benko* [2017] ILPr 29 (ECJ).

[66] ibid [36].

7.32 Based on the ECJ's case law discussed above, the contract between an issuer and the beneficiary of an unconfirmed letter of credit would fall within article 4(1)(b) because the issuing bank carries out certain tasks under the contract. These include arranging for another bank (the advising bank) to advise the beneficiary of the credit; arranging for another bank (the nominated bank) to receive documents presented under the credit and, if so authorised, to honour or negotiate a complying presentation; and receiving and examining the documents presented under the credit and, if the documents comply with the credit, making payment in accordance with the credit. In short, the services provided by the issuing bank lie in the transfer of a sum of money from the issuer to the beneficiary, as in *Kareda v Benco*. Moreover, the issuing bank provides these services in return for remuneration,[67] in the form of bank charges or commission. To be sure, in most cases, the remuneration is paid by the applicant, as opposed to the beneficiary. However, in view of the ECJ's expansive approach[68] discussed above, it matters not that the remuneration is not provided directly by the beneficiary, but comes from another source. The English common law rule of contract law that consideration must move from the promisee[69] is not relevant to the interpretation of the Regulation, which is a piece of EU legislation.

7.33 If, as suggested, an unconfirmed letter of credit is classified as a contract for the provision of services within article 4(1)(b) and the issuer is the party providing the services, then, under that provision, the law applicable to the credit is the law of the country where the issuer has its habitual residence, as defined in article 19 of the Regulation.[70] In that case, stop payment orders made in the issuing bank's country would be effective to defeat claims by beneficiaries in England even where, under the credit, documents are to be presented to, and payment made by, a nominated bank in another country.

7.34 However, if contrary to the view advanced above, an unconfirmed letter of credit is not a contract for the provision of services within article 4(1)(b), then the applicable law is determined by the rule in article 4(2). Under this provision, the applicable law is the law of the country where the party required to effect the characteristic performance has its habitual residence. In the case of the contract between the issuing bank and beneficiary under an unconfirmed credit, the issuing bank is the party effecting the characteristic performance.[71] Therefore, the law that governs the contract is the law of the country where the issuing bank has its habitual residence.[72] Consequently, stop payment orders made in the issuer's home country would have the same extended reach in England as in the case where article 4(1)(b) applied. This raises the question, however, as to whether this outcome can be avoided by

[67] ibid.

[68] *Corman-Collins v La Maison du Whisky* (n 61) [39]–[40].

[69] For the consideration provided by a beneficiary under a letter of credit, see ch 2 (Booysen) in this volume.

[70] Rome I Regulation (n 8), art 19(1) provides that the habitual residence of a natural person, acting in the course of his business activity, is his principal place of business. A letter of credit is, however, normally issued by a bank and most banks are companies. Rome I Regulation also provides that the habitual residence of a company is the place of its central administration. ibid art 19(2) further states that, where the contract is concluded in the course of the operations of a branch, agency, or other establishment, or if, under the contract, performance is the responsibility of such a branch, agency, or other establishment, then the place where the branch, agency, or other establishment is located shall be treated as the place of habitual residence. Therefore, under ibid art 19(2), where a letter of credit is issued by the London branch of a bank with its central administration in Japan, then England would be treated as the habitual residence of the bank.

[71] See Rome Convention (n 6), art 4(2) which is in similar terms and was discussed above.

[72] *Taurus Petroleum v State Oil Co of Iraq* (n 43). This aspect of the decision was not challenged on appeal: [2018] AC 690.

resorting to article 4(3) to displace the law of the issuer's country as the applicable law in favour of another country's law, as had been the practice under the Convention.

B. Can Article 4(3) Be Invoked to Displace the Law of the Issuer's Country?

It is well known that the architecture and language of article 4 of the Regulation are different from article 4 of the Convention. First, whereas the basic test in article 4(2) of the Convention is only a presumption, under articles 4(1) and (2) of the Regulation, the status of the basic position has been raised to a rule. Secondly, under article 4(3) of the Regulation, the law identified pursuant to the basic rule may be disregarded only where 'it is clear' that the contract is more closely connected with another country. Thirdly, under article 4(3), the contract must be 'manifestly' more closely connected to another country. What difference do these changes make in practice? In *Molton Street Capital LLP v Shooters Hill Capital Partners LLP*,[73] Popplewell J said that the revision of article 4 'suggests a higher threshold, which requires that the cumulative weight of the factors connecting the contract to another country must clearly and decisively outweigh the desideratum of certainty in applying the relevant test in Article 4(1) or 4(2)'. For this reason, his Lordship said that, when interpreting article 4 of the Regulation, decisions on article 4 of the Convention should be used with caution.[74] **7.35**

However, some commentators have gone further and have expressed the view that, in applying article 4(3) of the Regulation, it would not be 'legitimate to treat the place of performance as a more significant connecting factor than the territorial connections of the characteristic performer'.[75] Those commentators argue that, if the drafters of the Regulation had intended the place of performance to play a special role, this would have been specifically reflected in article 4. They accordingly conclude that it is not reasonable for a court to displace the law identified under article 4(1) or (2) on the basis of one connecting factor alone (namely the place of performance) and that article 4(3) should be used to displace the applicable law identified under article 4(1) or (2) only where a *combination* of factors lead to the conclusion that the contract is manifestly more closely connected with a country other than that identified by the primary rule.[76] Applying this approach in the context of letters of credit, it has been suggested that the decision of the Court of Appeal in *Marconi Communications*, discussed above, is no longer of much value under the Regulation,[77] because it accorded special weight to the place of performance. On the same facts, it is argued, a court would not be justified in coming to the same result under the Regulation.[78] **7.36**

If the Regulation were applied to the facts of *Marconi Communications*, the court would not displace the law of the issuing bank's country as the applicable law, so that a stop payment order made in the issuing bank's country would constitute a good defence to the **7.37**

[73] *Molton Street Capital LLP v Shooters Hill Capital Partners LLP* [2015] EWHC 3419 (Comm) [94].
[74] ibid [105].
[75] Hill and Shúilleabháin, *Conflict of Laws* (n 10) [4.70].
[76] ibid.
[77] ibid [4.72].
[78] ibid.

beneficiary's claim in England against the issuing bank. Consequently, cases such as *Power Curber* would be decided differently under the Regulation. This will result in a significant shift in the law's response to such orders. It would mean that, as the court explained in *NIDCO v BNP Paribas*,[79] 'a party who [has] opened a letter of credit could defeat the bank's payment obligation to pay by obtaining an injunction against the bank in its home jurisdiction'. The result in practice would be that, whereas at common law and under the Convention reliance on stop payment orders has been rare, under the Regulation such orders 'would soon become common place'.[80]

7.38 However, it is doubtful that the Regulation dictates this result. Whilst it is recognised that the changes introduced to article 4 of the Regulation mean that the threshold for disregarding the applicable law designated by the basic rule is higher than under the Convention, it does not necessarily follow that the threshold under the Regulation is radically different from that of the Convention. In certain respects, some of the new language in the Regulation simply reflect the practice of (continental European) national courts[81] and the ECJ under the Convention. For example, article 4(5) of the Convention does not stipulate, as does article 4(3) of the Regulation, that the law applicable under the basic rule may be disregarded only where it is 'clear' that the contract is more closely connected with another country. However, the ECJ had already decided that, under article 4(5) of the Convention, it had to be clear that the contract was more closely connected to another country.[82] In this respect, by inserting the word 'clear' into article 4(3) of the Regulation, the legislator is simply stating in express terms a standard that was already being applied by the ECJ under the Convention.

7.39 It is submitted that, in the particular context of letters of credit, it is likely that the place of performance will continue to weigh heavily when applying the 'escape clause' in article 4(3). First, one reason for the English courts' approach under the Convention is that '[t]he presumption contained in Article 4(2) is a blanket provision which falls to be applied across the entire field of contract law. It assumes the ability to identify a single party charged with the (single) performance characteristic of the contract. A letter of credit as such is not susceptible of such treatment.'[83] It is arguable that this statement applies equally to the new rules in articles 4(1)(b) and 4(2) of the Regulation. The former is a blanket provision covering all contracts for the provision of services and the latter is a blanket rule across the entire field of contracts other than those specifically listed in article 4(1). To that extent, the rationale for displacing the applicable law identified under the basic rule in the Convention continues to be relevant under the Regulation.

7.40 Secondly, in an unconfirmed credit under which documents are to be presented to, and payment made by, a nominated bank in the beneficiary's country, the usual expectations of the parties are that the law of that country would apply to the bank's undertaking to honour the credit in that country. In such a case, as Mance J explained in *Bank of Baroda*,[84] 'it would

[79] *NIDCO v BNP Paribas* (n 2) [17].
[80] ibid.
[81] Teun Struycken, 'Some Dutch Reflections on the Rome Convention, Art 4(5)' [1996] LMCLQ 18.
[82] *Intercontainer Interfrigo v Balkenende Oosthuizen BV* (n 45).
[83] *PT Pan Indonesia Bank v Marconi Communications* (n 32) [61].
[84] *Bank of Baroda v Vysya Bank* (n 46) 48.

be quite wrong to stop at [Article] 4(2)', since '[t]he Rome Convention was not intended to confuse legal relationships or to disrupt normal expectations'. Nor is the Regulation intended to do so. In a letter of credit transaction, where performance can take place in the issuing bank's home country or in a different country, if the parties concerned have agreed that performance should take place in a different country, the normal expectations of the parties is that the designated place of performance has a very strong connection to the contract.

Therefore, whilst it is recognised that the threshold for the 'escape clause' is higher under the Regulation, it is submitted that it is not so much higher that it would make a significant difference in the context of letter of credit transactions. Where, under a letter of credit, documents are to be presented to and payment made by a nominated bank in a country other than that of the issuing bank, a court would be justified in holding that, under article 4(3), the contract between the beneficiary and the issuing bank is manifestly more closely connected with the country where that nominated bank is located. On this basis, it is suggested that, in relation to letter of credit transactions in particular, the courts can and should continue to give the place of performance considerable weight in the application of article 4(3) of the Regulation. **7.41**

It is recognised that the position would be different in cases where performance is split between multiple countries, as where documents are to be presented in one country (for example, where the beneficiary is resident), but payment is to be made in a different country. Cases of this type are not very common, but an example may be found in *Taurus Petroleum Ltd v State Oil Marketing Co of the Ministry of Oil, Iraq*.[85] An unconfirmed credit[86] was issued by a bank in London and advised to the beneficiary in Iraq by an Iraqi bank. The beneficiary was to present documents to the advising bank in Iraq and these were to be forwarded to the issuing bank in London. However, for special reasons, payment was to be made by the issuing bank into a bank account in New York (in accordance with arrangements set up following the imposition of sanctions on Iraq by United Nations Security Council Resolution 1483 of 22 May 2003). It was held that, under article 4(2), the law that governed the contract between the issuing bank and the beneficiary was English law, since the characteristic performer (the issuing bank) was located in England. It does not appear to have been argued that, pursuant to article 4(3), English law should have been displaced in favour of the law of Iraq or New York, as the country of performance. It is submitted, however, that such an argument would have been difficult to sustain, as it is not clear that either Iraq or New York was 'manifestly' more closely connected to the contract than England. Whereas the beneficiary was resident in Iraq where its performance (presentation of complying documents) was to take place, the performance of the issuing bank (payment) was to be made in New York. The facts of *Taurus Petroleum* are different from those of the ordinary case where documents are to be presented to, and payment made at, a nominated bank in the beneficiary's country. In the ordinary case where, under the letter of credit, the performance of both the beneficiary and the issuing bank take place in the same country, then the courts are likely to displace the law of the country where the issuing bank is habitually resident in favour of the law of the country of performance. **7.42**

[85] *Taurus Petroleum v State Oil Co of Iraq* (n 43).

[86] The issuing bank requested the advising bank to confirm the credit, but the advising bank did not do so.

7.43 Another factor that the courts take into account in applying article 4(3) of the Regulation is 'whether the contract in question has a very close relationship with another contract or contracts'.[87] In the context of letters of credit, the contract between the beneficiary and the issuer will have a very close relationship with another contract or contracts where, for example, the credit authorises negotiation by another bank (as a contract will exist between the negotiating bank and the issuing bank). In such a case, the law that governs the contract between the negotiating bank and the issuing bank will be the law of the negotiating bank's country, either pursuant to article 4(1)(b) of the Regulation, on the basis that the negotiating bank is the party providing the services, or under article 4(2) of the Regulation, on the basis that the negotiating bank is the party carrying out the characteristic performance. As the negotiating bank's country is also the place of performance, it is unlikely that the court will displace that law pursuant to article 4(3).

7.44 Since the law of the negotiating bank's country would be the law that governs its contract with the issuing bank, when applying article 4(3) to the issuing bank's contract with the beneficiary, the court will take into account the fact that the latter contract has a very close connection with the former contract and accordingly will likely conclude that the issuing bank's contract with the beneficiary is manifestly more closely connected with the law of the negotiating bank's country than with the law of the issuing bank's country. On this basis, it is submitted that on the same facts, cases such as *Bank of Baroda* and *Marconi Communications* should be decided in the same way under the Regulation. If this approach were adopted by the courts, then under the Regulation stop payment orders made in the issuer's country would constitute no defence to a beneficiary's claim in England against the issuer. The position would be broadly similar to that under the Convention. Accordingly, the Regulation has not (even unintentionally) laid the foundation for a shift in the effect of foreign stop payment orders.

7.45 If, as suggested, the outcome in cases under the Regulation is likely to be similar to that under the Convention and at common law, then there would be no difficulties. However, if, contrary to the contention in this chapter, the court would stop at the first stage, under article 4(1) or 4(2), so that the law of the issuing bank's country would be the applicable law, then stop payment orders made in the issuer's country would be able to defeat beneficiaries' claims against issuing banks in England. This would create significant difficulties for beneficiaries/exporters. In such a case, the beneficiary may seek to argue that the court should nevertheless refuse to give effect to such an order on the basis that its application in England would be contrary to English public policy. It is by no means clear, however, that public policy would come to the rescue of the beneficiary in this context. This is considered in the next section.

VI. Any Role for the Public Policy Exception?

7.46 Both the Convention (article 16) and the Regulation (article 21) provide for a foreign applicable law to be excluded by the forum on the ground that its application in the particular

[87] Rome I Regulation (n 8), recital 20.

case would be contrary to the forum's public policy. A similar ground for excluding the governing law exists at common law. Thus, where a contract is valid under its governing law, the English courts may nevertheless refuse to apply that law and/or enforce the contract on the ground that enforcement in the particular case would be contrary to English public policy.[88] Similarly, where the performance of a contract is unlawful under its governing law, the English courts may rely on the public policy exception to exclude the governing law and enforce the contract in England. However, this public policy doctrine is normally used only in exceptional cases, such as where the foreign law, which prohibits performance of the contract, is an instrument of oppression or discrimination or otherwise constitutes a serious violation of human rights.[89] In the context of stop payment orders, if the order is discriminatory on the grounds of race, religion, or political belief, it is likely that an English court would refuse to recognise that order on the ground that its application would be contrary to English public policy. In the US case of *J Zeevi & Sons Ltd v Grindlays Bank (Uganda) Ltd*,[90] for example, a New York court refused to recognise an 'anti-Semitic' order issued by the Ugandan government prohibiting the issuing bank in Uganda from making payment under letters of credit issued in favour of Israeli beneficiaries. The New York court described the prohibition by the Ugandan government as 'confiscatory and discriminatory'.[91]

However, in the absence of any element of human rights violation, would an English court refuse to give effect to a stop payment order on the basis that English public policy favours enforcement of letters of credit? In *Cantrade Privatbank AG Zurich v Bangkok Bank Pub Co Ltd*,[92] a court in New York refused to recognise a Thai court injunction restraining an issuing bank in Thailand from paying under its letter of credit. In doing so, the New York court referred to 'New York's strong public policy in favour of enforcing letter of credit agreements according to their terms'.[93] However, such an application of the public policy exception is open to question. Courts should not resort to public policy merely because the policy of the law of the forum is different from that of the foreign governing law. The public policy exception should be used only where, as Justice Cardozo famously put it, application of the foreign law would 'violate some fundamental principle of justice, some prevalent conception of good morals, some deep-rooted tradition of the common weal'.[94] Thus, in a different US case, *Banco Amazonas SA v BNP Paribas (Suisse) SA*,[95] a New York court held that recognising a Swiss injunction restraining a Swiss issuing bank from making payment under a letter of credit would not offend the public policy of New York. The mere fact that the policy of New York law was in favour of enforcing letter of credit agreements was not enough to raise the public policy exception. That exception was normally invoked only in cases involving 'fundamental public policies'.[96] **7.47**

[88] See, for example, *Kaufman v Gerson* [1904] 1 KB 591 (CA) (decided at common law); *Duarte v Black & Decker Corporation* [2008] 1 All ER (Comm) (QB) (decided under the Rome Convention (n 6)), a restraint of trade clause in a contract of employment that is valid under its governing law may be refused enforcement in England on the basis that enforcement would be contrary to English public policy.

[89] *Oppenheimer v Cattermole* [1976] AC 249 (HL); *The Playa Larga* [1983] 2 Lloyd's Rep 171 (CA) 190; *Williams & Humbert Ltd v WH Trade Marks (Jersey) Ltd* [1986] AC 368 (HL) 428.

[90] *J Zeevi v Grindlays Bank* (n 36) 173.

[91] ibid.

[92] *Cantrade Privatbank v Bangkok Bank* (n 2).

[93] ibid citing *First Commercial Bank v Gotham Originals* (n 15) 298.

[94] *Loucks v Standard Oil Co*, 224 NY 99 (1918) 111.

[95] *Banco Amazonas v BNP Paribas* (n 28).

[96] ibid 3 citing, as an example, *J Zeevi v Grindlays Bank* (n 36), involving the 'anti-Semitic' prohibition.

7.48 It is submitted that the fact that the policy of English law is in favour of issuing banks honouring their obligations under their credits is unlikely to be a sufficient basis for an English court to invoke article 16 of the Convention or article 21 of the Regulation to refuse to give effect to a foreign stop payment order. In *Power Curber*, Lord Denning MR stressed 'the importance of letters of credit in international trade. They are the means by which goods are supplied all the world over. It is vital that every bank which issues a letter of credit should honour its obligations.'[97] Griffiths LJ also contrasted the approach of the Kuwaiti courts with the approach that would have been taken by an English court on similar facts. His Lordship said that, in the claim by the buyers in Kuwait, which was the basis of the stop payment order, there was no suggestion of fraud on the part of the US exporters. He further noted that, in the absence of fraud, an English court would not have interfered with the bank's obligation to pay under the credit and went on to state that 'the approach of the Kuwaiti court appears to be so out of step with that of our own courts and the courts of other trading nations that I fear we cannot recognise [the order]. The choice lies between upholding the world-wide practices of international commerce or the order of the Kuwaiti court. I choose the first option.'[98] These are strong statements. However, they do not go so far as to suggest that, if the law of Kuwait was the law that governed the contract between the beneficiary and issuing bank, the English court would have refused to give effect to the Kuwaiti order on the ground that its application would be contrary to English public policy.

VII. Claims by Correspondent Banks

7.49 In the case of a claim for reimbursement by a bank that has made payment under the letter of credit, a stop payment order made in the issuing bank's country normally affords the issuing bank no defence. As discussed below, the reason is that, in such a case, the law applicable to the contract between the issuing bank and claiming bank is usually the law of the home jurisdiction of the claiming bank, rather than that of the issuing bank's country. This is the case whether the claiming bank is a confirming bank or a nominated bank that has honoured or negotiated a complying presentation.

A. Confirming Bank

7.50 At common law, in the absence of choice, the proper law of the contract between a confirming bank and an issuing bank is the law of the country with which the contract has the closest and most real connection and that is usually the law of the country where the confirming bank carries on its business.[99] A similar position has been adopted by courts in other common law jurisdictions,[100] including Singapore.[101] Therefore, in the ordinary

[97] *Power Curber v National Bank of Kuwait* (n 2) 1241.
[98] ibid 1243.
[99] *European Asian Bank AG v Punjab and Sind Bank Ltd* [1981] 2 Lloyd's Rep 651 (QB) (hereafter *European Asian Bank v Punjab and Sind Bank*).
[100] For example, in the US, see *Bank of Cochin v Manufacturers Hanover Trust Co*, 612 F Supp 1533 (DCNY, 1985) aff'd 808 F 2d 209 (2nd Cir, 1986).
[101] *Kredietbank NV v Sinotani Pacific* (HC) (n 42); *Mizuho Corporate Bank Ltd v Cho Hung Bank* [2004] 4 SLR(R) 67 (HC) [7].

case where the issuing bank and confirming bank are in different countries, a stop payment order made in the issuing bank's country has no effect on the confirming bank's claim against the issuing bank in England.

The outcome is the same under the Convention, at least as applied in England. According to the English courts, under article 4(2) of the Convention, the performance that is characteristic of the contract between the issuing bank and the confirming bank is that of the confirming bank, in adding its confirmation to the letter of credit and honouring its undertaking given to the beneficiary at the request of the issuing bank. Therefore, the law of the country of the confirming bank's branch that is to honour the confirmation is the law applicable to the inter-bank contract.[102] However, that view is not universal. For example, in *Governor & Company of the Bank of Ireland v State Bank of India*,[103] the High Court of Northern Ireland took a different view and held that the characteristic performance is that of the issuing bank in making reimbursement. The court asked and answered the following questions:[104] **7.51**

> What is the performance that is characteristic of the contract? Essentially the characteristic performance is the reimbursement on receipt of the appropriate documents. Which party is to effect that characteristic performance? The defendant [issuing bank] as the reimbursing bank is the party making the payment that is the characteristic performance of the contract between the [confirming bank] and the [issuing bank].

This view is, with respect, questionable. The Northern Irish High Court appears to have misunderstood the full extent of the confirming bank's obligations under its contract with the issuing bank. Thus, the court stated: 'What are the performance obligations that arise in the contract between the issuing bank and the confirming bank? On one side the obligation is to furnish the appropriate documents. On the other side the obligation is to make payment on foot of the documents.'[105] The confirming bank's obligation to forward documents received under the credit is, however, incidental to its core obligation. As Mance J explained in *Bank of Baroda*,[106] confirmation by the confirming bank is 'the object or focus of the contract'. The confirming bank does this by adding its own undertaking to honour the credit and by honouring its undertaking thereby given to the beneficiary. In order to discharge that obligation, the confirming bank receives documents presented under the credit, examines them to determine whether they constitute a complying presentation,[107] and, if they do, honours the credit by making payment in accordance with its terms.[108] As a consequence of performing these important obligations, the confirming bank forwards the documents to the issuing bank for reimbursement and for remuneration by way of commission or bank charges. Therefore, the better view is that the characteristic performer is the confirming bank and that the applicable law is the law of the country where the confirming bank is located. Consequently, under the Convention, stop payment orders made in the **7.52**

[102] See, for example, *Bank of Baroda v Vysya Bank* (n 46) 47; *PT Pan Indonesia Bank v Marconi Communications* (n 32) [85]; *Arab Banking Corporation v First Union National Bank* [2001] 3 WLUK 252 (QB).
[103] *Governor & Company of the Bank of Ireland v State Bank of India* [2011] NIQB 22.
[104] ibid [24].
[105] ibid [23].
[106] *Bank of Baroda v Vysya Bank* (n 46) 46.
[107] UCP 600, art 14.
[108] ibid art 16.

issuer's country could not defeat claims by confirming banks in England. Since such orders have very limited reach under the Convention, attempts to use them as a defence against claims by confirming banks have been extremely rare.

7.53 It is submitted that the outcome is unlikely to be different under the Regulation. First, it is contended that the contract between the issuing and confirming bank is one for the provision of services within article 4(1)(b) of the Regulation,[109] and that the confirming bank is the party providing the services. Those services are the same as the characteristic performance outlined above and the confirming bank provides the services in return for remuneration in the form of a fee or commission. Secondly, if the contract is within article 4(1)(b), then its governing law is the law of the country where the confirming bank has its habitual residence. If the inter-bank contract is not one for the provision of services, so that article 4(2) applies, the result is still the same. Since article 4(2) of the Regulation is similar to article 4(2) of the Convention, it follows that the approach of the English courts to the former will be the same as that adopted in relation to the latter. The confirming bank is the characteristic performer. Therefore, the law of the country where the confirming bank has its habitual residence is the applicable law. Thus, whether the court applies article 4(1)(b) or 4(2) of the Regulation, the result would be the same; the law of the issuing bank's country is not the law that governs the contract between the issuing and confirming banks. Therefore, a stop payment order made in the issuer's country would afford the issuer no defence to a confirming bank's claim in England for reimbursement.

7.54 Would the court resort to the 'escape clause' in article 4(3) of the Regulation to displace the law of the confirming bank's country as the applicable law under article 4(1)(b) or 4(2)? It is submitted that this would be unlikely, especially in the ordinary case where the confirming bank's country is the place of performance, where the documents are to be presented and payment is to be made.[110]

7.55 However, the position may be different where the issuing bank is in one country (A), the confirming bank is in another country (B) that is different from that of the beneficiary (C) and, under the credit, documents are to be presented to and payment made by a nominated bank in the beneficiary's country (C). In such a case, the court is likely to proceed to invoke the 'escape clause' to displace the law of the confirming bank's country, in favour of the law of the nominated bank's country. This is on the basis of the very close connection between the confirming bank's contract with the issuing bank, on the one hand, and the confirming bank's contract with the nominated bank, on the other. Since the law applicable to the latter contract would be the law of the nominated bank's country, as explained below, this would weigh heavily in favour of the view that the same law should also apply to the former contract.[111] Yet, although in this scenario the applicable law is not the law of the confirming bank's country, nevertheless it is not the law of the issuing bank's country. Consequently, the result is the same, namely, that a stop payment order made in the issuing bank's country would not be effective in England to defeat the confirming bank's claim for reimbursement against the issuing bank.

[109] *Contra* Ebenezer Adodo, *Letters of Credit: The Law and Practice of Compliance* (OUP 2014) [11.69]–[11.73].
[110] Under the Rome Convention (n 6), the courts did not proceed to stage two in such cases.
[111] See the approach under the Rome Convention in *PT Pan Indonesia Bank v Marconi Communications* (n 32) [67], criticised in Christopher Hare, 'The Rome Convention and Letters of Credit' [2005] LMCLQ 417.

Thus, in the case of claims in England by confirming banks against issuing banks, stop payment orders made in the issuing bank's country have very limited reach at common law, under the Convention and under the Regulation. 7.56

B. Nominated Bank that Has Not Confirmed the Credit, but Has Honoured or Negotiated a Complying Presentation

At common law, in the absence of choice, the law that governs the contract between an issuing bank and a nominated bank that is authorised to honour or negotiate a complying presentation is the law of the country where, under the credit, the nominated bank is authorised to do so. On this basis, at common law, a stop payment order from the issuing bank's country is no defence to the nominated bank's claim in England for reimbursement.[112] It is interesting to observe that courts in the US arrived at a similar result through a different choice of law rule. The US courts, under common law rules, took the view that the law governing the contract between an issuing and negotiating bank was the law of the country where, under the credit, the negotiating bank was to obtain reimbursement.[113] Thus, where that country was different from the issuing bank's home jurisdiction, a stop payment order made in the issuing bank's country had no effect on the nominated bank's claim in the US.[114] 7.57

The position is similar under the Convention. In the contract between the issuing bank and the nominated bank, the characteristic performance is that of the nominated bank in honouring or negotiating a complying presentation.[115] Therefore, under article 4(2), the law of the nominated bank's country is the law that governs the contract.[116] Since the nominated bank's country is normally the country where, under the credit, documents are to be presented and payment made, the court would usually not proceed to the second stage in article 4 to displace that law, in favour of the law of a different country, as the applicable law.[117] Consequently, under the Convention, a stop payment order from the issuing bank's country provides the issuer with no defence against a nominated bank's claim in England. 7.58

The outcome is likely to be the same under the Regulation. First, it is submitted that the contract between the issuing bank and a nominated bank that has honoured or negotiated a complying presentation is a contract for the provision of services within article 4(1)(b) and that the nominated bank is the party providing the services.[118] If so, the law that applies to that contract is the law of the country where the nominated bank has its habitual residence. 7.59

[112] *European Asian Bank v Punjab and Sind Bank* (n 99).

[113] The English courts expressly rejected that approach: ibid 656; *Bank of Credit and Commerce Hong Kong Ltd v Sonali Bank* [1995] 1 Lloyd's Rep 227 (QB) 237.

[114] *J Zeevi v Grindlays Bank* (n 36) 226; *Cantrade Privatbank v Bangkok Bank* (n 2).

[115] *Gulf International Bank BSC v Albaraka Islamic Bank BSC*, 2003 WL 21729292, 24 July 2003 (QB (Comm)) [37] (hereafter *Gulf International Bank v Albaraka Islamic Bank*). The decision on this aspect of the case was not appealed: [2004] EWCA Civ 416.

[116] *PT Pan Indonesia Bank v Marconi Communications* (n 32) [65].

[117] *Gulf International Bank v Albaraka Islamic Bank* (n 115).

[118] The nominated bank carries out specific activities, including receiving documents presented under the letter of credit, examining the documents to determine whether they constitute a complying presentation (UCP 600, art 14(a)) and honouring or negotiating a complying presentation (ibid art 12(a)). The nominated bank carries out these activities in return for remuneration by way of bank charges or fees.

Secondly, even if the contract is not one for the provision of services under article 4(1)(b), the outcome would be the same under article 4(2), on the basis that the nominated bank is the characteristic performer,[119] and therefore the law applicable to the contract under article 4(2) is the law of the country where the nominated bank is habitually resident. Since that country is normally the country of performance, it is highly unlikely that the English courts will proceed to the second stage to displace that applicable law in favour of the law of another country. Since, in most cases, the law of the nominated bank's country will be the applicable law, a claim by a nominated bank in England against an issuing bank would be insulated from a stop payment order made in the issuing bank's country.

VIII. Conclusion

7.60 Longmore LJ recently observed that '[t]he whole point of [letters of credit] is that beneficiaries should be paid without regard to the merits of any underlying dispute between the beneficiary and its contractor'.[120] This commercial purpose of letters of credit would be seriously undermined if an importer who has arranged for a credit to be issued for the benefit of the exporter could prevent payment under the credit by obtaining a stop payment order against the issuing bank in its home country on the basis of a claim that the exporter has defaulted in his obligations under the underlying contract of sale. In examining the law's response to such orders, this chapter has shown that the common law allows such orders to have effect only in very limited instances: where the law of the issuing bank's country is the law that governs the credit or where under the credit the issuing bank's payment obligation is to be performed in its home jurisdiction. Where the credit is confirmed and the confirming bank is in another country, or where the credit is unconfirmed but documents are to be presented to and payment made by a nominated bank in another country, stop payment orders made in the issuing bank's country have afforded the issuing bank no defence at common law in England and other jurisdictions.

7.61 Under the Convention, such orders continued to have very limited effect on claims by a confirming bank against the issuing bank, or by a nominated bank that is not a confirming bank but has honoured or negotiated a complying presentation. This is because, under article 4(2), the law that governs the contract between the issuing bank and the claiming bank is the law of the claiming bank's country. It has been argued that, under the Regulation, the position should to be the same, whether one applies article 4(1)(b), as advocated in this chapter, or article 4(2).

7.62 In the case of a claim by the beneficiary of an unconfirmed credit, where documents are to be presented to and payment made by a nominated bank, under the Convention, the courts relied on article 4(5) to displace the law of the issuing bank's country, as the law applicable to the contract between the issuing bank and the beneficiary under article 4(2), in favour of the law of the place of performance (usually the nominated bank's country). That practice prevented foreign stop payment orders against issuers from defeating beneficiaries' claims in England. Under the Regulation, it has been argued in this chapter that, based on the

[119] See Rome Convention (n 6) art 4(2) which is discussed above.
[120] *NIDCO v Banco Santander* (n 2) [45].

jurisprudence of the ECJ, the contract between the issuing bank and beneficiary should be classified as one for the provision services within article 4(1)(b), that the issuing bank is the party providing the services and that therefore the prima facie applicable law is the law of the issuing bank's country. If article 4(1)(b) does not apply to this contract, then under article 4(2) the applicable law is the same. In either case, stop payment orders made in the issuing bank's country would defeat beneficiaries' claims against issuing banks in England and undermine the commercial purpose of letters of credit.

7.63 However, it has been argued that, under the Regulation, the law of the issuing bank's country is likely to be displaced in favour of the law of the place of performance and/or the law applicable to another contract (in the chain of letter of credit transactions) with which the contract between the issuing bank and the beneficiary has a very close relationship. Whilst, under article 4(3), the threshold for displacing the law identified under article 4(1) or (2) is apparently higher than under article 4(5) of the Convention, nevertheless, in the context of letters of credit, the place of performance continues to carry considerable weight and, in many cases, it will satisfy the higher threshold in article 4(3). Displacing the law of the issuing bank's country in this way would mean that a stop payment order made in the issuing bank's country would not constitute a defence to a claim in England in situations where they would not have been effective as a defence under the Convention. The Convention kept the door firmly shut on such orders. The Regulation has not opened that door. To do so would increase the likelihood that reliance on such orders would become commonplace, when under the Convention it has been rare.

8

Injunctions to Restrain Payment on Independent Guarantees

'Unconscionability' to Bolster the Fraud Exception

*Dora Neo**

I. Introduction

8.01 Independent guarantees are used in many fields, including international trade, to guarantee the performance of one party's obligations under a contract. The term 'independent guarantee' is a broad one which encompasses 'performance guarantees', 'performance bonds', and similar obligations known by various names, including 'demand guarantees', 'on-demand bonds', and 'standby letters of credit', depending on their precise use and geographical context.[1] These terms can often be used interchangeably, although more precise usage may be appropriate if the intention is to refer to a particular type of independent guarantee because its detailed and distinctive features are relevant to the transaction at hand.[2] In essence, they all refer to an autonomous obligation by the issuer of the guarantee or bond to pay a sum of money to the beneficiary provided that certain requirements are met (usually the making of a conforming demand). Without intending to connote any difference in the nature of the relevant obligations, this chapter uses the term 'independent guarantee' when discussing the general features of these instruments (to reflect generic terminology) and the term 'performance bond' when discussing Singapore and UK law (to reflect the terminology that is commonly used in these two jurisdictions).

8.02 The earliest UK cases on performance bonds established the proposition that the principles relating to these instruments are similar to those relating to commercial letters of credit ('commercial LCs').[3] In a commercial LC, the issuing bank must pay as long as the beneficiary presents documents that comply with the requirements of the credit,[4] regardless of any dispute between the buyer and the seller in the underlying sale contract. The equivalent principle in a performance bond is that the bank must honour its obligations under the

* I would like to thank Professor Christopher Hare for his comments on an earlier draft which have been very helpful in enhancing the final version of this chapter.

[1] For a discussion of the various terms that are used to refer to independent guarantees and similar undertakings, and their historical and geographical origin see Norbert Horn and Eddy Wymeersch, *Bank-Guarantees, Standby Letters of Credit and Performance Bonds in International Trade* (Kluwer 1990); Peter Ellinger and Dora Neo, *The Law and Practice of Documentary Letters of Credit* (Hart Publishing 2010) 303–05 (hereafter Ellinger and Neo, *Law and Practice of Documentary Credits*).

[2] See, eg *Kvaerner John Brown Ltd v Midland Bank Plc & Anor* [1998] CLC 446 (QB) 448, 489.

[3] See, eg *Howe Richardson Scale Co Ltd v Polimex-Cekop* [1978] 1 Lloyd's Rep 161 (CA), *Edward Owen Engineering Ltd v Barclays Bank International Ltd* [1978] QB 159 (CA) (hereafter *Edward Owen v Barclays Bank*).

[4] For a discussion on the requirements for determining a complying presentation in letter of credit transactions see ch 5 (Adodo) in this volume.

bond when a conforming demand is made, regardless of any dispute in the underlying contract between the obligor (referred to hereafter as the 'applicant') and the beneficiary. The parallel of presenting complying documents (such as bills of lading, insurance certificates, and commercial invoices) in a commercial LC is the making of a conforming demand (a simple written demand may be sufficient) by the beneficiary under a performance bond. This reflects the autonomy principle, traditionally to be departed from only in the event of fraud.[5] Where this exception applies, a court may grant an injunction to restrain the beneficiary from being paid on the bond even when he has presented a conforming demand.

In Singapore, the development of the unconscionability exception is a departure from the traditional position outlined above, a variation which the courts felt was justified by the special features of performance bonds, as discussed below. There is arguably no legal reason to apply exactly the same principles to performance bonds as to commercial LCs.[6] Performance bonds are relatively new instruments that first came to be used in the 1970s,[7] compared to commercial LCs with their hundreds of years of history. Within the broad framework of autonomy, courts should be able to refine the principles applying to commercial LCs to suit the different nature of the performance bond. As a Singapore judge has observed, '[a] performance bond is as good as cash as between [applicant] and [beneficiary] only because that is the effect of the English decisions and not because it is the cause of such decisions'.[8] It must be noted, as should be clear from the foregoing discussion, that the unconscionability exception in Singapore is applicable only to performance bonds and not to commercial LCs. **8.03**

This chapter examines the grant of injunctions to restrain calls on performance bonds on the basis of unconscionability,[9] focusing on the law and practice developed by the Singapore courts, and exploring this comparatively, particularly in relation to UK law. Because of Singapore's legal history, English cases are widely cited in Singapore, and the law is largely **8.04**

[5] Other exceptions to the autonomy principle that are still developing, such as nullity, unconscionability, illegality, and demand in breach of an agreement with the account party are discussed in Nelson Enonchong, *The Independence Principle of Letters of Credit and Demand Guarantees* (OUP 2011) (hereafter Enonchong, *Independence Principle*). See also Deborah Horowitz, *Letters of Credit and Demand Guarantees: Defences to Payment* (OUP 2010) (hereafter Horowitz, *Defences to Payment*).

[6] It has been suggested that performance bonds should logically be equated with other non-autonomous forms of security: Christopher Hare, 'On Autonomy' (NUS Centre for Maritime Law Working Paper Series No 18/03, April 2018) 4, 24 <https://law.nus.edu.sg/cml/pdfs/wps/CML-WPS-1803.pdf> accessed 31 August 2020 (hereafter Hare, 'On Autonomy'). See also Charles Debattista, 'Performance Bonds and Letters of Credit: A Cracked Mirror Image' [1997] JBL 289.

[7] They were referred to as 'a new business transaction' known as 'performance guarantee' or 'performance bond' in *Edward Owen v Barclays Bank* (n 3) 164. The growth in the use of performance bonds was probably fuelled by the superior bargaining power that came with oil-related wealth in the Middle East which enabled parties from these countries to insist that their counterparts procure performance guarantees in their favour. See *R D Harbottle (Mercantile) Ltd v National Westminster Bank Ltd* [1978] QB 146, 150 (hereafter *R D Harbottle v National Westminster Bank*); *Kono Insurance Ltd v Tins Industrial Co Ltd* [1988] 2 HKLR 36 (CA) 39; *Chartered Electronics Industries Pte Ltd v Development Bank of Singapore* [1992] 2 SLR(R) 20 (HC) [38] (hereafter *Chartered Electronics v DBS*).

[8] *Chartered Electronics v DBS* (n 7) [38] (per Chan Sek Keong J).

[9] See also Ramandeep Chhina, '"Unconscionability" as an Exception to the Autonomy Principle: How Well Is it Entrenched in Singaporean Jurisprudence?' [2016] LMCLQ 412 (hereafter Chhina, '"Unconscionability": How Well Entrenched?'); Roger J Johns and Mark S Blodgett, 'Fairness at the Expense of Commercial Certainty: The International Emergence of Unconscionability and Illegality as Exceptions to the Independence Principle of Letters of Credit and Bank Guarantees' (2011) 31 N Ill U L Rev 297; Agasha Mugasha, 'Enjoining the Beneficiary's Claim on a Letter of Credit or a Bank Guarantee' [2004] JBL 515.

similar in many areas of commercial practice, save for differences in detail.[10] One area of distinction is the willingness of the Singapore courts to grant injunctions to restrain calls on performance bonds based on unconscionability, which is a deliberate departure from the UK position where fraud is the only clearly established ground for doing so.

II. General Features of Independent Guarantees

8.05 Independent guarantees[11] are used to guarantee the performance of a range of obligations in various settings, including construction, finance, and international trade.[12] In international trade transactions, the sale or supply contract may provide that one party must procure a performance bond in favour of the other. For example, the seller may have to provide a performance bond to guarantee its proper performance of the sale contract; to guarantee that it will take up a tender if awarded (a 'tender bond'); or to ensure that any advance payments would be returned to the buyer if the contract is not performed (an 'advance payment bond'). Alternatively, the buyer, rather than the seller, may have to provide an independent guarantee. For instance, in a sale by open account, where the goods are shipped and delivered before payment is due, the buyer may have to procure a standby letter of credit to guarantee payment of the price.

8.06 Despite the use of the word 'guarantee' in some of the terms associated with such undertakings, they operate differently from the more familiar type of bank guarantees used in suretyship contracts, which are secondary obligations whereby the guarantor is liable to pay only if the principal debtor is in default. In contrast, in an independent guarantee, the bank's duty to pay is a primary obligation that is not conditional upon any default by the applicant. An important preliminary question in any dispute related to independent guarantees is whether the bank's payment obligation is a truly independent one. In other words, whether the obligation is conditional or unconditional. The discussion in this chapter applies only to unconditional guarantees, ie those that are independent of the underlying contract. Regardless of the label used, whether the bank's payment undertaking is conditional or not can only be determined by construing the terms of the undertaking itself.[13]

[10] See the Application of English Law Act (Cap 7A, 1994 Rev Ed) ('AELA') which was passed in 1993. Under the AELA, thirteen English commercial law statutes were specifically listed as being applicable in Singapore. The AELA also states that the common law of England (including the principles and rules of equity), so far as it was part of the law of Singapore before 12 November 1993, shall continue to be part of the law of Singapore, and shall continue to be in force in Singapore as long as it is applicable to the circumstances of Singapore and subject to such modifications as those circumstances may require.

[11] See Poh Chu Chai, *Guarantees and Performance Bonds* (3rd edn, LexisNexis 2017); Geraldine Andrews and Richard Millett, *Law of Guarantees* (7th edn, Sweet & Maxwell 2015) ch 16; Wayne Courtney, John Phillips, and James O'Donovan, *The Modern Contract of Guarantee* (3rd English edn, Sweet & Maxwell 2016) ch 13; Ali Malek and David Quest, *Jack: Documentary Credits* (4th edn, Tottel Publishing 2009) ch 12.

[12] See Roeland E Bertrams, *Bank Guarantees in International Trade* (4th edn, Wolters Kluwer 2010) ch 3.

[13] Careful drafting that reflects the intention of the parties is important. Ambiguous or contradictory language may send mixed signals: see *IE Contractors Ltd v Lloyds Bank Plc* [1990] 2 Lloyd's Rep 496 (CA) (hereafter *IE Contractors v Lloyds Bank* (CA)); *Gold Coast Ltd v Caja de Ahorros del Mediterraneo* [2002] 1 Lloyd's Rep 617 (CA); *Marubeni Hong Kong and South China Ltd v Mongolian Government* [2005] 1 WLR 2497 (CA); *Esal (Commodities) Ltd v Oriental Credit Ltd* [1985] 2 Lloyd's Rep 546 (CA) (hereafter *Esal v Oriental Credit*). The incorporation of standard rules that apply to independent guarantees and similar obligations into the bank's undertaking will indicate clearly that the undertaking is intended to be independent. The main sets of rules that are tailored for independent guarantees and/or standby letters of credit are: International Chamber of Commerce ('ICC'), *The International Standby Practices* (ICC Publication No 590, 1998) (hereafter ISP 98), which are used primarily with standby letters of credit; the ICC, *Uniform Rules for Demand Guarantees* (ICC Publication No 758, 2010) (hereafter

An independent guarantee transaction typically involves at least three contracts.[14] The first is the contract between the applicant and the beneficiary. This could be for the supply of goods or services, or for the payment of money ('the underlying contract'). Its terms will require the applicant to procure an independent guarantee in favour of the beneficiary, usually for a percentage of the contract price. This will guarantee proper performance of the applicant's obligations and the beneficiary can seek payment under the guarantee if the applicant breaches the contract. The second contract is between the applicant and the bank,[15] when the applicant approaches the bank to issue the required independent guarantee. In return, the applicant promises to reimburse the bank if the bank pays the beneficiary upon a conforming demand. The third contract is between the bank and the beneficiary. This is the independent guarantee itself. Here, the bank promises to pay the beneficiary if the latter makes a conforming demand. The requirements of a valid demand will be set out in the independent guarantee, and this will vary, according to the instructions given to the bank by the particular applicant. It is important to have an understanding of these different contracts in order to appreciate how the autonomy principle and the fraud or unconscionability exception operates. **8.07**

Three main situations in which issues related to the fraud exception may arise in litigation are: (i) where the beneficiary is suing the bank for a refusal to pay on the independent guarantee in the face of a complying demand; (ii) where the bank is seeking reimbursement from the applicant but the applicant asserts that the bank should not have paid as it had knowledge of the beneficiary's fraud; and (iii) where the applicant is seeking an injunction to restrain payment on the guarantee. The fraud exception applies in all three situations, although the rationale for its application and the standards of proof required may vary in each case. The usual justification for the fraud exception is stated to be the *ex turpi causa* doctrine. No action arises from a base cause, or fraud unravels all. The courts will not allow its processes to be used for fraud. This justification fits best with the first situation, where a fraudulent beneficiary will not succeed in suing the bank for a refusal to pay on a conforming demand. In the second situation, a bank that pays a beneficiary who has made a conforming demand, but whom the bank knows has been fraudulent, will not be entitled to reimbursement from the applicant. This is because the bank would have exceeded its mandate in paying on a demand which it knew was fraudulent. The most common situation that arises in litigation is probably the third one, where the applicant seeks an injunction to stop the beneficiary from receiving payment under the independent guarantee. The question here is whether the court will exercise its equitable powers to grant an injunction and intervene in the relationship between the parties. It must be highlighted that it is only in this third context that the Singapore courts have applied the unconscionability exception, **8.08**

URDG), which apply to demand guarantees; and the United Nations Convention on Independent Guarantees and Stand-by Letters of Credit (adopted 26 January 1996, UNGA Res 50/48, entered into force 1 January 2000) (hereafter UN Convention on IGs and Stand-by LCs), intended for use with all types of independent guarantees, including standby credits.

[14] Four parties will be involved in an international transaction where the applicant instructs its own bank to procure the issuance of an independent guarantee in favour of the beneficiary by a bank in the beneficiary's country. The instructing bank will issue a counter-guarantee in favour of the issuing bank whereby it agrees to reimburse the issuing bank if the latter has to pay out under the main guarantee.

[15] For convenience, the term 'bank' is used, but performance bonds may be issued by other entities, eg insurance companies.

to grant an injunction restraining payment on a performance bond despite a conforming demand. The issue of unconscionability has never arisen in relation to the first two situations. Returning to the contracts outlined in the previous paragraph, if the question to be decided by the courts is whether the bank has a contractual duty to pay the beneficiary on a conforming demand, the contract that takes centre stage is the one between the bank and the beneficiary. The autonomy principle applies, subject only to the fraud exception. On the other hand, if the question is whether the courts should intervene to grant an injunction, which is the focus of this chapter, the contract between the applicant and the beneficiary is also of relevance as this determines the obligations and expectations of the parties in relation to each other.

III. The Fraud Exception

8.09 The classic exposition of the fraud exception in relation to commercial LCs in the UK and Singapore is Lord Diplock's statement in *United City Merchants (Investments) Ltd v Royal Bank of Canada* that the fraud exception applies 'where the seller, for the purpose of drawing on the credit, fraudulently presents to the confirming bank documents that contain, expressly or by implication, material representations of fact that to his knowledge are untrue'.[16] An example might be where the documents, to the knowledge of the beneficiary, misstate the quantity of goods that have been shipped.

8.10 It is problematic to apply Lord Diplock's test of documentary fraud to performance bonds, where there is less focus on documents. Some performance bonds might require merely a written demand, with no prescription as to the form of words to be used. In such cases, no express representations of fact are made to which Lord Diplock's test can be applied; although it could be argued that there might be an implied representation, based on the presentation of the demand by the beneficiary, that the sums under the performance bond are due. A more detailed requirement might be for the beneficiary to make a written demand to the bank stating that the beneficiary has breached the underlying contract. This would be more in the nature of a statement of belief rather than one of fact. Nevertheless, it could be argued that a statement of whether one holds a particular belief could be regarded as a statement of fact,[17] and it would be a false statement if the person making the statement did not in fact hold the stated belief, ie that the applicant has breached the contract.[18]

[16] [1983] 1 AC 168 (HL) 183 (hereafter *United City Merchants v Royal Bank of Canada*).

[17] *Smith v Land and House Property Corp* (1884) 28 Ch D 7 (CA) 15; *Bisset v Wilkinson* [1927] AC 177 (PC) 182; *Tai Kim San v Lim Cher Kia* [2000] 3 SLR(R) 892 (HC) [37].

[18] Meeting the requirements of a valid demand in a performance bond could be seen as akin to the rule of strict compliance in commercial LCs, where the documents presented have to be exactly the same as what is required under the credit. The challenge in performance bond cases would lie in construing the bond to see what is required in order to make a valid demand, and this is a task that can be aided by a clear drafting. Cases addressing the issue of a valid demand in performance bonds in the UK and Singapore include: *Siporex Trade SA v Banque Indosuez* [1986] 2 Lloyd's Rep 146 (QB); *IE Contractors Ltd v Lloyds Bank Plc* [1989] 2 Lloyd's Rep 205 (QB); *IE Contractors v Lloyds Bank* (CA) (n 13); *Esal v Oriental Credit* (n 13); *Chartered Electronics v DBS* (n 7). In *Esal v Oriental Credit* (n 13) 550, the English Court of Appeal stated that it could be 'very salutary' to require a beneficiary to state the basis of his demand and to commit himself to claiming that the underlying contract has not been complied with, as this might help prevent the beneficiary from seeking, whether honestly or dishonestly, to apply the performance bond to the wrong contract, and help prevent abuses of the bond, such as a claim under the bond by the beneficiary when in fact none was justified.

A test of fraud that is more suited to performance bonds has been developed. In *State Trading Corporation of India Ltd v ED & F Man (Sugar) and the State Bank of India*, Lord Denning MR expressed the view that there was a term to be implied in a sale contract with regard to a performance bond that 'the buyer, when giving notice of default, must honestly believe that there has been a default on the part of the seller'.[19] In *GKN Contractors Ltd v Lloyds Bank plc*, Parker LJ stated that what was relevant was common law fraud, 'that is to say, a case where the named beneficiary presents a claim which he knows at the time to be an invalid claim, representing to the bank that he believes it to be a valid claim'.[20] In *United Trading Corporation SA and Murray Clayton Ltd v Allied Arab Bank Ltd,* the test of fraud was similarly expressed to be whether the beneficiary could not have honestly believed in the validity of its demand on the performance bond.[21] The Singapore Court of Appeal has accepted this statement and elaborated on it by incorporating the other elements of common law fraud set out in the classic English case of *Derry v Peek*,[22] and held that it would be fraudulent for the beneficiary to make a demand if it knows that the demand is invalid, had 'no honest belief' in its validity, or if it presented an invalid demand 'recklessly', that is 'indifferent to whether or not it is a valid demand'.[23] On the other hand, it must be emphasised that as the performance bond is meant to allow the beneficiary to obtain payment without waiting for the dispute in the underlying contract to be settled, the understanding between the parties must be that the beneficiary is entitled to call on the bond as long as it honestly believes that the applicant is in breach of contract, even if it may have been wrong in its assessment.[24] **8.11**

In addition to the concept of documentary fraud, discussed above, there is a broader version of the fraud exception that is accepted in some jurisdictions, known as 'fraud in the transaction',[25] although its limits are unclear.[26] There has been debate on the applicability of the 'fraud in the transaction' exception to commercial LCs, and the position in the UK has been described as not settled.[27] A strict reading of Lord Diplock's statement in *United City Merchants v Royal Bank of Canada*, which involved a commercial LC, that documentary fraud is the 'one established exception' to the autonomy principle suggests that in relation **8.12**

[19] *State Trading Corporation of India Ltd v ED & F Man (Sugar) and the State Bank of India* [1981] Com LR 235 (CA), referred to in *United Trading Corporation SA and Murray Clayton Ltd v Allied Arab Bank Ltd and Others* [1985] 2 Lloyd's Rep 554 (CA) 559 (hereafter *United Trading Corp v Allied Arab Bank*). Lord Denning's views have been adopted by the Singapore courts, see *Dauphin Offshore Engineering & Trading Pte Ltd v The Private Office of His Royal Highness Sheikh Sultan bin Khalifa bin Zayed bin Zayed Al Nahyan* [1999] SGHC 201 [24].

[20] (1985) 30 BLR 48 (CA) 53, 63.

[21] *United Trading Corp v Allied Arab Bank* (n 19) 561.

[22] (1889) 14 App Cas 337 (HL).

[23] *Arab Banking Corp (BSC) v Boustead Singapore Ltd* [2016] 3 SLR 557 (CA) [61], [63] (hereafter *BSC v Boustead Singapore*).

[24] *Cargill International SA v Bangladesh Sugar and Food Industries Corp* [1996] 2 Lloyd's Rep 524 (QB) 528 (per Morison J) (hereafter *Cargill International v Bangladesh Sugar*). This part of Morison J's judgment was not discussed when the case went up to the Court of Appeal, where the defendant's appeal was dismissed: [1998] 1 WLR 461 (CA).

[25] See ch 6 (Gao) in this volume, arguing for a different standard of fraud to be applied to documentary fraud as compared to 'fraud in the transaction'.

[26] Roy Goode, 'Abstract Payment Undertakings in International Transactions' in Peter Cane and Jane Stapleton (eds), *Essays for Patrick Atiyah* (OUP 1991) 211. It has questioned whether the scope of 'fraud in the transaction' means 'an unprincipled wholesale enquiry into the underlying transaction to determine what is "fair to do" or rather a limited enquiry into the underlying transaction to identify whether the demand for payment has been made with "no bona fide belief" or with 'no right to payment"': Chhina, '"Unconscionability": How Well Entrenched?' (n 9) 417.

[27] See Enonchong, *Independence Principle* (n 5) para 5.17.

to commercial LCs, 'fraud in the transaction' is not part of English law.[28] This restrictive interpretation of the meaning of 'fraud' in commercial LC cases is likely to be applied also in Singapore, where Lord Diplock's statement has been quoted and applied in case law.[29]

8.13 In relation to performance bonds, the fraud exception was applied in *Themehelp v West*, where the underlying contract was found to have been induced by fraudulent misrepresentation.[30] The English Court of Appeal upheld the High Court's decision to grant an injunction on the basis that the only reasonable inference that could be drawn from the circumstances was that the beneficiaries had been fraudulent. On its facts, this case can be classified as involving 'fraud in the transaction', since the fraud did not involve the documents. However, the Court of Appeal did not elaborate on the meaning of 'fraud' and the term 'fraud in the transaction' was not used in its judgment. The term 'fraud in the transaction' has similarly not been used in Singapore cases, but it can be observed that the question of whether there is 'fraud in the transaction' is consistent with the fraud test articulated above for performance bonds cases, of whether the beneficiary had no honest belief in the validity of its demands. The commonality between the two is that the 'no honest belief' test, like the 'fraud in the transaction' enquiry, does not look at the documents alone, but extends to considerations beyond the contents of the documents. It seems preferable, in relation to performance bonds, to use the 'no honest belief' formulation rather than to ask whether there was 'fraud in the transaction', as the 'no honest belief' test directs us squarely to the nub of the enquiry: did the beneficiary honestly believe it was entitled to call on the performance bond? It is possible that the scope of 'fraud in the transaction' is potentially wider than 'no honest belief', as the former could extend beyond questions of entitlement to call on the bond; and, if so, it would be desirable to limit the applicability of the fraud exception in performance bonds to cases where there is no honest belief in the validity of the call instead of using the broader concept of 'fraud in the transaction', so as not to stray too far from the autonomy principle.

8.14 In the US, both versions of the fraud exception are set out in § 5–109 of the Uniform Commercial Code ('UCC'), which applies equally to commercial and standby credits. Under this section, an injunction can be granted to prevent the issuer from honouring a demand 'if a required document is forged or materially fraudulent', or if honour of the presentation 'would facilitate a material fraud by the beneficiary on the issuer or the applicant', provided that certain conditions are satisfied. The first part of this provision corresponds roughly to the idea of documentary fraud, and the second part to the idea of 'fraud in the transaction', where a court could look beyond the documents at external matters, for example, whether a demand was made despite there being no breach in the underlying contract; or whether there was fraud in the procurement of the instrument or the underlying contract. The US approach in § 5–109 goes further than the UK or Singapore position in relation to commercial LCs, but it seems generally consonant with the 'no honest belief' approach in performance bonds, although the test of whether honour would 'facilitate a material fraud by

[28] *United City Merchants v Royal Bank of Canada* (n 16) 183.
[29] *Korea Industry Co Ltd v Andoll Ltd* [1989] 2 SLR(R) 300 (CA) (hereafter *Korea Industry v Andoll*).
[30] [1996] QB 84 (CA).

the beneficiary on the issuer or the applicant' makes the UCC rule more nuanced than the common law approach of 'no honest belief' adopted in the UK and Singapore.[31]

In deciding whether to grant an injunction restraining a bank from honouring a performance bond, courts in the UK and Singapore will look at whether there is clear evidence of the fact of fraud and as to the bank's knowledge.[32] The mere allegation of fraud will not be sufficient. The standard of proof that applies is the one articulated by Ackner LJ in *United Trading Corp v Allied Arab Bank*, to ask whether the applicant has shown that 'it is seriously arguable that on the material available, the only realistic inference is that [the beneficiary] could not honestly have believed in the validity of its demands on the performance bonds?'[33] Although the strict 'only realistic inference' standard of proof is still in use in Singapore, the courts have also accepted the less onerous standard of a 'strong prima facie case',[34] drawing guidance from the Canadian case of *CDN Research & Development Ltd v Bank of Nova Scotia*.[35] The reasons for adopting this more relaxed standard of proof for performance bonds are consonant with the reasons for developing the unconscionability exception, which are discussed below. **8.15**

In contrast with the UK approach towards the grant of interim injunctions, where the 'balance of convenience' test propounded in the case of *American Cyanamid Co Ltd v Ethicon Ltd*[36] is applied in determining whether to grant injunctions, the Singapore courts have dispensed with this test in cases involving commercial LCs and performance bonds, so that the question of whether there was fraud (or unconscionability in the case of performance bonds) was the sole consideration in applications for injunctions to be granted.[37] The view of the courts is that once fraud (or unconscionability) can be established, the question of 'balance of convenience' becomes superfluous, and 'it did not lie in the mouth of the defendant to claim that damages would still somehow be an adequate remedy'.[38] If this test were applicable, it would mean that the court would have to deal with both the equitable principle as well as the balance of convenience. In the opinion of the Singapore courts 'to require such a "double-barreled" test would be dichotomous and illogical'.[39] However, **8.16**

[31] The UCC approach could, on the one hand, be stricter than the common law test of 'no honest belief', because fraud that is not 'material' would not fall under § 5–109 (see ch 6 (Gao) in this volume). On the other hand, the test of whether honour of the letter of credit would facilitate a fraud by the beneficiary on the issuer or the applicant is potentially broader than the 'no honest belief' test and can be said to be more liberal.

[32] *Bolivinter Oil SA v Chase Manhattan Bank* [1984] 1 Lloyd's Rep 251 (CA) 257; *United Trading Corp v Allied Arab Bank* (n 19) 561; *Korea Industry v Andoll* (n 29) [19].

[33] *United Trading Corp v Allied Arab Bank* (n 19) 561; *BSC v Boustead* Singapore (n 23) [82]. This standard was applied by the Privy Council in *Alternative Power Solution Ltd v Central Electricity Board* [2015] 1 WLR 697 (PC) (hereafter *Alternative Power Solution v Central Electricity Board*).

[34] In *GHL Pte Ltd v Unitrack Building Construction Pte Ltd* [1999] 3 SLR(R) 44 (CA) and *Dauphin Offshore Engineering & Trading Pte Ltd v The Private Office of HRH Sheikh Sultan bin Khalifah* [2000] 1 SLR(R) 117 (CA) (hereafter *Dauphin Offshore v Private Office*), the Singapore Court of Appeal endorsed the strong *prima facie* standard propounded by the High Court in *Chartered Electronics v DBS* (n 7). Although this less onerous standard of proof was developed alongside the unconscionability exception, it applies to all situations where an interim injunction is sought to restrain payment on a performance bond, either based on the fraud or the unconscionability exception. Even after the 'strong prima face case' standard was developed, the 'only realistic inference' standard was applied in *BSC v Boustead Singapore* (n 23).

[35] (1982) 136 DLR (3d) 656 (HC).

[36] *American Cyanamid Co Ltd v Ethicon Ltd* [1975] AC 396 (HL) (hereafter *American Cyanamid v Ethicon*).

[37] *Brody, White and Co Inc v Chemet Handel Trading (S) Pte Ltd* [1992] 3 SLR(R) 146 (CA) [16], [20]; *Bocotra Construction Pte Ltd and others v Attorney-General* [1995] 2 SLR(R) 262 (CA) [44] (hereafter *Bocotra Construction v AG*).

[38] *Bocotra Construction v AG* (n 37) [46].

[39] ibid [45]

they have emphasised that dispensing with the balance of convenience did not make an injunction any easier to obtain, as the requirement to establish a clear case of fraud or unconscionability in interlocutory proceedings would apply a higher level of strictness, and mere allegations would be insufficient.[40] The Court did not explain this statement. If a balance of convenience test is applied to the grant of an injunction, the applicant faces two obstacles. At the first stage of the enquiry, as discussed above, the applicant must show a clear case of fraud, to satisfy the standards imposed by the 'only realistic inference' test, or the 'strong prima facie case' test.[41] Most applicants will fail at this stage as these standards are high. In Singapore, an applicant who passes this test will be granted an injunction. There are no further considerations. Although the result of the next step of the *American Cyanamid* test, whether damages would be an adequate remedy for the applicant, might in some cases cause a court to deny an injunction despite a finding of fraud in the first stage, this escape route is not available to a beneficiary in Singapore. The language quoted above, that 'it did not lie in the mouth'[42] of the beneficiary to claim that damages would still somehow be an adequate remedy, suggests that the court felt that it was justified to dispense with the second stage because the defendant had acted dishonestly (or unconscionably). In the UK, an applicant who succeeds in the herculean task of satisfying the standard of proof for fraud at the interlocutory proceedings, must still move on to the second stage of the enquiry, to show that the balance of convenience lies in its favour, and this might present an 'insuperable difficulty'.[43]

IV. The Unconscionability Exception

A. The Unconscionability Exception in Singapore

8.17 The unconscionability exception had a shaky start in Singapore,[44] before it was explicitly confirmed to be distinct from the fraud exception by the Court of Appeal in the case of *GHL Pte Ltd v Unitrack Building Construction Pte Ltd*.[45] Although the courts have resisted giving a definition of 'unconscionability', some broad guidance can be obtained from the cases. It is clearly less stringent that the test for fraud, as dishonesty is not required. An often-used

40 ibid [48].

41 See para 8.15 of this chapter.

42 See text accompanying n 38.

43 In *R D Harbottle v National Westminster Bank* (n 7) 155, Kerr J identified an 'insuperable difficulty' that the plaintiff would face in terms of the balance of convenience: if an injunction was not granted to restrain the bank from paying on the performance bond, and the beneficiary's call turned out to be in breach of contract, the bank would be able to satisfy the plaintiff's claims for damages; whereas if an injunction were granted against the bank, this might cause greater damage to the bank than the plaintiff might be able to pay. See also *Alternative Power Solution v Central Electricity Board* (n 33) [79]–[82], a case involving an irrevocable letter of credit, where the Privy Council accepted that the balance of convenience would almost always militate against the grant of an injunction. The force of this argument is particularly strong if the entity against whom the injunction is sought is willing to give an undertaking in damages that it had the means to honour. See also *Czarnikow-Rionda Sugar Trading Inc v Standard Bank London Ltd* [1999] 2 Lloyd's Rep 187 (QB) 202–04.

44 For example, in *New Civilbuild Pte Ltd v Guobena Sdn Bhd* [1998] 2 SLR(R) 732 (HC) [33] the judge expressed the view that the Court of Appeal in *Bocotra Construction v AG* (n 37) had 'in all likelihood, used the expression "unconscionability" interchangeably with "fraud" because it could not have made such a drastic departure from English law without giving any reason for it.'

45 *GHL Pte Ltd v Unitrack Building Construction Pte Ltd* [1999] 3 SLR(R) 44 (CA) (hereafter *GHL Pte Ltd v Unitrack*).

test is the one set on in *Raymond Construction Pte Ltd v Low Yang Tong*: Unconscionability 'involves unfairness, as distinct from dishonesty or fraud, or conduct of a kind so reprehensible or lacking in good faith that a court of conscience would either restrain the party or refuse to assist the party. Mere breaches of contract by the party in question ... would not by themselves be unconscionable.'[46] In *Eltraco International v CGH Development* ('*Eltraco*'), the Court of Appeal stated: 'In every instance of unconscionability there would be an element of unfairness. But the reverse is not necessarily true. It does not mean that in every instance where there is unfairness it would amount to "unconscionability".'[47] This emphasises that unfairness is just a factor, albeit an important one, to be considered in the assessment of the beneficiary's behaviour.[48] However, in appropriate circumstances, unfairness or a lack of bona fides could be sufficient to constitute unconscionability. The kind of situation that would amount to unconscionability would depend on the facts of each case and there is no pre-determined categorisation.[49] There can be overlap between fraud and unconscionability, but whilst 'in every instance where there is fraud there would have been a lack of bona fides or an element of unfairness, it does not follow that in every instance where the beneficiary of a performance bond lacks bona fides or behaves unfairly, there is necessarily fraud'.[50] Where there are genuine disputes between the applicant and the beneficiary, a call on the bond cannot be termed as abusive, as the beneficiary is entitled to protect their own interest.[51]

The juridical basis for adopting unconscionability as a ground for granting injunctions lies in the equitable nature of the injunction.[52] The Singapore courts have explained that just as considerations of conscience are applicable in relation to the use of injunctions in other areas of the law, these considerations should also be applied for the purposes of determining whether a call on a performance bond should be restrained in order to achieve a fair balance between the interests of the applicant and the beneficiary.[53] In determining whether a call on a bond is unconscionable, the entire picture must be viewed, taking into account all the relevant factors. Sufficient reasons must be given to the court to enable it to conclude that the beneficiary's conduct is so lacking in bona fides that an injunction is warranted, and these reasons must be drawn from a thorough consideration of the relevant facts as viewed in the entire context of the case, taking into account the parties' conduct leading up to the call on the bond.[54] It would be difficult for one single piece of evidence, read without the benefit of its context, to be definitive proof of a strong prima facie case of unconscionability.[55] **8.18**

A study by Professor Tang Hang Wu of the reported and unreported cases on unconscionability in Singapore between the years 2000 to 2015 identifies some factors **8.19**

[46] *Raymond Construction Pte Ltd v Low Yang Tong* [1996] SGHC 136, [5]-[6] (hereafter *Raymond Construction*).
[47] *Eltraco International Pte Ltd v CGH Development Pte Ltd* [2000] 3 SLR(R) 198 (CA) [30] (hereafter *Eltraco International v CGH Development*).
[48] ibid [30].
[49] *Dauphin Offshore v Private Office* (n 34) [42].
[50] ibid [35].
[51] *Shanghai Electric Group Co Ltd v PT Merak Energi Indonesia* [2010] 2 SLR 329 (HC) [39] (hereafter *Shanghai Electronic v PT Merak*), referring to *Eltraco International v CGH Development* (n 47) [32].
[52] *BS Mount Sophia v Join-Aim Pte Ltd* [2012] 3 SLR 352 (CA) [13] (hereafter *BS Mount Sophia v Join-Aim*).
[53] ibid.
[54] ibid [45]. See also *Eltraco International v CGH Development* (n 47) [31].
[55] *BS Mount Sophia v Join-Aim* (n 52) [45].

which the courts have taken into account in granting injunctions.[56] These factors include whether:[57] (i) the beneficiary of the bond has contributed to the delay in the works;[58] (ii) there is independent evidence, such as evidence from the architect, that there was no delay or defect in the works;[59] (iii) the claim for damages was time barred;[60] (iv) no performance was due on the sub-contract because the beneficiary's main contract had been terminated;[61] and (v) the call on the bond was not due to the applicant's poor performance, but based on ulterior motives, such as attempting to force the applicant to take over a contract.[62] This useful summary should be treated as just a rough indication, bearing in mind the general approach of the court stated in the previous paragraph that the context in which the facts occur is important.

B. The Unconscionability Exception in the UK and Other Jurisdictions

8.20 Although the inspiration for the development of the unconscionability exception in Singapore came from the English case of *Potton Homes Ltd v Coleman Contractors Ltd*,[63] this exception has hardly taken off in the UK. The case which is usually put forward as having recognised lack of faith as a ground for granting an injunction in the UK is *TTI Team Telecom International Ltd v Hutchison 3G UK Ltd* ('*TTI Team Telecom*'),[64] where the application for an injunction was based, inter alia, on the ground that the intended demand by the beneficiary was in bad faith. There, Judge Thornton QC accepted that in addition to fraud or dishonesty, 'lack of good faith has for a long time provided a basis to restrain a beneficiary' from calling on a performance bond,[65] but refused to grant the injunction as a lack of good faith on the part of the beneficiary could not be shown. The *TTI Team Telecom* case has hardly gained any judicial attention in the UK, and positioned as it is amidst the many well established English cases which state the fraud exception without any mention of the relevance of lack of faith, it is difficult to rely on this as an indication that the unconscionability exception is recognised in the UK.[66]

[56] Tang Hang Wu, 'Equity in the Marketplace: Reviewing the Use of Unconscionability to Restrain Calls on Performance Bonds' in Paul S Davies and James Penner (eds), *Equity, Trusts and Commerce* (Hart Publishing 2017) 67 (hereafter Tang, 'Reviewing the Use of Unconscionability to Restrain Calls on Performance Bonds'). This study found that 41% of the applications for injunctions were successful, but it cautioned that this may not give a complete picture as the practice in Singapore is that judges generally only write judgments when a party lodges a notice of appeal.

[57] These factors are reproduced from a fuller list found in ibid 68.

[58] *A1 Design & Build Pte Ltd v Neo Choon Seng* [2015] SGDC 86; *BS Mount Sophia v Join-Aim* (n 52); *Global Facade (S) Pte Ltd v Eng Lim Construction Company Private Limited* [2001] SGDC 325.

[59] *A1 Design & Build Pte Ltd v Neo Choon Seng* [2015] SGDC 86; *Polink Engineering Pte Ltd v Chen Hwei Lai & Ors* [2010] SGDC 36.

[60] *Econ Piling Pte Ltd v Aviva General Insurance Pte Ltd and another* [2006] 4 SLR(R) 501 (CA).

[61] *Prolian M&E Services Pte Ltd v Loh Lin Kett* [2001] SGDC 322.

[62] *Samwoh Asphalt Premix Pte Ltd v Sum Cheong Piling Private Limited and Another* [2001] 3 SLR(R) 716 (CA).

[63] *Potton Homes Ltd v Coleman Contractors (Overseas) Ltd* (1984) 28 BLR 19 (CA) 29. In this case, Eveleigh LJ did not accept that a performance bond was to be treated as cash between seller and buyer, or that a performance guarantee should be treated like a letter of credit, in all circumstances.

[64] [2003] 1 All ER (Comm) 914 (QB) (hereafter *TTI v Hutchison*).

[65] ibid [34].

[66] See Enonchong, *Independence* Principle (n 5) paras 7.16–7.28, where the author questioned the principal authorities relied upon to support the assertion in *TTI Team Telecom* that lack of good faith was a long established

Singapore and Australia are sometimes mentioned together as jurisdictions where the unconscionability exception applies. However, there are significant differences in the two jurisdictions. In Singapore, the unconscionability exception is a common law rule, whereas the unconscionability rule that applies in Australia[67] is based on statute.[68] The provision that is most relevant to unconscionability as an exception to the principle of autonomy in performance bonds is section 20 of the Australian Consumer Law found in schedule 2 of the Competition and Consumer Act 2010 (Cth).[69] Contravention of this section may result in judicial intervention by the grant of an injunction.[70] Section 20 is a broad provision which provides that a person '[m]ust not in trade or commerce, engage in conduct that is unconscionable, within the meaning of the unwritten law from time to time'. Australian courts have interpreted the predecessor of this section to mean that there should be an unconscionability exception relating to the beneficiary's conduct in seeking payment under a letter of credit or making a demand under a demand guarantee that has been issued in respect of an international trade transaction.[71] This means, in effect, that the statutory provision has made inroads into the principle of autonomy. As provided under section 20, unconscionable conduct is to be assessed according to the general law of unconscionability in Australia. This reveals two other significant differences between the unconscionability exception as applied in Singapore and Australia. The Australian statutory exception applies to both commercial LCs and performance bonds, whereas the Singapore common law exception applies to performance bonds only. And unlike in Australia, where the general law of unconscionability is well developed and can be referred to for guidance, Singapore law does not have a general doctrine of unconscionability and the substance of unconscionability must be tailored specially for restraining calls on performance bonds only. 8.21

In the USA, the law relating to letters of credit is found in the UCC.[72] These provisions apply to both commercial LCs as well as standby credits. Apart from §5–109 on fraud and forgery discussed above, there are no provisions in the UCC on unconscionability or good faith. 8.22

ground for granting an injunction, primarily *Elian and Rabbath (t/a Elian & Rabbath) v Matsas* [1966] 2 Lloyd's Rep 495 (CA); *Cargill International v Bangladesh Sugar* (QB) (n 24); and *Cargill International SA v Bangladesh Sugar and Food Industries Corp* [1998] 1 WLR 461 (CA). He concluded that it was an 'open question' whether English law 'recognised a general lack of good faith or unconscionable conduct exception separate from the fraud exception' (Enonchong, *Independence Principle* (n 5) para 7.28).

[67] For the position in Australia generally, see Horowitz, *Defences to Payment* (n 5) paras 6.17–6.42; Enonchong, *Independence Principle* (n 5) paras 7.37–7.49; Agasha Mugasha, *The Law of Letters of Credit and Bank Guarantees* (Federation Press 2003).

[68] In *Hortico (Australia) Pty Ltd v Energy Equipment Co (Australia) Pty Ltd* (1985) 1 NSWLR 545 (SC), Young J suggested that there might be some cases in which the unconscionable conduct may be so gross as to lead to the intervention of the court. However, in *Olex Focas Pty Ltd v Skodaexport Co Ltd* (1998) 3 VR 380 (SC), Batt J rejected 'gross unconscionability falling short of actual fraud' as a ground for an injunction under the general common law.

[69] This section replaced s 51AA of the Trade Practices Act 1974 (Cth) (Australia).

[70] Australian Consumer Law, s 232; in sch 2, Competition and Consumer Act 2020 (Cth) (Australia).

[71] See, eg *Olex Focas Pty Ltd v Skodaexport Co Ltd* (1998) 3 VR 380 (CA); *Boral Framework and Scaffolding Pty Ltd v Action Makers Ltd* [2003] NSWSC 557.

[72] For the US position generally, see John F Dolan, *The Law of Letters of Credit: Commercial and Standby Credits* (4th edn, LexisNexis A S Pratt 2007).

Although the provisions of §5–109 are relatively broad, the requirements of forgery or material fraud go beyond unconscionability or bad faith.

C. Policy Reasons for an Unconscionability Exception in Performance Bonds Cases

8.23 Two main reasons have been given by the Singapore courts for adopting a more lenient standard for the grant of injunctions in performance bonds cases, as compared to cases involving commercial LCs.[73]

8.24 The first reason stems from the inherent nature of the performance bond. As the beneficiary can get payment from the bank by presenting a written demand without having to show a breach of the underlying contract, this makes it relatively easy for the beneficiary to make an unmeritorious demand. In contrast, a beneficiary who seeks payment under a commercial LC will have to present conforming documents, which are usually produced by third parties. The greater danger of abusive calls in performance bond cases makes them a potentially 'oppressive instrument',[74] which may cause 'undue hardship' or 'unwarranted economic harm'[75] to the applicant thereby warranting a higher level of intervention by the court at an interlocutory stage.

8.25 The second reason relates to the function of performance bonds. Unlike the commercial LC which is a form of payment in exchange for goods, a performance bond is just a guarantee of performance. Even if the beneficiary is prevented from claiming on the bond initially, it will still be paid eventually if it wins the case. In the words of the judge in *Chartered Electronics v DBS*: 'A temporary restraining order does not affect the security nor the beneficiary's rights in it. It merely postpones the realisation of the security until the plaintiff is given an opportunity to prove his case.'[76]

8.26 These considerations are weighty ones, particularly the first. There is obviously moral hazard associated with a performance bond. An unscrupulous beneficiary can call on a performance bond issued in his favour without much effort.[77] That performance bonds are of this nature makes it important for the courts to be able to intervene to protect the applicant. That they are secondary in function minimises the ill effects of doing so. However, the assurance that a beneficiary who is restrained from receiving payment on a performance bond would still get paid later if his claim is proven gives cold comfort, as he expected to get paid immediately on demand.[78]

[73] See *Chartered Electronics v DBS* (n 7) [36], [39]; *GHL Pte Ltd v Unitrack* (n 45) [24].

[74] *GHL Pte Ltd v Unitrack* (n 45) [24].

[75] *JBE Properties Pte Ltd v Gammon Pte Ltd* [2011] 2 SLR 47 (CA) [11] (hereafter *JBE Properties v Gammon*).

[76] *Chartered Electronics v DBS* (n 7) [37] (Chan Sek Keong J).

[77] The risk of abuse can be reduced to some extent by the inclusion of provisions in the underlying contract to provide, for example, that the beneficiary should state the basis of its demand (see discussion of *Esal v Oriental Credit* (n 13) at n 18) or to stipulate that a particular document must be prepared by a third party. However, the extent to which an applicant can include protective terms in the underlying contract will depend on its bargaining power relative to the beneficiary.

[78] This was acknowledged by the Court of Appeal in *BS Mount Sophia v Join-Aim* (n 52) [22].

D. Assessing the Unconscionability Exception

8.27 It has been suggested that the relative ease of obtaining an injunction based on unconscionability[79] is liable to destroy the confidence in the performance bond as being cash in hand and undermine their commercial utility; that determining unconscionability would over-involve the court in disputes arising from the underlying contract; and that the concept of unconscionability is vague and could lead to uncertainty.[80] It has also been suggested that many of the cases that have been decided on the unconscionability principle could equally have been analysed under the fraud exception.[81]

8.28 Although it is easier to obtain an injunction based on unconscionability than on fraud, this does not mean that it is necessarily easy to obtain an injunction on the ground of unconscionability. Whether confidence in the performance bond as a commercial instrument will be destroyed does not depend so much on whether a particular jurisdiction recognises the unconscionability exception, but more on how the exception is applied by the courts. Although the understanding and practice relating to the unconscionability exception in Singapore took some years to stabilise from the 1990s to the 2000s, clear signals were given by the Court of Appeal in the 2010s emphasising that it would not be easy to obtain an injunction based on unconscionability and that it would be difficult for an applicant to show a strong prima facie case of unconscionability.[82] The courts have explained that the barrier for the grant of an injunction on the basis of unconscionability must be set at a high level to minimise the potentially harsh effects of this remedy on the beneficiary, who would '[i]n essence, be prevented from enforcing a substantive right which he had contracted for'.[83] Further, this strict approach was necessary in order not to undermine or erode the efficacy and '*raison d'être* of performance bonds—that they are to provide security for the performance of the obligor's obligations . . .'.[84]

8.29 There is a perennial tension between interests of the applicant and the beneficiary in the context of performance bonds.[85] On one hand, '[t]he right message should be communicated: that the courts will not condone any form of dishonesty or unconscionable behaviour on the part of beneficiaries'.[86] On the other hand, the principle of autonomy is important in international commerce, and '[i]t is vital that contracting parties . . . should be able to rely on the integrity of a bank's promise to pay upon an independent guarantee regardless of

[79] Thanuja Rodrigo, 'Theoretical Justifications for Restraining "Unconscionable" Demands under On-demand Guarantees' (2012) 40 ABLR 5.

[80] See Nelson Enonchong, 'The Problem of Abusive Calls on Demand Guarantees' [2007] LMCLQ 83, 104, discussed by Kelry Loi in 'Two Decades of Restraining Unconscionable Calls on Performance Guarantees: From *Royal Design* to *JBE Properties*' (2011) 23 SAcLJ 504, 508–14. See also Enonchong, *Independence Principle* (n 5) 7.34; Tang, 'Reviewing the Use of Unconscionability to Restrain Calls on Performance Bonds' (n 56) 58–60 and Ellinger and Neo, *Law and Practice of Documentary Credits* (n 1) 325–26.

[81] Horowitz, *Defences to Payment* (n 5) 6.43. One commentator has suggested that what is termed 'unconscionability' in Singapore is not very different from the wider 'fraud in the transaction' exception: Chhina, '"Unconscionability": How Well Entrenched?' (n 9). However, it would appear that the latter exception is stricter, as fraud involves dishonesty, unconscionability does not.

[82] See especially *BS Mount Sophia v Join-Aim* (n 52) [20]–[25]. Similar guidance was given in the earlier case of *Eltraco International v CGH Development* (n 47) [30].

[83] *BS Mount Sophia v Join-Aim* (n 52) [22].

[84] ibid [23].

[85] ibid [26]–[31].

[86] ibid [30], quoting from Ellinger and Neo, *Law and Practice of Documentary Credits* (n 1) 325–26.

disputes in the underlying contract.'[87] The decision to recognise the unconscionability exception is a policy trade-off which the Singapore courts have assessed to be worth making.[88] They have sought to alleviate the potential unfairness of denying the beneficiary's rights by ensuring that the court's discretion to grant a restraining injunction will be exercised sparingly. And, as will be discussed below, if the parties to the underlying contract do not wish the applicant to be able to restrain a call on the bond on the ground of unconscionability, they can provide accordingly in their contract.

8.30 The nature of a performance bond as a potentially oppressive instrument points to the need to protect the applicant from abusive calls. The fraud exception is inadequate to provide such protection. Abusive calls would be encouraged if the test to justify intervention by the court is one that can hardly ever be satisfied. Dishonesty is difficult to show in any context. This, coupled with the high standard of proof, makes obtaining an injunction on the basis of fraud exception almost an impossibility. When referring to 'the only realistic inference' is fraud test, the Singapore Court of Appeal stated that they expected 'that it would only be in truly exceptional circumstances that the account party would be able to discharge this high standard of proof'.[89] In *Edward Owen Engineering v Barclays Bank* ('*Edward Owen Engineering*'), Lord Denning MR observed that the possibility of an abusive call on a performance bond was so real that 'the ... supplier, if he is wise, will take it into account when quoting his price for the contract'.[90] This is certainly practical advice which makes business sense. But taken to its extreme, pricing in the risk of abuse will add to the cost of doing business. Beneficiaries who pay a higher price in the underlying contract may feel that they have paid for the privilege of calling on their performance bonds without fully assessing if their rights to do so have arisen; after all, the applicant half expects that the bond will be called upon. This may cause beneficiaries to call on performance bonds more lightly, with the awareness that fraud will be difficult to prove against them, which diminishes the usefulness of such bonds. It would be a pity if applicants must accept that there is little that they can do against abusive calls except to pre-empt this by the self-help remedy of charging more, especially if they fail to persuade beneficiaries to agree to provisions in performance bonds that require some form of third-party confirmation (such as the production of architects' certificates) before payment can be triggered under the respective bonds. In the face of the obstacles with the fraud exception, the unconscionability exception helpfully provides an additional tool to deal appropriately with abusive calls.

8.31 The unconscionability exception is able to catch unmeritorious behaviour that would otherwise have been condoned by the fraud exception. On the facts of *Edward Owen Engineering*, the buyer did not provide an irrevocable confirmed or confirmable letter of

[87] ibid.

[88] One consequence of such an approach might be that beneficiaries who are in a dominant position might insist that the law of a jurisdiction that is perceived to have stricter rules against the grant of injunctions is selected as the governing law of the contract. In *Shanghai Electronic v PT Merak* (n 51), English law was selected as the governing law. The case was heard in Singapore, where the courts were given non-exclusive jurisdiction to hear the dispute. The court had to decide whether the application for the grant of an injunction was a substantive right, in which case it would be governed by English law, or a procedural right to be governed by the *lex fori*. They decided it was the former. English law therefore applied, and the case was decided on the fraud exception alone.

[89] *BSC v Boustead* Singapore (n 23) [82]. As discussed above, the Singapore courts have accepted a more lenient standard of proof for performance bonds, requiring instead a 'strong prima facie case' of fraud. Even so, this is not an easy standard to satisfy.

[90] *Edward Owen v Barclays Bank* (n 3) 170.

credit as required by the contract.[91] It proceeded to call on the performance bond supplied by the seller, and the House of Lords did not intervene to prevent the buyer from claiming payment, as it could not be shown that the buyer was acting dishonestly in calling on the bond. A somewhat similar situation occurred in *Kvaerner Singapore Pte Ltd v UDL Shipping (Singapore) Pte Ltd*,[92] where the buyer was required to pay the balance of the purchase price by an irrevocable letter of credit. The buyer failed to provide the letter of credit despite reminders to do so, and eventually called on the performance bond. The court held that establishing the letter of credit was a precondition for calling on the performance bond. In the circumstances, an interlocutory injunction was granted to restrain payment under the bond. Although the word 'unconscionability' was not mentioned in this case, it was identified subsequently as illustrating a situation where payment would have been unconscionable.[93] The difference between an unconscionability approach and one based on fraud can be further illustrated by the way in which the Singapore courts viewed the facts in the English case of *Cargill International SA v Bangladesh Sugar and Food Industries Corp*.[94] There, the seller was unable to deliver sugar but the court did not restrain the buyer from receiving payment under the bond despite the fact that the buyer had bought sugar more cheaply elsewhere and had suffered no loss. Referring to this case, the Singapore Court of Appeal stated, in *Eltraco*, that if similar facts had occurred in Singapore, the courts might have granted an injunction based on unconscionability.[95]

The view that fraud is too difficult to prove was shared by the majority of a group of Singapore practitioners who participated in a survey on the law of performance bonds.[96] These practitioners were of the view that unconscionability was a positive development. They felt that fraud was almost impossible to prove, that the unconscionability exception allowed them to deal with abusive calls and that it evened out to some extent the inequality of bargaining power between the parties to the underlying contract. Otherwise, applicants would be powerless when faced with an abusive call on a performance bond. **8.32**

It has been suggested that the unconscionability exception in Singapore is equivalent to 'fraud in the transaction' and the law could have been developed by broadening the scope of the fraud exception to include 'fraud in the transaction' rather than formulating a new unconscionability exception.[97] This is an interesting suggestion, although applying a modified version of an existing label ('fraud', in the sense of 'fraud in the transaction') to cover an expanded fact situation, rather than formulating a new label ('unconscionability') does not solve the problem of having to define this expanded exception, however it is labelled. The meaning of 'fraud in the transaction' will have to be developed, just as the meaning of 'unconscionability' has to be explained. Ultimately, the main difference between these two approaches is that 'unconscionability' does not require dishonesty, whereas any form of **8.33**

[91] ibid.

[92] *Kvaerner Singapore Pte Ltd v UDL Shipping (Singapore) Pte Ltd* [1993] 2 SLR(R) 341 (HC) (hereafter *Kvaerner Singapore v UDL Shipping*).

[93] *Raymond Construction* (n 46) [5]; *GHL Pte Ltd v Unitrack* (n 45) [20].

[94] *Cargill International v Bangladesh Sugar* (QB) (n 24). In *Cargill*, the judge was of the view that the bond was not intended to represent an estimate of the amount of damages to which the buyer might be entitled for the seller's breach, but was a guarantee of due performance, and there was an implied term that the buyer would account to the seller for any amounts received under the bond that exceeded the amount of their actual loss.

[95] *Eltraco International v CGH Development* (n 47) [37]–[38].

[96] Tang, 'Reviewing the Use of Unconscionability to Restrain Calls on Performance Bonds' (n 56) 74.

[97] Chhina, '"Unconscionability": How Well Entrenched?' (n 9).

fraud, including 'fraud in the transaction' would, by definition, involve dishonesty. As discussed above, the idea of 'fraud in the transaction' is not particularly helpful in relation to performance bonds, where the 'no honest belief' test is preferable.

8.34 While it is true that parties must abide by the bargain that they have made and the risk allocation that they have agreed upon, their expectations arising from the contract are also relevant. An applicant who agrees to provide a performance bond accepts and expects that the beneficiary can claim on the bond when where is a dispute, without waiting for the dispute in the underlying contract to be settled. But unless there is something in the underlying contract indicating otherwise, the applicant would also expect the beneficiary to be honest in making the call, to act in good faith and to refrain from sharp practice. Indeed, the provisions of the underlying contract are relevant, not just in relation to the unconscionability exception, but also in the application of the fraud exception. It is only with reference to the underlying contract that the court can assess whether the beneficiary honestly believed that he had a valid claim when he made the call, or whether he was acting unconscionability. The underlying contract would typically contain an express or implied term that the beneficiary is only entitled to claim on the bond when there is a breach of contract by the applicant.[98] If the contract had intended for the beneficiary to call on the bond at its discretion, no issue of fraud or unconscionability would arise. It is therefore appropriate for a court of equitable jurisdiction to have regard to the underlying contract to understand the intentions and expectations of the parties when deciding whether to exercise its discretion to grant a restraining injunction.

V. The Underlying Contract

8.35 The discussion above emphasised the relevance of the parties' expectations in the underlying contract as a factor influencing the court's decision whether to grant an injunction based on the fraud or unconscionability exception. This section examines two situations where the courts had to decide whether to grant injunctions based on the express terms of the underlying contract: the first where the demand on the bond was contrary to the terms of the underlying contract, and the second where the application for an injunction by the beneficiary was not permitted under the terms of the underlying contract.

A. Demand in Breach of the Underlying Contract

8.36 Even in the UK, which has been very strict with the grant of injunctions, the idea that an injunction will be granted to restrain a beneficiary from being paid where the demand is in breach of a provision in the underlying contract that restricted the circumstances in

[98] When such a term is included in the contract, a call on the bond might be evidence of fraud if the beneficiary did not honestly believe he was entitled to call on the bond. Further, if the beneficiary calls on a performance bond where there is no breach of the underlying sale contract, this call would itself amount to a breach of the underlying contract by the beneficiary and may be seen by a court as a repudiatory breach which entitles the applicant to terminate the sale contract with the beneficiary: *Magenta Resources (S) Pte Ltd v China Resources (S) Pte Ltd* [1996] 2 SLR(R) 316.

which a performance bond might be called upon, has taken root independently of the fraud exception.

In *Sirius International Insurance Corp v FAI General Insurance Co Ltd* ('*Sirius v FAI*'),[99] the applicant and beneficiary agreed that the beneficiary would not draw down on the letter of credit unless certain conditions were satisfied. The English Court of Appeal was of the view that the conditions were not satisfied, and stated, *obiter*, that had the beneficiary demanded payment under the letter of credit in breach of the underlying contract despite not having satisfied these conditions, the Court would have granted an injunction to restrain the beneficiary from getting paid. When the case went up on appeal, the House of Lords was of the view that the conditions were satisfied, and did not consider the question whether a court may grant an injunction to restrain a beneficiary from demanding payment under a letter of credit on the basis that the demand would be a breach of a term in the underlying contract between the applicant and the beneficiary.[100] The Court of Appeal's opinion in *Sirius v FAI* was, however, relied upon in *Simon Carves Ltd v Ensus UK Ltd*,[101] where one of the conditions in the underlying contract was that the beneficiary would issue an Acceptance Certificate subject to the plant passing various performance tests. In connection with this, Special Condition 3.7 of the underlying contract stated: 'Upon the issue of the Acceptance Certificate the performance bond shall become null and void (save in respect of any pending or previously notified claims).' The English Technology and Construction Court decided that, where the parties had agreed to a provision that expressly prevented a beneficiary calling on the bond in certain circumstances and those circumstances had arisen, the call on the bond could be restrained by injunction. **8.37**

The cases discussed in the paragraphs above show that this exception to the autonomy principle, based on a demand in breach of the underlying contract, is capable of standing alone without having to rely on arguments based on fraud. Nevertheless, a typical fact situation in a case of this type might also support an application for an injunction based on fraud. This is because it is arguably a type of fraud when a beneficiary seeks to call on a performance bond when it knows, or can be taken to know, that the underlying contract forbids it from doing so (for example, because a condition precedent for the call is not satisfied, or because the entitlement to call has come to an end).[102] Making a demand in breach of the underlying contract is an exception that could potentially grow in importance as an alternative to the fraud exception, and this would free the applicant from having to show dishonestly on the part of the beneficiary. **8.38**

B. Contractual Clauses Excluding Unconscionability

One development in Singapore has been the use of contractual clauses in which the applicant agrees not to apply for an injunction to restrain payment on a performance bond except on grounds of fraud. The intention of such a clause is to prevent the applicant from **8.39**

[99] [2003] 1 WLR 2214 (CA).
[100] [2004] 1 WLR 3251 (HL).
[101] *Simon Carves Ltd v Ensus UK Ltd* [2011] EWHC 657 (TCC) (hereafter *Simon Carves v Ensus*). This exception has also been accepted by the Australian courts: see, eg *Lane-Mullins v Warrenby Pty Ltd* [2004] NSWSC 817 [53].
[102] *Simon Carves v Ensus* (n 101) [34]. See also *Kvaerner Singapore v UDL Shipping* (n 92).

seeking an injunction on the basis of unconscionability, although their effect is not limited to this situation. These clauses attracted widespread attention after the High Court and Court of Appeal decisions in *CKR Contract Services Pte Ltd v Asplenium Land Pte Ltd* ('*Asplenium*').[103] Clause 3.5.8 of the underlying construction contract provided as follows: 'The [applicant] agrees that except in the case of fraud, the [applicant] shall not for any reason whatsoever be entitled to enjoin or restrain (a) the [beneficiary] from making any call or demand on the performance bond or receiving any cash proceeds under the performance bond; or (b) the [bank] under the performance bond from paying any cash proceeds under the performance bond, on any ground including the ground of unconscionability.'[104] The applicant nevertheless applied for an injunction to restrain the beneficiary from being paid on the performance bond, claiming that the call was unconscionable, and justifying its action by arguing that Clause 3.5.8 was unenforceable. The High Court accepted the applicant's argument, but the Court of Appeal overturned the decision and decided that the clause was valid.[105] This meant that the applicant could only restrain a call on the performance bond in the event of fraud and was not entitled to do so on the ground of unconscionability. As there was no suggestion that any fraud was involved, the Court of Appeal allowed the beneficiary to claim payment on the bond.

8.40 Three propositions put forward in the High Court to show that the clause was unenforceable were rejected by the Court of Appeal. The first proposition was that the clause ousted the jurisdiction of the court and therefore should not be enforced for reasons of illegality and public policy. Whilst the Court of Appeal agreed that a clause which sought to oust the jurisdiction of the court would be void for public policy, it was of the view that the clause in question did not have this effect.[106] The clause merely placed limitations on the remedies the parties could seek, in the same way that exclusion clauses restricted the aggrieved party's rights to seek damages, which had never been treated as an ouster of the court's jurisdiction. For the same reason, the second proposition, that the power to grant injunctions flowed from the court's equitable jurisdiction which could not be circumscribed or curtailed by contract, was also rejected.[107] The parties had not been denied access to the court as such. The third argument was that the unconscionability exception was based on important policy considerations designed to strike a balance between party autonomy and the regulation of dishonest and unconscionable behaviour, and this could not be brushed aside by agreement. As this argument was made in the context of ousting the jurisdiction of the court, the Court simply highlighted that the policy reasons for developing the unconscionability exception in the context of abusive calls on performance bonds were quite different from the conceptions of public policy that led to contracts that sought to oust the jurisdiction of the court being found to be void and unenforceable.[108] However, the Court did not examine the question of whether the

[103] *CKR Contract Services Pte Ltd v Asplenium Land Pte Ltd* [2015] 3 SLR 1041 (CA) (hereafter *CKR Contract v Asplenium*). See also the High Court decision in *CKR Contract Services Pte Ltd v Asplenium Land Pte Ltd* [2015] 1 SLR 987 (HC). It would appear that these clauses had already begun to be used in Singapore in the early 2000s, as evidenced in a District Court case, *Scan-Bilt Pte Ltd v Umar Abdul Hamid* [2004] SGDC 274: see Tang, 'Reviewing the Use of Unconscionability to Restrain Calls on Performance Bonds' (n 56) 61–2.

[104] *CKR Contract v Asplenium* (n 103) [5].

[105] The position that the parties to a contract may exclude injunctive relief based on unconscionable conduct has been strongly criticised. See Lau Kwan Ho in 'Injunctive Relief: But Let's Agree Not To Have It?' (2016) 79(3) MLR 468 (hereafter Lau, 'Injunctive Relief').

[106] *CKR Contract v Asplenium* (n 103) [19], [22], [24], [36].

[107] ibid [37].

[108] ibid [41].

substance of the clause was against the public policy of regulating unconscionable behaviour in relation to performance bonds.

The Court of Appeal highlighted that the clause was something that the parties had voluntarily agreed to.[109] Further, the Court pointed out that the clause could potentially be subject to the usual common law and statutory controls that apply to exclusion clauses, such as the need for incorporation, or the Unfair Contract Terms Act ('UCTA').[110] This suggestion was put forward by the Court as an idea for further discussion, and it did not express any definite view on the matter, because the issue was not before it.[111] **8.41**

Asplenium decided that clauses in which the applicant agrees not to seek an injunction to restrain a call on a performance bond on grounds of unconscionability will not be struck down as being contrary to public policy. This meant that these clauses would only potentially be controlled by the law applying to exclusion clauses. But the Court of Appeal left open the question of whether such clauses would fall under section 3 of UCTA so as to be subject to the reasonableness test.[112] To bring no-injunction clauses within UCTA, the applicant (unless it is a consumer) must be dealing with the beneficiary's written standard terms of business. The beneficiary cannot, when itself in breach of contract (for example by calling on a bond when it is not entitled to do so), exclude or restrict the applicant's liability in respect of the breach, except in so far as the contract term satisfies the requirement of reasonableness.[113] Under UCTA, exclusion of liability includes excluding or restricting any remedy,[114] so the statute would potentially apply to excluding the applicant's right to seek the equitable remedy of an injunction based on unconscionability.[115] Assuming that UCTA applies, whether the no-injunction clause is reasonable will depend on all the circumstances of the case.[116] An indication of the potential judicial receptiveness to such a clause can be **8.42**

[109] ibid [36].

[110] Cap 396, 1994 Rev Ed (hereafter 'UCTA'). This statute is based on the English Unfair Contract Terms 1977.

[111] *CKR Contract v Asplenium* (n 103) [23].

[112] In the subsequent decision of *Bintai Kindenko Pte Ltd v Samsung C&T Corp* [2018] SGHC 191, [35] (hereafter *Bintai Kindenko v Samsung*) the High Court considered a similar type of clause, but did not examine the applicability of UCTA to the exclusion clause, save to refer to the view of the Court of Appeal in *CKR Contract v Asplenium* (n 103) that the clause might potentially be subject to UCTA, and concluded that it was 'not persuaded that the circumstances surrounding the Exclusion Clause in this case were so unreasonable as to render it unenforceable under UCTA'. When *Bintai Kindenko v Samsung* (n 112) went up to the Court of Appeal (see [2019] 2 SLR 295 (CA)) arguments on the issue of whether the clause was reasonable under UCTA were not allowed, for technical reasons.

[113] UCTA, s3 (n 110).

[114] ibid s 13(1)(b) provides: 'To the extent that this Part prevents the exclusion or restriction of any liability it also prevents ... excluding or restricting any right or remedy in respect of the liability.'

[115] An argument might be made that because the clause in *Asplenium* was one by which the applicant had agreed that the beneficiary should be able to claim on the performance bond even when the demand was unconscionable, this was in the nature of a 'basis clause' that defines the parties' liability rather than an exclusion clause, and should therefore not be caught by UCTA. This argument is unlikely to succeed in Singapore: see *Deutsche Bank AG v Chang Tse Wen* [2013] 4 SLR 886 (CA) [68], where the Singapore Court of Appeal stated that it is the substantive effect of a term that is important, so that the only question is 'whether a term or notice has the effect of excluding or restricting the imposition of a duty of care in law'. For the position in the UK on this point, see Mindy Chen-Wishart, *Contract Law* (6th edn, OUP 2018) para 11.5.4 (hereafter Chen-Wishart, *Contract Law*).

[116] UCTA, s 11(1) (n 110) provides: 'In relation to a contract term, the requirement of reasonableness ... is that the term shall have been a fair and reasonable one to be included having regard to the circumstances which were, or ought reasonably to have been, known to or in the contemplation of the parties when the contract was made.' In *Bintai Kindenko Pte Ltd v Samsung C&T Corp* [2019] 2 SLR 295 (CA) [70], the Court of Appeal rejected the proposition that all exclusion clauses which excluded an obligor's right to rely on the unconscionability exception were 'inherently unreasonable' because they excluded the court's ability to intervene in circumstances where intervention has already been deemed reasonable. The Court of Appeal also stated that such blanket assessment of all clauses of this type would have contradicted the clear principle laid down in *Koh Lin Yee v Terrestrial Pte Ltd* [2015]

seen from the Court of Appeal's reaction to the clause in *Asplenium*, where no negative comments were made about it. Further, in that case, the Court of Appeal commented that 'the policy underlying the operation of performance bonds ... does point (on a *prima facie* level at least) in favour of the reasonableness of such clauses', subject to the precise language and context of the clause.[117]

8.43 One puzzling aspect of the *Asplenium* case is the contradictory attitude of the Court towards unconscionability in two scenarios. An important policy reason for the unconscionability exception in Singapore was to protect the applicant against abusive calls on performance bonds. Yet at the same time, the indication from the *Asplenium* decision is that the Singapore courts will uphold a provision that allows the beneficiary to call on a bond even if this is unconscionable. One could argue that the policy of discouraging unconscionable behaviour is one that should be applicable to the question of whether to grant an injunction, as well as the question of whether to uphold a contractual clause that prevents the application for an injunction. However, under the principle of freedom of contract, contractual provisions will generally be upheld unless they fall into well-established situations that are policed by the courts. One of these is under the unfair contract terms legislation, discussed above. Contractual obligations that are against public policy will be policed under the general category of common law illegality. While it may be desirable for the courts to incorporate the policy of protection against abusive calls on performance bonds when it exercises its equitable jurisdiction to grant injunctions, it may not be equally justifiable to do so in order to render unenforceable a contractual provision that has been agreed to by the parties. The differing treatment of the two situations (the grant of an injunction versus the striking out of a contractual clause) confirms the assertion made earlier in this chapter that the courts look at the expectations of the parties in the underlying contract when deciding whether an injunction should be granted. In the absence of a restrictive clause, the applicant is entitled to expect the beneficiary to act in good conscience. On the other hand, if the applicant agrees for a restrictive clause to be included in the contract, he expects and accepts that it may be possible that the beneficiary may act unconscionably, but he is voluntarily giving up his rights to be protected against bad behaviour by the grant of an injunction on this basis. The inclusion of a no-injunction clause does not necessarily mean that the beneficiary has an intention to behave unconscionably, or that it wishes to give itself the option of doing so. Having to defend injunction proceedings which may be ill-conceived wastes time and resources, and it is understandable that a beneficiary may wish to avoid being subject to this.

8.44 *Asplenium* gives useful insight into the way in which the Singapore courts approach their jurisdiction to grant injunctions as well their attitude towards balancing fairness with the party autonomy and commercial certainty. The decision is a very significant one. It means that where a 'no-injunction' clause is incorporated into the underlying contract, the applicant will not be able to restrain the beneficiary's call on the performance bond even if this is unconscionable, the only remaining ground of restraint being fraud. If the use of this type of

2 SLR 497 (CA) [37] that 'whether or not a clause is (or is not) reasonable under the UCTA would depend not only on the various factors enunciated in the UCTA itself as well as in the case law ... but also (and perhaps more importantly) on the precise facts of the case itself'.

[117] *CKR Contract v Asplenium* (n 103) [23].

clause becomes widespread (which is a likely scenario, given that beneficiaries, who typically have more bargaining power, will favour it), the unconscionability exception may gradually lose its relevance in Singapore. However, a no-injunction clause of this type might not be as successful in other jurisdictions where the rule against unconscionability is a statutory one, depending on whether one is allowed to contract out of the relevant provision.

The use of this type of clause has potentially wider consequences than merely displacing the unconscionability exception. Because of the way in which the clause in *Asplenium* was drafted, the application for an injunction based on any ground other than fraud was excluded. This meant that other exceptions, such as the grant of an injunction to restrain the beneficiary from calling on the bond in breach of the underlying contract, as well as future exceptions that might be established or developed, were also excluded.[118] The effect of a clause such as the one in *Asplenium* is that fraud will have to be shown if an applicant is to be successful in obtaining an injunction in these other situations. **8.45**

VI. Change of Circumstances: Frustration and Force Majeure

The COVID-19 pandemic has led to increased awareness of the issues that might arise if obligations that are guaranteed by performance bonds are affected by frustration or force majeure. This section discusses whether the courts in the UK and Singapore might grant an injunction to restrain call on a performance bond by a beneficiary in a situation where the applicant is unable to perform its obligations in the underlying contract due to a change in circumstances; and also the potential effect of government action on the grant of such injunctions. **8.46**

A. General Principles

Whether the applicant has breached the underlying contract, or at least, whether the beneficiary believes that the applicant has done so, is crucial to the availability of an injunctive remedy. Non-performance would normally constitute a breach of contract, unless the non-performing party has a lawful excuse. Under the common law, a change in circumstances will excuse the applicant from its duty to perform if the underlying contract is frustrated (this is difficult to show),[119] or if the new situation falls within a force majeure clause which has the effect of releasing a party from its contractual obligations, either temporarily or permanently (this depends on the drafting and construction of the clause).[120] **8.47**

[118] Depending on what newly-established exception to the autonomy principle is asserted in a particular case, a clause that restricts an applicant from seeking an injunction restraining the beneficiary from calling on the bond on the basis of this new exception may not necessarily be enforceable. For example, if an illegality exception becomes established in the UK or in Singapore, it is not clear whether the courts will uphold a clause whereby the applicant contracts out of the ability to restrain illegal conduct. On the uncertain state of the illegality exception in the UK, see Enonchong, *Independence Principle* (n 5) paras 8.14–8.21.

[119] See Chen-Wishart, *Contract Law* (n 115); Andrew Phang and Goh Yihan, *Contract Law in Singapore* (Kluwer Law International 2012) ch 2; Burton Ong and Benjamin Wong, *Contract Law in Singapore: Cases, Materials and Commentary* (Singapore Academy Publishing 2019) ch 4.

[120] See generally Guenter Treitel, *Frustration and Force Majeure* (3rd edn, Sweet & Maxwell 2014).

8.48 Applying the doctrine of autonomy, the performance bond is separate from the underlying contract, and the bank has a duty to honour the call on the bond if a complying demand is made, regardless of what happens in the underlying contract. But would this still be the case if the underlying contract is frustrated, or the applicant is released from its obligations by a force majeure clause? Frustration discharges both parties from the contract, whereas the consequences of force majeure will depend on the provisions of the force majeure clause. If the contract has clearly been frustrated or performance has clearly been excused by a force majeure event, one could argue that it would be at least unconscionable, and possibly also fraudulent, for the beneficiary to call on the performance bond, and an injunction is likely to be ordered in these circumstances. However, the situation is rarely so clear cut. At the time of the call on the bond, the contracting parties would usually not have had the benefit of a judicial or arbitral ruling. They may not be sure whether the underlying contract has been frustrated or whether a force majeure clause has been activated.

B. Frustration

8.49 The law of frustration operates within narrow limits. In order for a contract to be frustrated, the performance of the obligation must be radically different from the performance that had been undertaken by the parties.[121] The courts in both the UK and Singapore have made it clear that the fact that performance of the contract has become more onerous or less profitable will not cause a contract to be frustrated.[122] In normal circumstances, if a performance bond guarantees proper performance of the seller's obligations under a sale contract, and the seller anticipates that the goods will be shipped from a certain port, but that port is closed, even if the seller claims that the contract has been frustrated, the buyer is likely to argue that the goods could still have been shipped through a different port. However, an event of the scale of the COVID-19 pandemic that has devastated countries across the globe, where transport, labour, and business activities are severely disrupted, is likely to make performance of the contract truly impossible and therefore be found to be a frustrating event. A contract would also be frustrated if performance becomes illegal,[123] which would be the case, for instance, if performance would contravene government regulations introduced to manage the pandemic. It may be that in the most obvious cases where it is clear that the contract cannot be performed, the court might find that the beneficiary did not honestly believe that the applicant was in breach of contract, and a call on the bond will be restrained as being fraudulent, or at least unconscionable; but this will usually not be the case. Whether a contract is frustrated is a matter of law, and it is difficult for the parties to be sure whether frustration has taken place until the courts have decided on the

[121] See the widely accepted UK House of Lords case, *Davis Contractors Ltd v Fareham Urban District Council* [1956] AC 696 (HL) 729 where Lord Reid stated: '[F]rustration occurs whenever the law recognises that without default of either party a contractual obligation has become incapable of being performed because the circumstances in which performance is called for would render it a thing radically different from that which was undertaken by the contract.'

[122] *Tsakiroglou & Co Ltd v Noblee Thorl GmbH* [1962] AC 93 (HL); *National Carriers Ltd v Panalpina (Northern) Ltd* [1981] AC 675 (HL); *Glahe International Expo AG v ACS Computer Pte Ltd* [1999] 1 SLR(R) 945 (CA); *Oversea-Chinese Banking Corp Ltd v Daewoo Singapore Pte Ltd* [2000] 2 SLR(R) 161 (HC).

[123] *Fibrosa Spolka Akcyjna v Fairbairn Lawson Combe Barbour Ltd* [1943] 1 AC 32 (HL).

matter. A beneficiary should, therefore, be able to justifiably call on the bond regardless of the applicant's assertions that the contract has been frustrated.[124]

C. Force Majeure

The uncertainty of the doctrine of frustration can be avoided by inserting a force majeure clause into a contract, providing for the obligations of the parties if an unexpected event happens that is outside their control. The relevant force majeure events and their consequences depend on how the clause is drafted. For example, the contract may provide that the obligations of the parties are to be suspended for a certain period, or that they are to enter into negotiations for an amicable settlement, or simply that the obligations will come to an end. Force majeure clauses are subject to interpretation, and it may not be clear whether a certain event falls within its scope. For instance, if the clause applies to acts of God, followed by a list of specific examples like floods, earthquakes, and typhoons, and does not include mention of virus outbreaks, it is not clear if a virus pandemic would be covered by the clause. It would be difficult for the applicant to show a strong prima facie case that the beneficiary had no honest belief that it was entitled to call on the bond, unless the relevant event is one that obviously fell within the force majeure clause and was the cause of the applicant's inability to perform. Obtaining an injunction based on the unconscionability exception is not necessarily easier, because calling on a bond when there is a genuine dispute whether the applicant's failure to perform is excused under the force majeure clause does not indicate sharp practice or a lack of bona fides. It would seem difficult to obtain an injunction based on either exception. **8.50**

Min Thai Holdings Pte Ltd v Sunlabel Pte Ltd ('*Min Thai*'),[125] a case that came before the High Court in Singapore, involved a force majeure situation. The seller of rice from China procured a performance guarantee that was payable to the buyer if the seller defaulted on delivering the rice within an agreed schedule. The seller gave notice that it was unable to deliver the rice on time because of severe flooding in China, to an extent that the country had not experienced in the last 100 years, and that this inability fell within the force majeure clause in the sale contract. The clause provided that a party was not liable for a failure to perform any of his obligations if he could prove that the failure was due to an impediment beyond his control.[126] Events such as 'floods' were explicitly identified as being included within the meaning of 'impediment'. The buyer nevertheless called on the performance guarantee. It asserted that due performance of the contract was not excused by the floods and typhoons, as the areas from which the rice was to be supplied were not affected and the seller was still able to source the rice. The High Court ordered the continuance of an interim injunction that had earlier been granted to restrain the buyer from receiving any money **8.51**

[124] A related question, beyond the scope of the discussion in this chapter, is whether the performance bond will itself be frustrated if the underlying contract is frustrated.

[125] *Min Thai Holdings Pte Ltd v Sunlabel Pte Ltd* [1998] 3 SLR (R) 961 (HC) (hereafter *Min Thai v Sunlabel*).

[126] The requirements for the operation of the force majeure clause in the underlying contract were that the party who was unable to perform must prove that the failure was due to an impediment beyond his control; that he could not reasonably be expected to have taken the impediment and its effects upon his ability to perform into account at the time; and that he could not reasonably have avoided or overcome it or at least its effects: see *Min Thai v Sunlabel* (n 125) [10].

under the guarantee. The Court found that it was unconscionable for the beneficiary to receive payment under the performance bond as there were serious issues to be tried between the parties, such as whether the contract was affected by force majeure and also whether the force majeure clause applied.[127]

8.52 The *Min Thai* decision requires further analysis. If indeed there were serious issues to be tried between the parties, this would seem to be precisely the situation in which a performance bond is needed, so that the beneficiary could be paid while waiting for the dispute to be settled. The question arises whether there are different expectations between the parties when the reason for non-performance is allegedly a force majeure event (rather than some other reason), which would require the beneficiary to wait until the dispute was settled before claiming on the bond. There was nothing in the reported judgment which pointed specifically to such different expectations in the *Min Thai* case.

8.53 Some guidance may be obtained from another Singapore case, *China Resources (S) Pte Ltd v Magenta Resources (S) Pte Ltd* ('*China Resources*'),[128] although this was not a decision involving the grant of an injunction as the beneficiary had already been paid under the performance bond. The contract here was for the sale of 'prilled urea of USSR origin'. The buyer was unable to meet the first shipment date provided in the contract and notified the seller that it was invoking the force majeure clause in the sale contract, on the basis of the political turmoil in Russia. The Singapore Court of Appeal was satisfied that the breakup of the former USSR fell within the force majeure clause, which explicitly extended to situations such as 'war, military action . . . etc'. The Court was of the view that the collapse of the Soviet Union 'had caused so much uncertainty, tension and chaos in the territories of the former Soviet Union that it was a situation akin to war and was capable of being a *force majeure* situation' within the contemplation of the force majeure clause.[129] The Court found that the seller had shown that their inability to ship the urea was due to the force majeure situation, that they informed the buyer immediately of the force majeure, and that they produced certification of the event that complied with the requirements of the clause.[130] The Court's decision that the buyer should not have called on the bond was reinforced by the fact any dispute could have been settled in accordance with the arbitration clause. The contract also provided that, in the event that the force majeure continued for more than 120 consecutive days, the parties were to 'discuss through friendly negotiation as soon as possible their obligation to continue to perform under the terms and conditions of the contract'.[131] The Court found that there was 'no justification for the buyers peremptorily to call on the performance bond in the way they did'.[132] The Court concluded that the wrongful call was a clear a repudiation of the sale contract by the buyers, and the sellers were entitled to accept the repudiation and claim for damages and a refund of the amount that had been paid to the buyers under the performance bond.

[127] The seller appealed against this decision, but its appeal was dismissed by the Court of Appeal with no written grounds of decision rendered.
[128] *China Resources (S) Pte Ltd v Magenta Resources (S) Pte Ltd* [1997] 1 SLR(R) 103 (CA) (hereafter *China Resources v Magenta Resources*).
[129] ibid [35].
[130] ibid [35].
[131] ibid [42].
[132] ibid [42].

8.54 An important question in situations involving a force majeure clause is whether the parties intended that the beneficiary should be able to make a demand on the performance bond even though the applicant who is unable to perform seeks relief under the force majeure clause.[133] This will be a deciding factor in the court's decision whether an injunction should be granted to restrain the beneficiary from calling on the bond in these circumstances. Given that the main purpose of a force majeure clause is to allocate risks if one of the parties is unable to perform as a result of a disruptive external event, the parties in a contract may well have intended that the provisions of the force majeure clause should first be applied to decide the obligations of the parties, before the performance bond was called on. This interpretation of the parties' intentions will be strengthened if the force majeure clause prescribes dispute settlement mechanisms, such as for arbitration or negotiation, as was the case in *China Resources*. One potential danger of this interpretation from the beneficiary's point of view is that its protection under the performance bond may be thwarted if the applicant frivolously claims relief under the force majeure clause in order to excuse a delay in performance. However, this situation can be dealt with by the court, even at an interlocutory stage. In deciding whether to grant an injunction to restrain payment, the court can consider the genuineness of the applicant's assertion of force majeure when it is assessing whether the beneficiary was acting dishonestly or unconscionably in calling on the bond.

8.55 For the sake of greater clarity, it might be a good idea for contracting parties to make their intentions clear, and state whether the beneficiary is entitled to call on the performance bond in circumstances where the applicant has invoked relief under a force majeure clause, or whether the right to call on the bond is to be suspended until the procedures set out in the force majeure clause have been exhausted. If there is a clause in the underlying contract that expressly suspends the beneficiary's right to call on the bond when the applicant has claimed relief under a force majeure clause, there may be an additional ground to apply for an injunction if the beneficiary makes a call in contravention of the clause. In these circumstances, restraint may be obtained on the basis of a breach of the underlying contract.[134]

D. Government Action

8.56 While the operation of performance bonds has been relatively undisturbed by government actions in the past, this cannot be taken for granted, as the examples from the UK and Singapore arising from the COVID-19 pandemic illustrate.

8.57 In May 2020, the UK government published Guidelines to strongly encourage 'all individuals, businesses (including funders) and public authorities to act responsibly and fairly in the national interest in performing and enforcing their contracts, to support the response to Covid-19 and to protect jobs and the economy'.[135] The Guidelines requested responsible

[133] This question could be analysed from an alternative point of view, based on the notions of good faith that are being developed in the English courts, which might in time grow in importance to become an additional exception to the autonomy principle: see *Yam Seng Pte Ltd v International Trade Corp Ltd* [2013] EWHC 111 (QB) (hereafter *Yam Seng v ITC*). However, it is worth noting that in Singapore, good faith is already a component of the concept of unconscionability in relation to performance bonds, although it has not been accepted as a general principle of contract law.

[134] See the discussion in [8.36]–[8.38].

[135] UK Cabinet Office, 'Guidance on responsible contractual behaviour in the performance and enforcement of contracts impacted by the Covid-19 emergency' (7 May 2020) <https://assets.publishing.service.gov.uk/

behaviour in relation to various matters including requesting, and giving, relief for impaired performance in respect of time for delivery of goods and completion of works and services and the making of payments; requesting, and allowing, extensions of time; making, and responding to, force majeure or frustration claims; and 'exercising remedies in respect of impaired performance, *including ... calling of bonds or guarantees* ... (emphasis added)'.[136]

8.58 A relevant question is whether an applicant could succeed in obtaining an injunction if a beneficiary called on the bond without regard to the Guidelines. It would be unlikely to succeed under the fraud exception. It would be difficult to show that the beneficiary did not honestly believe that it was entitled to make a demand under the bond, merely by virtue of the fact that it did not behave according to the Guidelines, as these are non-statutory guidance with no mandatory effect. They are expressly stated not to be intended to override contractual provisions or the law.[137] The applicant may stand a better chance of obtaining an injunction based on the unconscionability exception (if this exception applied in the UK). But even if the beneficiary is not willing to make concessions or renegotiate the contract to accommodate the other party as requested by the Guidelines, this may not mean that it is acting in a manner that is lacking in bona fides so as to justify the grant of an injunction.[138]

8.59 An example of a different response to the COVID-19 pandemic was seen in Singapore, where there was legislation to impose a moratorium (initially for a period of six months) on certain acts in relation to specific types of contracts if parties were unable to perform their obligations due to COVID-19.[139] This legislation did not excuse a breach of contract by the non-performing party, but merely prevented the aggrieved party from taking certain actions in relation to the scheduled contracts, such as bringing or continuing a court action or arbitration proceedings against the non-performing party, or terminating the contract, during the period of relief.[140] There were specific provisions that applied to performance bonds given in the context of international trade. These provisions prohibited the call on any performance bond given in relation to construction or supply contracts at any time earlier than seven days before the date of expiry of the bond; or where the term of the performance bond had been extended, earlier than seven days before the expiry following such extension.[141] Such legislative intervention clearly affected the rights of beneficiaries, but like interim injunctions, they were temporary, designed to preserve the applicant's liquidity and allow it some lead time before the beneficiary could call on the bond. The beneficiary's right to call on the bond was postponed but not otherwise affected. A beneficiary who called on a performance bond in contravention of the statute would be liable for an offence, and

government/uploads/system/uploads/attachment_data/file/883737/_Covid-19_and_Responsible_Contractual_Behaviour__web_final___7_May_.pdf> [1]. This was updated on 30 June 2020: <https://assets.publishing.service.gov.uk/government/uploads/system/uploads/attachment_data/file/899175/__Update_-_Covid-19_and_Responsible_Contractual_Behaviour_-_30_June__final_for_web_.pdf> accessed 21 August 2020.

136 ibid [15].

137 ibid [6]–[7].

138 Whilst this is the position based on the beneficiary's strict legal rights, a different standard of behaviour may be required if obligations of good faith are implied into the contract: see *Yam Seng v ITC* (n 133).

139 COVID-19 (Temporary Measures) Act 2020, s 5 (No 14 of 2020) (hereafter 'COVID-19 (Temporary Measures) Act').

140 ibid s 5(2).

141 ibid s 6(2); ibid s 6(3) requires issuers, upon application by the applicant, to extend the term of performance bonds to a date that is seven days after the end of the prescribed period or such other date as may be agreed.

the call would be void.[142] Interestingly, there was no similar moratorium or prohibition in Singapore applying to documentary presentations under commercial LCs. Presumably, the thinking was that if a seller had shipped goods, he was entitled to be paid. This is consistent with the policy distinction between performance bonds and commercial LCs in the development of the unconscionability exception in Singapore.

VII. Limits of Unconscionability and No-Injunction Clauses

A. Unconscionability Not Applicable to Commercial LCs

Will the unconscionability exception come to be applied in commercial LC cases in Singapore in future, and should it be? This author's view is that it will not, and should not be. The policy reasons for the development of the unconscionability exception in Singapore are based purely on the nature of performance bonds and will not justify applying the same exception to commercial LCs. Commercial LCs have been regarded for hundreds of years as 'the lifeblood of international commerce'[143] and treated as 'cash in hand',[144] and interfering with payment under a commercial LC would be equivalent to interfering with the primary obligation of the debtor to make payment under its contract with the beneficiary. For these reasons, the Singapore courts have reiterated that 'payment under a letter of credit should not be disrupted or restrained by the court in the absence of fraud',[145] and the author would respectfully agree. This is, however, different from the situation in countries like Australia, where the unconscionability exception applies to both performance bonds and commercial LCs. **8.60**

B. Unconscionability only Applicable to Injunctions

Three common situations in which the fraud exception in performance bonds might be relevant, and the different legal rules that apply to each situation, were discussed earlier in this chapter.[146] In contrast, it can be argued that the unconscionability exception is of more limited application in Singapore, as the rationale behind the exception suggests that it will only apply in situations where the applicant applies for an injunction to restrain payment on a performance bond despite a conforming demand by the beneficiary. This argument is supported by the view that the Singapore courts developed the unconscionability exception 'because in certain circumstances, even where the account party could not show that the beneficiary had been fraudulent in calling on the bond, it would nevertheless be unfair for the beneficiary to realise his security *pending resolution of the substantive dispute*'.[147] On this view, the unconscionability exception would not be relevant for settling **8.61**

[142] ibid ss 8(1) and (4).

[143] This phrase was first used by Kerr J in *R D Harbottle v National Westminster Bank* (n 7) 155 and quoted in many cases thereafter.

[144] *Intraco Ltd v Notis Shipping Corporation (The 'Bhoja Trader')* [1981] 2 Lloyd's Rep 256 (CA) 257; quoted in *Chartered Electronics v DBS* (n 7) [32].

[145] *JBE Properties v Gammon* (n 75) [10].

[146] See discussion at para 8.08.

[147] *BSC v Boustead Singapore* (n 23) [104].

the final dispute between the parties. Nor, as was postulated by *Arab Banking Corp (BSC) v Boustead Singapore Ltd*,[148] would it be applicable where the substantive dispute under the primary contract had been finally resolved. In the latter situation, there would no longer be any question of whether it would be fair to allow the beneficiary to receive payment under the performance bond, and the only remaining question would be whether the beneficiary is entitled to such payment.[149] Extrapolating from this, the unconscionability exception will not apply where the beneficiary is suing the bank for non-payment or where the bank is seeking reimbursement from the applicant after paying the beneficiary on the performance bond.

C. Excluding the Fraud Exception?

8.62 *Asplenium* confirmed that a beneficiary can enforce a clause in the underlying contract which prevents the applicant from applying for an injunction to restrain a call on the performance bond on grounds other than fraud. It is interesting to contemplate the parameters of this type of clause. In particular, would a clause that prevents the applicant from restraining a call on a performance bond based on the fraud exception be upheld by courts in Singapore or elsewhere? The possibility of a clause excluding an application for an injunction based on fraud was neither mentioned nor analysed in the *Asplenium* case. It has been suggested that indirect support for the position that a clause restricting a call on a bond on the basis of fraud would not be enforceable may be found in the principle that exclusion clauses would not naturally be construed to exclude liability for fraud.[150] However, this argument, based on the proper construction of exclusion clauses, is not squarely applicable in a situation where there is an express clause that prohibits injunctions based on the fraud exception. A direct argument would be that a contractual clause prohibiting the application for an injunction even where there is fraud will itself offend public policy because of the inherent egregious nature of fraud, and therefore be unenforceable. However, even if a clause excluding fraud was found not to be contrary to public policy, it is likely to fail at the next hurdle, which is that it must be found to be reasonable under UCTA.[151] On the other hand, if we return to the rule established in *Asplenium*, that the effect of this type of clause is to exclude a remedy, a contrary argument would be that a clause excluding the applicant from seeking the equitable remedy of an injunction based on the fraud exception may not be entirely objectionable as the applicant might still be able to seek other remedies to obtain redress for the beneficiary's fraud. Despite the theoretical arguments about whether a clause related to fraud would

[148] ibid.
[149] ibid.
[150] See Lau, 'Injunctive Relief' (n 105) 475, where the case of *Regus (UK) Ltd v Epcot Solutions Ltd* [2008] EWCA Civ 361 is discussed.
[151] It has been suggested that the fraud rule is part of international public policy and cannot be contracted away: Matti S Kurkela, *Letters of Credit and Bank Guarantees Under International Trade Law* (OUP 2008) 181. For arguments that it might be possible to contract out of the fraud exception in the context of commercial LCs, see Hare, 'On Autonomy' (n 6) 23–4. For the proposition that a contracting party cannot exclude liability for fraudulent misrepresentation, see *HIH Casualty General Insurance Ltd v Chase Manhattan Bank* [2003] 2 Lloyd's Rep 61 (HL) [16], [24], [76], [121], [122]. In *Jiang Ou v EFG Bank AG* [2011] 4 SLR 246 (HC), the High Court in Singapore indicated that it would be unreasonable under UCTA for a bank to use a verification clause to exclude liability for the fraud of its employee.

be enforceable, it would seem most unlikely that a clause to this effect would find its way into many contracts. Such a clause is likely to cause the relationship between the parties to start off badly, and also will hardly be necessary given how difficult it is to obtain an injunction based on the fraud exception.

VIII. Conclusion

Whether the courts of a particular jurisdiction should intervene to issue injunctions to restrain unconscionable calls on performance bonds is a policy decision. The relative ease of making conforming demands on performance bonds makes them potentially oppressive instruments. The traditional fraud exception is very difficult to establish and provides insufficient protection from abusive calls. The unconscionability exception supplements the traditional fraud exception to help better balance the interests of the applicant and the beneficiary. Such intervention will not erode confidence in the use of performance bonds as commercial instruments if the discretion to grant injunctions is exercised sparingly. On the contrary, this could inculcate a culture of integrity in the use of performance bonds. Although the concept of unconscionability is not susceptible to exact definition, this flexibility is also its strength and judges in established legal systems should be well equipped to adjudicate on the issue of unconscionability in a wide range of situations. Where the applicant claims that it should be excused from non-performance as the underlying contract has been frustrated or affected by a force majeure event, and the beneficiary nevertheless calls on performance bond, it may be difficult to assess whether the beneficiary was acting dishonestly or unconscionably. Particularly where force majeure is concerned, it may not be clear if the parties intended the beneficiary to be able to call on the bond after notice of force majeure had been given by the applicant. To avoid uncertainty, it would be useful to add a clause in the underlying contract providing for this situation. **8.63**

The practice relating to the grant of injunctions to restrain calls on performance bonds in Singapore reflects many of the features mentioned in the paragraph above. The Singapore courts have stated that the threshold of unconscionability that had to be established before a court would grant an injunction restraining call on a bond was a high one. An injunction would be granted only if the entire context of the case was 'particularly malodorous', and the applicant was able to show a strong prima facie case of unconscionability, which should not be easy to do.[152] A noteworthy development in Singapore is the use of a clause in the underlying contract where the applicant agrees not to seek an injunction to restrain a call on the performance bond except on the ground of fraud, thereby ruling out an application on the basis of unconscionability. The fact that this type of clause has been upheld by the Singapore courts reflects their policy of balancing the interests of the parties. The use of this type of clause would result in less protection for the applicant, but as it had voluntarily agreed to this, the principle of freedom of contract would generally apply. **8.64**

152 *BS Mount Sophia v Join-Aim* (n 52) [21].

PART II
TRADE FINANCE TECHNOLOGY

Whilst the previous part considered some of the difficulties that have dogged documentary trade finance, Part II looks to the future. Given the technological advances that have occurred since the advent of the documentary letter of credit, the former is increasingly threatening to eclipse the latter. In a sector where ease, speed and cost-effectiveness are prized, it is unsurprising that technological solutions to perennial trade finance problems are attracting renewed interest. That said, attempts to digitize trade finance are not novel. Over the years, there have been numerous (usually unsuccessful) initiatives in this direction. Most notable is the International Chamber of Commerce's attempt to update the UCP regime with the e-UCP, which has simply not gained the traction that many had expected. The reasons why the achievements have never really matched the desire in the trade finance sector are threefold. First, it is simply not possible to digitize trade finance until trade documents, namely bills of lading, bills of exchange and cargo insurance documents, can be created, transferred and stored electronically. Without this step, any solution will still involve moving bundles of paper around the world. Secondly, the trade finance community will simply not move towards the digitization of trade documents until there is an effective legal framework guaranteeing that electronic data are as reliable as, and equivalent to, paper-based documents. In this regard, digitization will not happen until the legal framework can provide enough assurance to a sufficiently large portion of the trade finance sector. Thirdly, there seems little point spending the time and effort developing a legal framework until there is a technological framework capable of dealing with the requirements for digital trade. Technological know-how appears to have reached that point. These three concerns are addressed in Part II and, although there remains scope for healthy scepticism about the ability of technology to transform trade finance overnight, there are a series of more modest market-based, legal and technological developments that incrementally and cumulatively may take trade finance into its digital future.

9

The Electronic Bill of Exchange and Its Use in International Trade

*Benjamin Geva**

I. Introduction

9.01 In an international sale of goods, the seller typically draws a bill of exchange ('bill') payable to itself. The seller 'discounts' the bill by indorsing it to its bank ('the remitting bank') for value received in the form of immediate provisional credit to the seller's account. The remitting bank then forwards the bill for presentment to the drawee. In a typical case, the drawee is either the buyer or the buyer's bank. In such a situation, the presenting bank is usually the buyer's bank. Where the drawee is a bank, the remitting bank could act as the presenting bank. Otherwise, the itinerary from the remitting bank to the presenting bank could pass through intermediary bank(s), each indorsing the bill to the next one for value. Any bank involved in the collection, other than the remitting bank (but including the presenting bank), is a collecting bank. Where the bill is payable at a future time, so that it is a 'term draft', the drawee who accepted the bill may return it to the presenting bank, which can then continue to negotiate it for value. Where the drawee/acceptor is the buyer, the instrument is a trade acceptance. Where the drawee/acceptor is a bank, it is a bank acceptance. Either way, on the due date, the drawee pays the bill to the holder and money moves back to the remitting bank, at which point the credit to the seller's account finalises. Conversely, if the bill is dishonoured, the presenting bank may either attempt to enforce it against the acceptor (if the bill has been accepted) or return the bill backward towards the remitting bank, which will in turn reverse the provisional credit previously given to the seller.

9.02 Bills remain important in international trade because they are both payment and credit instruments, while also providing assistance in the facilitation of liquidity. At the same time, in international trade - and, in fact, always between distant parties to a sale transaction - the physical transportation of bills from place to place may be slow, not completely safe, and certainly inefficient. However, a bill must be something tangible, on which words could be written so as to create a permanent tangible record, and physically deliverable from hand to hand in order to confer and acquire rights thereon.

9.03 The chapter does not endeavour to propose a uniform law recommended for all jurisdictions to adopt. Rather, it discusses revisions for domestic laws designed to move the law of negotiable instruments to the electronic age. Nor does the chapter address changes to

* For research assistance in the final preparation of the manuscript I am grateful to Damian Lu, Alexander Davis, and Simona Ristic of Osgoode Hall Law School.

conflict of laws rules—other than pointing at the functional equivalents for existing requirements premised on paper-based environment such as signature and delivery.

9.04 The chapter thus discusses various aspects of the electronification of bills. Section II presents the legal requirements for both written and electronic formats as either applied or as may be applied to bills. Section III addresses the electronic presentment of a paper bill. Section IV deals with the legal status of a substitute paper bill created out of an electronic image. Section V analyses the handling of an electronic image of a bill. Section VI focuses on a bill created and evolving electronically. Section VII addresses the option of having bills either in paper or electronic format immobilised by means of a deposit to a clearing house where they are to be transferred by means of making appropriate entries in its records. The concluding observation of section VIII is that it is both desirable and feasible for the law to accommodate not only an electronic bill but also the potential conversion of a physical bill to an electronic one and vice versa in the life of one such an instrument.

II. Physical and Electronic Formats for Bills: Legal Requirements

9.05 The following provisions of the UK's Bills of Exchange Act 1882[1] ('BEA') support the conclusion that a bill must be something tangible, on which words could be written so as to create a permanent tangible record, and physically deliverable from hand to hand in order to confer and acquire rights thereon. To begin with, under section 3(1) of the BEA:

> (1) A bill of exchange is an unconditional order in writing, addressed by one person to another, signed by the person giving it, requiring the person to whom it is addressed to pay on demand or at a fixed or determinable future time a sum certain in money to or to the order of a specified person, or to bearer.

9.06 'Written' is defined in section 2 to 'include . . . printed' and 'writing' to 'include . . . print.' This is a non-exhaustive definition, which is arguably expanded by another non-exhaustive definition in schedule 1 to the Interpretation Act 1978,[2] under which:

> 'Writing' includes typing, printing, lithography, photography and other modes of representing or reproducing words in a visible form . . .

9.07 With respect to the requirement of a signature, section 91 of the BEA provides:

> (1) Where, by this Act, any instrument or writing is required to be signed by any person it is not necessary that he should sign it with his own hand, but it is sufficient if his signature is written thereon by some other person by or under his authority.
> (2) In the case of a corporation, where, by this Act, any instrument or writing is required to be signed, it is sufficient if the instrument or writing be sealed with the corporate seal.

9.08 A creative interpretation might treat words in a permanent record that are 'visible' on a computer screen as satisfaction of the writing requirements.[3] To that end, the signature

[1] UK Bills of Exchange Act 1882 (hereafter BEA).
[2] UK Interpretation Act 1978.
[3] Leif Gamertsfelder, 'Electronic Bills of Exchange: Will the Current Law Recognize Them?' (1998) 21 University of New South Wales Law Journal 566.

requirement is not drafted so as necessarily to be limited to a handwritten one. However, several other provisions militate against any attempt to bypass the requirement that a bill must be written on a tangible item.

For example, a 'bearer', to whom a bill may be payable, is defined in section 2 of the BEA to 'mean ... the person in possession of a bill or note which is payable to bearer'. Otherwise, under section 3(1) of the BEA, which is reproduced above, a bill is payable 'to the order of a specified person,' namely the 'payee'. For his or her part, under section 2 of the BEA, 'the payee or indorsee of a bill or note who is in possession of it, or the bearer thereof' is termed the 'holder.' According to the same provision,[4] 'indorsement' means an indorsement completed by delivery; 'issue' means the first delivery of a bill or note, complete in form to a person who takes it as a holder; and 'delivery' in turn means transfer of possession, actual or constructive, from one person to another. **9.09**

Furthermore, according to BEA, s 21(1), with the exception of the acceptance, '[e]very contract on a bill, whether it be the drawer's, the acceptor's, or an indorser's, is incomplete and revocable, until delivery of the instrument in order to give effect thereto' and, under BEA, s 31, '[a] bill is negotiated when it is transferred from one person to another in such a manner as to constitute the transferee the holder of the bill';[5] '[a] bill payable to bearer is negotiated by delivery';[6] and 'a bill payable to order is negotiated by the indorsement of the holder completed by delivery'.[7] **9.10**

Finally, BEA, s 52(4) provides that '[w]here the holder of a bill presents it for payment, he shall exhibit the bill to the person from whom he demands payment, and when a bill is paid the holder shall forthwith deliver it up to the party paying it'. **9.11**

Needless to say, in the present electronic age, the adequacy and fitness of a method of payment and credit premised on writing and delivery has been questioned. Way back in 1985, at the dawn of electronic funds transfers ('EFTs'), Peter Ellinger wrote a seminal article in which he purported to review 'two questions ... linked to the making of deferred payment undertakings by means of EFT networks'.[8] The first was concerned with the feasibility of such arrangements at that time. The second concerned 'the future of negotiable instruments in light of the advent of EFTs'. At the time of his article, Peter Ellinger identified the latter question as 'a plan for the future'.[9] **9.12**

Indeed, then and now, it has been possible for a customer to authorise its bank to either pay or collect on designated dates. Hence, the crux of the issue has been the second question - namely the desirability of, or need for (as well as the feasibility of), an electronic negotiable instrument. Peter Ellinger was hesitant as to the desirability of, or need for, an electronic negotiable instrument, as he doubted that the operation of the bills market 'in London and elsewhere ... [was] so defective as to call for an expensive and fundamental reform'.[10] As for **9.13**

[4] BEA (n 1) s 2.
[5] ibid s 31(1).
[6] ibid s 31(2).
[7] ibid s 31(3).
[8] Peter Ellinger, 'Electronic Funds Transfer as a Deferred Settlement System', in R M Goode (ed), *Electronic Banking: The Legal Implications* (London: The Institute of Bankers and Centre for Commercial Law Studies of Queen Mary College University of London 1985) 29 (hereafter Ellinger, 'Electronic Fund Transfers').
[9] ibid (n 8) 29 (all cites in this paragraph).
[10] ibid 44.

its feasibility, he was of the opinion that it may 'be possible to create' or dispatch 'a bill of exchange or promissory note by the use of an EFT network'.[11] However, he concluded that:[12]

> Once such an instrument reached its destination it would have to be treated as a document. To be used as a negotiable instrument, it would have to be transferred by indorsement and delivery; it would have to be presented for acceptance and for payment, and if dishonoured, might have to be protested.... The true question is whether such instrument may be replaced altogether by deferred payment EFTs of a negotiable character. Such an EFT would then be produced, transmitted, transferred and retired through the relevant network.

9.14 To that end, Peter Ellinger identified four legal problems or objections.[13] The first is that 'a bill ... embodies a string of contracts,' each undertaken by a successive party. The second is the requirement of delivery or physical transferability. The third is that 'a negotiable instrument constitutes an item of property' for whose ownership possession may be required 'and not just a string of contracts'. The fourth objection is 'procedural', relating to requirements such as presentment and protest that require physical handling of the instrument.

9.15 'Electronification'—namely, the elimination of physical processing and delivery—will enhance efficiency and speed. While it introduces its own risks (such as hacking), the chance is that, particularly if proper technology is used, electronification will also enhance security and reduce errors. Accordingly, at this point in time, a strong case can be made for the desirability of bringing the negotiable instrument into the ambit of electronic banking as much as possible.[14] The four issues raised by Peter Ellinger relate to two points. First, the perceived incompatibility among the hardware systems required for the negotiable instrument to evolve from its issue, indorsement, acceptance, presentment, and protest. Second, the legal requirements as to the tangible nature of the instrument. As for the first point, technology has made enormous headway, so far translated into projects relating to cheques. As for the second, the law need not remain static and ought to be adjusted to changing circumstances.

9.16 One area in which 'signature' and 'delivery' play a fundamental role is in the conflict of laws rules applicable to bills of exchange. In principle, according to BEA, s 72, '[w]here a bill drawn in one country is negotiated, accepted, or payable in another', both the validity 'as regards requisites in form' and 'interpretation' of the contract on a bill is determined by reference to the law of the place where the contract is made. As for the identification of such a place, '[t]he mere signature does not make a contract. To constitute a contract on an instrument there must be a delivery over the instrument by the

[11] ibid 39.
[12] ibid.
[13] ibid 41–43 (from which all cites in this paragraph are taken).
[14] Arguments in support of such a move have been floating for quite a long time. See, eg James A Newell and Michael R Gordon, 'Electronic Commerce and Negotiable Instruments (Electronic Promissory Notes)' (1995) 31 Idaho Law Review 819; Gonzalo Villata Puig, 'Electronic Bills of Exchange and Promissory Notes in Australia' (2000) 7 Murdoch University Electric Journal of Law 27. For recommending caution (due to security concerns) while still recognising that '[n]o one can resist progress', see Anastasia Tsakatoura, 'E-finance—bills of exchange, promissory notes, documentary credits, forfaiting' (*Lex E-Scripta*, 22 June 2002) <http://www.inter-lawyer.com/lex-e-scripta/articles/e-finance1.htm> accessed 04 February 2021; cf Jianhong Fan and Yang Tao, 'Negotiable Instruments, in Particular Bills of Exchange in Macau, China' (2007) 2 Journal of Commercial Law and Technology 83, where the authors indicate that drafting 'a complete electronic negotiable instruments law was deemed premature' in Macau.

[signer] for a good consideration: and as soon as these circumstances take place the contract is complete'.[15] In the United States, §214 of the Second Restatement of the Law of Conflicts of Laws[16] provides that the law of the place of delivery determines the obligations of a drawer and indorser and the law of the place of payment determines the obligations of the acceptor. For its part, article 4(1) of the Convention for the Settlement of Certain Conflicts of Laws in Connection with Bills of Exchange and Promissory Notes,[17] like the US Restatement, states that '[t]he effects of the obligations of the acceptor of a bill . . . are determined by the law of the place in which these instruments are payable'. At the same time, article 4(2) provides that '[t]he effects of the signatures of the other parties liable on a bill . . . are determined by the law of the country in which is situated the place where the signatures are affixed'. Hence, to establish certainty for the law that will govern the electronic bill, functional equivalents to both 'signature' and 'delivery' must be formulated.

A preliminary question is whether UNCITRAL Model Law on Electronic Commerce[18] ('LEC') does not provide a framework for addressing the issue at hand. Thus, according to article 5, '[i]nformation shall not be denied legal effect, validity or enforceability solely on the grounds that it is in the form of a data message' and, under article 6(1), '[w]here the law requires information to be in writing, that requirement is met by a data message if the information contained therein is accessible so as to be usable for subsequent reference'. Furthermore, article 7(1) goes on to provide that:[19] **9.17**

> Where the law requires a signature of a person, that requirement is met in relation to a data message if:
>
> (a) a method is used to identify that person and to indicate that person's approval of the information contained in the data message; and
> (b) that method is as reliable as was appropriate for the purpose for which the data message was generated or communicated, in the light of all the circumstances, including any relevant agreement.

Finally, article 8 goes on to provide that: **9.18**

> (1) Where the law requires information to be presented or retained in its original form, that requirement is met by a data message if:

[15] *Abrey v Crux* (1869) LR 5 CP 37, 42.

[16] Restatement (Second) of Conflict of Laws 1971 (US).

[17] Convention for the Settlement of Certain Conflicts of Laws in Connection with Bills of Exchange and Promissory Notes, 7 June 1930, 143 LNTS 319 (entered into force 1 January 1934).

[18] *UNCITRAL Model Law on Electronic Commerce with Guide to Enactment 1996*, GA Res 51/162, UNCITRAL, UN Doc A/51/628 (1998) <http://www.uncitral.org/pdf/english/texts/electcom/V1504118_Ebook.pdf> accessed 04 February 2021 (hereafter *Model Law on Electronic Commerce*).

[19] To that end, see also the following provisions of *UNCITRAL Model Law on Electronic Signatures with Guide to Enactment 2001*, GA Res 56/80, UNCITRAL, UN Doc A/56/588 (2001) <http://www.uncitral.org/pdf/english/texts/electcom/ml-elecsig-e.pdf> accessed 04 February 2021 (hereafter *Model Law on Electronic Signatures*) art 2(a) of the *Model Law on Electronic Signatures* states: '"Electronic signature" means data in electronic form in, affixed to or logically associated with, a data message, which may be used to identify the signatory in relation to the data message and to indicate the signatory's approval of the information contained in the data message.' According to art 6(1), '[w]here the law requires a signature of a person, that requirement is met in relation to a data message if an electronic signature is used that is as reliable as was appropriate for the purpose for which the data message was generated or communicated, in the light of all the circumstances, including any relevant agreement.'

(a) there exists a reliable assurance as to the integrity of the information from the time when it was first generated in its final form, as a data message or otherwise; and
(b) where it is required that information be presented, that information is capable of being displayed to the person to whom it is to be presented.

...

(3) For the purposes of subparagraph (a) of paragraph (1):
(a) the criteria for assessing integrity shall be whether the information has remained complete and unaltered, apart from the addition of any endorsement and any change which arises in the normal course of communication, storage and display; and
(b) the standard of reliability required shall be assessed in the light of the purpose for which the information was generated and in the light of all the relevant circumstances.

9.19 According to the Guide to Enactment of the UNCITRAL Model Law on Electronic Commerce,[20] '[a]rticle 8 is pertinent to ... negotiable instruments, in which the notion of uniqueness of an original is particularly relevant'. Accordingly, this statutory framework resolves any doubt not only as to the mere possibility of an electronic bill but also as to its possible compliance with the 'writing' and 'signature' requirements as well. However, this statutory framework does not address the issues pertaining specifically to negotiable instruments, including bills of exchange, such as possession and delivery. True, a sympathetic court could treat exclusive control of the electronic bill as the equivalent of possession and the irrevocable electronic transmission as tantamount to physical delivery; nonetheless, this approach may not be adequate to accommodate the diverse requirements governing the electronification of bills.

9.20 Regrettably, negotiable instruments are excluded from the coverage of *the United Nations Conventions on the Use of Electronic Communications in International Contracts (2007).*[21] The drafters observed that 'issues raised by negotiable instruments ... in particular the need for ensuring their uniqueness, go beyond simply ensuring the equivalence between paper and electronic forms'[22] so that 'special rules would need to be devised' to resolve 'the particular difficulty of creating an electronic equivalent of paper-based negotiability'.[23] They thus concluded that 'finding a solution for this problem requires a combination of legal, technological and business solutions, which had not been fully developed and tested'.[24]

9.21 Accordingly, the useful starting point for the 'electronification' of bills of exchange in particular is UNCITRAL's Model Law on Electronic Transferable Records ('LETR').[25]

[20] *Model Law on Electronic Commerce* (n 18) [63].
[21] See *United Nations Convention on the Use of Electronic Communications in International Contracts*, 23 November 2005, art 2(2) <https://www.uncitral.org/pdf/english/texts/electcom/06-57452_Ebook.pdf> accessed 04 February 2021 (hereafter *UN Convention on the Use of Electronic Communications*).
[22] See Explanatory Notes to *UN Convention on the Use of Electronic Communications* (n 21) 35.
[23] ibid 14.
[24] ibid 35.
[25] *Model Law on Electronic Transferable Records*, GA Res 72/114, UNCITRAL, UN Doc A/72/458 (2017) <http://www.uncitral.org/pdf/english/texts/electcom/MLETR_ebook.pdf> accessed 04 February 2021 (hereafter *UNCITRAL Model Law on Electronic Transferable Records*). See further the discussion in ch 11 (Davidson) of this volume.

Ironically, a footnote to article 1(3) leaves open the possibility of excluding bills from what otherwise seems to be a proper framework for the creation and transfer of an electronic bill. Thus, under article 2 of the LETR, an 'electronic record' is defined to mean 'information generated, communicated, received or stored by electronic means'. According to article 10(1), this then becomes an 'electronic transferable record', when:

(a) [It] contains the information that would be required to be contained in a transferable document or instrument; and
(b) A reliable method is used:
  (i) to identify that electronic record as the electronic transferable record;
  (ii) to render that electronic record capable of being subject to control from its creation until it ceases to have any effect or validity; and
  (iii) to retain the integrity of that electronic record.

Pursuant to article 8, a legal writing requirement is satisfied where the information contained in an electronic transferable record 'is accessible so as to be usable for subsequent reference' and, under article 9, a legal signature requirement is met 'if a reliable method is used to identify that person and to indicate that person's intention in respect of the information contained in the electronic transferable record'. According to article 11, 'possession' is satisfied by the exclusive control of the transferable record and consequently a transfer of control is tantamount to the transfer of delivery. Finally, for our purposes, under article 15, an 'endorsement' requirement is met where the required information 'is included in the electronic transferable record' and 'is compliant with the requirements set forth in articles 8 and 9' as to writing and signature. **9.22**

Starting from this perspective, the ensuing discussion as to the need for statutory and regulatory changes is however inspired primarily by legislative innovations made in the US focusing on the cheque, being a bill of exchange drawn on a bank and payable on demand.[26] The cheque experience teaches us that it is too simplistic to deal with the issues at hand as involving a choice between the physical or electronic bill, or even, as to whether an electronic bill can be accommodated by law while still retaining all the features of a negotiable instrument. Rather, the infinite number of participants spread throughout the globe and their diverse stage of technological development militates against the feasibility of a common, universal, and worldwide technological platform. Hence, the law ought to accommodate not only the possibility of an electronic bill but also the potential conversion of a physical bill to an electronic one and vice versa in the life of such an instrument. **9.23**

It is noteworthy that a deferred EFT in the form of electronic Deferred Payment Undertaking ('DPU') already exists as a payment and credit instrument in international trade. However, the DPU is also known as a Deferred Payment Credit ('DPC') and has been used in lieu of an accepted bill in a letter of credit transaction, particularly with the view of avoiding stamping requirements on bills.[27] In *Banco Santander v Banque* **9.24**

[26] See BEA (n 1) s 73 and UCC § 3–104, cl (f) ('Check' is defined as 'a draft . . . payable on demand and drawn on a bank', and 'draft' is defined in § 3–104(e), by reference to § 3–104(a), being the same as a bill of exchange).

[27] See John F Dolan, 'Negotiable Obligations for Discount: Notes, Acceptances, DPUs and BPOs' (2013) 29 Banking & Finance Law Review 103; André Casterman, 'Modernising Global Trade Finance Practices' (2012) 6 Journal of Payments Strategy & Systems 225; International Chamber of Commerce, 'Bank Payment Obligation' <http://icc.tobb.org.tr/docs/Bank%20Payment%20Obligation.pdf> accessed 04 February 2021; Mohd Hwaidi, 'The Implications of *Banco Santander v Bayfern Ltd* on Deferred Payment under Documentary Credit in UCP

Paribas,[28] when the issuing bank's DPU's fell due, having taken an assignment of proceeds from the beneficiary upon a complying documentary presentation (so as to effectively discount the issuing bank's DPC and prepay the beneficiary), the confirming bank was refused reimbursement by the issuing bank on the basis of the beneficiary's fraud. The Court of Appeal upheld the issuing bank's defence, thereby treating it as a mere assignee of the credit's proceeds and not in the position of a holder in due course.

9.25 UCP 600[29] purported to overrule *Banco Santander* by providing in article 12(b) that 'by nominating a bank to . . . incur a deferred payment undertaking, an issuing bank authorizes that nominated bank to prepay or purchase . . . a deferred payment undertaking incurred by that nominated bank'. Article 7(c) goes even further by providing that 'an issuing bank undertakes to reimburse a nominated bank that has honoured or negotiated a complying presentation and forwarded the documents to the issuing bank. Reimbursement for the amount of a complying presentation under a credit available by . . . deferred payment is due on maturity, whether or not the nominated bank prepaid or purchased before maturity. An issuing bank's undertaking to reimburse a nominated bank is independent of the issuing bank's undertaking to the beneficiary.' In the United States, UCC § 5–109(a)(1) is to the same effect:

> (a) If a presentation is made that appears on its face strictly to comply with the terms and conditions of the letter of credit, but a required document is forged or materially fraudulent, or honour of the presentation would facilitate a material fraud by the beneficiary on the issuer or applicant:
>
> (1) the issuer shall honour the presentation, if honour is demanded by (i) a nominated person who has given value in good faith and without notice of forgery or material fraud, (ii) a confirmer who has honoured its confirmation in good faith, (iii) a holder in due course of a draft drawn under the letter of credit which was taken after acceptance by the issuer or nominated person, or (iv) an assignee of the issuer's or nominated person's deferred obligation that was taken for value and without notice of forgery or material fraud after the obligation was incurred by the issuer or nominated person.

9.26 However, at the most, these provisions provide limited negotiability on a DPU in favour of a nominated bank in a letter of credit transaction. Neither full negotiability nor negotiability outside this specific letter of credit context is envisaged.

600' (2011) 5 International Business Law Journal 569; Klaus Vorpeil, 'Bank Payment Obligations: Alternative Means of Settlement in International Trade' [2014] International Business Law Journal 41; Koji Takahashi, 'The Introduction of Article 12(b) in the UCP 600: Was it Really a Step Forward?' [2009] Journal of International Banking Law and Regulation 285; Carlo R W de Meijer and Manoj Menon, 'Bank Payment Obligation: The Missing Link?' (2012) 6 Journal of Payments Strategy & Systems 232; Giovanni Profazio, and Jason Chuah, 'An Analysis of Acceptance and Deferred Payment Credits in Civil and Common Law' (2007) 13 Journal of International Maritime Law 330; and Alan L Tyree, 'Deferred Payment Letters of Credit' (2013) 24 Journal of Banking and Finance Law and Practice 66.

28 [2000] All ER (D) 246 (CA).

29 International Chamber of Commerce, 'Uniform Customs and Practice for Documentary Credits' (ICC Publication No 600, 2007) (hereafter 'UCP 600').

In contrast, this chapter, even as it focuses on international trade, is designed to address the issue of negotiability for electronic bills in a comprehensive way as a matter of the law of negotiable instruments. Its argument is premised on the enhanced role of party autonomy, provided by the quickening pace of innovative technological developments, that must be accommodated by reformed harmonised national laws. It is written with the view of enhancing the potential of the existing framework within which international trade finance has been conducted. **9.27**

III. Electronic Presentment of a Bill

Electronic presentment is provided for in the US by UCC § 4–110. Thereunder, the presentment of an 'item' may be made pursuant to an interbank agreement for presentment. 'Item' is defined in UCC § 4–104(a)(9) to mean 'an instrument or a promise or order to pay money handled by a bank for collection or payment'. This is broader than a cheque and hence may be taken to apply to bills as well. **9.28**

Under UCC § 4–110, '[a]greement for electronic presentment' could be in the form of an agreement, clearing-house rule, or Federal Reserve regulation or operating circular.[30] The agreement is to provide 'that presentment ... may be made by the transmission of an image of an item or information describing [it] ... rather than delivery of the item itself'. The transmission of the image or information constitutes a 'presentment notice'; its receipt is the actual presentment. Other elements that may be covered by the agreement for electronic presentment are 'procedures governing retention ... payment, dishonor and other matters ... '. Arguably, return procedures fall within the ambit of the agreement. An interbank voluntary agreement may be either bilateral or multilateral.[31] In any event, as per the language quoted above, 'agreement for electronic presentment' under UCC § 4–110 may not **9.29**

[30] See, eg Collection of Checks and Other Items By Federal Reserve Banks and Funds Transfers through Fedwire, 12 CFR § 210 (1980) (hereafter 'Regulation J'), defining 'item' in § 210.2(i) to include 'electronic item,' such as an electronic image of a cheque or any other paper item. See also Federal Reserve Banks, *Collection of Cash Items and Returned Checks* (Operating Circular No 3, 01 January 2019) <https://www.frbservices.org/assets/resources/rules-regulations/010119-operating-circular-3.pdf> accessed 09 February 2021, in which electronic access to the Reserve Bank's cheque services is governed by Section 5 and Appendices E (MICR Presentment Services), E1 (Truncation Service), E2 (MICR Presentment Plus Service), and E3 (Basic MICR Presentment Service). The Board recently proposed to delete the definition of 'electronic item' and revise the definition of 'item' in § 210.2(i) to include a cheque and an electronic cheque, defined in Regulation CC. A companion amendment would clarify that the term 'item' does not include an electronically-created item. See further: Board of Governors of the Federal Reserve System, *Collection of Checks and Other Items by Federal Reserve Banks and Funds Transfers Through Fedwire*, 83 Fed Reg 11431 (2018) <https://www.federalregister.gov/documents/2018/03/15/2018-04486/collection-of-checks-and-other-items-by-federal-reserve-banks-and-funds-transfers-through-fedwire> accessed 09 February 2021. The Board's proposal came into force with the implementation of the final rule: *Collection of Checks and Other Items by Federal Reserve Banks and Funds Transfers Through Fedwire*, 83 Fed Reg 61509 (2019) <https://www.federalregister.gov/documents/2018/11/30/2018-25267/collection-of-checks-and-other-items-by-federal-reserve-banks-and-funds-transfers-through-fedwire> accessed 09 February 2021.

[31] One such multilateral agreement is under the rules of the cheque truncation program of the National Automated Clearing House Association ('NACHA') for electronic images of truncated cheques placed into the Automated Clearing House ('ACH') Network. Cheque truncated items placed into the ACH Network are TRC/TRX entries referred to as a category of Payment Applications in NACHA Operating Guidelines s 1(2)(c) (as well as in Section (C)(3) of the 'ACH Primer' preceding the NACHA Operating Rules) and are governed by NACHA Operating Rules, art 10. See also the NACHA Check Safekeeping Guidelines and Rules.

be entirely consensual; however, this is in line with UCC § 4–103(b), under which 'Federal Reserve regulations and operating circulars, clearing-house rules, and the like have the effect of agreements ... whether or not specifically assented to by all parties interested in items handled'.

9.30 Similarly, in the UK, BEA, s 89A(1) deals with presentment of instruments by electronic means. Thereunder, 'presentment for payment of an instrument ... may be effected by provision of an electronic image of both faces of the instrument, instead of by presenting the physical instrument, if the person to whom presentment is made accepts the presentment as effective'. According to BEA, s 89B(1), excluding banknotes, section 89A applies to:

(a) a cheque, or
(b) any other bill of exchange or any promissory note or other instrument—
  (i) which appears to be intended by the person creating it to enable a person to obtain payment from a banker indicated in it of the sum so mentioned,
  (ii) payment of which requires the instrument to be presented, and
  (iii) which, but for section 89A, could not be presented otherwise than by presenting the physical instrument.[32]

9.31 BEA, s 89B(1)(b)(i) covers not only a bill drawn on a banker, but also any bill payable at a bank regardless on whom it is drawn. It thus covers a trade acceptance drawn on a buyer, as long as it 'appears to be intended by the person creating it to enable a person to obtain payment from a banker.' Perhaps a broader provision may be required in the BEA, allowing the transmission of an electronic image to any party who agreed to receive an electronic presentment. Under another proposed amendment, the presenter ought to be taken to warrant that the image sent accurately represents the bill, as well as undertake to indemnify any person who suffered loss as a result of not presenting the original bill.

9.32 A drawee ought to be entitled to transmit back its acceptance to the presenting bank on an electronic image. The drawee will then be taken to make all warranties and incur all indemnification liabilities made and incurred by the drawer of an electronic bill, as discussed further in section VI below.

9.33 For their part, the ICC's uniform rules for the collection of bills in international trade[33] address the issue of 'presentation', being under article 5(a), 'the procedure whereby the presenting bank makes the documents available to the drawee as instructed'. However, form of presentation is not provided for and thus the general law, as discussed above, applies with regards to bills.[34]

[32] BEA (n 1) s 89E(1) provides for compensation in cases of presentment by electronic means 'for any loss of a kind specified by the regulations'.

[33] *Uniform Rules for Collections* (1995 Revision, ICC Publication No. 522, 1995) <https://www.law.kuleuven.be/personal/mstorme/URC522.pdf> accessed 09 February 2021 (hereafter 'URC 522').

[34] Regardless, albeit by reference to the earlier (1979) version of the URC, according to Sam Maduegbuna in 'The Collection of Bills in International Trade' (1993) 8 Banking & Finance Law Review 155, 161–62: '[i]t is doubtful ... whether the rules bind a drawee or importer, because the rules are incorporated neither into the bill nor into the underlying contract between the exporter and importer. Besides there is no practical advantage in the rules binding on the importer... [who] is not a party to the contract of collection ...'.

IV. The Substitute Paper Bill

An elaborate statutory and regulatory scheme providing for the 'substitute check', replacing an electronic image of the original cheque, exists in the US under the Check Clearing for the 21st Century Act ('Check 21 Act'),[35] which has been implemented by Regulation CC.[36] In essence, the Check 21 Act authorises a collecting bank[37] to create a substitute cheque,[38] being a paper reproduction of the original cheque, for further negotiation or presentment. Having agreed to receive a cheque in an electronic form, a collecting bank that received the electronic cheque image or information is authorised under the Check 21 Act to create a substitute cheque. Upon compliance with specified requirements, the substitute cheque is to become 'the legal equivalent of an original check for all persons and all purposes'.[39] The Check 21 Act further includes warranty and indemnity provisions.[40] 9.34

In practice, the creation of a substitute cheque by a collecting bank is predicated upon the existence of two preconditions. First, the creating bank must have received the transmission of an image of the original cheque instead of the cheque itself. The sender of that transmission will be a customer, the holder of the cheque (in which case the creating bank is the depositary bank in the chain), or a prior collecting bank (in which case the creating bank is an intermediary bank). Second, the bank receiving the substitute cheque, being either a collecting/intermediary bank or the drawee bank, must not have agreed to accept electronic transmission of an image, which would likely be the case for a small bank that does not have the required processing equipment. 9.35

Stated otherwise, the Check 21 Act does not require banks to accept electronic transmission of cheque information or image. Rather, it authorises a collecting bank that agreed to accept the electronic transmission, whether from its customer or a prior collecting bank, to issue a substitute cheque, to be processed onward as if it were the original cheque. A bank, whether a subsequent collecting/intermediary bank or the drawee bank, must accept the substitute cheque as the equivalent of the original cheque. By the same token, a customer who received original cheques with the periodic statement, cannot object to receiving substitute cheques in lieu of original cheques that have been so truncated in the collection process.[41] 9.36

By truncating paper cheques, the Check 21 Act eliminates the long-distance transportation of the physical cheques, though it does not eliminate or bypass intra-city or local 9.37

[35] Check Clearing for the 21st Century Act, 12 USC § 5001 (2003) (hereafter Check 21 Act).

[36] Subpart D of Availability of Funds and Collection of Checks, 12 CFR § 229 (2017) (hereafter Regulation CC).

[37] In the cheque collection process, a collecting bank is every bank other than the drawee or payor bank.

[38] An explicit purpose of the Check 21 Act was '[t]o facilitate check truncation by authorizing substitute checks'. See Check 21 Act (n 35) § 2(b)(1).

[39] ibid § 4(b). See also Regulation CC (n 36) § 229.51(a).

[40] For a comprehensive overview, though written prior to the promulgation of the final text for subpart D of the Regulation CC, see Paul S Turner, *Analysis of the Check Clearing for the 21st Century Act* (LexisNexis 2004) (hereafter Turner, *Check 21*) For more on the background to the Check 21 Act, see *Availability of Funds and Collection of Checks*, 69 Fed Reg 1470 (2004); *Availability of Funds and Collection of Checks*, 69 Fed Reg 47290 (2004); Federal Reserve, *Press Release* (26 July 2004) <https://www.federalreserve.gov/boarddocs/press/bcreg/2004/20040726/default.htm> accessed 09 February 2021; Federal Reserve, *Press Release* (22 October 2004) <https://www.federalreserve.gov/boarddocs/press/bcreg/2004/20041022/default.htm> accessed 09 February 2021.

[41] An agreement of the recipient is dispensed with for a substitute cheque deposited, presented, sent for collection, or returned, 'so long as a bank has made the warranties in section 5 with respect to such substitute check': see Check 21 Act (n 35) § 4(a).

transportation. The following hypothetical example will demonstrate the circumstances governed by the Check 21 Act. Suppose a drawer has a bank account with a payor bank in New York. The drawer sends a cheque drawn on that account to the payee in California, who deposits the cheque in his or her account with a Californian depositary bank. The latter is a large institution that has equipment for the transmission of the image of the cheque. At the same time, the payor bank is a small institution that does not have processing equipment capable of receiving the electronic transmission of a cheque. There is nothing in the UCC, the Check 21 Act, or any other instrument, to force the payor bank to accept electronic transmission; hence, electronic presentment is not an option for the depositary bank. Rather, the depositary bank may transmit the image of the cheque to an intermediary bank in New York, which is capable of accepting such transmission.[42] In effect, this is an electronic negotiation of the cheque. Having agreed to accept the electronic transmission, the New York intermediary bank is now required under the Check 21 Act to create a paper substitute cheque. The Act further requires the payor bank to accept the presentment of the substitute cheque as if it were the original cheque. Finally, any requirement, either by statute or agreement, to provide the cancelled cheque, as under the contract between the drawer and the payor bank, is to be satisfied under the Check 21 Act by providing the substitute cheque.

9.38 A substitute cheque is a paper production of the original cheque that contains the image of that cheque's front and back; the substitute also bears a MICR (Magnetic Ink Character Recognition) line containing the information appearing on the MICR line of the original cheque, and conforms, particularly in paper stock, dimension, and otherwise, with generally applicable industry standards for substitute cheques. It must be suitable for automated processing in the same manner as the original cheque.[43] To be the legal equivalent of the original cheque, a substitute cheque must 'accurately represent ... all of the information on the front and back of the original check as of the time the original check was truncated' and bear the legend: 'This is a legal copy of your check. You can use it the same way you would use the original check.'[44]

9.39 As in the example above, a substitute cheque is typically created by a collecting intermediary bank. However, it can also be created by the depositary bank, where it has agreed to receive the deposit of the cheque from the payee/holder by means of electronic transmission. Furthermore, a substitute cheque may even be created by the payee/holder. For example, such would be the case for a large organisation that receives cheques in various locations, but would prefer to deposit them in one place. The organisation may then arrange for the electronic transmission of cheque images to one place where substitute cheques will be created for deposit. Alternatively, through the use of a mobile device, even an individual may transmit a cheque image to a depositary bank. In general, a cheque could be transformed

[42] Interbank settlement between the Californian depositary bank and the New York intermediary bank may take various forms. For example, it may be either bilateral (on a correspondent account one bank has with the other), or part of multilateral clearing house settlement. If the cheque is collected through the Reserve Banks, settlement will take place on the books of the Reserve Banks. Check 21 Act does not deal with interbank settlement arrangements.

[43] Check 21 Act (n 35) § 3(16) implemented by Regulation CC (n 36) § 229.2(aaa).

[44] ibid § 4(b); Regulation CC (n 36) § 229.51(a).

from electronic form to substitute-cheque form several times throughout the course of the collection and return process.

One can attempt to derive from the above discussion of the Check 21 Act the provisions that should be included in a (future) statute governing the electronic transmission (effectively, negotiation) of an electronic image of a bill to a collecting bank and the procedures that should be followed. That proposed statute should define a substitute bill as a paper production of the original bill that contains the image of the front and back of the original bill. The proposed statute should further provide that the substitute bill should: (i) conform, particularly in paper stock, dimension, and otherwise, with generally applicable industry standards for substitute bills, and (ii) be suitable for automated processing in the same manner as the original bill.[45] As well, under the proposed statute, in order to be the legal equivalent of the original bill, a substitute bill must 'accurately represent . . . all of the information on the front and back of the original [bill] as of the time the original [bill] was truncated' and bear an appropriate legend identifying it as a legal copy of the original bill.[46] **9.40**

In connection with a substitute bill, the proposed statute should also provide for warranties and an indemnity. The warranties should be, first, that the substitute bill meets the requirements for legal equivalence, and second, against double payment on the original bill or any other representation of it.[47] The indemnity should be 'to the extent of any loss incurred . . . due to the receipt of a substitute [bill] instead of the original [bill]'. Other than for costs, expenses, and reasonable attorney's fees, the amount to be indemnified is to the extent of loss proximately caused by the breach of warranty. In the absence of a breach of a warranty, the amount of any indemnity is limited though to the amount of the substitute bill. Either way, the amount of loss to be indemnified ought to be reduced by an amount representing any loss resulting 'from the negligence or failure to act in good faith on the part of an indemnified party'.[48] An example of loss incurred notwithstanding the lack of any breach of warranty is the case where forgery, proof of which would have allowed a purported signer to avoid liability, cannot be proved on the substitute bill, but allegedly could have been proved on the original. Thus, an effective method to determine the authenticity of a manual signature is by measuring the pen pressure input by the signer. This feature does not carry over to the copy of the bill and certainly not to a substitute cheque created from the image of the bill. **9.41**

The proposed statute should provide that substitute bill warranties are to be given by each bank 'that transfers, presents, or returns a substitute [bill] and receives consideration for the [bill]'. In turn, indemnity liability should be incurred by '[a] reconverting bank and each bank that subsequently transfers, presents, or returns a substitute [bill] in any electronic or paper form, and receives Page 1–69 (Rel 22) consideration for such transfer, presentment, or return . . . '.[49] A 'reconverting bank' should be defined as the bank that creates the substitute bill or, where the substitute bill is created by the indorser to the remitting bank, the first bank that transfers or presents the substitute bill, namely, the remitting bank.[50] Arguably, **9.42**

[45] Check 21 Act (n 35) § 3(16), implemented by Regulation CC (n 36) § 229.2(aaa).
[46] cf ibid § 4(b); Regulation CC (n 36) § 229.51(a) (legend to appear on a substitute cheque).
[47] Check 21 Act (n 35) § 5; Regulation CC (n 36) § 229.52(a).
[48] Check 21 Act (n 35) § 6. See also Regulation CC (n 36) § 229.53.
[49] Check 21 Act (n 35) §§ 5 and 6 respectively. See also Regulation CC (n 36) §§ 229.52 and 229.53 respectively.
[50] Check 21 Act (n 35) § 3(15).

having been listed as a party liable to indemnify for loss caused by the breach of warranty, the reconverting bank ought also to be listed as one of the warrantors.[51]

9.43 The proposed statute should further provide that both substitute bill warranties and the indemnity are to be stated to run to the benefit of the transferee, any subsequent collecting or returning bank, the remitting bank, the drawee, the drawer, the payee and any indorser.[52] Since a bill could be transformed from electronic form into a substitute bill several times in the course of the collection and return process, it is possible that there could be multiple substitute bills, and thus multiple reconverting banks, with respect to the same payment transaction. A subsequent participant may thus benefit from the warranties and indemnities of more than one reconverting bank. As well, a remitting bank receiving an electronic representation of a substitute (rather than original) bill will both receive and pass on the reconverting bank's warranty and indemnity protections.

9.44 The proposed statute might also cover the unusual case where a paper bill is drawn to a payee's, and not the drawer's order, and it is the payee (or any subsequent holder) who converts it into an electronic image transmitted to the remitting bank.[53] In such a case, in the footsteps of Regulation J,[54] a sender of an electronic bill derived directly from the original paper bill is to make for it two sets of warranties. To begin with, the first set covers the transfer warranties that apply as if the electronic bill were a paper bill governed by bills of exchange law. Under English law, this corresponds to precluding the sender from denying what falls under the transfer warranties in the UCC.[55] The second is a warranty that applies as if the electronic bill were a substitute bill. Accordingly, to cover the case where an electronic image has been created from an original bill that was deficient in some respect, an end-to-end combined liability structure is provided.[56]

9.45 Finally, the proposed statute ought to explicitly authorise transacting with the substitute bill by indorsement and otherwise. While this derives from the legal equivalency principle, it is important to be explicit in asserting that such legal equivalency is dynamic and not static, so that it is not limited to the status of the bill as it was originally converted.

[51] The reconverting bank can hardly be described as a 'bank that transfers ... a substitute check', unless 'transfer' is to include the first delivery or issue; this indeed appears to be the view of the Federal Reserve: see Regulation CC (n 36) Appendix E to Part 229, XXXI(A)(1), which states that 'the reconverting bank starts the flow of warranties when it transfers, presents, or returns a substitute check . . .'. The reference in the Check 21 Act (n 35) § 5 (a provision that does not purport to cover the reconverting bank, which is separately referred to in § 6) to '[a] bank that transfers', as opposed to 'each bank that subsequently transfers' as in § 6, re-enforces this interpretation; yet, the Act would have been clearer had it distinguished between the issue of a substitute cheque and its subsequent transfer.

[52] Check 21 Act (n 35) §§ 5 and 6 respectively.

[53] Where the sender is the drawer or payee, the bill is originally created electronically, a situation addressed in section V of this chapter.

[54] Regulation J (n 30) §§ 210.2–210.6 and 210.12.

[55] Transfer warranties are provided under UCC § 4-207, roughly corresponding to the indorser's preclusions under BEA (n 1) s 55(2).

[56] For background on Regulation J (n 30), see *Collection of Checks and Other Items by Federal Reserve Banks and Funds Transfers Through Fedwire*, 69 Fed Reg 62553 (2004) and Federal Reserve Bank of New York, 'Final Amendment to Regulation J: Collection of Checks and Other Items', Circular No 11653 (25 October 2004) <https://www.newyorkfed.org/banking/circulars/11653.html> accessed 09 February 2021.

V. Interbank Negotiation and Exchange of Bill Images

In the US, there are three principal sets of interbank image exchange rules. Essentially, each endeavours to equate the position of cheque images to that of the cheques themselves under existing legislation and other sources of law. In fact, they extend the legal framework of Check 21 Act[57] to cover image exchanges. The first set of image exchange rules is contained in subpart A of Regulation J,[58] governing interbank exchange through Federal Reserve Banks. Further implemented by Operating Circular No 3, it specifically deals with the collection of cheques and other items by Federal Reserve Banks. Thereunder, an 'item' is broadly defined to cover a cheque, including one in an electronic format.[59] While it is not limited to cheques, it does not extend beyond items collected by Federal Reserve Banks. **9.46**

The second set is contained in the Electronic Check Clearing House Organization ('ECCHO') Rules.[60] ECCHO is 'a national not-for-profit "rule-making organization" owned entirely by its member banks'.[61] ECCHO was established in 1990 primarily to address the increased risk resulting from the introduction of tight funds availability schedules for cheques under Regulation CC.[62] The use of electronics expedited both the forward presentment and return processes, so as to allow banks to meet the tight statutory schedules. The organisation has five membership classes (Full Members, Affiliate Members, Participating Members, Associate Members, and Sponsored Members), which reflect variations in Members' roles in the corporate governance of the organisation. A Member must establish the technological and communication methods for exchanging electronic cheque transactions with another Member. As 'an association of banks or other payors regularly clearing items', ECCHO is a clearing house under UCC § 4–104(a)(4) even though it does not process payments at all. Rather, it develops rules governing electronic exchanges of cheque images. Such rules qualify as 'clearing-house rules' under UCC § 4–103(b) and govern bilateral and multilateral exchanges of member banks which choose to adhere to them. According to that provision, 'all parties interested in' the cheques are bound by such rules governing their exchange. Accordingly, while the ECCHO Rules do not constitute customer agreements, they bind customers a by virtue of UCC § 4–103(b). **9.47**

The ECCHO Rules provide the legal framework for both forward presentment and return of an electronic cheque, being the image and related information derived from the paper cheque. The ECCHO Rules do not apply to the substitute cheques that reproduce cheque images. Substitute cheques, and to some extent electronic cheques derived from substitute cheques, are governed by the Check 21 Act[63] and the provisions of subpart D of Regulation CC[64] implementing it. The ECCHO Rules govern only electronic cheque **9.48**

[57] Check 21 Act (n 35).
[58] Regulation J (n 30) § 210.
[59] ibid § 210.2(i)(1)(ii) in conjunction with § 210.2(h).
[60] The text below draws in large part on the ECCHO Rules Summary of July 2018 (of which a copy is in the author's hands) as well as on the content from the ECCHO website <https://www.eccho.org/> accessed 10 February 2021. The earlier version of the ECCHO Rules Summary is that of December 2016 and is available online: https://www.eccho.org/cc/rules/Rules%20Summary_December-2016-2.pdf accessed 10 February 2021. See also Viveca Y Ware, *Check Image Exchange: Covering Legal Bases* (The Independent Community of Bankers of America 2008).
[61] Alvin C Harrell, 'Electronic Checks' (2001) 55 Consumer Finance Law Quarterly Report 283.
[62] Regulation CC (n 36).
[63] Check 21 Act (n 35).
[64] Regulation CC (n 36).

transactions between two Members. A Member is not required, by virtue of its membership to send and receive electronic cheque transactions with another Member. The 2012 ECCHO Rule summary specifically addressed Member agreements, sometimes referred to as Banking Practice Agreements ('BPAs') that may designate a particular electronic-communication switch or a cheque-image archive to exchange electronic cheque images. Such agreements, that may also establish a 'bridge' or link between private networks/archives, are outside the ECCHO framework. While supporting a number of processes for cheque-image exchange, ECCHO Rules do not establish the rules for accessing or using private networks/archives.

9.49 Under the ECCHO Rules, the cheque itself is not sent to the receiving Member. In turn, Page 1–73 (Rel 22) states that the electronic cheque is an 'item', as well as a 'check', under the UCC and Regulation CC.[65] ECCHO Rules also provide for the time and manner in which presentment is actually made and further address diverse matters such as indorsements, as well as storage and retrieval of the original cheque. To protect the receiving Member in each electronic cheque transaction, the ECCHO Rules provide for indemnifications, but rely on electronic cheque warranties provided under Regulation CC, discussed below. An additional warranty and related indemnity as to the compliance with ECCHO Rules are specifically provided.[66]

9.50 The third principal set of interbank image exchange rules governs the regulatory framework in the US covering the exchange of cheque images under Regulation CC.[67] Following a proposal of the Federal Reserve Board ('Board') from 2013,[68] the final version of § 229.30(a) (dated 15 June 2017 and effective on 1 July 2018)[69] states that unless otherwise agreed by the sending and receiving banks,[70] electronic images of cheques and electronic information related to cheques that banks send and receive by agreement would be subject to subpart C of Regulation CC as if they were paper cheques. Accordingly, a bank that transfers or presents for value an electronic cheque and electronic returned cheque, each defined in § 229.2(ggg) as 'an electronic image of, and electronic information derived from, a paper check or paper returned check, respectively,' gives all the cheque warranties and indemnities.[71] According to § 229.34(a)(1), which is effective from 1 July 2018,

[65] ibid.

[66] Prior to July 2018, there were additional warranties as to the accuracy and quality of the image as well as against double payment, all of which is now provided by Regulation CC (n 36).

[67] Regulation CC (n 36).

[68] *Availability of Funds and Collection of Checks*, 79 Fed Reg 6673 (2014) (to be codified at 12 CFR § 229) <https://www.federalregister.gov/articles/2014/02/04/2013-30024/availability-of-funds-and-collection-of-checks> accessed 09 February 2021 (hereafter 'FRS Availability Proposal').

[69] *Availability of Funds and Collection of Checks*, 82 Fed Reg 27552 (2017) (to be codified at 12 CFR § 229) <https://www.federalregister.gov/documents/2017/06/15/2017-11379/availability-of-funds-and-collection-of-checks> accessed 09 February 2021 (hereafter *Availability of Funds and Collection of Checks*).

[70] FRS Availability Proposal (n 68) would permit a sending and receiving bank to vary, by agreement,the warranties the sending bank makes to the receiving bank for electronic cheques and electronic returned cheques. Such an agreement could provide, for example, that the bank transferring the electronic cheque does not warrant that the electronic image or information are sufficient to create a substitute cheque. The agreement would not, however, vary the effect of the warranties with respect to banks and persons not bound by the agreement: see FRS Availability Proposal (n 68) 6684.

[71] Under the revised Regulation CC (n 36) § 229.34(c), (d), and (e), such warranties relate to (i) the settlement amount, encoding, and offset; (ii) returned checks; and (iii) notice of non-payment.

additional 'Check-21-like warranties'[72] are specifically given with respect to electronic cheques and electronic returns:

> Each bank that transfers or presents an electronic check or electronic returned check and receives a settlement or other consideration for it warrants that—
>
> (i) The electronic image accurately represents all of the information on the front and back of the original check as of the time that the original check was truncated and the electronic information includes an accurate record of all MICR line information required for a substitute check ... and the amount of the check, and
>
> (ii) No person will receive a transfer, presentment, or return of, or otherwise be charged for an electronic check or electronic returned check, the original check, a substitute check, or a paper or electronic representation of a substitute check such that the person will be asked to make payment based on a check it has already paid.

This provides a double warranty for not only the accuracy and completeness of the electronic record, but also against double payment of the cheque. For the purposes of this double warranty, § 229.34(a)(2) provides that the beneficiary is '[in] Page 1-75 (Rel. 22) the case of transfers for collection or presentment, the transferee bank, any collecting bank, the paying bank, and the drawer' and '[i]n the case of transfers for return, the transferee returning bank, any subsequent returning bank, the depositary bank, and the owner'.[73] **9.51**

Such a scheme governing the exchange and indorsement of cheque images could be made to apply to bill images. Under such a proposed scheme, images of electronic bills are to be treated as bills or bill substitutes for the purpose of both forward collection and return. The computer program underlying the proposed scheme could be made to facilitate the transmission of an encrypted version of the imaged 'bill' to which the 'handwritten' drawer's and indorser's signatures—both made on a trade acceptance by the seller of the goods, as well each successive indorsement—are attached. The double warranty for the accuracy and completeness of the electronic record and against double payment are to be given by each sender. **9.52**

The key to the proposed scheme is legal equivalency in the electronic world for acts and situations existing in the paper-based world. However, in the final analysis, practically speaking, legal equivalency works best when it goes hand in hand with technological feasibility: it is only where technology facilitates the change of control of the electronic image from one person to the other that legal equivalency of the image can work. In the alternative situation, in which parallel control remains in a sender's hands, warranties and indemnities against double payments are as good to the recipient as the creditworthiness of the sender that gives them. **9.53**

[72] *Availability of Funds and Collection of Checks* (n 69), as originally proposed in the FRS Availability Proposal (n 68) 6683.

[73] The Board requested comment on whether the drawer (under sub-paragraph (i)) or owner (under sub-paragraph (ii)) should be required to make a claim against his or her bank before making a breach of warranty claim against a prior collecting bank. The Final Rule and its Commentary neither mentions nor reflects any such comment.

VI. Electronic Bill (EB) as 'Paperless Bill'

9.54 Broadly speaking, in the absence of a statutory (or other precise) definition, an electronically issued payment order that otherwise has all the characteristics of a cheque and is treated as a 'paperless cheque' is known as an 'Electronic Payment Order' ('EPO')[74] or 'Electronic Cheque'.[75] Like a paper cheque,[76] an EPO is issued by the drawer/payer and is addressed to the drawee/payor bank, ordering it to pay on demand a sum certain in money to the payee (or bearer), to whom the order is issued. This is both feasible technologically and efficient economically: it is indeed said that as an equivalent to a cheque, the EPO possesses features such as 'speed, finality, relatively low cost, and ubiquity'.[77]

9.55 Certainly, the same can be said about the 'electronic bill' ('EB'). A software bill program can create a visual image of both the front and the back of the 'bill' and take a screenshot of the image. The program could then transmit to the remitting bank an encrypted version of the imaged 'bill' to which the 'handwritten' drawer's and indorser's signatures, both the seller of the goods ('seller'), are attached. The program could further facilitate the successive indorsements and the acceptance on the bill. However, in the absence of an existing comprehensive statutory, as well as regulatory, framework, private agreements are required to fill the gap and determine legal issues involving the EB. A natural inclination is to resort to the UCC (or BEA), as well as the Check 21 Act. The passage of a comprehensive statute in that direction is thus highly recommended.

9.56 Purporting to address the collection of EPOs,[78] the Board noted that not being derived from an original paper cheque, an electronically-created cheque image cannot be used to create a substitute cheque that meets the requirements of the Check 21 Act and Regulation CC. The Board, however, observed that as a practical matter, a collecting bank receiving an electronically-created cheque image cannot distinguish it from an image of a paper cheque that it receives electronically. Such a bank may transfer the image as if it were derived from a paper cheque or produce a paper item that is indistinguishable from a substitute cheque. Under the proposed revision to § 229.34 of Regulation CC, a bank that transfers an image

[74] On the 'Electronic Payment Order' ('EPO'), see eg Katy Jacob et al, Federal Reserve Bank of Chicago Financial Markets Group, *Digital Checks as Electronic Payment Orders* (Policy Discussion Paper Series, PDP 2009-5, 2009) <http://www.chicagofed.org/digital_assets/publications/policy_discussion_papers/2009/PDP2009-5.pdf> accessed 09 February 2021; Mary Kepler, 'A Summary of the Electronic Payment Order Forum' (Federal Reserve Bank of Atlanta 2013) <http://www.frbatlanta.org/documents/rprf/rprf_pubs/130521_summary_paper.pdf> accessed 09 February 2021 (hereafter Kepler, 'Summary of the EPO Forum'); 'EPO: The Next Frontier of a Check' (ECCHO 2017) <https://www.eccho.org/wordpress/wp-content/uploads/ECIfinal.pdf> accessed 09 February 2021; Phyllis Meyerson, 'Electronic Payment Orders (EPOs)' (ECCHO 17 June 2013).

[75] See *Availability of Funds and Collection of Checks* (n 69) 27579, § 229.2(ggg): 'Electronic check and electronic returned check mean an electronic image of, and electronic information derived from, a paper check or paper returned check, respectively, that—(1) Is sent to a receiving bank pursuant to an agreement between the sender and the receiving bank; and (2) Conforms with ANS X9.100–187, unless the Board by rule or order determines that a different standard applies or the parties otherwise agree.'

[76] 'Paper-check' (as defined in UCC § 3–104(f) in conjunction with UCC §§ 3–103(a)(8) and 3–104(e)) is used in this section in the sense of a 'check' in order to distinguish it from the EPO.

[77] Kepler, 'Summary of the EPO Forum' (n 74).

[78] *Availability of Funds and Collection of Checks*, 76 Fed Reg 16862 (2011) (to be codified at 12 CFR § 229) <https://www.federalregister.gov/documents/2011/03/25/2011-5449/availability-of-funds-and-collection-of-checks> accessed 09 February 2021. Note that these proposed amendments were implemented with the final rule of *Availability of Funds and Collection of Checks* (n 69) (effective since 1 July 2018).

in the collection system would make all warranties that the bank would make if the image were derived from a paper cheque.

Since the source of the electronic image is unknown, the Board proposed that a bank receiving a warranty claim relating to an electronic collection item, electronic return, or a nonconforming substitute cheque, would be able to pass back its liability for the item to the bank from which it had received the electronically-created image and information. Although the first bank to make the warranty may also be unaware of whether an image or information came from a paper instrument, the Board nevertheless expressed its view that that bank is in the best position to know and protect itself contractually against the risk. Indeed, the warranty given is that the appearance of an electronic image conforms with that of the physical cheque from which it is derived. Thus, according to the version of § 229.34(a)(1) effective from 1 July 2018, and reproduced above in section V, the warranty given by '[e]ach bank that transfers or presents an electronic check or electronic returned check and receives a settlement or other consideration for it' applies to the accuracy of the electronic image and against double payment. **9.57**

In particular, these warranties purport to cover all losses that would have been caused by warranty breaches had the electronically created item been derived from a paper cheque. It also covers losses caused by the absence of paper at any stage of the life of the payment item, a fact of which the drawee bank may be unaware. Furthermore, following proposed § 229.34(b) of the Board's Availability Proposal,[79] § 229.34(g) is an indemnity provision under which:[80] **9.58**

> Each bank that transfers or presents an electronically-created item[81] and receives a settlement or other consideration for it shall indemnify, ... each transferee bank, any subsequent collecting bank, the paying bank, and any subsequent returning bank against losses that result from the fact that—
> (1) [t]he electronic image or electronic information is not derived from a paper check;
> (2) [t]he person on whose account the electronically-created item is drawn did not authorize the issuance of the item in the amount stated on the item or to the payee stated on the item ...; or
> (3) [a] person receives a transfer, presentment, or return of, or otherwise is charged for an electronically-created item such that the person is asked to make payment based on an item or check it has already paid.

The indemnity under § 229.34(g) would not flow to the drawer, payee, or the depositary bank. The Board rationalised that 'the payee and the depositary bank are in the best position to know whether an item is electronically created and to prevent the item from entering the check collection system'. As well, the Board went on to explain, the depositary bank can contractually pass the risk to the payee. Finally, it is the drawer who introduced 'items **9.59**

[79] See note 78 (above).
[80] *Availability of Funds and Collection of Checks* (n 69) 27582.
[81] Under § 229.2(hhh), 'electronically-created item' means 'an electronic image that has all the attributes of an electronic check or electronic returned check but was created electronically and not derived from a paper check'. See also *Availability of Funds and Collection of Checks* (n 69) 27579.

electronically created by the [drawer]' into the check collection system.[82] Under § 229.34(i)(1), the indemnity amount shall not exceed the sum of:

(i) [t]he amount of the loss of the indemnified bank, up to the amount of the settlement or other consideration received by the indemnifying bank; and
(ii) [i]nterest and expenses of the indemnified bank (including costs and reasonable attorney's fees and other expenses of representation).

9.60 However, under § 229.34(i)(2)(i), and without reducing 'the rights of a person under the UCC or other applicable provision of state or federal law',[83] if such loss 'results in whole or in part from the indemnified bank's negligence or failure to act in good faith, then the indemnity amount ... shall be reduced in proportion to the amount of negligence or bad faith attributable to the indemnified bank'. The Board rationalised the ultimate adoption of 'these protections as indemnities ... rather than warranties, as there would not likely be a difference in the damage calculation as between an indemnity and a warranty, and the rule permits a comparative negligence claim for indemnities, which may be appropriate in some cases for these items'.[84]

9.61 Such indemnities should also be provided in connection with the EB. As in connection with the EPO, those indemnities ought not to flow to the seller and remitting bank. As in the case of the electronic image, practically speaking, legal equivalency of the EB can best work hand in hand with technological feasibility: it is only where technology facilitates the change of control of the EB from one person to the other that legal equivalency of the EB can work. In the alternative situation, in which parallel control remains in a sender's hands, warranties and indemnities against double payments are as good to the recipient as the creditworthiness of the sender who gives them.

VII. Depository Bills

9.62 Participants in international trade transactions may consider the establishment of a clearing house to which holders of instruments, namely bills (including those in the form of substitute bills and EPOs), may negotiate respective instruments that they hold for deposit. Subsequent transfers of a deposited instrument will be effected by making appropriate entries in the records of the clearing house. For a deposited instrument, the clearing house will be deemed to attorn for the participant to whose account the instrument is credited at the time. Effectively, under this practice, instruments deposited with the clearing house will be immobilised so that a participant in whose favour a transaction is effected will be deemed to be in possession of the depository bill. Instructions under which the clearing house will be authorised and bound to act by making appropriate entries in its records must originate exclusively from that participant or from a party acting under that participant's authority. Consequently, a transfer recorded by the clearing house will have the effect of a constructive delivery from the transferor to the transferee. Discharging payments will be

[82] FRS Availability Proposal (n 68) 6696.
[83] Regulation CC (n 36) § 229.34(i)(2)(ii).
[84] *Availability of Funds and Collection of Checks* (n 69) 27569.

made to the clearing house which will be obligated to pay the 'holder', namely, the participant to whose account the instrument is credited at the time. Dishonour by the drawee will require a secondary party to make payment to the clearing house, which in turn will pay the holder.

Such a scheme will be modelled on the Canadian Depository Bills and Notes Act,[85] dealing with depository debt securities. However, the Canadian scheme is limited to instruments that, prior to their deposit, are written bills and notes, while the proposed scheme for bills used in international trade is designed to also cover substitute bills and EPOs deposited with a clearing house. As well, the proposed scheme will have to address a transfer from the clearing house to a holder who may not be a participant. **9.63**

VIII. Concluding Observations

With the view of accommodating both manual and electronic handling of bills of exchange by the various participants in payments in international trade, particularly in the footsteps of US legislation and regulation addressing cheques, it is possible to provide, through legislation, an extremely flexible scheme, covering diverse situations and facilitating maximum freedom of movement between paper and image, and original and copy. Indeed, an environment in which one set of rights and duties is embodied in original paper, its copy(ies), and its electronic image, all of which co-exist (albeit not necessarily in the same hands), is quite unsafe. It is bound to create an 'explosive' mixture leading to conflicting legitimate expectations. Moreover, a warranty against double payment has its own limitations. First, as already indicated, it is as good and as reliable as the sender who gives it. Second, it would not cover the payment of an instrument fraudulently 'manufactured' out of an image of an authentic instrument.[86] However, technological innovations are inevitable and ought to be addressed by comprehensive, balanced legislation taking into account the legitimate expectations of all participants. **9.64**

In the final analysis, a move towards complete electronification from end-to-end is premature. A fully electronic bill transaction is a functional equivalent with a one-time negotiable deferred electronic debit transfer. From that perspective, the convergence between the laws that govern those transactions ought to be seriously considered. A cohesive forward-looking legal framework, consisting of statutory, regulatory, and contractual sources, ought to address debit transfers as a distinct form of payment. However, the deferred EFT is effectively an electronic bill. As indicated, the infinite number of participants spread throughout **9.65**

[85] Depository Bills and Notes Act SC 1998, c 13. For an Australian proposal in that direction, see: Working Group Officials, *National Competition Policy Review of the Bills of Exchange Act 1909* (Canberra ACT July 2003) 84.

[86] As to the burden of proving whether the instrument was not counterfeit compare *Wachovia Bank, NA v Foster Bancshares, Inc.* 457 F 3d 619 (7th Cir 2006) (holding that drawee ought to prove payment of an authentic instrument) and *Chevy Chase Bank, FSB v Wachovia Bank, NA* 2006 US App LEXIS 29944 (4th Cir 2006) (entitling drawee to benefit from a presumption of authenticity). The Board amended Regulation CC (n 36) by adding a new § 229.38(i) following the former case: see *Availability of Funds and Collection of Checks*, 83 Fed Reg 46849 (2018) <https://www.federalregister.gov/documents/2018/09/17/2018-20029/availability-of-funds-and-collection-of-checks> accessed 09 February 2021, which amends subpart C of Regulation CC (n 36) effective from 1 January 2019.

the globe and their diverse stages of technological development militates against the feasibility of a common and worldwide technological platform. Hence, the law ought to accommodate not only the possibility of an electronic bill, but also the potential conversion of a physical bill to an electronic one, and vice versa, in the life of one such instrument. The BEA ought to be revised to provide for such a robust and flexible framework.

10

Digitalisation of Shipping and Insurance Documents

Implications for Trade Finance

Miriam Goldby

I. Introduction

The use of documentary credits in support of cross-border trade transactions has been declining in recent decades, mainly for reasons to do with the associated costs. A letter of credit can in fact be an expensive form of finance, as it requires an assessment of the risks involved in individual transactions or courses of dealing, as well as burdensome and resource-intensive manual checking of multiple documents. Thus, fees can range from 0.75% to 1.5% of the transaction's value,[1] and a number of additional charges may apply, including for handling discrepancies.[2] These costs can be significantly reduced if technology were harnessed to ease the risk-assessment process by giving banks greater visibility into business relationships and transaction flows, as well as automating the checking process; but this would require paper documents to be replaced by electronic data. Given that the bank's position as secured creditor tends to be tied at law to its holding certain documents, however, the legal effects of this transition need to be carefully assessed. Accordingly, this chapter analyses the legal implications for banks of replacing trade documents that have a bearing on its position as secured creditor with electronic data. The focus is upon bills of lading and cargo insurance certificates. This chapter argues that, while considerable certainty as to the bank's legal position may be achieved through careful contractual arrangements, some question marks inevitably remain that can only be resolved through legislative action. **10.01**

II. Background: The Presentation of Paper Documents under Documentary Letters of Credit with Special Focus on Bills of Lading and Insurance Certificates

Where financing of a cross-border sale occurs through a letter of credit, the seller will be required to produce documents of a certain type that comply with the letter of credit's requirements. In these instances, the bank as creditor will require collateral, which will usually come in the form of a pledge over the goods being sold. In order to effect this pledge, an original bill of lading will usually be required among the documents presented to the bank **10.02**

[1] Patrick Gleeson, 'What is the fee for a letter of credit?' (*Zacks*, 28 January 2019) <https://finance.zacks.com/fee-letter-credit-10533.html> accessed 1 August 2020.

[2] Institute of Export and International Trade, 'A Guide to Letter of Credit Charges' (*Open to Export*, 6 February 2015) <https://opentoexport.com/blog/a-guide-to-letter-of-credit-charges/> accessed 1 August 2020.

in compliance with the letter of credit. Indeed, because bills of lading are documents of title,[3] if a bill of lading is pledged to a bank as security for the credit advanced, the bank will have a pledge over the actual goods that the document represents. Assuming that it is made with the appropriate intention, the transfer of the bill of lading constitutes a pledge of the goods that it represents (by transferring a special property), as opposed to transferring their ownership (or the general property).[4]

10.03 A pledge is a form of consensual security and consists of the actual or constructive delivery of possession[5] of an asset to the creditor by way of security.[6] It can be viewed as a type of bailment that carries with it a mandate of sale on default of payment.[7] Under English law, there is no need to have recourse to a court of law for authority to sell on the default of the debtor-pledgor.[8] The operation of a letter of credit agreement is such that the bank does not pay out money before it has had the negotiable bill of lading delivered to it (in the case of a bearer bill) or indorsed in its favour (in the case of an order bill), either of which, if the appropriate intention is present, is sufficient to create a pledge. If the bill is non-negotiable (or 'straight'), the bank would need to be designated as consignee in the bill in order to obtain constructive possession of the goods,[9] and therefore a pledge over them.

10.04 If it rejects the bill of lading, the bank does not become its holder;[10] but, if the beneficiary fails to resume possession of the document, the bank remains in a position to take it up, provided that the bank has the beneficiary's consent to do so, and it is not necessary for a fresh presentation to be made.[11] While in the period between the bill of lading's rejection and the bank taking up the documents, the legal rights and obligations that the physical possession of the bill of lading confers upon the bank may be ambiguous, in practice, the physical possession by the bank of a full set of bills of lading, whether negotiable or not,[12] precludes any other person from lawfully claiming delivery of them from the carrier.[13] This gives the bank effective control over the goods, or a remedy against the carrier, if they are delivered in the absence of the bill.[14] Once the bill of lading has been pledged to the bank, the latter becomes the holder for the purposes of sections 2 and 5 of the Carriage of Goods by Sea Act 1992 ('COGSA 1992');[15] although the bank is not liable to the carrier under section 3 of COGSA 1992, unless it takes or demands delivery from the carrier of any of the goods to which the bill of lading relates or makes a claim under the contract of carriage against the carrier in

[3] *Enichem Anic SpA v Ampelos Shipping Co Ltd (The Delfini)* [1990] Lloyd's Rep 252 (CA) 268 (hereafter *The Delfini*).

[4] *Hibbert v Carter* (1787) 1 TR 745; *Sewell v Burdick* (1884) 10 App Cas 74 (HL) (hereafter *Sewell v Burdick*); *Brandt v Liverpool, etc, Steam Navigation Co* [1924] 1 KB 575 (CA).

[5] For the nature of the pledgee's interest in the subject matter of the pledge, see *Bassano v Toft* [2014] EWHC 377 (QB) [49], [57]. The pledgee's interest is not defeated by every parting of possession (ibid [50]–[57]).

[6] Louise Gullifer (ed), *Goode and Gullifer on Legal Problems of Credit and Security* (6th edn, Sweet & Maxwell 2017) [1.47]. See also *Donald v Suckling* (1866) LR 1 QB 585.

[7] On the position of those purchasing the pledged assets from the pledgee, see *Bank St Petersburg v Arkhangelsky* [2015] EWHC 2997 (Ch) [36]–[40].

[8] *The Odessa* [1916] 1 AC 145 (PC) 157–59.

[9] *JI MacWilliam Co Inc v Mediterranean Shipping Co SA (The Rafaela S)* [2005] 2 AC 423 (HL) (hereafter *The Rafaela S*). See also Carriage of Goods by Sea Act 1992 (UK) (hereafter 'COGSA 1992'), s 2(1)(b).

[10] *Standard Chartered Bank v Dorchester LNG (The Erin Schulte)* [2014] EWCA Civ 1382 (hereafter *The Erin Schulte*) [28].

[11] ibid [33], [51]–[52].

[12] *The Rafaela S* (n 9).

[13] *Sucre Export SA v Northern River Shipping Ltd (The Sormovskiy 3068)* [1994] 2 Lloyd's Rep 266 (QBD) 274.

[14] *The Erin Schulte* (n 10) [53], [56]. See also s 2(2), COGSA 1992 (n 9).

[15] *Primetrade AG v Ythan Ltd* [2005] EWHC 2399 (Comm) [65]–[78].

respect of those goods.[16] Furthermore, the bank obtains an insurable interest under the Marine Insurance Act 1906 ('MIA').[17]

It is common for banks to have the cargo insurance rights assigned to them, when they act as pledgees,[18] in order to protect the value of their collateral if the goods are lost or damaged. The bank acquires these rights through the assignment of an insurance document, usually a cargo insurance certificate, which would normally be one of the documents required to be presented under the letter of credit. Having been designed by the insurance industry specifically for use in the international sales of goods, cargo insurance certificates were conceived as documents granting rights to the holder.[19] The assignment of such a certificate was discussed briefly in *Koskas v Standard Marine Insurance Co*,[20] in which the argument was initially raised by the insurers that the cargo insurance certificate had not been properly indorsed. The insurers later withdrew the argument, and the court commented that 'the underwriters have very properly decided not to press that point'[21] because the language of the certificate was not sufficiently clear specifically to require indorsement. Thus, it would seem that indorsement is only necessary to effect assignment of a cargo insurance certificate where this is explicitly required by the certificate itself. *Koskas* also suggests that the courts were happy to accept that being the holder of the certificate conferred standing to claim against the insurer.[22] 10.05

Thus, bills of lading and cargo insurance certificates are not just documents that the bank checks to verify their compliance with the credit. They are also essential steps in the mechanism whereby the bank obtains collateral for its security interest and protects the value of that collateral. If paper documents are dispensed with and replaced by data, new mechanisms need to be devised to put the bank in an equivalent position. 10.06

III. The Digital Alternatives Landscape: State of Play and Perceived Benefits

A report published by the Boston Consulting Group ('BCG') in 2017 observed that '[p]rocesses that currently support the global trade finance ecosystem are labour-intensive and predominantly paper-based. They are estimated to generate four billion pages of documents annually.'[23] It is not, therefore, surprising that much effort has been made across the financial industry to harness new technologies towards the more efficient use of resources 10.07

16 *Fortis Bank v Indian Overseas Bank* [2011] EWHC 538 (Comm) [59].

17 Marine Insurance Act 1906 ('MIA'), s 8. Similar rules apply in jurisdictions that have modelled their laws on the MIA: see, for example, Canadian Federal Marine Insurance Act 1993, s 10; Australian Marine Insurance Act 1909, s 11. For an overview of the similar position in the US, see Donald T Rave and Stacey Tranchina, 'Marine Cargo Insurance: An Overview' (1991–92) 66 Tulane Law Review 371, 382–4.

18 With respect to assignment, see MIA (n17) ss 15, 50–51.

19 Miriam Goldby, *Electronic Documents in Maritime Trade: Law and Practice* (2nd edn, OUP 2019) [7.21] (hereafter Goldby, *Electronic Documents*).

20 *Koskas v Standard Marine Insurance Co* (1927) 27 Ll L Rep 59 (CA) (hereafter *Koskas v Standard Marine*).

21 ibid 61.

22 On the assignment of cargo insurance certificates, see further Goldby, *Electronic Documents* (n 19) [7.32].

23 Sukand Ramachandran, Jarryd Porter, Rony Kort, Ravi Hanspal, and Huny Garg, 'SIBOS 2017: Digital Innovation in Trade Finance: Have We Reached a Tipping Point?' (*The Boston Consulting Group ('BCG')*, October 2017) 2 <https://www.swift.com/news-events/news/digital-innovation-in-trade-finance-have-we-reached-a-tipping-point> accessed 1 August 2020 (hereafter Ramachandran, 'SIBOS 2017').

in this sector. The BCG report finds sixty to eighty[24] unique data-fields are captured in the (ten–twenty)[25] documents that are typically involved in a trade finance transaction and that, in 85–90% of around 5,000 interactions with these data-fields that can occur within a single transaction,[26] the players involved generally ignore the data and simply transmit them to the next party in the supply-chain.[27] The BCG report also notes that the sixty to eighty unique data-fields 'are reused across documents some 8–10 times, and many of the documents are duplicated, increasing the risk of discrepancies, which can add significant delays to an already lengthy two-to-four-week process'.[28] The report notes additionally that the Internet of Things ('IoT') will create a 'wave of new data fields' relating to the traded goods that are generated by sensors and that '[w]ithout digitising existing processes, players will struggle to react to this new information flow'.[29] It is easy to see how new possibilities may open up if, rather than being contained within the silos of individual paper documents, these data fields were to be digitised, and if redundant activities could be minimised (for example, through automation by using 'smart contracts'). The labour (and costs) associated with checking hundreds of pages of documents manually for compliance with the credit could be eliminated. The possibility of negotiating better financing terms may also open up because digitalisation would give the bank greater visibility into its client's business relationships and transaction flows.

10.08 The presentation of data rather than documents in compliance with a letter of credit depends on the availability of suitable avenues for the communication of those data. The Society for Worldwide Interbank Financial Telecommunication ('SWIFT') has taken various steps over recent years to facilitate trade finance. Besides being involved in the development and launch of the Bill of Lading Electronic Registry Organization ('Bolero'),[30] which is discussed further below, it has developed a number of important tools that may be used in the processing of trade data, including the SWIFTNet Trade Services Utility ('TSU'), a platform for the matching of data in bank payment obligation ('BPO') transactions.[31]

10.09 'SWIFT for Corporates' is a service that allows non-financial institutions (that is, banks' corporate clients) to use the SWIFT network for communication with their banks. 'SWIFT for Corporates' provides a gateway, whereby businesses can communicate with multiple banks over a single platform by using a single personal digital signature.[32] SWIFT runs a certification programme that assesses business applications and middleware against SWIFT requirements.[33] It has also embraced 'ISO 20022', which is not only a message standard in itself using the international and widely used 'eXtensible Markup Language' ('XML') syntax, but also a methodology for creating consistent message standards across all of the financial

[24] ibid 6.
[25] ibid 3.
[26] ibid 3.
[27] ibid 3–5.
[28] ibid 4.
[29] ibid 7.
[30] Goldby, *Electronic Documents* (n 19) [10.22].
[31] ibid [4.18]–[4.23].
[32] SWIFT, 'SWIFT for Corporates' <https://www.swift.com/node/4361> accessed 1 August 2020. In relation to the personal digital signature, see SWIFT, 'SWIFT Launches 3SKey Digital Identity Solution', Press Release (*SWIFT*, 26 October 2010) <http://www.swift.com/press_releases/3skey_launch> accessed 25 March 2013.
[33] SWIFT, 'SWIFT Certified Applications deliver an extra level of confidence' <https://www.swift.com/about-us/partner-programme/swift-certified-applications> accessed 1 August 2020.

industry's business processes. 'ISO 20022' is designed to achieve interoperability between different messaging standards; existing standards, including SWIFT's own proprietary MT messages, can be mapped to 'ISO 20022'. Both of these developments open the door to digital communication between banks and non-banks without compromising the security standards required by the financial sector.

In view of the fact that bills of lading and cargo insurance certificates are such crucial cogs in the trade-finance machinery, the focus of this section is to give some insight into the efforts made in recent decades to replace those documents with digital alternatives. **10.10**

A. Digital Alternatives to Bills of Lading

At the time of writing, six electronic systems providing digital alternatives to paper bills of lading have been approved by the International Group of Protection and Indemnity Clubs ('IGP&I'), making them acceptable alternatives for international cargo carriers.[34] Of these six systems, Bolero and essDOCs' CargoDocs Document Exchange ('CargoDocs'), which are discussed below, have been in operation for longest. A third system, 'e-Title', was approved in 2015,[35] and a fourth, 'edoxOnline',[36] was approved in early June 2019.[37] Two further systems have been approved since then, namely the 'WAVE Network' and 'CargoX'.[38] The last three systems to be approved are blockchain-based systems.[39] While the multipartite contractual frameworks underpinning the blockchain-based systems have not all yet been placed in the public domain, the approval of these systems by the IGP&I would suggest that their legal underpinnings share essential features with those underlying the Bolero and CargoDocs systems, discussed further below. **10.11**

Both Bolero and CargoDocs permit non-bank-to-bank communication. Bolero provides certain services through a cloud-based 'software as a service' ('SaaS') model.[40] This consists of a set of web applications that may be used (amongst other things) to apply for, receive **10.12**

[34] Goldby, *Electronic Documents* (n 19) [6.02].

[35] UK P&I Club, 'Electronic (Paperless) Trading Systems', (Circular 12/15, October 2015) <https://www.ukpandi.com/news-and-resources/circulars/2015/circular-1215-electronic-paperless-trading-systems/> accessed 1 August 2020. See also UK P&I Club, 'Electronic (Paperless) trading systems—Electronic Shipping Solutions & Bolero International Ltd—Updated ESS DSUA Version 2013.1' (Circular 6/13, March 2013) <https://www.ukpandi.com/news-and-resources/circulars/2013/circular-613-electronic-paperless-trading-systems--electronic-shipping-solutions--bolero-internation/> accessed 1 August 2020.

[36] See 'Global Share, through the renowned edoxOnline platform, announces the launch of the long-awaited 'Electronic Bill of Lading under Blockchain technology' <https://www.globalshare.com.ar/news/global-share-through-the-renowned-edoxonline-platform-announces-the-launch-of-the-long-awaited-electronic-bill-of-lading-under-blockchain-technology/> accessed 1 August 2020.

[37] UK P&I Club, 'Electronic (Paperless) Trading' (Circular 7/19, 11 June 2019) <https://www.ukpandi.com/knowledge-publications/publications/article/circular-7-19-electronic-paperless-trading-148894/> accessed 1 August 2020.

[38] UK P&I Club, 'Electronic Paperless Trading—Approval of Cargo X' (Circular 3/20, 18 February 2020) <https://www.ukpandi.com/knowledge-publications/article/circular-3-20-electronic-paperless-trading-approval-of-cargox-151443/> accessed 1 August 2020; UK P&I Club, 'Electronic (Paperless) Trading' (Circular 16/19, 23 December 2019) <https://www.ukpandi.com/knowledge-publications/publications/article/circular-16-19-electronic-paperless-trading-151105/> accessed 1 August 2020.

[39] For a useful insight into the working of these schemes, see UK P&I Club, 'Electronic Bills of Lading—An Update Part I' (26 March 2020) <https://www.ukpandi.com/knowledge-publications/article/electronic-bills-of-lading-an-update-part-i-151842/> accessed 1 August 2020.

[40] Bolero, 'Company Overview' <http://www.bolero.net/home/company-overview/> accessed 1 August 2020.

advice about, and making electronic presentations under, letters of credit.[41] Messages are exchanged over the Bolero Core Messaging Platform ('BCMP'). Among the documents that may be presented electronically is the Bolero Bill of Lading ('BBL').[42] This is an electronic alternative to a paper bill, the legal underpinnings of which (as discussed further below) are provided by the Bolero Rulebook, a multipartite contractual instrument to which all users must subscribe. Indeed, Bolero is a closed (that is, members-only) system, which requires a would-be user to register as a member before using it. The system relies on Internet communications, and secures these communications through the use of digital signatures,[43] Bolero itself acting as a certification authority ('CA').[44] The system makes use of both the authentication and encryption functions of 'PKI'.[45] This makes it extremely secure against fraud.[46] It also helps to ensure the accuracy of the registry records, whereby the holder exercises exclusive control over the electronic record constituting the bill of lading.[47] 'Holdership'[48] of the BBL by the shipper to whom it is issued, and by subsequent transferees, is registered in the Bolero Title Registry ('BTR') until the BBL reverts back to the issuer (namely, the carrier) upon surrender. Importantly, the Bolero system also provides for the addition of a 'Pledgee Holder', which is defined as 'a User who is or becomes Designated as both Pledgee and Holder simultaneously',[49] and whose rights and obligations over the BBL are exercised only when the pledge is enforced.

10.13 CargoDocs is an electronic shipping document exchange developed by a company called essDOCS Exchange Limited ('essDOCS') (previously Electronic Shipping Solutions ('ESS')). As is the case with Bolero, its service is only open to members linked together by becoming party to the ESS-Databridge Services and Users Agreement ('DSUA').[50] Like Bolero, CargoDocs also uses digital signatures to ensure messages' integrity and source. In producing transport documents, parties communicate over the system with the shipper

[41] Bolero, 'Letters of Credit Management' <http://www.bolero.net/home/guarantee-management/> accessed 7 March 2019.

[42] See Bolero International, 'Bolero Rulebook' (2013) <http://www.bolero.net/wp-content/uploads/2020/04/Bolero-Insights-The-Bolero-Rulebook-NW.pdf> accessed 1 August 2020 (hereafter 'Bolero Rulebook') rule 1.1(11), which defines the Bolero Bill of Lading ('BBL') as 'a BBL Text with its related Title Registry Record'. According to the Bolero Rulebook, rule 1.1(6), a 'BBL Text' is 'a document which: (a) is sent into the Core Messaging Platform and recorded in the Title Registry as the documentary component of the Bolero Bill of Lading; and (b) acknowledges the receipt of goods by a Carrier for carriage by sea'. Rule 1.1(55) defines a 'Title Registry Record' as 'the structured information kept in the Title Registry linked to the BBL Text, and derived from Title Registry Instructions involving the related Bolero Bill of Lading'.

[43] Goldby, *Electronic Documents* (n 19) [2.35]–[2.38].

[44] For an explanation of how digital signatures are used within the Bolero system, see Bolero, 'Operating Procedures Manual' (Version 2.4, 1999–2000) 16–24 ('Security Tutorial' and 'Digital Signatures in the Bolero System') (hereafter Bolero, 'Operating Procedures Manual') <http://www.bolero.net/en/Newsdownloads/articlesordownloads.aspx> accessed 8 July 2012.

[45] In the Bolero system, the second function described is optional: see Bolero, 'Operating Procedures Manual' (n 44) 24: '... the effectiveness of modern encryption techniques in rendering digital communications secret raises national security and law enforcement concerns that have led some countries to regulate the import-export supply and use of encryption technology. In implementing a local User System, a User is well advised to inform itself of any applicable restrictions on the use of encryption technology ...'.

[46] Christopher Reed, *Internet Law: Text and Materials* (2nd edn, Cambridge University Press 2004) 185: 'All encryption can be broken given sufficient time and computing resources. The effectiveness of encryption as a method of signing electronic documents relies on the fact that it is *computationally infeasible* to break the encryption method, and thus become able to forge the signatures, within a reasonable period of time.'

[47] For analysis of the concept of 'exclusive control' in the UNCITRAL Model Law on Electronic Transferable Records, see ch 11 (Davidson) in this volume.

[48] Bolero Rulebook (n 42) rule 1.1(33).

[49] ibid rule 1.1(42).

[50] See section III of this chapter.

supplying information and the carrier or his agent completing the issue of the bill. In the process, documents may be collaboratively reviewed, amended, or corrected where necessary. The system provides electronic options for dealing with documents, including 'sign', 'issue', 'amend' (with the consent of the shipper and the carrier), 'send', 'return' (used when the intended indorsee rejects the documentation or if it is sent to the wrong party), 'indorse', 'print convert' (used when it is necessary to convert the electronic document to paper),[51] 'produce', and 'accomplish' (a familiar phrase to users of paper bills issued in three sets, all of which carry the legend 'one being accomplished the other to stand void'). The ability to use the different functionalities will depend on the user's authority and capabilities with respect to the transaction in question. For example, only the user who is in control of the original bill of lading (whether because it was issued to it or subsequently transferred to it) will be able to indorse it to another user. Once the indorsement is effected, and unless the indorsee decides to return the documents, the indorser loses control and only retains access to an electronic document marked 'copy' for record-keeping purposes. The system may be used for the creation of the full set of documents required for shipments of container, energy, and bulk cargoes.[52] Creators of certificates of origin, quality, and quantity can be given access to the system, with authority to create, sign, and issue these documents in electronic form. Documents created and traded using CargoDocs can be presented to banks in accordance with the Electronic Supplement to the Uniform Customs and Practice for Documentary Credits ('eUCP') and may be accepted or rejected by banks in the same manner. CargoDocs can thus enable the electronic presentation of documents to banks.[53] It may also be used to automate the creation of BPO baselines and datasets and submissions between corporates and banks via SWIFT's TSU in accordance with the Uniform Rules on Bank Payment Obligations (URBPO), as well as automating the release of the electronic bill of lading, which is held in escrow until data is matched.[54]

Since blockchain technology burst on the scene, its potential to be used in developing digital 10.14
alternatives to bills of lading has been widely discussed and publicised. Indeed, there are a number of systems being piloted and trialled in the international transport community.[55] As was observed above, a number of blockchain-based platforms enabling the replacement of paper bills of lading with digital alternatives and performing the same (perhaps enhanced) functions have been approved by the IGP&I. There is every sign that more will be developed and launched in the wake of the coronavirus pandemic, which has highlighted the difficulties in moving bundles of paper documents around the world.[56] In the container-shipping

[51] Electronic Shipping Solutions ('ESS'), 'eB/Ls: DSUA Overview' (16 December 2010) states that this command '... requires the carrier or the carrier's agent receiving [it]... to print off the eB/L and manually sign it. The trade log (identifying the previous transfers in the form of an endorsement chain) is attached to the (now) paper bill ... A carrier is obliged to comply with the request to Print Convert.'

[52] essDOCS Exchange Limited ('essDOCS'), 'Markets' <https://www.essdocs.com/network/markets> accessed 1 August 2020.

[53] essDOCS, 'Capabilities' <https://www.essdocs.com/capabilities/path-to-paperless> accessed 1 August 2020.

[54] CargoDocs, 'Bank Payment Obligation Plus' <https://www.essdocs.com/solutions/banks/bank-payment-obligation-plus> accessed 1 August 2020. See also SWIFT, 'Distributed Ledgers, Smart Contracts, Business Standards and ISO 20022' (Information Paper) (September 2016) 7 <https://www.swift.com/sites/default/files/documents/swift_info_paper_distributedledgerstandards.pdf> accessed 1 August 2020 (hereafter SWIFT, 'Distributed Ledgers'), discussing the possibility of automating payments by means of 'smart contract' technology.

[55] Goldby, *Electronic Documents* (n 19) [6.46], [11.43]–[11.52].

[56] See ICC Academy, 'How Banks Digitize Their Trade Business' (Briefing Webinar) (27 May 2020) <https://www.youtube.com/watch?v=V2IkoR9pVil> accessed 21 August 2020, in which representatives from Bolero, essDOCs, and OGY Docs, the provider of the WAVE BL, all reported accelerated take-up of their digital

space, the Digital Container Shipping Association (which, at the time of writing, consists of nine large liner carriers) has been set up with the remit of adopting common open-digital standards for the container shipping industry in order to facilitate these developments.[57]

B. Digital Cargo Insurance Certificates

10.15 Platforms enabling cargo insurance certificates to be issued electronically have been available to the international business community for a number of years now. These certificates are usually issued pursuant to a declaration made under an open-cover agreement, whereby an insurer undertakes to cover all shipments declared by the assured that fall within the scope of the open-cover terms.[58] Accordingly, the assured, or its agent, simply needs to complete an online template, created on the basis of the open-cover terms, with details of the cargo and voyage in order for a certificate to be issued. The certificate, which is issued instantaneously and contains the authorised facsimile signature of the insurer, can then be presented to the bank under a letter of credit agreement.[59]

10.16 Significantly, none of the available platforms appears to possess the functionality to assign certificates, so if the bank requires an assignment of the assured's rights against the insurer, the certificate may need to be printed out and assigned in the usual way.[60] As the insurance industry looks to harness technologies, such as distributed-ledger technologies ('DLT'), 'smart contracts', IoT, and machine-learning, however, it may well become commercially expedient to integrate assignment functionalities into those platforms that enable the electronic issue of certificates, thereby tokenising the rights against the insurer that are represented by the certificate.[61]

C. Trade Finance Communication Networks and Platforms

10.17 At the time of writing, several solutions are being developed with the objective of harnessing DLT and 'smart contracts' in developing trade and supply-chain finance solutions.[62] Of

alternatives as a result of restrictions resulting from the coronavirus pandemic. See also International Chamber of Commerce ('ICC'), 'ICC Memo to Governments and Central Banks on Essential Steps to Safeguard Trade Finance Operations' (3 April 2020) <https://iccwbo.uk/products/icc-memo-to-governments-and-central-banks-on-essential-steps-to-safeguard-trade-finance-operations> accessed 21 August 2020.

[57] See Gavin van Marle, 'Digital Standards for Container Shipping on the Starting Blocks' (*gCaptain*, 21 June 2019) <https://gcaptain.com/digital-standards-for-container-shipping-on-the-starting-blocks/?utm_source=feedburner&utm_medium=feed&utm_campaign=Feed%3A+Gcaptain+%28gCaptain.com%29&goal=0_f50174ef03-eea0c33445-169948733&mc_cid=eea0c33445&mc_eid=3cf70423bc> accessed 1 August 2020. See also Digital Container Shipping Association, 'DCSA takes on eBL standardisation' <https://dcsa.org/wp-content/uploads/2020/05/20200519-DCSA-taking-on-eBL.pdf> accessed 21 August 2020.

[58] Goldby, *Electronic Documents* (n 19) [7.13]–[7.14].

[59] ibid [12.19]–[12.32].

[60] ibid [8.40]–[8.44].

[61] Miriam Goldby, Christopher Reed, Michaela MacDonald, Katie Richards, and Lucy Stanbrough, 'Triggering Innovation: How Smart Contracts Bring Policies to Life', Lloyd's Emerging Risk Report 2019: Understanding Risk (Lloyd's of London 2019) section 3 <https://reaction2.lloyds.com/REACTION/Home/RSForm?RSID=5EPUNCZzxlH7nSBS3W59A6XEhcl40XwjpavcZzL9MbgBeEyMbO5FD-Vrvoryt3tQ> accessed 24 June 2019.

[62] Ramachandran, 'SIBOS 2017' (n 23) 13.

particular note is 'Contour', which is built using 'Corda'[63] and which focuses on digitising letter of credit transactions. Under its previous name 'Voltron', Contour was used in November 2018 to run a pilot transaction enabling the digital transfer of title to goods on the blockchain by integrating Bolero's solution.[64] It was rebranded as 'Contour' in 2020 and has since been fully commercialised.[65] Also interesting are two platforms: 'we.trade',[66] a European digital trade finance platform, and 'eTradeConnect',[67] a similar platform based in Hong Kong and serving the Asian market, both of which are built using Hyperledger Fabric.[68] The two platforms joined forces through a memorandum of understanding on 31 October 2018, whereby they would become interconnected.[69] we.trade is focused on supporting open-account trades, rather than letters of credit,[70] but there is no reason why in future it could not be adapted to electronic presentation under a letter of credit in accordance with the eUCP. When using the we.trade platform, a financing bank enters into a legally binding Bank Payment Undertaking ('BPU'), which is enforced through a 'smart contract' upon satisfaction of the applicable settlement conditions defined therein,[71] among which could be the submission of bill of lading and cargo insurance certificate data, as well as the transfer of the rights necessary to put the bank in the position of pledgee and assignee. The BPU has similarities with the Bank Payment Obligation ('BPO'),[72] except that in the BPU the issuing bank undertakes to make payment directly to the seller, rather than the seller's bank as in the BPO.[73] Finally, in response to the restrictions resulting from the coronavirus pandemic, the Bankers Association for Finance and Trade ('BAFT') has developed the Distributed Ledger Payment Commitment ('DLPC'), which is 'a digital instrument to

[63] For a comprehensive discussion of 'Corda', see Richard G Brown, 'The Corda Platform: An Introduction' (May 2018) <https://www.corda.net/content/corda-platform-whitepaper.pdf> accessed 1 August 2020. See also Nicky Morris, 'Trade finance blockchain consortia: how they differ' (*Ledger Insights*, June 2018) <https://www.ledgerinsights.com/trade-finance-blockchain-consortium/> accessed 1 August 2020.

[64] Sanne Wass, 'Second HSBC-ING blockchain transaction sees bill of lading integrated with Voltron platform' (*Global Trade Review*, 6 November 2018) <https://www.gtreview.com/news/fintech/second-hsbc-ing-blockchain-transaction-sees-bill-of-lading-integrated-on-voltron-platform/> accessed 1 August 2020.

[65] Eleanor Wragg, 'Voltron moves into full commercialisation and rebrands as "Contour"' (*Global Trade Review*, 28 January 2020) <https://www.gtreview.com/news/fintech/voltron-moves-into-full-commercialisation-rebrands-as-contour/> accessed 21 August 2020. See also <https://www.contour.network> accessed 21 August 2020.

[66] we.trade is a blockchain-based trade-finance platform launched in June 2018 which has fourteen major European banks among its partners: see we.trade, 'Banking Partners' <https://we-trade.com/banking-partners> accessed 12 March 2019.

[67] 'eTradeConnect' is a blockchain-based trade-finance platform initiated by a consortium of twelve banks in Hong Kong, which launched in September 2018: see eTradeConnect, 'What is eTradeConnect' <https://www.etradeconnect.net/Portal> accessed 1 August 2020.

[68] Hyperledger is 'an open source collaborative effort created to advance cross-industry blockchain technologies. It is a global collaboration, hosted by The Linux Foundation, including leaders in finance, banking, Internet of Things, supply chains, manufacturing and Technology': see Hyperledger, 'About Hyperledger' <https://www.hyperledger.org/about> accessed 1 August 2020.

[69] we.trade, 'Announcement on collaboration between we.trade and eTradeConnect' (Press Release) (31 October 2018) <https://cms.we-trade.com/app/uploads/we.trade-and-HKTFPCL-Joint-press-release-FINAL.pdf> accessed 1 August 2020.

[70] Nicky Morris, 'Trade finance blockchain race is about to start' (*Ledger Insights*, June 2018) <https://www.ledgerinsights.com/wetrade-trade-finance-blockchain-race/> accessed 1 August 2020.

[71] we.trade, 'Frequently Asked Questions (FAQ): Business' <https://we-trade.com/faq> accessed 1 August 2020 (hereafter we.trade, 'FAQ'), in particular the answers to the questions, 'What are the benefits of the we.trade platform for my business?' and 'How is Bank Payment Undertaking regulated, to what laws or regulations would it be subject?'.

[72] Goldby, *Electronic Documents* (n 19) [4.18]–[4.23].

[73] we.trade, 'FAQ' (n 71), in particular the answer to the question, 'How is Bank Payment Undertaking regulated, to what laws or regulations would it be subject?'. See also Goldby, *Electronic Documents* (n 19) [4.21].

ensure that payment commitments *in digital form on any platform or network* are legally binding and enforceable in accordance with their terms, irrespective of the platform/network, or the trade finance instrument, out of which the payment commitment arises'.[74] This can be implemented using blockchain technology.

10.18 Thus, efforts to harness new technologies intended to replace paper can be observed across the various sectors engaged in international trade activity. In particular, the full digitalisation of the two types of document essential to the bank's status as secured creditor in a documentary credit transaction is now possible in technological terms. It is, therefore, worthwhile to examine the legal framework within which these developments have been occurring in order to gauge its readiness to accommodate those technological changes.

IV. Legal Framework Supporting the Use of Digital Alternatives to Paper Documents in Documentary Credit Arrangements: Gaps and Uncertainties

10.19 The legal framework relating to the performance of obligations under a letter of credit arrangement may be found in the terms of the various contracts between the parties as interpreted and enforced in light of the applicable domestic law. Documentary credit agreements almost invariably incorporate the terms of the Uniform Customs and Practices on Documentary Credits 2007 ('UCP 600').[75] The UCP 600 contain various provisions focused on the requirements to be satisfied by documents in general[76] (and certain documents in particular, most notably invoices,[77] transport documents,[78] and cargo insurance documents[79]) in order to be deemed compliant with the credit. Since the adoption in 2002 of the eUCP, which is the electronic presentation supplement to the UCP,[80] it has been permissible to present to banks under a letter of credit, electronic documents in place of paper ones. Article e1(b) of the eUCP provides that the eUCP shall apply as a supplement to the UCP 600 where the letter of credit indicates that it is subject to the eUCP. Article e2 provides that the eUCP operates alongside the UCP 600, whose provisions therefore remain in effect; that the eUCP prevails in case of conflict with the UCP 600; and that, where permitted by the credit, the beneficiary may elect to present only paper documents, in which case the eUCP will be ousted. Where the eUCP is incorporated into a letter of credit, therefore, the presentation of digital alternatives to paper documents is permitted and may even be required by the credit. Where the credit permits or requires the submission of data, rather than documents, two questions arise. First, what happens if the data submitted do not exactly match

[74] Bankers Association for Finance and Trade ('BAFT'), DLPC Working Group of the Innovation Council, 'BAFT DLPC—Distributed Ledger Payment Commitment: Business Best Practices (Initial Release)' (June 2020) <https://baft.org/docs/default-source/2020/06/baft-dlpc-business-bps-final.pdf?sfvrsn=5fad20e1_6> accessed 21 August 2020 (emphasis in original).
[75] ICC, 'Uniform Customs and Practice for Documentary Credits' (ICC Publication No 600, 2007) (hereafter 'UCP 600').
[76] ibid arts 14, 17.
[77] ibid art 18.
[78] ibid arts 14(c), 19–27.
[79] ibid art 28.
[80] ICC, 'Supplement for UCP for Electronic Presentation, Version 1.1' (ICC Publication No 639, 2007); ICC, 'eUCP Version 2.0' (2019).

the requirements of the credit? Secondly, does the submission of electronic data achieve the same legal effects as those achieved by the presentation of the paper documents being replaced? These questions are answered next.

A. Content Compliance

Article 14(d) of the UCP 600 provides that '[d]ata in a document, when read in context with the credit, the document itself and international standard banking practice, need not be identical to, but must not conflict with, data in that document, any other stipulated document or the credit'.[81] Thus, that provision does not require an exact match, but merely an absence of conflict. Where electronic data is being used in place of paper documents and where the checking is being undertaken by a matching-engine rather than a human agent, however, consideration might need to be given to whether this approach is still optimal. The application of article 14(d) as it presently stands would require the matching-engine to be programmed to declare a match where data from different sources is non-conflicting, although not identical; such an option is only likely to become possible with advances in machine-learning. Alternatively, manual checking of any non-matches by a human agent would need to take place in order to determine whether the 'non-match report' was issued as a result of an actual conflict in the data or simply as a result of slightly different, but not conflicting, wording used by different data-issuers. This would mean, however, that the potential benefits of a digital presentation would not be reaped to the full. 10.20

Pending the development of artificial intelligence technologies that are able to recognise actual conflicts, a final option would be to revise the eUCP so that payment is only due upon a transaction-matching application reporting an exact match. This is similar to article 10 of the URBPO, under which, in the case of a mismatch, payment becomes conditional upon a mismatch acceptance. As indicated above,[82] collaborative digital document-preparation over electronic platforms, whereby the same data can be used by multiple issuers of documents relating to the same transaction, is already available. In the future, this capability may well evolve to the extent that identical wording in the different documents (or different data sources) becomes the norm. Should this occur, there is an even stronger argument for adopting the URBPO approach of requiring an exact match, subject to any mismatches being waived by human agents. 10.21

Another question raised by documentary compliance in electronic presentation derives from the signature requirement in the UCP 600, which applies to both the bill of lading[83] and the insurance certificate.[84] The signature requirement is there to ensure that the 10.22

[81] UCP 600, art 14(d). This is a change of terminology from the UCP 500 (ICC, 'Uniform Customs and Practice for Documentary Credits' (ICC Publication No 500, 1993)), which used the term 'not inconsistent'. Art 14(d) applies a less strict standard, such that 'a purely linguistic inconsistency does not justify refusal of the presentation': see Michael Bridge (ed), *Benjamin's Sale of Goods* (10th edn, Sweet & Maxwell 2017, with 2018 supplement) [23–119].

[82] See section II(A) of this chapter.

[83] UCP 600, art 20(a)(i), under which bills of lading 'must appear to ... be signed' by the carrier, by the master or by a named agent on behalf of either of them.

[84] ibid art 28(a) , according to which '... an insurance certificate or a declaration under an open cover, must appear to be issued and signed by an insurance company, an underwriter or their agents or their proxies'.

document presented appears to derive from a particular source (the carrier, in the case of the bill of lading; and the insurer, in the case of the cargo insurance certificate). In the digital world, this question is determined through a process of authentication. Indeed, article e6(f) of the eUCP provides that, in order to be acceptable under the eUCP, the data submitted must be capable of being authenticated. As indicated in the ICC Guide to the previous version of the eUCP,[85] a higher level of authentication than is possible for paper documents may be achieved when electronic data are being used, in the sense that determining reliably the source of digitally signed data is achievable with a higher degree of certainty. In other words, if bill of lading data purports to originate from a carrier, the bank would be able to check that the relevant digital signature is one actually associated with that carrier. However, the eUCP drafters attempted to adapt the standard of facial compliance applicable to paper documents to electronic data with the result that article 3b(iii) of the eUCP refers to the 'apparent identity' of the data's sender and the 'apparent source' of the data, and article e7(d)(i) provides that the bank is only obliged to check the 'apparent authenticity' of the data. Thus, where an electronic presentation is made under the eUCP, the bank's right to reject for non-compliance may give rise to more uncertainty than it would in the paper world, in view of the grey area surrounding 'authentication'. This raises various questions. What is the meaning of 'apparent' authenticity when it relates to electronic data? What steps is the bank either obliged, or entitled, to take in order to establish such authenticity? What would be the position if the bank uncovered evidence that the data were false or forged in that they do not derive from the source from which they purport to derive (for example, transport data which are not originated by a bona fide carrier)? Could the bank reject the documentary presentation as non-compliant? Could the beneficiary challenge the rejection on the basis that the data were 'apparently' authentic when the beneficiary itself was not aware of any lack of authenticity?[86]

10.23 If the letter of credit requires digitally signed data, thereby enabling the easy verification of the data's source as part of the compliance check, then arguably the data should fail the compliance test if it purports to derive from a source other than its actual originator. However, the reference to 'apparent' authenticity may muddy the waters in such circumstances and, in the absence of further guidance on this question being provided by the ICC, banks would do well to build appropriate provision into the credit itself.

[85] James Byrne and Dan Taylor, 'ICC Guide to the eUCP: Understanding the Electronic Supplement to the UCP 500' (ICC Publication No 639, 2002) 75–6.

[86] With respect to paper documents, see *Montrod Ltd v Grundkotter Fleischvertreibs GmbH* [2002] 1 WLR 1975 (CA), suggesting that the bank would be obliged to accept the presentation, although the Court of Appeal's decision has been widely criticised: see Michael Bridge, 'Documents and Contractual Congruence in International Trade' in Sarah Worthington (ed), *Commercial Law and Commercial Practice* (Hart Publishing 2003) 213, 237. See also L Y Chin and Y K Wong, 'Autonomy–A Nullity Exception at Last?' [2004] LMCLQ 14. This issue was decided differently by the Singaporean courts: see *Beam Technology (Manufacturing) Pte Ltd v Standard Chartered Bank* [2003] 1 SLR(R) 597 (CA). In both the English and Singaporean cases, the question was framed in terms of the fraud exception to the autonomy principle, not in terms of whether a forged (and therefore null) document could ever be compliant with the requirements of the credit: see Ewan McKendrick, *Goode on Commercial Law* (5th edn, Penguin 2016) [35.116]. See also the obiter dictum in *Mees Pierson NV v Bay Pacific (S) Pte Ltd and Others* [2000] 2 SLR(R) 864 (HC) [42].

B. Legal Effects

The UCP 600 also lays down particular requirements that specific paper documents, including bills of lading[87] and cargo insurance certificates,[88] need to satisfy in order to be deemed compliant. In particular, both articles 20 and 28 of the UCP 600 require, where documents are issued in sets of more than one original, that the full set of originals be presented to the bank.[89] This requirement is in line with banks' need to receive the documents not only for the purpose of checking them for compliance, but also to have transferred to them rights pertinent to their position as secured creditor. The transfer of such rights occurs by operation of laws determining the legal effects of being the 'holder' of the paper documents in question; laws that enjoy a certain uniformity throughout the world. Unfortunately, laws determining the legal effects of transacting over an online platform have not (yet) been adopted in the majority of jurisdictions. **10.24**

Nor does the eUCP specify how the transfer of rights is to be effected where electronic data are being presented in place of paper documents, as the need for the data's originality simply creates a requirement in article e9 for the information to be presented as originally issued. Thus, the eUCP does not address how important rights, normally received by the bank pursuant to the transfer of a bill of lading or the assignment of a cargo insurance certificate, are to be acquired when data rather than documents are being presented. The method for transferring those rights, therefore, needs to be carefully considered when entering into the letter of credit arrangement, and must be built into such arrangements on a case-by-case basis. This will need to be done irrespective of legislation being adopted that recognises the effects of using communication platforms to provide digital alternatives to transferable documents (as discussed in section V below), although the adoption of legislation would arguably provide the bank with greater clarity than it would otherwise be able to achieve without such legislation. **10.25**

V. Filling in the Gaps: Contractual Frameworks and their Limitations

While the technology to achieve widespread digitalisation, in particular DLT, is developing rapidly, the absence of supporting legal frameworks and widely recognised standards for its implementation and use may prove a stumbling block to rapid adoption.[90] Like the laws of many other jurisdictions, English law does not make explicit provision for electronic alternatives to bills of lading or cargo insurance certificates, either in statute[91] or case law; **10.26**

[87] UCP 600, art 20.

[88] ibid art 28.

[89] ibid arts 20(a)(iv), 28(c), although presentation of less than a full set of bills of lading is contemplated in ICC, *International Standard Banking Practice for the Examination of Documents under UCP 600* (ICC Publication No 745E 2013). ibid art A29(c).

[90] Goldby, *Electronic Documents* (n 19) [2.47]. See also Ramachandran, 'SIBOS 2017' (n 23) 7, 14, 20; SWIFT, 'Distributed Ledgers' (n 54) 7–8.

[91] In this regard, the provisions of the Carriage of Goods by Sea Act 1971 ('COGSA 1971'), which gives the force of law in the UK to the International Convention for the Unification of Certain Rules of Law relating to Bills of Lading 1924 (hereafter 'Hague Rules'), as amended by the Brussels Protocol 1968 (hereafter 'Hague-Visby Rules'), applies only to 'contracts of carriage covered by a bill of lading or any similar document of title, in so far as such document relates to the carriage of goods by sea': see COGSA 1971, s 1(4); Hague-Visby Rules, art I(b). COGSA

thus, there cannot be absolute certainty that their use will achieve the desired effects in legal terms. Pending the emergence of appropriate laws, solutions under development must rely on private contractual frameworks to establish the parties' rights and duties and to allocate any risks and liabilities. Indeed, all the electronic platforms discussed in section III above rely on such contractual frameworks to achieve the necessary legal effects. In this section, the focus shall be on how these frameworks can achieve the transfer to the financing bank of the rights that such a bank must receive in order to obtain a pledge over the goods financed by the documentary credit arrangement, as well as a direct claim against the insurer should such goods be lost or damaged.

A. Contractual Rights Against the Carrier and Rights Over the Goods Themselves

10.27 Any contractual framework governing the use of digital alternatives to bills of lading must ensure that the transferee receives rights against the carrier, including the same contractual rights as would have been received upon the transfer of a paper bill and the same proprietary rights involving the constructive possession of the underlying goods. The first of these requires action to be taken on two fronts. First, because there is no certainty that the international conventions regulating contracts of carriage (among them the Hague-Visby Rules)[92] would apply on their own terms to contracts of carriage that never contemplated the issue of a paper bill of lading,[93] the multipartite contracts that govern the relationships among users of electronic platforms will normally contain clauses incorporating as contractual terms the provisions of the various conventions that would otherwise have applied to the contract as a matter of law.[94] Secondly, to ensure that the transferee receives rights of suit against the carrier, the actions undertaken over the relevant electronic system with the object of transferring rights must be such as to amount to a novation—a contract law concept whereby one party to a contract is replaced by a third party, who thus becomes the new party to the contract.[95]

1992, s 1(5) (n 9), which gives the lawful holder of a bill of lading rights of suit against the carrier under English Law, provides that the legislation can be made applicable to digital alternatives through the issue of regulations by the Secretary of State. As no such regulations have been issued, this provision is liable to create considerable uncertainty as to whether COGSA 1992 could ever apply to digital alternatives in their absence. Note that at the time of writing the Law Commission of England and Wales is in the course of preparing a consultation paper, which it expects to publish in spring 2021, proposing law reforms intended to recognize the legal effect of documents of title and negotiable instruments issued in electronic form. See Law Commission, *Digital Assets Project*, online at <https://www.lawcom.gov.uk/project/digital-assets/> accessed 20 February 2021.

[92] Hague-Visby Rules (n 91).

[93] A combined reading of ibid art III(2) and the proviso to ibid art VI might suggest that those rules were intended to apply to all ordinary commercial shipments. See also *The Rafaela S* (n 9) [18]. See further Miriam Goldby, 'The Impact of New Commercial Practices on Liner Contracts of Carriage: New Wine in Old Skins?', in Jason Chuah (ed), *Research Handbook on Maritime Law and Regulation* (Edward Elgar 2019) ch 10.

[94] See, for example, Bolero Rulebook (n 42) rule 3.2(4).

[95] At common law, novation terminates an old contract between two contracting parties and substitutes that contract with a new contract involving one of the original contracting parties and a new contracting party. A novation, therefore, not only transfers rights, but also the original contracting party's obligations to the new contracting party who replaces him: see *Argo Fund Ltd v Essar Steel Ltd* [2005] EWHC 600 [60]–[66], aff'd [2006] 2 Lloyd's Rep 134 (CA). See also Malcolm Clarke, 'Transport Documents: Their Transferability as Documents of Title; Electronic Documents' [2002] LMCLQ 356, 366–68, explaining how the English courts are likely to address the issue of consideration necessary for a valid novation. See further Bolero Rulebook (n 42) rule 3.5.

As to the second issue raised above, an important function of the paper bill of lading is its ability, as a document of title, to enable its holder to exercise property rights over the underlying goods and/or to express its intention to transfer (or accept the transfer) of those property rights. The paper bill of lading can perform this function because its 'holder' is deemed to have constructive possession of the underlying goods.[96] Depending upon the intention with which the transfer is effected, delivery of (constructive) possession can transfer to the recipient general or special property rights.[97] In the absence of a document of title, constructive possession may be transferred in English law by an attornment.[98] Attornment essentially works as follows: the person entitled to possession of the goods (usually the shipper) communicates to the carrier the intention to transfer the goods to a third party, whereupon the carrier notifies the third party that it is now holding the goods for that third party. From that time, the third party has constructive possession of the goods[99] and can accordingly transfer the goods to another third party, and so on. 10.28

The property rights themselves are not dealt with in the multipartite contracts as these rights are obtained by operation of the transferee's contract with the transferor (whether a contract of sale or pledge) wherein the relevant intention is expressed. As an attornment by the carrier to the bank would transfer constructive possession of the goods to the bank,[100] attornment can put the bank in the position of a pledgee,[101] thereby making a document of title superfluous. Of course, transfer by this method requires the intervention of the carrier (or its agent) upon each transfer, but, as all transfers are taking place through digital communications, this intervention can be achieved more easily. 10.29

Thus, at least where English law applies, the great majority of the uncertainties surrounding the bank's position as secured creditor when the paper document of title is abandoned can be addressed by a well-conceived contractual framework and an electronic system designed in full awareness of the steps needed to achieve not only the application of the international conventions regulating contracts of carriage, but also the valid novation and attornment of contractual and proprietary rights. 10.30

[96] *Barber v Meyerstein* (1870) LR 4 HL 317, 329–30; *Sanders Bros v Maclean* (1883) 11 QBD 327 (CA) 341; *Sewell v Burdick* (n 4) 105; *The Delfini* (n 3) 268. See also Goldby, *Electronic Documents* (n 19) [5.38].

[97] *Lickbarrow v Mason* (1787) 2 TR 63, 100 ER 35; *Hibbert v Carter* (1787) 1 TR 745.

[98] The principle of attornment has its basis in medieval land law: see William Holdsworth, *Historical Introduction to the Land Law* (OUP 1927) 129–30.

[99] It would appear from *The Future Express* [1993] 2 Lloyd's Rep 542 (CA) 550 that express acknowledgement is necessary for an attornment to take place, since the Court of Appeal noted that 'the bill of lading is the one exception to the rule that a change in the right to possession of goods in the keeping of a third party requires [the latter] to attorn'. See, more recently, *Mercuria Energy Trading v Citibank* [2015] EWHC 1481 (Comm) [59]–[60], holding that, in the absence of attornment, the transfer of warehouse receipts, which are not documents of title, does not constitute constructive delivery of the goods to the transferee.

[100] For the effect of an attornment to a financing bank, see Clyde & Co, 'The Legal Status of E-Bills of Lading' (17 October 2018) <https://www.clydeco.com/insight/reports/the-legal-status-of-e-bills-of-lading> accessed 1 August 2020: 'The carrier [who has attorned to a bank], as bailee of the goods, owes a duty to deliver the goods to the order of the bank. Accordingly, the bank will be able to enforce that obligation against the carrier, subject to a) the terms of the attornment, b) the contractual provisions pursuant to which the carrier holds the goods and c) whether the property in the goods had already passed from the previous holder to the borrower [to whom the bank has extended credit] at the time of insolvency [of the e-bill's previous holder].'

[101] See Richard King, *Gutteridge and Megrah's Law of Bankers' Commercial Credits* (8th edn, Europa Publications 2001) [8–805]: '… delivery of possession [by way of pledge] may take the form of the actual handing over of the goods to the pledgee or of a symbolical or constructive delivery. Symbolical or constructive delivery may be effected *by an agreement on the part of the owner of the goods, or some person holding the goods on his behalf, to hold them as bailee on behalf of the pledgee*, a device which is deemed to change the nature of the original possession of the goods, so as to amount to a constructive delivery' (emphasis added).

10.31 Some uncertainties may remain. Determination of the applicable law would depend on the forum in which any dispute regarding the goods is being decided, and that law may be hard to ascertain in a digital environment with respect to goods that are being transported across borders over long distances. Moreover, whatever the relevant applicable law, it would need to recognise the effects of novation and attornment in order for the suggested solution to operate effectively. In addition, it is uncertain whether, in terms of capital adequacy requirements,[102] the letter of credit permitting electronic documents would be treated in the same way as if the pledge over the goods were taken through transfer of a paper-based document of title. These uncertainties can only really be resolved if appropriate legislation is adopted. This is the subject of the discussion in section VI.

B. Direct Claim Against the Insurer

10.32 Once a bank has obtained a pledge over the goods, the bank also has an insurable interest in them.[103] The bank would normally obtain a direct claim against the insurer as a result of the assignment to the bank of a paper cargo insurance certificate,[104] and, as already noted, even certificates issued electronically are normally printed out and assigned in this way. However, if the full benefits of digitalisation are to be achieved, a method of transferring rights without relying on paper must be devised. Can the desired legal effect (namely, giving the transferee a direct claim against the insurer) be achieved if paper is abandoned?

10.33 Various routes may be open under English law to ensuring that the bank has a direct claim against the insurer. First, where an open-cover insurance contract is in place, in order for it to cover a particular shipment of goods, a declaration of that shipment needs to be made under the open cover.[105] In the event that the identity of the particular financing bank is known ahead of that declaration being made and the certificate issued, its name can be entered as assured or as an additional assured, so that assignment will not be necessary. Secondly, under section 23(1) of the MIA, the policy must specify the name of the assured *or of some other person affecting insurance on his behalf*. This indicates that, even if the cover is taken out in the name of another person, the bank, as principal, may be considered an assured if the person effecting the insurance intends to contract as agent on the bank's behalf[106] at the time that the risk is

[102] Most jurisdictions impose capital requirements on internationally active banks in line with the Capital Adequacy Framework adopted by the Basel Committee on Banking Supervision ('BCBS'). The most recent (third) edition of the Framework was adopted in 2011, with subsequent additions and revisions: see Bank for International Settlements, 'Basel III: A global regulatory framework for more resilient banks and banking systems—revised version' (June 2011) <https://www.bis.org/basel_framework/> accessed 1 August 2020 (hereafter Basel III). Implementation is under way and progress is being monitored in the twenty-eight BCBS member states: see Bank for International Settlements, 'Sixteenth progress report on adoption of the Basel regulatory framework' (May 2019) <https://www.bis.org/bcbs/publ/d464.htm> accessed 1 August 2020. Treatment of credit-risk mitigation under Basel III may be found in the section on Calculation of Risk-Weighted Assets for Credit Risk ('CRE'). See in particular Chapter CRE 20 'Standardised Approach: Individual Exposures', para 20.44.

[103] MIA (n 17), s 8. Similar rules to these apply in jurisdictions that have modelled their laws on the MIA.

[104] Goldby, *Electronic Documents* (n 19) [7.32].

[105] MIA (n 17) s 29. See also Goldby, *Electronic Documents* (n 19) [7.13]–[7.14].

[106] Jonathan Gilman, Claire Blanchard, Mark Templeman, Philippa Hopkins, and Neil Hart, *Arnould: Law of Marine Insurance and Average* (19th edn, Sweet & Maxwell 2018) [8–809]: 'Whether it is necessary that the "agent" should have had any particular person in mind as his principal is a matter on which conflicting opinions have been expressed, and the cases are not easily reconciled. It is submitted, however, that it is sufficient to show that the person effecting the policy was intending to insure on behalf of persons having an insurable interest of the

bound,[107] and has authority to act as such.[108] Where the agent enters into the contract of insurance without authority from his principal, that principal may ratify the contract pursuant to section 86 of the MIA, even after he is aware of the loss. For that provision to apply, however, the insurer needs to have been aware that the agent was, or at least might have been, acting for another, because an undisclosed principal cannot ratify.[109] However, even if the bank is not identified at the time of the declaration pursuant to which the certificate is issued, the bank may nevertheless qualify as an assured by being a member of the class indicated.[110]

Statutory law contemplates two other routes to giving the assured a direct claim: an assignment under section 50 of the MIA or an assignment effected in accordance with section 136 of the Law of Property Act 1925 ('LPA 1925'). As regards the MIA route, two questions may create uncertainty, namely whether, and under what circumstances, electronic data would be considered to constitute a 'policy' for the purposes of section 50 of the MIA;[111] and whether that provision would apply at all to a certificate issued pursuant to a declaration under an open cover.[112] Provided that the digital evidence of cover is accepted to be a 'policy' for the purposes of section 50 of the MIA, there is no reason why it could not be assigned by a method other than indorsement, so long as one is able to show that there was an intention to assign[113] and that this method was a 'customary manner' of **10.34**

same nature as that of the person who later seeks to ratify, or acquiring such an interest at some time during the risk.' (hereafter Gilman et al, *Arnould.)* Indeed, in the US, policies may be written 'for the account of whom it may concern', in which case, 'if it was the intent of the person taking out the insurance that the interest of the party seeking indemnity be covered, that party actually had an insurable interest, and indemnity is due by the insurer to that party': see Thomas J Schoenbaum, *Admiralty and Maritime Law* (5th edn, West 2011) [19–3]. However, by express agreement a person may exclude his ability to rely on a policy intended to cover as assureds a class of persons of which he forms part: see *Haberdashers' Aske's Federation Trust v Lakehouse Contracts* [2018] EWHC 558 (TCC). Nor will the person attempting to claim under the insurance contract succeed if the insurance purports to compensate a class of persons of which he does not form part, even if he is named as co-insured: see *Cruise and Maritime Services International v Navigators Underwriting Agency (The Marco Polo)* [2017] EWHC 843 (Comm), where it was held that the general sales agent of a ship's time charterer could not claim under a policy where it was named as co-insured, as the policy was expressed as indemnifying the assured for 'losses, costs and expenses incurred as charterers' (ibid [21]). The court noted that the claimant's name had been added to the insurance policy 'at no additional premium' and 'without any real thought' (ibid [28]).

[107] *Siu Yin Kwan v Eastern Insurance Co Ltd* [1994] 1 AC 199 (PC). Privity-of-contract rules would prevent anyone, on whose behalf the broker did not intend to contract, from obtaining rights against the insurer through this method: see *Iraqi Ministry of Defence v Arcepey Shipping Co SA (The Angel Bell)* [1979] 2 Lloyd's Rep 491 (QBD) 497 (hereafter *The Angel Bell*); *Canadian Imperial Bank of Commerce v Insurance Corp of Ireland Ltd* (1991) 75 DLR (4th) 482 (BCCA).

[108] *Keighley, Maxted & Co v Durant* [1901] AC 240 (HL).

[109] ibid.

[110] For evidence that this option is, in fact, being adopted to some extent, see Law Commission, *Insurance Contract Law: Post Contract Duties and Other Issues* (Law Com CP No 201, 2011) <https://www.lawcom.gov.uk/document/insurance-contract-law-post-contract-duties-and-other-issues-consultation/> accessed 1 August 2020 (hereafter Law Commission, *Insurance Contract Law*) [16.40]: 'We were told by a leading cargo insurer that under their contractual terms of insurance the assured includes not only the name stated in the schedule but also "any party to whom insurable interest in the subject matter insured hereunder passes under a contract of sale". This means that the insurance is assigned automatically as soon as insurable interest in the goods passes. All that is required is that the assignor provides the assignee with details of the cover.' Of course, where a bank is involved as financer, the clause would need to specify pledge agreements and not just contracts of sale.

[111] See Law Commission, *Reforming Insurance Contract Law Issues Paper 9—The Requirement for a Formal Marine Policy: Should Section 22 Be Repealed?* (October 2010) [4.18]–[4.22] <https://www.lawcom.gov.uk/document/insurance-contract-law-issues-papers/> accessed 1 August 2020.

[112] The view was expressed in *Diamond Alkali Export Corp v Fl Bourgeois* [1921] 3 KB 443 (KBD) 457, that MIA (n 17), s 50 would not apply to certificates; however, this contention has not been repeated since and certificates are assigned as a matter of course in practice. See further *Koskas v Standard Marine* (n 20).

[113] *Safadi v Western Assurance Co* (1933) 46 Ll L Rep 140 (KBD) 144.

assigning.[114] Where the MIA route is taken, and a claim is made by the bank, the insurer may raise defences that it would have been entitled to raise if the action had been brought in the name of the person by whom, or on behalf of whom, the policy was effected, but only if those defences arise out of the contract itself.[115]

10.35 Where the LPA 1925 route is selected, the benefit of the insurance contract will be transferred to the assignee, allowing the latter to sue in its own name. The assignment must be absolute and must transfer to the assignee all the legal title to the benefit of the promise assigned.[116] The assignment does not create a new contract between the insurer and the transferee, but simply entitles the transferee to the benefit of the insurer's promise under the insurance contract.[117] An assignment of this kind must observe certain formalities[118] and is subject to equities that have priority over the assignee's right,[119] meaning that the insurer may raise against the assignee any defence or right of set-off valid as against the assured, making this route less attractive to an assignee than that available under the MIA, although the same uncertainties do not arise with respect to the application of the LPA 1925.

10.36 Assignment is, therefore, by no means precluded if the paper cargo insurance certificate is abandoned, provided that the appropriate procedural steps are built into the design of the electronic system and the supporting contractual framework identifies the parties' intentions with respect to the effect of each of those steps.

C. Trade Finance Platforms: The Bank's Legal Position

10.37 There are other legal issues that need to be addressed where data are being presented to a financing bank, rather than documents. In particular, consideration must be given to the best way of meeting confidentiality and data-protection obligations. Communication platforms over which authenticated data is shared and where contractual and proprietary entitlements are recorded, as well as the contractual frameworks supporting them, will need to be designed with a view to achieving not only the desired legal effects equivalent to those attendant upon the issue and transfer of relevant documents, but also the fulfilment of any other legal or statutory obligations. For example, in order to transact over we.trade, users

[114] There are suggestions in the case law that, for these purposes, it may not be as hard to show that a particular market practice is 'customary': see *The Angel Bell* (n 107) 497; cf Law Commission, *Insurance Contract Law* (n 110) [2.49].

[115] MIA (n 17), s 50(2). See also *Baker v Adam* (1910) 15 Com Cas 227. Examples of defences arising out of the insurance contract include non-disclosure of material facts by the assured at the time the contract was concluded (see *William Pickersgill & Sons Ltd v London & Provincial Marine & General Insurance Co Ltd* [1912] 3 KB 614 (KBD)) or any breach of the duty of utmost good faith or fraud on the part of the original assured (see *Black King Shipping Corp v Massie (The Litsion Pride)* [1985] 1 Lloyd's Rep 437 (QBD) 519). See also *Graham Joint Stock Shipping Co Ltd v Merchants Marine Insurance Co Ltd (The Ioanna) (No 1)* [1924] AC 294 (HL) 297; cf *P Samuel & Co Ltd v Dumas* [1924] AC 431 (HL), in which the mortgagee was a party to the policy in his own right, rather than as assignee.

[116] In *Hughes v Pump House Hotel (No 1)* [1902] 2 KB 190 (CA) 194, Mathew LJ described such an assignment as 'one under which all the rights of the assignor in respect of the moneys payable under the building contract were intended to pass to the assignees, and not one which purports to be by way of charge only'.

[117] *Raiffeisen Zentralbank Osterreich AG v Five Star General Trading LLC (The Mount I)* [2001] QB 825 (CA) [74].

[118] Law of Property Act 1925 (hereafter 'LPA 1925'), s 136(1) requires that the assignment must be effected in writing by the assured and express written notice must be given to the insurer. The assignment must also not be conditional, but absolute.

[119] ibid.

must sign up to the we.trade rulebook,[120] and buyers/sellers obtain access to we.trade via a member bank with whom they have to enter a contractual agreement.[121] Transactions taking place over the platform are not broadcast to the whole network, but, thanks to a feature in Hyperledger Fabric called 'Channels', they are transmitted only to those peers who are members of a particular channel, so that information about a particular trade will be uploaded to a channel of which only the buyer and seller bank nodes are members.[122] This safeguards confidentiality. Further, personal data is never stored on the blockchain, and only a reference to attached documents (and not the documents themselves) is stored on the blockchain,[123] enabling compliance with privacy and data-protection requirements.[124]

VI. Filling in the Gaps: Legislation

The legislative route to recognising the ability of electronic records and processes to have equivalent effects to the issue and transfer of certain trade documents could, of course, preclude the need by parties to have resort to the incorporation of convention terms, novation, and attornment within contractual frameworks underlying digital alternatives. Legislation would also address any uncertainties that cannot be resolved contractually. Two major projects of the United Nations Commission on International Trade Law ('UNCITRAL') have attempted to provide avenues for nations to adopt legislation in this space. **10.38**

The United Nations Convention on Contracts for the Carriage of Goods Wholly or Partly by Sea 2008 ('the Rotterdam Rules') includes provisions on negotiable electronic transport records:[125] provided certain requirements are satisfied,[126] these electronic records are treated as equivalents of negotiable transport records[127] (or transferable paper bills of lading). The Rotterdam Rules also provide for procedures[128] to transfer rights against a carrier that make no reference to any paper document.[129] Both of these sets of provisions can support the replacement of the paper bill of lading with electronic data and processes, precluding the distinct legal treatment of any electronic alternative as long as it complies with relevant requirements. At the time of writing, twenty-five states have signed the Rotterdam Rules, and five have ratified them. The Rotterdam Rules will not come into force until they have gained twenty ratifications,[130] but in the meantime those provisions could provide legislators, who **10.39**

[120] we.trade, 'FAQ' (n 71), in particular the answer to the question, 'How are orders and transactions proved?'. The contents of the we.trade rulebook are not publicly available.

[121] ibid in particular the answer to the question, 'How is the onboarding of each type of client in the platform carried out?'.

[122] ibid; in particular the answer to the question, 'What data is uploaded to blockchain?'.

[123] ibid.

[124] Regulation (EU) 2016/679 of the European Parliament and of the Council of 27 April 2016 on the Protection of Natural Persons with Regard to the Processing of Personal Data and on the Free Movement of Such Data, and Repealing Directive 95/46/EC (General Data Protection Regulation) [2016] OJ L119/1, which came into force on 25 May 2018 by virtue of art 99.

[125] United Nations Convention on Contracts for the Carriage of Goods Wholly or Partly by Sea (adopted 11 December 2008 UNGA Res 63/122) arts 1(10)(b), 1(18), 1(21), 1(22), 3, 8 (hereafter 'Rotterdam Rules').

[126] ibid arts 9, 38(2).

[127] ibid arts 3, 8.

[128] These procedures require a means of 'designating, a means of 'notifying', a means of 'identifying' and (impliedly) a means of recording who is currently the controlling party: ibid art 51(1).

[129] ibid arts 50, 51(1).

[130] For the status of the Rotterdam Rules, see <https://treaties.un.org/Pages/ViewDetails.aspx?src=IND&mtdsg_no=XI-D-8&chapter=11&clang=_en> accessed 1 August 2020.

wish to adopt rules recognising digital equivalents to paper bills of lading, with a reference point.

10.40 Another reference point may be found in the UNCITRAL Model Law on Electronic Transferable Records 2017 ('MLETR'),[131] which sets out the requirements that electronic alternatives must satisfy in order to be recognised as capable of achieving the same legal effects, in terms of parties' rights and liabilities, as paper documents of title and negotiable instruments. If domestic legislation were to be modelled on the MLETR's provisions and its requirements were fulfilled, then the legal status of digital alternatives to both paper bills of lading and cargo insurance certificates would be clarified. The principle of technological neutrality ensures that so long as the relevant functional equivalence requirements are satisfied, any technology may be used, including DLT.

VII. Conclusion

10.41 This chapter discusses the implications that replacement of paper bills of lading and paper cargo insurance certificates with digital alternatives would have on a financing bank within the current legal environment. It also examines the steps that can be taken to resolve any uncertainties as to such a bank's legal position as secured creditor. This chapter argues that the majority of these uncertainties may be addressed through carefully designed contractual frameworks. The current embryonic state of the law should not, therefore, stall efforts to introduce, and transact on the basis of, digital alternatives to these commonly used paper documents. This transition is desirable in view of its potential to reduce the costs and delays that diminish the attractiveness of the letter of credit as a financing tool.

[131] UNCITRAL, 'Model Law on Electronic Transferable Records' (2017) UN Publication No E.17.V.5 <https://uncitral.un.org/sites/uncitral.un.org/files/media-documents/uncitral/en/mletr_ebook_e.pdf> accessed 20 August 2020. See further ch 11 (Davidson) in this volume.

11

Implementation and Implications of the UNCITRAL Model Law on Electronic Transferable Records in Trade Finance

Alan Davidson

I. Introduction

The background to the Model Law on Electronic Transferable Records ('ML-ETR') requires an appreciation of the approach taken in, and the purposes underlying, the previous texts promulgated by Working Group IV (Electronic Commerce) of UNCITRAL.[1] UNCITRAL was formed by resolution of the United Nations General Assembly in December 1966. The purpose of UNCITRAL is to further the progressive harmonisation and unification of the law of international trade.[2] UNCITRAL currently has six Working Groups involved in drafting Conventions, Model Laws, Legislative Guides and Recommendations, Contractual Texts, and Explanatory Texts. In the 1990s, UNCITRAL expressed its belief that national legislatures would significantly benefit from enhancing their existing legislation governing the use of alternatives to paper-based methods of communication and storage of information, and from formulating such legislation where none currently existed. UNCITRAL's aim was to address the growing concern, doubt, and legal uncertainty arising from the increase in electronic commerce. **11.01**

In 1996, UNCITRAL released what is currently the most popular model law for ensuring consumer and commercial protection in an electronic environment. The UNCITRAL Model Law on Electronic Commerce ('ML-EC')[3] provides nations with a template of internationally acceptable and robust rules that would remove legal obstacles to electronic commerce and create a more secure legal environment for those participating in such activity. The ML-EC was intended to facilitate the use of electronic forms of communication and the digital storage of information in electronic records. **11.02**

To this end, the ML-EC provides standards to assess the legal force of electronic messages and legal rules for electronic commerce in specific areas, such as the carriage of goods. In relation to the former, the ML-EC incorporates the fundamental principles of functional equivalence and non-discrimination. That is, where the electronic form is functionally **11.03**

[1] The author has been an active delegate to all sessions of the United Nations Commission on International Trade Law ('UNCITRAL') Working Group IV (Electronic Commerce) since 2014.

[2] Establishment of the United Nations Commission on International Trade Law ('UNCITRAL'), UNGA Res 2205 (XXI) (17 December 1966).

[3] UNCITRAL, 'Model Law on Electronic Commerce with Guide to Enactment 1996 with additional article 5 *bis* as adopted in 1998' (1999) UN Publication No E.99.V.4 <https://uncitral.un.org/sites/uncitral.un.org/files/media-documents/uncitral/en/19-04970_ebook.pdf> accessed 20 August 2020 (hereafter UNCITRAL, 'ML-EC').

equivalent to the traditional paper-based form, it should be treated equally by the law; and the law should not discriminate against transactions because of their electronic form. These core principles permeate virtually all domestic legislation based on the ML-EC. An additional principle underlying the ML-EC is that of technology neutrality. This term was chosen in response to the recognition that technology is constantly developing. For example, as the term 'electronic mail' connotes a particular medium of communication, the ML-EC uses the more generic expression 'data message' to avoid that concept and its descriptive language becoming anachronistic.

11.04 More specifically, the ML-EC addresses the legal recognition of data messages; the notion of 'writing' in the electronic sphere; the legal validity of electronic signatures; the recognition of an electronic record as an 'original' record; the legal admissibility of, and evidentiary weight to be attributed to, data messages; the retention of data messages; the formation and validity of contracts by electronic means; the recognition by parties of data messages; the attribution of data messages to particular parties; the acknowledgement of receipt for data messages; and the determination of the time and place of dispatch and receipt of data messages.[4]

11.05 The ML-EC represented a significant step forward in relation to the regulation of electronic commerce and largely achieved its objectives of removing legal obstacles, promoting commercial certainty, providing a more secure legal environment for electronic commerce, and being 'of use to individual users of electronic commerce in the drafting of some of the contractual solutions that might be needed to overcome the legal obstacles'.[5] The ML-EC has gained significant international acceptance, being incorporated into legislation in more than 150 jurisdictions.[6] The drafting process was attended by representatives of over fifty nations and ten international organisations. Notwithstanding this global success and adoption, the ML-EC represents 1990s thinking and reflects the limited understanding of the issues at that time. It has become dated with the advent of newer technology and the even greater uptake of that technology. More significantly, case law has closely scrutinised the provisions and revealed flaws.[7]

11.06 In 2005, the United Nations released the UN Convention on the Use of Electronic Communications in International Contracts ('the Electronic Communications Convention').[8] The Electronic Communications Convention is intended to assure commercial parties and financial institutions internationally that contracts negotiated electronically

[4] ibid, arts 5–15.

[5] UNCITRAL, 'Guide to Enactment of the UNCITRAL Model Law on Electronic Commerce (1996)' UN (1999) Publication No E.99.V.4 [2] <https://uncitral.un.org/sites/uncitral.un.org/files/media-documents/uncitral/en/19-04970_ebook.pdf> accessed 20 August 2020.

[6] See UNCITRAL, 'UNCITRAL Model Law on Electronic Commerce (1996)—Status' <https://uncitral.un.org/en/texts/ecommerce/modellaw/electronic_commerce/status> accessed 20 August 2020.

[7] For example, with respect to confusion about 'time of receipt', see *Austar Finance Group Pty Ltd v Campbell* [2007] NSWSC 1493; and *Reed v Eire* [2009] NSWSC 678; and, with respect to the signature provisions, see *SM Integrated Transware Pte Ltd v Schenker Singapore (Pte) Ltd* [2005] 2 SLR(R) 651 (HC); and *Golden Ocean Group Ltd v Salgaocar Mining Industries Pvt Ltd* [2012] EWCA Civ 265. See also Alan Davidson, *Social Media and Electronic Commerce Law* (Cambridge University Press 2016) chs 11–12.

[8] Convention on the Use of Electronic Communications in International Contracts (adopted 23 November 2005 UNGA Res 60/21, entered into force 1 March 2013) <https://uncitral.un.org/sites/uncitral.un.org/files/media-documents/uncitral/en/06-57452_ebook.pdf> accessed 20 August 2020 (hereafter UNCITRAL, 'Electronic Communications Convention').

are as valid and enforceable as traditional paper-based transactions. The provisions build on and improve both the ML-EC and the UNCITRAL Model Law on Electronic Signatures promulgated in 2001.[9]

The Electronic Communications Convention implemented several improvements to the ML-EC. First, certain definitions were refined and extended. For example, 'communication' and 'electronic communication' were added to expand the limited meaning of 'data message'. 'Communication' now includes 'any statement, declaration, demand, notice or request, including an offer and the acceptance of an offer, that the parties are required to make or choose to make in connection with the formation or performance of a contract'.[10] 'Automated messaging system' was inserted to address the issue of transactions and messaging being generated by a computer program without human review or intervention. 'Originator' and 'addressee' were refined to apply to the expanded meaning of electronic communications. **11.07**

Second, the test for the functional equivalence of a 'signature' was expanded. The ML-EC test invoked only a 'reliability test', namely that the electronic signature must be 'as reliable as appropriate' to be deemed the functional equivalent of a manuscript signature. Whilst this provided greater flexibility, it also produced more uncertainty. UNCITRAL expressed its concern that a party might seek to 'invoke the 'reliability test' to repudiate its signature in cases where the actual identity of the party and its actual intention could be proved'.[11] The 'reliability test' should not be used to 'lead a court or trier of fact to invalidate the entire contract on the ground that the electronic signature was not appropriately reliable' where there is no dispute regarding the identity of the signatory or the fact of signing.[12] Hence, the Electronic Communications Convention inserted an alternative test for validating the method of signature where that method is 'proven in fact' to have identified the signatory and indicated the signatory's intention in respect of the information contained in the electronic communication. **11.08**

Third, the test for determining the time of dispatch and receipt was outmoded. The ML-EC test for ascertaining the time of dispatch did not take into account the possibility that the sender might retain the ability to retrieve a sent message. The ML-EC test for determining time of receipt referred to a communication entering a 'designated information system' without any further explanation. As regards email, courts were unsure whether 'designated information system' meant the Internet generally, the recipient's internet service provider or the recipient's email inbox. This was rectified by the Electronic Communications Convention using the expression 'capable of being retrieved'.[13] **11.09**

[9] UNCITRAL, 'Model Law on Electronic Signatures with Guide to Enactment' (2001) UN Publication No E.02.V.8 <https://uncitral.un.org/sites/uncitral.un.org/files/media-documents/uncitral/en/ml-elecsig-e.pdf> accessed 20 August 2020.

[10] UNCITRAL, 'Electronic Communications Convention' (n 8) art 4.

[11] UNCITRAL, 'Explanatory note by the UNCITRAL secretariat on the United Nations Convention on the Use of Electronic Communications in International Contracts' (2007) UN Publication No E.07.V.2 [164] <https://www.uncitral.org/pdf/english/texts/electcom/06-57452_Ebook.pdf> accessed 20 August 2020 (hereafter UNCITRAL, 'Explanatory note (2007)').

[12] ibid.

[13] UNCITRAL, 'Electronic Communications Convention' (n 8) art 10(2).

11.10 Fourth, the Electronic Communications Convention introduced provisions governing contracts involving electronic communications in order to deal with invitations to make offers, the use of automated message systems for contract formation and for the correction of errors in electronic communications.[14] The Convention also removes any legal obstacles that may arise from treaty provisions concluded before the widespread use of electronic communications. In that regard, the Convention also provides for the retrospective treatment and re-interpretation of earlier United Nations Conventions, including the Convention on the Recognition and Enforcement of Foreign Arbitral Awards 1958 ('the New York Convention') and the United Nations Convention on Contracts for the International Sale of Goods 1980 ('CISG').[15] To date, the Electronic Communications Convention has been signed by many nations, and ratified by fifteen.[16]

11.11 The ML-EC and the Electronic Communications Convention were intended to apply to electronic forms of writing, signatures, transactions, and contracts. They were not intended to apply to negotiable instruments, documents of title, and similar trade documents. Indeed, Article 2(2) of the Electronic Communications Convention specifies certain exclusions, which include:

> [B]ills of exchange, promissory notes, consignment notes, bills of lading, warehouse receipts or any transferable document or instrument that entitles the bearer or beneficiary to claim the delivery of goods or the payment of a sum of money.[17]

11.12 The reason for this deliberate exclusion was a concern regarding the potential consequences of unauthorised duplication of documents of title and negotiable instruments. Indeed, any transferable instrument that entitles the bearer or beneficiary to claim the delivery of goods or the payment of a sum of money makes it necessary to develop mechanisms to ensure the 'singularity' of those instruments. Additionally, the issues raised by negotiable instruments and similar trade documents involve considerations that go beyond merely ensuring the equivalence between paper-based and electronic forms. In particular, the Working Group IV (Electronic Commerce) determined that it would need to deal with the question of the 'uniqueness' of electronic instruments. In this regard, UNCITRAL stated:

> [F]inding a solution for this problem required a combination of legal, technological and business solutions, which had not yet been fully developed and tested.[18]

11.13 The Working Group quite deliberately put aside the thorny issues of the functional equivalence of electronic transferable records until a later time. That time came in 2011 when UNCITRAL held a colloquium 'with a view to identifying a roadmap for future work by the Commission in the area of electronic commerce, with particular regard to legal issues

[14] ibid arts 11, 12, and 14.

[15] ibid art 20.

[16] The nations that have ratified or acceded to the Electronic Communications Convention (n 8) are Azerbaijan, Bahrain, Benin, Cameroon, Congo, Dominican Republic, Fiji, Honduras, Kiribati, Montenegro, Paraguay, Russian Federation, Singapore, and Sri Lanka. Australia has stated that it will ratify the Convention; although Australia has now incorporated the terms of the Convention into its domestic legislation.

[17] Although this exclusion does not specifically refer to letters of credit or bank payment obligations, it could be interpreted *euisdem generis* to include such other trade instruments.

[18] UNCITRAL, 'Explanatory Note (2007)' (n 11) [80]–[81].

relating to electronic transferable records'.[19] As a result of that colloquium, UNCITRAL mandated Working Group IV (Electronic Commerce) with drafting rules concerning electronic transferable records. In the first few sessions, the delegates debated whether the work should take the form of a convention, a model law or some other form of text. The Working Group eventually settled on a model law.

II. Model Law on Electronic Transferable Records 2017

A. Purpose

In making the ML-ETR available, UNCITRAL intends to provide a platform for ensuring harmonisation, legal certainty, and commercial predictability for the increased participation in electronic commerce. The purpose of the ML-ETR[20] is to facilitate the legal use of 'electronic transferable records' ('ETRs') domestically and internationally. ETRs ought to be fundamental in the world of electronic commerce and contribute to trade facilitation. The ML-ETR applies to ETRs that are functionally equivalent to paper-based transferable documents or instruments. Article 2 defines a 'transferable document or instrument' as 'a document or instrument issued on paper that entitles the holder to claim the performance of the obligation indicated in the document or instrument and to transfer the right to performance of the obligation indicated in the document or instrument through the transfer of that document or instrument'. Such 'transferable documents and instruments' are vital in international trade, in particular transport, logistics, and trade finance (popularly referred to as 'fintech') and would typically include bills of lading, bills of exchange, promissory notes, consignment notes, and warehouse receipts (in developing countries). In other words, the concept of the 'transferable document or instrument' covers those instruments previously excluded by the Electronic Communications Convention and would also extend to those obligations owed to beneficiaries under commercial and standby letters of credit and independent guarantees.[21] The principle of technological neutrality entails adopting a system-neutral approach, enabling the use of a variety of technological models, whether based on registry, token, distributed ledger, or other technology. By using such technology, the commercial risks become more than acceptable for commercial parties in dealings that involve significant transaction value, the transfer of property rights and the imposition of obligations. Transactions can also proceed with greater efficiency, speed, and security. **11.14**

[19] UNCITRAL, Colloquium on Electronic Commerce (14-16 February 2011, New York) <https://uncitral.un.org/en/colloquia/electronic_commerce/2010> accessed 20 August 2020. The writer was an invited speaker at the colloquium.

[20] UNCITRAL, 'Model Law on Electronic Transferable Records' (2017) UN Publication No E.17.V.5 <https://uncitral.un.org/sites/uncitral.un.org/files/media-documents/uncitral/en/mletr_ebook_e.pdf> accessed 20 August 2020 (hereafter UNCITRAL, 'ML-ETR').

[21] ibid. UNCITRAL, 'ML-ETR' would deal with the issue, transfer, and amendment of letters of credit and independent guarantees, but not the presentation of documents by the beneficiary. However, the e-UCP, which is the electronic supplement to the UCP 600, is intended to deal with electronic presentation: see ICC, 'eUCP Version 2.0' (2019).

11.15 This potential framework for regulation will also provide some comfort to commercial parties developing blockchain technology.[22] Blockchains can passively and faithfully store records and information or can be used actively as a mechanism for facilitating commercial transactions. An example of the latter use is the 'smart contract'. In essence, a 'smart contract' is an agreement or part of an agreement converted into code. A 'smart contract' permits the increased use of automation in the commercial world, computer systems are effectively trusted with greater autonomy through artificial-intelligence platforms and the expanding use of blockchain or distributed-ledger technology. To form a 'smart contract' using such technology,[23] parties encrypt a message or messages, forming a block of data, using precise and predetermined protocols, which then 'inform' all the nodes on the network of the new block. The nodes validate the transaction by rigorously verifying the parties' identity and then record the acceptance of the block on the ledger. This process is shared (or 'distributed') amongst the nodes. In due course, an additional encrypted block of data is typically added to the ledger (after it has been verified with the same level of rigour) after the previously verified block, thereby forming a chain of blocks. All network nodes continue verification and authentication of each new submission of a block. The integrity of the ledger is said to be immutable.[24] The 'smart contract' can be self-executing, which belies the underlying complexity. In that regard, the Ethereum system permits tokens to represent and incorporate smart contracts; and most importantly to be self-executing and self-enforcing.

11.16 Any number of contracts can be put into 'smart' form. One example is an option agreement: where the requirements of the option are satisfied, the 'smart contract' is activated and the necessary consequential actions are automatically taken, including execution and payment. Each step is recorded on the blockchain. In the international trade context, payment under the sale contract may be triggered when the vessel reaches a set GPS position, or a financial penalty might be automatically imposed should the vessel fail to reach that position by a specified time and date. Such technology can also facilitate the financing of international trade and can be used in connection with letters of credit, independent guarantees, bills of exchange, promissory notes, and so forth. This trade finance innovation is facilitated by the advent of ETRs and the introduction of the ML-ETR.

B. Operation

11.17 The ML-ETR builds on the core principles of non-discrimination against the use of electronic means of transacting, the functional equivalence of paper-based and electronic methods and technology neutrality underpinning all UNCITRAL texts on electronic commerce. In regard to the last issue, Working Group IV (Electronic Commerce) barely

[22] For the use of blockchain technology in relation to electronic bills of lading and cargo insurance certificates, see ch 10 (Goldby) in this volume. For scepticism over the use of blockchain technology in trade finance, see ch 12 (Winn) in this volume.

[23] The expression originates from the seminal article by Satoshi Nakamoto where the expression used is a 'chain of blocks': see Satoshi Nakamoto, 'Bitcoin: A Peer-to-Peer Electronic Cash System' <https://bitcoin.org/bitcoin.pdf> accessed 20 August 2020.

[24] See, for example, Christopher Millard, 'Blockchain and Law: Incompatible Codes?' (2018) 34 Computer Law & Security Review 843.

discussed the underlying technology involved, since the delegates and observers were typically lawyers. Indeed, there was an underlying, unspoken assumption that the technical experts regarded any issues concerning the originality or duplication of ETRs as resolved. Accordingly, the text of the ML-ETR remains largely neutral in its references to the underlying technology, although the Explanatory Note to the ML-ETR does refer to 'enabling the use of various models whether based on registry, token, distributed ledger or other technology'.[25] The reference to a 'registry' could include a centralised, decentralised, or distributed registry. Accordingly, the ML-ETR does not represent an abandonment of the idea of using a central registry for its purposes, even though experimentation with centralised registries has had mixed results. The reference to distributed-ledger technology clearly envisages the possible use of blockchain technology, which involves a ledger that is available to all, immutable, and supplemented by stringent crypto-methods. That said, no attempt is made in the explanatory notes to consider how, where, or when blockchain technology should or could be utilised, so the matter has been left to merchants and financiers to implement this in due course. Finally, the reference to 'other' technologies in the explanatory notes provides for the possibility of future technologies that commercial parties may develop and incorporate into their dealings. Ultimately, the ML-ETR may acclimate various forms of technology, including registries, tokens, and distributed ledgers.

Chapter II of the ML-ETR contains provisions on the 'functional equivalence' of paper- **11.18**
based and electronic methods. More specifically, articles 8 and 9 provide for the functional equivalence of electronic writing and electronic signatures,[26] so that writing and signatures should be treated equally by the applicable law whether in electronic or paper-based form. Whilst many nations have already enacted electronic writing and signature provisions in conformity with the ML-EC, the Working Group recognised the potential for a jurisdiction to adopt the ML-ETR without previously having enacted the equivalent of the ML-EC or the Electronic Communications Convention. In relation to trade finance, most financial institutions are members of SWIFT,[27] which since 1975 has provided a secure electronic network for financial institutions to send, receive, and authenticate information about financial transactions. It could be regarded as financial institutions own secure private intranet, which existed prior to the Internet. Recognising the advantages of such a network, banks became early adopters. If the domestic law of a specific jurisdiction casts doubt upon the validity of electronic transactions concluded through SWIFT, the adoption of the ML-EC, Electronic Communications Convention, and now the ML-ETR will effectively settle that issue. This will facilitate the more widespread adopting of electronic trade finance.

The key provision of the ML-ETR is article 10.[28] Where the law requires a transferable docu- **11.19**
ment or instrument, that requirement is met by an electronic record where two conditions are met. First, the electronic record must contain the information that would be required to be contained in the corresponding paper-based transferable document or instrument.

[25] UNCITRAL, 'Explanatory Note to the UNCITRAL Model Law on Electronic Transferable Records' (2017) UN Publication No E.17.V.5 [18] <https://uncitral.un.org/sites/uncitral.un.org/files/media-documents/uncitral/en/mletr_ebook_e.pdf> (hereafter UNCITRAL, 'Explanatory Note (2017)').

[26] UNCITRAL, 'ML-ETR' (n 20) arts 8–9.

[27] SWIFT is an acronym for the 'Society for Worldwide Interbank Financial Telecommunication' <swift.com> accessed 20 August 2020.

[28] UNCITRAL, 'ML-ETR' (n 20) art 10.

Second, a 'reliable method' must be used 'to identify that electronic record as *the* electronic transferable record'; 'to render that electronic record capable of being subject to control from its creation until it ceases to have any effect or validity'; and 'to retain the integrity of that electronic record'.

11.20 The first of those conditions recognises the necessity to comply with the applicable substantive law for the relevant transferable document or instrument. The second condition imposes requirements concerning identity, control, and integrity upon the validity and effectiveness of the ETR. These elements will be considered in turn.

1. Reliable Method

11.21 The ML-ETR uses the expression 'reliable method' in several key provisions to establish the standard to be met by electronic forms for functional equivalence to operate. This expression is used in the key articles that define ETRs (article 10); define the notion of 'control' (article 11); permit the use of electronic signatures (article 9); deal with indications of time and place in ETRs (article 13); allow the amendment of ETRs (article 16); permit the replacement of a transferable document or instrument with an ETR (article 17); or permit the replacement of an ETR with an equivalent paper-based transferable document or instrument (article 18). The expression 'reliable method' is nebulous and flexible. As described above, a similar approach was taken with regard to the functional equivalence of electronic signatures in the ML-EC,[29] where the expression used was that the method had to be 'as reliable as appropriate'. Without any further guidance, this expression was unclear, difficult to apply and could lead to unintended results. Some courts expressed concern, if not bewilderment at its interpretation.[30] The Explanatory Note to the Electronic Communications Convention attempted to provide some assistance in determining what might be considered 'as reliable as appropriate' in the context of article 9 of that Convention (concerning electronic signatures):

> Legal, technical and commercial factors that may be taken into account in determining whether the method used … *is appropriate*, include the following: (a) the sophistication of the equipment used by each of the parties; (b) the nature of their trade activity; (c) the frequency at which commercial transactions take place between the parties; (d) the kind and size of the transaction; (e) the function of signature requirements in a given statutory and regulatory environment; (f) the capability of communication systems; (g) compliance with authentication procedures set forth by intermediaries; (h) the range of authentication procedures made available by any intermediary; (i) compliance with trade customs and practice; (j) the existence of insurance coverage mechanisms against unauthorized

[29] UNCITRAL, 'ML-EC' (n 3) art 7(1) provides: 'Where the law requires a signature of a person, that requirement is met in relation to a data message if: (a) a method is used to identify that person and to indicate that person's approval of the information contained in the data message; and (b) that method is *as reliable as was appropriate for the purpose for which the data message was generated or communicated, in the light of all the circumstances, including any relevant agreement*' (emphasis added).

[30] For example, in *Getup Ltd v Electoral Commissioner* [2010] FCA 869 [14]–[17], the Federal Court of Australia was required to hear an issue concerning 'reliability' in circumstances where there was no doubt that the electronic signature was that of the signatory, who had signed with the requisite intention. The court expressed some frustration at having to apply a 'reliability' test in those circumstances. In particular, Perram J stated that 'because s 10(1)(b) (the reliability test) is pitched at a very high level of generality it understandably eschews identifying any of the parties to the communication at all.' Accordingly, his Honour concluded: 'I cannot accept that the slightly pixilated nature of Ms Trevitt's signature rendered it unreliable for the Commissioner's purposes.'

communications; (k) the importance and the value of the information contained in the electronic communication; (l) the availability of alternative methods of identification and the cost of implementation; (m) the degree of acceptance or non-acceptance of the method of identification in the relevant industry or field both at the time the method was agreed upon and the time when the electronic communication was communicated; and (n) any other relevant factor.[31]

The difficulty of interpreting, implementing, and applying the notion of 'reliability' by reference to the multi-factorial approach in these explanatory notes is, however, immediately apparent. Indeed, those drafting the notes immediately recognised the problem, describing it thus: **11.22**

> [T]he courts in some States might be inclined to consider, for instance, that only signature methods that employed high-level security devices are adequate to identify a party, despite an agreement of the parties to use simpler signature methods.... The requirement that an electronic signature needs to be 'as reliable as appropriate' should not lead a court or trier of fact to invalidate the entire contract on the ground that the electronic signature was not appropriately reliable *if there is no dispute about the identity of the person signing or the fact of signing*, that is, no question as to authenticity of the electronic signature. *Such a result would be particularly unfortunate* ...[32]

The solution to this problem was to incorporate an additional and alternative control or test that operated to limit the potentially negative consequences of the more open-textured approach to the notion of 'reliability'. Accordingly, in the context of electronic signatures, article 9 of the Electronic Communications Convention went on to provide that, where the technological method for inserting an electronic signature is '[p]roven in fact to have fulfilled the functions [required] by itself or together with further evidence',[33] then it is to be regarded as functionally equivalent to a manual signature. This addition prevents electronic signatures becoming too susceptible to legal challenge on technological grounds. **11.23**

The ML-ETR unsurprisingly duplicated this approach. Hence, article 12 of the ML-ETR establishes a 'general reliability standard' for determining whether the technological method used for an ETR is 'as reliable as appropriate'.[34] That provision commences with a non-comprehensive list of seven factors to guide the determination of whether a particular method is 'as reliable as appropriate': **11.24**

> [T]he method referred to shall be: (a) *As reliable as appropriate* for the fulfilment of the function for which the method is being used, in the light of all relevant circumstances, which may include: (i) Any operational rules relevant to the assessment of reliability; (ii) The assurance of data integrity; (iii) The ability to prevent unauthorized access to and use of the system; (iv) The security of hardware and software; (v) The regularity and extent of audit by an independent body; (vi) The existence of a declaration by a supervisory body, an accreditation body or a voluntary scheme regarding the reliability of the method; (vii) Any applicable industry standard ...[35]

[31] UNCITRAL, 'Explanatory Note (2007)' (n 11) [162] (emphasis added).
[32] ibid [163]–[164] (emphasis added).
[33] UNCITRAL, 'Electronic Communications Convention' (n 8) art 9(3)(b)(ii).
[34] UNCITRAL, 'ML-ETR' (n 20) art 12.
[35] ibid art 12(a) (emphasis added).

11.25 As in the Electronic Communications Convention, there is then an alternative approach to demonstrating the reliability of the technological method, namely if it can be 'proven in fact to have fulfilled the function by itself or together with further evidence'.[36] Most likely, it will be the latter test that is invoked in future disputes and analysis, as it bolsters the extent to which commercial parties may rely upon ETRs.

2. Identity

11.26 The nature of electronic duplication is that digital copies can be made that are indistinguishable from the original. The latest technologies available to commercial parties, however, provide solutions in a modern commercial context to minimise the risk of duplication of the electronic record. Working Group IV (Electronic Commerce) recognised this difficulty, and took expert advice, initially through the 2011 Colloquium, about what technical and practical solutions were available. Both the Working Group and the Explanatory Note to the ML-ETR considered expressions such as 'uniqueness' and 'singularity' when addressing this issue.[37] Despite the fact that electronic commerce will arguably reduce, rather than increase, the commercial and instrument risk that has been part of the use of paper-based documents, the Note explains, however, that 'uniqueness is a relative notion that poses technical challenges in an electronic environment, as providing an absolute guarantee of non-replicability may not be technically feasible'.[38] Of course, in the paper-based world, such a guarantee is not required. Even when forgery and fraud remain an ever-present risk, the *original* paper-based document or instrument may still be described as being unique. Centuries of commercial practice have permitted sophisticated trade parties to weigh and balance the underlying risks of forgery and fraud and to take appropriate, if not full-proof, actions. Indeed, such practices have developed to the point where, in the paper-based world, some instruments no longer need to be 'unique'. For example, bills of lading are commonly issued in triplicate. Each is valid and acceptable, but not necessarily 'unique'.[39] Accordingly, the Explanatory Note adopts the term 'singularity' in preference to the term 'unique' and explains that the former term 'requires reliable identification of the electronic transferable record that entitles its holder to request performance of the obligation indicated in it, so that multiple claims of the same obligation would be avoided'.[40] The other effect of the notion of singularity is 'the prevention of unauthorised replication of an electronic transferable record by the system'.[41]

11.27 Linked to the issue of 'singularity' is how the ETR can be transferred without duplication of the record. Working Group IV (Electronic Commerce) discussed in particular how an 'electronic record' could become an 'electronic transferable record' without undermining that record's 'singularity'. For a short time, the Working Group used the expression the 'operative electronic transferable record' to distinguish it from a non-operative copy of that record. Later, the expression 'authorised electronic transferable record' was debated. In the end, it was determined that no additional descriptor was necessary and that it sufficed for

[36] ibid art 12(b).
[37] UNCITRAL, 'Explanatory Note (2017)' (n 25) [81]–[85], [94]–[96], [112].
[38] ibid [82].
[39] See Miriam Goldby, 'A Re-Assessment of the CMI Rules for Electronic Bills of Lading in the Light of Current Practices' [2008] LMCLQ 56; Nick Gaskell, 'Bills of Lading in an Electronic Age' [2010] LMCLQ 233.
[40] UNCITRAL, 'Explanatory Note (2017)' (n 25) [84].
[41] ibid [85].

reference to be made simply to 'the' electronic transferable record, which was then defined and described as containing the features required by article 10. Indeed, the Explanatory Note to the ML-ETR makes clear that the '[i]nsertion of a further qualifier might create uncertainty'.[42] Using the definite article 'the' did, however, cause concern for those nations in the session whose language did not have a corresponding word, but this issue was left to the translating personnel (and not considered further by the Working Group per se).[43] On the basis of these discussions, 'electronic record' was defined as 'information generated, communicated, received or stored by electronic means, including, where appropriate, all information logically associated with or otherwise linked together so as to become part of the record, whether generated contemporaneously or not'.[44] An 'electronic transferable record' was in turn defined as 'an electronic record that complies with the requirements of article 10'.[45]

3. Control, Exclusive Control, and Transfer of Control

In the paper-based world, possession, including constructive possession, of the transferable document or instrument typically confers specific rights, economic value, legal possession, and/or ownership upon the holder. The concept of 'control' was intended by Working Group IV (Electronic Commerce) to be the electronic functional equivalent of the paper-based notion of possession. In essence, the notion of 'control' focuses upon 'the use of a reliable method to identify the person in control of the electronic transferable record'.[46] Indeed, given the concerns over the uniqueness of the ETR, the requirement of control must necessarily involve the exercise of *exclusive* control. 11.28

This issue is dealt with in article 11 of the ML-ETR. Sub-article 11(1) provides that, 'where the law requires or permits the possession of a transferable document or instrument, that requirement is met with respect to an electronic transferable record if a reliable method is used ... [t]o establish *exclusive control* of that electronic transferable record by a person; and to identify that person as the person in control'.[47] The Explanatory Note to the ML-ETR considers that the reference to 'exclusive' control in this provision is for reasons of 'clarity', although in a somewhat circular (and unclear) manner then states that 'the notion of "control", similarly to that of "possession", implies exclusivity in its exercise'.[48] Furthermore, the Note explains that the 'concept of "control" does not refer to "legitimate" control, since this is a matter of substantive law'.[49] Furthermore, the Note provides that the notions of 'control' and 'singularity' (considered above) in the ML-ETR operate independently and should be distinguished from one another, since 'it is possible to conceive of exclusive control over a multiple record', as well as 'non-exclusive control over a single record'.[50] Accordingly, in the absence of more concrete guidance in the Explanatory Note, the notion of exclusivity 11.29

[42] ibid [93], [97].
[43] ibid [96].
[44] UNCITRAL, 'ML-ETR' (n 20) art 2.
[45] ibid.
[46] UNCITRAL, 'Explanatory Note (2017)' (n 25) [84].
[47] UNCITRAL, 'ML-ETR' (n 20) art 11(1) (emphasis added).
[48] UNCITRAL, 'Explanatory Note (2017)' (n 25) [111].
[49] ibid.
[50] ibid [112].

of control will essentially be a question of fact and depend to a large degree on the precise technology used.

11.30 Despite the lack of clarity over the determination of control over the ETR, this notion also underpins sub-article 11(2), which deals with the 'transfer' of control. This is the functional equivalent of transferring possession of a paper-based document or instrument. In the paper-based world, transferable documents and instruments are typically those that evidence or create some form of property right that is capable of transfer. In such cases, the transfer of possession typically occurs by the simple delivery, or the endorsement and delivery, of the relevant document. In that regard, sub-article 11(2) provides that '[w]here the law requires or permits the transfer of possession of a transferable document or instrument, that requirement is met with respect to an electronic transferable record by the transfer of control over the electronic transferable record'.[51] How precisely this transfer occurs will depend upon the nature of the technology used; but, whatever the precise mechanism, it must simultaneously satisfy the 'exclusive control' and 'identity' requirements in article 11(1) with respect to the transferee.

4. Integrity

11.31 As well as ensuring the 'singularity' of the ETR, the ML-ETR also addresses the need to maintain the integrity of the ETR in the sense of ensuring that it is not subject to any unauthorised alteration. According to the Explanatory Note to the ML-ETR, '[t]he notion of integrity is an absolute one', since '[i]t refers to a fact, and as such, is objective, i.e. either an electronic transferable record retains integrity or it does not'.[52] In this regard, sub-article 10(2) provides the 'criterion for assessing integrity' of an ETR, namely 'whether information contained in the electronic transferable record, including any authorized change that arises from its creation until it ceases to have any effect or validity, has remained complete and unaltered apart from any change which arises in the normal course of communication, storage and display'.[53] Accordingly, the ETR's integrity will usually depend upon the security features of the underlying technology.

C. Implementation

11.32 Despite the obvious advantages of the ML-ETR for international trade generally, and trade finance in particular, implementation is likely to be slow and cautious. Typically, paper-based transferable documents or instruments were used to transfer significant value or property rights. Accordingly, traders will initially be circumspect with respect to their own property and that of their clients. Similarly, banks will be concerned that their rights of recourse and rights as pledgee under the trade documents are not diminished. Accordingly, for the ML-ETR to be a worthwhile venture, a few nations need to be 'pioneers'[54] by

[51] UNCITRAL, 'ML-ETR' (n 20) art 11(2).
[52] UNCITRAL, 'Explanatory Note (2017)' (n 25) [100].
[53] UNCITRAL, 'ML-ETR' (n 20) art 10(2).
[54] For the term 'pioneer' as connoting an entity involved in the spread of innovation and ideas, see Everett Rogers, *Diffusion of Innovations*, (5th edn, Simon and Schuster 2003); Myles McGregor-Lowndes and Alan Davidson, *The Internet for Lawyers* (LBC Sydney 1997) ch 2.

embracing the new ML-ETR. In that regard, nations such as Singapore have already commenced the process.

Broadly, there are three possible approaches to implementing the ML-ETR. First, the principles of the ML-ETR could be enacted in new or existing generic legislation dealing with the issue of electronic transactions.[55] Second, industry- or sector-specific legislation could be amended to allow ETRs as a substitute for particular paper-based instruments. For example, legislation dealing with the carriage of goods by sea could be amended to permit ETRs in place of a bill of lading; and bills of exchange legislation could be amended to allow for a similar step in respect of those instruments. Third, a combination of these approaches could be used to ensure both the specific and general application of the ML-ETR. The disadvantage of the first approach, however, is that it does not signal to any particular industry or sector the specific changes in practice that the legislative amendment is intended to encourage. Traders, lawyers, financiers, and insurers will typically only make themselves aware of the specific legislation, regulations, and amendments that are applicable to that particular industry or sector. If the pertinent electronic standard appears in, for example, generic electronic transactions legislation, questions will remain as to the legislature's intention behind the changes. It may be cogently argued that, if it is Parliament's intention to alter established common law principles in a particular area, then such changes should be made directly in industry-, sector-, or instrument-specific legislation. These specific amendments are more likely to encourage the use of ETRs by 'pioneers' and accordingly promote the diffusion of innovation. Accordingly, it is submitted that the principles of control, identity, and transfer in the ML-ETR, as well as the definitions of 'electronic record' and 'electronic transferable record', would be more appropriately incorporated into domestic legislation dealing specifically with, for example, bills of lading or bills of exchange.[56] That said, the third possible approach is to combine the first two suggestions. This is the view preferred in this chapter. This will have the advantage of both targeting particular industries or sectors and providing a general platform for all electronic transactions and instruments across the board. The result would be to embrace functional equivalence fully, to promote electronic media and trade, and to align economic and trade concerns with commercial realty. 11.33

III. Conclusion

The universal implementation of the ML-ETR will enhance international and domestic trade by facilitating the incorporation of electronic instruments and communications. As well as encouraging business and enterprises to engage in international trade, the ML-ETR will support ancillary enterprises providing transport, logistics, finance, and insurance. Implementation of the ML-ETR would almost certainly improve the speed and security of trade-finance transactions and would facilitate the development of self-executing, 'smart' finance contracts. Moreover, the ML-ETR will facilitate technological innovation and electronic design, providing clarity and certainty regarding the use of ETRs in trade finance, whether bills of lading, bills of exchange, promissory notes, or warehouse receipts. ETRs are likely to prove fundamental to the future of the trade finance environment. 11.34

[55] Such legislation exists in more than 150 jurisdictions. See, for example, the Electronic Transactions Act 1999 (Cth) in Australia, and the Electronic Transactions Act (Cap 88, 2011 rev ed) in Singapore.

[56] See further ch 9 (Geva) and ch 10 (Goldby) in this volume.

12

Will Blockchain Transform Trade Finance?

*Jane K Winn**

I. Introduction: Why Transforming Trade Finance is Hard

12.01 Ever since someone using the pseudonym, Satoshi Nakamoto, published a white paper entitled, 'Bitcoin: A Peer-to-Peer Electronic Cash System' in 2008, there has been enormous interest in business and technology circles about the possibility of developing new commercial applications for cryptography. Excitement surrounding new uses for encryption technology eventually fuelled a speculative bubble for 'initial coin offerings' ('ICOs') that blossomed quickly in 2017 and just as quickly collapsed in 2018.[1] Interest in cryptocurrencies is likely to continue to wax and wane for a variety of reasons unrelated to their economic fundamentals, leading one economist to recommended treating investments in cryptocurrencies as the equivalent of buying lottery tickets.[2]

12.02 While cryptocurrencies may be the most visible new commercial application for encryption technologies, they are by no means the only one. The term 'blockchain' is used to describe technologies that incorporate some design elements of cryptocurrencies, while avoiding others that generally make cryptocurrencies unsuitable for use in conventional commerce.[3] *The Economist* magazine defined blockchain as 'a database designed to be distributed among many users, to be immutable, to work without oversight from any central authority and to dispense with the need for its users to trust each other'.[4] The Gartner consulting firm has defined blockchain as 'an expanding list of cryptographically signed, irrevocable transactional records shared by all participants in a network'.[5] In 2017, Gartner speculated that blockchain technologies might 'generate an annual business value of over $175 billion by 2025 and rise to over $3 trillion by 2030'.[6]

* Many thanks to Professors Dora Neo and Christopher Hare for their feedback on earlier drafts.

[1] Nellie Bowles, 'Everyone Is Getting Hilariously Rich and You're Not' (*The New York Times*, 13 January 2018) <https://www.nytimes.com/2018/01/13/style/bitcoin-millionaires.html> accessed 1 August 2020; Oscar Williams-Grut, '"Unsustainable" crypto startup funding bubble has burst' (*Yahoo Finance UK*, 15 November 2018) <https://uk.finance.yahoo.com/news/unsustainable-crypto-startup-funding-bubble-burst-080005455.html> accessed 1 August 2020.

[2] Kenneth Rogoff, 'Cryptocurrencies are like lottery tickets that might pay off in future' (*The Guardian*, 10 December 2018) <https://www.theguardian.com/business/2018/dec/10/cryptocurrencies-bitcoin-kenneth-rogoff> accessed 1 August 2020.

[3] United Nations Economic Commission for Europe ('UNECE') Centre for Trade Facilitation and Electronic Business, 'Blockchain in Trade Facilitation: Sectoral challenges and examples' (28 March 2019) ECE/TRADE/C/CEFACT/2019/INF.3 <https://www.unece.org/fileadmin/DAM/cefact/cf_plenary/2019_plenary/CEFACT_2019_INF03.pdf> accessed 1 August 2020 (hereafter UNECE, 'Blockchain in Trade Facilitation').

[4] See 'What to make of cryptocurrencies and blockchains' (*The Economist*, 30 August 2018) <https://www.economist.com/technology-quarterly/2018/08/30/what-to-make-of-cryptocurrencies-and-blockchains> accessed 1 August 2020.

[5] Rajesh Kandaswamy and David Furlonger, 'Gartner Blockchain Primer for 2018' (*Gartner Group*, 1 February 2018) 2.

[6] John-David Lovelock, Martin Reynolds, Bianca Granetto, and Rajesh Kandaswamy, 'Forecast: Blockchain Business Value, Worldwide, 2017–2030' (*Gartner Group*, 2 March 2017).

Trade finance looks to some observers like an ideal use case for blockchain because they believe it could radically lower transaction costs and remove barriers to entry in trade-finance markets.[7] The administration of cross-border trade remains dominated by complex, old-fashioned, hybrid human-computer-paper systems long after disruptive innovations have transformed commerce in many other domains.[8] Interest in blockchain is driven by the desire to cut through the 'Gordian knot' of complex, fragmented, anachronistic legacy trade-finance systems now in use. Blockchain advocates believe it is superior to the legacy database technologies currently in use in all important transaction-processing systems and designed to work within hierarchically networked computer systems controlled by large organisations. **12.03**

To other observers, however, blockchain looks more like a mass delusion similar to that generated by the fraudulent biotech company, Theranos.[9] This is because explanations of how blockchain can be used in commerce usually make the most sense when presented with the least detail. Once the effort to integrate blockchain into real-world transaction processing systems begins, it quickly becomes apparent that, far from making commerce simpler and easier to carry out, they make it more complex and difficult.[10] The most positive thing sceptics can find to say about blockchain is that it has focused unprecedented levels of attention on the problems of legacy back-office computer systems, which in turn might mobilise enough resources to overcome some of the collective action problems that have made those legacy systems so resistant to change.[11] **12.04**

The process of sorting through all the conflicting claims being made about blockchain is complicated by the fact that most organisations have been very aggressive about announcing the beginning of blockchain projects, but almost no one has any incentive to admit publicly that their blockchain experiments have failed.[12] The lack of a universally accepted definition for the term 'blockchain' further complicates matters. For example, after Facebook described 'Libra', the new cryptocurrency that it announced in 2019 it would launch, as a **12.05**

[7] World Economic Forum, 'The future of financial infrastructure: An ambitious look at how blockchain can reshape financial services' (*World Economic Forum*, August 2016) 74 (hereafter World Economic Forum, 'The Future of Financial Infrastructure').

[8] Felix Vemmer, 'How Blockchain Technology Could Revolutionize International Trade' (*Global Economic Dynamics Project*, 2 March 2017) <https://ged-project.de/videos/international-trade/changes_in_global_value_chains/how-blockchain-technology-could-revolutionize-international-trade/> accessed 1 August 2020.

[9] Kai Stinchcombe, 'Don't believe the hype: There are no good uses for blockchain' (*American Banker*, 2 January 2018) <https://www.americanbanker.com/opinion/dont-believe-the-hype-there-are-no-good-uses-for-blockchain> accessed 1 August 2020; Avi Asher Schapiro, 'What the Theranos Documentary Misses' (*The New Republic*, 29 March 2019) <https://newrepublic.com/article/153419/theranos-documentary-misses> accessed 1 August 2020.

[10] Jeff Loehr, 'Blockchain is a waste of time, energy and mental space—please stop' (*Hackernoon.com*, 18 March 2018) <https://hackernoon.com/blockchain-is-a-waste-of-time-energy-and-mental-space-please-stop-db4cbe35058f> accessed 1 August 2020.

[11] Matt Levine, 'Blockchain for Banks Probably Can't Hurt: It's certainly better than scurrying around for 20 days looking for your fax machine' (*Bloomberg*, 1 September 2015) <https://www.bloomberg.com/opinion/articles/2015-09-01/blockchain-for-banks-probably-can-t-hurt> accessed 1 August 2020; Rajesh Kandaswamy and David Furlonger, 'Blockchain Technology Spectrum: A Gartner Theme Insight Report' (*Gartner Group*, 8 October 2018).

[12] Lawrence H White, 'Central bank digital currency might be fool's gold' *American Banker* (*American Banker*, 1 December 2018) <https://www.americanbanker.com/opinion/central-bank-digital-currency-might-be-fools-gold> accessed 1 August 2020; Nick Roquefort-Villeneuve, 'Why 98% of B2B Blockchain Projects Have Failed?' (*Medium.com*, 22 March 2019) <https://medium.com/predict/why-98-of-b2b-blockchain-projects-have-failed-5147c0651af9> accessed 1 August 2020.

'blockchain technology', some critics noted that it incorporated neither the 'blocks' nor the 'chains' characteristic of blockchain.[13]

12.06 Just as there is no canonical definition of blockchain, there is no canonical definition of business process reengineering. The term 'business process reengineering' is often used to refer to the process of setting organisational goals; describing an 'as is' or current situation that will have to be changed; describing a 'to be' or 'happy' state that is the target; and developing a process for moving from the 'as is' state to the 'to be' or 'happy' state.

12.07 Most of the claims being made to justify investments in blockchain make more sense if understood as justifications for investing in business process reengineering. For example, in blog post on *Medium.com*, Noumaan Kaleem states:[14]

> Many banks are looking towards reducing costs and increasing efficiency by replacing the use of paper with technology. With Blockchain, the industry would have the ability to streamline trade finance progress.

12.08 The author appears unaware that organisations such as the International Chamber of Commerce in Paris, the global funds transfer network SWIFT, the World Customs Organisations, and the United Nations Conference on Trade and Development ('UNCTAD') have been making steady progress for decades streamlining trade finance with legacy technologies. Kaleem also appears unaware that this trend accelerated after the World Trade Organisation Trade Facilitation Agreement ('WTO TFA') was concluded in 2013.

12.09 Migrating existing trade finance systems to newer technology architectures constitutes business process reengineering whether or not it involves blockchain. The idea of business process reengineering was originally popularised by the 1993 book with that title written by management consultants, Michael Hammer and James Champy.[15] Similar strategies for business process transformation have been popularised with other names, including total quality management, continuous improvement, lean, agile, Six Sigma, adaptive management, or even design thinking.[16] No matter who undertakes business process reengineering, or why, there is a broad, general consensus that the odds of the effort succeeding are low. Hammer and Champy estimated the failure rate for business process reengineering efforts to be from 50% to 70%, and later studies have repeatedly validated that estimate.[17]

[13] Jemima Kelly, 'Facebook's Libra: blockchain, but without the blocks or chain' (*Financial Times*, 18 June 2019) <https://ftalphaville.ft.com/2019/06/18/1560849057000/Facebook-s-Libra--blockchain--but-without-the-blocks-or-chain/> accessed 1 August 2020.

[14] Noumaan Kaleem, 'How Blockchain Will Revolutionize Trade Finance' (*Medium.com*, 30 March 2019) <https://medium.com/@nakaleem2003/how-blockchain-will-revolutionize-trade-finance-ff519b25a35> accessed 1 August 2020.

[15] Michael Hammer and James Champy, *Reengineering the Corporation: A Manifesto for Business Revolution* (Harper Collins 1993).

[16] In American legal education, this process is known as 'outcome-based assessment'.

[17] Thomas H Davenport, 'The Fad That Forgot People' (*Fast Company*, 31 October 1995) <https://www.fastcompany.com/26310/fad-forgot-people> accessed 1 August 2020 (67% of reengineering efforts were judged as producing mediocre, marginal, or failed results); John Kotter, *Leading Change* (Harvard Business School Press 1996) (70% of change efforts fail); Michael Beer and Nitin Nohria, 'Cracking the code of change' *Harvard Business Review* (May–June 2000) 133–41 ('The brutal fact is that about 70% of all change initiatives fail'); Charlie C Chen, Chuck C H Law, and Samuel C Yang, 'Managing ERP Implementation Failure: A Project Management Perspective' (2009) 56(1) IEEE Transactions on Engineering Management 157 (more than 50% of reengineering efforts fail).

The goal of reengineering trade finance is to create value for trade finance suppliers and users. Indeed, Peter Drucker famously asserted '[t]here is only one valid definition of business purpose: to create a customer … It is the customer who determines what a business is'.[18] Choosing the technology that will be used to pursue a business goal in advance of mapping out the "as is" analysis of the current situation, the "to be" analysis of the target, and a migration plan for the transition only increases the already high odds that the business process reengineering effort will fail. It is clearly true that the value of conventional trade-finance services, such as letters of credit, to the parties engaged in cross-border trade is eroding because they are complex, burdensome, and anachronistic. That fact by itself does not, however, demonstrate that blockchain will work better than any other technology in rationalising those processes. 12.10

Many of the claims being made for how blockchain can transform trade finance appear to be fuelled by the same kind of magical thinking that sustained Theranos for many years.[19] Just as it eventually became obvious that Theranos simply could not do what its executives claimed it could do, at some point it is likely to become clear to everyone, except the most committed blockchain ideologues, that it simply cannot do what some have claimed it could do.[20] Although most blockchain investments may ultimately prove to be no more valuable than those made in Theranos, blockchain investors may be in a better position to hide their losses if they mischaracterise whatever technology they end up using as being blockchain, even though it is not—a practice known as 'blockchain washing'.[21] 12.11

II. Believing in Blockchain

According to a 2016 report by the World Economic Forum on the potential impact of blockchain on financial services, the 'value driver' for blockchain adoption in trade finance would most likely be increased operational efficiency.[22] If trade finance could be transformed from an expensive, slow, paper-intensive, anachronistic process to a simple, quick, modern, efficient process, then transaction costs in cross-border trade might be significantly reduced. 12.12

Blockchain can be understood as a form of group record-keeping, in which a group of individuals get together and agree to keep joint records, rather than delegating record-keeping responsibility to just one member of the group. Each member of the group runs the same software simultaneously and each maintains separate copies of all transaction records. Ownership rights and the validity of transfers of ownership are determined by a group-consensus process. This distributed structure eliminates the need to ensure that the party 12.13

[18] Peter F Drucker, *Management: Tasks, Responsibilities, Practices* (Harper Collins 1973) 61.

[19] World Economic Forum, 'Blockchain could boost global trade by $1 trillion' (*World Economic Forum*, 19 September 2018) <https://www.weforum.org/agenda/2018/09/blockchain-set-to-increase-global-trade-by-1-trillion/> accessed 1 August 2020.

[20] Bernard Marr, 'Is this the end of blockchain?' (*Forbes.com*, 10 December 2018) <https://www.forbes.com/sites/bernardmarr/2018/12/10/is-this-the-end-of-blockchain/> accessed 1 August 2020.

[21] Ray Valdes, David Furlonger, and Fabio Chesini, 'The Bitcoin Blockchain: The Magic and the Myths' (*Gartner Report*, 8 April 2016) 5.

[22] World Economic Forum, 'The Future of Financial Infrastructure' (n 7) 21.

maintaining the system-of-record version of a database is trustworthy, replacing a central authority with a combination of processes and group consensus.

12.14 The 'block' to which blockchain refers is a data structure that corresponds to an entry in a paper ledger book. Each block has a time stamp and a hashed (ie, tamper-resistant) link to a previous block, thus creating a 'chain' of blocks. If someone tried to modify an older transaction, the chain connecting it to newer transactions will break, making it nearly impossible to hide any attempt at modifying a block.

12.15 In a conventional database system, one computer system within a network may be designated as the authoritative 'system of record' in the event that there is any inconsistency among the different copies of the data in the database. In a blockchain system, the database of records is maintained by members of the group and, if there is ever any disagreement about what information belongs in the database, it is resolved by consensus among the network participants. New information is added onto existing blockchains; it does not overwrite or alter existing information. Once new information has been validated by consensus and added to the database, it should be nearly impossible for anyone to alter or remove it. For this reason, it is common to describe information stored in a blockchain as being 'immutable', or 'permanent', or 'tamper-proof'.[23]

12.16 Bitcoin and most initial coin offerings are based on a 'public' or 'permission-less' blockchain design, while 'private' or 'permissioned' blockchain systems would be more likely to replace conventional trade-finance mechanisms, such as letters of credit. The bitcoin system is considered public or permission-less because there is no central authority deciding who may or may not participate. New bitcoins are created and added to the database by 'miners' who must solve a difficult computational challenge known as a 'proof-of-work' problem. The first miner to solve one of these problems is rewarded with the value of the new bitcoin.

12.17 Many features of public blockchain systems make them ill-suited for use in conventional commerce. One major challenge is their appeal to people engaged in illegal or criminal activity because they offer something close to the anonymity of paying with cash. Another is blockchain's poor performance compared to conventional transaction-processing technologies: because all nodes on a blockchain network participate in creating consensus every time a block is updated and because the kind of cryptographic calculations that must be performed to achieve consensus are very computationally intensive, transaction processing in public blockchain systems may grow slower as the number of participants increases. The visibility of all the information in a public blockchain to anyone who chooses to investigate may be incompatible with the privacy or confidentiality requirements of many prospective users.

12.18 Private or permissioned blockchains are designed to overcome these challenges while still preserving the decentralised consensus process and the immutability of transaction information associated with bitcoin. By restricting access to the system, those wishing to engage in unlawful conduct anonymously can be excluded from participating and the privacy or confidentiality requirements of individuals wishing to participate in the system

[23] Angela Walch (transcribed interview), 'Blockchain Applications to International Affairs: Reasons for Skepticism' (2018) 19 Georgetown Journal of International Affairs 27.

for legitimate purposes can be met. The computational load of processing transactions can be reduced by restricting the number of nodes on the network participating in the process, which in turn would increase the processing speed and scalability of the system. If blockchain does achieve widespread adoption in trade finance, it would most likely be in the form of a private blockchain, not a public one.[24]

In cross-border trade transactions, contracting parties usually cannot deal with each other face-to-face, and the need to move goods across borders instead of within a domestic market increases the time and expense required to complete transactions. Among the risks that may be amplified in cross-border trade compared to domestic trade are the risks of fraudulently duplicated paper documents or errors in the manual processing of paper documents. These sources of increased uncertainty and delay in turn increase the risk that one of the contracting parties will default. Intermediaries, such as commercial banks, have traditionally assisted parties engaged in cross-border trade to mitigate these risks in exchange for hefty fees. **12.19**

Replacing paper-based processes in trade finance with blockchain applications might permit data to be entered only once into a computer system before being accurately duplicated across the network.[25] Delays caused by the need to collect many different paper documents, then manually review them, could be reduced or eliminated. Delays caused when non-conforming documents are rejected, and then must be revised and resubmitted, might also be reduced. The total number of intermediaries involved in each transaction could be reduced in addition to reducing or eliminating manual document-review processes. Compliance burdens now borne by the trading parties and the commercial banks in processing the payments could be reduced as a result of the transparency and immutability of blockchain digital records.[26] In other words, in the best case scenario following the adoption of blockchain in trade finance, the cost of trade finance might drop, while its effectiveness might be increased. **12.20**

In a 2019 report on global trade-management system software, Gartner listed the following examples of cross-border trade technologies being developed with blockchain: 'Universal Trade Network' is developing interoperability standards for different financial blockchain networks; 'Marco Polo Network' combines the R3 enterprise blockchain platform with 'TradeIX' blockchain trade-finance solutions; 'Voltron' offers a blockchain-based digital letter of credit service; the 'Blockchain in Transport Alliance' ('BiTA') is a standard-setting organisation developing standards for the use of blockchain in logistics, with more than 500 members in freight, transportation, logistics, and software industries; 'TradeLens' is an open, neutral platform based on blockchain and developed by IBM and Maersk with more than 100 companies participating; and 'Global Shipping Business Network' is an open, neutral platform based on blockchain and developed by 'CargoSmart', together with nine ocean carriers and terminal operators, that competes with 'TradeLens'.[27] After noting that these **12.21**

[24] David Groombridge and Chrissy Healey, 'Blockchain Trials Show Pragmatism Emerging Across Industries' (*Gartner Report*, 15 May 2019).

[25] World Economic Forum, 'The Future of Financial Infrastructure' (n 7) 74–82 (Section 5.4, 'Deposits and Lending: Trade Finance').

[26] Luc Publiatti and Bill Gain, 'Can blockchain revolutionize trade?' (*World Bank Blog*, 5 June 2018) <https://blogs.worldbank.org/trade/can-blockchain-revolutionize-trade> accessed 1 August 2020.

[27] William McNeill and Oscar Sanchez Duran, 'Market Guide for Global Trade Management Software' (*Gartner Report*, 10 July 2019).

efforts are still in an early stage of development, Gartner warned that '[d]espite the recent advancements, use caution when considering blockchain. Right now, it should be viewed as a potential complementary technology, not as a wholesale replacement'.[28]

III. Some Realism about Blockchain

12.22 For a variety of reasons, it now appears that early reports of blockchain's potential to disrupt commerce were exaggerated. Even blockchain entrepreneurs acknowledge that parallels can be drawn between the wave of enthusiasm for blockchain and the dot-com bubble of the late 1990s.[29] Although the results of blockchain pilot projects are rarely shared with the public, the few that have been disclosed have not been encouraging. For example, in 2019, the German Bundesbank revealed that a pilot project it had launched in 2016 with Deutsche Boerse AG demonstrated that using blockchain to transfer and settle securities transactions was slower and more expensive than processing the same transactions using more conventional computer technology.[30]

12.23 The idea that the adoption of new technology tends to occur within a 'hype cycle' of excessive enthusiasm followed by excessive pessimism before widespread adoption is finally achieved was first suggested by Howard Fosdick in 1992.[31] Fosdick's thesis was that the amount of publicity a new technology receives was inversely related to its usability, so that, by the time a technology came into widespread use, it was receiving virtually no publicity at all. This trade-off was later popularised by the Gartner management consulting firm under the rubric 'hype cycle'.[32] The Gartner hype cycle is divided into five phases—technology trigger, peak of inflated expectations, trough of disillusionment, slope of enlightenment, plateau of productivity—but for a technology featured in a Gartner hype cycle report to progress through all phases is exceptional.[33] Most overhyped technologies, such as Desktop Linux for Business, Web Services-Enabled Business Models, or Broadband over Power Lines, make brief appearances, then disappear without a trace, or are discarded as 'obsolete before plateau'. The ultimate fate of blockchain—perhaps repurposed under a new label, such as 'peer-to-peer computing'—will not be known for many years, and even then can only be confirmed with hindsight.

12.24 Given the dearth of concrete results to support most of the claims being made on behalf of blockchain, something else must have been driving the bubble. Part of the answer is clearly spillover effects from the bubble in cryptocurrencies.[34] In addition, blockchain was often

[28] ibid.

[29] Ben Dickson, 'Are We in a Blockchain Winter?' (*PC Magazine*, 6 April 2019) <https://sea.pcmag.com/opinion/32222/are-we-in-a-blockchain-winter> accessed 1 August 2020.

[30] Izabella Kaminska, 'Blockchain officially confirmed as slower and more expensive' (*Financial Times*, 29 May 2019) <https://ftalphaville.ft.com/2019/05/29/1559146404000/Blockchain-officially-confirmed-as-slower-and-more-expensive/> accessed 1 August 2020.

[31] Howard Fosdick, 'The Sociology of Technology Adoption' *Enterprise Systems Journal* (September 1992).

[32] See, for example, David Furlonger and Rajesh Kandaswamy, 'Hype Cycle for Blockchain Technologies 2018' (*Gartner Report*, 25 July 2018).

[33] Michael Mullany, '8 Lessons from 20 Years of Hype Cycles' (*LinkedIn.com*, 7 December 2016) <https://www.linkedin.com/pulse/8-lessons-from-20-years-hype-cycles-michael-mullany/> accessed 1 August 2020.

[34] Michael J Casey, 'Crypto Winter Is Here and We Only Have Ourselves to Blame' (*Coindesk.com*, 3 December 2018) <https://www.coindesk.com/the-crypto-winter-is-here-and-we-only-have-ourselves-to-blame> accessed 1 August 2020.

portrayed as a radically new and different way to process transactions. These claims were clearly overstated:[35]

> There is a mania surrounding the blockchain technology which underlies cryptocurrencies—it is surrounded by a boundless enthusiasm, and based on the breathless excitement, one might believe that it is the cure for cancer, Alzheimer's disease, and the common cold, all in one. Allow me to inject some reality into this conversation: Yes, even though someone recently told you about how critical blockchain is for your future life in the same breathless excited voice with which your parents told you bedtime stories like the three little pigs, Cinderella, or read you the Very Hungry Caterpillar; the truth remains that blockchain is *just a tamper-resistant way of recording transactions into a digital ledger*.

Computer security experts also cast doubts on claims that there is anything particularly original about the security features of blockchain:[36] **12.25**

> Private blockchains are completely uninteresting. In general, they have some external limitation on who can interact with the blockchain and its features. These are not anything new; they're distributed append-only data structures with a list of individuals authorized to add to it. Consensus protocols have been studied in distributed systems for more than 60 years. Append-only data structures have been similarly well covered. They're blockchains in name only, and—as far as I can tell—the only reason to operate one is to ride on the blockchain hype.

Many with hands-on experience of working with business information systems found blockchain advocates' enthusiasm hard to fathom. For example, a supply chain management company IT manager noted: 'I have a hard time getting too excited about [blockchain] because it's just going to be a new form of messaging … It's going to have some advantages, like better security around the messaging, but I just don't see it as being something deeply transformative'.[37] **12.26**

The positive tone of many status updates on blockchain pilot projects can often be attributed to conflating the benefits attributable to the unique characteristics of blockchain with those attributable to any digital transformation or business process reengineering effort. Other times, the positive tone of reports on blockchain success stories is mere puffery. For example, David Gerard analysed a report about the World Food Programme's pilot projects in Pakistan and in Jordan that recorded cash and benefits disbursed to vulnerable families and then reconciled those disbursements with the families' entitlements.[38] Gerard noted that the pilot was carried out using a system that lacked almost all the hallmarks of blockchain **12.27**

[35] Brian Tankersley, 'Blockchain is a Database, Get Over It' (*CPA Practice Advisor*, 22 March 2018) <https://www.cpapracticeadvisor.com/accounting-audit/article/12402865/blockchain-is-a-database-get-over-it> accessed 1 August 2020 (emphasis in original).

[36] Bruce Schneier, 'There's no good reason to trust blockchain technology' (*Wired.com*, 6 February 2019) <https://www.wired.com/story/theres-no-good-reason-to-trust-blockchain-technology/> accessed 1 August 2020.

[37] Roberto Michel, 'The Digital Supply Chain Takes Shape' (*Logistics Management*, 10 May 2019) <https://www.logisticsmgmt.com/article/the_digital_supply_chain_takes_shape> accessed 1 August 2020.

[38] David Gerard, 'The World Food Programme's much-publicised "blockchain" has one participant—i.e., it's a database' (*Attack of the 50 Foot Blockchain*, 26 November 2017) <https://davidgerard.co.uk/blockchain/2017/11/26/the-world-food-programmes-much-publicised-blockchain-has-one-participant-i-e-its-a-database/wfp-building-blocks/> accessed 27 August 2019.

technology, and that '[l]iterally all the benefits of the scheme are stated as possibilities—"could," "can," "aims to," "potential to"—rather than anything that had been tangibly realised in the pilots'.

12.28 One possible reason that the most extravagant claims for blockchain could ricochet around the Internet encountering little resistance is that people who understand the weakness of the claims being made for blockchain have little incentive to try to persuade committed blockchain-boosters that they are mistaken. Those with subject-matter expertise in enterprise computing systems usually have better things to do with their time than try to reason with zealots and ideologues. Once an enterprise realises that its own blockchain pilot failed, its managers have no incentive to tell their shareholders or competitors what really happened. Those responsible for launching those projects would not want to call the attention of their own directors and shareholders to their own missteps, nor would they want to tip off competitors poised to make their own investments in blockchain, allowing them to avoid making the same costly mistakes.

12.29 Management consulting firms seeking to make a quick profit from the current high level of interest in blockchain have a strong incentive to be very selective about what kind information they disclose to prospective clients about other blockchain pilot projects that they have worked on. In a competitive market for management consulting services, such a strategy might maximise short-term profits, but backfire in the long term if clients later blame the consultants for money squandered on unsuccessful blockchain projects. Some management consulting firms with a longer-term client relationship strategy are seeking to build creditability by warning clients to avoid blockchain projects:[39]

> The majority of enterprise blockchain projects do not actually need blockchain technology and would be better off using conventional technologies ... While there are several dozen nascent supply-chain-related blockchain initiatives, none are fully operational. Significant concerns remain regarding the foundational technology, with regard to scalability, flexibility, confidentiality of data, efficiency, governance and interoperability.

12.30 In July 2018, internet pioneer Vint Cerf weighed into this debate by posting to *Twitter* a photograph of a simple flow-diagram containing only two boxes: the first box contains the question, 'Do I need a Blockchain?'; and then an arrow points to the second box with the answer, 'No'.[40]

12.31 A recent attempt to collect and analyse information about forty-three publicly announced blockchain projects failed because no one associated with any of the projects would answer any of the researchers' questions.[41] The researchers were careful to note that the mere fact that no one would answer any of their questions did not prove those projects had failed. They did, however, highlight the irony of evangelists for more transparent and accountable

[39] Andrew Stevens, John Johnson, Noha Tohamy, C Klappich, 'Seven Things That Supply Chain Leaders Need to Know About Blockchain' (*Gartner Report*, 24 February 2017).

[40] Vinton G Cerf, 'Simple flowchart' (19 July 2018) <https://twitter.com/vgcerf/status/1019987651301081089> accessed 1 August 2020.

[41] Wayan Vota, 'Blockchain Use Case Failure: 43 Projects and Zero Impact Found' (*ICTWorks.org*, 10 December 2018) <https://www.ictworks.org/blockchain-impact-failure/> accessed 1 August 2020.

technology systems refusing to cooperate with efforts to make their own operations more transparent and accountable.

One heuristic that can help to distinguish between mere preliminary explorations of a new technology, on the one hand, and success in achieving widespread adoption of a new technology, on the other, is simply to ask whether or not what is being discussed is a pilot project. If the person promoting a new technology does not understand the question, or refuses to answer it, then that is usually a good indication that what is being discussed is, in fact, only a pilot project. If the response is that, following a successful pilot, the technology is now gaining widespread adoption, a second heuristic can be used to assess the credibility of this type of claim: the ratio of the transaction volume for the new technology over the total volume for that type of transaction. For example, the fact that $25 million of electronic fund transfers were being processed on a monthly basis using a blockchain technology might sound impressive until that total is compared to the trillions of dollars of electronic fund transfers that are executed on a daily basis using legacy systems. **12.32**

Even as scepticism about the plausibility of claims that blockchain will transform commerce grows, many reputable organisations continue to churn out ponderous publications trying to guess what impact blockchain might have in the future.[42] The dry, abstract, ponderous tone of a 2019 UN development agency report gives no clear indication that its authors realised that their informants were only talking about pilot projects, not real commercial transaction processing systems:[43] **12.33**

> In the case of private or permissioned ledgers, blockchain technology provides for the immutability and auditability of transactions entered by the authorized parties and, thereby, satisfies the requirements of legal systems for considering digital evidence as being valid. In addition, the tamper proof nature of data recorded using blockchain technology, usually in a chronological order and/or with time stamps further enhances the reliability of and authenticity of the recorded transactions, thus lending credibility to, and increasing the admissibility of, the electronic data being submitted as evidence.

The empirical research for this report appears to have consisted of asking blockchain promoters to disclose information about their products and business models in a standardised format. Its authors tried to signal their commitment to neutrality and objectivity by including this disclaimer in the abstract of the report:[44] **12.34**

> This document is a work in progress. It is presented to the Plenary in order to share the state of advancement of this work. It does not constitute a position of any kind of UN/CEFACT or the UNECE Secretariat.

Such a disclaimer is insufficient to offset the authors' failure to distinguish 'vaporware' from commercial success. **12.35**

[42] See, for example, Emmanuelle Ganne, *Can Blockchain Revolutionize International Trade?* (World Trade Organization 2018); World Economic Forum, 'Trade Tech: A New Age for Trade and Supply Chain Finance' (White Paper) (January 2018) <http://www3.weforum.org/docs/WEF_White_Paper_Trade_Tech_.pdf> accessed 1 August 2020 (substituting the term 'distributed ledger technology' for 'blockchain').

[43] UNECE, 'Blockchain in Trade Facilitation' (n 3) 14.

[44] ibid 1.

12.36 By contrast, a Gartner report published around the same time highlights the growing disillusionment of enterprise technology managers with blockchain:

> For many, blockchain is a technology looking for a problem. Much of the resulting disillusionment is due to the misalignment of blockchain with the requirements of enterprise projects. But it also is due to complete blockchain technology—with features such as decentralized consensus, elimination of central authorities, tokenization, data confidentiality, scalability, manageability, security services and more—still not being ready for enterprise use. In 2019, IT leaders, including CIOs, trying to embrace blockchain face a confusing array of technology questions. They seek to understand: how it works, why they need it, what value it offers over legacy database or other technologies, what use cases are most appropriate and how to work with their peers in a consortium. They also need to understand how to integrate blockchain into their existing systems and processes.[45]

12.37 Management consultants, such as Gartner analysts, have access to different kinds of information about commercial practice than do researchers in government, non-governmental organisations, and academia, but that does not mean that researchers who are not management consultants cannot find ways to dig below the surface of self-serving statements by technology developers.

12.38 Researchers working outside of management consulting firms or enterprise IT departments can still be expected to make an effort to assess the credibility of information they receive from industry sources. For example, in November 2017, BBVA issued a press release announcing its intention to revolutionise trade finance by collaborating with Wave, a blockchain startup.[46] Applying the first heuristic, it is clear that the press release described a pilot project. Before moving on to the second heuristic, there must be evidence that the pilot was completely successful and that efforts are underway to secure widespread adoption of the new technology; but there are no subsequent press releases from BBVA about its collaboration with Wave. In 2019, a blockchain enthusiast disclosed the following information in a blog: 'At present, Barclays is the only company exploring the potential of the Wave platform. But they also want to collaborate with other banks or financial institutions to fully utilise the potential of this wonderful trade finance blockchain.'[47] The most obvious inference that can be drawn from these two sources is that BBVA abandoned its effort to collaborate with Wave, presumably because the outcome of the pilot project was not acceptable to BBVA.

12.39 Although blockchain may ultimately end up together with Desktop Linux for Business, Web Services-Enabled Business Models, or Broadband over Power Lines in the graveyard of technology solutions that went straight from being overhyped to being irrelevant, many blockchain promoters' criticisms of the current fragmented, archaic state of trade finance are well taken. Many blockchain advocates appear, however, to be unaware of the slow,

[45] Avivah Litan and Adrian Leow, 'Blockchain Primer for 2019' (*Gartner Report*, January 2019) 3.

[46] Luz Fernández Espinosa, 'BBVA and Wave carry out the first blockchain-based international trade transaction between Europe and Latin America' (*BBVA*, 27 November 2017) <https://www.bbva.com/en/bbva-and-wave-carry-first-blockchain-based-international-trade-transaction-europe-and-latin-america/> accessed 1 August 2020 (hereafter Espinosa, 'BBVA and Wave').

[47] Hasib Anwar, 'Trade Finance Blockchain: Redesigning The World of Trades and Businesses' (*101blockchains.com*, 30 April 2019) <https://101blockchains.com/trade-finance-blockchain/> accessed 1 August 2020.

steady progress in modernising the technology of trade finance that is being made using legacy technologies.

IV. Transforming the Architecture of Global Trade Systems

In the decades since the Uruguay Round of negotiations ended and the World Trade Organisation ('WTO') began operations in 1995, the contours of a new technological architecture for the global trade system have been taking shape. The legal foundation for this new global trade system architecture was formally laid in 2013 when the Doha Round of negotiations concluded with the WTO TFA, which is the first multilateral trade treaty to be concluded since the creation of the WTO itself. Unlike other multilateral trade treaties, the WTO TFA focuses on issues related to the operational efficiency of cross-border trade, rather than economic relations between member states.[48] As the WTO/GATT framework generally rests on consensus decision-making—albeit there are periodic lapses into organised hypocrisy, as needed to hold the system together—the WTO TFA framework for rationalising and modernising the operations of trading nations builds incrementally on current practice.[49] 12.40

On 17 February 2017, the WTO TFA entered into force following its ratification by two-thirds of the WTO's 164 members. The WTO has defined trade facilitation as the 'simplification, modernisation, and harmonisation of export and import processes'.[50] Countries that ratified the WTO TFA commit to streamlining processes for clearing goods through customs; publishing information about their import and export procedures; increasing the use of electronic payments and electronic documents; increasing the transparency with which fees are set and penalties imposed; providing a single point of contract for dealing with government agencies; and permitting consultation for proposed customs rules, and a right of appeal for customs administration decisions. 12.41

The roots of the WTO TFA can be traced back through decades of work by the World Customs Organisation ('WCO') to standardise and harmonise customs administration processes around the world and the work of United Nations economic development agencies, such as the United Nations Economic Commission for Europe ('UNECE'), to develop consensus standards for electronic commerce. The WTO TFA requirement that countries set up a single point of contact for traders' interactions with government agencies is often referred to as a 'single-window' requirement. In 2004, UNECE issued 'Recommendation 33' urging all trading nations to develop a single window, namely, a 'facility that allows parties involved in trade and transport to lodge standardized trade-related information and/or documents to be submitted once at a single entry point to fulfil all import, export, and transit-related regulatory requirements'.[51] Advanced economies with the capacity to move 12.42

[48] Jane K Winn, 'The Promise of Global Digital Trade Facilitation Platforms' in Jane K Winn and Sheela Rai (eds), *Trade Facilitation and the WTO* (Cambridge Scholars Publishing 2019).

[49] Richard H Steinberg, 'In the Shadow of Law or Power? Consensus-Based Bargaining and Outcomes in the GATT/WTO' (2002) 56 International Organization 339.

[50] World Trade Organization, *World Trade Report 2015* (World Trade Organisation 2015) 34.

[51] UNECE Centre for Trade Facilitation and Electronic Business, 'Recommendation and Guidelines on establishing a Single Window' (July 2005) ECE/TRADE/352 UN Publication No 05.II.E.9 <http://www.unece.org/fileadmin/DAM/cefact/recommendations/rec33/rec33_trd352e.pdf> accessed 1 August 2020.

their own government operations in this direction began providing technical assistance in support of this recommendation to emerging economies that often lacked that capacity.

12.43 Before countries can establish a successful national single-window system, they must engage in the public sector equivalent of business process reengineering in order to bring different government agencies working with processes and technologies under a single, unified framework designed to be easy for importers and exporters to understand. In the 1990s, the US Treasury led the development of an 'International Trade Data System' ('ITDS') that would serve as the foundation for a single-window system. In addition, US Customs launched its own 'Automated Commercial Environment' ('ACE') to integrate all the information being collected by various government agencies for analysis and tracking. In the face of Congressional reluctance to fund both systems, the decision was taken to merge them and run the combined program on US Customs computer systems. The decision was also taken not to run the ITDS/ACE system as a separate computer system, but instead to require all forty-eight federal agencies within its scope to modify their existing computer systems to conform to ITDS/ACE standards.

12.44 While US Customs made steady progress towards creating a single window, it was not particularly successful in persuading other federal agencies to make the same effort to ensure the success of the single-window project. In 2006, the US Congress noted the slow progress and included in the Security and Accountability for Every Port Act ('SAFE Port Act') a mandate to the Secretary of the Treasury to get all forty-eight federal agencies engaged in clearing goods across US borders into the ITDS/ACE system. After that proved to be an insufficient incentive to get laggard agencies on board, President Obama issued an executive order setting a deadline of 31 December 2016 for all relevant government agencies to participate fully in the ITDS/ACE system.[52]

12.45 US Customs staggered the deadlines for different agencies to comply in an effort to minimise the disruption to traders, but some agencies still failed to meet their deadlines. For example, the Department of Homeland Security ('DHS') was rumoured to be $1 billion over budget and woefully behind schedule, just weeks before its own February 2016 deadline to connect to the ITDS/ACE system.[53] Although nominally the newest major federal agency created in almost half a century, DHS was actually an amalgamation of pre-existing agencies, each with their own legacy IT systems, so it is not surprising that DHS was struggling to demonstrate its compliance with ITDS/ACE standards. As some agencies fell behind schedule with their implementation plans, US importers, exporters, freight forwarders, and customs brokers were left struggling to ascertain how they were supposed meet the deadline to comply with ITDS/ACE requirements.

12.46 In the 1980s, Singapore began work on its national single-window system known as 'TradeNet'. The Singapore government established a private firm, CrimsonLogic, to host the TradeNet system, which went live in 1989.[54] Since its inception, TradeNet has been a model

[52] Executive Order No 13659, 'Streamlining the Export/Import Process for America's Businesses' 3 CFR 222 (2014).

[53] Industry Tap, 'New Government ACE System Not Ready For February 28th Deadline' (4 February 2016) <http://www.industrytap.com/new-government-ace-system-not-ready-february-28th-deadline/34281> accessed 1 August 2020.

[54] UNECE Centre for Trade Facilitation and Electronic Business, *Case Studies on Implementing a Single Window* (United Nations 2005) 57–68.

of efficiency and transparency. Other countries that have successfully launched single-window systems with less controversy and foot-dragging than the US include Finland, Mauritius, Germany, and Sweden. In 2005, the Finns summarised with disarming frankness the challenges they faced when they began constructing their system in the 1990s:

> The first system operated with a central database and dumb terminals, it was very rigorous and nothing could be changed without huge cost. There were no [single-window] interfaces to replace at that time. A Windows SW interface was added later, without great success, because it was exceptionally badly designed … [When the SW system was first launched in] 1992 nobody knew what we were doing; hence the solution was left to the state-owned software company VTTK to resolve. The result was a rather clumsy, inflexible and expensive system. It was, however, a useful learning experience. The pressure to build a completely new system mounted and when it was realised, in 1998, that the system was not Y2K proof, we had a good excuse to make a fresh start. We now knew what we wanted and the design phase involved everybody who wanted to have a say. The present system is easy to learn and use, but its age has started to show.[55]

Once a government has brought all of the computer systems it uses in connection with clearing goods for import and export into a single, integrated system and created a single-user interface for traders, it does not require much of a leap of imagination to think of such a system as a 'platform'.[56] For example, much of the information required by government agencies is the same information that intermediaries handling logistics or financing require to provide their services to trading parties. While the first priority for single-window systems remains making it easier for traders to work with governments, countries whose efforts to launch single windows were successful soon turned to trying to make those single-window systems attractive to private intermediaries as well. In the 2000s, Hong Kong launched its 'Digital Trade & Transportation Network', South Korea launched its 'u-TradeHub', and Singapore launched its 'TradeXchange' to draw private parties, such as transportation, warehousing, trade-finance and insurance companies, into their national single-window systems.[57] **12.47**

Comparing the costs and benefits of trade-finance reform based on blockchain with that based on building out from a national single-window system, it quickly becomes obvious why the national single-window systems are a more attractive option for most parties involved in international trade. For most parties, the cost of coming into compliance with national single-window standards represents a sunk cost. Expanding the range of activities that can be streamlined and modernised using national single-window technologies is a low-cost, high-benefit strategy for many parties, even though this usually requires continued use of legacy computer systems. Any attempt to implement a blockchain trade finance system would be a very risky investment, even if the cost to one organisation of **12.48**

[55] ibid 7.

[56] For the description of the ITDS/ACE system as a platform, see Laura Siegel Rabinowitz, 'Importers Beware: US Customs in Enforcement Mode' (*Law360*, 21 November 2016) <https://www.kelleydrye.com/getattachment/463e06c6-a758-48ee-a8f2-1d97b14965fc/attachment.aspx> accessed 28 August 2019.

[57] Jonathan Koh Tat Tsen, 'Ten Years of Single Window Implementation: Lessons Learned for the Future' (Global Trade Facilitation Conference, Geneva, December 2011) 14.

making such a move is relatively small, because the investment would have little or no value if few other parties involved in trade made similar investments.

12.49 Both the appeal of national single-window systems and the failure of blockchain systems to gain enough momentum to take off reflect the economics of standards and networks. According to Metcalfe's Law, services delivered over computer networks become more valuable to each user as the total number of users increases.[58] The benefit that network users derive from others also using the same network is described as an 'externality' in economics because neither the network operator nor any individual user will compensate other users for the contribution that they make to the value of the network. The externalities associated with computer networks are referred to as 'network effects'.[59]

12.50 Network effects may have a negative, as well as positive, effect on users of a network. Efforts to create a network for the first time often suffer from a chicken-and-egg problem because users will be reluctant to join until they feel certain that everyone else will join the same network. Private sector sponsors of new networks may have to create a bandwagon effect to inspire prospective users to join. Public sector sponsors of new networks may have the luxury of simply mandating participation—a 'taxation by regulation' strategy.[60]

12.51 Once a network achieves widespread adoption, then its users may become 'locked in' to that network if their fear of losing the positive network externalities that the existing network provides makes them unwilling to join a newer, better network. The tendency of network users to want to participate in the same network as everyone else in order to enjoy positive network externalities, and then to become locked into the first network that they join, may confer an economic benefit on the operator of that network known as a 'first mover advantage'.[61]

12.52 One way that regulators and users can reduce the risk that a network operator will benefit unfairly from lock-in is to favour networks based on open standards that ensure interoperability across the network and competition among network service-providers at the same time. Government agencies involved in national single-window systems would have few incentives to invest the time and effort in developing standards open enough to level the playing field between conventional trade-finance parties, on the one hand, and disruptive innovators offering trade-finance services based on blockchain technologies, on the other. Therefore, once a national single-window system is in place and conventional trade-finance parties, such as banks, factors, and trade-credit insurance companies, have joined it, something like a public sector 'first mover advantage' sheltering the incumbents is likely to make it very difficult for disruptive blockchain trade-finance services to gain any traction in trade-finance markets.

12.53 The current systems of trade finance operate as a kind of virtual global network because the legal system of every trading nation will enforce obligations growing out of common

58 See generally, Pam Woodall, 'Untangling e-conomics' (*The Economist*, 23 September 2000) <https://www.economist.com/special-report/2000/09/21/untangling-e-conomics> accessed 1 August 2020.

59 Carl Shapiro and Hal Varian, *Information Rules: A Strategic Guide to the Network Economy* (Harvard Business School Press 1998) 15 (hereafter Shapiro and Varian, *Information Rules*).

60 Richard A Posner, 'Taxation by Regulation' (1971) The Bell Journal of Economics and Management Science 22.

61 Shapiro and Varian, *Information Rules* (n 59) 29.

trade-finance mechanisms, such as letters of credit, prepayment, open account, and factoring and because employees of financial institutions and trading parties understand how to use those systems. Blockchain innovators are in effect challenging a 'first mover advantage' that accrued to traditional trade-finance sources, even before national single windows began operation. In the case of letters of credit, this 'first mover advantage' was established centuries ago. The network is embodied in the tacit and explicit knowledge of millions of bank employees, carrier staff, and trading party staff working in trading nations around the world.[62] Each prospective adopter of a blockchain solution must not only be convinced that a critical mass of other participants will make the same move, but they must also be willing to write off the tacit and explicit knowledge that permits them to manoeuvre in the old system and must also commit to creating new forms of tacit and explicit knowledge of blockchain systems to replace their prior knowledge.[63]

Migration from an existing network to a new challenger can be accelerated by subsidising **12.54** the use of the new network. The theory of platforms explains how such a subsidy can be created by the organisers of a 'two-sided platform' who can divide prospective users into different 'sides' and find a way to get one side to subsidise the participation of the other. For example, when the Visa and MasterCard payment card networks were established in the late 1960s, the network operators were consortia of banks: one side of the 'two-sided platform' was the cardholders and the merchants were the other side. Card networks, such as Visa and MasterCard, tend to charge merchants relatively high fees for access to their networks, and they turn over part of those fees to cardholders in the form of frequent flyer miles, cash back, or other incentives to use their cards more often.[64] In a similar way, Google, as a platform operator, charges advertisers high fees that it then uses to subsidise user access to search results.

No blockchain innovators have yet uncovered a strong enough value proposition to gen- **12.55** erate the surpluses required to convince one 'side' of a two-sided trade finance platform to begin subsidising new users of their systems. By contrast, when governments commit to expanding the operation of their national single-window system to include the participation of private trade intermediaries, offering an interface that is easy to use could help increase the rate of voluntary, private sector participation.

Cross-border trade today takes place within a complex, diffuse ecosystem populated by **12.56** millions of participants, including exporters, importers, carriers, customs brokers, banks, and government agencies in every country around the world. At some point in the future, all the different national single windows for trade facilitation may be linked together into a global single-window network or platform. If an integrated global trade facilitation emerges through the development of open standards, then trading parties would enjoy the benefits of competition among private trade intermediaries in the form of reduced risk of lock-in to proprietary trade facilitation standards, as well as lower prices for better service from private trade intermediaries. But in the absence of a global platform operator capable of setting

[62] Ikujiro Nonaka, 'Dynamic Theory of Organizational Knowledge Creation' (1994) 5 Organization Science 14.
[63] Diane Coutu, 'The Anxiety of Learning' *Harvard Business Review* (March 2002).
[64] Jean-Charles Rochet and Jean Tirole, 'Platform Competition in Two-Sided Markets' (2003) 1 Journal of the European Economic Association 990.

up a two-sided platform and compelling one side to subsidise the participation of another side, progress towards a globally interoperable trade facilitation system may be slow.

V. Transforming the Workflow of Global Trade Transactions

12.57 Blockchain appears to be an attractive solution compared to sorting out the mess with many of the legacy computer systems upon which conventional forms of trade finance, such as letters of credit, depend because many legacy computer systems are in such a state of disrepair.[65] Even if blockchain does not transform trade finance in quite the way some of its promoters have suggested, however, the excitement about blockchain may nevertheless make 'boring back-office coordination sexy, which means that it might actually get done'.[66]

12.58 Banks are by no means the only large organisations struggling to bring legacy computer systems up to par with computer systems designed today. Industry experts estimate that 80% of the world's corporate data reside on, or originate from, mainframe computers.[67] A major reason that it took twenty years for US federal agencies to build a national single-window system is that so many federal computer systems are woefully out-of-date and very difficult to maintain.[68] Most banks are in a similar position: a recent academic study of bank legacy migration problems estimated that banks are spending around 75% of their ICT budgets merely keeping their legacy systems up and running.[69]

12.59 The diversity and complexity of the 'as is' state of these legacy systems, the lack of a clear consensus regarding the appropriate 'to be' state that these systems should be moving towards, and the desire of those operating them not to make public the challenges they face in keeping them running, create significant collective action problems. A collective action problem arises whenever the result of actors making rational decisions in response to the incentives they face as individuals produces a collective outcome that no individual wants.[70] Some private sector efforts, such as the 'Banking Industry Architecture Network', are trying to help overcome these collective action problems by developing voluntary, consensus interoperability standards for financial services information systems, but progress in implementing such strategies remains slow.[71]

12.60 Cross-border trade transactions also tend to be much more complex than similar transactions carried out within a single country. A study of the export of sugar from Thailand to Bangladesh identified nineteen distinct steps required to successfully complete the entire

[65] Zulfikar Abbany, 'Fail by design: Banking's legacy of dark code' (*DW*, 3 May 2018) <https://www.dw.com/en/fail-by-design-bankings-legacy-of-dark-code/a-43645522> accessed 1 August 2020.

[66] Matt Levine, 'Executive Pay and Blood Trouble' (*Bloomberg*, 11 July 2016) <https://www.bloomberg.com/opinion/articles/2016-07-11/executive-pay-and-blood-trouble> accessed 1 August 2020.

[67] Levi Norman, 'The FutureScape of IT' (*IBM IT Infrastructure Blog*, 8 February 2018) <https://www.ibm.com/blogs/systems/the-futurescape-of-it/> accessed 1 August 2020.

[68] US Government Accountability Office, 'Federal Agencies Need to Address Aging Legacy Systems', GAO-Report 16–468 (May 2016).

[69] James Crotty and Ivan Horrocks, 'Managing Legacy System Costs: A Case Study of a Meta-assessment Model to Identify Solutions in a Large Financial Services Company' (2017) 13 Applied Computing and Informatics 175.

[70] Mancur Olson, *The Logic of Collective Action: Public Goods and the Theory of Groups* (Harvard University Press 1965).

[71] Penny Crosman, 'PNC Puts Industry Tech Blueprint to the Test' (*American Banker*, 9 February 2015) <https://www.americanbanker.com/news/pnc-puts-industry-tech-blueprint-to-the-test> accessed 1 August 2020.

transaction,[72] approximately thirty-one separate documents were required to complete the cross-border transaction and thirteen different stakeholders were involved. A sale by a Thai sugar-producer to a Thai customer would normally involve many fewer steps and stakeholders. As a result of their greater complexity, formality, and diversity of stakeholders, the challenges of business process reengineering for cross-border trade processes are usually much greater than those for commerce carried out within only one country.

The division of labour was first identified by the economist Adam Smith in 1776 as a necessary step towards increasing economic productivity.[73] Labour segmented into many separate tasks could be combined with inflexible machine processes to produce enormous gains in productivity in the nineteenth and twentieth century. In the twenty-first century, however, the rigid segmentation of work into discrete tasks was often seen as a source of inefficiency and waste. For this reason, business process improvement normally begins by breaking through thickets of 'functional silos' of rigidly segmented tasks in order to see the underlying 'end-to-end' business process.[74] **12.61**

Even when the steps in business process improvement have been decided, it does not follow that it will be easy to execute them successfully. On the contrary, the conventional wisdom in management circles is that from 50% to 70% of attempts at business process improvement fail.[75] Common causes of the failure of process improvement efforts include poor integration with an organisation's most important strategic goals; insufficient attention to the needs of stakeholders, such as customers; superficial, high-level analyses that fail to identify the challenges accurately; and poor communication.[76] Variations in the capacity to engage in the process of 'process improvement' or 'quality engineering' can play a major role in the success or failure of business process reengineering efforts. 'Process improvement' refers to ideas first described by Walter Shewhart in 1924 and later set out in detail in his 1931 book.[77] Shewhart's protégé, Edwards Deming, developed the plan-do-study-act method for implementing Shewhart's basic idea of creating a feedback loop to assist in monitoring any process that is repeated. A 2015 survey by McKinsey & Company demonstrated the continued relevance of process improvement in business: they showed that the odds of success for a 'business transformation' project increased from 26% to 79% when managers consistently followed the engineering discipline of process improvement.[78] **12.62**

[72] Somnuk Keretho and Saisamorn Naklada, 'Analysis of Export and Import Processes of Selected Products in Thailand' (Asia-Pacific Research and Training Network on Trade Working Paper No 103, United Nations June 2011) <https://www.unescap.org/sites/default/files/AWP%20No.%20103_0.pdf> accessed 1 August 2020.

[73] Adam Smith, *Inquiry into the Nature and Causes of the Wealth of Nations* (W Strahan and T Cadell 1776).

[74] Alec Sharp and Patrick McDermott, *Workflow Modelling: Tools for Process Improvement and Applications Development* (2nd edn, Artech House 2009) 19 (hereafter Sharp and McDermott, *Workflow Modelling*).

[75] Hans Pruijt, 'Multiple Personalities: The Case of Business Process Reengineering' (1998) 11 Journal of Organizational Change Management 260.

[76] James Proctor, 'Why Do BPR Initiatives Often Fail to Deliver Results?' (*Inteq Blog*, 21 March 2019) <https://www.inteqgroup.com/blog/why-do-business-process-reengineering-initiatives-fail> accessed 1 August 2020.

[77] Walter A Shewhart, *Economic Control of Quality of Manufactured Product* (Martino Fine Books 2015) vii (Preface): 'Broadly speaking, the object of industry is to set up economic ways and means of satisfying human wants and in so doing to reduce everything possible to routines requiring a minimum amount of human effort.' The first edition of this book was published in 1931 and it remains in print in 2019.

[78] McKinsey & Company, 'How to Beat the Transformation Odds' (*McKinsey*, 1 April 2015) <https://www.mckinsey.com/business-functions/organization/our-insights/how-to-beat-the-transformation-odds> accessed 1 August 2020.

12.63 Trying to accelerate the pace of business process improvement by tinkering with bits and pieces of existing processes, rather than doing the hard work of isolating and analysing the end-to-end process that underlies many smaller functional processes, is a recipe for failure. This is because trying to optimise individual parts of a process is not the same as trying to optimise the whole process and may be worse than doing nothing at all.[79] Technological change can intensify this problem, rather than ameliorating it. As Bill Gates observed, '[t]he first rule of any technology used in a business is that automation applied to an efficient operation will magnify the efficiency. The second is that automation applied to an inefficient operation will magnify the inefficiency.'[80] The slow progress in getting disparate federal agencies to reach agreement on common data standards for an integrated single-window system, and then actually to implement them, illustrate how difficult it can be to overcome these challenges.

12.64 Blockchain technologies enclose information in a secure wrapper, but cannot themselves guarantee the quality of the information that goes into the wrapper.[81] In order to ensure that the quality of information used is the same, or better, quality after changing the technology for trade finance as it was before that change, a thoughtful, deliberate effort at business process reengineering must be undertaken. This includes establishing process context, scope, and goals; analysing the current or 'as-is' process by modelling its workflow and identifying factors that have an impact on process performance; designing the new or 'to-be' process'; and developing the process for moving from 'as-is' to 'to-be', often at the same time as maintaining current operations.[82]

12.65 The 'to-be' state for many businesses engaged in cross-border trade includes a version of enterprise resource management software that combines software to manage logistics, supply chain operations, risk management, and compliance.[83] In 2018, the Gartner consulting firm noted that 'global trade management' ('GTM') was emerging as a distinct market for business software products that combine logistics, trade compliance, and finance functions. Many of the anachronistic features of cross-border trade, and much of the complexity that blockchain proponents believed blockchain could alleviate, are already being alleviated by more conventional software applications that are compatible with both legacy IT systems and emerging IT systems.

12.66 Global trade management software systems may help large trade intermediaries, such as global third-party logistics services and large enterprises engaged in cross-border trade, but they are too expensive and demanding for many small traders and intermediaries to be able to use, especially those in emerging economies. While no open-source, lightweight global trade management software is yet widely available for smaller intermediaries and traders in emerging economies, UNCTAD has developed an open-source software program to

79 Sharp and McDermott, *Workflow Modelling* (n 74) 17.

80 Christopher Stancombe, 'Tempted to rewrite Bill Gates' rules on automation?' (*Capgemini*, 2 January 2015) <https://www.capgemini.com/2015/01/tempted-to-rewrite-bill-gates-rules-on-automation/> accessed 1 August 2020.

81 Mike Orcutt, 'Blockchain smart contracts are finally good for something in the real world' (*MIT Technology Review*, 19 November 2018) <https://www.technologyreview.com/s/612443/blockchain-smart-contracts-can-finally-have-a-real-world-impact/> accessed 1 August 2020.

82 Sharp and McDermott, *Workflow Modelling* (n 74) 65.

83 William McNeill, 'Market Guide for Global Trade Management Software' (*Gartner Report*, 25 May 2018).

help automate customs functions in emerging economies. In 2019, UNCTAD's Automated System for Customs Data ('ASYCUDA') had been adopted in ninety countries, or more than half of emerging economies.[84] As more emerging economies begin constructing single-window systems in order to come into compliance with their WTO TFA obligations, the number of emerging economies implementing ASYCUDA is likely to increase.

Efforts to modernise cross-border trade workflows have been underway for decades and are beginning to show results. The WTO TFA creates a framework within which efforts to solve longstanding collective action problems, such as migrating legacy computer systems to newer technology architectures and expanding the scope of automated processes by standardising workflows, are making progress using legacy technologies. The unique features of technologies based on blockchain—consensus decision-making and secure, tamper-resistant records—do not appear to address the most important issues in the business process reengineering of cross-border trade flows that would have emerged if a serious workflow modelling effort had been undertaken. When the chief operating officer of a blockchain trade-finance platform resigned in 2019, he publicly voiced doubts about the relevance of blockchain solutions to meeting industry challenges: 'I have not yet seen something that shows the ultimate benefit of the technology . . . We are building solutions that are perceived as valuable by the providers of the solutions, not the users.' **12.67**

VI. Transforming Trade Finance Incrementally

In many discussions of the potential impact of blockchain on trade finance, the focus is on letters of credit both because they are such an anachronism and because letters of credit are presumed to be 'the most common payment system in international trade transactions'.[85] While the former point is clearly correct, the latter point is clearly incorrect. Industry experts have long recognised that 'documentary letters of credit' used to finance trade transactions were dying out.[86] In 2008, one industry expert estimated that, while as much as 80% of cross-border trade transactions were once covered by letters of credit and 20% covered by other mechanisms, the proportions had reversed with only 20% of trade transactions being financed with a letter of credit and 80% with other mechanisms.[87] More recent estimates of the proportion of cross-border trade financed by letters of credit are even lower: 12.5% in 2016,[88] and 10% in 2019.[89] In other words, one of the primary use cases for blockchain in trade finance—replacing letters of credit—may be illusory. The role of banks in providing trade finance was already in steep decline as a result of changing business models in **12.68**

[84] See 'ASYCUDA: User Countries' <https://asycuda.org/en/user-countries/> accessed 1 August 2020.

[85] See Espinosa, 'BBVA and Wave' (n 46).

[86] As nationally chartered banks in the US have the power to issue letters of credit, but lack the power to issue guarantees per se, they use 'standby letters of credit' to achieve the functional equivalent of a guarantee, but, as standby letters of credit have nothing to do with cross-border trade, they are outside the scope of this discussion.

[87] Dominic Broom, 'Banks and the Global Supply Chain—A Tipping Point for Global Trade?' (*The Global Treasurer*, 4 March 2008) <https://www.theglobaltreasurer.com/2008/03/04/banks-and-the-global-supply-chain-a-tipping-point-for-global-trade/> accessed 1 August 2020.

[88] Friederike Niepmann and Tim Schmidt-Eisenlohr, 'Trade finance around the world' (*VoxEU CEPR*, 11 June 2016) <https://voxeu.org/article/trade-finance-around-world> accessed 1 August 2020.

[89] Finbarr Bermingham, 'Banks signal the decline of traditional trade finance' (*Global Trade Review*, 5 July 2017) <https://www.gtreview.com/news/global/banks-signal-the-death-of-traditional-trade-finance/> accessed 1 August 2020.

cross-border trade and improvements in legacy technologies long before blockchain was invented.

12.69 Alternatives to letters of credit include sales on open account (exporter extends credit to importer), prepayment (importer extends credit to exporter), trade credit insurance, factoring (lending secured by accounts receivable based on the borrower's creditworthiness), and reverse factoring (lending secured by accounts receivable based on the borrower's customer's creditworthiness). In advanced market economies, vendors commonly extend credit to their customers for thirty, sixty, or ninety days depending on industry custom and information gathered about the borrower's creditworthiness. Granting trade credit for cross-border transactions is riskier because reliable, objective information about a prospective borrower's creditworthiness may not be available and the legal remedies available to the exporter in the importer's national legal system in the event of default may be unsatisfactory. At the other extreme from open account, in which the exporter bears the full risk of non-payment by the importer, is prepayment, in which the importer bears the full risk of non-performance by the exporter. Only an exporter with significant market power would demand prepayment because such unfavourable trade terms will drive away many prospective customers.

12.70 A letter of credit requires one or more banks to become deeply involved in the administration of the transaction, but the independence and strict compliance principles of letter of credit law restrict the scope of a bank's participation to the analysis of supporting documents. When parties engaged in trade had few choices other than prepayment/open account or letter of credit as payment mechanisms, these doctrines contributed to the profitability of the banks' trade finance operations.

12.71 The use of paper-based supporting documents has been declining in recent years as global supply chains have continued to expand and investment in trade-facilitation processes has increased. Supporting documents, such as certificates of origin, inspection certificates, and insurance binders, are often provided in electronic form today. Bills of lading as documents of title have long posed unique digitisation challenges, but those may also be less daunting than they once were.[90] For example, a US retailer might decide that the volume of its purchases in China justifies maintaining its own logistics facilities at ports in both China and the US and entering into 'volume contracts' with trans-Pacific carriers. When the retailer's agents in China receive container-loads of goods at a Chinese port, the retailer would thus become the outright legal owner of the goods before they are ever loaded on ships bound for the US. Within such a framework, the retailer could easily dispense with paper bills of lading, relying instead on data exchanged between the Chinese subsidiary and the US parent company to track the movement of the goods through its global supply chain.

12.72 If both banks and traders expect the proportion of trade transactions financed by letters of credit to continue declining, it is hard to see how any blockchain-enabled version of the letter of credit could ever gain enough momentum to achieve widespread adoption. The difficulty of convincing uncertain users to make the leap to a new collective solution increases if most users expect a market to shrink in the future, instead of growing.

[90] See ch 10 (Goldby) in this volume.

VII. Conclusion

On 25 February 2000, General Motors, Ford, and DaimlerChrysler announced their intention to form a combined business-to-business Internet marketplace, where vendors and purchasers in the US automotive industry could all transact business with each other simultaneously. Renault and Nissan soon joined, as did the software providers Oracle, SAP, and Commerce One. The name 'Covisint' was created to express their aspirations for the marketplace ('co' stands for cooperation and communication, 'vis' for visibility and visions, and 'int' for Internet and international).[91] Construction of the Internet marketplace began as soon as the Federal Trade Commission issued a no-action ruling on its antitrust dimensions.[92] **12.73**

The collaborators' original vision was nothing if not breath-taking: General Motors speculated that, as soon as 2001, vehicle production time could be cut from forty-five to ten days and costs cut by 6% once the combined $300 billion dollar spent by all five manufacturers with their 30,000 suppliers could be channelled through the Internet marketplace.[93] The fundamental flaws in the strategy surfaced almost immediately. Scarcely a year later, a Gartner analyst described the ensuing mess in the following terms:[94] **12.74**

> Laying out the relationships in Covisint is like reading a soap opera script. It's full of intrigue, love triangles, affairs, fights, and more publicity stunts than a Hollywood premiere ... SAP, Oracle, and Commerce One partnering will be like three angry pit bulls tearing each other apart in a fenced yard. Everyone wants to stop and help, but at the same time they're caught up in morbid curiosity.

In 2005, Thomas Stallkamp, former president of Chrysler Corp, offered an even bleaker assessment: 'Covisint was a horrible idea. Nobody thought it through. Data exchanges are fine, but Covisint and the way it was done was an absolute failure—it never got off the ground.'[95] **12.75**

Even after its spectacular and very public collapse only a couple of years after its founding, however, Covisint never closed its doors. Within a few years, it had successfully transformed itself into a provider of secure collaboration technologies for both public and private sector users. It was acquired by Compuware in 2004, and after shelving plans for an initial public offering in 2008, it was eventually spun off in 2013 as a cloud computing company. It quickly staked a claim to being an 'Internet of Things'/connected car service provider, which then led to its being acquired for more than $100 million in 2017 by OpenText, a technology services company offering integrated cloud, 'Internet of Things', and supply chain optimisation services. **12.76**

[91] Bart Kemper, 'Just what does Covisint mean, anyway?' (*the fabricator*, 13 March 2001) <https://www.thefabricator.com/article/shopmanagement/just-what-does-covisint-mean-anywayr> accessed 1 August 2020.

[92] United States of America Federal Trade Commission, 'FTC Terminates HSR Waiting Period for Covisint B2B Venture' (Press Release) (11 September 2000) <https://www.ftc.gov/news-events/press-releases/2000/09/ftc-terminates-hsr-waiting-period-covisint-b2b-venture> accessed 1 August 2020; United States of America Federal Trade Commission Staff, 'Entering the 21st Century: Competition Policy in the World of B2B Electronic Marketplaces' (Federal Trade Commission October 2000) <https://www.ftc.gov/sites/default/files/documents/reports/entering-21st-century-competition-policy-world-b2b-electronic-marketplaces/b2breport_0.pdf> accessed 1 August 2020.

[93] Lauren Gibbons Paul, 'B2B e-commerce: The biggest gamble yet' (*Computerworld.com*, 10 July 2000)..

[94] Kevin Prouty, 'SAP Buys Into the Confusion That Is Covisint' (*Gartner Consulting*, 16 June 2000).

[95] David Blanchard, 'Covisint Follows the Road Less Traveled' (2005) 9 Logistics Today 14.

12.77 Covisint's experience is common for many start-up companies: after making a splash by promising to do one thing, they must reinvent themselves, after it becomes clear that their original plan is not feasible. Covisint's experience is uncommon only in the intensity of the global scrutiny it received from its inception until its original strategy flamed out spectacularly on the world stage, as well as for its success in repeatedly reinventing itself in the two short decades of its existence.

12.78 Once John Carreyou exposed the scale of the fraud at Theranos, financial market commentators abruptly shifted from praising Theranos to asking how so many smart people could have been so wrong:[96]

> The Theranos scandal clearly illustrates the risk of market failure in markets for highly innovative products and services: over nearly a decade, sophisticated investors gave $900 million in start-up funding to a company without noticing that the company had never been able to develop a successful commercial product.

12.79 Elizabeth Holmes' ability to inspire the confidence of sophisticated investors and to manage the image Theranos presented to the public no doubt contributed quite a bit to Theranos' success. In that regard, Elizabeth Holmes successfully crafted a 'David and Goliath' narrative about breaking through barriers erected by an entrenched oligopoly that both the public and quite a few investors found difficult to resist. Many blockchain pilots are being marketed in a similar manner. Such narratives are likely to appeal to business leaders who, like Theranos investors, know little about the technology that is ostensibly driving the success of the venture. They are less likely to appeal to business leaders who are comfortable with the measured pace, shared control, and inherent uncertainty characteristic of the discipline of process improvement.

12.80 Most blockchain pilots undertaken within financial market segments, such as trade finance, will probably be allowed to fade into obscurity, far from the glare of the world media spotlight, because they began their lives with much less fanfare than Covisint. If the teams of software developers and business analysts working on those projects persevere with the same tenacity as the management of Covisint, they may also be able to survive long enough to participate in the successful launch of a new business, albeit not the same one that they originally set out to create.

12.81 In his autobiography, Henry Ford wrote, '[f]ailure is only the opportunity to begin again, this time more intelligently'.[97] If the irrational exuberance characteristic of most blockchain pilot projects can eventually be redirected towards more productive uses, then lessons learned from those pilot projects could contribute to the success of the much larger effort now underway to transform trade finance within the emerging digital global trade system.

[96] Andrew Hill, 'Fresh blood: Why everyone fell for Theranos' (*Financial Times*, 18 March 2018) <https://www.ft.com/content/a45ffdf0-2850-11e8-b27e-cc62a39d57a0> accessed 1 August 2020.

[97] Henry Ford and Samuel Crowther, *My Life and Work* (Page & Co 1922) 19.

PART III
INNOVATION AND TRADE-FINANCE CHALLENGERS

The previous two parts have focused upon the challenges for documentary trade finance and how some, but not all of those challenges might be met by technology, principally through the mechanism of digitizing trade documents. Whilst there can be no doubt that such digitization could dramatically reduce costs and processing times, such a solution simply swaps paper-based documents for digital "documents" within the existing trade-finance frame of reference. Part III examines the extent to which trade finance might be able to escape from current practical and analytical frameworks by developing entirely novel ones. In this regard, trade parties could abandon the notion of "documents" altogether (whether paper-based or electronic) by simply transmitting key data as part of the financing structure; they could abandon reliance on bank-based trade finance by meeting their financing and liquidity requirements through more bespoke non-bank options; they could abandon generic trade finance structures by developing specialized trade finance mechanisms for particular trade sectors; or they could abandon traditional notions of payment by linking different sale transactions together. Whilst each of these options involves trade finance in the broadest sense of that term, the development of such innovative financing and payment structures enables trade finance to be moulded so that it serves the interests of trade parties, rather than those of the banks. Undoubtedly, such innovation can be facilitated by technological developments, but that is not necessarily the case: technology and innovation do not quadrate perfectly. Accordingly, Part III focuses on trade finance innovation.

13

The Bank Payment Obligation as a Signal Step in the Evolution of Digital Trade Finance

*Agasha Mugasha**

I. Introduction

The bank payment obligation ('BPO') is a new digital financial instrument used by banks to facilitate cross-border trade. It is issued electronically by the buyer's bank (the obligor bank) to the seller's bank (the recipient bank) to ensure payment to the seller, mitigate the performance risk for the buyer, and finance the trade transaction. It was created to address the drawbacks of documentary credits, which include a relatively high cost, slow payment process and subjective judgment on the decision to honour the credit, on the one hand; and open account transactions, which offer minimal security and financing options to the contracting parties, on the other hand. Launched in 2013, it has been hailed as 'the biggest innovation to have taken place in the trade finance world since the letter of credit came into common use in the 17th century;'[1] objectively, however, it is one among a few promising modern techniques such as electronic letters of credit and blockchain-executed letters of credit that can facilitate trade finance. **13.01**

Inspired by the long and successful history of documentary credits, the BPO is an irrevocable and autonomous bank undertaking whose honour is conditional on the performance of the conditions prescribed in the undertaking.[2] Whereas the bank's undertaking in a documentary credit runs in favour of the exporter, the undertaking in a BPO runs in favour of the exporter's bank. Furthermore, whereas the bank undertaking in a documentary credit is conditional on the presentation of compliant documents to the nominated bank, the undertaking in a BPO is conditional on the successful matching of structured **13.02**

* I owe a debt of gratitude to Professor Dora Neo, Professor Christopher Hare, and all the participants at the Trade Finance for the 21st Century Symposium held in March 2018 at the Faculty of Law, National University of Singapore.

[1] David Hennah, 'BPO: A Digital Instrument for a Digital Age' February 2018 Documentary Credit World 25 (hereafter Hennah, 'BPO: Digital Instrument'); see also Staff Editors, 'Trade Finance: The State of Play and Recent Trends' (2014) 28 Journal of Taxation and Regulation of Financial Institutions 55, 59 (hereafter Staff Editors, 'Trade Finance: State of Play and Recent Trends'), where the BPO is described as one of the most important innovations in recent years. The first rules were drafted following a memorandum of understanding between the ICC and SWIFT in September 2011 and were adopted in 2013: see David Meynell and Gary Collyer, 'BPO: A Reintroduction' (*Trade and Forfaiting Review*, 29 March 2017) accessed 28 February 2018 (hereafter Meynell and Collyer, 'BPO: A Reintroduction').

[2] The key books on documentary credits include John F Dolan, *The Law of Letters of Credit: Commercial and Standby Credits* (4th edn, LexisNexis A.S. Pratt 2007) (hereafter Dolan, *Law of Letters of Credit*); Peter Ellinger and Dora Neo, *The Law and Practice of Documentary Letters of Credit* (Hart Publishing 2010) (hereafter Ellinger and Neo, *Law and Practice of Documentary Letters of Credit*); Ali Malek and David Quest, *Jack: Documentary Credits* (4th edn, Tottel Publishing 2009); Agasha Mugasha, *The Law of Letters of Credit and Bank Guarantees* (Federation Press 2003) (hereafter Mugasha, *Law of Letters of Credit and Bank Guarantees*).

trade data on an independent electronic platform.[3] It differs, therefore, from a documentary credit which is an obligation of the issuing bank directly to the exporter and depends on the examination of documents by the banks.[4] Thus, according to the Uniform Rules for Bank Payment Obligations ('URBPO'),[5] a bank payment obligation is 'an irrevocable and independent undertaking of an Obligor Bank to pay or incur a deferred payment obligation and pay at maturity a specified amount of money to a Recipient Bank following submission of all Data Sets required by an Established Baseline resulting in a Data Match or an acceptance of a Data Mismatch . . . '.[6] The irrevocable undertaking, once communicated to the recipient bank, constitutes a legally binding, valid, and enforceable payment obligation of an obligor bank to a recipient bank under the appropriate standard of law and is enforceable in accordance with its terms. Specifically, the seller is assured of payment if it meets its obligations, while the buyer is assured that payment will only be made if the conditions of payment in the BPO are met. In business terms, the BPO is a form of a guarantee from the buyer's ('obligor') bank to seller's ('recipient') bank and is intended to offer a level of security to the seller's bank so that it supports the financing of open account transactions.[7] Furthermore, it is conceptually a new financial instrument and it is neither a 'lite' letter of credit nor an electronic letter of credit.[8] The BPO is different from the electronic letters of credit that are envisaged in the Supplement to the Uniform Customs and Practice for Documentary Credits for Electronic Presentation (Version 1.1), which is better known by its acronym 'eUCP'.[9] Whereas the eUCP caters for the electronic presentation of paper documents to the bank to trigger payment, the BPO framework only envisages the extraction of trade data from the trade documents for electronic presentation and the electronic matching of that data on a specified matching application.[10] The dematerialisation of trade, in this instance through the use of digital trade information instead of paper-based information, and the use of e-commerce platforms for the exchange of information instead of the manual examination of documents, are intended to improve working capital and financial processes for the trading parties and generate income and efficiencies for the banks involved.[11] The BPO conforms to the market trend of the digitisation of trade flows and the conduct of business generally, including the use of communication platforms for the exchange of information among different parties using structured messages.

[3] SWIFT Corporate and Supply Chain Market Management Team, 'Bank Payment Obligation: A new payment method' (*SWIFT*, July 2016) 6 <https://www.swift.com/node/35051#:~:text=SWIFT %20is%20a%20member%2Downed,with%20speed%2C%20certainty%20and%20confidence.&text=What%20is%20BPO%3F,for%20risk%20mitigation%20and%20financing!> accessed 22 June 2020 (hereafter SWIFT, 'Bank Payment Obligation: A new payment method').

[4] See UCP 600, art 7.

[5] *Uniform Rules for Bank Payment Obligations* ICC No. 750E (hereafter URBPO).

[6] URBPO (n 5) art 3. The corresponding provision is UCP 600, art 2 which defines a credit as an arrangement that is irrevocable and thereby constitutes a definite undertaking of the issuing bank to honour a complying presentation.

[7] See Croner-I, 'Using the Bank Payment Obligation rather than Letter of Credit' (*Croner-i*, 2019) <https://app.croneri.co.uk/questions-and-answers/using-bank-payment-obligation-rather-letter-credit?product=32> accessed 22 June 2020.

[8] Meynell and Collyer, 'BPO: A Reintroduction' (n 1).

[9] They are formally provided for in the eUCP (Version 1.1 Supplement to UCP 600, 2007).

[10] David J Hennah, *ICC Guide to the Uniform Rules for Bank Payment Obligations* (International Chamber of Commerce 2013) 88 (hereafter David Hennah, *ICC Guide to Uniform Rules for BPO*).

[11] See generally, Benjamin Geva, 'Banking in the Digital Age—Who Is Afraid of Payment Disintermediation?' (2018) European Banking Institute Working Paper Series 23/2018 (hereafter Geva, 'Banking in the Digital Age').

Conceptually, the BPO is positioned between documentary letters of credit, which require the banks to receive documents and make decisions basing on those documents before payment is made, on the one hand; and open account transactions, where the banks' role is limited to transmitting documents and making payment without making any decisions on the documents, on the other hand. The banks' role in BPOs consists of the receipt of electronic trade data and its transmission to a transaction matching application ('TMA') that determines if the data matches a previously determined data set. The obligor bank's undertaking introduces the security and legal features of a documentary credit, while the TMA's electronic matching of data introduces the element of efficiency found in open account trading.[12] Currently, the BPO is bank-centric because it was designed by banks to intermediate in the supply chain finance where they were not significant players[13]and operates on the matching platform to which only banks have access. Its operations centre around the TMA, currently, the Trade Service Utility platform ('TSU') operated by SWIFT, which makes decisions on data matches or mismatches; and the use of structured messages based on the ISO20022 XML standard. Furthermore, the rules governing the BPO only cover the bank-to-bank relationships leaving the relationship between the banks and the underlying parties to bilateral agreements.[14] **13.03**

This chapter considers the business case for, and the legal aspects of, the BPO, and makes two main points. First, the legal aspects of the BPO are familiar, since its starting point is to create a secure instrument similar to a documentary credit and apply it in the open account space. Secondly, the commercial factors that led to the creation of the BPO constrain its growth and wide acceptability at the same time. The BPO was created as digital innovation and yet it faces competition from other digital initiatives that are products of the same technological innovations; furthermore, it was created to fill the gap between documentary credits and open account transactions; and yet, each one of these techniques has a stable customer base and will not be easily displaced. Therefore, the BPO can only thrive in the limited digital space not occupied by documentary credits, open account transactions, and its digital competitors. Following this introduction, section II of this chapter outlines the factors that led to the creation of the BPO as well as its contractual setting, thereby shedding light on its intended role in trade finance. It will point out that, as a digital solution to the payment for and financing of trade, its unique value lies in the technological innovation to adapt the security and financing features of the documentary credit to the open account space. This part also provides the benchmarking evidence for evaluating the future role of the BPO, which will be undertaken later in this chapter. SectionIII focuses on the legal aspects, as extracted from the applicable URBPO (also called 'the Rules' in this chapter), with a view to placing the rules governing the new instrument in the context of the general rules governing the well-established finance instruments. Thus, in pertinent places, the chapter lightly compares the provisions in the URBPO to the better-known rules for documentary credits, the Uniform Customs and Practice for Documentary Credits ('UCP'), to **13.04**

[12] See Global Supply Chain Finance Forum, 'Definition Bank Payment Obligation' <http://supplychainfinanceforum.org/techniques/bank-payment-obligation-bpo/> accessed 22 June 2020 (hereafter Global Supply Chain Finance Forum, 'Bank Payment Obligation').

[13] John Bugeja, 'A Split Personality' (*Trade and Forfaiting Review*, May 2015) <https://www.trade-advisory.com/wp-content/uploads/2015/08/BPO-A-split-Personality-no-marks.pdf> accessed 22 June 2020 (hereafter Bugeja, 'A Split Personality').

[14] Bugeja, 'A Split Personality' (n 13) 2.

elucidate the key principles governing the BPO. Section IV postulates on the sustainability of the new financial instrument and observes that, notwithstanding the advantages of the BPO over the more established documentary credits and open account transactions, there has been a slow adoption of the new financial instrument and that the older financial instruments have been resilient in the face of the challenger instrument. Nonetheless, there is a niche market in cross-border trade where the BPO plays an important part and that could be the springboard for its sustainability as an additional trade finance instrument. The BPO has progressed further in international recognition than earlier electronic initiatives because it was supported by international rules from the outset, which rules relied on the familiar legal principles used in documentary credits, and was launched via an international banking network. Arguably, it points to the way of the future and might inspire the development of other instruments in the further digitalisation of trade finance.[15]

II. The Business Case and Contractual Setting for the Bank Payment Obligation

13.05 The banks spearheaded the creation of the BPO early in the twenty-first century due to the perceived need for a digital payment instrument that addressed the drawbacks of letters of credit and open account transactions. That need for a digital instrument had arisen due to a convergence of several factors in trade, finance, and technology.

13.06 First, documentary credits were generally perceived as inefficient, costly, and subjective since they required the manual transportation and processing of documents which was slow, time consuming, and inherently subjective, leading to avoidable disputes.[16] One case study reported that replacing the manual document checking process with the BPO could abridge the payment process by seven days, reduce the documentation for the seller by at least 30%, and enhance accuracy and objectivity in examining the documents.[17] Furthermore, the bank intermediation fees and the regulatory cost of capital for documentary credits, which were passed on to the customer, made this traditional financing instrument expensive. Since the documentary credit creates a contingent liability on the part of the bank issuer and any bank that incurs a payment obligation, a regulatory cost is incurred and then passed on to the applicant of the letter of credit. Furthermore, since the bank is required to hold capital against that obligation, it makes credit more expensive and reduces the amount of available capital for lending.[18] Because of these drawbacks, there was a perceived need for a more efficient, cheaper, and objective instrument. That need was partly

[15] See David Meynell, 'ICC Rules to Facilitate the Widespread Digitalisation of Trade Finance' (*International Chamber of Commerce United Kingdom*, 13 November 2018) <https://iccwbo.uk/blogs/press-releases/icc-rules-to-facilitate-the-widespread-digitalisation-of-trade-finance> accessed 22 June 2020 (hereafter David Meynell, 'ICC Rules'); David Hennah, 'BPO: Digital Instrument' (n 1).

[16] Staff Editors, 'Trade Finance: The State of Play and Recent Trends' (2014) 28 Journal of Taxation and Regulation of Financial Institutions 55, 56.

[17] Thomas Tan, 'Bank Payment Obligation: A New Trade Payment Instrument' (*Global Trade Review*, April 2015) 7 <http://www.gtreview.com/wp-content/uploads/2015/04/Thomas-Tac_CIMB.pdf> accessed 22 June 2020 (hereafter Thomas Tan, 'Bank Payment Obligation'); David Hennah, *ICC Guide to Uniform Rules for* BPO (n 10) 30.

[18] According to the Basel regulatory framework for capital adequacy, letters of credit are characterised as off-balance sheet commitments before they are called upon and still attract margining provisions: see generally, Simon Gleeson, *Gleeson on the International Regulation of Banking* (3rd edn, OUP 2018).

met by the migration of some business to the open account method, as discussed in the next paragraph, and partly by the creation of the BPO, which was structured to increase the operational efficiency and objectivity of the documentary credit payment process.

Secondly, by the beginning of the twenty-first century there was a near global shift in world trade payment methods to open account terms, which grew exponentially, while traditional finance methods, such as documentary credits, grew only modestly.[19] Open account transactions are those where the trade between seller and buyer is not supported by any banking instrument or financing facility and the bank's role is limited to making payment.[20] That shift to open account transactions was partly attributable to the increased share of trade between related parties, which do not require the strong security features of the documentary credit,[21] and partly because open account transactions are cheaper and faster than documentary credits since the banks are only payment facilitators without making any undertaking to pay the seller and without any duty to examine documentary compliance for the benefit of the buyer.[22] Open account transactions, however, have the inherent limitation that they secure neither payment for the seller nor performance for the buyer and, thus, leave the parties exposed to payment and performance risks.[23] Furthermore, open account sales offer limited financing options and typically, the finance is limited to receivables or payables financing—essentially, post-shipment finance when the goods have been accepted and the invoices approved.[24] Yet, suppliers frequently require pre-shipment finance before any invoices have been generated.[25] These were important factors in the development of the BPO, which is intended to offer a wider menu of financing options across the supply chain. **13.07**

Thirdly, by the beginning of the twenty-first century, globalisation had significantly extended supply chains for trade in commodities across the developing and emerging markets[26] at a time when there was a significant contraction in the liquidity available for **13.08**

[19] See Global Supply Chain Finance Forum, *Standard Definitions for Techniques of Supply Chain Finance* (BAFT, EBA, FCI, ICC, and ITFA, 2016) 17 <https://www.iccgermany.de/fileadmin/user_upload/Content/Banktechnik_und_-praxis/Standard_Definitions_for_Techniques_of_Supply_Chain_Finance_Global_SCF_Forum_2016.pdf> accessed 22 June 2020 (hereafter *Standard Definitions for Techniques of Supply Chain Finance*). By 2012, over 80% of global trade was conducted on open account transactions and that trend was set to continue: Michael Quinn, Imre Gorzsas, and Bilge Ozisik, 'Bank Payment Obligation: Financial Instruments to Manage Risk in the Open Account Trade' <https://www.ifc.org/wps/wcm/connect/e2be7c004d0e681887d6c7f81ee631cc/GFM-TSC-BPM5-Quinn.pdf?MOD=AJPERES> accessed 19 August 2019 (hereafter Quinn, Gorzsas, and Ozisik, 'BPO: Financial Instruments to Manage Risk in the Open Account Trade'). Open account terms had emerged earlier in merchant-to-merchant trade: see, eg John F Dolan, *Fundamentals of Commercial Activity: A Lawyers Guide* (Little, Brown & Co 1991) 21–9 (hereafter Dolan, *Fundamentals of Commercial Activity*).

[20] See *Standard Definitions for Techniques of Supply Chain Finance* (n 19) 24.

[21] Committee on the Global Financial System, 'Trade finance: developments and issues' (CGFS Paper No 50, Bank for International Settlements, 2014) <https://www.bis.org/publ/cgfs50.pdf> 14–15 accessed 22 June 2020 (hereafter Committee on the Global Financial System, 'Trade finance: developments and issues'). For instance, in 2016, 42.4% of international trade in the US occurred between related parties (see US Census Bureau: Economics and Statistics Administration, 'US Goods Trade: Imports and Exports by Related-Parties' (*US Census Bureau*, 6 July 2017) <https://www.census.gov/foreign-trade/Press-Release/2016pr/aip/related_party/rp16.pdf> accessed 22 June 2020) and that share was 40.8% in 2010 (US Census Bureau, 'US Goods Trade: Imports & Exports by Related-Parties 2010') (*US Census Bureau*, 11 May 2011) <https://www.census.gov/foreign-trade/Press-Release/2010pr/aip/related_party/rp10.pdf> accessed 22 June 2020.) Related-party trade includes trade by US companies with their subsidiaries abroad as well as trade by US subsidiaries of foreign companies with their parent companies.

[22] Dolan, *Fundamentals of Commercial Activity* (n 19) 21–6.

[23] For the disadvantages of open account sales see *Standard Definitions for Techniques of Supply Chain* Finance (n 19).

[24] SWIFT, 'Bank Payment Obligation: A new payment method' (n 3).

[25] ibid.

[26] See eg, Quinn, Gorzsas, and Ozisik, 'BPO: Financial Instruments to Manage Risk in the Open Account Trade' (n 19).

trade finance coupled with increased regulation that required higher margining requirements.[27] Typically, the suppliers were small- and medium-sized enterprises ('SMEs') with varying funding requirements and practices by industry or region, and they required innovative solutions to keep trade flowing and to remain afloat.[28] At the time of increasing global trade, however, SMEs were severely constrained in raising working capital from banks, which were the traditional lenders for trade finance. They, thus, had to look for alternative ways of funding and that resulted in the larger corporate buyers seeking new ways of assisting their suppliers obtain finance.[29] Innovative financing solutions led to the creation of the BPO. Supply chain finance was required to provide more funds for working capital, mitigate risk, and enhance the multitude of business processes. Effected properly, supply chain finance could facilitate trade by giving the suppliers more finance options for enhancing liquidity while giving the buyers extended payment terms.[30] The BPO met that need by making financing potentially available from the time the seller obtains a purchase order and before it produces any goods or services. The BPO, especially the deferred payment type, also increased the financing options for the supplier who required working capital. By assuring the seller of payment upon receipt of the purchase order, the instrument formed the basis on which pre-shipment finance could be based, much like an advance payment letter of credit, and generates crucial working capital. It is noteworthy, however, that the BPO has the same capital requirements as documentary credits since they are also characterised as contingent liability; that is, the obligor bank commits itself to make a payment when there is a data match with an established baseline or a mismatch that has been accepted.[31] That is one significant factor why the BPO has not made significant inroads into the documentary credit territory, as will be seen later.

13.09 The fourth and critical factor for the creation of the BPO was the development of new and innovative technologies by banks, specialised financial institutions, and independent providers that increased the digitalisation of trade, including the transmission and processing of messages on electronic platforms. The technology was based on the familiar concepts of eDocumentation and ePlatforms and aimed to deliver trade-finance products more efficiently and cost effectively.[32] The BPO is one such financial product which adapts technology and the familiar legal features of the documentary credit in trade finance by utilising banking channels to mitigate risk and assure efficient and cost-effective payment.[33]

[27] See Ross P Buckley, Douglas W Arner, and Rebecca L Stanley, 'Trade Finance in East Asia: Potential Responses to the Shortfall' (2014) 15 Melbourne Journal of International Law 1, 1–6.

[28] 'ICC Banking Commission's fourth SCF summit launches new definitions' (*Trade and Forfaiting Review*, 15 March 2016) (hereafter 'ICC Banking Commission launches new definitions').

[29] Clifford Chance, 'An Evolution of Trade Receivables Financing' (*Clifford Chance*, April 2016) <https://www.cliffordchance.com/content/dam/cliffordchance/briefings/2016/04/an-evolution-in-trade-receivables-financing.pdf> accessed 22 June 2020.

[30] 'ICC Banking Commission launches new definitions' (n 28); and generally, Iris H-Y Chiu, 'A New Era in Fintech Payment Innovations? A Perspective from the Institutions and Regulation of Payment Systems' (2017) 9 Law, Innovation and Technology 190.

[31] David Hennah, *ICC Guide to Uniform Rules for BPO* (n 10) 40.

[32] SWIFT, 'Bank Payment Obligation: A new payment method' (n 3); 'ICC Banking Commission launches new definitions' (n 28).

[33] A comparable new payment technique is blockchain: see ch 12 (Winn) in this volume.

A. Transaction and Contractual Setting

The BPO serves the same purposes of assurance of payment and performance as the documentary credit which, of course, is a well-known financial instrument. Like the confirmed documentary credit, the BPO in the four-corner model for supply chain finance, involving two banks and the two counter-parties to the trade transaction, is most suited to cross-border trade. This model reduces Know-Your-Customer and other compliance requirements for each bank because the trading counterparties would normally be customers of the bank.[34] In that model, the first relationship is the contract for the sale of goods and their shipment between the buyer and seller, for which they directly exchange the trade documents. That transaction forms the basis for, but is not part of, the BPO. It is not a standardised transaction. However, the International Chamber of Commerce has a template in the form of the ICC Model International Sale Contract.[35] The second relationship is that between the banks and their respective customers, the buyer and seller. That relationship, too, is not standardised, but the International Chamber of Commerce ('ICC') has launched the Guidelines for the Creation of BPO Customer Agreements.[36] In the performance of their duties under that relationship, the seller and buyer respectively extract and send the trade data to their respective banks, which, in turn send it to the TMA. When the seller's data matches the pre-agreed data received from the buyer, there is an established baseline on which the TMA would, subsequently, base its decision regarding whether there is a match of data to trigger payment. The third relationship is the one between the TMA and the two respective banks. Since the TMA plays a central role in the BPO transaction, the involved banks must subscribe or participate in the same TMA[37] and be subject to its rules.[38] Presently, all BPOs use the Trade Services Utility ('TSU'), which is the TMA at SWIFT. Furthermore, as seen above, the contractual framework for the BPO requires the use of industry standards in the transmission of structured digital messages among the banks and the TMA. The advantage of using industry standards is that any party can exchange data by using a trade transaction matching scheme, and that eventually, the BPO can be used by any TMA that uses the same standards.[39] Thus, according to the URBPO, the use of the ISO 20022 Trade Services Management ('TSMT') messages is mandatory and the use of any other message type is outside the scope of the Rules.[40] If there is a successful match of the trade data by the TMA, the TMA sends the match report to the two banks, at which point the BPO becomes payable according to its terms (at sight or deferred payment). Copies of **13.10**

[34] SWIFT, 'Bank Payment Obligation: A new payment method' (n 3) 5; see also Geoffrey L Wynne and Hannah Fearn, 'The Bank Payment Obligation: Will it Replace the Traditional Letter of Credit—Now, or Ever?' (2014) 29 Butterworths Journal of International Banking and Financial Law 102 (hereafter Wynne and Fearn, 'The Bank Payment Obligation').

[35] International Chamber of Commerce Policy and Buin, 'ICC International Sale Model Contract' (*UN Trade Facilitation Implementation Guide*) <http://tfig.unece.org/contents/icc-model-international-sale-contract.htm> accessed 22 June 2020.

[36] International Chamber of Commerce Policy and Business Practices, 'ICC Guidelines for the Creation of BPO Customer Agreements' (*International Chamber of Commerce*, August 2015) <https://cdn.iccwbo.org/content/uploads/sites/3/2015/08/ICC-Guidelines-for-the-Creation-of-BPO-Customer-Agreements.pdf.> accessed 22 June 2020.

[37] URBPO (n 5) art 1(a).

[38] Each bank is subject to the SWIFT TSU Rulebook.

[39] See David Hennah, *ICC Guide to Uniform Rules for BPO* (n 10) 32–33.

[40] URBPO (n 5) art 2(c)(i). The ISO 20022 messaging standards 'facilitate the technological integration of trade, payment and cash management data'.

the match report are relayed to the buyer and seller by their respective banks, and payment is then made to the seller by the seller's bank.

III. Salient Features of the Legal Framework for the BPO

13.11 The legal framework for BPOs largely follows the principles governing documentary credits as encapsulated in the UCP. In the absence of decided court cases on the BPO, therefore, analogies with the law documentary credits are most pertinent.

A. Applicable Rules and Notable Exclusions

13.12 The structure and terminology of the URBPO relate back to familiar language used in the UCP and adapt it for digital communication. The application of the URBPO, therefore, like the UCP, is predicated upon the agreement of the parties. So, the URBPO only apply when the payment segment of an established baseline expressly states that it is subject to the Rules or when each involved bank agrees in a separate agreement that the Rules apply to the BPO.[41] When the URBPO are incorporated in the established baseline, the Rules apply in their entirety and bind the banks. However, it is still open to the banks to expressly modify or exclude some specifically agreed rules through the established baseline or by separate agreement.[42] There is no precedent for the use of the BPO without incorporating the URBPO. In that event, the court would arguably apply general principles of law and thereby end up applying the URBPO as the most advanced and authoritative statement of the applicable industry standards.

13.13 By design, the URBPO do not include all the contractual relationships that one normally encounters in the practice of documentary credits, and some of these exclusions have inhibited the use and growth of the BPO instrument. Since the URBPO only cover the bank-to-bank relations, or what is termed the 'collaborative space' for banks, the relations between the seller or buyer and their respective banks, or what is termed the 'competitive space' for banks is left to each individual bank. As seen above, however, the competitive space is covered by a set of guidelines to assist the banks in the creation of customer contracts or agreements.[43] Secondly, since there is no prospect of presenting documents to the bank or the TMA, there are no rules for the presentation of documents in the URBPO, which contrasts with the extensive provisions concerning documents in the UCP.[44] The URBPO also do not provide for the basis for determining whether the data matches or does not match to trigger the payment or rejection of a presentation. That role and what it entails, which are the equivalent to the determination of documentary compliance under documentary credits,

[41] URBPO (n 5) art 2(a).

[42] ibid.

[43] It was envisaged from the outset of the drafting that subsequent versions of the URBPO would expand coverage of the Rules to include the relations in the competitive space: Meynell and Collyer, 'BPO: A Reintroduction' (n 1); but subsequent thinking might have reduced that ambition: see David Meynell, 'ICC Rules' (n 15).

[44] UCP 600 arts 17–28.

are left to the TMA and its relations with the subscribing banks.[45] Similarly, since the BPO is the obligor bank's direct undertaking to the recipient bank, there are no provisions in the Rules for advice or confirmation of the undertaking.

B. Establishment of the BPO and Amendment of an Established Baseline to Add a BPO

As a payment method, the BPO, just like the documentary credit, will be agreed upon in the trade transaction and its terms and conditions will be communicated to and among the banks at the outset. It would then be part of the established baseline and would give the buyer and the seller the whole range of financing options along the different segments of the trade transaction; for instance, pre-shipment, post-shipment, approved trade receivables, and buyer finance. Furthermore, the BPO can be issued by amendment to the established baseline later in the lifecycle of the trade transaction and for an amount that differs from the value of the goods since some of the services relating to the goods would have been performed earlier in the cycle. It would then provide post-shipment financing based on the receivables.[46] This flexibility is useful where the seller identifies a financing requirement based on receivables that will not provide liquid funds for a while, and yet the commercial and transport data had been submitted to its bank. A delay in issuing the BPO also reduces the cost of capital for the buyer whose credit lines remain free until the BPO is issued.[47] **13.14**

According to the URBPO, a baseline incorporating the BPO only becomes an established baseline, ie effective, when each bank has accepted its role through the TMA. When there is only one obligor bank that submitted a baseline to the TMA and there are zero mismatches between that baseline and the baseline submitted by the recipient bank, the BPO will become established when the TMA sends a baseline match report with zero mismatches with the status 'established' and affirming a match between the data submitted by the two banks.[48] At that point, the obligor bank is irrevocably bound by the BPO. If there are other obligor banks, for instance when the obligor bank is not the buyer's bank or there are multiple obligor banks, the BPO is established when the TMA sends to each bank a role and baseline acceptance notification following a baseline match report with zero mismatches.[49] Similarly, any amendment either to the established baseline that incorporates the BPO or to incorporate the BPO requires the consent of each involved bank.[50] The amendment is entirely an inter-bank matter and may be requested by the obligor bank or the recipient bank by sending a baseline amendment request to the TMA and it is accepted by the counterparty bank sending an amendment acceptance to the TMA.[51] The amendment becomes **13.15**

[45] URBPO (n 5) art 1(b). In contrast, the UCP, first, in art 2 defines a complying presentation as one that is in accordance with the terms and conditions of the credit, the provisions of the UCP and international banking practice; and second, in art 14 lays down the standard for the examination of documents.

[46] David Hennah, *ICC Guide to Uniform Rules for BPO* (n 10) 33.

[47] ibid 36–7.

[48] URBPO (n 5) arts 9(d)(i) and 10(a)(i).

[49] ibid, arts 9(d)(ii) and 9(d)(iii). The above provisions are similar to the provisions of the UCP 600 where, first, the undertaking of the bank is binding when it leaves the sphere of control of the bank issuing it (UCP 600, art 7 (b)).

[50] URBPO (n 5) art 11(a).

[51] ibid art 11(b)(i).

effective when the TMA sends to the obligor bank an amendment acceptance notification following such acceptance or when the TMA sends to any other involved bank a role and baseline acceptance notification confirming that such bank has accepted its role as specified in the baseline contained in the full push through report.[52] According to the URBPO, a requested amendment will be rejected and the established baseline will remain in place if any involved bank rejects the amendment request. If this happens, the TMA sends an amendment rejection or a role and baseline rejection to each other involved bank.[53]

C. Expiry Date

13.16 An established baseline must state an expiry date for the BPO; that is, the date by which all the data sets must be submitted to the TMA. The BPO remains in effect until it either expires before submission of all the data sets required by the established baseline, the established baseline is amended so as to release the obligor bank from its undertaking, or the BPO is fully paid in accordance with its terms, whichever happens earliest.[54] The URBPO eschews the problem of different time zones across the globe by standardising the determination of the expiry date. It does this by adopting the Universal Time Coordinated ('UTC') as the basis for computing the time of the expiry date.[55] Under this approach, all expiry periods are specified using the same time reference, the UTC, which approximates the Greenwich Meridian Time.[56]

D. Honour of the Undertaking

13.17 The undertaking of the obligor bank in the BPO is to pay at sight or incur a deferred payment undertaking and pay it at maturity in accordance with the terms of the BPO and following the submission of the required data sets and a data match or a data mismatch that has been accepted by each involved bank.[57] Thus, the pre-requisite for triggering payment under a BPO is that there is a data match on the TMA or a mismatch that has been accepted following the submission of the data by the recipient bank. In a departure from the UCP which anticipates that the nominated bank will examine the required set of documents as soon as it is presented,[58] the URBPO requires the submission of all data sets to the TMA before a data match is made. When the match is made, the TMA sends a data set match report simultaneously to all the involved banks of either a data match or data mismatch.[59] In

[52] ibid arts 10(a)(ii) and 11(c)(i)–(c)(iii).

[53] ibid art 11(d). These are similar to the practices captured in UCP 600, art 10.

[54] URBPO (n 5) art 11(f).

[55] ibid arts 8(a) and 8(b). These are similar to UCP 600, art 6(d)(i).

[56] David Hennah, *ICC Guide to Uniform Rules for BPO* (n 10).

[57] URBPO (n 5) art 10c. This is similar to documentary credits: UCP 600, arts 7(b), and art 2 (the definition of 'honour').

[58] See UCP 600 art 14(b).

[59] URBPO (n 5) art 8(c). This brief procedure avoids the lengthy and discretionary processes of the paper-based process in documentary credits. Under UCP 600, art 16(c), a bank that declines payment must give notice to the presenter expeditiously, but not later than five banking days. The bank may hold documents at the disposal of the presenter (cf *Fortis Bank SA/NV v Indian Overseas Bank* [2011] EWCA Civ 58 for liability if the bank wrongfully detains documents). The issuing bank may seek a waiver from the applicant (UCP 600 art 16(b)) or may pay under reserve: *Banque de l'Indochine et de Suez SA v JH Rayner (Mincing Lane) Ltd* [1983] QB 711 (CA).

case of a data mismatch, the obligor bank has an immediate discretion to accept or reject the mismatches.[60] This differs significantly from the process in documentary credits where the nominated bank has, first, to use its judgment to determine compliance with the terms of the credit; and if the documents do not comply, secondly, to decide whether or not to contact the buyer to seek a waiver of discrepancy.[61] Thus, the procedure under the BPO is rigorous, efficient, and objective, and indeed, a major attraction of the BPO is that it releases banks from the cumbersome processes of document examination and exercising discretions on honour and payment. In practice, though, waivers of mismatches in BPOs are requested and often granted because of the relationships among the contracting parties.[62]

E. Duties of the Bank

An involved bank is required to act on the messages received from the TMA without delay. It must also ensure that any data it submits to the TMA relating to the underlying transaction accurately reflects the data received from the buyer or seller in the underlying transaction.[63] When a message is received during the time when a bank is normally closed, the message will be deemed to have been received on the next banking day. **13.18**

F. The Independence Principle: Separate and Independent Contracts

Article 6 of the URBPO provides for the independence or autonomy of the BPO from the underlying and related transactions thus: **13.19**

> Article 6 Bank Payment Obligations v. Contracts
>
> (a) A BPO is separate and independent from the sale or other contract on which the underlying trade transaction may be based. An Involved Bank is in no way concerned with or bound by such contract, even if any reference whatsoever to it is included in an Established Baseline. Consequently, the undertaking of an Obligor Bank is not subject to claims or defences by the buyer resulting from its relationship with an Involved Bank or the seller.
>
> (b) A Recipient Bank can in no case avail itself of the contractual relationship existing between the buyer and the Buyer's Bank or an Obligor Bank other than the Buyer's Bank.[64]

This principle imposes a singular duty on the obligor bank to pay under the BPO if there is a data match or a mismatch that has been accepted. The independence principle is reinforced in article 10e of the URBPO which provides that the obligor bank's duties do not depend on its right or ability to obtain reimbursement from any other party. The above provisions **13.20**

60 URBPO (n 5) art 10(c); David Hennah, *ICC Guide to Uniform Rules for BPO* (n 10) 30.
61 See UCP 600, art 16.
62 Wang Shiyong, 'BPO: Still a Long Way to Go' February 2018 Documentary Credit World 20, 22 (hereafter Wang, 'BPO: Still a Long Way to Go').
63 URBPO (n 5) arts 9(a)–(c).
64 It corresponds to UCP 600, art 4 and has been adapted to suit the digital context.

are similar to those that apply to documentary credits, on which there is a body of well-developed literature, together with a growing number of exceptions to that principle, the most known of which is the fraud exception.[65]

13.21 A pertinent issue is, therefore, whether the fraud exception to the independence principle in documentary credits similarly applies to the BPO.[66] It ought to be recalled that the fraud exception in documentary credits is a creature of domestic law because the ICC deliberately left it to each jurisdiction to develop that exception according to its local circumstances.[67] In Anglo-American jurisdictions, the fraud exception is principally based on the overriding public policy of *ex turpi causa non oritur actio*, or, 'fraud unravels all', which applies as a general principle of law.[68] The same is true for the widely acknowledged illegality exception,[69] which is not specific to documentary credits but, rather, applies as a general principle of law, that the courts of law will not be used to perpetuate an illegal purpose or transaction.[70] In principle, therefore, the fraud exception applies to BPOs, as does the illegality exception and other private law[71] or public law principles which might affect the application of the autonomy principle, such as sanctions, anti-corruption measures, price escalation clauses, or Islamic law compliance issues.[72] The courts are likely to reason by analogy to documentary credits, applying specific legislation where it exists, for example in China,[73] or case law where it is relevant.

13.22 The digital element of the BPO is a double-edged sword as far as the fraud exception is concerned. While the electronic transmission of information to the banks isolates the banks further from the underlying transaction, making it even harder for the them even to suspect fraud in the underlying transaction or the documents,[74] certain types of fraud, for example

[65] See, eg Nelson Enonchong, *The Independence Principle of Letters of Credit and Bank Guarantees* (OUP 2011) (Enonchong, *Independence Principle*); Xiang Gao, *The Fraud Rule in the Law of Letters of Credit: A Comparative Study* (Kluwer Law International 2002); Mugasha, *Law of Letters of Credit and Bank Guarantees* (n 2); Ellinger and Neo, *Law and Practice of Documentary Letters of Credit* (n 2).

[66] Classic cases on the fraud exception include *Stejn v J Henry Schroder Banking Corp*, 31 NYS 2d 631 (NYSC, 1941); *United City Merchants (Investments) Ltd v Royal Bank of Canada* [1983] 1 AC 168 (HL) (hereafter *United City Merchants v Royal Bank of Canada*); *Bank of Nova Scotia v Angelica-Whitewear* (1987) 36 DLR (4th) 161 (SCC). A similar issue would be whether illegality in the underlying transaction would excuse the obligor bank from paying, similar to letters of credit where a bank is enjoined from paying a letter of credit that is underpinned by an illegal transaction (see eg, *Society of Lloyd's v Canadian Imperial Bank of Commerce* [1993] 2 Lloyd's Rep 579 (QB); and *Mahonia v JP Morgan Chase Bank* [2003] EWHC 1927 and [2004] EWHC 1938 (Comm)). The same could be asked of the possible exceptions to the autonomy principle, such as unconscionability and an express or implied agreement not to draw on the credit: *Olex Focas Pty Ltd v Skodaexport Co Ltd* [1998] 3 VR 380 (SC); *Dornell Properties v Renansa* 2011(1) SA 70 (SCA); and *ALYK (HK) Limited v Caprock Commodities Trading Pty Limited* [2012] NSWSC 1558.

[67] Dolan, *Law of Letters of Credit* (n 2).

[68] See eg, Ross Cranston et al, Principles of Banking Law (3rd edn, OUP 2017) 535; Mugasha, *Law of Letters of Credit and Bank Guarantees* (n 2) 138–40.

[69] See eg, *Group Jose Re v Walbrook Insurance Co Ltd* [1996] 1 WLR 1152 (CA) (per Staughton LJ); *Mahonia Ltd v JP Morgan Chase Bank* [2003] EWHC 1927 (Comm) (hereafter *Mahonia Ltd v JP Morgan Chase Bank*).

[70] *Mahonia Ltd v JP Morgan Chase Bank* (n 69) [68] (per Colman J).

[71] See eg, *SAFA Ltd v Banque Du Caire* [2000] 2 All ER (Comm) 567 (CA) for a credit procured by misrepresentation can be rescinded *ab initio*; and *Solo Industries UK Ltd v Canara Bank* [2001] 2 All ER (Comm) 217 (CA) for authority that a bank can refuse payment if the beneficiary was complicit in a fraudulent misrepresentation by the applicant.

[72] For an excellent monograph dedicated to the exceptions to the independence principle, see Enonchong, *Independence Principle* (n 65).

[73] See Supreme People's Court of the People's Republic of China, 'The Provisions on Several Issues Concerning the Trial of Disputes over Letters of Credit' Interpretation of the Supreme People's Court [2005] No. 13.

[74] Still, the fraud exception can be invoked by any interested party (eg guarantor or applicant's financier) and is not necessarily limited to the bank or the applicant: see, for example, *Contronic Distributions Pty Ltd v Bank of New South Wales* [1984] 3 NSWLR 110 (SC); *O'Sullivan v National Australia Bank* [1998] NSWSC 303.

a collusion between the buyer and seller, are easier to perpetrate when the electronic transmission is limited to trade data. Notwithstanding these practical nuances, the application of many of the exceptions to the autonomy principle is a matter of public policy and would, therefore, apply to the BPO.

G. Data Supremacy in a Digital Bank-to-Bank Instrument

Since the BPO is a digital instrument, the undertaking of the obligor bank to the recipient bank is conditional on the matching of data sets required by an established baseline on the TMA.[75] While there would usually be an underlying trade transaction that generated the documents between seller and buyer, the BPO itself as a bank obligation towards another bank and the information flow among the banks and the TMA are exclusively digital. Thus, article 7 of the URBPO provides that: **13.23**

> Article 7 Data v. Documents, Goods, Services or Performance
>
> An Involved Bank deals with data and not with documents, or the goods, services or performance to which the data or documents may relate.[76]

The digital nature of the BPO is the cornerstone to its efficiency and cost-effectiveness. It, however, raises several concerns that have thwarted the widespread acceptance of the BPO.[77] First, the isolation of banks from the underlying transaction limits their compliance with their internal procedures on checking the genuineness of the transaction and complying with the law on know-your-customer requirements.[78] While the banks involved in documentary credits rely on the documents relating to the underlying transaction to check the genuineness of that transaction, the relevant documents are not routed through the banks in the BPO arrangement, thus depriving the banks of this avenue for playing their oversight function and complying with the law. Secondly, and related to this, the trade documents in a documentary credit transaction, such as the bill of lading, constitute the collateral for bank financing and a potential source of reimbursement or loss mitigation for the bank. Their absence in the BPO transaction deprives the banks of this type of security and risk-mitigation technique.[79] Thirdly, the digital nature of the BPO technically increases the potential for the perpetration of some types of fraud; for example, where the parties to the underlying transaction collude to present false data to their respective banks. This contrasts with documentary credits which typically require a set of different types of documents generated by different unrelated parties, thus embedding some basic protections against fraud by the parties to the underlying transaction.[80] Together with some legal and deliberate choices made by the banks, these reasons have constrained the wide acceptance of the BPO by the banks. **13.24**

[75] URBPO (n 5) art 3.

[76] This is similar to UCP 600, art 5, which provides for documentary supremacy that banks deal with documents and not with goods, services, or performance to which the documents may relate.

[77] See Wang, 'BPO: Still a Long Way to Go' (n 62).

[78] ibid 21.

[79] ibid 21.

[80] See eg, *United City Merchants v Royal Bank of Canada* (n 66).

H. The Boilerplate Provisions

13.25 The URBPO contain the standard disclaimer clauses that the involved bank will not be liable or responsible for the effectiveness of the data received from the seller or buyer or any documents or acts by a third party (article 12); for force majeure acts—those beyond its control (article 13); and the unavailability of the transaction matching application (article 14). By way of limiting the application of the force majeure event, the obligor bank is required to pay on the resumption of business and the recipient bank is entitled to payment if the BPO expired during the force majeure event and all the data sets required by the established baseline had been submitted before the force majeure event.[81]

I. Assignment of Proceeds (Article 16)

13.26 The recipient bank is permitted to assign the proceeds of the BPO, in similar fashion to the assignment of proceeds under the article 39 of the UCP. There is, however, a logical difference with the provisions of the UCP where the beneficiary is typically the seller of goods or services. Thus, the URBPO require the recipient bank to obtain consent of the obligor bank for an effective assignment of proceeds.[82] Reasoning by analogy to the requirement for consent for the transfer of a documentary credit, it would seem that express consent to transfer a BPO must be obtained.[83] Similarly, it would also be expected that such consent would be readily forthcoming in most cases when it is requested because consent should not be withheld unless there is a good reason.[84]

J. Applicable Law

13.27 Article 15a of the URBPO provides that the governing law of a BPO will be that of the location of the branch or office of the obligor bank. According to article 15b, the preceding provisions in the URBPO supplement the applicable law to the extent not prohibited by that law. These unsurprising provisions provide clarity from the outset while concealing the trap created by the fact that many countries do not have mature laws or a wide experience on BPOs or electronic transactions. It would be expected that recourse would be had to the law of documentary credits, but still, this is underdeveloped in certain crucial respects, such as the application of the fraud exception; so, this means that the law applicable to the BPO may be uncertain.[85] Ultimately, the URBPO might apply to any gaps in the law since it is the most developed legal instrument on BPOs and because it would not be prohibited by law.

[81] URBPO (n 5) art 13(b).
[82] ibid art 16(b).
[83] See *Bank Negara Indonesia 1946 v Lariza (Singapore) Pte Ltd* [1988] AC 583 (PC).
[84] See Mugasha, *Law of Letters of Credit and Bank Guarantees* (n 2) 225–26.
[85] Wang, 'BPO: Still a Long Way to Go' (n 62) 22.

IV. Evaluation

The BPO is a digital financial product that was designed by the banks for the banks to intermediate in the open account space. It adds a welcome flexibility to cross-border trade finance by extending the financing options potentially available for each of the segments of that transaction and permitting the banks to enter at any of those stages in the supply chain; for example, when the purchase order is created, or when the goods have been produced, shipped, or delivered. Thus, a BPO can be issued for a trade transaction already underway and does not have to be issued at the outset. Its superiority over documentary credits lies in its speed in executing payment and the objectivity and automaticity in determining whether payment should be made. **13.28**

The BPO has succeeded as a new financial instrument that has captured a sizeable, even though not overwhelming, proportion of the market.[86] In this, it fared better than some of its earlier e-commerce predecessors that had more localised or shorter application.[87] This is partly because of the adoption of global standards in the form of the URBPO, which are technically astute and, ideally, should facilitate the adoption of the new financial instrument globally. The structure and content of the URBPO are familiar, since they are based on the template of the UCP and other documents authored by the ICC, even though the URBPO are significantly shorter because of the limited topics covered. As seen previously, the URBPO neither cover the relations between the banks and their customers, which means that the customers cannot initiate a BPO transaction, nor the relationships between the TMA with its bank clients. It was envisaged from the outset of the drafting of the URBPO that there would be a second phase of developing the Rules whereby the relations between the underlying parties, that is, the buyer and seller and their respective banks, would be added to the URBPO framework and it was also subsequently hoped that such a development might kickstart the widespread use of the BPO.[88] Since the BPO is a relatively new financial instrument on which there is very little judicial or other commentary, the legal relationships that it establishes have not been tested and one can only reason by analogy to documentary credits, electronic communication, and general principles of modern commercial law. **13.29**

To date, the BPO has found a challenge in establishing its strong short- or medium-term value to displace the existing payment methods across the network of recipient banks, obligor banks, sellers, and buyers.[89] The lack of widespread commercial application of the BPO illustrates, therefore, that astute rules, by themselves, do not create sufficient real value **13.30**

[86] It has succeeded in countries such as Japan, Germany, and Turkey (see Hennah, 'BPO: Digital Instrument' (n 1)) and it had earlier been predicted in 2014 that it would capture 10% of the trade-finance market by 2020: see Staff Editors, 'Trade Finance: State of Play and Recent Trends' (n 1) 60.

[87] A good example is electronic data interchange (EDI) that held so much promise about thirty years ago but was ultimately underwhelming because of business perceptions, the costs of initial set up, a shortage of personnel with relevant technical skills, and the emergence of new technology.

[88] Meynell and Collyer, 'BPO: a Reintroduction' (n 1).

[89] One year after the adoption of the URBPO, fifty-eight banks had adopted the BPO and there were more than thirty corporates on the BPO/TSU, but transaction volumes were still very small: see David Gustin 'SWIFT's Bank Payment Obligation continues to struggle' (*Spend Matters*, 4 August 2014) <http://spendmatters.com/tfmatters/swifts-bank-payment-obligation-continues-to-struggle/> accessed 22 June 2020. There were forty early adopters and only three aggressive promoters (JP Morgan, RBS, and Standard Chartered) and this has not changed substantially: see Wang, 'BPO: Still a Long Way to Go' (n 62).

in the eyes of the business entities targeted by the new financial instrument.[90] Several factors explain this lack of widespread acceptance. First was the negative publicity for the BPO on its launch, since there was a general, but mistaken, perception that the BPO was created to replace the popular documentary credit.[91] Documentary credits, despite being document intensive, and, therefore, slow, expensive, and prone to error, have held their own not only because of the inertia by the banks but also because they provide the effective security that is not available in other financial instruments. Thus, they tend to be the instrument of choice in trade covering long distances, newly formed trade relationships and in countries with weaker contractual enforcement, less financial development, and higher political risk.[92] They are also popular in some countries because of historical preferences and regulatory regimes that require the use of letters of credit.[93] Furthermore, the letter of credit rules, including the UCP and its supplement for the electronic presentation of documents ('eUCP 1.1'), are better known among banking and commercial practitioners. In contrast, the BPO is just as expensive as a documentary credit in terms of bank capital because the bank substitutes its credit for the customer's credit and the bank assumes an obligation on behalf of its client and, yet, there are no documents that serve as collateral in the hands of the bank. Open account transactions have also largely retained their share of business, thus fending off the competition from the BPO, because, first, whereas the BPO increases the finance options for corporations, some of them had found alternative financing solutions before the advent of the BPO, for instance using supplier networks.[94] Secondly, the BPO was marketed exclusively to highly creditworthy customers, meaning that it was deprived of a critical mass since it was not generally available for use by all bank customers.[95]

13.31 The novel feature about the BPO is that it is an electronic payment and security mechanism to facilitate trade finance. Its boon is also its bane. In the twenty-first century, technological innovation in commercial transactions is rampant where banks and financial technology companies are competing and at the same time cooperating in investing in multifarious transactional applications and payment methods.[96] There is, thus, stiff competition for investment capital and acceptability among the BPO and other different technological innovations. Its advantages overlap with those offered by the distributed ledger technology, commonly known as blockchain, which was introduced in 2014, one year after the launch of the BPO. The first trade-finance transaction with blockchain was completed in 2016.[97] Blockchain, like the BPO and other digital innovations, has technology-based operational

[90] See David Gustin, 'Will SWIFT's Bank Payment Obligation ever become a real option for corporates?' (*Spend Matters*, 9 June 2014) <http://spendmatters.com/tfmatters/47766/> accessed 22 June 2020 (hereafter Gustin, 'SWIFT's Bank Payment Obligation').

[91] Earlier writings alluded to the anticipated competition between the two instruments: see eg, Wynne and Fearn, 'The Bank Payment Obligation' (n 34).

[92] Committee on the Global Financial System, 'Trade finance: developments and issues' (n 21) 9.

[93] ibid 10.

[94] See Jason Busch, Pierre Mitchell, and David Gustin, 'E-Invoicing 2014 Forecast: Customer Recommendations and Vendor Shortlists' (*Spend Matters*, 12 February 2014) <http://spendmatters.com/2014/02/12/e-invoicing-2014-forecast-customer-recommendations-vendor-shortlists/> accessed 22 June 2020.

[95] Wang, 'BPO: Still a Long Way to Go' (n 62) 22.

[96] The prominent methods in the early twenty-first century include blockchain and smart contracts.

[97] See Barclays, 'Blockchain Revolution in Trade Finance' (*Barclays Corporate*, 30 September 2016) <https://www.barclayscorporate.com/insights/innovation/blockchain-revolution-in-trade-finance/> accessed 22 June 2020; Martin Arnold, 'European Banks to Launch Blockchain Trade Finance Platform' (*Financial Times*, 26 June 2017) <https://www.ft.com/content/6bb4f678-5a8c-11e7-b553-e2df1b0c3220> accessed 22 June 2020.

requirements,[98] many advantages,[99] and a wavering support in the commercial marketplace.[100] At their core, blockchain and similar techniques intend to combine efficiency, cost-effectiveness, and security of their transactions, which are the same values at the core of BPOs. Some innovations will thrive, others may develop into some inter-operable systems or see their advantages parsed out throughout the financial industry to improve different systems, while some will wither.

Currently, the BPO operates best in the niche market where the traders have prioritised the electronic presentation of data.[101] It will also be useful for traders involved in emerging markets and using the open account method when they could usefully benefit from having payment protection that they do not currently have.[102] That niche market is small and more effort is required from the banks and corporate customers to give it clout in the market. Alternatively, the instrument may develop into something else with equivalent or enhanced values.[103] **13.32**

V. Conclusion

As we have seen, the BPO is a digital conditional payment instrument that relies on structured electronic messages that are sent to a TMA that automatically determines whether the terms of payment have been met. It combines the security and legal features of a letter of credit with the efficiency of open account trading whereby payment is triggered by the electronic matching of data.[104] Thus, its purpose is not new since it seeks to mitigate the usual trade risks; namely, uncertainty of payment (liquidity risk) and uncertainty of performance (market risk) by the trading counterparties. It competes for the commercial market with other payment and security methods such as documentary credits, open account, standby letters of credit,[105] and credit insurance[106] while borrowing some legal and practical features from them. **13.33**

The BPO is a signal innovation in trade finance because it has successfully established itself as an independent instrument. Furthermore, it is a frontrunner in the era of digitalisation as it encapsulates some key commercial advantages for any digital instrument; namely, efficiency and security. It truly illustrates that technological innovation is the future of trade **13.34**

[98] See ch 12 (Winn) in this volume.

[99] The advantages include the reduction in operational costs, traceability, and provenance, transparency, digital uniqueness, and the elimination of fraud: see Barclays, 'Blockchain: what is it and how will it impact your business?' (*Barclays Corporate*, 11 November 2019) 4 <https://www.barclayscorporate.com/content/dam/barclayscorporate-com/documents/insights/innovation/blockchain.pdf> accessed 22 June 2020.

[100] See Izabella Kaminska, 'Growing Scepticism Challenges the Blockchain Hype' (*Financial Times*, 20 June 2017) <https://www.ft.com/content/b5b1a5f2-5030-11e7-bfb8-997009366969> accessed 22 June 2020; Andrew Hill, 'Blockchain Man and Woman Will Have to Wait: Companies Are Not Ready For Them' (*Financial Times*, 30 October 2017) <https://www.ft.com/content/52fbdb80-b999-11e7-9bfb-4a9c83ffa852> accessed 22 June 2020.

[101] Top commodity traders (eg Glencore and BHP) have made electronic trading a priority, but not mid-level manufacturers or technology companies: see Gustin, 'SWIFT's Bank Payment Obligation' (n 90).

[102] The alternatives could be credit insurance and standby credits.

[103] Hennah, 'BPO: Digital Instrument' (n 1) 26.

[104] Global Supply Chain Finance Forum, 'Bank Payment Obligation' (n 12).

[105] See eg, Dolan, *Fundamentals of Commercial Activity* (n 19) 28.

[106] In a credit insurance facility, the credit insurer underwrites the risk of non-payment in consideration of a premium.

finance, but its capital regulatory treatment also teaches that the regulators should give capital relief to payment instruments for them to thrive. Like other innovations, it builds on familiar business techniques and legal concepts to serve certain identified business needs. Most notably, it releases the banks from the cumbersome documentary processes while maintaining bank support.[107] It, therefore, adds something new to the existing array of payment and financing methods by serving a distinct market of corporate buyers in the supply chain who prioritise the use of electronic payment assurance and those suppliers in emerging and other markets who wish to access the liquidity and efficiency options it offers.

13.35 The lack of a widespread adoption of the BPO leads to a direct comparison with documentary credits which, of course, have been very successful globally. While the epochs in which the two methods were created vary immensely and direct comparisons do have limitations, there are several reasons for the slow adoption of the BPO regardless of its own technical merits. First, it could plausibly be argued that the BPO did not have a substantial underlay of commercial demand as the documentary credit had. It was, instead, created as a financial product in search of a market. As has been noted, the trading community does not understand the range and benefits of supply chain finance because supply chain finance itself and its terminology are still developing.[108] It has been noted, in particular, that the BPO sits in the bank-to-bank space and that many corporate clients are not aware of its full potential. In this light, a technological innovation and well-crafted rules will not cure the matter of commercial demand. As has been perceptively noted, technology is not a driver, it's only an enabler.[109] Secondly, the uptake depends on the commercial and technological competition. As seen above, the competing financial techniques of documentary credits and open account transactions have largely held on to their respective shares of the market. That inertia is partly due to the comfort of the familiar and profitable documentary credit, and a reticence to invest in new technology for an untested market. In sum, the low rate of adopting the BPO by corporates encapsulates the technological, legal, risk, and compliance barriers and a lack of critical mass.[110]

13.36 As seen above, the novelty with the bank payment obligation lies in the technological sphere—that it is a wholly digital bank-to-bank instrument centred around a TMA—and not in the legal or regulatory domain. The legal principles involved, while not identical to those found in letters of credit, will be familiar to those educated on documentary credits. The judges, lawyers, and scholars of trade-finance law are well-placed to play a key role in the development of the new financial instrument.

[107] Wang, 'BPO: Still a Long Way to Go' (n 62).
[108] 'ICC Banking Commission launches new definitions' (n 28) 2.
[109] See ch 12 (Winn) in this volume.
[110] Gustin, 'SWIFT's Bank Payment Obligation' (n 90).

14

Something Old, Something New

Open Account, Prepayment, and Supply Chain Finance

*Christopher Hare**

I. Introduction

14.01 The traditional documentary letter of credit has had huge success in facilitating international sale and supply transactions. There are a number of reasons behind this success: the development by an international body of a uniform set of contractual default principles (in the form of the UCP 600) reflecting and harmonising market practice; the adoption of fundamental principles (namely strict compliance and autonomy) that limit the defences to payment under the letter of credit, thereby inspiring parties' confidence in the unimpeachability of banks' payment obligations; and the utilisation of a network of banks to ensure that a beneficiary's entitlements are governed as far as possible by its own domestic legal principles. That said, the iron grip that the letter of credit has had over trade finance is arguably loosening, in just the same way as the bill of exchange became less popular in a previous era. Indeed, it is the letter of credit's demise that has created the space for alternative trade-finance mechanisms. Accordingly, section II will examine the reasons that lie behind this shift away from bank-dependent documentary finance. The consequence, however, is that trade parties have turned to simpler, quicker, and cheaper solutions to finance their sale transactions. Most significant has been the meteoric rise of the simplest possible payment terms, namely that the sale be on 'open account' terms (when shipment occurs before payment) or on 'prepayment' or 'cash-in-advance' terms (in the converse situation). Such payment terms alone are relatively high-risk, however, since they require parties to trust one another and can leave a party with real cash-flow difficulties if its counterparty's performance is not immediately due. To this end, banks and other finance-providers have attempted to provide liquidity through various forms of Supply Chain Finance ('SCF') to address those trust and liquidity issues. Whilst there have always existed finance techniques designed to address these concerns, their increasing popularity and use has brought them out of the shadows and placed them firmly centre-stage. Accordingly, section III will examine traditional techniques designed to provide liquidity to trade parties within the context of documentary letters of credit, before considering the more modern SCF techniques associated with open-account and pre-payment trade terms. Section IV concludes.

* My thanks to Professor Dora Neo for her comments on an earlier draft; these have much improved the final version.

II. The Letter of Credit's Demise

14.02 The demise of the letter of credit is intimately linked with the growth in popularity of 'open-account' and prepayment terms, which has in turn been driven by a renewed interest in SCF. Whilst it is unclear whether the increased use of 'open-account' and prepayment terms is a cause or consequence of letters of credit becoming less popular (or, more likely, both), the data is clear: trade parties' use of letters of credit has reduced steadily over time and 'the slump continues', with the volume of letters of credit being issued through SWIFT falling by a further 3.9% in 2019 alone.[1] That said, the drop in documentary trade finance is not uniform. A more fine-grained analysis of the data highlights a number of variations:[2] in terms of the type of instrument, letters of credit available by negotiation continue to represent the lion's share of documentary trade instruments;[3] import letters of credit were used far more extensively in the Asia-Pacific region (in particular China, India, South Korea, and Bangladesh), followed by the Eurozone and the Middle East some way behind (with the United Kingdom and Germany seeing particularly sharp declines in use);[4] and the use of export letters of credit has largely followed the same pattern with the Asia-Pacific region leading the pack, followed by the Eurozone and non-eurozone Europe lagging behind (with Italy and Switzerland experiencing notable drops in letter of credit use).[5] These regional variations in letter of credit use may be explained in part by whether the particular jurisdiction is economically developed or developing, by a variety of geographical factors (such as the distance to major commercial centres or trading partners),[6] and by the presence (or otherwise) of international banks within the particular jurisdiction.[7] That said, whilst the outlook for the letter of credit is generally grim, a silver lining of the global coronavirus pandemic has been that documentary trade finance has proved popular with trade parties seeking a proxy for counterparty trust. Indeed, in the context of the current pandemic, the International Chamber of Commerce ('ICC') has indicated that '[t]he risk mitigating properties of documentary trade may grow in popularity (reversing the ongoing shift to open account trade), although this may be less pronounced than in previous crises as more attention has been placed on how to apply risk mitigation to SCF'.[8] Accordingly, like the Global Finance Crisis before it, the coronavirus outbreak has 'reversed the trend in recent years in which revenues have shifted from documentary to open account trade'.[9] The ICC's current prediction is, however, that this is a '*temporary* shift away from open account trade and back to documentary trade'.[10] The reason for this view is that '[t]he Covid-19 environment

[1] International Chamber of Commerce Banking Commission ('ICC Banking Commission'), '2020 ICC Global Survey on Trade Finance' (July 2020) 40 (hereafter ICC Banking Commission, '2020 Global Survey').

[2] Bank for International Settlements ('BIS'), 'Trade Finance: Developments and Issues', Report Submitted by a Study Group Established by the Committee on the Global Financial System (January 2014) 9, 16 (hereafter BIS, 'Trade Finance').

[3] ICC Banking Commission, '2020 Global Survey' (n 1) 46.

[4] ibid 41–2.

[5] ibid 42–4.

[6] Friederike Niepmann and Tim Schmidt-Eisenlohr, 'Banks in International Trade Finance: Evidence from the US', Federal Reserve Bank of New York Staff Reports (No 633, 2013) (hereafter Niepmann and Schmidt-Eisenlohr, 'Banks in International Trade Finance').

[7] BIS, 'Trade Finance' (n 2) 11–12.

[8] ICC Banking Commission, 'ICC Trade Register Report: Global Risks in Trade Finance' (May 2020) 8 (hereafter ICC Banking Commission, 'Trade Register Report 2020').

[9] ibid 16.

[10] ibid 21 (emphasis added). For the general collapse in trade in 2020 during the global pandemic, see OECD, *Covid-19 and International Trade: Issues and Actions* (12 June 2020) <http://www.oecd.org/coronavirus/

may have finally convinced everyone that paper-based trade is outdated and unsustainable accelerating the move to digitisation'.[11] As a result, whilst it may be too early to speak of a 'new normal' heralding a resurgence of documentary letters of credit, the longer the global pandemic and the Sino-US trade tensions continue,[12] the more uncertainty in the supply chains will drive traders to precisely such 'safe haven' trade-finance instruments. Like so much with the coronavirus pandemic, its impact on trade finance remains a guessing game.

Assuming that, once the global coronavirus pandemic is over, the letter of credit continues its steady decline, it is important to determine the causes behind this phenomenon. Some of the causes are not difficult to identify and have already been considered in earlier chapters. **14.03**

A. Technology

In a world that has become so conscious about transaction speed, there appears to be little future for documentary trade finance.[13] Indeed, in an era of social distancing and sanitisation, it seems almost incomprehensible why the participants in an international sale would want to pass bundles of documents from hand to hand and jurisdiction to jurisdiction. Whilst the ICC introduced the eUCP to facilitate the letter of credit's transition from a paper-based world to the digital era,[14] this has not proved a great success: trade parties have been reluctant to digitise the documents that would be required for an electronic presentation under a letter of credit, as a result of concerns about increased fraud and how bills of exchange and lading could be effectively transmuted into electronic form.[15] There also remains a heathy degree of scepticism about how transformative technology might be, in particular whether distributed ledger technology can live up to its hype.[16] That said, there are increasingly the technological[17] and legal[18] frameworks in place to make digital trade finance a reality. Whether the letter of credit is able to survive depends upon its adaptability to this new electronic environment. **14.04**

B. Regulation

In recent years, banks have faced something of a regulatory onslaught. This only accelerated in the period following the Global Financial Crisis. Trade finance has been no exception. **14.05**

policy-responses/covid-19-and-international-trade-issues-and-actions-494da2fa/> 22 February 2021. See also ICC, *Trade Financing and Covid-19* (May 2020).

[11] ibid 23.

[12] ibid 16.

[13] Whilst technological advances are likely to have a significant impact on trade finance, there are also risks associated with such a development, namely computer system failures, vulnerability to cyber-attacks and the possibility that machine-learning programmes might become so sophisticated that they replicate human error: see ICC Banking Commission, 'Trade Register Report 2020' (n 8) 24.

[14] For the current version, see ICC, 'eUCP Version 2.0' (2019).

[15] Peter Ellinger, 'The Uniform Customs and Practice for Documentary Credits (UCP): Their Development and the Current Revisions' [2007] LMCLQ 152, 158.

[16] See ch 12 (Winn) in this volume.

[17] See ch 10 (Goldby) in this volume.

[18] See chs 9 (Geva) and 11 (Davidson) in this volume.

Accordingly, banks issuing and confirming letters of credit face an increasingly heavy regulatory burden that has driven up their compliance costs and has made letters of credit increasingly inaccessible to trade parties lacking an established trading relationship with a particular bank. There are three particular areas in which the regulatory burden has fallen particularly heavily.

14.06 The first area of regulatory activity concerns the prudential supervision of banks, in particular how the Basel capital adequacy and liquidity regimes should apply to banks' trade-finance operations. Indeed, as the regulatory requirements of the Basel regimes have increasingly intensified over time, so has uncertainty grown about their application to letters of credit in particular. Initially, under the Basel I regime, bank assets were risk-weighted according to the borrower's default risk, which in turn determined how much capital a bank had to set aside (no less than an 8% minimum capital ratio of riskier assets' notional value), so that banks could cover any potential losses in straitened times.[19] The Basel I regime, however, recognised the low-risk character of trade-finance liabilities,[20] by providing a more favourable regulatory environment for 'short-term self-liquidating trade-related contingencies (such as documentary credits collateralised by the underlying shipments)'. Pursuant to this more liberal regime, banks only needed to carry 20% of the capital that they would otherwise have had to carry if the same amount had simply been advanced as a loan.[21] Accordingly, as letters of credit were considered to involve a low-risk exposure, the 'capital cost' for a bank's trade financing activities was relatively low compared to other forms of lending. Under the Basel II regime, the basic position remained the same, although there was an increased recognition of the cyclical nature of business activity with the result that a bank's particular credit risk had to be determined by reference to a wider set of economic risk categories. Of particular concern to the trade finance area was the fact that banks had to use 'country risk' (rather than 'counterparty risk') in calculating their capital ratios, at least when the former was higher than the latter. This was the so-called 'sovereign floor' principle. As a result of this principle, trade finance (including traditional letters of credit) became comparatively expensive for banks (when compared to other forms of lending) in terms of 'capital cost' when the letter of credit was issued by a bank on behalf of an applicant in a 'high-risk' country, such as one in recession or one that had recently defaulted on sovereign debt.[22] The other difficulty, besides the operation of the 'sovereign floor principle', was that Basel II also operated a one-year 'maturity floor' for all lending commitments,[23] which meant that trade-finance instruments, despite generally having a shorter maturity than one year, nevertheless attracted a 'capital cost' appropriate to longer-term commitments.[24] This

[19] Basel Committee on Banking Supervision ('BCBS'), 'International Convergence of Capital Measurement and Capital Standards' (Basel, July 1988) [28]–[44] (hereafter BCBS, 'Basel I').

[20] For consideration of the low default risk in trade instruments, see generally ICC Banking Commission, 'ICC Trade Register Report: Global Risks in Trade Finance' (2017).

[21] BCBS, Basel I (n 19) [42(c)].

[22] Marc Auboin, 'Trade Finance under the Current Basel Regulatory Framework: What Are the Issues?', in Jean-Pierre Chauffour and Mariem Malouche (eds), 'Trade Finance During the Great Trade Collapse' (World Bank 2011) 385, 386–87 (hereafter Auboin, 'Trade Finance'). See also International Chamber of Commerce ('ICC'), 'Recommendations on the Impact of Basel II on Trade Finance' (Banking Commission Document 470/1119, 2009): 'The capital intensity of lending to mid-market companies under Basel II is four to five times higher than for equivalent transactions under Basel I.'

[23] BCBS, 'International Convergence of Capital Measurement and Capital Standards: A Revised Framework' (Basel June 2004) [320] (hereafter BCBS, 'Basel II').

[24] Auboin, 'Trade Finance' (n 22) 385, 387–88.

latter concern was mitigated to some extent by national regulators being given the discretion to disapply the one-year 'maturity floor' for 'short-term exposures with an original maturity of less than one year that are not part of a bank's ongoing financing of an obligor',[25] but there was no guarantee that such a discretion would be exercised.

Both the 'sovereign floor principle' and the one-year 'maturity floor' were subsequently addressed by the Basel Committee for Banking Supervision in October 2011, when it agreed to waive the former principle for trade-finance activity with low-income countries and to disapply the latter *as a rule* for short-term trade-finance instruments, rather than leaving this to the discretion of national regulators.[26] This position has now been crystallised under Basel III. The Basel Committee on Banking Supervision has confirmed that the original one-fifth risk-weighting from Basel I (without either of the earlier qualifications)[27] 'will be applied to both the issuing and confirming banks of short-term self-liquidating trade letters of credit arising from the movement of goods (e.g. documentary credits collateralised by the underlying shipment)'.[28] This has now been implemented into the new Basel Framework when determining the 'capital cost' for banks of risk-weighted assets.[29] The concern over the application of the Basel III regime to trade finance has, however, lain in a different direction, namely the requirement that regulators supplement risk-based capital requirements with a leverage ratio. For the purposes of this ratio, banks must apply a considerably higher risk-weighting to off-balance-sheet liabilities. The leverage ratio's underlying rationale is clear: banks are discouraged from accumulating off-balance-sheet items (such as derivative exposures) that might ultimately become toxic and damage the wider financial system. Despite this good sense, however, a possible 'unintended consequence' of the leverage ratio was to make the issuance and confirmation of letters of credit far more 'costly' for banks in capital terms.[30] As letters of credit are only moved onto a bank's balance sheet following the verification of the presented documents,[31] they are effectively off-balance sheet items before that time. Accordingly, concerns were expressed that the 'capital cost' of letters of credit might increase by as much as 40%,[32] and that, as margins for such instruments are generally low, banks would tend to divest themselves of trade-finance business in favour of more profitable activity.[33] This position was finally regularised on 12 January 2014, however, when the Basel Banking Committee indicated that it would reverse its previous position, so that the 14.07

[25] BCBS, 'Basel II' (n 23) [321]–[322].

[26] BCBS, 'Treatment of Trade Finance under the Basel Capital Framework' (October 2011) 3–4.

[27] BCBS, 'Basel III: Finalising Post-crisis Reforms' (December 2017) [111] (hereafter BCBS, 'Post-crisis Reforms').

[28] ibid [83]. A higher risk-weighting applies to default undertakings such as performance bonds and standby letters of credit: ibid [81].

[29] BCBS, 'Basel Framework' (15 December 2019) CRE 32.46: 'The one-year floor does not apply to the following exposures: (1) Short-term self-liquidating trade transactions. Import and export letters of credit and similar transactions should be accounted for at their actual remaining maturity; (2) Issued as well as confirmed letters of credit that are short term (ie having a maturity below one year) and self-liquidating' (hereafter BCBS, 'Basel III').

[30] Marc Auboin and Isabella Blengini, 'The Impact of Basel II on Trade Finance: The Potential Unintended Consequences of the Leverage Ratio' (CESIFO Working Paper No 4953) 2, 5 (hereafter Auboin and Blengini, 'The Impact of Basel II').

[31] Auboin, 'Trade Finance' (n 22) 385, 389.

[32] Gilles Thieffry, 'The Impact of Basel III on Commodity Trade Finance: Legal and Regulatory Aspects' (2011) 9 JIBLR 455, 457.

[33] Duygu Tavan, 'Basel III Reshapes Trade Finance' (*The Banker*, 1 March 2013) <https://www.thebanker.com/Transactions-Technology/Trading/Basel-III-reshapes-trade-finance?ct=true> 22 February 2021 (hereafter Tavan, 'Basel III').

obligations of issuing and confirming banks would from 2018 be given a lower weighting under Basel III for the purposes of the leverage ratio.[34] This has now been implemented into the new Basel Framework when determining the leverage ratio,[35] so that letters of credit are once again relatively 'cheap' for banks in capital terms. Unfortunately, this beneficial change has arguably come too late, as the uncertainty over the years has caused traditional banks to restrict their letter-of-credit activity or to exit the sector altogether.[36] The regulatory impact on the shape of the trade finance sector will be considered further below.

14.08 The second regulatory area concerns the application of domestic anti-money laundering and anti-terrorist financing legislation,[37] both of which are generally derived from the recommendations of the Financial Action Task Force ('FATF'),[38] to the trade-finance area, in particular letters of credit. From an early stage, FATF perceived trade-based money laundering (or 'TBML') as a particular problem requiring an international response.[39] As well as conducting the usual 'know your customer' checks in relation to their instructing party, banks that issue or confirm letters of credit must be alert to certain 'red flags' indicating the existence of TBML in relation to the underlying sale transaction.[40] These include deviations from a trade party's usual business patterns; related-party transactions; transactions with frequent documentary changes, multiple discrepancies or missing information; the use of complex financial or corporate structures; the future-dating of bills of lading; trade-party reticence to provide information; and even the fact that goods are dual-use or shipped via an unusual route.[41] Whilst technology can certainly assist banks in carrying out these anti-money laundering checks more efficiently,[42] the very fact that such checks need to be carried out at all strikes at the heart of the letter of credit. According to the UCP 600, the foundational principles of letters of credit are that '[a] credit by its nature is a separate transaction from the sale or other contract on which it may be based'[43] and that '[b]anks deal with documents and not with goods, services or performance to which the documents may relate'.[44] TBML requires banks, however, to do precisely the opposite. Not only does this increase the time and costs associated with examining and processing documents under letters of credit, but it also raises the spectre of civil or criminal liability for banks who rely on the letter of credit's traditional autonomy as a justification for not investigating matters too much. Moreover, at common law, banks can only generally refuse payment under a letter of credit when it is 'clearly established at the interlocutory stage that the

[34] Auboin and Blengini, 'The Impact of Basel II' (n 30) 7. See also BCBS, 'Post-crisis Reforms' (n 27) Annex: Leverage Ratio [13].

[35] BCBS, 'Basel III' (n 29) LEV 30.51: 'For short-term self-liquidating trade letters of credit arising from the movement of goods (eg documentary credits collateralised by the underlying shipment), a 20% CCF will be applied to both issuing and confirming banks'.

[36] Tavan, 'Basel III' (n 33).

[37] See, for example, Proceeds of Crime Act 2002 (hereafter 'POCA 2002'), Pt VII; Money Laundering, Terrorist Financing and Transfer of Funds (Information on the Payer) Regulations 2017, SI 2017/692.

[38] Financial Action Task Force ('FATF'), 'International Standards on Combating Money Laundering and the Financing of Terrorism and Proliferation' (October 2003).

[39] See generally FATF, 'Best Practices on Trade Based Money Laundering' (20 June 2008).

[40] Bankers Association for Finance and Trade ('BAFT'), 'Guidance for Identifying Potentially Suspicious Activity in Letters of Credit and Documentary Collections' (March 2015).

[41] Monetary Authority of Singapore, 'Guidance on Anti-Money Laundering and Countering the Financing of Terrorism Controls in Trade Finance and Correspondent Banking' (October 2015).

[42] ICC Banking Commission, 'Trade Register Report 2020' (n 8) 24.

[43] ICC, 'Uniform Customs and Practice for Documentary Credits' (ICC Publication No 600, 2007) (hereafter 'UCP 600') art 4(a).

[44] ibid art 5.

only realistic inference is ... that the bank was aware of the fraud';[45] yet, in England, a bank is required to make an authorised disclosure on the mere ground that it 'suspects' another to be engaged in money laundering.[46] There is no requirement that the bank's suspicion be reasonable, although 'the suspicion so formed should be of a settled nature',[47] in the sense that there should be a sufficiently strong evidentiary basis for the suspicion that it cannot simply be dismissed. In such circumstances, the bank's disclosure to the relevant authorities suspends (and potentially terminates altogether) the issuing or confirming bank's obligation to pay,[48] until the appropriate consent is forthcoming from those authorities.[49] Accordingly, the regulation of TBML risks weakening the twin pillars of strict compliance and autonomy; contradicting the safeguards carefully erected by the courts around the fraud (and other) exception; and undermining the basic irrevocable nature of commercial credits. In such a regulatory environment, it is hardly surprising that the letter of credit has come under such strain.

The third area of regulation impacting upon letters of credit stems from the sanction regimes imposed by the United Nations, the EU Council, or individual countries to achieve various political and economic ends. Not only does the violation of such sanctions invalidate the banks' payment undertakings under a letter of credit, but those banks may also become subject to significant criminal penalties. Just as with TBML, issuing and confirming banks may no longer just deal with the documents alone and ignore all extraneous matters;[50] rather, banks must nowadays inform themselves about the details of the underlying sales transactions (particularly the ultimate destination of the goods and funds to be disbursed under the credit) in order to determine whether honouring the letter of credit would potentially violate a particular sanctions regime.[51] Indeed, the high number and broad range of applicable sanctions regimes now requires banks to carry out extensive and onerous checks before honouring a letter of credit. This is at odds with the essentially ministerial task envisaged by the UCP regime[52] and represents a significant inroad into the autonomy and irrevocability of such instruments.[53] Indeed, in order to facilitate their task, some banks have developed a practice of inserting a 'sanctions clause' into their letters of credit. The ICC has, however, objected to such a practice: to the extent that the 'sanctions clause' simply performs an 'advisory' function by informing counterparties of the relevant bank's intention to comply with applicable sanctions regimes, the ICC has stated the clause to be unobjectionable;[54] but, where (as is increasingly the case) the clause purports to confer a discretion upon the issuing or confirming bank **14.09**

[45] *Alternative Power Solution Ltd v Central Electricity Board* [2015] 1 WLR 697 (PC) [59]. See also *National Infrastructure Development Co Ltd v Banco Santander SA* [2017] 1 CLC 37 (CA) [20]–[24]. Established bank knowledge is similarly a pre-condition of a bank seeking to justify a refusal to pay of its own motion: see *United City Merchants (Investments) Ltd v Royal Bank of Canada* [1983] AC 168 (HL).

[46] POCA 2002 (n 37) ss 328, 338.

[47] *K Ltd v National Westminster Bank plc* [2007] 1 WLR 311 (CA) [14]–[23] (hereafter *K v National Westminster Bank*). See also *Shah v HSBC Private Bank (UK) Ltd* [2009] 1 Lloyd's Rep 328 (QB) [23]; *N v Royal Bank of Scotland plc* [2017] 1 WLR 3938 (CA) [64]; *Lonsdale v National Westminster Bank plc* [2018] EWHC 1843 (QB) [56].

[48] *K v National Westminster Bank* (n 47) [9]–[12].

[49] POCA 2002 (n 37) s 335.

[50] UCP 600, art 5.

[51] Consider BAFT, 'Guiding Principles for Sanctions Issues Related to Shipping and Financial Products' (February 2017).

[52] UCP 600, arts 5, 14(a).

[53] ibid arts 1, 4–5.

[54] ICC, 'Guidance Paper on the Use of Sanctions Clauses in Trade Finance-Related Instruments Subject to ICC Rules' (Document No 470/1238, 2014) [2.1]–[2.2] (hereafter ICC, 'Guidance Paper'). Although there is no standard form for such clauses, an example might be: 'Presentation of document(s) that are not in compliance with

whether or not to honour its commitment in light of relevant sanctions regimes,[55] or allows such banks to refer to their own 'internal sanctions-related policy',[56] the ICC has declared the clause to be fundamentally at odds with the traditional approach to letters of credit. Whilst these clauses undoubtedly differ in formal terms, it may be wondered whether in practice the first type of clause is any more consistent with traditional letter of credit principles given that it may still provide a basis for an issuing or confirming bank refusing to honour a letter of credit following investigation into the surrounding circumstances. In light of such difficulties, banks have unsurprisingly abandoned letters of credit.

C. Competition

14.10 As a consequence of technological advances and the increased regulatory burden in the trade-finance area, letters of credit have been subjected to increased competition. This takes two forms. First, the letter of credit increasingly faces competition from cheaper, quicker, and technologically more advanced payment mechanisms, with the 'Bank Payment Obligation' or 'BPO' being the most obvious recent example.[57] Indeed, the development of 'open-account' trading and SCF has been greatly facilitated by the development of electronic platforms that enable the parties to deal with one another, as well as facilitating a degree of automation. Technology is not, however, the whole story. Other trade-finance mechanisms have similarly displaced the letter of credit where they are better adapted to serving particular sections of the trading community (such as financing that respects Islamic principles)[58] or assisting trading parties *in extremis* (such as countertrade).[59] One observable consequence of these competitors seizing the territory previously occupied by the letter of credit is that the latter instrument has increasingly been re-purposed for other uses. This has led to the development of 'synthetic' or 'structured' letters of credit. According to *Calderon v US Department of Agriculture, Foreign Agricultural Service*,[60] such instruments have certain hallmarks, including the letter of credit indicating that documents would be considered acceptable 'despite any and all discrepancies' or 'acceptable as presented'; that photocopies would be acceptable in place of originals; and that the letter of credit's issue date is later than the date on the bill of lading. Although 'synthetic' letters of credit may take a number of different forms and have a number of different specific aims, they tend to share one key feature: although the transaction resembles a letter of credit, there is in fact no *underlying* sale transaction, since the credit's primary aim is simply to provide a loan or liquid funds to a particular entity,[61] rather than to effect

the applicable anti-boycott, anti-money laundering, anti-terrorism, anti-drug trafficking, and economic sanctions laws and regulations is not acceptable.'

[55] ICC, 'Guidance Paper' (n 54) [2.4], [3.1(c)], [4.1]–[4.2].
[56] ibid [2.5], [3.1(b)], [4.1]–[4.2].
[57] See ch 13 (Mugasha) in this volume.
[58] See ch 15 (Ercanbrack) in this volume.
[59] See ch 16 (Hare) in this volume.
[60] *Calderon v US Department of Agriculture, Foreign Agricultural Service*, 236 F Supp 3d 96 (DCDC, 2017) (hereafter *Calderon v US*). See also *Grains and Industrial Products Trading Pte Ltd v Bank of India* [2016] 3 SLR 1308 (CA) [119].
[61] Through these 'synthetic' structures, 'US banks [were] knowingly extending no-strings-attached loans to foreign banks in order to provide those banks with liquid capital': see *Calderon v US* (n 60). See also *Re Champion*

payment for goods. That is not to say, however, that there is *never* a sale contract in the background: the drawdown of the funds will usually be conditioned upon a documentary presentation, although the required documents may be from a completed sale contract between the parties or merely documents that have been recycled on a number of occasions from earlier sale transactions. The rationale for adopting such a synthetic structure is to take advantage of the letter of credit's (now) more favourable regulatory treatment under Basel III, which was considered above. Despite this apparent evasion of the Basel III regime, there is some judicial support for the validity of synthetic letters of credit. In *Fortis Bank (Nederland) NV v Abu Dhabi Islamic Bank*,[62] Schweitzer J indicated that '[t]he fact that [the transaction] was 'structured' as a trade financing, while perhaps unusual, is not by itself a fraudulent or illegal scheme'. It is less clear whether national bank regulators would agree with such a characterisation given that the documents perform a security function under a traditional letter of credit, which is patently not the case with a synthetic structure. Ultimately, however, traditional letters of credit may become tainted by association with such evasive practices, which may in turn further damage their standing.

Secondly, as well as there being increased competition from other payment mechanisms, banks have equally become subject to increased competition from other finance-providers. The reason why this has impacted upon the documentary letter of credit is because such trade finance instruments are generally viewed as ones that only banks can issue. Indeed, under the UCP 500, the ICC made clear that, whilst it was not possible for the UCP to proscribe non-bank entities entirely from issuing letters of credit, this was certainly not desirable and should be strongly discouraged. According to the ICC Banking Commission:[63] **14.11**

> The UCP reflects that state of practice, namely a situation where the issuer or other actor on a letter of credit is a bank. As a result, although there is no affirmative rule in the UCP prohibiting entities that are not banks from issuing confirming, paying, negotiating or advising letters of credit, its vocabulary ('issuing bank', 'confirming bank', etc) assumes that these entities are banks. This assumption is based on the recognition that there are three principal advantages to bank issuance and handling of letters of credit: namely that banks have the operational expertise to handle issuance and presentation under letters of credit in a professional manner, that they have the tradition of independence from the underlying transaction which is the basis of the commercial reputation of the letter of credit, and that in virtually all countries banks are specially regulated with a view toward protecting those who rely on their undertakings. These matters are of considerable importance to the integrity of the letter of credit as an instrument of commerce and to its dependability as an instrument of payment.

Similarly, according to the UCP 600, a 'credit' is defined as 'any arrangement, however named or described, that is irrevocable and thereby constitutes a definite undertaking of the issuing bank to honour a complying presentation'.[64] As a result of the uncertainty over

Enterprises Inc, Bankr Lexis 2720 (BC Del, 2010); *Re Allied System Holdings Inc*, 556 BR 581 (DC Del, 2016); *Re Ashnic Corporation*, 683 Fed Appx 131 (3d Cir, 2017).

[62] *Fortis Bank (Nederland) NV v Abu Dhabi Islamic Bank*, 936 NYS 2d 58 (NYSC, 2010).
[63] ICC Banking Commission, 'When a Non-bank Issues a Letter of Credit' (30 October 2002) 2.
[64] UCP 600, art 2.

the capital treatment of letters of credit and the application of money-laundering and sanction regimes, banks have become increasingly reluctant or unable to issue letters of credit in order to meet the demands of trade parties, resulting in the so-called 'trade finance gap' of US$1.6 trillion.[65] The position is particularly acute in relation to SMEs, as the regulatory burden on banks is heaviest when dealing with such counterparties.[66] Some traditional banks have simply exited the trade-finance sector altogether, whilst others have suffered capacity-constraints meaning that they are unable to service trade parties' needs. As a consequence, a raft of alternative finance-providers (including insurance companies, pension funds, and 'shadow banks', which are not directly affected by the Basel regime) have effectively stepped into the breach by filling the trade financing void left behind by the traditional banking sector.[67] Fintech companies and other technology-based start-ups in particular have been active in using technological solutions to address the 'trade finance gap'.[68] Given that these alternative finance-providers are not considered by the ICC to be sufficiently creditworthy to issue letters of credit subject to the UCP regime, these entities have instead sought to provide the necessary finance through other cheaper, faster, and more flexible means, in particular SCF. Accordingly, as a result of the 'trade finance gap', it is almost inevitable that there should be a growth in alternative forms of trade finance and, as trade parties become accustomed to those alternatives, it is equally inevitable that the demand for letters of credit would become more constrained. Indeed, having seen the opportunities presented by SCF, banks themselves are now embracing this as an alternative.

D. Efficiency

14.12 The causes of the letter of credit's demise are not, however, entirely exogenous. Besides being documentary in nature, letters of credit have increasingly suffered from their own limitations. The high fees associated with the issue, confirmation, and amendment of letters of credit make them an expensive form of finance;[69] indeed, as occurred during the Global Financial Crisis, those fees are likely to track even higher during the coronavirus pandemic as banks become increasingly risk-averse and seek to protect their own balance-sheets.[70] Moreover, given that letters of credit are designed to provide beneficiaries with a reliable paymaster, the high discrepancy rates and rejection rates associated with such instruments make them far less reliable than intended.[71] This erodes confidence in their use. In no small part, this position has not been helped by the doctrine of strict compliance: as originally conceived, this doctrine represented one of the letter of credit's real strengths, since it enabled banks to deal with documents rapidly and in a purely ministerial capacity;

[65] ICC, 'Re-thinking Trade and Finance' (July 2017) 105 (hereafter ICC, 'Re-thinking Trade and Finance').
[66] ibid 17, 25.
[67] ICC, 'Re-thinking Trade and Finance' (n 65) 31. See also Tavan, 'Basel III' (n 33).
[68] ICC, 'Re-thinking Trade and Finance' (n 65) 207; ICC Banking Commission, 'Trade Register Report 2020' (n 8) 26–8.
[69] See ch 10 (Goldby) in this volume, indicating that 'fees can range from 0.75%–1.5% of the transaction's value, and a number of additional charges may apply, including for handling discrepancies'.
[70] ICC Banking Commission, 'Trade Register Report 2020' (n 8) 23.
[71] Peter Ellinger, 'Rejection of Documents Tendered under a Letter of Credit' [2013] LMCLQ 1, 4 (hereafter Ellinger, 'Rejection of Documents'). In recent times, default rates under documentary letters of credit have remained largely stable, and even improved slightly, although there has been a recent spike in default rates in relation to import letters of credit: see ICC Banking Commission, 'Trade Register Report 2020' (n 8) 8, 34.

increasingly, however, the doctrine's strictness is effectively providing banks with a discretion (usually acting upon their customer's instructions) whether or not to make payment in a particular case, since it would be unusual for documents to contain no discrepancy at all. As a consequence, discrepancy rates were high when the UCP 600 was adopted[72] and, as 'the ICC's attempt to introduce uniformity as regards details of compliance—made in the International Standard Practice (known as 'ISBP')—has not achieved its object',[73] rejection levels have remained stubbornly elevated.

III. The Rise of Open Account, Prepayment, and Supply Chain Finance

A. Open Account and Prepayment Terms

As letters of credit have become increasingly unattractive, unmanageable, and unavailable to banks and trade parties, the space for alternative technologies, financing mechanisms, and finance-providers has opened up. Accordingly, it is within that space (or 'trade finance gap') that trade parties have turned to 'open account' and 'prepayment' terms. The former refers to the situation where the seller has agreed to ship the goods, giving the buyer a period of credit before payment becomes due (usually thirty or ninety days after shipment or delivery); the latter refers to the buyer agreeing to pay for the goods in advance, usually so that the seller can use those funds to acquire the goods in question. As explained by the Global Supply Chain Finance Forum ('GSCFF'):[74] **14.13**

> Open account trade refers to trade transactions between a seller and a buyer where transactions are not supported by any banking or documentary trade instrument issued on behalf of the buyer or seller. The buyer is directly responsible for meeting the payment obligation in relation to the underlying transaction. Where trading parties supply and buy goods and services on the basis of open account terms an invoice is usually raised and the buyer pays within an agreed time frame. Open account terms can be contrasted with trading on the basis of cash in advance, or trading utilising instruments such as Documentary Credits, as a means of securing payment.

Over the last decade, open account and prepayment trading have usually been reported as accounting for anything between 45%[75] and 60%[76] of global trade-finance terms, although some surveys have put the figure even higher.[77] Whatever the precise figure, the modelling

[72] Just before the UCP 600 was adopted, average rejection rates were between 52% and 56% for import and export letters of credit respectively: see Institute of International Banking Law and Practice, 'DC-PRO 2005 LC Market Intelligence Survey', in James Byrne and Christopher Byrnes (eds), *Annual Survey of Letter of Credit Law and Practice Handbook* (The Institute of International Banking Law & Practice 2006) 231.
[73] Ellinger, 'Rejection of Documents' (n 71) 3.
[74] Global Supply Chain Finance Forum ('GSCFF'), 'Standard Definitions for Techniques of Supply Chain Finance' (2016) 8 (hereafter GSCFF, 'Standard Definitions').
[75] ICC Banking Commission, 'Trade Register Report 2020' (n 8) 22.
[76] International Monetary Fund ('IMF') and BAFT, 'IMF-BAFT Trade Finance Survey. A Survey Among Banks Assessing the Current Trade Finance Environment' (2009); IMF, BAFT, and International Financial Services Association, 'A Survey Among Banks Assessing the Current Trade Finance Environment. Trade Finance Services: Current Environment and Recommendations: Wave 3' (2010).
[77] ICC, 'ICC Global Trade and Finance Survey' (2009); BIS, 'Trade Finance' (n 2) 9.

suggests that open account trading's market-share will 'grow at 2% [compound annual growth rate] over the coming decade, dependent on macroeconomic factors, including industry recovery from COVID-19'.[78] This growth is expected to be at the expense of documentary trade finance, although (as indicated above) the global coronavirus pandemic has caused a shift back to lower-risk letters of credit. In some respects, the phenomenal rise of open-account and prepayment terms turns the trade-finance clock back almost a century, since these payment terms are about the simplest, quickest, and most straightforward ones that trading parties could use.

14.14 There are, however, limits upon the use of such payment terms. First, open-account and prepayment terms carry considerable risk of non-payment for the seller in the former situation and of non-delivery for the buyer in the latter. In many ways, such terms involve little more than crossing one's fingers and hoping for the best. Accordingly, such payment terms are only generally appropriate when a trade party has confidence in its counterparty's ability and willingness to perform. This will usually be the case when trade parties have dealt with each other successfully on previous occasions; already have an established and ongoing legal or commercial relationship; and/or for some other reason trust each other (whether as a result of the counterparty's size, reputation, or jurisdiction in which it is based). In such circumstances, there seems little point in the trade parties incurring the additional expense and uncertainty of interposing one or more banks between themselves. Where the trade parties are strangers to one another, however, they are likely to employ the risk-mitigating features of the letter of credit.[79] Nevertheless, even in trade with unknown counterparties, the desire to enter or expand into highly competitive markets or to secure a particular customer may compel a trade party to accept a higher risk of non-payment or non-delivery by offering particularly favourable payment terms.[80] In such circumstances, a seller may seek to mitigate its risk by employing state-backed credit-default mechanisms (such as an export credit guarantee) or private export credit insurance against the full range of circumstances that might result in non-payment, whether insolvency, war, nationalisation, or currency inconvertibility. On the buyer's side, a performance bond or first-demand guarantee from a bank may provide the requisite degree of assurance.

14.15 Secondly, even when the parties deal without any financial intermediary, there remain concerns for trade parties about compliance with anti-money laundering legislation and trade sanctions regimes.[81] 'Open account' and 'prepayment' terms require trade parties to be self-reliant in this regard by carrying out the necessary checks and bearing any compliance costs.[82] Whether these costs are higher for the trade parties than for the banks will depend upon the circumstances: on the one hand, as trade parties are not as accustomed or as well adapted as banks in performing these checks, this factor may drive the costs up; on

[78] ICC Banking Commission, 'Trade Register Report 2020' (n 8) 22, 26.

[79] Unsurprisingly, data have revealed that the parties are more likely to resort to payment mechanisms that interpose a bank when involved in a newly formed trade relationship: see Niepmann and Schmidt-Eisenlohr, 'Banks in International Trade Finance' (n 6).

[80] United States Department of Commerce, International Trade Administration, *Trade Finance Guide* (2012) ch 5.

[81] GSCFF, 'Standard Definitions' (n 74) 15.

[82] See the Wolfsberg Group, ICC, and BAFT, 'Trade Finance Principles' (2017) [1.5] Appendix IV, indicating that, even in open-account transactions that have minimum bank involvement, there will be a need to perform basic 'know your customer' checks.

the other, the fact that trade parties will be much better placed than issuing and confirming banks to understand the particular trade sector, the particular counterparty, and the particular transaction may operate to reduce those costs. Indeed, by dealing with the same counterparties on a repeat basis, trade parties can avoid the need for extensive compliance checks, although this will obviously be a problem if trade parties are seeking to access new markets or customers.

Thirdly, 'open-account' or 'prepayment' terms will usually involve the buyer or seller granting their counterparty a reasonable period of credit before payment or delivery is required.[83] This can, however, create a liquidity problem for the person granting credit, as the seller may be looking to those funds in order to pay the price for the goods to its own supplier or to fund its operations more generally; whilst the buyer may have prepaid the seller, but may not be entitled to receive payment from its own sub-buyer until it has delivered the goods in question. Just as the parties are able to mitigate the risks of non-payment or non-delivery by seeking third-party protection under performance bonds or credit insurance, so too have trade parties developed a range of techniques designed to mitigate the risks of a liquidity crunch or supply-chain failure. Those liquidity-enhancing techniques are considered in the next subsection. **14.16**

B. Supply Chain Finance

SCF is an umbrella term that has widespread commercial currency, even if it is not a legal term of art. According to the ICC, SCF can be defined compendiously as 'the use of financing and risk mitigation practices and techniques to optimise the management of the working capital and liquidity invested in supply chain processes and transactions'.[84] As considered above, whilst there are a number of reasons for the current popularity of open-account and prepayment terms, trade parties' ability to use SCF in achieving their risk-mitigation and liquidity aims has undoubtedly contributed to this state of affairs. SCF does, however, come with a couple of health warnings. First, as indicated above, there is little trust in times of crisis. Trust is critical to the attractiveness and use of open-account terms and consequently SCF. Accordingly, the longer the global coronavirus pandemic persists, the greater the impact on this type of financing, although it is not presently envisaged that the current downturn in SCF's use is likely to be permanent.[85] **14.17**

Secondly, there is an opacity around the accounting treatment of traders' SCF liabilities: for example, when Carillion collapsed in 2018 owing £500 million to banks through SCF facilities, 'this was not immediately clear from its balance sheet: as per common practice, SCF debts were listed as money "owed to creditors" (ie "trade receivables") rather than bank debt'.[86] Whilst such favourable accounting treatment no doubt makes SCF more attractive **14.18**

[83] For example, the average contractual maturity for trade finance products is '111 days for import [letters of credit], 129 days for export [letters of credit], 133 days for loans for import/export, and 625 days for performance guarantees': see ICC Banking Commission, 'Trade Register Report 2020' (n 8) 34.
[84] GSCFF, 'Standard Definitions' (n 74) 8.
[85] ICC Banking Commission, 'Trade Register Report 2020' (n 8) 21.
[86] ibid 29.

to trading parties, its association with a number of corporate collapses[87] has tarnished its reputation and risks the heavy hand of regulation having a chilling effect on SCF activity.[88]

14.19 Thirdly, the willingness of banks to engage in SCF activity has been driven by their ability to manage their own risk by selling securitised trade-finance assets to investors who have generally perceived these as being low-risk assets.[89] The novelty of this market may make SCF-based securitised investments less attractive in the current uncertain climate, which in turn may make banks more reticent to engage in SCF activity if they are no longer able to offload their risk through securitisation structures.

14.20 Finally, as described above, the favourable regulatory treatment of letters of credit for bank capitalisation purposes was a battle a long time in the winning. In the end, the Basel III regime applied a favourable one-fifth risk-weighting for bank capital purposes to 'documentary credits collateralised by the underlying shipment'.[90] Similarly, the one-year maturity floor has now been automatically disapplied for 'import and export letters of credit and similar transactions',[91] and the leverage ratio no longer applies to 'short-term self-liquidating trade letters of credit arising from the movement of goods (e.g. documentary credits collateralised by the underlying shipment)'.[92] None of this is apt to cover SCF transactions, which accordingly do not appear to be automatically exempt from the operation of the one-year 'maturity floor' or the leverage ratio. Instead, national regulators have been given the discretion whether or not also to exempt '[s]ome trade finance transactions that are not [automatically] exempt' from the one-year maturity floor.[93] As regards the application of the leverage ratio, SCF might qualify as a 'transaction-related contingent item'[94] or (if it involves an 'off-balance sheet securitisation exposure') as an 'eligible liquidity facility', but only if the stringent conditions set out in the Basel Framework are met.[95] In short, there remains a considerable amount of uncertainty regarding SCF's capital treatment under Basel III: whilst this may ultimately have a chilling effect upon banks' willingness to engage in such activity, the non-bank sector is likely to flourish in its stead given that alternative finance-providers are not usually impacted by Basel III to the same extent, if at all.

14.21 Whilst the excitement surrounding SCF might suggest that its aims are entirely novel, devices aimed at improving trade parties' liquidity are far from new. Even when trade finance was almost entirely dependent upon documentary letters of credit, techniques had already developed to address trade parties' lack of liquidity. Accordingly, the first part of this subsection will analyse the letter of credit's traditional liquidity-enhancing devices and consider the difficulty and confusion that has long surrounded (and still does) their operation. It is no doubt for that reason that the market has developed more straightforward mechanisms. Accordingly, the second part of this subsection will consider the various modern techniques that SCF nowadays uses to achieve broadly the same aims. Once again, adding

[87] ibid.
[88] See generally International Trade and Forfaiting Association, 'A Guide to Accounting and Legal Issues under IFRS 9 for the Trade Receivables and Supply Chain Finance Industry' (May 2019).
[89] ICC Banking Commission, 'Trade Register Report 2020' (n 8) 30.
[90] BCBS, 'Post-crisis Reforms' (n 27) [83].
[91] BCBS, 'Basel III' (n 29) CRE 32.46.
[92] ibid LEV 30.51.
[93] ibid CRE 32.47(2).
[94] ibid LEV 30.49.
[95] ibid LEV 30.53.

the soubriquet 'SCF' might suggest that something innovative is being attempted, but the reality is that the term 'SCF' largely involves a re-labelling and re-purposing of familiar commercial concepts and techniques for the trade-finance context specifically. Accordingly, the legal difficulties associated with some of these devices are well-documented and are unlikely to disappear simply because they are employed in a different context. These problems will be highlighted in the third part.

C. Traditional Liquidity-Enhancing Techniques

When trade parties employ a letter of credit as the means of payment, there are several liquidity-enhancing devices that they can employ. Some of these rely upon third parties to provide the necessary assurance or funds. For example, the seller might arrange for an export credit guarantee, which is issued by a state-sponsored body in order to support, encourage, and facilitate trade transactions in particular sectors that are considered strategic in the broader national interest. Similarly, a performance bond may be issued at the seller's request to incentivise the buyer to open a letter of credit or at the buyer's request to incentivise the seller to ship the goods. In essence, the export credit guarantee or performance bond provides the seller with a fall-back position in the event that the letter of credit fails to produce payment. These third-party devices are beyond the present analysis, which focuses more on the way trade parties may structure their dealings in order to convert the illiquid letter of credit into liquid funds, namely by using a transferable letter of credit, a trust receipt arrangement, or a back-to-back letter of credit. As these devices have not often be subjected to detailed judicial scrutiny, their nature and effect remains somewhat obscure, even today. **14.22**

1. Transferable Letters of Credit

A transferable letter of credit enables the seller to cede a portion of the existing credit issued in its favour to its own supplier.[96] In essence, where a letter of credit is stated to be 'transferable', the beneficiary is able to instruct the confirming or nominated bank (termed, for these purposes, the 'transferring bank')[97] to issue a further letter of credit on 'the terms and conditions specified in the original Credit' (subject to a number of exceptions relating to the credit's amount and expiry date)[98] to the seller's own supplier (termed the 'second beneficiary'). The second beneficiary is entitled to present the documents required by the credit, including his own invoice, to the transferring bank in return for payment of the amount owed by the credit's first beneficiary. That beneficiary is entitled to substitute its own invoice and documents for the second beneficiary's documents held by the transferring bank and to receive payment of its profit on resale to the credit applicant. The transferring bank will then transmit the first beneficiary's substituted documents for reimbursement by the issuing bank and applicant. In this way, a seller can employ a letter of credit as a means of paying for the goods without having to find the necessary funds, thereby ameliorating any potential cash-flow problems. **14.23**

[96] UCP 600, art 38(b).
[97] ibid art 38(b).
[98] ibid art 38(h).

14.24 Whilst the procedure governing transferable letters of credit is comprehensively set out in the UCP 600,[99] there are a number of practical difficulties arising from these instruments that flow from the uncertainty regarding their doctrinal underpinnings. In functional terms at least, there appears to be a transfer of rights from the first beneficiary to the second, but the juridical nature of the transfer mechanism remains obscure. In particular, it is unclear whether the transfer of a letter of credit can be analogised with other legal mechanisms that operate to transfer rights. Whilst a number of theories have been posited to explain how letters of credit are transferred, two suggestions may be given short shrift. The first such suggestion is that a transferable letter of credit involves the second beneficiary vicariously performing the first beneficiary's obligations.[100] Whilst vicarious performance may explain the second beneficiary's entitlement to present documents under a transferable credit, it does not explain its entitlement to be paid directly by the transferring bank. This is because an entity performing obligations vicariously does not generally acquire any rights by virtue of that performance, as it does not become a party to the agreement in question. The second suggestion that can be confidently dismissed is that the transfer of a letter of credit involves its negotiation to the second beneficiary. Whilst a letter of credit may well require the presentation of bills of exchange, which are then capable of being negotiated to third parties, the letter of credit itself is not a negotiable instrument that may be transferred by indorsement and delivery.[101] This view is supported by the UCP 600, which makes clear that a transferable credit (or any part thereof) may only be transferred once; a negotiable instrument may be negotiated on any number of occasions.[102] As a result, commentators have generally rejected this view.[103]

14.25 A possible theoretical explanation of a letter of credit's transfer might be that it involves nothing more than an equitable assignment of the rights under that credit.[104] There are a number of indications that the concepts of transfer and assignment are in fact distinct. First, an equitable assignment will be effective without the obligor's prior consent,[105] whereas it

[99] There are some issues, however, that are not contained in the UCP 600 and have been interpolated by domestic courts, such as the duty of confidentiality owed by the transferring bank: see *Jackson v Royal Bank of Scotland* [2005] 1 WLR 377 (HL). See further Christopher Hare, 'Transferable Letters of Credit: Responsibility, Remoteness and Loss of a Chance' [2005] LMCLQ 350.

[100] Contrast A N Oelofse, *The Law of Documentary Letters of Credit in Comparative Perspective* (Interlegal 1997) 486–87 (hereafter Oelofse, *Law of Documentary Letters of Credit*) analysing the problem in terms of 'a substitutionary performance by the issuing bank within its relationship with the first beneficiary'.

[101] *Shaffer v Brooklyn Park Garden Apartments*, 311 Minn. 452, 250 NW 2d 172 (Minn 1977) (hereafter *Shaffer v Brooklyn Park*): 'Authorities agree, however, that a letter of credit is not in itself a negotiable instrument although a draft presented under it may be.'

[102] UCP 600, art 38(d).

[103] Michael Smith, 'Transmitting the Benefit of a Letter of Credit' [1991] JBL 447, 449, 452 (hereafter Smith, 'Transmitting the Benefit'). See also Richard King, *Gutteridge & Megrah's Law of Bankers' Commercial Credits* (8th edn, Routledge 2001) [5–20] (hereafter King, *Gutteridge & Megrah*). Although the letter of credit is not a negotiable instrument, both instruments are autonomous in nature: see Clive Schmitthoff, 'The Transferable Credit' [1988] JBL 49, 50 (hereafter Schmitthoff, 'The Transferable Credit').

[104] A transfer would have to be an equitable (rather than legal or statutory) assignment as only part of the first beneficiary's contractual rights are transferred: see *Walter & Sullivan Ltd v J Murphy & Sons Ltd* [1955] 2 QB 584 (CA). The assignment of part of a debt falls outside the scope of Law of Property Act 1925, s 136(1): see *Cotton v Heyl* [1930] 1 Ch 510; *Williams v Atlantic Assurance Co* [1933] 1 KB 81 (CA); *Deposit Protection Board v Dalia* [1994] 2 AC 367 (HL) 392; *Raiffeisen Zentralbank Osterreich AG v Five Star General Trading LLC* [2001] 1 Lloyd's Rep 597 (CA) [75] (hereafter *Raiffeisen Zentralbank v Five Star*).

[105] Although the obligor is not required specifically to consent to the assignment, it is a precondition of a statutory assignment that the obligor be given notice in writing pursuant to Law of Property Act 1925, s 136(1). See also Smith, 'Transmitting the Benefit' (n 103) 452.

is not possible to transfer a letter of credit without obtaining the specific consent of the transferring bank.[106] Secondly, some of the second beneficiary's rights may be altered upon transfer,[107] whereas the assignee's rights are identical to those of the assignor.[108] Thirdly, the UCP 600 makes clear that the beneficiary of a non-transferable letter of credit may nevertheless assign the actual proceeds of that credit, although it is less clear whether there can also be an assignment of the right to receive those proceeds.[109] Fourthly, following a valid assignment, the first beneficiary must still present the documents required by the letter of credit, whereas a transferee steps into the transferor's shoes and is accordingly entitled to present the documents and demand payment in its own right. In essence, to describe the operation as a 'transfer' is probably a misnomer: no chose in action is in fact transferred, but rather the second beneficiary obtains for the first time 'a contractual right to engender a debt by presentation of the documents'.[110] Accordingly, there is little academic support for the assignment theory as the underlying explanation for transferable letters of credit.[111]

A further theoretical explanation might be that the transferable letter of credit operates by way of an attornment or acknowledgement by the transferring bank in favour of the second beneficiary. An attornment occurs when one party instructs another, who is holding a fund on his behalf, to hold all or part of that fund for the benefit of a designated third party. If the fundholder consents to this instruction and informs the relevant third party accordingly, that third party will be entitled to receive the attorned portion of the fund.[112] The notion of a 'fund' for these purposes has received an expansive definition. In *Shamia v Joory*,[113] a 'fund' was held to include the fundholder's liabilities to its instructing party. Accordingly, as the fundholder's liability need not have accrued in order to constitute a 'fund', the concept could include the transferring bank's future liability to pay the first beneficiary upon the presentation of conforming documents.[114] On this basis, a direction by the first beneficiary to the effect that a transferring bank should pay some or all of the credit's proceeds to the second beneficiary could arguably amount to an attornment, provided the bank consents. There are a number of reasons, however, why the attornment theory is unsatisfactory. First, the inclusion of debts and other liabilities within the concept of a 'fund' not only appears inconsistent with previous authority,[115] but also has been subjected to trenchant **14.26**

[106] UCP 600, art 38(a).

[107] ibid art 38(g).

[108] Smith, 'Transmitting the Benefit' (n 103) 452.

[109] UCP 600, art 39. See also *Marathon Electrical Manufacturing Corp v Mashreqbank PSC* [1997] 2 BCLC 460 (QB) 465 (hereafter *Marathon Electrical v Mashreqbank*). That transfer and assignment involve different processes has been clearly articulated by the US courts: see *Algemene Bank Nederland NV v Soysen Tarim Urunleri Dis Tiscaret Ve Sanayi AS*, 748 F Supp 177 (1990) (hereafter *Algemene Bank v Soysen*); *Studwell Inc v Korean Exchange Bank*, 55 Cap App 4th 1185 (1997).

[110] *The Hong Kong and Shanghai Banking Corporation v Kloeckner & Co AG* [1989] 2 Lloyd's Rep 323 (QB) (hereafter *HSBC v Kloeckner*). See generally ICC Banking Commission, 'Transferable Credits and the UCP 500' (30 October 2002).

[111] Smith, 'Transmitting the Benefit' (n 103) 452; Alan Ward and Gerard McCormack, 'Assignment and Documentary Credits' [2000] JIBL 138, 140 (hereafter Ward and McCormack, 'Assignment').

[112] John Davies, '*Shamia v Joory*: A Forgotten Chapter in Quasi-Contract' (1959) 75 LQR 220, 228 (hereafter Davies, '*Shamia v Joory*').

[113] *Shamia v Joory* [1958] 1 QB 448, 459 (hereafter *Shamia v Joory*), considered in *Myers v Design Inc (International) Ltd* [2003] 1 WLR 1642 (Ch) [7]–[9]. See also *Israel v Douglas* (1789) 1 Hy Black 239; *Hamilton v Spottiswoode* (1849) 4 Exch 200; *Griffin v Weatherby* (1868) LR 3 QB 753 (hereafter *Griffin v Weatherby*).

[114] *Shamia v Joory* (n 113) 459. For the apparently contrary suggestion that an attornment will only be of relevance after the presentation of conforming documents: see Smith, 'Transmitting the Benefit' (n 103) 450.

[115] In *Liversidge v Broadbent* (1859) 4 H&N 603 it was held that the transfer of a debt had to be effected by means of an assignment, rather than by attornment, and consequently had to be supported by consideration moving

criticism.[116] If these criticisms are sound, the concept of attornment can have little application in the letter of credit context.[117] Secondly, even if those criticisms are unsound, the concept of attornment alone cannot explain *all* of the rights acquired by the second beneficiary: an attornment could potentially justify the second beneficiary's ability to receive payment under the credit, but cannot explain its right to present the documents required by the credit. The effect of an attornment is limited to the creation of an entitlement to a fund, rather than the creation of any wider rights, such as the right to present conforming documents. Thirdly, it seems tolerably clear from the authorities that, following an attornment, the fundholder holds the relevant fund to the use of the attornee, who thereby acquires a proprietary right. Accordingly, if the fundholder refuses to pay the attornee, the latter can seek restitution of the attorned sum as money had and received;[118] otherwise, the fundholder would be unjustly enriched at the attornee's expense. It has never really been doubted, however, that the second beneficiary's rights under a transferred letter of credit, including its right to claim payment, are simply contractual in nature. As a result, the analogy with attornment does not seem convincing.

14.27 A seemingly more fruitful theoretical explanation than assignment or attornment equates the operation of a transferable letter of credit to a novation of rights from the first to the second beneficiary.[119] A novation takes place when the obligor under a contract enters into a new contract with a third party on the same terms as its original contract with the obligee. At first sight, this is strikingly similar to how a transferable letter of credit operates: the first beneficiary will return the original credit to the transferring bank, so that it can issue a new credit in favour of the second beneficiary in largely identical terms (albeit for a smaller sum). The original credit, however, remains available for the balance remaining after the second beneficiary has drawn under the transferred credit,[120] with the result that the transferring bank remains liable to pay those sums to the first beneficiary. This continuing ability on the first beneficiary's part to present substituted documents under the credit potentially distinguishes the transferable letter of credit's operation from a novation of rights. Following a novation, the obligor will ordinarily be released from *all* its obligations to the original obligee.[121] Whilst a possible reconciliation might be to suggest that a transferable credit involves only a *partial* novation that extinguishes only *some* of the transferring bank's original obligations, this cannot explain why the first beneficiary's right to claim the full amount due under the credit will revive in the event that the second beneficiary allows the credit to expire unused. In such a case, the first beneficiary's rights appear at first to be merely *suspended*, with those rights only being extinguished when the transferring bank pays the

from the assignee. See also *Walker v Rostron* (1842) 9 M&W 411; *Seasymbol Marine Ltd v BMM Shipbrokers Ltd*, unreported, 27 November 1995; cf *Banque de la Mediterranée v Streeters of Godalming Ltd*, unreported, 9 July 1980, where Parker J suggested that *Liversidge* did not undermine the correctness of *Shamia v Joory* (n 113). The term 'fund' in CPR r 25.1(1)(l), does not include a debt or other liability: see *Myers v Design Inc (International) Ltd* [2003] 1 All ER 1168 (Ch).

[116] *Nerva v RL&G Ltd* [1995] IRLR 200 (QB).

[117] Smith, 'Transmitting the Benefit' (n 103) 450.

[118] *Griffin v Weatherby* (n 113) 758–59; *Shamia v Joory* (n 113). See also Davies, '*Shamia v Joory*' (n 112) 225–29.

[119] Smith, 'Transmitting the Benefit' (n 103) 452–53; Ward and McCormack, 'Assignment' (n 111) 140. See also King, *Gutteridge & Megrah* (n 103) [5–20].

[120] Ward and McCormack, 'Assignment' (n 111) 140.

[121] *Re Burton Marsden Douglas (a firm)* [2004] 3 All ER 222 (Ch) [21], where Lloyd J stated that the effect of a novation is 'to extinguish the original contract and to replace it by the new one'.

second beneficiary.[122] Accordingly, novation does not provide a satisfactory theoretical explanation of the transferable letter of credit.

As the transferable letter of credit is difficult to explain by reference to the ordinary mechanisms in English law for the transmission of rights, it might be tempting to view the transferable letter of credit as a *sui generis* institution that was designed specifically for the needs of international trade finance[123] and is incapable of classification according to domestic law criteria. Such a characterisation, however, merely begs the question. A better approach might be to analyse the matter through the lens of domestic contractual principles. The suspension of the first beneficiary's right to payment under the transferred portion of a credit might be explained by reference to the equitable doctrine of promissory estoppel.[124] This is because the first beneficiary's request that the transferring bank cede part of the credit to the second beneficiary constitutes a clear and unequivocal representation to the issuing and confirming banks (through the agency of the transferring bank) that the first beneficiary will not insist on payment of the transferred part of the credit. Moreover, by undertaking fresh obligations to the second beneficiary, those banks have clearly relied upon the first beneficiary's representations. Accordingly, as it would be inequitable for the first beneficiary to revert to its original rights, it would be estopped from doing so. Those rights will, however, be finally extinguished when the second beneficiary receives payment according to the terms of the transferred credit.[125] In the event that the transferred part of the credit lapses unused and the second beneficiary remains unpaid, the first beneficiary may then resume its rights to receive full payment under the credit. As regards the creation of the new rights in favour of the second beneficiary, this might be explained by applying basic agency principles. By issuing a transferable credit, the issuing bank authorises the transferring bank to act as its agent in any dealings with the designated second beneficiary. By agreeing to the terms of a particular transfer, the transferring bank acts as the agent of the issuing bank and any confirming bank in creating a direct contractual relationship with the second beneficiary.[126] Accordingly, the second beneficiary is effectively put in the same position as that originally enjoyed by the first beneficiary in relation to the transferred part of the credit and to that extent enjoys the same undertakings from the issuing and confirming banks as the first beneficiary.[127] Conversely, those banks owe the same duties to the second beneficiary with respect to the examination of tendered documents as they owe to the first beneficiary. Any documentary examination will accordingly need to comply with the procedures in the 14.28

[122] Oelofse, *Law of Documentary Letters of Credit* (n 100) 487.

[123] Schmitthoff, 'The Transferable Credit' (n 103) 51.

[124] For the generally suspensory nature of promissory estoppel, see *Central London Property Trust Ltd v High Trees House Ltd* [1947] KB 130.

[125] *In re AOV Industries Inc*, 64 BR 933 (Bankr D Dist Col, 1986). For the potentially extinctive nature of a promissory estoppel, see *Collier v P&MJ Wright (Holdings) Ltd* [2007] EWCA Civ 1329; *Rock Advertising Ltd v MWB Business Exchange Centres Ltd* [2016] EWCA Civ 553.

[126] For acceptance of this view in the US, see *Banca del Sempione v Provident Bank of Maryland*, 160 F 3d 992 (1998) (hereafter *Banca del Sempione v Provident Bank*); *Integrated Measurement Systems Inc v International Commercial Bank of China*, 757 F Supp 938 (1991) (hereafter *Integrated Measurement Systems v CBC*). See also *Algemene Bank v Soysen* (n 109) 181–82; *Banca del Sempione v Provident Bank of Maryland*, 75 F 3d 951 (1996) 964. A similar conclusion has been reached by the Singaporean courts: see *Agritrade International Pte Ltd v Industrial and Commercial Bank of China* [1998] 1 SLR(R) 322 (HC); cf King, *Gutteridge & Megrah* (n 103) [5–20].

[127] *National Bank & Trust Co v JLM International Inc*, 421 F Supp 1269 (1976).

UCP 600.[128] Like any other agent, the transferring bank does not undertake any direct contractual obligations to the second beneficiary.[129]

14.29 Whilst estoppel and agency principles adequately explain the operation of transferable letters of credit, there are two objections to this theoretical approach. The first objection is that this contract-based approach represents a distinctly English one to the issue and that reliance upon overtly domestic concepts is inappropriate in such an international context. Given that the UCP 600 does not deal comprehensively with all the issues concerning transferable letters of credit, however, the only solution is to fall back onto domestic law principles. Indeed, the ICC Banking Commission seems content with this position.[130] The second objection is that this contract-based approach provides little assistance in resolving the more controversial issues surrounding transferable letters of credit. There are three such controversies. The first controversy concerns whether the second beneficiary's rights against the issuing and confirming banks are affected by any claims that those banks might have against the first beneficiary, such as a right of set-off[131] or a defence based upon the first beneficiary's fraud. Certainly, the answer would have been negative if the transfer of a letter of credit had involved negotiation.[132] The same position would arguably have pertained if such a transfer had operated by way of novation,[133] but not if it had involved an assignment.[134] A contract-based solution does not, however, provide any ready answer to this question. Nevertheless, it is possible to arrive at a solution from first principles: as each contractual relationship engendered by a letter of credit is autonomous,[135] the relationship between the issuing bank and the second beneficiary is independent of that between the issuing bank and the first beneficiary, so that equities arising from the latter relationship should not infect the former. Indeed, in *Banca del Sempione v Provident Bank of Maryland*, the second beneficiary was not precluded from enforcing a transferred letter of credit by virtue of the first beneficiary's fraud against the issuing bank,[136] although the position may be different if the second beneficiary were shown to be privy to the fraud.[137] The second

[128] UCP 600, arts 14–17. In *Creaciones Con Idea SA v Mashreqbank PSC*, 38 UCC Rep Serv 2d (Callaghan) 946 (1999), Motley J appears to have accepted that the examination and rejection of documents presented by the second beneficiary had to follow the same procedures as are applicable to documents presented by the first beneficiary.

[129] *Integrated Measurement Systems v CBC* (n 126). See also *Sound of Market Street Inc v Continental Bank International*, 819 F 2d 384 (1987).

[130] In the context of transferable credits, it would appear that national law will determine a bank's liability for breaching the terms of ICC, 'Uniform Customs and Practice for Documentary Credits' (ICC Publication No 500, 1993) (hereafter 'UCP 500') art 48, as well as the available remedies: see ICC Banking Commission Opinion R 386 (ICC Publication No 632) 44. Domestic law also governed the extent to which fraud might affect the obligations under a transferable letter of credit: see ICC Banking Commission Opinions R 202 & R341 (ICC Publication No 632) 53, 257.

[131] *HSBC v Kloeckner* (n 110); *Safa Ltd v Banque du Caire* [2000] 2 Lloyd's Rep 600 (CA).

[132] For the protection afforded to a 'holder in due course', see Bills of Exchange Act 1882 (hereafter 'BEA 1882'), ss 29(1), 38(2). A holder is presumed to be a 'holder in due course': see BEA 1882, s 30(2).

[133] Smith, 'Transmitting the Benefit' (n 103) 450–51, although this conclusion will depend upon the precise terms of the novation. For the contrary view, see *Graiseley Properties Ltd v Barclays Bank plc* [2013] EWCA Civ 1372 [32]–[37].

[134] Whilst an assignee would be bound by any defences available against the assignor involving illegality, mistake, or misrepresentation (see *Marathon Electrical v Mashreqbank* (n 109) 469–70), there has been uncertainty as to whether the same position pertains in the case of a fraudulent misrepresentation: see *Stoddart v Union Trust Ltd* [1912] 1 KB 181; cf *Banco Santander SA v Bayfern Ltd*, unreported, 25 February 2000.

[135] UCP 600, arts 4–5.

[136] *Banca del Sempione v Provident Bank* (n 126). See also *Cromwell v Commerce & Energy Bank*, 464 So 2d 721 (1985) 732, 736; *Brown v United States National Bank*, 371 NW 2d 692 (1985) 700.

[137] *Shaffer v Brooklyn Park* (n 101), where the second beneficiary was enjoined from drawing upon the credit on account of the fact that it had presented a certificate containing materially false statements of fact.

controversy concerns how one might determine the priority between two beneficiaries to whom the same part of the credit has been transferred.[138] Whilst assignment, negotiation, and novation would certainly provide a ready solution to this problem,[139] the contract-based solution can similarly provide an answer by reference to first principles: as the UCP 600 provides that a credit may only be transferred once, the first transfer in time should have priority. The third controversy concerns how the law governing the transfer of a credit is determined: given that the choice of law principles applicable to negotiable instruments and assignments are not without their legal difficulties, adopting a contract-based approach would enable a court to apply the contractual choice of law rules, which are relatively settled and much more straightforward to operate.

2. Trust Receipt Arrangements

Whilst the transferable letter of credit is a traditional way of providing liquidity to a seller so that it can pay its own supplier, a buyer may equally face cash-flow difficulties if its obligation to reimburse the issuing bank matures before the buyer has received the funds from on-selling the relevant goods. Part of the difficulty arises from the fact that the issuing bank will have a pledge over the goods as security for the buyer's reimbursement obligation, but the bank's rights as pledgee depend upon its continued possession of the bill of lading. Once that document is released, the bank's pledge ends. Accordingly, the issuing bank will not wish to transfer the bill of lading until it has been paid, but the buyer cannot sell the goods in order to reimburse the bank without the bill of lading. Accordingly, there is an impasse. The solution is for the bank to release the bill of lading to the buyer pursuant to a trust-receipt arrangement: this effectively sub-divides possession into its actual and constructive elements, so that the bank's rights as pledgee continue despite its losing physical control of the bill of lading.[140] Accordingly, the issuing bank has continuing protection by virtue of the trust receipt from the consequences of the buyer's insolvency.[141] This is clear from *Northwestern Bank Ltd v John Poynter, Son & Macdonalds*,[142] in which the House of Lords held that a bank was entitled to claim the proceeds from the sale of goods under a trust receipt in priority to the buyer's unsecured creditors. **14.30**

Whilst trust receipts are far from uncommon, there remains a degree of uncertainty surrounding the nature of the issuing bank's rights under such arrangements, as well as their susceptibility to legal challenge. Most of the legal difficulties surrounding trust receipts arise from their drafting. There are two key issues. The first drafting challenge arises from the fact that the issuing bank's rights as pledgee are only preserved when the bill of lading is released for a specific or limited purpose. Accordingly, the bank must carefully define how the buyer may use the bill of lading. If that document is released for general or unspecified purposes, then the issuing bank will lose its security interest.[143] The second drafting challenge **14.31**

[138] This could potentially occur as a result of a fraud perpetrated from within the transferring bank or when two different transferring banks transfer the whole or part of a credit without reference to one another.

[139] For example, in the assignment context, priority is determined by the order in which notice is given to the obligor: see *Dearle v Hall* (1823) 3 Russ 1 (hereafter *Dearle v Hall*).

[140] Given that the issuing bank will nowadays have contractual rights against the carrier as 'holder' of the bill of lading under the Carriage of Goods by Sea Act 1992, the bank's rights as pledgee may be less important in the future: see *Standard Chartered Bank v Dorchester LNG (2) Ltd (The Erin Schulte)* [2014] EWCA Civ 1382.

[141] *Official Assignee of Madras v Mercantile Bank of India Ltd* [1935] AC 53 (PC) 63, 64; *Askrigg Pty Ltd v Student Guild of the Curtin University of Technology* (1989) 18 NSWLR 738 (SC) 745–46 (hereafter *Askrigg v Student Guild*).

[142] *Northwestern Bank Ltd v John Poynter, Son & Macdonalds* [1895] AC 56 (HL).

[143] *TEA 1983 Ltd v Uniting Church (NSW) Trust Association* [1985] VR 139 (SC) 140–41.

arises out of the fact that banks will often attempt to extend their security rights beyond the goods themselves to other forms of property that represent those goods, whether the proceeds from their re-sale, the receivables to which the re-sale gives rise or other property into which the goods are subsequently incorporated. Each of these difficulties will be considered in turn.

14.32 Given that the whole purpose underlying the trust receipt is to enable the buyer to re-sell the goods, the simplest form of trust receipt usually contains a recital recognising the continuing validity of the bank's rights as pledgee over both the goods and the proceeds of their sale.[144] In addition, the trust receipt may also purport to give the bank security over the receivables from the resale of the relevant goods. Whilst the bank's property rights can undoubtedly survive in such proceeds, the bank's interest over the receivables or proceeds cannot be a pledge.[145] Accordingly, the question has arisen as to whether the bank might instead have a fixed or floating charge over the buyer's book debts and their proceeds.[146] If the bank's interest were indeed characterised as a charge, then there is a risk that the charge would need to be registered in order to bind the buyer's liquidator.[147] English law currently requires that a 'charge' created by a company[148] must be registered within twenty-one days of its creation.[149] If the charge is not registered, then it will be absolutely void as against the buyer's liquidator or administrator or any of its creditors.[150] In *Re David Allester Ltd* ('*David Allester*'),[151] which concerned a trust receipt whereby the buyer undertook 'to hold the goods when received, and their proceeds when sold as your trustees',[152] Astbury J held that the trust receipt did not create any new independent security interest over the goods themselves, but merely acknowledged and evidenced the bank's pre-existing pledge.[153] Moreover, as regards the bank's interest over the proceeds, these were held on trust by the

[144] *Lloyds Bank Ltd v Bank of America National Trust and Savings Association* [1937] 2 KB 631, 632–33, aff'd [1938] 2 KB 147 (CA) 157–58. For a more detailed trust receipt, see *Fairfax Gerrard Holdings Ltd v Capital Bank plc* [2008] 1 Lloyd's Rep 297 (CA) [11], [32]. See also *Askrigg v Student Guild* (n 141) 741, 745; *United Malayan Banking Corporation Bhd v Aluminex* [1993] 3 MLJ 587 (SC, Kuala Lumpur) (hereafter *United Malayan v Aluminex*) 595; *Bank of Tokyo-Mitsubishi Ltd v Baskan Gida Sanayi Ve Pazarlama AS* [2004] 2 Lloyd's Rep 395 (Ch) [21]; *Re Far East Structural Steelwork Engineering Ltd* [2005] 654 HKCU 1, [8] (hereafter *Re Far East Structural*).

[145] Whilst an individual banknote may be pledgeable (see *Taylor v Chester* (1869) LR 4 QB 309, 314), a fund of money is not generally so susceptible.

[146] Whether a charge over receivables will be characterised as a floating charge will depend upon the degree of control that the buyer may exercise over the receivables' proceeds: see *Siebe Gorman & Co Ltd v Barclays Bank Ltd* [1979] 2 Lloyd's Rep 142 (Ch). The charge will be fixed if the trust receipt requires the proceeds of the receivables to be paid into a blocked account and they are in fact so paid: see *Re Keenan Bros Ltd* [1986] BCLC 242 (SC, Ireland); *Agnew v IRC* [2001] 2 AC 710 (PC) [48] (hereafter *Agnew v IRC*); *National Westminster Bank plc v Spectrum Plus Ltd* [2005] 2 AC 680 (HL) [56], [117], [140] (hereafter *National Westminster Bank v Spectrum Plus*). A degree of freedom on the part of the applicant to deal with the proceeds is not necessarily inconsistent with the charge being characterised as fixed: see *ABN Amro Bank NV v Chiyu Banking Corp Ltd* [2000] 3 HKC 381.

[147] *Re Far East Structural* (n 144) [47].

[148] A charge includes a mortgage, but not a pledge: see Companies Act 2006 (hereafter 'CA 2006'), s 859A(7).

[149] ibid s 859A(4).

[150] ibid s 859H(3).

[151] *Re David Allester Ltd* [1922] 2 Ch 211 (hereafter *Re David Allester*). The application in *David Allester* was made pursuant to the Companies (Consolidation) Act 1908, s 93. See also *Re Harwick, ex parte Hubbard* (1886) LR 17 QBD 690, 697, 698, 701.

[152] *Re David Allester* (n 151) 212.

[153] ibid 216. See also *United Malayan Banking Corp Bhd v Lim Kang Seng* [1994] 2 SLR 787 (HC) 797 (hereafter *United Malayan v Lim Kang Seng*); *Re Far East Structural* (n 144) [26], [27]. See further Hans Tijo, 'Personal Property Security Interests in Singapore and Malaysia' (1995) 16 Co Lawyer 28 (hereafter Tijo, 'Personal Property Security Interests') 29; Peter Ellinger, 'Trust Receipt Financing' (2003) 18 JIBLR 305, 305 (hereafter Ellinger, 'Trust Receipt Financing').

buyer for the bank.[154] According to Astbury J, '[t]he object of these letters of trust was not to give the bank a charge at all, but to enable the bank to realise the goods over which it had a charge in the way in which goods in similar cases have for years and years been realised in the City and elsewhere'.[155] It followed that the trust receipt in *David Allester* did not require registration under the bills of sale legislation then in force. Albeit decided on slightly different grounds to *David Allester*,[156] this approach was similarly adopted by the English Court of Appeal in *Re Hamilton, Young & Co*.[157] That said, there are other decisions both in England and abroad suggesting that the issuing bank does have a registrable charge under a trust receipt arrangement.[158] Accordingly, given that the decided cases have concerned the interpretation of foreign or domestic legislation that has since been repealed,[159] there remains some uncertainty as to how the courts would approach this question under more modern legislation, such as the Companies Act 2006.[160]

Where the trust receipt is drafted in even wider terms, so that the issuing bank seeks to assert an interest in any finished product resulting from the pledged goods being subjected to some manufacturing process,[161] the bank's interest is at even greater risk of being characterised as a charge over the mixed or processed goods. Certainly, in the context of retention of title clauses, attempts by a seller to retain an interest in any subsequent products have suffered precisely this fate in order to prevent the seller receiving a windfall at the buyer's expense.[162] Upon such a characterisation, the charge would require registration in order to retain its validity against the buyer's liquidator, administrator, and creditors.[163] Moreover, as the buyer is likely to be free to deal with the processed goods by selling them in the ordinary course of business, the charge is likely to be floating in nature.[164] Traditionally, floating charges have been subjected to additional grounds of invalidity that are not otherwise **14.33**

[154] *Re David Allester* (n 151) 218–19.

[155] ibid 218.

[156] Whilst *David Allester* decided that the trust receipt did not require registration on the grounds that it was not a bill of sale within the relevant legislation in the first place, the trust receipt in *Re Hamilton, Young & Co* [1905] 2 KB 772 (hereafter *Re Hamilton, Young*) was considered a 'document used in the ordinary course of business as proof of the control of goods' (see Bills of Sale Act 1878, s 4) and accordingly excluded from the scope of the legislation, which would otherwise have been applicable. See also *UDI (HK) Ltd v Fantana Ltd*, HCCW No 19 of 1976, 3 May 1978.

[157] *Re Hamilton, Young* (n 156) 785, 788, 789, 790, aff'ing [1905] 2 KB 382, 389, 390. This decision arguably turned upon the precise wording of the trust receipt at issue in that case: see *Re Far East Structural* (n 144) [44], [45].

[158] *Ladenberg & Co v Goodwin, Ferreira & Co Ltd* [1912] 3 KB 275 (hereafter *Ladenberg v Goodwin*) 280, 281; *Re Far East Structural* (n 144) [40], [47]. See also Ellinger, 'Trust Receipt Financing' (n 153) 306. For the proposition that a trust receipt may create a charge of a more general nature, see *United Malayan v Lim Kang Seng* (n 153) 797. See also Tijo, 'Personal Property Security Interests' (n 153) 29, suggesting that this is implicit in the Malaysian Supreme Court's decision in *United Malayan v Aluminex* (n 144).

[159] In *Re David Allester* (n 151) 217–19, Astbury J concluded that the trust receipt was not a charge within Companies (Consolidation) Act 1908, s 93(1), as it did not constitute a bill of sale. This conclusion is accordingly impliedly supported by *Re Hamilton, Young* (n 156).

[160] Ellinger, 'Trust Receipt Financing' (n 153) 306. See also *Ladenberg v Goodwin* (n 158).

[161] Ellinger, 'Trust Receipt Financing' (n 153) 307.

[162] Consider *Re Bond Worth Ltd* [1980] Ch 228, 248; *Borden (UK) Ltd v Scottish Timber Products Ltd* [1981] Ch 25, 46; *Re Peachdart Ltd* [1984] Ch 131, 142–43; *Clough Mill Ltd v Martin* [1985] 1 WLR 111 (CA) 120, 125. One possible argument to circumvent this result might be to rely upon the principles governing claims to mixed funds following a successful tracing exercise, since an innocent contributory has a choice between claiming a proportionate share of the fund or asserting a charge for the contribution made to the fund: see *Foskett v McKeown* [2001] 1 AC 102 (HL). If a bank were to assert an interest under a trust, this would not have to be registered under the Companies Act 2006.

[163] CA 2006 (n 148) ss 859A, 859H.

[164] *National Westminster Bank v Spectrum Plus* (n 146).

applicable to fixed charges.[165] One way to avoid this conclusion might be to use language indicating an intention to create some form of interest in the product (such as a beneficial interest under a trust) other than a charge.[166] It may be dangerous, however, to place too much reliance upon such drafting techniques, given the English courts' willingness to re-characterise property rights if the language used for their creation does not reflect the true nature of the interest created.[167] Accordingly, in the absence of modern judicial guidance regarding the application of the current regime for registering security interests, an issuing bank that insists on security over the products of the original goods should probably err on the side of caution by taking steps to register their interest.

14.34 The legal uncertainty over trust receipts has effectively undermined their reliability, which may in large part explain the absence of recent judicial consideration.[168] It is possible that the development of the electronic bill of lading may make the trust receipt mechanism more attractive to trade parties.[169] Digitisation of the shipping documents would enable the trade parties to employ blockchain technology to provide a permissioned platform that records the interests of the various parties involved in a trade transaction in a manner that is visible to all: as the bank's rights would no longer be dependent upon possessing a piece of paper, the buyer would be able to deal with the bill of lading subject to the bank's rights, which would be protected by means of a ledger entry in the electronic record.[170] Replacing a paper-based trust receipt with a straightforward ledger entry showing that the bank retained virtual possession of the bill of lading would certainly simplify matters for a bank seeking to retain its rights against the goods themselves, the receivables arising on their resale or the proceeds of those receivables. After all, as stated in *David Allester*,[171] '[t]he letters of trust merely record the terms on which the pledgors were to realize the goods on behalf of the pledgees'. Accordingly, it should matter little whether that 'record' is paper-based or electronic. That said, it is less clear that technology can solve the legal difficulties concerning the need to register security interests over the products of the goods in question.

3. Back-to-Back Letters of Credit

14.35 The final mechanism that sellers might employ to enhance their liquidity position is the 'back-to-back' letter of credit. In a similar fashion to the transferable letter of credit considered above, the 'back-to-back' letter of credit involves a seller (who is also the beneficiary

[165] Insolvency Act 1986, s 245.

[166] Ellinger, 'Trust Receipt Financing' (n 153) 306. In this regard, it would be advisable to avoid using global trust receipts.

[167] *Agnew v IRC* (n 146) [32]; *National Westminster Bank v Spectrum Plus* (n 146) [119], [141].

[168] There are also significant uncertainties regarding how choice of law principles might apply to trust receipts. Given that the trust receipt relates to property rights over tangible property, the *lex situs* will generally apply (see *Winkworth v Christie Manson & Woods* [1980] Ch 496; *Macmillan Inc v Bishopsgate Investment Trust plc (No 3)* [1995] 1 WLR 978 (Ch)), although a different principle may apply when the finance-provider is seeking to assert a claim to receivables or proceeds of sale (see *Raiffeisen Zentralbank v Five Star* (n 104)). There is some uncertainty, however, regarding whether the *lex situs* might be disapplied in favour of a contractual law governing the trust receipt: see *Glencore International AG v Metro Trading International Inc* [2001] 1 Lloyd's Rep 284 (QB) (hereafter *Glencore v Metro Trading*). Assuming the *lex situs* represents the applicable principle, it is unclear whether the relevant *situs* would be the physical location of the goods, the location of the bill of lading, or the location of the proceeds (assuming the pledged goods have been sold). Moreover, the *situs* may change over time, making it important to be able to track the documents, goods, and proceeds (whichever is relevant) at all times.

[169] See ch 10 (Goldby) in this volume.

[170] For the discussion of 'electronic transferable records', see ch 11 (Davidson) in this volume.

[171] *Re David Allester* (n 151) 214.

under one letter of credit) arranging for its bank to issue a second letter of credit on the same terms in favour of the seller's own supplier. The seller's bank is usually content to issue this second credit against an undertaking that the proceeds of the first credit will be paid into the seller's account held with that bank. Accordingly, without actually receiving payment, a seller is able to use its illiquid letter of credit to fund its acquisition of the goods, thereby avoiding a potential credit-crunch if there is a mismatch between its own supplier's credit terms and those of its buyer. Whilst the two letters of credit in a 'back-to-back' arrangement bear a high degree of resemblance, the reality is that there is no legally enforceable link between them. Indeed, in *PT Adaro Indonesia v Rabobank*,[172] the Singapore High Court made clear that, even if both letters of credit relate to the same cargo and have the same documentary requirements, they remain legally separate transactions. As a result, even though the letters of credit are expressed to be 'back-to-back', payment (or the failure to pay) under one credit does not necessarily trigger payment or default under the other credit. Accordingly, the absence of an enforceable linking mechanism means that 'back-to-back' letters of credit provide rather weak legal protection.

D. Modern SCF Techniques

Given the legal uncertainty and practical difficulties surrounding the traditional liquidity-enhancing devices considered above, the development of more flexible financing techniques under the umbrella of 'SCF' is unsurprising. As well as being a 'holistic concept', SCF is also a dynamic one, covering 'a broad range of established and evolving techniques for the provision of finance and management of risk'.[173] Moreover, different SCF techniques can be used in a standalone fashion or in combination. SCF is also 'event-driven' in that the particular liquidity-enhancing technique employed by the parties 'is driven by an event or "trigger" in the physical supply chain'.[174] Accordingly, there is considerable scope for automation of the SCF processes, especially as the SCF-providers require visibility of the underlying trade flows.[175] **14.36**

Such high-level sentiments are not, however, particularly helpful in identifying the detail of those transactions that might arguably fall within the broad notion of SCF. On one level, any loan, overdraft or security could be described as a form of SCF if it is used to finance the sale or purchase of goods or services internationally. It is because of the potentially broad and nebulous nature of SCF that the GSCFF[176] concluded that there was a need to define more closely the 'core' SCF techniques being used by trade parties and to develop standard market-wide definitions to facilitate dialogue around the refinement of current SCF techniques and the development of new ones. Moreover, given the uncertainty described above surrounding the financial reporting and regulation of SCF, a common nomenclature for **14.37**

[172] *PT Adaro Indonesia v Rabobank* [2002] 2 SLR(R) 79 (HC).
[173] GSCFF, 'Standard Definitions' (n 74) 8.
[174] ibid.
[175] ibid.
[176] The GSCFF was established in January 2014 by a number of SCF-industry associations and was facilitated by the ICC 'to address what has been recognised as a need to develop, publish and champion a set of commonly agreed standard market definitions for Supply Chain Finance and for SCF-related techniques': see GSCFF, 'Standard Definitions' (n 74) 11.

'core' SCF techniques can only assist in clarifying how such transactions should be treated for regulatory purposes.[177] To that end, the GSCFF has divided the SCF area into three broad categories:, namely 'Receivables Purchase SCF'; 'Loan or Advance-based SCF'; and 'Enabling Frameworks for SCF'. As regards the last category, the prime example is the Bank Payment Obligation (or 'BPO'); as the BPO has been considered more fully elsewhere,[178] it will not be analysed further below. Accordingly, the present focus is on the first two categories.

1. Receivables Purchase SCF

14.38 The hallmark of the SCF techniques that fall within this first category is that they involve the seller obtaining financing by selling all or part of its receivables to a finance-provider by way of an assignment or transfer in return for the face-value of the receivables, minus a margin or deduction (to reflect the quality of the receivables) and finance charges (reflecting the service provided). Accordingly, the financial institution makes a profit on the transaction and the trader obtains immediate access to liquid funds in place of its illiquid assets. Overall, using the standard terminology suggested by the GSCFF, there appear to be four architype transactions that constitute the category of 'Receivables Purchase SCF', although these transactions do not exist in watertight categories and there will naturally be market variations on the broad themes considered next.

(a) Receivables Discounting

14.39 Sellers may engage in 'receivables discounting', which involves a transaction between a seller and (usually) its bank, whereby the former agrees to 'sell individual or multiple receivables (represented by outstanding invoices) to [the] finance provider at a discount'.[179] The transaction may contemplate the transfer of a single receivable or multiple receivables on a seasonal or continuous basis (sometimes termed 'block discounting'), and in the latter case the facility may be made available to the seller on a committed or uncommitted basis. The transaction will ordinarily be structured as a 'true sale' of the receivables, in the sense that there is an outright assignment to the finance-provider upon the seller providing a certified copy of the relevant invoice or invoice data set.[180] Accordingly, receivables discounting enables the seller to manage its balance sheet.[181] Assuming the buyer is aware of the discounting arrangement, it may be asked to provide validation to the finance-provider of the receivables' existence and genuineness, as well as acknowledging the fact of their assignment.[182] When the receivables fall due, they may be collected by the finance-provider itself (with payment being made directly by the buyer) or by the seller, acting as the finance-provider's agent (with payment being made into an account in the seller's name against which the finance-provider would have special drawing rights).[183] If the receivables are sufficiently high in quality (so that the likelihood of the buyer's default remains sufficiently low), the finance-provider may agree to purchase them without the possibility of having any further

[177] GSCFF, 'Standard Definitions' (n 74) 14.
[178] See ch 13 (Mugasha) in this volume.
[179] GSCFF, 'Standard Definitions' (n 74) 28.
[180] ibid 29. The finance-provider will have to carry out 'know your customer' and anti-money laundering checks at the outset of the transaction and periodically throughout its relationship with the seller: ibid 30.
[181] ibid 32.
[182] ibid 29.
[183] ibid.

recourse against the seller; otherwise, the finance-provider may retain such rights expressly in the discounting agreement to protect against the receivables defaulting. In non-recourse receivables discounting, the finance-provider may manage its own risk through credit-default insurance or by off-loading risk through securitisation, participation, or syndication structures.

Receivables discounting does, however, give rise to three particular practical and legal difficulties, namely whether or not the discounting can occur on a confidential basis and without notice to the buyer (in case this impacts unfavourably upon the seller's continuing business relationship with the buyer); whether the contracts underlying the receivables contain provisions restricting their assignment (as the buyer might wish to retain control over the identity of its creditor); and how the law applicable to the assignment of the receivables is determined. These difficulties will be explored further below.[184] **14.40**

(b) Forfaiting

The seller may seek to improve its liquidity position through 'forfaiting', which will usually involve a 'forfaiting agreement' for existing instruments, or a 'master forfaiting agreement' for existing and future instruments, between the seller and a finance-provider.[185] The parties often choose to subject their forfaiting transaction expressly to the Uniform Rules for Forfaiting ('URF 800'),[186] which is a standard set of rules governing forfaiting agreements in much the same way as the UCP 600 governs documentary letters of credit. The URF 800 also contains annexes setting out template agreements for use in the primary forfaiting market.[187] According to the URF 800, the forfaiting agreement should set out the documents that the seller has to provide to the finance-provider and the price payable for the transferred instruments, as well as the time-frame for presenting the relevant documents and making payment.[188] **14.41**

Like receivables discounting, forfaiting ordinarily operates by way of an outright transfer. That said, forfaiting usually differs from receivables discounting in a number of ways, albeit that particular transactions may involve a degree of convergence between those two types of financing. First, whilst receivables discounting may occur on a recourse or non-recourse basis, the hallmark of forfaiting is non-recourse financing,[189] although the URF 800 recognises exceptions to this core principle when the seller knows of defects in the payment instruments; is not the owner of the instrument; has failed to transfer the instrument properly; has breached the underlying agreement with the buyer; or is guilty of fraud.[190] If the agreement allows the finance-provider to have recourse against the seller, then it cannot be properly classified as an example of forfaiting. Secondly, forfaiting is traditionally limited to the transfer of instruments embodying a payment undertaking (usually bills of exchange and promissory notes, but potentially even letters of credit), rather than 'pure' **14.42**

[184] See subsection E in this chapter.
[185] GSCFF, 'Standard Definitions' (n 74) 35.
[186] ICC, 'Uniform Rules for Forfaiting' (ICC Publication No 800E, 2013) (hereafter 'URF 800').
[187] ibid Annexes 1 and 2.
[188] ibid art 5.
[189] ibid art 4(a): 'On the settlement date, the seller sells to the buyer and the buyer purchases from the seller the payment claim without recourse. The buyer will have no claim against the seller or any prior seller for the non-payment of any amount due in respect of the payment claim . . .'
[190] ibid art 13(b).

non-documentary receivables. Increasingly, 'forfaiting' can extend to non-documentary receivables,[191] but only if the financing is provided on a non-recourse basis. Thirdly, whilst it is always possible for finance-providers to mitigate their exposure to receivables discounting by engaging in various risk-mitigating operations, there happens to be a deep and liquid secondary forfaiting market,[192] which means that finance-providers can dispose of any payment instruments quickly and cheaply to other financial institutions, without having the additional expense of purchasing or negotiating risk-mitigation mechanisms. The reason for these differences between the forfaiting and receivables discounting markets stems from the reification[193] of the payment obligation in a document that is negotiable in character:[194] not only does the finance-provider generally take the instrument free of prior defects in title and the buyer's own equities, but these benefits can equally be passed on to third parties making such instruments highly transmissible. Accordingly, a number of the disadvantages associated with receivables discounting simply do not apply to forfaiting activity,[195] although there certainly remain some difficult choice of law issues. That said, the principal disadvantage of forfaiting is that it still relies upon paper-based instruments that require endorsement and delivery unless in bearer form;[196] if the electronic bill of exchange can be developed successfully,[197] then forfaiting will become a much more attractive option.

(c) Factoring

14.43 'Factoring' may be employed by the seller to manage its cash-flow.[198] In many ways, factoring resembles receivables discounting, since the agreement between the seller and the finance-provider involves an outright transfer of the receivables in return for a discounted payment on a recourse or non-recourse basis.[199] In general, the seller will receive two payments from the factor: upon sending a copy of the relevant invoice to the factor, the seller will receive prepayment of part of the price (usually around 80%); and, upon the buyer paying the invoice, the factor will then transfer the remainder of the price, less any fees and financing charges.[200]

14.44 There are, however, two key differences between factoring and receivables discounting. First, beyond the assignment of the receivables themselves, factoring usually involves 'the finance provider [becoming] responsible for managing the debtor portfolio and collecting payment of the underlying receivables', as well as offering credit insurance protection against the buyer's insolvency.[201] Indeed, the UNIDROIT Convention on International

[191] ibid art 2, which indicates that, according to the definition of 'payment claim', the harmonised rules are not limited to payment undertakings embodied in an instrument. See also GSCFF, 'Standard Definitions' (n 74) 34.

[192] The secondary forfaiting market is so well-developed that the URF 800 contains specific rules governing secondary-market operations: see URF 800 (n 186) arts 8–10.

[193] One consequence of this reification (albeit one frequently described as an anomaly) is that bills of exchange (especially cheques) are susceptible to claims in the tort of conversion: see *OBG Ltd v Allan* [2008] 1 AC 1 (HL).

[194] BEA 1882 (n 132) ss 54, 55.

[195] See subsection E in this chapter.

[196] BEA 1882 (n 132) s 31(3).

[197] See chs 9 (Geva) and 11 (Davidson) in this volume.

[198] In international factoring, an alternative is to use 'a two-factor system' with a factor in each of the buyer's and seller's jurisdictions with the contractual or correspondent relationship to service the buyer and the seller respectively subject to the General Rules for International Factoring promulgated by Factors Chain International: see GSCFF, 'Standard Definitions' (n 74) 43.

[199] ibid; in addition, '[l]imited recourse may be maintained however, to ensure that the seller delivers against specific warranties that are a condition of payment'.

[200] ibid 41.

[201] ibid 39.

Factoring 1988 ('UCIF')[202] makes clear that to qualify as a 'factoring contract' not only must the seller assign the receivables to the finance provider, but the latter must also 'perform at least two of the following functions: finance for the supplier, including loans and advance payments; maintenance of accounts (ledgering) relating to the receivables; collection of receivables; protection against default in payment by debtors'.[203] Accordingly, it is the package of management and collection services beyond the bare provision of financing that makes the finance-provider a factor. Indeed, factoring has become such a specialised branch of SCF that certain financial institutions focus almost exclusively on such activity. Secondly, whilst receivables discounting may occur on a confidential basis, the additional management and collection services provided by a factor usually mean that the assignments will have to be notified to the buyer, as debtor. Indeed, according to the UCIF, a transaction only counts as a 'factoring contract' if 'notice of the assignment of the receivables is to be given to debtors'.[204] The practical consequence is that, under a factoring arrangement, the proceeds of the receivables will generally be paid directly to the factor (although it is possible to have 'non-notification factoring' when the proceeds of the receivables will be paid into the seller's account or an escrow account for forward transmission to the finance-provider).[205] Given these additional services offered by the finance-provider, factoring may attract higher fees that can only be justified if a large number of receivables is involved. In terms of legal difficulties, the requirement of notification to the debtor means that at least one of the legal difficulties associated with receivables discounting (as considered further below) is not relevant; the other legal problems remain the same.

(d) Payables Finance

14.45 The seller's liquidity might be managed through a 'payables finance' structure. Unlike the three types of financing considered above, payables finance is initiated by the buyer rather than the seller, provided that the buyer has established a contractual payables-finance programme with one or more finance-providers. By providing a programme under which sellers can enhance their liquidity, the buyer hopes to attract business. When the buyer concludes a sale contract with a seller, the former will encourage the seller to use the payables-finance programme to obtain immediate payment of its receivables from specified finance-providers.[206] The decision whether to do so or not lies entirely with the seller. If the seller does require liquidity enhancement, it will conclude a contract with the finance-provider to assign its receivables in return for immediate payment of their full value, subject to financing fees and charges. Funds are released to the seller, when the buyer gives its unconditional approval of the particular invoice; this constitutes an unconditional commitment by the buyer to pay the relevant receivables directly to the finance-provider on maturity.[207] Electronic invoicing and automated reconciliation can facilitate this process.[208] As the

[202] According to the UNIDROIT Convention on International Factoring (Ottawa, 28 May 1988) (hereafter 'UCIF') art 14(1), the Convention came into force on 1 May 1995. As there are only currently nine contracting states, the Convention is unlikely to have significant application, as the buyer, seller, and factor must all have places of business in contracting states or the contract must be governed by the law of a contracting state: ibid art 2.

[203] ibid art 1(2)(b).

[204] ibid art 1(2)(c).

[205] GSCFF, 'Standard Definitions' (n 74) 43.

[206] ibid 45.

[207] ibid 46.

[208] ibid 47.

finance-provider is relying upon the buyer's assurances and creditworthiness, the financing will often be provided without recourse to the seller.[209] A 'softer' version of payables finance is 'reverse factoring', where the buyer does not give the finance-provider an irrevocable commitment to pay the invoices, but does furnish the finance-provider with information regarding the invoices that it considers to be valid and accurate.[210] Given that in legal terms the resulting transaction between the seller and the finance-provider is indistinguishable from receivables discounting, the same difficulties apply as are considered further below.

2. Loan or Advance-based SCF

14.46 The hallmark of this category of SCF is that, rather than the finance-provider purchasing receivables or payment instruments from the seller, the finance is advanced in the form of a term loan or revolving facility to provide working capital for the seller's trade-related activities. There are four types of transaction that fall within this broad category.

14.47 First, the seller could obtain a loan or advance against the receivables from its trade activity. Unlike receivables discounting, which requires an outright assignment of the receivables, this form of SCF involves taking security over those receivables, or even simply lending on an unsecured basis in the expectation that the receivables will produce sufficient funds to service the loan.[211] Although granting security over the receivables will reduce the financing costs for the seller and increase the finance-provider's protection, some of the legal difficulties considered below will apply to such a transaction.

14.48 Secondly, rather than lending against the seller's receivables, a finance-provider may secure a loan or advance to either the buyer or seller against the inventory in their warehouse. Whilst the transaction normally takes the form of secured lending, it is possible to structure the transaction as a 'true sale' under a repo agreement. Inventory financing can extend to raw materials (such as minerals, metals, or agricultural products), work-in-progress, and finished products.[212] A pledge and/or charge over the inventory and its proceeds can be created by the delivery of negotiable warehouse receipts when the goods are in storage or the bills of lading (or other transport document) when they are in transit. If the buyer or seller is entitled to use the inventory or their proceeds in the ordinary course of business, then the security will likely take the form of a floating (rather than fixed) charge. Whilst inventory financing is not generally problematic, there is at least one legal difficulty that it entails as considered further below.

14.49 Thirdly, the requisite liquidity may be provided through 'pre-shipment finance', which involves a contract between the finance-provider and seller to provide the funds 'for the sourcing, manufacture or conversion of raw materials or semi-finished goods into finished goods and/or services, which are then delivered to a buyer'.[213] Pre-shipment finance looks similar to loan-based SCF against the seller's receivables, which was considered above, especially as pre-shipment finance can also involve security over the seller's receivables. There is, however, one key difference: lending against receivables involves the finance-provider

[209] ibid 45.
[210] ibid 48.
[211] ibid 49.
[212] ibid 56.
[213] ibid 60.

creating post-shipment liquidity on the strength of the receivables that have already arisen; whereas pre-shipment finance is aimed at providing the working capital needed to produce the goods in question, with the security over the receivables being purely incidental to that core purpose. Similarly, pre-shipment finance differs from loan-based SCF against inventory, which was considered above: inventory-based lending can involve advances to either seller or buyer (according to the location of the relevant inventory); whereas pre-shipment finance can only be advanced to the seller, as it aims to assist with the production of the goods that will subsequently be shipped. Moreover, inventory-based financing necessarily involves taking security over the borrower's inventory, whereas pre-shipment finance may involve other forms of security or even no security at all. Nevertheless, despite these differences, pre-shipment finance is sufficiently close to the other two forms of loan-based SCF considered above that the same types of legal difficulty arise, as considered further below.

Finally, the finance-provider may provide 'distributor finance'. This may be distinguished from the other forms of loan-based SCF, as it is exclusively offered to the buyer. In essence, distributor finance is designed to provide entities purchasing goods with a means of managing their cash-flow, given that there may be a significant period of time between the short credit terms imposed by a large manufacturer and the longer period of time to on-sell the goods in question.[214] The reason why this type of financing deserves special treatment is because it usually involves the large manufacturer entering into a 'master distributor finance agreement' with a finance-provider, which then enters into individual financing arrangements with individual distributors by offering better terms than those entities would have been able to arrange for themselves. Accordingly, such an arrangement is advantageous for the distributor (which can access cheaper finance) and the manufacturer (with which distributors are encouraged to deal). Whilst the finance-provider will often take security over the distributor's receivables or inventory, the manufacturer may also enter into some risk-mitigating or risk-sharing arrangement with the finance-provider. As with other forms of loan-based SCF, the processing speed for transactions can be facilitated through web-based platforms and automated processes. **14.50**

E. Problems

There are three particular legal difficulties that arise from SCF, especially when the technique in question concerns the assignment of receivables whether outright or by way of security for advances. **14.51**

1. Prohibitions or Restrictions on Assignment

The first difficulty arises when an international sale contract (and accordingly the receivable to which it gives rise) contains a provision prohibiting its assignment or transfer. On its face, such a clause would appear to prevent recourse to assignment-based SCF techniques. Indeed, such non-assignment clauses have been held valid in English law as a matter of public policy at the highest level.[215] Accordingly, if there was an attempt by the **14.52**

[214] ibid 52.

[215] *Linden Gardens Trust Ltd v Lenesta Sludge Disposals Ltd* [1994] 1 AC 85 (HL).

seller to transfer the right to payment under a receivable in violation of a non-assignment clause, not only would this constitute a breach by the seller of the underlying sale agreement, but the assignment would not confer any rights upon the finance-provider against the buyer.

14.53 That said, there are techniques that a finance-provider might employ in order to sidestep (or at least minimise) the impact of a non-assignment clause. First, rather than taking an assignment of the right to be paid the receivables' proceeds, the assignment could simply relate to the proceeds themselves: the seller would still retain the *right* to payment, but would be obliged to hand over the *proceeds*, once received, to the finance-provider. From the finance-provider's perspective, such a solution is sub-optimal: as well as having no direct rights against the buyer, the finance-provider's proprietary rights in the proceeds will only 'bite' once the funds are received by the seller, with the result that the finance-provider is effectively bearing a double risk that either the buyer or seller may become insolvent. Whilst this risk can be mitigated to a degree by the finance-provider taking security over the seller's other assets, this is only likely to make SCF more costly and slower than desired. Secondly, rather than taking a direct assignment of the right to be paid the receivable, a seller could declare a trust over that right or its proceeds in favour of the finance-provider. Whilst a trust over the proceeds similarly suffers from the disadvantage that the finance-provider's rights only attach at the moment that the funds are received by the seller, a trust over the chose in action representing the right to payment does not suffer from this weakness, as it is existing rather than future property. As recognised by the English Court of Appeal in *Barbados Trust Co Ltd v Bank of Zambia*,[216] a declaration of trust would appear to confer upon the finance-provider many of the advantages that would derive from a direct assignment: the finance-provider would be entitled to use the *Vandepitte* procedure[217] to bring proceedings against the buyer directly if necessary;[218] and the finance-provider might be able to compel the seller to transfer the legal title to the right to payment pursuant to the rule in *Saunders v Vautier*.[219] Accordingly, despite the non-assignment clause, a declaration of trust over the right to receive payment would effectively operate as the functional equivalent of an assignment. Indeed, given that a trust arrangement will generally destroy the mutuality needed for a set-off to operate, the trust mechanism may even place the finance-provider in a stronger position than if an assignment were actually permitted. Thirdly, as recognised in *First Abu Dhabi Bank PJSC v BP Oil International Ltd*,[220] the finance-provider may seek to protect itself by securing a warranty from the seller that none of the receivables arise from non-assignable contracts. Whilst this may not confer upon the finance-provider any proprietary rights to a particular receivable, such a clause would at least confer upon the finance-provider some possibility of recourse in the event that the receivables are in fact non-assignable.

[216] *Barbados Trust Co Ltd v Bank of Zambia* [2007] 1 Lloyd's Rep 495 (CA) [43], [88] (hereafter *Barbados Trust v Bank of Zambia*). See also *Don King Productions Inc v Warren* [2000] Ch 291 (hereafter *Don King v Warren*) 321; *First Abu Dhabi Bank PJSC v BP Oil International Ltd* [2018] EWCA Civ 14, [28] (hereafter *First Abu Dhabi Bank v BP Oil*).

[217] *Vandepitte v Preferred Accident Insurance Corp of New York* [1933] AC 70 (PC).

[218] *Barbados Trust v Bank of Zambia* (n 216) [44]–[46], [98]–[119].

[219] *Saunders v Vautier* (1841) 4 Beav 115. For a rejection of this contention, see *Don King v Warren* (n 216) 321.

[220] *First Abu Dhabi Bank v BP Oil* (n 216). See also Peter Turner, 'Prohibitions on Assignment: Intellectualism v Law' (2018) 134 LQR 532.

The confusion that has resulted from the English courts simultaneously upholding and undermining non-assignment clauses in equal measure has led to legislative intervention. On a domestic level, assuming the issue is governed by English law, section 1 of the Small Business, Enterprise and Employment Act 2015 allows the Secretary of State to enact regulations invalidating any term preventing or restricting the assignment of receivables that arise out of 'a contract for goods, services or intangible assets (including intellectual property)' when 'at least one of the parties has entered into [the contract] in connection with the carrying on of a business'.[221] Those regulations have now been enacted, providing that 'a term in a contract has no effect to the extent that it prohibits or imposes a condition, or other restriction, on the assignment of a receivable arising under that contract or any other contract between the same parties'.[222] Whilst on their face, the Business Contract Terms (Assignment of Receivables) Regulations 2018 ('the Regulations') would apply to facilitate SCF in the trade finance context, the statutory avoidance of non-assignment clauses does not operate when the seller qualifies as a 'large enterprise'.[223] This important qualification means that the Regulations will only generally operate when SCF is provided to sellers and buyers that qualify as an 'SME'. Nevertheless, where the seller qualifies as a 'large enterprise', the UCIF might operate to invalidate a non-assignment clause, since it provides that '[t]he assignment of a receivable by the supplier to the factor shall be effective notwithstanding any agreement between the supplier and the debtor prohibiting such assignment'.[224] The rationale for these legislative interventions is clear: SCF would become inordinately expensive and slow if finance-providers had to perform due diligence on all the relevant receivables. Accordingly, the direction of travel (both at common law, in domestic legislation, and under international instruments) is to facilitate SCF by enabling the free transfer of receivables, regardless of any contractual restrictions. **14.54**

2. Notice to the Buyer

Secondly, where the particular SCF technique involves an assignment that is notified to the buyer, then the transaction may fall within the scope of section 136(1) of the Law of Property Act 1925, provided that the relevant notice is given in writing. Statutory assignments cause few legal difficulties. In the event that the seller and finance-provider choose not to notify the buyer, the assignment can only be effective in equity.[225] Whilst notice to the buyer may not be a precondition of a valid equitable assignment, it is nevertheless advisable from the finance-provider's perspective to give notice for three reasons. **14.55**

The first reason concerns priority. In the event that the seller were to assign the same receivable twice to different finance-providers (whether as part of a fraudulent scheme or simply because the SCF arrangements with different finance-providers happen to overlap), the priority of claims to the receivable will be determined according to the order in which notice has been given to the buyer.[226] Accordingly, a finance-provider who has not given notice of an equitable assignment runs the risk of losing priority to other finance parties. The second **14.56**

221 Small Business, Enterprise and Employment Act 2015, s 1(3).
222 Business Contract Terms (Assignment of Receivables) Regulations 2018, SI 2018/1254, reg 2(1).
223 ibid reg 3.
224 UCIF (n 202) art 6 (1).
225 *Gorringe v Irwell India Rubber and Gutta Percha Works* (1886) 34 Ch D 128.
226 *Dearle v Hall* (n 139).

reason concerns discharge. Until notice is given to the buyer of the assignment, the buyer is free to discharge its liability by paying the seller; whereas, if the buyer does so after receiving notice, it can be made to pay the same amount again to the finance-provider.[227] The third reason concerns the equities that the buyer might be able to raise. Once notice of an assignment has been given to a debtor, no further set-offs that that debtor might acquire against the assignor after that date can be raised against the assignee.[228] Furthermore, the buyer and seller are no longer free to modify the underlying agreement.[229] Accordingly, by not giving notice, a finance-provider risks the value of the receivables that it has acquired being eroded by the seller's continued dealings with the buyer. To counter this risk, the finance-provider is likely to increase its fees and retain some form of recourse against the seller, including taking security over its other assets. Alternatively, the seller can arrange for the receivables to be embedded in a negotiable instrument and enter into a forfaiting arrangement with the finance-provider: the concept of negotiability would protect the finance-provider from further equities regardless of whether or not notice has been given to the buyer.[230] Accordingly, where there is a desire or need to keep the SCF arrangements confidential from the buyer, forfaiting may provide a better route for achieving the parties' commercial aims.

3. Choice of Law

14.57 Thirdly, there are real choice of law difficulties that arise out of SCF. In the case of loan-based SCF, the position ought to be relatively straightforward, as the respective rights of the seller and finance-provider will generally be determined by the law that the parties have chosen or that is otherwise applicable in the absence of party choice.[231] That said, where the finance-provider takes security over the buyer's or seller's inventory, the validity and effect of that security interest will normally be governed by the *lex situs* of the relevant inventory;[232] whilst this is unproblematic when the inventory is located in the same jurisdiction, the position is more difficult when the inventory is scattered across a number of jurisdictions. In such circumstances, a court would have to apply multiple different laws to the finance-provider's rights over the inventory and the finance-provider would potentially have to perfect or register its security interest in a number of different jurisdictions. To avoid this difficulty, the courts may choose to apply a single, global law to the inventory wherever it is located (most likely the law applicable to the contract between the seller and finance-provider).

14.58 Similar difficulties arise when security is taken over receivables or they are transferred outright to the finance-provider. Whilst the initial view was that the choice of law rule for the

[227] *Brice v Bannister* (1878) 3 QBD 569 (hereafter *Brice v Bannister*).
[228] *Marathon Electrical v Mashreqbank* (n 109).
[229] *Brice v Bannister* (n 227).
[230] BEA 1882 (n 132) ss 29(1), 30(2), 38(2).
[231] Council Regulation (EC) 593/2008 of 17 June 2008 on the Law Applicable to Contractual Obligations [2008] OJ L177/6 (hereafter 'Rome I Regulation') arts 3–4. From 1 January 2021, the Rome I Regulation will continue to apply in the United Kingdom to contracts concluded before 31 December 2020: see Agreement of 12 November 2019 on the Withdrawal of the United Kingdom of Great Britain and Northern Ireland from the European Union and the European Atomic Energy Community [2019] OJ CI384/1, art 66. For contracts concluded after 31 December 2020, the Rome I Regulation will continue to apply in the United Kingdom as part of "retained" EU law: see European Union (Withdrawal) Act 2018, s 3(2)(a). For the amendments to the Rome I Regulation to take account of 'Brexit", see the Law Applicable to Contractual Obligations and Non-Contractual Obligations (Amendment etc) (EU Exit) Regulations 2019, SI 2019/834.
[232] *Glencore v Metro Trading* (n 168).

transfer of intangibles should be their *lex situs* (which would effectively be the jurisdiction where the debtor was located),[233] the modern trend is that an intangible should be governed by the law of the contract that engenders it.[234] Whichever approach is applied, given that the seller will be financing sales to many different buyers, neither provides a satisfactory solution in the SCF context. Accordingly, a special choice of law rule appears to be necessary when dealing with global assignments of receivables, whether by way of security or outright.[235] As in the context of inventory financing, the most obvious candidate is the law applicable to the agreement between the seller and finance-provider.

That said, the choice of law position may be more straightforward when the parties use a negotiable instrument in place of a pure intangible. With respect to bills of exchange, it is tolerably clear that the *lex situs* governs the transfer of negotiable instruments,[236] although it is less certain whether that principle operates by virtue of the statutory choice of law rule in section 72 of the Bills of Exchange Act 1882 or general choice of law principles.[237] Whatever the source of the *lex situs* principle in this context, the *lex situs* would likely be the place where the bill of exchange was endorsed and delivered by the seller to the finance-provider. As this is likely to be the same place for any bills of exchange in the seller's hands, there is no need to develop a special choice of law rule to govern global transfers of such instruments to a finance-provider under a forfaiting arrangement. **14.59**

IV. Conclusion

There can be little doubt that the letter of credit has been on the decline in recent years. Whilst it is possible that the global coronavirus pandemic might lead to their greater use in the short term, the increase in regulation, technology, and innovation will impact upon the continued utility of the letter of credit in the long term. The space left behind has been replaced by trade parties reverting to open-account and prepayment terms and by banks and other finance-providers supporting their customers with various SCF techniques. The current prediction is that trade parties' reliance on SCF will increase year on year. Whilst, as considered above, there are some uncertainties regarding the application of the financial reporting and prudential supervision requirements to SCF, that form of financing should continue to prosper once those uncertainties are resolved. **14.60**

233 Mark Moshinsky, 'The Assignment of Debts in the Conflict of Laws' (1992) 109 LQR 591.

234 Rome I Regulation (n 231) art 14. See also *Raiffeisen Zentralbank v Five Star* (n 104); *WestLB AG v Philippine National Bank* [2012] 4 SLR 894 (HC), aff'd [2014] 1 SLR 1389 (CA). See also Pippa Rogerson, 'The *Situs* of Debts in the Conflict of Laws: Illogical, Unnecessary and Misleading' (1990) 49 CLJ 441.

235 Lord Collins et al (eds), *Dicey, Morris and Collins on the Conflict of Laws* (15th edn, Sweet & Maxwell 2018) vol 2, rule 126(2) (hereafter Collins, *Conflict of Laws*).

236 *Alcock v Smith* [1892] 1 Ch 238; *Embiricos v Anglo-Austrian Bank* [1904] 2 KB 870; *Koechlin et Cie v Kestenbaum Bros* [1927] 1 KB 889 (CA).

237 Collins, *Conflict of Laws* (n 235) vol 2, rule 224(2).

15

Islamic Trade Law and the Smart Contract Revolution

*Jonathan Ercanbrack**

I. Introduction

15.01 Islamic finance was conceptualised as a post-colonial assertion of cultural and religious diversity in the increasingly integrated and harmonised market practices of the global economy. Interest-free (*riba*)[1] banking would help pious Muslims through everyday acts to develop an Islamic communitarian ethos in which everybody gained and in which transparency, honesty, and fairness prevailed. The amalgamation of individual Islamic acts would contribute to restoring Islamic civilisation to its rightful place amongst the community of nations.

15.02 Despite the industry's postcolonial origins, many of the contracts which the industry uses as a conceptual basis derive from Islamic jurisprudence or the body of Islamic law known as sharia. The sharia comprises the holy sources of Islam including the Qur'an which Muslims believe originated from the Prophet Muhammad's revelation of the word of God in the early seventh century CE. However, Islamic jurisprudence (*fiqh*) was developed over the course of nearly two centuries and eventually was applied as a governing legal system throughout the Near and Middle East from around the ninth century CE.[2] This status persisted until the Ottomans undertook a series of reforms known as the *tanzimat*, which preceded the dissolution of the Ottoman Empire as well as the abandonment of the sharia throughout the empire's former territories. Whereas Islamic family law continues to play a role in many Muslim majority jurisdictions, with the possible exception of Saudi Arabia, the commercial rules of the sharia, were almost entirely discarded in favour of secular commercial law.[3] The

* I would like to thank Josh Baker for his excellent research assistance. Thanks also to the steadfast support of Raj Brown and Sara Cattarin for their helpful comments and suggestions. I also benefited from an email exchange with Umar Oseni and thank him for his expertise.

[1] *Riba,* in the Arabic, has been simply defined to convey an unjustified enrichment in which a party receives a monetary advantage without giving a countervalue in return. However, there is considerable scholarly debate as to what this exactly means. The Arabic root of *riba* is *r.b.w.*, which means to increase, to grow or to augment. Yet the technical word for interest is (*fa'ida*). The opacity of *riba*'s meaning resulted in a complex jurisprudence, which created different categorisations of *riba* according to the type of transaction undertaken. For an in-depth analysis see Nabil Saleh, *Unlawful Gain and Legitimate Profit in Islamic Law: Riba, Gharar and Islamic Banking* (Cambridge University Press 1986) (hereafter Saleh, *Unlawful Gain and Legitimate Profit in Islamic Law*).

[2] Technically, the sharia consists of the holy sources: the Qur'an, the Sunna, ijma' (consensus) and *qiyas* (analogical reasoning). Whereas *fiqh* is the 'understanding' of these sources, the jurisprudence which derives therefrom. Scholars increasingly refer to sharia as an umbrella term for both of these meanings. This is the meaning of the term, which I will employ throughout this chapter.

[3] One of the most influential scholars of Islamic law in our time even concludes that 'traditional sharia can surely be said to have gone without return'. See Wael Hallaq, 'Can the Sharia Be Restored?' in Yvonne Y Haddad and Barbara F Stowasser (eds), *Islamic Law and the Challenge of Modernity* (Altamira Press 2004) 42. See also Wael Hallaq, 'Hegemonic Modernity: the Middle East and North Africa During the Nineteenth and Early Twentieth Centuries' in *Shari'a: Theory, Practice, Transformations* (Cambridge University Press 2009) 396.

reasons for this diminished role are complex and numerous but must include the impact of the West and its modernising project, which began with 'legal colonialism'.[4]

The first modern Islamic finance project began in the Nile Delta region of Egypt, where, in 1963, it was implemented to include under-banked and often poor farmers in an equitable and religiously compatible way.[5] Since these modest beginnings, it has become one of the fastest growing financial sectors, comprising over US$2 trillion in assets, and is now facilitated in over sixty countries worldwide. The IMF considers the Islamic finance industry systemically important in more than fourteen jurisdictions.[6] The industry's success, however, has come at the cost of Islamic finance's traditional emphasis on financial inclusion, equitable outcomes, and the avoidance of interest and excessive risk. The invisible hand of the global economy has co-opted Islamic finance in its stream of increasingly harmonised financial practices.[7] The legal and economic substance of Islamic financial products which emerges in global financial markets reflects the neoliberal economic paradigm in which the global economy operates.[8] **15.03**

Paradoxically, the technological revolution may allow Islamic finance to rediscover aspects of its trade-finance roots, helping it to develop trade practices that are cheaper, financially inclusive, transparent, less risky, more efficient and which transfer a greater share of the risk to sellers. Fintech may help the industry to realise Islamic commercial principles to a greater extent. Technologies such as blockchain or distributed ledger technology ('DLT')—a decentralised database infrastructure for storing data and managing software applications—may increase the transparency of supply chains, accelerate the digitalisation of trade processes, and automate trade finance contracts. Other technologies such as the internet of things—everyday devices which communicate with other devices by means of sensors and other processes—enable the tracking of products along the supply chain and help to prevent equipment breakdowns. Artificial intelligence enables machines and computers to perform cognitive functions normally associated with humans. Robots direct warehouse storage, machines package products, and corporations mine big data to determine consumer preferences and behaviour for customised selling. These and other technologies are bringing the world closer together in a 'New Digital Revolution' which promises to enact technology-driven structural change in the trade-based global economy.[9] **15.04**

The general principles of Islamic trade finance have been discussed broadly in the voluminous literature. Most accounts deal with the different modes of facilitating finance including the *murabaha* (cost mark-up sale), *mudaraba*, *musharaka* (both profit- and **15.05**

[4] Muslims refer to legal colonialism as *isti'mar qanuni*. Aharon Layish, 'Islamic Law in the Modern World: Nationalization, Islamization, Reinstatement' (2014) 21 Islamic Law. & Society 276, 277–78.

[5] For a fascinating account by the progenitor of this project, see the German-trained economist, Ahmed El Naggar's, *Zinslose Sparkassen: Ein Entwicklungsprojekt im Nil-Delta* (2nd edn, Al-Kitab Verlag 1982).

[6] Ghiath Shabsigh et al, 'Ensuring Financial Stability in Countries with Islamic Banking' (IMF Country Report No 17/145, International Monetary Fund 2017).

[7] For an analysis of the legal and market mechanisms which drive the standardisation of Islamic financial law, see Jonathan Ercanbrack, 'The Standardization of Islamic Financial Law: Lawmaking in Modern Financial Markets' (2019) 67(4) American Journal of Comparative Law 825 (hereafter, Ercanbrack, 'Standardization of Islamic Financial Law').

[8] Jonathan Ercanbrack, *The Transformation of Islamic Law in Global Financial Markets* (Cambridge University Press 2015) (hereafter Ercanbrack, *Transformation of Islamic Law in Global Financial Markets*).

[9] World Trade Organization, 'World Trade Report 2018' (World Trade Organization 2018) (hereafter 'WTO Report 2018').

loss-sharing partnerships), *wakala* (agency), and *kafala* (guarantee) contracts. Surprisingly, there are very few accounts of the effects of blockchain and smart contracts on Islamic trade finance and its underlying Islamic principles. One pioneering work does not grapple with the transformation of Islamic trade law, nor does it delve into the legal and sharia-related issues that these technologies bring forth.[10] There are several works that deal broadly with the innovative capacity that fintech can provide to Islamic finance in more or less a general sense. This chapter explores the commercial origins and contemporary practice of Islamic trade finance, highlighting its conceptual and practical transformation, and its blockchain- and smart contract-based future. The chapter examines the principles of Islamic trade finance, charting their transformation from the classical past to the present digital era. The chapter argues that the industry's ethical and social mission may be realised to a greater extent by looking to future-oriented technologies such as blockchain for trade finance.

15.06 Using comparative law methodology, which calls for the examination of multiple systems of law and is geared towards the development of new and divergent legal trends, this chapter is organised in the following way: First, a short history of trade and commerce in the Islamic tradition is examined; second, the chapter investigates the development of modern Islamic finance; third, the principles of Islamic commercial law are introduced, followed by fourth, a discussion of the *murabaha* for trade finance; fifth, the way in which English courts have dealt with Islamic financial transactions are considered; and, finally, blockchain and smart contracts for Islamic trade finance are introduced, highlighting its mechanisms, legal, and sharia-related considerations, and their potential to help Islamic trade finance realise its ethical aspirations and efficiency concerns. The conclusion follows.

II. Trade in the Muslim World—Then and Now

15.07 Trade—and its financing—has always been central to the economy of the Muslim world. As land was mostly unfit for agricultural production in southern Arabia, Arabs tended to become traders, manufacturers, navigators, transporters, and middlemen. The dominant

[10] Leisan Safina and Umar A Oseni, 'The Potentials of Smart Contract in Islamic Trade Finance' in Umar A Oseni and S Nazim Ali (eds) *Fintech in Islamic Finance: Theory and Practice* (Routledge 2012) 226 (hereafter, Safina and Oseni, 'Potentials of Smart Contract in Islamic Trade Finance') is the only other account that deals with blockchain, smart contracts, and Islamic trade finance. The article, while pioneering, does not grapple with the wholesale transformation of Islamic trade law, nor does it go into detail regarding legal and sharia-related issues. Hazik Mohamed and Hassnian Ali, *Blockchain, Fintech, and Islamic Finance* (Walter de Gruyter 2019) (hereafter Mohamed and Ali, *Blockchain, Fintech and Islamic Finance*) focus on the wide array of fintech technologies including artificial intelligence, big data, blockchain, machine learning, internet of things devices and more, highlighting the innovative capacity of these technologies for the Islamic finance industry. The book is the first to introduce the topics in any depth and is an important source of further research. See also Islamic Financial Stability Board, 'IFSB Stability Report 2017' (IFSB 2017) (hereafter 'IFSB Report 2017'), which provides a brief analysis of blockchain for cryptocurrency and the interaction of blockchain-based smart contracts with sharia. Furthermore, a number of articles have addressed the compatibility of cryptocurrencies and sharia such as Mohammed Motlaq Assaf, 'Cryptocurrency According to the Objectives of Islamic Law: Bitcoin as a Case Study' (2019) 36 Journal of College of Sharia & Islamic Studies 21, which argues that cryptocurrencies cannot be considered currencies from a sharia perspective; and Mohd Ma'Sum Billah, 'Islamic Cryptocurrency? A Model Structure' (2019) 35 Journal of Islamic Banking & Finance 20, which introduces the 'model' sharia-compatible cryptocurrency in relation to conventional cryptocurrencies such as Bitcoin. Imtiaz Mohammad Sifat and Azhar Mohamad, 'Revisiting Fiat Regime's Attainability of Shari'ah Objectives and Possible Futuristic Alternatives' (2018) 38 Journal of Muslim Minority Affairs 1 is an interesting paper, which briefly sketches the merits of cryptocurrencies for purposes of realising Islam's higher objectives (*maqasid al-sharia*).

historical account indicates that prior to the advent of Islam, the trade activities of the Arabs had acquired significance as the agropastoral economy had merged with the commercial economy of the market towns.[11] Therefore, Islam likely originated in a dynamic trading culture, which at the time was ruled by a wealthy tribe known as the Quraysh. The Qur'an itself has been described as the embodiment of the relations between man and God of a 'strictly commercial nature'. Allah is the merchant and the universe his reckoning, where all is counted, and everything measured. His institution is the Qur'an and He establishes a pattern of honest dealing. Life is a business in which man gains or loses.[12] Indeed, the sharia is highly attuned to the benefits of trade. The Qur'an states, 'let there be among you traffic and trade by mutual good will'[13] and a number of prophetic traditions attest to the merchant's exalted role in the afterlife, such as Muhammad's proclamation that: '*the merchant who is sincere and trustworthy will (at Judgment Day) be among the prophets, the just and the martyrs*'.[14] Indeed, the Prophet Muhammad is to have been the agent of a *qirad* investment with his future wife Khadija and is considered to have been a successful trader in his own right.[15] Furthermore, it is estimated that over 75% of jurists that lived during the ninth and tenth centuries engaged in commerce or handicrafts or had family who did.[16] In fact, the founder of the Hanafi school of Sunni Islam, Abu Hanifah, was a partner in a venture involving the export of silk from Kufa to Baghdad.[17]

The commercial impulse of Islam, which may distinguish the religion amongst the mono- **15.08**
theistic faiths, was evidenced in the practice of medieval trade. Buying and selling on credit was an accepted commercial practice, allowing international and long-term trade to flourish and solving the problem of transporting large sums of money across perilous lands. Credit, in combination with other contracts, was also an effective means of sharing commercial risk.[18] According to a study of the Cairo Geniza records, which document classical Middle Eastern civilisation between the tenth and sixteenth centuries, trade was carried out via mostly informal partnerships in the area between Morocco and Mesopotamia.[19] Partnerships were used for practically every economic activity as they substituted for contracts of employment and loans on interest.[20] Indeed, it is believed that Arabs developed complex credit facilities up to four centuries before the Europeans,[21] and that one of the earliest forms of business association practiced in Europe—the *commenda*—was received

[11] Ziaul Haq, 'Inter-Regional and International Trade in Pre-Islamic Arabia' (1968) 7 Islamic Studies 207, 209–10. For a contrary view which holds that most Arab trade in pre-Islamic Mecca served the domestic needs of southern Arabia, rather than the surrounding empires, see Patricia Crone, *Meccan Trade and the Rise of Islam* (Basil Blackwell 1987).

[12] Charles Torrey, *The Commercial-Theological Terms in the Koran* (EJ Brill 1892) 48.

[13] *The Qur'an*, translated by M A S Abdel Haleem (OUP 2008) 4:29 (hereafter '*The Qur'an*').

[14] Sunan al-Darimi, XVIII, 8. Cf Maxime Rodinson, *Islam and Capitalism* (Allen Lane 1974) 16.

[15] Abraham L Udovitch, *Partnership and Profit in Medieval Islam* (Princeton University Press 1970) 175 (hereafter Udovitch, *Partnership and Profit in Medieval Islam*).

[16] Hayyim Cohen, 'The Economic Background and the Secular Occupations of Muslim Jurisprudence and Traditionalists in the Classical Period of Islam' (1970) 13 Journal of the Economic & Social History of the Orient, 16, 39–40 (hereafter Cohen, 'Economic Background and Secular Occupations of Muslim Jurisprudence').

[17] ibid 26.

[18] Abraham L Udovitch, 'Reflections on the Institutions of Credits and Banking in the Medieval Islamic Near East' (1975) 41 Studia Islamica 5, 2.

[19] Ercanbrack, *Transformation of Islamic Law in Global Financial Markets* (n 8) 79.

[20] S D Goitein, *A Mediterranean Society: the Jewish Communities of the Arab World as Portrayed in the Documents of the Cairo Geniza* (vol 1, Economic Foundations, University of California Press 1967).

[21] Udovitch, *Partnership and Profit in Medieval Islam* (n 15) 77.

by Southern Europe from Arabia following Islamic conquests and was based on the pre-Islamic *qirad*.[22]

15.09 In the modern world, trade within the Muslim world has only grown in importance, with over 20% of all trade between Organisation of Islamic Cooperation ('OIC') countries in 2015 being with other OIC states.[23] In 2005, such trade only constituted 15% of the total,[24] which demonstrates that intra-OIC trade is of ever-increasing importance to the Muslim world. Yet, contrary to its historical prominence, the Middle East and North Africa ('MENA') region has generally been seen as one which under-trades with other countries, relative to its GDP and a number of other factors.[25] In 2017, the MENA region contributed only 5% of global exports and 4.3% of total imports. Non-tariff barriers in the region are seen as particularly high including burdensome technical regulations, import authorisation procedures, cumbersome customs clearance, and border controls. Moreover, there is little transparency, harmonisation, or standardised procedures for cross-border trade facilitation in the region, amongst other structural shortcomings. Heavy investment in trade-related infrastructure and logistics, trade facilitation, and digitalisation of the economy are seen as imperative if the region hopes to meet its contemporary challenges.[26]

15.10 Islamic trade finance is seen as having great potential in this context, but it is important not to overstate the current importance of sharia-compliant trade finance to intra-OIC trade. While the International Islamic Trade Finance Corporation was set up by the Islamic Development Bank to facilitate sharia-compliant trade finance and has successfully used sharia-compliant trade financing in projects from Kazakhstan[27] to Burkina Faso,[28] sharia-compliant trade finance accounts for only 1.14% of intra-OIC trade according to a 2018 article.[29] Therefore, while the Islamic finance industry—including Islamic trade finance—is growing, it remains a niche market in all economies apart from those which have fully Islamised their banking systems or in which Islamic banking and finance have become systemically important.[30] Nonetheless, the industry provides a useful case study for examining

[22] The *qirad* is a profit- and loss-sharing partnership, similar to the *mudharaba*, and is used to finance trade. See Udovitch, *Partnership and Profit in Medieval Islam* (n 15) 172; Abraham L Udovitch, 'At the Origins of the Western Commenda: Islam, Israel, Byzantium?' (1962) 37 Speculum 198, 207.

[23] Emmy Abdul Alim, 'What Is the Value of Trade Among the Mostly Muslim-Majority 57 OIC Countries?' (*Salaam Gateway*, 25 October 2017) <https://www.salaamgateway.com/en/story/what_is_the_value_of_trade_among_the_%20mostly_muslimmajority_57_oic_countries-SALAAM25102017072648/> accessed 4 June 2019.

[24] Organisation of Islamic Cooperation, 'OIC-2025: Programme of Action' (OIC) <https://www.oic-oci.org/docdown/?docID=16&refID=5> accessed 4 June 2019.

[25] Alberto Behar and Caroline Freund, 'The Trade Performance of the Middle East and North Africa' (Forum for Research in International Trade, July 2011) <https://freit.org/WorkingPapers/Papers/TradePatterns/FREIT321.pdf> accessed 4 July 2019.

[26] Nasser Saidi and Aathira Prasad, 'Trade and Investment Policies in the MENA Region' (Background Note) (MENA-OECD Working Group on Investment and Trade, 28 November 2018) 5–7.

[27] International Islamic Trade Finance Corporation, 'ITFC's Investment of Wheat in Kazakhstan' (*International Islamic Trade Finance Corporation*) <http://www.itfc-idb.org/en/content/itfcs-investment-wheat-kazakhstan> accessed 4 June 2019.

[28] International Islamic Trade Finance Corporation, 'ITFC Supports Burkina Faso's Cotton Sector With €85 Million Syndicated Murabaha Financing' (*International Islamic Trade Finance Corporation*) <http://www.itfc-idb.org/en/content/itfc-supports-burkina-fasos-cotton-sector-eu85-million-syndicated-murabaha-financing-1> accessed 4 June 2019.

[29] Arno Maierbrugger, 'Islamic Trade Finance Has Much More Potential' (*Gulf Times*, 20 March 2018) <https://www.gulf-times.com/story/585900/Islamic-trade-finance-has-much-more-potential> accessed 4 June 2019.

[30] Iran, Sudan, Brunei, Saudi Arabia, Kuwait, Qatar, Malaysia, the United Arab Emirates, Bangladesh, Djibouti, Jordan, and Bahrain comprise Islamic banking and financial assets of 15% or more of total banking and financial assets in their respective economies. See Islamic Financial Services Board, 'Islamic Financial Services Stability Report 2018' (IFSB 2018) 9.

modern Islamic trade-finance mechanisms, their classical roots, and the implications of technological development.

III. The Development of the Modern Islamic Finance Industry

To understand Islamic trade finance, it is necessary to briefly examine the history of Islamic finance as a concept. In the classical period, as mentioned above, trade and its finance were conducted through informal partnerships, but the concept of modern finance was introduced to the Muslim world alongside colonialism.[31] From the middle of the nineteenth century colonialism caused almost all Muslim countries to adopt Western laws and legal systems, and this was particularly apparent in the commercial sphere.[32] Furthermore, the concept of the nation state, previously alien to Muslims, was introduced and took control from the jurists who had always served as a counterbalance to rulers.[33] The sharia's inherent pluralism and its base in unchanging texts meant that codification of its principles further distorted it and gradually removed it from the lives of Muslims.[34] By the end of the nineteenth century, these developments had combined to ensure that the financial systems of most Muslim countries were Westernised and secularised,[35] as can be seen in the fact that interest was permitted in the Egyptian Civil Code.[36] 15.11

Such developments caused inevitable discontent amongst some Muslims, with the influential Iraqi Shia mufti, Muhammad Baqir Al-Sadr, denouncing the 'long, bitter history of exploitation and struggle' that the Muslim world had faced under colonialism.[37] Similarly, the activist and founder of the Muslim Brotherhood, Hassan Al-Banna, claimed that Western social principles had failed as they had not helped man reach 'rest and tranquillity'.[38] Thinkers such as Al-Banna and Al-Sadr advocated a return to Islam,[39] seeing it as a third way that would aid the development of the Muslim world more than either capitalism or communism.[40] This would be done through 'Islamic economics': the creation of 15.12

[31] Ibrahim Warde, *Islamic Finance in the Global Economy*, (Edinburgh University Press 2000) 49 (hereafter Warde, *Islamic Finance in the Global Economy*).

[32] Habib Ahmed, 'Islamic Law, Adaptability, and Financial Development' (2006) 13 Islamic Economic Studies 79, 85. From the mid-nineteenth century the sharia was largely abandoned in favour of European law codes, mainly from France. Upon independence, many states in the MENA region adopted the Egyptian or Kuwaiti law codes but these were derived from European civil law influences, primarily the French Civil Code. In particular, the Egyptian Civil Code of 1948 influenced the civil codes of many Arab countries. See David Suratgar, 'The Development of the Legal Systems of the Middle East; Islamic Law and the Importance of Civil Law to the Process of Modernisation' in Brian Russell (ed), *An Introduction to Business Law in the Middle East* (Drake Publishers 1975) 9.

[33] Wael B Hallaq, '"Muslim Rage" and Islamic Law' (2003) 54 Hastings Law Journal 1705, 1710–11 (hereafter Hallaq, '"Muslim Rage" and Islamic Law').

[34] ibid 1713; Haider Ala Hamoudi, 'The Muezzin's Call and the Dow Jones Bell: On the Necessity of Realism in the Study of Islamic Law' (2008) 56 America Journal of Comparative Law 423, 434–35 (hereafter Haider A Hamoudi, 'Muezzin's Call and the Dow Jones Bell').

[35] Warde, *Islamic Finance in the Global Economy* (n 31) 36.

[36] ibid 49.

[37] Muhammad Al-Sadr, 'The Psychological Role of Islam in Economic Development' in John J Donohue and John L Esposito (eds), *Islam in Transition: Muslim Perspectives* (OUP 2007) 252 (hereafter Al-Sadr, 'Psychological Role of Islam in Economic Development').

[38] Hassan Al-Banna, 'The New Renaissance' in John J Donohue and John L Esposito (eds), *Islam in Transition: Muslim Perspectives* (OUP 2007) 60 (hereafter Al-Banna, 'The New Renaissance').

[39] ibid 62; Al-Sadr, 'The Psychological Role of Islam in Economic Development' (n 37) 254, 258.

[40] Charles Tripp, *Islam and the Moral Economy: The Challenge of Capitalism* (Cambridge University Press 2006) 111 (hereafter Tripp, 'Islam and the Moral Economy').

the idealised *Homo Islamicus*, whose pious actions would build an alternative system to the capitalist one built on the greed of *Homo Economicus*.[41] And what better to represent the inherent greed of capitalist economics than the charging of interest? Interest is prohibited in classical Islamic law, and yet in the modern era jurists had allowed interest to be paid.[42] Islamic economists saw the charging of interest as an injustice as it kept money in the hands of the moneyed classes and disincentivised the assumption of risk in equity-based investments as interest on a loan is payable regardless of the success of the venture in question.[43] Moreover, some opponents of interest denounced as a 'fraud' the ability to make money out of nothing by demanding interest be paid alongside the principal.[44]

15.13 In resisting interest in the modern world, Islamic finance now had a purpose, a 'desire to articulate a form of political, economic and social order that resists the dominant global paradigms and creates a separate, self-defined Islamic identity resting on unique ethical and moral bases'.[45] Yet, without the quadrupling of oil prices between 1973 and 1974, and the attendant talk of a new international economic order that this generated, perhaps Islamic finance would not have come into existence.[46]

15.14 In the 1970s, the first commercial Islamic banks were formed, with the purpose of creating a more socially valuable banking system. In practice, this meant a two-tier partnership, where individuals invested in the bank, and the bank invested in ventures, and profits and losses were shared in proportion to the amount invested.[47] Unfortunately, this proved unpopular with clients who had become used to the minimal risk of loss present in conventional deposits, and the cost of monitoring all the bank's investments proved too high to be practicable.[48] Thus, the idealism of the early Islamic finance industry began to fade, and instead the industry had to adapt to survive.[49] Meanwhile, the dreams of a new economic order began to fade as oil prices fell sharply in 1986.[50] This, combined with the end of the Cold War, the rise of neoliberalism, and the growing importance of technology, meant that a new type of Islamic finance was born out of necessity.[51] Islamic financial institutions have gradually moved away from profit and loss sharing structures towards structures more akin to conventional products.[52] One of those products, the *murabaha* agreement, is of particular importance to Islamic trade finance and will be examined shortly. First, the principles of classical Islamic commercial law—which modern Islamic finance still relies on for legitimacy—will be introduced.

[41] ibid 122.
[42] ibid 127.
[43] Haider A Hamoudi, 'Muezzin's Call and the Dow Jones Bell' (n 34) 453–54.
[44] Tarek El Diwany 'Travelling the Wrong Road Patiently' *Middle East Banker* (September 2003).
[45] Haider Ala Hamoudi, 'Muezzin's Call and the Dow Jones Bell' (n 34) 425.
[46] Warde, *Islamic Finance in the Global Economy* (n 31) 93.
[47] Haider A Hamoudi, 'Muhammad's Social Justice or Muslim Cant?: Langdellianism and the Failures of Islamic Finance' (2007) (40) Cornell International Law Journal 89, 116–17 (Haider A Hamoudi, 'Langdellianism and the Failures of Islamic Finance').
[48] ibid.
[49] Tripp, 'Islam and the Moral Economy' (n 40) 142.
[50] Warde, *Islamic Finance in the Global Economy* (n 31) 78.
[51] ibid 78–80.
[52] Haider A Hamoudi, 'Langdellianism and the Failures of Islamic Finance' (n 47) 118–19.

IV. Principles of Islamic Commercial Law

A. Ownership and its Limits

Ownership (*al-milkiyyah*) is an Islamic legal relationship between a human being and property, which specifically attaches the said property to him/her. An owner is entitled to deal in his property unless there is a legal restriction which prevents him/her from doing so. Yet to speak of 'ownership' in the Western context with regards to Islamic law is somewhat misleading. In fact, all property is owned by God, evidenced by the verse: 'To Allah does belong the dominion of the heaven and the earth, and all that is therein.'[53] To be the owner of a piece of property is thus to be a trustee and vice-regent of the said property—'and spend out of that whereof He has made you heirs'.[54] In Islam property is not to be considered an end in itself but simply a means of satisfying human needs and wants. Indeed, humans are warned of the dangers of excessive consumption in an earlier verse: 'Eat not up your property among yourselves in vanities, but let there be among you traffic and trade in good will.'[55] All property rights in Islam should be viewed in the light of this verse, and constrained to avoid causing harm to others. 15.15

B. The Nature of Property

Property (*mal*) was not defined in either the Qur'an, or the Sunna, and as such its definition has been left to juristic interpretation.[56] While there are some differences between the schools regarding what constitutes *mal*, some general principles can be abstracted, which may affect the types of trade that can be financed Islamically: 15.16

1. To qualify as mal, something must be naturally desired by man. In modern terms, this can be defined as having commercial value.
2. It must also be capable of being owned and possessed. So, for example, fish in the sea or birds in the sky are not mal as it is impossible to possess them.
3. It must be capable of being stored.
4. It must be beneficial in the eyes of the sharia. Hence, poisonous substances and carrion are not considered mal. Additionally, there appears to be a *de minimis* threshold here, as small amounts of any good which are incapable of benefiting wider society, such as single ears of corn, are not considered mal.
5. Finally, the ownership of the thing must be assignable and transferable.[57]

As a result of this taxonomy, Islamic law makes a distinction between material things (*'ayn*) and immaterial things (*dayn*). *Dayn* is often considered to be a debt, but can be described as something which is not present, yet to be paid or completed, but is already owned by the creditor under a contract.[58] *Dayn* cannot be described to be in the creditor's possession; 15.17

[53] *The Qur'an* (n 13) 5:120.
[54] ibid 57:7.
[55] ibid 4:29.
[56] Muhammad W Islam, 'Al-Mal: The Concept of Property in Islamic Legal Thought' (1999) 14 Arab Law Quarterly 361, 362 (hereafter W Islam, 'The Concept of Property in Islamic Legal Thought').
[57] ibid 365.
[58] Ercanbrack, *Transformation of Islamic Law in Global Financial Markets* (n 8) 64.

instead, *dayn* is embedded within their human capacity.[59] As such, Foster equates *dayn* with the common law concept of a 'chose in action'.[60]

15.18 One area in which this debate has surfaced in modern Islamic finance is in relation to intellectual property rights. If these rights are seen as dependent on corporeal matter, then they would be considered *'ayn*. If not, then due to the prohibition of *riba* described below, they could only be exchanged at par value.[61] Furthermore, the distinction proves vastly important to the debt-oriented modern finance industry as the sale of a debt for another debt at a discount (*bay'al-dayn bi al-dayn*) is not valid.[62] Therefore, debt may only be traded or assigned at par value. An oft-cited Hadith supported this prohibition: 'The Messenger of God forbade sale of the delayed obligation (*al-kali'*) for a delayed obligation'.[63]

C. *Riba*

15.19 The prohibition of *riba* is perhaps the most widely known principle of Islamic commercial law. *Riba* literally means 'increase' and has been defined as an unjust enrichment in which one party to an agreement receives a monetary advantage without giving a countervalue in return.[64] The Qur'an exhorts generosity and the avoidance of exploitation of those worse off.[65] In theory, the prohibition of *riba* serves to replace zero-sum transactions with more just and equitable ones, as by removing the possibility of charging money for a loan transaction, only charitable loans—either gifts or loans requiring no interest—are available to lenders and these cannot be the source of commercial profitmaking.[66]

15.20 *Riba's* prohibition can be traced to several verses of the Qur'an, including 'You who believe, do not consume usurious interest, doubled and redoubled [. . .] beware of the Fire prepared for those who ignore [this],'[67] and 'God has allowed trade and forbidden usury.'[68] Through *qiyas* the principle of *riba* gradually expanded. In Islamic commercial law, *riba* encompasses two related phenomena. First, *riba al-fadl*, which can be described as the inequality of countervalues in a given exchange of items of the same type—for example, trading an amount of gold for a larger amount of gold or silver,[69] or trading one *dayn* for another *dayn* at a discount.[70] More relevant to modern financial practices is the prohibition of *riba al-nasi'a*, which can be defined as the deferred completion of such an exchange, regardless of whether the deferment is accompanied

[59] ibid.
[60] Nicholas H D Foster, 'Transfers of Rights and Obligations in the U.A.E: A Comparative Analysis in the Light of English Law, French Law and the Shari'a' in Eugene Cotran (ed) *Yearbook of Islamic and Middle Eastern Law*, vol VII (Brill 2000–2001) 41 (hereafter Foster, 'Transfer of Rights and Obligations in the UAE').
[61] Ercanbrack, *Transformation of Islamic Law in Global Financial Markets* (n 8) 65.
[62] Wahbah Al-Zuhayli, *Financial Transactions in Islamic Jurisprudence* (translated by Mahmoud A El-Gamal, vol I, Dar al-Fikr 2003) 81 (hereafter Al-Zuhayli, *Financial Transactions in Islamic Jurisprudence*).
[63] Foster, 'Transfer of Rights and Obligations in the UAE' (n 60) 43.
[64] Joseph Schacht, *An Introduction to Islamic Law* (Clarendon Press 1964) 145.
[65] See for example, *The Qur'an* (n 13) 30:39 which compares *ribawi* loans unfavourably with charitable giving.
[66] Ercanbrack, *Transformation of Islamic Law in Global Financial Markets* (n 8) 71.
[67] *The Qur'an* (n 13) 3:130.
[68] ibid 2:275.
[69] Saleh, *Unlawful Gain and Legitimate Profit in Islamic Law* (n 1) 17.
[70] Al-Zuhayli, *Financial Transactions in Islamic Jurisprudence* (n 62) 81.

by an increase to one of the countervalues.[71] This prohibits charging a time value for money.[72]

All four major schools differ in their rules regarding when a transaction will be considered *ribawi* in nature, but it should be noted that over time there has been a trend towards a more rigid and conservative definition of *riba*.[73] This remains true to this day, although the translation of *riba* in modern editions of the Qur'an has been changed to 'usury', which may reflect a narrower focus on the prohibition of interest in modern Islamic finance when compared to its more expansive prior definitions.[74] **15.21**

D. *Gharar*

Gharar is another important prohibition of Islamic commercial law. It was developed by analogy from the Quranic prohibition of gambling and can be defined as the prohibition of risk, uncertainty, and speculation.[75] Its effect is to prohibit so-called zero-sum contracts where one party stands to gain at the expense of another's loss.[76] As Hassan notes, the rationale for the prohibition is a belief that a just profit should be the result of one's labour, time, and expenditure, and not simply 'winning' a speculative transaction.[77] As with the prohibition of *riba*, this appears to be Islamic law's attempt to create mutually beneficial contracts, and to prevent the exploitation of the weak by the strong.[78] It is important to note that Islamic law has no problem with a contract having an unequal result, if that result was not inherent to the contract itself in the form of *gharar*. What is important is that profit derives from the assumption of liability (*al-kharaj bi al-kharaj*). Without taking on commercial risk, the basis for profit-making in Islamic law does not exist. **15.22**

With respect to the sales contracts that form the backbone of Islamic trade finance, *gharar* in a transaction can take many forms. Ibn Rushd, a Maliki scholar, wrote that *gharar* in sales transactions causes the buyer to suffer damage for want of knowledge which affects either of the countervalues to the contract. As such, he specified five conditions that had to be met for *gharar* to be averted. These are: **15.23**

1. The price and the subject matter of the contract must be in existence. This is related to the rules on the nature of property discussed above.
2. The characteristics of the above countervalues must be known.
3. The amount of the countervalues must be determined.
4. The parties must have full control over both countervalues, to ensure that the transaction can take place.

[71] Saleh, *Unlawful Gain and Legitimate Profit in Islamic Law* (n 1) 17.
[72] Ercanbrack, *Transformation of Islamic Law in Global Financial Markets* (n 8) 76.
[73] Fazlur Rahman, 'Riba and Interest' (1964) 3 Islam Studies 1, 13.
[74] Haider A Hamoudi, 'Muezzin's Call and the Dow Jones Bell' (n 34) 460.
[75] Ercanbrack, *Transformation of Islamic Law in Global Financial Markets* (n 8) 62.
[76] Nayla Comair-Obeid, *The Law of Business Contracts in the Arab Middle East* (Kluwer Law International 1996) 55 (hereafter Comair-Obeid, *The Law of Business Contracts in the Arab Middle East*).
[77] Hussein Hassan, 'Contracts in Islamic Law: The Principles of Commutative Justice and Liberality' (2002) 13 Journal of Islamic Studies 257, 280.
[78] Sami Al-Suwailem, 'Towards an Objective Measure of Gharar in Exchange' (2000) 7 Islamic Economic Studies 61.

5. If any part of the contract is to be performed on a future date, that date must be defined.[79]

15.24 Throughout the history of Islamic law, commercial necessity has dictated that the rigidities of *gharar* be avoided in certain instances. For example, the bartering of livestock for meat was tolerated even though the unknown differences of the countervalues in the transaction violated both *gharar* and *riba*.[80] There has always been some element of *gharar* inherent to all trading, with respect to at least one portion of the transaction. For this reason, modern jurists such as Sanhuri saw *gharar* as more of a sliding scale than something to be completely eradicated from all commercial dealings.[81] Excessive *gharar* is to be completely prohibited, while more trivial instances of *gharar* are to be tolerated, although what constitutes excessive *gharar* is for each jurist to decide.

E. Freedom of Contract and the System of Islamic Nominate Contracts

15.25 In Islam, all obligations to which human beings are subjected arise out of the covenantal encounter between man and God.[82] This can be seen in several passages of the Qur'an, for example, 'verily those who swear allegiance to thee, swear allegiance really to God',[83] and 'Fulfil the covenant of God when ye have entered into it and break not your oaths after ye have confirmed them.'[84] The importance of fulfilling one's obligations is made more explicit in the command: 'Ye who believe! Fulfil all obligations!'[85] These passages are the source of the principle of the sanctity of contract in Islamic law.

15.26 Traditionally, Islamic law recognised no specific freedom of contract. Instead, by reference to the Qur'an and the Sunna (the sayings and doings of the Prophet Muhammad exemplified in written traditions known as *hadith*), and the application of *qiyas* (analogical reasoning) by jurists, a system of nominate contracts was developed.[86] Nominate contracts are a set of contracts in which jurists developed specific names and concise rules. The Islamic jurist's casuistic approach elicited subtle rules pertaining to specific contracts rather than formulating broad theories such as a general theory of obligations. The majority of scholars focused on the contract of sale as a kind of model for contracts. A sale contract can be defined as an immediate and concurrent exchange for a fixed price in cash or kind. The delivery of the goods cannot be delayed so that the contract resembles a barter transaction. The sale contract requires an exchange of offer (*ijab*) and acceptance (*qabul*) but these are not promissory. Offer and acceptance are understood as performatives, as 'constitutive, dispositive utterances', which to indicate finality, are to be phrased in the past tense. Therefore, the parties create immediate entitlements in each other, so that the goods pass

[79] Ibn Rushd, *The Distinguished Jurist's Primer, a Translation of Al-Bidayat Al-Mujtahid* (translated by Imran A K Nyazee, vol II, Garnet Publishing Limited 1996) 148, 172.
[80] Ercanbrack, *Transformation of Islamic Law in Global Financial Markets* (n 8) 67–68.
[81] Saleh, *Unlawful Gain and Legitimate Profit in Islamic Law* (n 1) 68.
[82] Bernard Weiss, *The Spirit of Islamic Law* (University of Georgia Press 1998) 26–31.
[83] *The Qur'an* (n 13) 48:10.
[84] ibid 16:91.
[85] ibid 5:1.
[86] Susan E Rayner, *The Theory of Contracts in Islamic Law* (Arab and Islamic Laws Series, Graham & Trotman 1991) 100.

to the buyer as soon as the contract has been concluded.[87] It would seem that the objective of the immediate exchange in the contract of sale is to avoid *riba* and *gharar* as discussed above.[88] Characteristically, the focus is on the subject matter of the contract as opposed to any obligation to which the contract gives rise. However, in practice the system was much more varied. Due to the requirements of business, the exceptions and qualifications far outnumber the rule. Such exceptions came to be known as innominate contracts. An example is the *bay' al-salam* or forward sale in which the subject matter does not yet exist, but the seller undertakes to make it available at a later date to the purchaser. The non-existent subject matter is a promise given in exchange for immediate payment. This kind of sale would normally be unlawful as the seller sells what is not in existence.[89]

Similarly, the extent to which parties to a contract may append conditions (*shurut*) to an agreement has been the subject of much debate, with some schools adopting a more conservative approach than others.[90] For the purposes of modern Islamic finance, the liberal view articulated by the Hanbali scholar Ibn Taymiyyah, that 'the parties decide as they wish the content of their juridical acts and determine the effects on the condition that these effects are not contrary to public order and morals',[91] has been adopted. While this gives the appearance of greater party contractual freedom, there are still some important limitations. The most important such limitation in Islamic trade finance is the inability to combine two contracts together, or to make fulfilment of one contract necessary in the fulfilment of another.[92] **15.27**

Due to what has been described as the inherently common law nature of Islamic finance, the industry looks to the old nominate contracts to legitimise modern financial practices.[93] Now that the sources and general principles of Islamic trade financing law have been enumerated, the way in which a traditional nominate contractual form has been adapted for modern trade financing purposes will be described. **15.28**

V. Islamic Trade Finance in Practice: The *Murabaha* Contract

While many, if not all, of the nominate contractual forms available to Islamic finance practitioners can be used as trade financing mechanisms, for reasons of space they cannot all be discussed here. Instead, the most used contractual form in the Islamic finance industry—the *murabaha*, which according to most estimates accounts for over 80% of the Islamic banking business[94]—will be examined. **15.29**

[87] Aron Zysow, 'The Problem of Offer and Acceptance: A Study of Implied-in-Fact Contracts in Islamic Law and the Common Law' (1985-86) 34 Cleveland State Law Review 69, 76 (hereafter Zysow, 'Problem of Offer and Acceptance').

[88] Noor Mohammed, 'Principles of Islamic Contract Law' (1988) 6 Journal of Law and Religion 115, 123 (hereafter Mohammed, 'Islamic Contract Law').

[89] See Nabil Saleh, 'Definition and Formation of Contract under Islamic and Arab Laws', (1990) 5 Arab Law Quarterly 101; Comair-Obeid, *The Law of Business Contracts in the Arab Middle East* (n 76).

[90] See Ercanbrack, *Transformation of Islamic Law in Global Financial Markets* (n 8) 59–62 for an overview.

[91] Comair-Obeid, *The Law of Business Contracts in the Arab Middle East* (n 76) 38.

[92] Noel J Coulson, *Commercial Law in the Gulf States* (Graham & Trotman 1984) 54. This restriction has been overcome in Islamic trade finance through 'Promises to Purchase' and other such undertakings.

[93] Mahmoud A El-Gamal, *Islamic Finance: Law, Economics and Practice* (Cambridge University Press 2006) 64.

[94] Warde, *Islamic Finance in the Global Economy* (n 31) 133.

15.30 The *murabaha* has been defined as 'a fiduciary credit sale with a fixed and disclosed profit margin over the cost of the subject matter of the sale'.[95] It has a pre-Islamic origin and its original purpose appears to have been to assist less knowledgeable purchasers in determining a fair price for unfamiliar goods.[96] Thus, it was more a form of trade rather than a method of trade finance.[97] However, the inherent flexibility of the *murabaha* structure means that it can be used to approximate many conventional financial transactions, which makes it the perfect mode of finance for the acquisition of assets, goods, or commodities.[98] As well as serving a trade-finance purpose, the *murabaha* can also be used for other purposes including liquidity and risk management and the raising of capital,[99] which explains why it lies at the core of much of the current Islamic finance industry's business. The basic features of the *murabaha* as a means of trade finance will now be discussed.[100]

A. Structure, Profit, and Fees

15.31 Like many nominate contractual forms, the *murabaha* is based on the contract of sale, and therefore must first meet the requirements of a sale contract under Islamic law. Those requirements can be summarised as being: a buyer and seller; an object—both the price of the contract and the consideration provided for this price; and an expression of offer and acceptance.[101] Several *shurut* are also read into sale contracts, meaning that the contract will not be valid if one of the parties is a child, or is not sane, or if the offer and acceptance are not given during the same contract session.[102]

15.32 In its most basic form in relation to trade finance, the *murabaha* involves a financial institution and a customer. The customer wishes to purchase an asset from a third party and engages the financial institution to do this. The financial institution (seller) then acquires title to the asset from the third party before entering into a sales contract with the customer (purchaser) where the seller discloses the initial purchase price of the asset and both parties agree upon a profit margin which the purchaser agrees to pay to the seller in addition to the initial purchase price and in consideration for the asset. Deferred payment terms are agreed and then title to the asset is transferred from the seller to the purchaser.

15.33 The disclosure of the price of the asset and the agreement of a profit margin are fundamental to the *murabaha* structure, which is categorised as a type of trust sale (*bay' al-amanah*). Without this step, the contract is a normal type of sale contract (*musawamah*). In addition to disclosing the initial price of the asset, the seller must also disclose whether

[95] Craig R Nethercott, '*Murabaha and Tawarruq*' in Craig R Nethercott and David M Eisenberg (eds) *Islamic Finance: Law and Practice* (OUP 2012) 193 (hereafter Nethercott, '*Murabaha* and *Tawarruq*').

[96] ibid 192–93.

[97] ibid 193.

[98] ibid.

[99] ibid 200–05 contains some case studies of the different uses of the *murabaha*.

[100] Subsections A–F below are based on the detailed description of the *murabaha* found in Nethercott, '*Murabaha* and *Tawarruq*' (n 95) at 193–97. Where other sources are used in addition, they will be referenced.

[101] Umar F Moghul and Arshad A Ahmed, 'Contractual Forms in Islamic Finance Law and *Islamic Inv. Co. of the Gulf (Bahamas) Ltd. v. Symphony Gems N.V. & Ors.*: A First Impression of Islamic Finance' (2003) 27 Fordham International Law Journal 150, 167 (hereafter Moghul and Ahmed, 'Contractual Forms in Islamic Finance Law').

[102] ibid, 167–68.

they obtained the asset in question on deferred payment terms.[103] Once the price has been agreed it cannot be modified under any circumstances due to the prohibition on *riba* discussed above. Similarly, there can be no uncertainty as to the price, for that would amount to *gharar*.

There is debate between the schools as to how the cost price of the asset may be calculated. For example, and importantly in the trade-finance context, can expenses such as insurance, transportation, and packing be included within the cost price? The Accounting and Auditing Organization for Islamic Financial Institutions ('AAOIFI'), a respected standard setting body for the industry, follows the Hanbali view that any expenses such as those mentioned above can be added to the cost price, if they are disclosed by the seller and both parties to the transaction agree to it.[104] However, if such an expense is 'customarily considered as normal' to the transaction at hand, then it can be included in the cost price without disclosure to the purchaser.[105] The cost price must not include a conventional upfront fee or facility fee in consideration for the transaction,[106] which is an important difference between the *murabaha* and conventional trade finance methods such as the letter of credit. **15.34**

B. Payment Schedule

The pre-agreed price may be paid at any time on a deferred basis, either in instalments or as a lump sum. There is no restriction as to the timing of the payments—parties are free to contract according to their commercial requirements—except that the payment timings be agreed as part of the sale transaction.[107] **15.35**

C. Title to the Asset

The seller must obtain the title to the asset before it can be transferred to the purchaser. The ownership of the title to the asset must be real—although it can be actual or constructive depending on the nature of the asset[108]—and the seller need not take physical possession of the goods prior to selling them. **15.36**

D. Agency

It is permissible for the financial institution to authorise an agent, other than the purchase orderer (customer), to carry out the purchase. Only in 'dire need' should the customer be appointed to act as an agent. The agent must not sell the asset to himself. Rather the **15.37**

[103] It is not permissible to carry out a *murabaha* on deferred payment terms where the asset involved is gold, silver, or currencies. See Accounting and Auditing Organization for Islamic Financial Institutions, 'Shari'ah Standard No (8) (Murabahah)' (AAOIFI, 2015) 2/2/6 (hereafter AAOIFI, 'Shariah Standard').

[104] ibid 4/4/3.

[105] ibid.

[106] ibid 2/4/1–2/4/2.

[107] ibid 4/8.

[108] ibid 3/2.

institution must first acquire title to the asset and then sell it to the agent turned customer, by allowing 'an interval of time between the performance of the agency contract and the execution of the contract of *murabahah*'.[109]

E. Possible Syndication

15.38 Like a letter of credit, a *murabaha* may be bilateral (involving only the purchaser and the selling financial institution) or may be syndicated. In a syndicated *murabaha* the seller would act as a *mudarib* (partner) alongside other financial institutions.

F. Actual Sale

15.39 It is a requirement of the *murabaha* transaction that the sale between the seller and purchaser be a valid one. Hence, it is not permissible for a purchaser to use a *murabaha* transaction to raise funds over an asset which they already own.[110] If there has been any dealing between the third-party supplier of the asset and the purchaser, that must be excluded from the *murabaha*,[111] and it is not permissible for an existing contract between the third-party supplier and the purchaser to be assigned to the financial institution so that it can be used in a *murabaha* transaction.[112] It is also not permissible to enter into a *murabaha* transaction if the customer wholly owns or owns a majority share of the supplier of the item.[113] This restriction is meant to prevent the so-called *bay' al-'inah* (a legal stratagem in which a person sells an asset to another for a deferred payment. Thereafter, the seller buys back the asset for a cash payment before having made full payment of the deferred price). AAOIFI forbids the contract as it views the stratagem as a means of avoiding the *riba* prohibition. However, the Sharia Advisory Council of the Malaysian Securities Commission and the National Sharia Advisory Council of Bank Negara Malaysia—the central bank—have made the *bay' al-'inah* a lawful Islamic standard.[114] Finally, the sale of the asset may not be concluded prior to the seller gaining title to it.[115]

G. Subject Matter and Liability for Defects

15.40 Regarding the subject matter of the *murabaha*, the rules on the nature of property discussed above apply. For example, it would be impermissible to conduct a *murabaha* agreement in relation to pork products for they are considered *haram*. Cash is also not permitted to be the subject of a *murabaha* as that would amount to *riba*, meaning that the refinancing of an initial *murabaha*,[116] or creating a *murabaha* over gold, silver, or other *ribawi* goods, is

[109] ibid 3/1/3–3/1/5.
[110] ibid 2/2/1.
[111] ibid 2/2/2.
[112] ibid.
[113] ibid 2/2/3.
[114] Ercanbrack 'Standardization of Islamic Financial Law' (n 7) 16. Notably, the stratagem is regularly used throughout the industry in an important financing contract known as the *tawarruq*.
[115] AAOIFI, 'Shariah Standard' (n 103) 3/1/1.
[116] ibid 2/2/7.

not permitted.[117] The seller may sell the goods without liability for defects provided that if the seller does not do so, liability remains for latent defects after the execution of the contract. This would entitle the buyer to sue the seller for any defects.[118] In practice, Islamic financial institutions acting as sellers will allocate the risk of defects to the purchaser which would then preclude any such action. Furthermore, the buyer is not able bring an action against the supplier as they are a third party to the supply of the goods. This latter aspect distinguishes the Letter of Credit from the *murabaha* for trade finance. However, in general, the *murabaha* approximates the balance of risks in the transaction that are found in a conventional letter of credit arrangement.[119] The following section sets out the steps of the *murabaha* agreement, highlighting the contractual structure and the risks that this poses to the financier and the buyer.

H. Phases of the *Murabaha* Agreement

There are five phases to a typical *murabaha* agreement. First, there is the documentation phase where the seller and purchaser first enter into an agreement. This agreement will detail the seller's financial commitment under the *murabaha* and will include representations and warranties by the purchaser as to its credit and credit-related events, trading activity (as seen in a conventional financing facility), positive and negative undertakings as to its activities during the term of the *murabaha*, and events of default which would permit the termination and acceleration of the purchase price.[120] Within this agreement, the mechanics of the other stages of the *murabaha* will be set out and perhaps specimen forms will be attached which represent the said phases.[121] **15.41**

The conditions precedent to the seller's obligations under the *murabaha* will also be set out in this phase.[122] They will be very similar to those found in an equivalent conventional finance transaction—for example they are likely to include legal opinions on the legality and enforceability of the *murabaha*, and copies of corporate authorisations and authority.[123] An important condition precedent unique to Islamic finance in general is the requirement that a *fatwa* be delivered stating that the proposed *murabaha* is Sharia-compliant.[124] Finally, this documentation phase will include information on the place and time of payment, clauses relating to the resolution of disputes and the governing jurisdiction of the agreement, and other clauses that operate in the same way as their conventional finance equivalents.[125] **15.42**

The second phase of the *murabaha* agreement is the request phase, when, after all conditions precedent are met, the purchaser notifies the seller of the asset that it wishes to purchase.[126] **15.43**

117 ibid 2/2/6.
118 ibid 4/9–4/10.
119 Kilian Bälz, 'A Murabaha Transaction in an English Court: The London High Court of 13th February 2002 in *Islamic Investment Company of the Gulf (Bahamas) Ltd v Symphony Gems NV & Ors*' (2004) 11 Islamic Law and Society 117, 122 (hereafter Bälz, 'A Murabaha Transaction in an English Court').
120 Nethercott, '*Murabaha* and *Tawarruq*' (n 95) 198.
121 ibid.
122 ibid.
123 ibid.
124 ibid.
125 ibid.
126 ibid.

The seller then arranges to purchase the said asset and notifies the purchaser of the cost price and the proposed profit. This is done in the form of an offer to sell which is conveyed to the purchaser.[127]

15.44 Following receipt of this offer, the purchaser in turn delivers a 'promise to purchase' the asset at a certain price.[128] Traditionally a promise was not considered legally enforceable in Islamic law as the proto-typical sale contract is characterised as an immediate exchange of countervalues and therefore is not promissory. Known as *wa'd* in Arabic, the promise in Islamic law is unilateral and future-oriented and while the fulfilment of promises is commendable, only Allah determines whether it will happen. Therefore, the majority of classical jurists have deemed the *wa'd* as non-binding.[129] However, as many modern Islamic financial structures depend on the *wa'd* to accommodate modern finance structures, albeit according to the form of classical Islamic rules, minority opinions that view the *wa'd* as legally binding have been appropriated. This is the case with the *murabaha* as a non-binding promise from the purchaser would be unacceptable to the selling financial institution which has to buy assets at the request of the purchaser. As a result, some jurists allow that the purchaser is liable to the seller for any losses caused by a failure to complete the *murabaha*, although this remains subject to debate among scholars and practitioners.[130] If documented as a purchase undertaking, however, the promise is enforceable in modern municipal legal systems.

15.45 In the fourth phase of the *murabaha*, the seller purchases the asset detailed in the offer to sell and the promise to purchase and takes title to it. Then the asset is resold to the purchaser.[131] Importantly, and as discussed above, the seller need not have actual possession of the goods. Constructive possession is satisfactory. The important element of possession is the assumption of risk that the asset may be lost or damaged between the purchase and resale. Of course, this is mitigated by having the period in which the seller possesses the asset in question be very small in duration.[132] After the above phases are all complete, the sale transaction is regulated in its operation phase by the terms of the *murabaha* agreement.[133]

I. Ensuring Performance

15.46 Prior to the completion of the transaction, the seller may take money in the form of a security deposit known as *hamish jiddiyyah* which may be drawn upon if the customer breaches his/her binding promise to purchase the asset.[134] In the case of breach, the institution is

[127] ibid.
[128] ibid.
[129] Marjan Muhammad, Hakimah Yaacob, and Shabana Hasan, 'The Bindingness and Enforceability of a Unilateral Promise (Wa'd): An Analysis from Islamic Law and Legal Perspectives' (2011) 30 International Shari'ah Research Academy for Islamic Finance 1, 4–7 (hereafter Muhammad et al, 'Bindingness and Enforceability of a Unilateral Promise'). The Ottoman *Majalla* of the mid-nineteenth century, which included the Hanafi School of Islamic contract law, defined contract as 'the obligation and engagement of two parties with reference to a particular matter', indicating that it had opted for validating the exchange of promises for future performance whereas the premodern jurists had refused to countenance this understanding of the law. See Mohammed, 'Islamic Contract Law' (n 88) 127–28.
[130] Nethercott, '*Murabaha* and *Tawarruq*' (n 95) 198–99.
[131] ibid 199.
[132] Haider A Hamoudi, 'Jurisprudential Schizophrenia: On Form and Function in Islamic Finance' (2007) 7 Chicago Journal of International Law 605, 612 (hereafter Hamoudi, 'On Form and Function in Islamic Finance').
[133] Nethercott, '*Murabaha* and *Tawarruq*' (n 95) 199.
[134] AAOIFI, 'Shariah Standard' (n 103) 2/5/3–2/5/4.

limited to deducting only the amount of actual damage incurred as a result of the breach. A charge for the lost profit is not permissible.[135] However, this security cannot cover loss or damage to the goods which is suffered whilst the goods are in the possession of the seller.[136] The seller alone bears these risks which, according to sharia, cannot be offloaded to the buyer prior to the transfer of title. Moreover, according to sharia, the seller's liability extends to any defects of the goods as the seller must bear the responsibility of ownership. In practice, however, financial institutions regularly exclude liability for the risks of defects in *Murabaha* contracts despite the clear contravention of ownership responsibilities per the sharia. Notably, it is permissible for the financial institution to obtain a personal guarantee from the purchaser of the good performance of the supplier when the purchaser has suggested a particular source of supply for the item that is the subject matter of the contract.[137] Ostensibly, 'good performance' would exclude the risks of defective goods, thus providing a means of limiting risk in these circumstances. Regarding the security (*hamish jiddiyyah*), it cannot be used to cover loss or damage to the goods which is suffered while the goods are in the possession of the seller.[138] During the operations phase, the seller can receive a third party guarantee of the purchaser's obligations which can be called upon if there is a default event or if the purchase price needs to be accelerated.[139] It is also common practice to take security over the purchaser's other collateral to secure the purchaser's obligation under the *murabaha* agreement.[140]

J. Default and Restructuring

As the purchase price is fixed in a *murabaha* agreement, there can be no penalty for late payment in the form of an increase to the amount due.[141] However, AAOIFI Standards allow for such a late penalty if it is put to a charitable purpose.[142] Non-penalty charges such as enforcement and recovery costs are recoverable from the purchaser.[143] **15.47**

The acceleration of charges in the event of a default is possible in a *murabaha* agreement.[144] In the event of a default, any security may be realised and the subject matter of the *murabaha* may be repossessed, although both of those remedies are subject to availability within the enforcement jurisdiction specified in the initial *murabaha*.[145] **15.48**

One of the limits of the nominate contractual system is the lack of freedom to amend contractual terms, which severely limits the ability of defaulting *murabaha* purchasers to restructure their initial agreement through variation of terms.[146] Such a restriction is not present in a conventional trade financing scenario. **15.49**

135 ibid.
136 ibid 2/5/2.
137 ibid 2/5/1.
138 Nethercott, '*Murabaha* and *Tawarruq*' (n 95) 200. See also AAOIFI, 'Shariah Standard' (n 103) 2/5/2.
139 AAOIFI, 'Shariah Standard' (n 103) 2/5/2.
140 Nethercott, '*Murabaha* and *Tawarruq*' (n 95) 200.
141 ibid 207.
142 AAOIFI, 'Shariah Standard' (n 103) 5/6 and Appendix D.
143 Nethercott, '*Murabaha* and *Tawarruq*' (n 95) 207.
144 ibid 208.
145 ibid.
146 ibid.

VI. Islamic Trade Finance in English Courts

15.50 Now that the theory behind the *murabaha* agreement and its potential application in a trade-finance transaction has been discussed, it is worth examining what happens when such an agreement breaks down and is subject to litigation. Do certain defences apply in the event of a default which are unavailable to defaulting parties in a conventional trade-finance transaction? Is non-compliance with the features of a classical *murabaha* agreement grounds for the revocation of the agreement? To answer those questions, it will be necessary to analyse the relevant case law in this area.

A. The *Symphony Gems* Case

15.51 *Islamic Investment Company of the Gulf (Bahamas) Ltd v Symphony Gems NV and others*[147] was the first instance of an English court ruling on a *murabaha* transaction used for trade-finance purposes,[148] and, although it is not an authoritative judgment, it is a useful case study on how English courts approach such transactions.[149]

15.52 According to the facts of the case, Islamic Investment Company of the Gulf (Bahamas) Ltd ('IICG') and Symphony Gems had entered into an agreement on 27 January 2000, the structure of which was very similar to that described above. IICG was defined as the 'Seller' and Symphony Gems as the 'Purchaser', and the intent was to grant Symphony Gems 'a revolving purchase and sale facility whereunder the Seller shall purchase supplies and immediately sell them on to the purchaser on deferred payment terms subject to conditions contained within the agreement'.[150] The other defendants in the case signed as guarantors of Symphony Gems' obligations under the agreement.[151]

15.53 To make use of this revolving facility, the Purchaser was to request through an irrevocable offer that the Seller buy supplies from a specified supplier. After receiving this offer, the Seller was to confirm the offer by sending an acceptance to the Purchaser, before purchasing the supplies requested and reselling them to the Purchaser on deferred payment terms.[152]

15.54 Under this agreement, two offers were made by the Purchaser, which involved the purchase of a total of US$15 million worth of rough diamonds from a supplier based in Hong Kong and trading as Precious (HK) Ltd. The initial cost price of the diamonds was US$7.5 million per transaction, which—after the agreed profit margin was applied—meant that Symphony Gems owed IICG US$7,917,450 per transaction. This was to be paid in three instalments, due in July, September, and November of 2000.[153] For some reason, the diamonds were never delivered to Symphony Gems, so they were unable to pay any of the money owed. Following a lengthy correspondence between both parties, IICG brought the matter to court to recover the money owed, plus interest pursuant to a liquidated damages clause in

147 [2002] All ER (D) 171 (Transcript) (QB) (hereafter *Symphony Gems*).
148 Bälz, 'A Murabaha Transaction in an English Court' (n 119) 118.
149 Ercanbrack, *Transformation of Islamic Law in Global Financial Markets* (n 8) 224.
150 *Symphony Gems* (n 147).
151 ibid.
152 ibid.
153 ibid.

the *murabaha* agreement, and damages, minus US$7.5million that had already been recovered from a bank guarantee that had been realised.[154]

15.55 Various defences to IICG's claim were raised, the most important being the non-delivery of the goods, since that strikes at the heart of the difference between a *murabaha* and a letter of credit arrangement. Under a conventional arrangement, payment obligations are autonomous, meaning that the risk of non-delivery is borne by the purchaser alone.[155] The *murabaha* agreement attempted to imitate such a risk profile by stating that title to the supplies would pass immediately from the Seller to the Purchaser as soon as the Seller gained title.[156] Similarly, clause 4.4 provided that the instalments due were payable notwithstanding the Seller breaching any of its obligations—which, per Tomlinson J, must include a failure to deliver.[157] Ultimately, Tomlinson J noted that the defendants had failed to raise the defence of non-delivery at any point before the trial and had in fact taken up the issue of non-delivery with the supplier of the goods and not IICG.[158] This aided him in deciding that the defendants were responsible for arranging the delivery of the goods in question, and that the *murabaha* agreement was in fact 'a financing agreement facilitating or apparently facilitating the purchase of supplies by the purchaser'.[159]

15.56 A second defence raised by the defendants was the illegality of the *murabaha* agreement, both because its inclusion of a liquidated damages clause was in breach of the principle of *riba* and because the contract was to be performed in Saudi Arabia, where it would be illegal. Tomlinson J held that the contract did not require performance in Saudi Arabia and was able to avoid pronouncing on the legality of the *murabaha* agreement itself because clauses 25.1 and 26 of the agreement made reference to English law being the sole governing law of the agreement.[160] Thus, this case became a case requiring the interpretation of a contract under English law,[161] and as such expert evidence stating that the *murabaha* agreement was not a true *murabaha* agreement could be ignored.[162]

B. *Shamil Bank v Beximco*

15.57 Although it is not a trade-finance case, it is worth briefly discussing the later case of *Beximco Pharmaceuticals Ltd & Others v Shamil Bank of Bahrain EC* due to its authority in relation to the use of non-national legal systems as the governing law of a contract.[163] Here it was argued that a contractual clause stating that 'Subject to the principles of the Glorious Sharia'a, this Agreement shall be governed by and construed in accordance with the laws of England'[164] should incorporate Sharia principles such as the prohibition of *riba* and

154 ibid.
155 Bälz, 'A Murabaha Transaction in an English Court' (n 119) 124.
156 *Symphony Gems* (n 147).
157 ibid.
158 ibid.
159 ibid.
160 ibid.
161 Ercanbrack, *Transformation of Islamic Law in Global Financial Markets* (n 8) 225.
162 Bälz, 'A Murabaha Transaction in an English Court' (n 119) 124.
163 [2004] EWCA Civ 19 (hereafter *Beximco Pharmaceuticals v Shamil Bank*).
164 ibid [1].

the proper nature of a *murabaha* contract into agreements between the parties.[165] In response to this argument the Court of Appeal stated that mere reference to the Sharia was not enough to incorporate such specific provisions.[166] However, had the parties specifically incorporated such provisions into their agreements the defendants would have been likely to succeed.[167]

15.58 A further, and perhaps unintended, consequence of the *Beximco* decision was its definition of the *murabaha* as a sales contract.[168] Potter LJ states that both parties were content to 'dress up' the transaction as a *murabaha* 'sale [...] whilst taking no interest in whether the proper formalities [...] were actually complied with'.[169] Thus, with respect to Islamic nominate contractual agreements, English courts will look to their substance and purpose through the lens of English contractual principles, absent any expressly incorporated Islamic legal principles to the contrary, rather than looking to the nominate contract system's rules.[170] This provides legal certainty to Islamic financial institutions contracting under English law that their bargains will be enforced even if they depart from the rules of the *murabaha* discussed above, but it also reduces the Sharia element of such contracts from a matter of law to being merely a private matter of compliance where parties are free to structure their transaction in accordance with sharia or not.[171] This has been criticised by those who see the *murabaha* transaction as having converged excessively with its conventional finance alternatives, differing only in form but not in effect.[172] Perhaps the case law cited above evidences their view that Islamic trade finance is based on mimicry, or perhaps it simply reflects the modern commercial reality that trade finance is trade finance, regardless of the religion of the parties involved.

VII. The Future: Blockchain for Islamic Trade Finance

15.59 Blockchain technology is a new infrastructure for storing data and managing software applications. It is essentially a database comprising records of multiple transactions which are collected into a block. A block of entries is recorded in electronic form and contains a cryptographic hash of the preceding block, which allows the blockchain to be linked together. These are stored as a ledger and can be distributed globally without a central repository.[173] Essentially, anyone with an internet connection can retrieve information stored on a blockchain, allowing parties to engage directly with one another for a number of reasons including storing information, transferring value, and coordinating social or economic

[165] ibid [49].
[166] ibid [52].
[167] ibid [55].
[168] Jason C T Chuah, 'Islamic Principles Governing International Trade Financing Instruments: A Study of the Morabaha in English Law' (2006–2007) 27 Northwestern Journal of International Law and Business 137, 149.
[169] *Beximco Pharmaceuticals v Shamil Bank* (n 163) [47].
[170] Ercanbrack, *Transformation of Islamic Law in Global Financial Markets* (n 8) 229.
[171] ibid 232; see also Kilian Bälz, 'Sharia Risk? How Islamic Finance Has Transformed Islamic Contract Law' (Islamic Legal Studies Program, Harvard Law School, Occasional Publications, September 2008) <https://pil.law.harvard.edu/wp-content/uploads/2019/12/Sharia_Risk_by_Kilian_Balz.pdf>.
[172] See, for example Hamoudi, 'On Form and Function in Islamic Finance' (n 132) 613.
[173] Margo Tank, David Whitaker, and Patricia Fry, 'Smart Contracts, Blockchain, and Commercial Law' in *Smart Contracts: Is the Law Ready?* (Smart Contracts Alliance and Chamber of Digital Commerce, September 2018) 112–13 (hereafter Tank et al, 'Smart Contracts, Blockchain and Commercial Law').

activity. Furthermore, the transnational peer-to-peer networks upon which blockchain relies enable people to store non-repudiable data pseudonymously and in a transparent manner. When data is stored on a blockchain, its distributed network and consensus mechanisms and other characteristics, make it exceptionally hard to change or delete. No single party has the ability to modify or revise information once it has been recorded, lending it a great deal of transparency. However, the use of digital signatures and public-private key cryptography allows persons storing information on a blockchain to engage in transactions privately, without revealing their identity.[174]

Trade-finance transactions can be given effect through blockchain-based smart contracts.[175] Smart contracts are computer programmes that, once information has been given as an input, process that information according to rules set out in a contract and carry out actions as a result. Consisting of binary 'if . . . then' statements, terms are given as an input which, when fulfilled, are given effect. Smart contracts are automatically self-enforcing, meaning that they are able to carry out these actions without the intervention of a third party, reducing or possibly even eliminating the need for human oversight. Importantly, even though parties may have different incentives and are located in disparate countries, no single party can affect the execution of the smart contract's code. In this way, the parties can be assured that the contract will be performed irrespective of their trust in the other party. They must only trust the blockchain, which is capable of enforcing the parties' contractual terms.[176] Smart contracts can be used to deal with basic economic transactions at a lower cost, higher speeds, and with greater reliability.[177] Blockchain used in combination with a smart contract will create a trade, logistics, and supply chain infrastructure which incentivises Islamic trade finance to become significantly more efficient and transparent. These technologies will compel the industry to overcome its attachment to legal artifice in favour of adopting substantive trade practices that are more closely aligned with Islamic commercial principles. **15.60**

Trade finance, in particular letter of credit transactions, involves multiple stakeholders and is highly labour and paper intensive. Trade transactions are not yet digitalised in spite of a spate of recent efforts. A single shipment of roses from Kenya to Rotterdam generates a pile of paper 25cm high, while the cost is higher than the shipment of containers. On average more than 100 stakeholders are involved in this type of shipment.[178] These interactions are highly costly and have led a number of banks to explore blockchain as a means of automating the process, improving efficiency and enhancing security. Numerous proofs of concept have been developed successfully in the last few years and blockchain's commercial application is imminent. For example, in 2016, the Bank of America Merill Lynch, HSBC, and the Infocomm Development Authority of Singapore developed a prototype **15.61**

[174] Primavera De Filippi and Aaron Wright, *Blockchain and the Law: Rule of Code* (Harvard University Press 2018) (hereafter De Filippi and Wright, *Blockchain and the Law*).

[175] See also ch 12 (Winn) in this volume.

[176] Max Raskin, 'The Law and Legality of Smart Contracts' (2017) 1 Georgetown Technology Review 305, 319–20 (hereafter Raskin, 'Law and Legality of Smart Contracts').

[177] Michael Casey et al, 'The Impact of Blockchain Technology on Finance: A Catalyst for Change' (International Center for Monetary and Banking Studies, Centre for Economic Policy Research, 2018).

[178] Ian Allison, 'Shipping Giant Maersk Tests Blockchain-Powered Bill of Lading' (*International Business Times*, 14 October 2016) <https://www.ibtimes.co.uk/shipping-giant-maersk-tests-blockchain-powered-bills-lading-1585929?webSyncID=6ccc1e6b-089a-2b6d-810d-e60990b22563&sessionGUID=8871313c-992a-4279-3293-95100716e18d> accessed 14 August 2019.

using blockchain which mirrored a paper-intensive letter of credit transaction. Information between exporters, importers, and their respective banks was shared on a permissioned blockchain, which was then executed through a series of smart contracts.[179] The prototype transaction illustrated that blockchain can streamline financial flows and enhance the security, transparency, speed, and reliability of supply chain financing. Smart contracts will help to streamline trade finance transactions, particularly those related to conventional letter of credit transactions and its nearly identical Islamic alternatives. The technology will make the role of some involved parties, such as correspondent banks, redundant.[180] Notably, however, a *murabaha* transaction for trade-finance purposes still necessitates the involvement of the bank as a seller as a loan with interest is not permissible under sharia. In sum, blockchain has the potential of levelling the playing field in relation to logistics and related party costs, which would be particularly helpful as companies from developing countries are faced with costs almost double that of their developed country peers.[181] These costs are the result of extensive paperwork and the fact that a wide array of stakeholders involved in border and customs procedures.

15.62 Islamic trade finance, not unlike its conventional counterpart, has traditionally catered to mid- and large-sized businesses. The complexity and cost of *murabaha*-based trade finance has limited its scope as the industry has not been able to extend its sources of revenue. *Murabaha*-based transactions include complex contractual drafting including numerous security documents, multiple legal opinions, seller-issued *fatwas* (Islamic legal opinion), and credit and payment services comprising a higher level of counterparty risk. These processes have made them unaffordable for smaller businesses, particularly those in developing countries where SME access to finance is particularly low.[182] The use of blockchain may open up the industry to these smaller players by creating a marketplace that is open to any importer or exporter. Blockchain reduces the degree of coordination effort amongst numerous stakeholders involved in a trade financing transaction by allowing all of the trade-finance information to be brought into one trusted environment that can be accessed by the interested parties. Typically, stakeholders act in silo and in a sequential manner. Records, such as those of shippers, export brokers, import customs, banks, and transportation providers, are kept separately. Any party can alter them, which makes the process vulnerable to fraud.[183] Where multiple authorisations are required for the export of a product, blockchain allows an exporter to submit the information just once. Agencies involved with the platform would then be able to validate the transaction or issue relevant documents.

15.63 A smart contract can easily be programmed to give effect to a *murabaha*-based trade-finance agreement between the buyer (importer) and seller (Islamic bank). The *murabaha*

[179] The Bank of America Merill Lynch, HSBC, and the Infocomm Development Authority of Singapore, 'BofAML, HSBC, IDA Singapore Build Pioneering Blockchain Trade Finance App' (News Release) (10 August 2016) <https://www.about.hsbc.com.sg/-/media/singapore/en/press-releases/160810-blockchain-letter-of-credit.pdf> accessed 14 Aug 2019.

[180] Safina and Oseni, 'Potentials of Smart Contract in Islamic Trade Finance' (n 10) 226.

[181] WTO Report 2018 (n 9) 45.

[182] According to the WTO, tariffs accounted for 9% on average in 2013. A 2015 WTO study found that trade costs can amount to a 134% ad valorem tariff on a product in high-income countries and a 219% tariff in developing countries. These costs are largely the result of paperwork and the number of agencies involved in border procedures. See Emmanuelle Ganne, 'Can Blockchain Revolutionize International Trade?' (World Trade Organization 2018) 28–29 (Ganne, 'Can Blockchain Revolutionize International Trade').

[183] ibid 31.

sales agreement, including security documents, *fatwas*, and legal opinions, can be recorded on a smart contract and shared between the importer (buyer) and the exporter (seller) and the supplier. The smart contract also allows for recording the details of any agency agreement between the buyer and the seller in relation to the purchase of the asset or commodity. In real-time the Islamic bank or its buyer/agent will have the capability to review the agreement and to carry out the purchase of the goods on behalf of the importer/buyer. Once the goods are purchased, the seller can initiate a second smart contract detailing the sale of the goods to the buyer. As Islamic commercial law requires a separate meeting of the minds for each contract of sale, an entirely self-executing smart contract would contravene its rules, which are meant to provide clarity to contracting parties and thereby avoid *gharar*. Therefore, smart contracts incorporating *murabaha* transactions would require the same binding promise (*wa'd*) which, while putatively allowing the transactions to be carried out individually, binds the buyer to a legally enforceable purchase undertaking. The parties' agreement would still be required prior to each sales transaction, which, while slowing the execution of the smart contract, does not wholly denude the technology of its numerous advantages.[184] Blockchain's facilitation of easy access to data and end-to-end transparency of the entire value chain would create a level playing field for all parties involved in a trade transaction. The exchange of trade data including the trader's credit history increases the speed, efficiency, and security of financing.[185] Other events along the supply chain such as a customs agent's confirmation of approval or the approval of a bill of lading would not require action by the bank.

The code of a smart contract is remarkably similar to many terms and conditions normally found in a contract. There has been a good deal of debate amongst legal scholars as to whether a smart contract constitutes a legally valid contract.[186] The balance of arguments now weighs heavily in favour of smart contracts being fully capable of giving rise to a legally binding contract under English and American common law as well as Spanish civil law legal systems.[187] A judicial taskforce of the United Kingdom has concluded the same in a much anticipated public statement.[188] The sharia is capable of viewing smart contracts similarly as Islamic jurists are primarily concerned with the avoidance of prohibited elements in transactions, ie *riba* and *gharar* as well as what is recognised as legitimate property, eg excluding alcohol, pork, pornography, and armaments. The rules of contract formation, **15.64**

[184] Contrary to the position as expressed in IFSB Report 2017 (n 10) 116, which envisions trade finance as merely the seller's offer and the buyer's acceptance, rather than the complex chain of stakeholder interactions that take place over the course of a trade finance transaction. This is not the sole issue of sharia that may conflict with blockchain technology. A comprehensive analysis of the compatibility of sharia and blockchain is beyond the scope of this chapter.

[185] Mohamed and Ali, *Blockchain, Fintech and Islamic Finance* (n 10) 145.

[186] A comprehensive legal analysis is beyond the remit of this chapter. For a brief analysis which argues that smart contracts should not be equated with a binding contract, see Richard Howlett, 'A Lawyer's Perspective: Can Smart Contracts Exist Outside the Legal Structure?' (*Bitcoin Magazine*, 2016) <https://bitcoinmagazine.com/articles/a-lawyer-s-perspective-can-smart-contracts-exist-outside-the-legal-structure-1468263134> accessed 21 August 2020. See also Raskin, 'Law and Legality of Smart Contracts' (n 176), who argues that traditional legal jurisprudence will not be displaced and can help craft simple rules to accommodate this technology.

[187] Miren B Aparicio Bijuesca, 'The Challenges Associated with Smart Contracts: Formation, Modification, and Enforcement' in *Smart Contracts: Is the Law Ready?* (Smart Contracts Alliance and Chamber of Digital Commerce, September 2018) 21–22 (hereafter Aparicio Bijuesca, 'Challenges Associated with Smart Contracts').

[188] A UK Taskforce has publicly declared that a smart contract is capable of satisfying the basic requirements of an English law legal contract. See UK Jurisdiction Taskforce, 'Legal Statement on Cryptoassets and Smart Contracts' (UK Jurisdiction Taskforce, November 2019) [136].

vitiating factors, and remedies have largely been outsourced to municipal systems of law such as English and New York law which are the vehicular legal systems in which cross-border Islamic finance contracts are given effect. Jurists have been prepared to treat Islamic contractual rules far more flexibly than these seemingly fixed prohibitions as reflected in numerous contractual practices including the binding promise (*wa'd*) discussed above. Subsidiary rules can change with time and place and societal developments such as technological advancement.[189] Moreover, legal stratagems known as *hiyal* are widely viewed as necessary tools which allow Islamic law to adapt to modern financial markets.[190] *Hiyal* are the means by which legal theory can be put into practice, narrowing the gap between ideals and reality.[191] Classical Hanafi jurists, in particular, viewed *hiyal* as the means by which one could make lawful that which otherwise is unlawful; to create what the Hanafis called '*makharij*' (singular: *makhraj*) or 'exits'.[192]

15.65 Some have argued that an agreement to execute the code could be legally valid so long as the terms of the code was expressed in human language.[193] Indeed, more abstract legal concepts such as 'force majeure' or 'good judgement' may require a broader contractual framework, particularly in relation to complex transactions and associated definitions of non-operational clauses such as choice of law, competent jurisdiction, or any dispute resolution mechanisms.[194] Furthermore, a written agreement has the advantage of providing a roadmap of the parties' contractual intentions as these may need to be investigated should the code give effect to unwanted outcomes. This is particularly so given the irreversibility of smart contracts which makes it nearly impossible for the code to be changed or stopped once the process has been activated. The outcome is recorded on the blockchain and is immutable.[195] While the immutability of the code is designed to minimise or even abolish disputes, inevitably human language which feeds into code is prone to error or ambiguity and disputes will arise. Because smart contracts are either in the process of being executed or have already been executed, the aggrieved party will need to go to the court to remedy a contract. In all cases, the remedy must come after the execution of the contract and reference to an agreement in human language will be necessary.[196] The sharia is capable of accommodating these operational requirements so long as its major principles remain intact.

15.66 A number of legal, regulatory, and interoperability issues must be addressed, particularly in less developed countries, for the technology to deliver its potential. While a more detailed

[189] Mohamad Akram Laldin and Hafas Furqani, 'Fintech and Islamic Finance: Setting the Shari'ah Parameters' in Umar A Oseni and S Nazim Ali (eds) *Fintech in Islamic Finance: Theory and Practice* (Routledge 2019) 115.

[190] ibid.

[191] Joseph Schacht, '*Das Kitab Al-Hijal Fil-Fiqh (Buch der Rechtskniffe) Des Abu Hatim Mahmud Ibn Al-Hasan Al-Qazuini*' (Orient-Buchhandlung Heinz Lafaire 1924) 6.

[192] Satoe Horii, 'Reconsideration of Legal Devices (Hiyal) in Islamic Jurisprudence: The Hanafis and Their "Exits" (Makharij)' (2002) 9 Islamic Law & Society 312, 312–13. Historically, *hiyal* were employed in nearly all facets of life. Their use dealt with matters that extended far beyond strictly legal transactions to everyday aspects of life. However, the chapters of the *fiqh* devoted to spiritual matters (*'ibadat*) comprise a much smaller proportion of *hiyal*, indicating that ritual worship is more closely aligned with the ideals of the law. See Joseph Schacht, 'Die Arabische Hijal-Literatur: Ein Beitrag Zur Erforschung Der Islamischen Rechtspraxis' (1926) XV Der Islam 211, 213.

[193] Volker Nienhaus, 'Blockchain Technologies and the Prospects of Smart Contracts' in Umar A Oseni and S Nazim Ali (eds) *Fintech in Islamic Finance: Theory and Practice* (Routledge 2019) 198 (hereafter Nienhaus, 'Blockchain Technologies and the Prospects of Smart Contracts').

[194] Aparicio Bijuesca, 'Challenges Associated with Smart Contracts' (n 187) 24.

[195] Nienhaus, 'Blockchain Technologies and the Prospects of Smart Contracts' (n 193) 198.

[196] Raskin, 'Law and Legality of Smart Contracts' (n 175) 322.

analysis is beyond the scope of this chapter, one final observation regarding electronic communications legislation is warranted due to its significance. Legislation recognising the validity of e-signatures, e-documents, and e-transactions including blockchain transactions is essential.[197] A robust regulatory framework for the digital market is crucial in supporting consumer trust. Yet many developing countries have lagged behind in promulgating e-commerce legislation and other aspects of their legal systems such as consumer protection laws and data protection laws, which may explain why many consumers in developing countries actively engage in social media while they abstain from online shopping.[198]

VIII. Conclusion

The pace at which the technological revolution is reshaping the global economy is like nothing the world has ever experienced. It may provide technological solutions to the development of industries or even entire countries which hope to 'leapfrog' their historical underdevelopment to the most modern technological stage. Perhaps the most famous example is Africa's use of mobile phones for banking and remittances, which almost entirely bypassed fixed-line technology.[199] **15.67**

The digitalisation of Islamic trade finance via blockchain and smart contracts will help Islamic finance to standardise its financial practices, as the technology itself requires increased standardisation and platform interoperability for it to function optimally. While religious and ethical considerations must be given to this market-driven development,[200] there is undoubtedly much to applaud about blockchain's potential for streamlining inefficient trade-finance practices, creating a level playing field, increasing transparency and reducing opportunities for fraud. That technological innovation would help Islamic finance to realise its commercial principles is not what its theorisers had in mind when they set out to create an Islamic economy. Perhaps this paradox says something important about the monumental changes that Islamic financial law has undergone in the modern, globalised world. It would seem that innovation of the kind we are on the cusp of experiencing in Islamic trade finance may be conducive to generating more ethical and transparent trade-finance processes. **15.68**

Furthermore, the eventual success of blockchain for Islamic and conventional trade finance can help the states of the MENA region to seize the technological moment, radically transforming their state-led, oil-dependent economies so as to meet their citizens' increasing social and economic demands. Whether this becomes reality depends on the extent to which data can be standardised across blockchain platforms, so that disparate parties **15.69**

[197] Ganne, 'Can Blockchain Revolutionize International Trade' (n 182) xiii.

[198] WTO Report 2018 (n 9) 45. An example of an Electronic Communications Statute that recognises, enables, and enforces the use of smart contracts is the Uniform Electronic Transactions Act in the United States. See Tank et al, 'Smart Contracts, Blockchain and Commercial Law' (n 173).

[199] David Pilling, 'Are Tech Companies Africa's New Colonialists?' (*Financial Times*, 5 July 2019) <https://www.ft.com/content/4625d9b8-9c16-11e9-b8ce-8b459ed04726> accessed 14 August 2019.

[200] See Ercanbrack, 'Standardization of Islamic Financial Law' (n 7) for an account of the market and legal mechanisms underlying standardisation and the ethical questions which arise therefrom. Further research concerning the compatibility of Islamic commercial law and smart contract technology is necessary, in particular.

communicate with one another using a similar data format. Standardised data sets relating to import, export, transit, transport, and finance are the prerequisites to the exchange of information.

15.70 Moreover, the complexity of international trade cannot be simplified unless the underlying trade finance and customs clearing processes as well as bills of lading are completely digitalised. While some previous attempts at creating electronic bills of lading systems failed, notably SEADOCS,[201] blockchain may offer a route to managing data in this particular area. Blockchain technology has been used to issue and transfer electronic bills of lading. The challenges of implementing blockchain and smart contracts for trade finance are significant but with concerted effort, surmountable and revolutionary.

[201] Ganne, 'Can Blockchain Revolutionize International Trade' (n 181) 44.

16

Countertrade as Finance

Christopher Hare

I. Introduction

Until the last decade or so, there could be little doubt that the letter of credit was the pre-eminent financing tool for the international sale of goods. More recently, this dominance has been challenged by the availability of cheaper financing mechanisms, the advent of more rapid technological solutions and the increase of banking regulation that undermines the fundamental tenets of letter of credit law.[1] Beyond these modern challenges, there have always been two significant limitations upon the letter of credit's utility and reach. First, using a letter of credit assumes that a seller is content to receive monetary consideration in return for its goods. A seller may have compelling economic reasons for preferring to receive non-monetary consideration. Those reasons may result from national or international economic pressures, such as '[h]ard currency shortages, dramatic changes in the world energy situation and ever-present pressures to reduce trade deficits',[2] or from a desire by developing countries to acquire goods, services, or technology from developed countries that would not otherwise be possible.[3] Secondly, using a letter of credit assumes that the trade parties to the underlying sale are based in a jurisdiction that is economically and politically stable, such that it has a sufficiently well-developed banking or financial system to support the issue of letters of credit.[4] Where a jurisdiction lacks a minimum level of financial, economic, or political infrastructure, using a letter of credit may simply not be feasible. Even when the letter of credit is an option, any weakness or instability in the domestic banking system may make a letter of credit's use undesirable in the circumstances; such a payment instrument can only operate as an effective proxy for trust between trade parties if it constitutes a reliable source 16.01

[1] In particular, the introduction of anti-money laundering legislation and the imposition of international sanctions means that banks cannot realistically just 'deal with documents and not with goods, services of performance to which the documents may relate' as indicated by UCP 600, art 5. Instead, banks must now concern themselves with the details of the underlying transaction in order to comply with their regulatory requirements.

[2] Thomas McVey, 'Countertrade and Barter: Alternative Trade Financing by Third World Nations' (1981) 6 Maryland J Int L 197, 219 (hereafter McVey, 'Countertrade and Barter'). See also San-Rim Choi and Adrian Tschoegl, 'Currency Risks, Government Procurement and Counter-Trade: A Note' (2003) 13(12) Applied Financial Economics 885. When countertrade is driven by economic constraints, banks may still perform an intermediary or advisory role or provide financing to one of the countertrade parties: see Oleg Sviridenko, 'Countertrade Operations with the Republics of the Former USSR' (1992) 1 IBLJ 69, 73 (hereafter Sviridenko, 'Countertrade Operations').

[3] Christopher Kerres, 'A Report on Countertrade' (1991) 1 U Miami Int & Comp L Rev 173, 175; Ruben Berrios and Josephine Olson, 'Countertrade as a Form of Debt Payment; Peru's Experience with the Soviet Union and Commercial Banks' (1995) 25 Nordic J of Latin American Studies 3, 5–6 (hereafter Berrios and Olson, 'Countertrade as a Form of Debt Payment').

[4] Although it is possible for non-bank entities to issue a letter of credit, these will not necessarily provide the same security of payment as a bank and the credit itself will not be subject to the UCP regime: see ICC Commission on Banking Technique and Practice ('ICC Banking Commission'), 'When a Non-bank Issues a Letter of Credit' (30 October 2002).

of payment.[5] It is when the letter of credit is unavailable, inappropriate, or undesirable that trade parties might use one of the established forms of 'countertrade' as the mechanism for financing their respective sales.[6] In essence, 'counter-trade products can take on the guise of a payment method' that provides a rapid and cost-effective way of gaining entry to new markets or dominance in existing ones,[7] since countertrade is 'a viable financing alternative in international transactions ... [and] a way of supplementing traditional finance in trade'.[8]

16.02 According to the United Nations Commission on International Trade Law ('UNCITRAL'),[9] a countertrade transaction is one 'in which one party supplies goods, services, technology or other economic value to the second party, and, in return, the first party purchases from the second party an agreed amount of goods, services, technology or other economic value'. Accordingly, the hallmark of countertrade operations is that trade parties enter into matching and opposite trade transactions with the result that goods and services are effectively supplied in return for other goods or services.

16.03 Although countertrade is not new, it has always been the poor relation, since economic or political upheavals have been the usual driver for countertrade activity.[10] Accordingly, the economic crises in the 1920s and the Great Depression in the 1930s saw a growth in international countertrade activity, as domestic currencies suffered from exchange weakness or volatility; hyperinflationary pressures (as in Austria, Germany, Poland, and Russia) eroded the value of money; and domestic currency exchange regulations limited cross-border capital flows.[11] Certainly, between the two World Wars and in the aftermath of the Second World War, countertrade became the conventional method for conducting international trade in Germany, with Central and Eastern European countries following suit during the 1950s and 1960s in relation to East-West trade.[12] That growth continued during the 1970s (as a result of the oil crisis) and 1980s (as a result of the 'Cold War'), with estimates being that countertrade accounted for between 10%[13] and 15%[14] of global trade

[5] Whilst letters of credit will often be preferred to open account terms in jurisdictions 'with weaker contractual enforcement, less financial development and higher political risk' (see Bank for International Settlements, 'Trade Finance: Developments and Issues' (Report submitted by a Study Group established by the Committee on the Global Financial System, January 2014) 9), there will usually be a tipping point at which the degree of legal, economic, or financial instability will make letters of credit unattractive to trade parties.

[6] For the view that countertrade can be justified in economic terms, see Tore Ellingsen, 'A Model of Countertrade' (London School of Economics Discussion Paper No EI/3, March 1991).

[7] Sviridenko, 'Countertrade Operations' (n 2) 70–71. For a potential disadvantage of countertrade linked to its eligibility for support from the Export Credit Guarantee Department, see Edgar Herzfeld, 'Countertrade on Capital Projects: Problems of Linkage' [1987] JBL 196 (hereafter Herzfeld, 'Countertrade on Capital Projects'); Clive Schmitthoff, 'Countertrade' [1985] JBL 115 (hereafter Schmitthoff 'Countertrade') 117.

[8] Berrios and Olson, 'Countertrade as a Form of Debt Payment' (n 3) 5. See also John Parsons, 'A Theory of Countertrade Financing of International Business' (Alfred P Sloan School of Management Working Paper, March 1985) 4.

[9] United Nations Commission on International Trade Law ('UNCITRAL'), 'Legal Guide on International Countertrade Transactions' (United Nations, 1993) (hereafter UNCITRAL, 'Legal Guide') 5.

[10] For a detailed discussion of countertrade's development, see Thomas McVey 'Countertrade: Commercial Practices, Legal Issues and Policy Dilemmas' (1984) 16 Law and Policy in International Business 1, 6–14 (hereafter McVey 'Countertrade: Commercial Practices').

[11] See Bretton Woods Agreement, art VIII(2)(b), incorporated into English law by the UK Bretton Woods Agreement Order in Council (1946) SR &O 1946 No 36.

[12] Jerzy Rajski, 'Some Legal Aspects of International Compensation Trade' (1986) 35 ICLQ 128, 135 (hereafter Rajski, 'Legal Aspects'); Murat Sumer and Jason Chuah, 'Emerging Legal Challenges for Countertrade Techniques in International Trade' [2007] Int TLR 111, 111–12 (hereafter Sumer and Chuah, 'Emerging Legal Challenges').

[13] Sumer and Chuah, 'Emerging Legal Challenges' (n 12) 112.

[14] Sviridenko, 'Countertrade Operations' (n 2) 69.

at that time (and potentially even as much as one third),[15] although official statistics are difficult to obtain.[16] Whilst countertrade's popularity continued in the immediate aftermath of the Soviet Union's collapse in the 1990s due to the ensuing currency-exchange and inflationary challenges,[17] this gradually changed as the former Eastern bloc countries developed more liberal economies.[18] That said, countertrade has never really gone away:[19] it continues to be used in South American countries faced with currency devaluations;[20] in countries, such as India, China,[21] and Indonesia, to fire their development;[22] and is commonplace in the oil market. Indeed, countertrade has had something of a renaissance in recent years as a result of the economic, financial, and banking instability engendered by the Global Financial Crisis[23] and has increasingly been viewed as an effective vehicle for Islamic trade finance.[24]

Countertrade (like gold) has traditionally operated as a safe port in times of crisis. **16.04** Accordingly, some level of resurgence is likely in a global pandemic that has seen global trade collapse,[25] especially when there was already a rise in nationalist and protectionist tendencies and higher levels of international financial regulation that make bank-based financing options increasingly expensive and cumbersome. Whilst some of these problems might be alleviated by developing new trade-finance techniques (such as the Bank Payment Obligation ('BPO')), or by the inexorable march of technology, the aim of this chapter is to examine an old trading technique that might be re-purposed into a straightforward and cost-effective trade-finance mechanism. Indeed, the 'self-help' nature of countertrade and its freedom from bank oversight is certainly consistent with the growth of open-account and prepayment transactions, as well as the increasing popularity of blockchain technology as a solution to the paper-based problems of trade finance.

That said, countertrade will only flourish to the extent that its legal consequences are reliable and secure. **16.05** In this regard, section II will consider the different forms of countertrade transaction, before section III considers some of the potential legal difficulties associated with such operations. Some concluding remarks will be offered in section IV.

[15] William Renforth and Constance Bates, 'Does Countertrade Help Small Business Exports?' (Proceedings of the 1986 Academy of Marketing Science Annual Conference, 1986) 465. See also Michael Rowe, *Countertrade* (3rd edn, Euromoney Publishing 1997) 1. As countertrade has not often been considered from a financing perspective, it is difficult to assess accurately the significance of countertrade when compared with other forms of trade finance, rather than as a part of global trade. Extrapolating from one set of data to the other, however, the impact is likely to be significant.

[16] Berrios and Olson, 'Countertrade as a Form of Debt Payment' (n 3) 4.

[17] Sviridenko, 'Countertrade Operations' (n 2) 70, 72.

[18] Sumer and Chuah, 'Emerging Legal Challenges' (n 12) 112.

[19] See Richard Fletcher, 'A Holistic Approach to Countertrade' (1998) 27 Industrial Marketing Management 511. See also Schmitthoff 'Countertrade' (n 7) 116; Sumer and Chuah 'Emerging Legal Challenges' (n 12) 113.

[20] Berrios and Olson, 'Countertrade as a Form of Debt Payment' (n 3) 6–7.

[21] See generally Aspy Palia and Oded Shenkar, 'Countertrade Practices in China' (1991) 20 Industrial Marketing Management 57.

[22] Berrios and Olson, 'Countertrade as a Form of Debt Payment' (n 3) 6.

[23] Sander de Vries, Countertrade: A New Perspective for an Old Practice?' (*Zanders*, 17 November 2011) <https://zanders.eu/nl/latest-insights/countertrade-a-new-perspective-for-an-old-practice/> accessed 30 August 2020.

[24] Sumer and Chuah, 'Emerging Legal Challenges' (n 12) 113, 123–24. See further ch 15 (Ercanbrack) in this volume.

[25] See, for example, Jon Grevatt, 'Covid-19: Indonesia looks to expand countertrade options' (*Janes*, 17 July 2020) <https://www.janes.com/defence-news/news-detail/covid-19-indonesia-looks-to-expand-countertrade-options> accessed 30 August 2020.

II. Forms of Countertrade

16.06 As introduced above, countertrade operations in essence cover any contractual structure that involves goods moving in opposite directions between two trading partners. Although countertrade does not on its face involve the provision of finance, the premise of this chapter is that countertrade essentially involves one supply transaction being used as the means of financing a matching transaction.[26] Indeed, the 'distinctive feature of [countertrade] transactions is the existence of a *link* between the supply contracts in the two directions in that the conclusion of the supply contract or contracts in one direction is conditioned upon the conclusion of the supply contract or contracts in the other direction'.[27] Indeed, if no such 'link' existed between the opposing sale transactions, then they would hold little interest from a trade finance perspective, as they would simply be independent (albeit coincidental) transactions. Accordingly, it is the 'link' (whatever its form) that makes these transactions legally interesting,[28] and that qualifies them as a form of financing: the 'link' effectively means that the price for goods is paid by means of the matching sale transaction, rather than the direct payment of currency. In that regard, there appear to be four broad types of countertrade operation.[29]

16.07 The first type of countertrade is the barter transaction. A true barter involves only one contract between the trade parties.[30] Obviously, in its very simplest form, a barter transaction could simply involve a one-off transaction where goods or services are exchanged for other goods or services. Whilst such a simple and straightforward international transaction is certainly possible, it is unlikely to give rise to many of the difficulties considered further below.[31] A more complex variation is the 'valued barter', which similarly involves the exchange of goods or services, but a balancing payment is made into a settlement account to reflect the difference in relative value between the respective goods or services.[32] Barter is not, however, simply limited to the type of transaction that might occur in under-developed economies or between unsophisticated trading parties, but may extend to 'an intergovernmental agreement addressing mutual trade in particular goods between identified partners, or to countertrade in which trans-border flow of currency is eliminated or reduced or where a single contract governs the mutual shipment of goods'.[33] Accordingly, whilst barter was particularly common in post-War East-West trade,[34] more sophisticated, complex, and longer-term barter-like transactions have developed subsequently.[35] Accordingly, the type of barter transaction that is potentially legally problematic is when there is a framework

[26] McVey, 'Countertrade and Barter' (n 2) 202.

[27] UNCITRAL, 'Legal Guide' (n 9) 1 (emphasis added).

[28] A further complicating feature of countertrade operations is that there may often be a public law element if governmental regulations promote or restrict certain types of countertrade or payment under such contracts; if the contracts are concluded through state trading agencies; or if the countertrade is designed to achieve some broader sovereign function (such as purchasing military equipment or in pursuit of some broader diplomatic agenda): see UNCITRAL, 'Legal Guide' (n 9) 7.

[29] For a detailed analysis of the different forms of countertrade, see Sumer and Chuah, 'Emerging Legal Challenges' (n 12) 115–23.

[30] Schmitthoff 'Countertrade' (n 7) 120.

[31] See section III of this chapter. See also Schmitthoff 'Countertrade' (n 7) 119–20.

[32] Schmitthoff 'Countertrade' (n 7) 120.

[33] UNCITRAL, 'Legal Guide' (n 9) 8.

[34] Rajski, 'Legal Aspects' (n 12) 130.

[35] ibid.

agreement covering a series of current and future deliveries of goods and/or services in both directions between two trading parties,[36] without funds being exchanged at all or only being used to balance out any disparity in the value of the goods provided on either side.

16.08 This more complex type of barter transaction does, however, start to resemble (and, indeed, may in some circumstances be indistinguishable from) the second (more modern) form of countertrade transaction, namely counter-purchase. In contrast to barter or barter-like contracts (which in its truest form involves only one contract between the parties),[37] 'counterpurchase [is a] multi-contractual arrangement effected on the basis of two or more interrelated contracts which provide for mutual performance by the parties of an agreed value, based on independent payment mechanisms'.[38] As counter purchase involves parallel, albeit independent, contracts of sale: it is 'a transaction in which the parties, in connection with the conclusion of a purchase contract in one direction enter into an agreement to conclude a sales contract in the other direction'.[39] Accordingly, the hallmark of a counter-purchase transaction is a provision in the first transaction to the effect that a second matching and opposite transaction will be concluded at some future time. Whilst counter-purchase can be used in respect of discrete matching sale transactions,[40] it is not unusual for the parties to conclude 'a framework agreement indicating the principal rules under which the future export contracts are to be concluded',[41] or at the very least the parties may enter into a non-binding 'memorandum of understanding' with respect to future transactions.[42]

16.09 A variation of the counter-purchase transaction is the third broad type of countertrade, namely the buy-back transaction. This typically involves a long-term arrangement under which one party supplies the raw materials, equipment, technology, or know-how for the production of defined goods or the building of a production facility,[43] the necessary work being done by the counterparty on condition that the supplier of those materials purchases any finished product. This form of countertrade often involves a single over-arching framework transaction with each party obtaining funding through their own bank for the acquisition of the raw materials or the production facility used to create the finished product.[44] Given its long-term character, it is important to include in the framework agreement provision for the relationship to be adjusted to accommodate changing circumstances.[45]

16.10 A variation on the buy-back transaction is the fourth type of countertrade, namely the direct off-set transaction:[46] the difference between the buy-back and off-set transaction is

[36] It has been suggested that a true barter arrangement only covers a one-off transaction, whereas a series of barters is better viewed as a counter-purchase transaction: see Sumer and Chuah, 'Emerging Legal Challenges' (n 12) 115.

[37] Schmitthoff 'Countertrade' (n 7) 120.

[38] Rajski, 'Legal Aspects' (n 12) 131.

[39] UNCITRAL, 'Legal Guide' (n 9) 8.

[40] McVey, 'Countertrade and Barter' (n 2) 202.

[41] Rajski, 'Legal Aspects' (n 12) 131.

[42] For potential legal difficulties, see Koh, 'Countertrade: The Problem of Linkage in International Counterpurchase Agreements' [1990] ICCLR 97.

[43] It is unclear whether such transactions would fall within the scope of the United Nations Convention on Contracts for the International Sale of Goods 1980 (United Nations, 2010, Publication No. E.10.V.14) (hereafter 'Vienna Convention') art 3.

[44] UNCITRAL, 'Legal Guide' (n 9) 9.

[45] Rajski, 'Legal Aspects' (n 12) 134.

[46] Guido Nassimbeni, Marco Sartor, and Guido Orzes, 'Countertrade: Compensatory Requests to Sell Abroad' (January 2014) J for Global Business Advancement.

that 'in a direct offset *both* parties commit themselves to purchase over a period of time goods from each other, whereas under a buy-back transaction the party that has supplied the production facility commits itself to purchase goods resulting from the production facility'.[47] In some respects, the direct off-set transaction resembles the more complex forms of barter described above in that, like the buy-back transaction, there will usually be an overarching framework transaction regulating the individual dealings between the parties.

16.11 That said, the categories of countertrade are not watertight and parties may develop their own individualised variations on the four structures described above.[48] Moreover, the above description was premised upon the notion that the dealings were purely bilateral, but there are usually contractual mechanisms in countertrade transactions allowing third parties to join the contractual framework. Moreover, multiple parties may engage in more complex forms of countertrade that perform the same basic financing function as bilateral arrangements. These include the 'switch' or 'swap' transaction:[49] the former involves one of the parties to a bilateral arrangement looking to a third party for the provision of hard currency; and the latter involves three or more parties utilising a 'merry-go-round' arrangement to swap goods amongst themselves.[50]

16.12 Thus far, the forms of countertrade considered have involved the supply obligations in independent, but matching, transactions being used as the finance mechanism for the equivalent obligation in the opposing contract. It is also possible, however, for the necessary link to operate not on the supply obligation, but the payment obligation. By linking the payment obligations, the parties may avoid having to provide the necessary hard currency, having to tackle exchange control difficulties or having to rely too extensively on an unreliable banking or financial system. There are effectively two broad types of linked counter-payment.

16.13 The first type is the 'blocked account',[51] which involves one party paying the price in respect of goods that they have purchased into a designated account, which the other party may then access when they have shipped their own goods and satisfied any conditions attached to the account (any balance being left in the account to finance future transactions between the parties). This mechanism is only likely to be helpful when the parties can agree on a jurisdiction with an effective banking system, have established clearly defined conditions for withdrawal of the funds from the account, and want to avoid the expense, risk, and delay that may result from using a letter of credit. Where these practical concerns can be overcome, a 'blocked account' device may prove helpful in avoiding currency exchange issues or legislative or governmental restrictions on capital flows.

[47] UNCITRAL, 'Legal Guide' (n 9) 9.

[48] Rajski, 'Legal Aspects' (n 12) 129. The forms of countertrade transaction have been described as 'infinite and [varying] from country to country and case to case': see Schmitthoff 'Countertrade' (n 7) 118. There may also be variations on the private law model of countertrade when a sovereign state or some other public entity engages in the activity, as the relevant obligations may be incorporated in a treaty or some other international instrument, such as a commodity exchange agreement: see McVey, 'Countertrade and Barter' (n 2) 203.

[49] UNCITRAL, 'Legal Guide' (n 9) 77. See also McVey, 'Countertrade and Barter' (n 2) 203–04.

[50] Cedric Guyot, 'Countertrade Recent Legal Developments and Comparative Study' (1986) 8 IBLJ 759, 763. See also Schmitthoff 'Countertrade' (n 7) 121–22.

[51] UNCITRAL, 'Legal Guide' (n 9) 92. A more complex structure that achieves the same broad aim (when payment is to be made by letter of credit rather than liquid funds) is 'crossed letters of credit', where the documents required under the letter of credit issued on behalf of one trade party requires that one of the documents to be presented proves that the beneficiary has issued an opposite and matching letter of credit: ibid 99–101.

The second type is a payment set-off structure,[52] which, like the countertrade transactions considered above, avoids the need for either party to transfer significant funds to their counterparty, with only the balance being transferred to one party or the other. The set-off arrangement may relate to a single pair of matching transactions or may provide a framework for a series of ongoing bilateral trades between the parties. The advantage of this arrangement is that the set-off is capable of covering payment obligations that are otherwise expressed in different currencies (provided there is the requisite mutuality), as well as accommodating multi-party set-off when a 'set-off account' or multi-party netting arrangement is used.[53] 16.14

III. Legal Problems of Countertrade

Countertrade activity has given rise to a number of public law concerns regarding its compatibility with competition, anti-dumping, taxation, and fair-trading principles,[54] as well as policy concerns over accountability when countertrade is used as a development tool. This section will, however, focus on the private law difficulties that may arise. 16.15

A. The Nature and Effectiveness of the Transactional 'Link'

For a countertrade transaction to achieve its commercial purpose, there must be an effective 'link' between the matching, but opposite, transactions. The strongest form of 'link' is one that arises automatically between the parties as a matter of law. An example would be the situation where there are mutual debts that arise under matching sales transactions, so that one liquidated sum will automatically reduce or extinguish the amount of the other, provided that there is the requisite mutuality between the parties. Whilst equitable set-off extends the reach of that doctrine beyond mutual liquidated debts, this type of legal 'link' is not, however, a panacea: there are limits upon the types of claim that may be subject to an equitable set-off and the circumstances in which such a right might be asserted. 16.16

A more common (albeit weaker) form of 'link' is one that depends upon the parties taking action to establish it, rather than the 'link' arising automatically. In the countertrade context, the 'linking' mechanism will generally be contractual in nature.[55] As regards its form, there are three broad options. First, where the two sale agreements are concluded simultaneously and the goods supplied at the same time,[56] each contract may contain a provision linking the supply of goods in one direction to the equivalent obligation in the other direction. Effectively, by inserting a common provision into each transaction a 'bridge' is created between the two independent transactions. Depending on how that provision is drafted, this 'two-way' link may make the validity or performance of each sale contract dependent 16.17

[52] ibid 92.
[53] ibid 101–05.
[54] For a detailed analysis, see McVey, 'Countertrade: Commercial Practices' (n 10) 35–56. See also Schmitthoff 'Countertrade' (n 7) 116–17.
[55] Rather than using a contractual 'linking' device, the parties could potentially use some form of proprietary 'link', such as an assignment or security; but this type of 'link' is not generally viewed as a countertrade transaction.
[56] UNCITRAL, 'Legal Guide' (n 9) 12.

upon the other.[57] Alternatively, where the contracts are concluded simultaneously, but one party is to supply the goods before the other, it may only be necessary to include a 'linking' provision in one of the sale contracts. Secondly, where only one of the sale contracts is concluded,[58] that contract might contain a commitment by the purchaser of those goods to enter into further contracts in the future to supply different goods in the opposite direction. Including such a commitment in the sale contract itself is common when that commitment is intended to be limited in scope or duration. Thirdly, where the trade parties wish to commit to future corresponding sale contracts on a longer-term basis (as with an on-going barter, counter-purchase or direct off-set transaction), the parties may draft an overarching agreement that seeks to provide a framework for their ongoing dealings.[59] Whilst there is naturally a degree of standardisation in such bridging or framework arrangements,[60] their effectiveness as a linking mechanism is far from automatic and depends very much on the way the arrangement is drafted and how tightly it draws together the commitments on either side.[61]

16.18 Whatever the precise form of the contractual 'link', its content will depend upon the drafting process. At one end of the scale, the closest possible link is when the two sale contracts are made interdependent. Whilst UNCITRAL has certainly encouraged trading parties 'to include in the countertrade agreement clauses indicating the extent of interdependence of obligations',[62] care must be taken. In particular, it is important to specify whether it is simply the contractual performances under the matching sales that are interdependent or whether it is the validity of the contracts themselves that may be impacted.[63] Moreover, it is important to specify the types of non-performance in one contract that will justify non-performance or trigger invalidity in the opposing contract; otherwise, an excusable failure to perform may trigger unintended legal consequences.[64] As indicated above, the contractual interdependence will usually relate to the parties' respective supply obligations, but (especially in a counter-purchase arrangement) may equally relate to their payment obligations. Accordingly, one party may deposit the price for goods in a 'blocked account', with those proceeds being subject to the 'flaw' that they may only be withdrawn when its counterparty has performed its own supply obligation under the opposite sale contract.[65] At the other end of the scale is the bridging provision or framework agreement typically used in counter-purchase transactions,[66] pursuant to which a party commits to concluding one or more future sale contracts moving in the opposite direction.[67] Whilst the parties will

[57] Rajski, 'Legal Aspects' (n 12) 131.
[58] UNCITRAL, 'Legal Guide' (n 9) 12.
[59] ibid.
[60] Sumer and Chuah, 'Emerging Legal Challenges' (n 12) 114.
[61] Rajski, 'Legal Aspects' (n 12) 132.
[62] UNCITRAL, 'Legal Guide' (n 9) 142.
[63] Rajski, 'Legal Aspects' (n 12) 132.
[64] Herzfeld 'Countertrade on Capital Projects' (n 7) 197. See also Rajski, 'Legal Aspects' (n 12) 131.
[65] For recognition of 'flawed asset' arrangements, see *Re Bank of Credit and Commerce International SA (No 8)* [1998] AC 214 (HL).
[66] Rajski, 'Legal Aspects' (n 12) 133.
[67] It has been suggested that one of the reasons why parties may wish that the contractual 'link' remain weak in counter-purchase transactions is because, if the two matching sales transactions started 'merging into one', this might undermine the ability of one of the parties to secure other forms of traditional financing since 'a bank which would normally be interested in financing the conventional portion of the transaction (the first agreement) will most likely opt not to do so if the second agreement is legally connected to the first': see McVey, 'Countertrade and Barter' (n 2) 205.

obviously seek to map out the nature and contents of any subsequent contract as closely as possible, a mere undertaking to enter into future transactions must inevitably represent a weaker form of 'linkage' than when the parties have actually entered into the matching transaction already.[68] Indeed, assuming that such a commitment is valid at all, the remedies for breach would only ever sound in damages, as no English court would be likely to specifically enforce such a framework arrangement given the need for ongoing supervision.[69] It is because of the relative legal weakness of such future commitments that countertrade parties frequently seek to strengthen their legal protection by also concluding a co-operation agreement,[70] by inserting a liquidated damages clause,[71] or by demanding a performance bond as security.[72]

The difficulty in drafting an effective contractual 'link' in countertrade transactions is highlighted by the decision of the Court of Appeal in *The State Trading Corporation of India v M Golodetz Ltd* ('*Golodetz*'),[73] which concerned a contract for the sale of 12,600 metric tons of South Korean sugar by M Golodetz Ltd ('Golodetz') to the State Trading Corporation of India Ltd ('STC') on C&F terms to an Indian Port. At the time of the sale contract, the cargo of sugar was already afloat on *The Sara D*. Payment was to be made by an irrevocable sight letter of credit to be opened within seven days of the contract's conclusion. The sale contract also contained a 'countertrade' provision for the export by Golodetz within the following six months of unspecified goods with a value equivalent to 60% of the stowed sugar. As security for its obligation, Golodetz was required to provide STC with a performance bond 'for 3% of the value of export leg of countertrade within seven days of finalisation of import contract' ('the Countertrade Performance Bond'). Unfortunately, the day after the sale contract's conclusion, *The Sara D* sank and the cargo was declared a total loss. As Golodetz had effectively supplied the relevant goods, it pressed in vain for the letter of credit to be opened and eventually terminated the sale contract on the basis of STC's repudiatory breach by failing to open the credit.[74] 16.19

Golodetz submitted its damages claim to arbitration by the Council of the Refined Sugar Association. In its turn, STC sought to rely upon Golodetz's failure to issue the Countertrade 16.20

[68] The 'link' in such a situation is arguably even weaker than in the context of 'back-to-back' letters of credit. As indicated by the Singapore High Court in *PT Adaro Indonesia v Rabobank* [2002] 2 SLR(R) 79 (HC), even if both matching letters of credit relate to the same cargo and have the same documentary requirements, they are separate transactions, so that the existence of the 'back-to-back' credit, or the fact of payment thereunder, does not necessarily trigger payment under the original credit.

[69] See generally *Co-op Insurance Society Ltd v Argyll Stores Holdings Ltd* [1998] AC 1 (HL).

[70] Rajski, 'Legal Aspects' (n 12) 133.

[71] Schmitthoff 'Countertrade' (n 7) 122. Countertrade parties are specifically encouraged to include liquidated damages clauses for breach of the sale contracts and the framework agreement: see UNCITRAL, 'Legal Guide' (n 9) 142. In drafting such a clause, countertrade parties are encouraged to consider the legal consequences of invoking a liquidated damages clause and whether that party 'is precluded from also claiming the fulfilment of the countertrade commitment': see UNCITRAL, 'Legal Guide' (n 9) 119–20. Care should be taken to ensure that the clause does not infringe the penalty jurisdiction in English law: see generally *Cavendish Square Holding BV v El Makdessi* [2016] AC 1172 (SC). Similarly, there is encouragement to include a force majeure clause or other provision dealing with exoneration from performance: see UNCITRAL, 'Legal Guide' (n 9) 142.

[72] Where the countertrade parties use a performance bond, rather than conditional guarantee, they are encouraged to set out in the framework agreement the details of the performance bond to be issued and the circumstances in which it can be called upon: see UNCITRAL, 'Legal Guide' (n 9) 130. For discussion of performance bonds, see ch 8 (Neo) in this volume.

[73] *The State Trading Corporation of India v M Golodetz Ltd* (EWCA, 8 June 1989) (hereafter *STCI v Golodetz* (CA)).

[74] See *Jaks (UK) Ltd v Cera Investment Bank SA* [1998] 2 Lloyd's Rep 89 (QB).

Performance Bond as excusing its own failure to open the letter of credit. As the sale contract was largely silent as to the inter-relationship between the Countertrade Performance Bond and the principal letter of credit, the issue arose as to whether the former was a condition precedent of the latter, so as to excuse STC what would otherwise constitute a breach of contract. The arbitrators decided that this was not the case, as the sale contract did not expressly subject the letter of credit's opening to the existence of the Countertrade Performance Bond. Moreover, the sale contract was largely silent as to the form of the Countertrade Performance Bond, the bank at which it was to be opened, and its precise terms.[75] This decision was reversed by Evans J,[76] who concluded that 'the obligation of [STC] to open the credit was conditional on [Golodetz] taking "appropriate steps" to ask the bank to issue the [Countertrade Performance Bond]'.[77] Schmitthoff has expressed his disagreement with this conclusion: given that the parties' respective obligations to open the Countertrade Performance Bond and the letter of credit were in fact to be performed simultaneously, he has suggested that '[t]he correct answer would have been that each financial obligation was conditional on the other, and, that in the this simultaneous situation both parties were in default'.[78]

16.21 No doubt as a consequence of this academic critique, there was a further appeal. In that regard, Kerr LJ indicated that, as 'the opening of the [Countertrade Performance Bond] was not expressed to be a condition precedent to STC's obligation—admittedly in the nature of a condition—to open the letter of credit within seven days',[79] he had to make a 'value judgment' about whether this was implicitly the case by reference to the commercial significance of the Countertrade Performance Bond. In this regard, his Lordship concluded:[80]

> [The Countertrade Performance Bond] was not a condition precedent to anything under the express terms of the contract, and I can see no reason for concluding that it had this character by implication. It did not relate to the main and immediate transaction, but to another one which did not fall to be performed for a further six months. It was relatively unimportant in terms of money.... [T]here was no similar agreed proforma for the [Countertrade Performance Bond]. Its terms might well have required negotiation quite apart from those of the countertrade transaction itself.... STC required the [Countertrade Performance Bond] as a security to ensure that the export contract would in fact materialise. But ... this is not an argument in favour of treating the timeous opening of the [Countertrade Performance Bond] as a condition of the sugar contract. On the contrary, the undefined nature of the countertrade transaction may well militate against this contention. But in any event, the commercial significance of the [Countertrade Performance Bond] was only a matter of a relatively small sum of money.... For all these reasons I can see no basis for concluding that the sellers' obligation concerning the [Countertrade Performance Bond] had the character of a condition, let alone of a condition precedent to STC's obligation to open the letter of credit. Indeed, since the prescribed time limits for both obligations were the same, viz 'not later than seven days after the conclusion of the

[75] *STCI v Golodetz* (CA) (n 73).
[76] *The State Trading Corporation of India v M Golodetz Ltd* [1988] 2 Lloyd's Rep 182 (QB).
[77] Clive Schmitthoff, 'Financial Arrangements in Countertrade Transaction' [1988] JBL 502, 502.
[78] ibid 503.
[79] *STCI v Golodetz* (CA) (n 73).
[80] ibid.

contract' in the case of the letter of credit and 'within seven days of finalisation of import contract' in relation to the [Countertrade Performance Bond], it seems unarguable that the parties could have intended that performance of either obligation was to be a condition precedent to the performance of the other.

Given the range of differing views in *Golodetz*, the salutary lesson to draw is that, whatever the nature of the contractual 'link' between the opposite and matching transactions, its terms need to be clearly drafted, not only with respect to the content of each party's countertrade obligation, but also the time-frame within which those obligations must be discharged, the sequence of each party's performance, and ideally the consequences of breach. As *Golodetz* exemplifies, sloppy drafting in a countertrade transaction can cost the parties dear. **16.22**

B. Certainty and Completeness

Whilst *Golodetz* highlights the commercial and practical consequences of failing to specify the parties' countertrade obligations with sufficient clarity in on-going barter, counter-purchase, and direct off-set transactions,[81] there may come a tipping point where the drafting failures are so extensive that they impact upon the countertrade's legal validity.[82] It is hornbook law that in order to constitute a valid contractual commitment, an agreement must be sufficiently certain in its undertakings, and sufficiently complete in its coverage, to be enforceable by the courts. Accordingly, vague, meaningless, or contradictory terms in a contract risk falling afoul of the former concern[83] and a failure to agree on essential or material matters the latter.[84] In the countertrade context, UNCITRAL has recognised the dangers of the commitments in countertrade operations not being held enforceable by national courts and has warned about the need to ensure that the matching contract is defined closely enough.[85] That said, the problems are not necessarily always associated with drafting failures, but may be the product of the parties deliberately leaving matters vague, such as the quantity and type of goods to be supplied in the future;[86] the relative value to be ascribed to the goods passing between the parties;[87] and the time-frame within which the relevant goods are to be delivered. These are not mere matters of detail that can legitimately be left open, but relate to core contractual matters.[88] **16.23**

[81] UNCITRAL, 'Legal Guide' (n 9) 10–11.

[82] Rajski, 'Legal Aspects' (n 12) 132.

[83] *G Scammell & Nephew v Ouston* [1941] AC 251 (HL) (hereafter *Scammell v Ouston*), although this has subsequently been described as a 'rare case' of such uncertainty: see *Scammell v Dicker* [2005] EWCA Civ 405. Where such a vague phrase is included in a contract, it may be possible to sever the offending part or phrase, so that it is not the whole contract that fails for want of certainty: see *Nicolene Ltd v Simmonds* [1953] 1 QB 543 (CA).

[84] *Bols Distilleries BV v Superior Yacht Services Ltd* [2006] UKPC 45 [35].

[85] UNCITRAL, 'Legal Guide' (n 9) 11.

[86] As UNCITRAL has recognised, '[p]recision as to type, quality and quantity [of goods] increases the likelihood that the intended supply contract will be concluded': see UNCITRAL, 'Legal Guide' (n 9) 52. Even if the parties want to leave the nature and quantity of goods for later determination, it would be advisable at least to provide a list of goods that would discharge the obligations under the countertrade arrangement: ibid.

[87] UNCITRAL has recognised the risk of a countertrade arrangement being invalidated if the price is not specified, and accordingly parties are encouraged to provide a clear mechanism, external standard, or third-party expert for ascertaining the price to be paid in the future, if not explicitly stated: see UNCITRAL, 'Legal Guide' (n 9) 64.

[88] *Teekay Tankers Ltd v STX Offshore and Shipbuilding Co Ltd* [2017] EWHC 253 (Comm).

16.24 This legal risk is apparent from the subtext in *Golodetz*. Whilst the appeal in that case was focused on the narrow question of whether Golodetz's obligation was a condition precedent to STC's obligation, Kerr LJ was alive to the significant uncertainty in the countertrade provision when he indicated that 'the [terms of the Countertrade Performance Bond] might well have required negotiation quite apart from those of the countertrade transaction itself'.[89] Accordingly, his Lordship observed that counsel had 'rightly accepted ... that [Golodetz's] commitment to the countertrade transaction might not be enforceable in law, but only as a matter of commercial morality, because a number of essential terms would clearly require negotiation and agreement, in particular the description and price of the goods to be exported'.[90] Given that *Golodetz* arguably represents the leading countertrade decision in English law, it is a matter of some concern that this fundamental issue has been left hanging in this way.

16.25 Increasingly, however, English law has recognised that commercial parties may wish to regulate their long-term relationships by concluding framework contracts that are surprisingly light on detail in order to maximise flexibility as the trading relationship develops.[91] Accordingly the English courts have shown a degree of tolerance in this regard,[92] no longer insisting on absolute clarity or certainty and being prepared to enforce agreements in which the details may be supplied at some future stage.[93] UNCITRAL has similarly expressed the desire that countertrade arrangements should be enforced by national courts, despite those transactions being relatively open-textured.[94] To this end, in *RTS Flexible Systems Ltd v Molkerei Alois Muller GmbH & Co KG*,[95] the United Kingdom Supreme Court emphasised that, provided there is at least agreement 'upon all the terms which [the parties] regarded or the law requires as essential for the formation of legally binding relations', it is not fatal that 'certain terms of economic or other significance have not been finalised'.[96] This approach has been endorsed by the Supreme Court even more recently in *Wells v Devani*.[97] Despite this more liberal modern approach and the English courts' traditional reluctance to condemn commercial transactions as being too uncertain,[98] it is not at all clear that the contractual

89 *STCI v Golodetz* (CA) (n 73).

90 ibid. See also Schmitthoff 'Countertrade' (n 7) 122.

91 *RTS Flexible Systems Ltd v Molkerei Alois Muller GmbH & Co KG* [2010] 1 WLR 753 (SC) [48] (hereafter *RTS v Molkerei*).

92 *Hillas & Co Ltd v Arcos Ltd* (1932) 147 LT 503 (HL) 514 (hereafter *Hillas v Arcos*).

93 *Fletcher Challenge Energy Ltd v Electricity Corporation of New Zealand Ltd* [2002] 2 NZLR 433 (CA).

94 UNCITRAL, 'Legal Guide' (n 9) 26.

95 *RTS v Molkerei* (n 91) [45], [61]–[70]. See also *Bear Stearns Bank plc v Forum Global Equity Ltd* [2007] EWHC 1576 (comm).

96 The price has traditionally been considered an essential term (see *May & Butcher v R* [1934] 2 KB 17), although the Sale of Goods Act 1979 (UK) (SGA 1979), s 8(2) does contain a statutory mechanism to the effect that '[w]here the price is not determined ... the buyer must pay a reasonable price'. This suggests that a failure to agree on price may not always be fatal, although a countertrade transaction will not always involve 'a money consideration' as required by SGA 1979, s 2(1) in order to qualify as a contract of sale: see Schmitthoff 'Countertrade' (n 7) 115. Similarly, whilst not all countertrade transactions will necessarily fall within its scope, the Vienna Convention (n 43), art 14(1) requires that a contract's terms be "sufficiently definite", which means that "it indicates the goods and expressly or implicitly fixes or makes provision for determining the quantity and price". That said, any gaps in the contract may be filled by reference to the Vienna Convention's underlying "general principles" or "any usage to which [the parties] have agreed and ... any practices which they have established between themselves": ibid arts 7(2) and 9.

97 *Wells v Devani* [2020] AC 129 (SC) [17].

98 *Scammell v Ouston* (n 83) 268; *Petromec Inc v Petroleo Brasileiro SA* [2006] 1 Lloyd's Rep 121 (CA) [121]; *Whitecap Leisure Ltd v John H Rundle Ltd* [2008] 2 Lloyd's Rep 216 (CA) [21]; *Durham Tees Valley Airport Ltd v BMIbaby Ltd* [2011] 1 All ER (Comm) 731 (CA) [88].

'link' in countertrade transactions would necessarily pass the requisite legal threshold: as *Golodetz* highlights, without the price or the goods having been identified, there is little to enforce. Whilst the fact that the parties have acted on an alleged agreement,[99] or have provided some objective benchmark[100] or machinery[101] to resolve any uncertainty, will point against an agreement being uncertain or incomplete, *Golodetz* shows that this is not an absolute truth. Accordingly, the mere fact that commercial persons wish to embrace contractual fluidity does not per se remove the legal risk that an English court might strike down an agreement on grounds of uncertainty or incompleteness;[102] there comes a tipping point when doctrinal matters can no longer simply be sacrificed on the altar of commercial expediency. This is not contractual paternalism, but simply the pragmatic recognition that contractual remedies will be limited in what they can achieve if it is unclear what the court is being asked to enforce. Indeed, what separates a contract from an agreement is the willingness of a court to deploy its judicial armoury in its support. That said, given that countertrade transactions are not always concluded for purely commercial reasons, but may be concluded by state actors in order to achieve high-level development, political, or military goals, agreements may instead take the form of an international treaty (and so not be subject to domestic contractual principles) or may be susceptible to sovereign immunity claims (which would take the agreement outside judicial purview in any event). Indeed, unless countertrade can provide the necessary legal certainty, it may become states alone, rather than commercial parties, that employ this mechanism in the future.

Those forms of countertrade that employ a bridging or framework structure for their sale contracts may also be susceptible to a related form of legal vulnerability, namely that the 'link' mechanism is nothing more than an 'agreement to agree' or a 'contract to contract'. The reason for treating this as a separate concern from certainty and completeness is that an agreement can be invalidated on this ground, even if it would otherwise be sufficiently certain and complete to be enforced. For example, in the counter-purchase context, there might be a very straightforward concluded trade agreement, which contains a provision to the effect that a clearly defined matching trade transaction for specified goods at a specified price will be entered into at some future date. In terms of its content and the obligations created, this agreement would appear to be sufficiently certain and complete;[103] and yet English law has always had a deep-seated hostility to agreements to agree.[104] As Lord Ackner stated, in *Walford v Miles*,[105] '[t]he reason why an agreement to negotiate, like an agreement to agree, is unenforceable, is simply because it lacks the necessary certainty'. **16.26**

That said, there seems to be an increasing recognition that any such uncertainty can be cured by inserting a provision indicating an objective standard against which the undertaking to make a further agreement can be measured, whether a standard of 'reasonable **16.27**

[99] *RTS v Molkerei* (n 91) [47], [61].

[100] *Hillas v Arcos* (n 92) 514; *Didymi Corporation v Atlantic Lines & Navigation Co Inc* [1987] 2 Lloyd's Rep 166 (QB) 169.

[101] *Sudbrook Trading Estate Ltd v Eggleton* [1983] 1 AC 444 (HL) 482–487.

[102] Consider *Alfred McAlpine Construction Ltd v Panatown Ltd* [2001] EWCA Civ 485 [35]; *Maple Leaf Volatility Master Fund v Rouvroy* [2009] EWHC 257 (Comm) [223].

[103] McVey, 'Countertrade and Barter' (n 2) 204–06.

[104] *Von Hatzfeldt-Wildenburg v Alexander* [1912] 1 Ch 284, 289; *Courtney & Fairbairn Ltd v Tolaini Brothers (Hotels) Ltd* [1975] 1 WLR 297 (CA) 301–02. See also *North v Wilkinson* [2018] EWCA Civ 161 [14].

[105] *Walford v Miles* [1992] 2 AC 128 (HL) 138.

endeavours'[106] or potentially 'best efforts', or 'best endeavours'. Even where no explicit standard is stipulated, there are growing signs that English law may finally be ready to recognise the utility of good faith as a standard against which contractual performance might be measured;[107] if the performance of an 'agreement to agree' can be measured against an implicit good faith standard, then these become far less objectionable. Such a notion of good faith is more likely to be implied into 'certain categories of long-term contract',[108] where the parties have made a substantial, longer-term commitment to one another involving a high degree of communication and co-operation based upon mutual trust and confidence. As this category of 'relational' contract seems apt to cover countertrade transactions, it is possible that English courts in future will use notions of good faith to avoid striking down such transactions.

16.28 Alternatively, if English law were to persist in the view that all countertrade transactions (or at least certain categories) are likely to be too uncertain, it might nevertheless be possible to treat countertrade transactions as belonging to an intermediate category of arrangement that has commercial (albeit not legal) force. Examples of such arrangements include letters of intent[109] and comfort letters,[110] upon which commercial parties are accustomed to rely, despite such arrangements being unenforceable in legal terms. Whilst such a classification would be cold comfort to parties who are forced to litigate a dispute, analogising some countertrade transactions to comfort letters might at least explain why they operate effectively in the market, despite uncertainties over their legal enforceability.[111]

C. Nature and Effect of 'Blocked Accounts'

16.29 As explained above, rather than using a contractual provision or framework arrangement to 'link' the sale contracts or the delivery obligations thereunder, the parties may seek to 'link' the payment obligations arising under matching sales. This may be achieved by way of an express set-off arrangement: if a clause in the parties' arrangement makes clear that sums should be set-off against each other, even if English law would not ordinarily recognise such a set-off, then the courts will nevertheless give effect to that arrangement.[112] Such a contractual set-off is equally likely to be recognised abroad. Alternatively, the parties might 'link' their respective payment undertakings through the mechanism of a 'blocked account' into which the proceeds of any sale must be paid and out of which the funds may only be withdrawn by either party when defined conditions have been satisfied. Whilst this mechanism is commonly used for a range of commercial transactions, care needs to be taken to ensure that the conditions for withdrawal are sufficiently clearly stated. Moreover, as it is

[106] *Astor Management AG v Atalaya Mining plc* [2017] EWHC 425 (Comm) (hereafter *Astor Management v Atalaya*); cf *Dany Lions Ltd v Bristol Cars Ltd (No 2)* [2014] 2 All ER (Comm) 403 (QB).

[107] See generally *Yam Seng Pte Ltd v International Trading Corp Ltd* [2013] EWHC 111.

[108] *Compass Group UK and Ireland Ltd v Mid Essex Hospital Services NHS Trust* [2013] EWCA Civ 200 [105]; *Globe Motors Inc v TRW Lucas Varity Electric Steering Ltd* [2016] EWCA Civ 396 [67]–[68]. See also *Astor Management v Atalaya* (n 106); *Ilkerler Otomotiv Sanayai ve Ticaret Anonim Sirketi v Perkins Engines Co Ltd* [2017] 4 WLR 144 (CA); *Nehayan v Kent* [2018] EWHC 333 (Comm).

[109] *Kleinwort Benson Ltd v Malaysia Mining Corporation* [1989] 1 All ER 785 (CA).

[110] *Associated British Ports v Ferryways* [2009] 1 Lloyd's Rep 595 (CA) [24].

[111] Rajski, 'Legal Aspects' (n 12) 135.

[112] *Grenda Investments Ltd v Barton* [2017] EWHC 2371 (Comm).

possible for the 'blocked account' to be established and operated in a number of different ways, care must be taken to define the nature of the parties' rights to the account funds. For example, it is necessary to determine whether the legal title to the chose in action representing the account is held in joint names or only one parties' name. In the latter case, it will also need to be determined whether the legal accountholder also holds the equitable title to the account-funds on trust for the parties (and, if so, in what proportions); whether the legal accountholder also holds the entire beneficial interest, subject to defined contractual drawing rights in favour of the other party; or whether the accountholder's rights are subject to a charge or 'flawed-asset' arrangement in favour of the other party.

Indeed, the difficulty in characterising the nature of the parties' rights under a joint-account arrangement, when it is not properly documented, was highlighted in *Whitlock v Moree*:[113] the issue concerned whether the beneficial interest in an account, which was held solely in the name of the party who had contributed all the funds, was held entirely for himself pursuant to a presumed resulting trust or was held jointly with his friend, so that rights of survivorship arose. Ultimately, the Privy Council resolved the difficulty by focusing on the parties' indications in the account-opening documents. **16.30**

Even on the relatively straightforward facts of *Moree*, the legal issues were difficult; that is only likely to be magnified in the much more complex context of countertrade. Indeed, there are additional considerations that arise when a 'blocked account' is used in the context of an international transaction. Where the 'blocked account' is held with an English bank or the English branch of a foreign bank, then English law will determine whether the parties' rights are proprietary (whether arising under a trust or charge) or contractual in nature. Once one moves the account to a civilian jurisdiction, one faces the risk that an intended trust mechanism is either not respected[114] or morphs into a trust-like concept, such as the *fiducie* in French Law. Whilst none of this is insurmountable with careful thought about the nature of the parties' rights and the location of the account, there could be significant insolvency consequences of not paying sufficient attention to such issues from the outset. **16.31**

D. Choice of Law Issues

Besides the concerns relating to the nature and validity of the 'link' mechanism in countertrade transactions considered above and the issue of whether any disputes should be submitted to arbitration or judicial determination (and, if so, where),[115] there may also be real choice of law difficulties. Some of the issues are likely to relate to the proper characterisation of the 'link' mechanism in question for choice of law purposes. This was already considered above in relation to 'blocked accounts', which can take a number of different juridical forms. Once the transaction has been properly characterised,[116] there are three particular choice **16.32**

113 *Whitlock v Moree* [2017] UKPC 44.

114 Consider the UK Recognition of Trusts Act 1987, implementing the Convention on the Law Applicable to Trusts and on their Recognition (adopted 1 July 1985, entered into force 1 January 1992) (hereafter 'Recognition of Trusts Act 1987').

115 UNCITRAL, 'Legal Guide' (n 9) 169–70. See also Schmitthoff 'Countertrade' (n 7) 122–23.

116 See generally *Macmillan Inc v Bishopsgate Investment Trust plc* [1996] 1 All ER 585 (CA).

of law issues that may arise in the countertrade context depending upon the nature of the 'link' employed.

16.33 First, where the 'link' between the sale contracts is contractual in nature (as in the case of a framework agreement), most of the difficulties in this area could be cured by the simple expedient of expressly choosing an applicable law.[117] Given that each party will wish its own law to govern the transaction, it may not be possible to choose a law that governs each sale contract, as well as the bridging, framework or 'link' arrangement.[118] Accordingly, it is not beyond the realms of possibility that no law will have been chosen for all or some of the relevant transactions, or even that each independent transaction is governed by a separate law.[119]

16.34 As the various contractual relationships are by definition 'linked', one issue concerns the extent to which the law applicable to each independent contract does or should 'infect' that applicable to other contracts. Whilst the common law was prepared to submit related contracts to a similar legal system when the link in question was particularly close (as in the case of a performance bond and counter-guarantee),[120] it was certainly not the automatic judicial response and there had to be a clear commercial justification for subjecting the various contracts to a single law.[121] The English courts unsurprisingly continued the same broad approach under the Rome Convention when determining the applicable law in the absence of choice: the presumptively applicable law under article 4(2) would be displaced under article 4(5), so that all networks of contracts, even those characterized as 'autonomous', tended to be subjected to a single law.[122] As recognised by the European Court of Justice,[123] the commercial imperative for subjecting contractual networks to a uniform law did not alter when the Rome Convention was introduced; nevertheless, the difference in structure between the choice of law principles at common law and under the Rome Convention did sometimes result in the English courts taking their willingness to displace the presumptively applicable law too far.[124] Whilst article 4 of the Rome I Regulation[125] now makes clear that the presumptively applicable law should not be displaced on a whim, but only when there is a 'manifestly' more closely connected legal system,[126] it is clear that such displacement is still likely to occur when there is a contractual network (albeit potentially less frequently than under the Rome Convention).[127] Indeed, Recital 20 of the Rome I Regulation states

[117] UNCITRAL, 'Legal Guide' (n 9) 160.
[118] ibid 161. See also Schmitthoff 'Countertrade' (n 7) 122.
[119] Herzfeld, 'Countertrade on Capital Projects' (n 7) 198.
[120] *Turkiye Is Bankasi AS v Bank of China* [1993] 1 Lloyd's Rep 132 (QB).
[121] *Bank of Credit & Commerce Hong Kong Ltd v Sonali Bank* [1995] 1 Lloyd's Rep 227 (QB).
[122] *Bank of Baroda v Vysya Bank Ltd* [1994] 2 Lloyd's Rep 87 (QB).
[123] *Haeger & Schmidt GmbH v MMA IARD* [2015] QB 319 (ECJ) [49].
[124] *Marconi Communications International Ltd v PT Pan Indonesia Bank TBK* [2005] EWCA Civ 442, criticised in Christopher Hare, 'The Rome Convention and Letters of Credit' [2005] LMCLQ 417.
[125] Council Regulation (EC) 593/2008 of 17 June 2008 on the Law Applicable to Contractual Obligations [2008] OJ L177/6 (hereafter 'Rome I Regulation') art 3. From 1 January 2021, the Rome I Regulation will continue to apply in the United Kingdom to contracts concluded before 31 December 2020: see Agreement of 12 November 2019 on the Withdrawal of the United Kingdom of Great Britain and Northern Ireland from the European Union and the European Atomic Energy Community [2019] OJ CI384/1, art 66. For contracts concluded after 31 December 2020, the Rome I Regulation will continue to apply in the United Kingdom as part of "retained" EU law: see European Union (Withdrawal) Act 2018, s 3(2)(a). For the amendments to the Rome I Regulation to take account of 'Brexit", see Law Applicable to Contractual Obligations and Non-Contractual Obligations (Amendment etc) (EU Exit) Regulations 2019, SI 2019/834.
[126] *Intercontainer Interfrigo SC (ICF) v Balkenende Oosthuizen BV* [2010] QB 411 (ECJ).
[127] *Molton Street Capital LLP v Shooters Hill Capital Partners LLP* [2015] EWHC 3419 (Comm) [94].

that 'account should be taken, *inter alia*, of whether the contract in question has a very close relationship with another contract or contracts'. For obvious reasons, this possibility has particular relevance to countertrade involving 'linked' transactions: in the absence of any clearly expressed choice that different parts of the contractual network should be governed by different laws, there is a real risk that they will all be subjected to some uniform law. Accordingly, countertrade parties should think carefully about the choice of law implications of 'linking' their otherwise independent transactions.

Secondly, where the relevant 'link' involves a set-off between the parties' payment obligations, the contractual choice of law principles discussed above may also potentially be significant. According to article 17 of the Rome I Regulation, '[w]here the right to set-off is not agreed by the parties, set-off shall be governed by the law applicable to the claim against which the right to set-off is asserted'. This suggests that the parties are free to choose the law applicable to any set-off, although it is not clear how this possibility will assist countertrade parties who are at odds over the law governing their relationship more generally. Where there is no express choice, article 17 provides that the law applicable to the set-off is the same as that applicable to the underlying right; but, where two contractual claims governed by different laws are set-off against one another, article 17 will be difficult to apply, as the law applicable to the set-off ought not be determined solely by the identity of the party asserting the right of set-off. Otherwise, the set-off would be governed by the law of whichever party raised the argument first. Accordingly, an English court will likely fall back onto determining 'the country with which [the contract] is most closely connected' under article 4(4) of the Regulation. The uncertainty regarding how the Rome I Regulation applies to set-off, however, undermines countertrade transactions employing such a 'linking' device. **16.35**

Thirdly, if the parties choose to 'link' their transaction through a 'blocked account', the different possible characterisations of the account (as considered above) may alter the law applicable to its operation. Where a party's rights take the form of drawing rights or a 'flawed asset arrangement' over the account, the existence and scope of those rights is likely to be determined by the law applicable to the contract under which those rights were granted; whereas the enforceability of those rights against the bank in question will be determined by the law applicable to the account contract.[128] Where a party is granted a charge or some other form of security over the account, its validity, scope, and enforceability will similarly be determined by the law applicable to the account contract. Where a trust has, however, been created over the 'blocked account', the beneficiary's rights under that trust will be governed by the law chosen by the settlor,[129] or, in the absence of choice, by 'the law with which a trust is most closely connected'.[130] In making that determination, a court should examine the place for the trust's administration designated by the settlor, the *situs* of the trust assets, the trustee-bank's place of business, and the place where the trust's objects are to be fulfilled. These factors may point to the law applicable to the account contract, but that is not necessarily the case. **16.36**

[128] See *Sierra Leone Telecommunications Co Ltd v Barclays Bank plc* [1998] 2 All ER 821 (QB).
[129] Recognition of Trusts Act 1987 (n 114) art 6, sch 1.
[130] ibid art 7.

IV. Conclusion

16.37 This chapter's aim was to act as an antidote to the relentless focus of trade finance on technological solutions. Whilst it is not the intention to deny the significance that technological advances are likely to have in reducing the costs and increasing the efficiency of trade-finance operations, technology alone cannot do all the work. It is also necessary to examine alternative commercial and legal frameworks within which technology can achieve its aims. Whilst open account trading and supply-chain financing techniques appear to be eclipsing more traditional financing frameworks,[131] such as the documentary letter of credit, both of these techniques are based upon certain assumptions about the political, economic, and financial context in which trade parties are dealing. In circumstances where these assumptions come under strain, such as in times of national or international crisis, there may be other financing techniques, such as countertrade, that may serve trade parties' interests better. Standing on the precipice of an unprecedented economic, social, and health crisis, the time may be right to consider repurposing old financing techniques to deal with new problems.

[131] See ch 14 (Hare) in this volume.

Index

For the benefit of digital users, indexed terms that span two pages (e.g., 52–53) may, on occasion, appear on only one of those pages.